Farewell Spit
ganui Inlet
Golden Bay
D'Urville I
Marlborough Sounds
Kahurangi Point
Tasman Bay
Nelson
NELSON
Vernon Lagoon
Blenheim
L Grassmere
Cape Campbell
Westport
Cape Foulwind
L Rotoroa
MARLBOROUGH
L Elterwater
L Rotoiti
Paparoa Ra
Punakaiki
Seaward Kaikoura Ra
Lewis Pass
Greymouth
Kaikoura
L Sumner
WEST COAST
Arthur's Pass
Motunau I
Okarito Lagoon
Southern Alps
Ashley Estuary
Avon-Heathcote Estuary
Christchurch
Banks Peninsula
CANTERBURY
L Ellesmere
Open Bay Is
Jackson Head
Haast
L Tekapo
L Pukaki
MACKENZIE BASIN
Washdyke Lagoon
Wainono Lagoon
Milford Sound
L Wanaka
Waitaki River
Queenstown
Oamaru
L Wakatipu
Moeraki Point
Secretary I
Te Anau
FIORDLAND
L Te Anau
OTAGO
Breaksea I
Taiaroa Head
L Manapouri
Otago Peninsula
esolution I
Dunedin
SOUTHLAND
Catlins
Invercargill
Puysegur Point
Solander Is
Muttonbird Is
Codfish I
Stewart Island
Muttonbird Is

The Field Guide to the BIRDS *of* NEW ZEALAND

The Field Guide to the BIRDS *of* NEW ZEALAND

Barrie Heather & **Hugh Robertson**
Illustrated by **Derek Onley**

PENGUIN BOOKS

To Rosemary & Lea

PENGUIN

UK | USA | Canada | Ireland | Australia
India | New Zealand | South Africa | China

Penguin is an imprint of the Penguin Random House group of companies, whose addresses can be found at global.penguinrandomhouse.com.

Penguin Random House New Zealand

First published by Penguin Books (NZ) Ltd in 1996
This revised and updated edition published by Penguin Random House New Zealand, 2015

7 9 10 8 6

Cover and text design by Anna Egan-Reid © Penguin Random House New Zealand
Typeset in Minion and Amasis by Anna Egan-Reid
Endpaper maps by Chris Edkins
Colour separation by Image Centre Ltd
Printed and bound in China by 1010 Printing

A catalogue record for this book is available from the National Library of New Zealand.

ISBN 978-0-143-57092-9

penguinrandomhouse.co.nz

CONTENTS

FOREWORD TO THIS EDITION

New Zealanders have always had a high level of interest in the natural history of our unique part of the world, and a reputation for innovative and committed conservation action. The long isolation of our biota, which evolved in the absence of browsing, grazing or predatory mammals, made Aotearoa New Zealand a special place, but it was a biota set to fail once humans eventually made their way to these shores with our insatiable appetites and baggage of attendant mammals.

The first wave of extinctions followed the arrival of Maori, kiore (Pacific rat) and kuri (dog) about 1000 years ago; this included the disappearance of the entire radiation of moa, and many other flightless bird species and large-bodied insects. A second wave of extinctions followed the arrival of European settlers as they cleared most of the remaining lowland forest, drained swamps and introduced many more mammals that took their toll on palatable plants and vulnerable birds.

Fortunately, some early naturalists such as Thomas Potts and, somewhat reluctantly, Sir Walter Buller, recognised what was happening and started the fight to preserve what was left after hundreds of years of plundering and neglect. From these efforts rose a strong conservation movement: Tongariro National Park became the world's fourth national park; three island wildlife sanctuaries – Resolution, Little Barrier and Kapiti – were established in the 1890s; and in 1923, the Royal Forest and Bird Protection Society was formed to advocate for protection of our natural biota.

New Zealand conservation has been well served with a range of excellent identification guides to our flora and fauna, among which *The Field Guide to the Birds of New Zealand* by Barrie Heather and Hugh Robertson (in all four editions) stands proud. This book not only contains splendid artwork by Derek Onley and concise field identification information opposite each plate, but also a handbook section with much more detail about each species.

What makes this book perhaps unique among bird guides worldwide is the 'Conservation' section for most native species. This feature shows the importance of conservation to the New Zealand psyche, and celebrates the many successes, won through intensive management, translocations and pest control. It also highlights our ongoing problems.

The remarkable stories of the recovery of Black Robins, Chatham Islands Taiko and Little Spotted Kiwi, among others, are summarised along with worrying news about ongoing declines, especially of many seabirds and Arctic waders. Despite innovative mitigation measures to reduce accidental bycatch from fisheries operations, many mollymawks and petrels are still killed, and this, combined with climate change affecting their food supplies, has led to many major population reductions. Arctic waders, which undergo amazing long-distance flights lasting up to a week, are reliant on good food supplies at their stopover sites where they refuel before their next migration leg. Unfortunately, much of the intertidal habitat they rely on in northeastern Asia has been destroyed in recent decades in the name of economic growth, as thousands of hectares of rich mudflats have been converted into container ports or aquaculture ponds.

The last two plates, depicting species lost since 1900, just after the awakening of the conservation ethos in New Zealand, serve to remind us that much still needs to be done to maintain our indigenous birdlife. The challenge is to keep those plates restricted to those eight species. With well-funded research, monitoring and management, the development of further innovative solutions, growing community group efforts to control pests, and public support to improve the state of our waters, forests and other natural habitats, this can and must be done.

Kevin Hackwell, 2015
Group Manager, Campaigns and Advocacy
Forest & Bird

FOREWORD TO THE FIRST EDITION

The development of the field guide has been the key to the advance of recreational birdwatching and has contributed to many essential aspects of scientific ornithology; in turn, other disciplines – plant life, mammals, invertebrates – have produced their field guides. But the lead given by birdwatchers and ornithologists in this field of practical natural history remains unchallenged.

Our first New Zealand bird guide – with which my own association with the then-burgeoning art of the field guide as pioneered by Roger Tory Peterson began – appeared in 1966. Dr D. L. Serventy, in introducing a later Australian bird field guide, said: 'The virtue of a field guide is that it contains all the information necessary, in pictures and text, to identify a bird. But no more. Authors should resist the temptation to include extra data.'

Our 1966 *Field Guide* strayed from Dom Serventy's somewhat uncompromising formula. But we felt that – especially with respect to our comparatively few native passerines – a little extra information on life history and other aspects would not go amiss and would, in fact, probably serve to stimulate the observer. The 1966 *Field Guide*, in its numerous editions and, later, improved plates succeeded beyond our expectations and has surely fulfilled its aim of being a usable and practical guide.

A new guide to New Zealand birds is now timely. First, the art of the field guide – that essential blend of illustrations and information – has steadily reached greater perfection: new methods have been produced by bird artists to enable species to be compared at rest and in flight, and new standards of typography and book design aimed at ease of identification have been achieved. Then there is all the new material – as Dick Sibson said in his editorial Preface to the 1966 *Field Guide*, the decision to produce such a book was timely, for 'the last few decades have been exciting'. This is ever truer for the present stage!

In the 30 years since 1966 there has been much discussion on the reliability of important field characters and much rigorous checking of plumage and behavioural characteristics. Together with a wealth of new information, this has led inevitably to the decision to produce a completely new *Field Guide*. In Derek Onley, a keen amateur ornithologist, an artist has been found capable of translating the now impressive art of bird illustration into the needs of a modern field guide.

I would like to take this opportunity of congratulating both authors on their mastery of the technique required in condensing and expressing field information: the facing-page text is utility natural history writing at its best. The main text provides an excellent summary of what is known of each species and should satisfy the inquiring minds of field naturalists and professional ornithologists alike. In particular, I know how much thought and inspiration the authors have contributed towards developing the idea of this new field guide, and how much sheer hard work goes into writing such a guide.

Dr Hugh Robertson belongs to the new school of ornithologist, coupling a strong scientific training and career in ornithology with a love of birdwatching.

Like every New Zealand author of ornithological material, I was deeply indebted to Barrie Heather for his editorial skill during his period as voluntary editor of *Notornis*, and have benefited from his high standards of accuracy and scientific expression: he can be justly proud of this book and of having done so much to launch New Zealand ornithology on its latest phase.

E. G. Turbott, 1996
Past President
Ornithological Society of New Zealand

INTRODUCTION

The fourth edition of *The Field Guide to the Birds of New Zealand* aims to help you to identify wild birds seen anywhere in the New Zealand region, including the Ross Sea sector of Antarctica. It follows the same format as the first edition and the various revised editions of its predecessor, *A Field Guide to the Birds of New Zealand* by Falla, Sibson and Turbott, in providing the reader with a brief and informative summary of what is known about the birds of New Zealand.

HISTORY

In 1959, the Council of the Ornithological Society of New Zealand asked Dr Robert Falla, Dick Sibson and Graham Turbott to collaborate in compiling a practical field guide to the birds in the New Zealand region. Their first edition, with 18 colour plates by Chloë Talbot Kelly, was published in 1966 and revised in 1970. In 1979, a further revision of the text was made and this new edition contained 48 colour plates by Elaine Power.

These various editions of Falla, Sibson and Turbott served as the 'bible' for a generation of birdwatchers in New Zealand, not only as a practical guide for identifying birds, but as a ready source of information on the distribution and habits of New Zealand birds.

The first edition of our book, *The Field Guide to the Birds of New Zealand*, was published in 1996. With our publishers, we decided to base its general layout on the very popular *Field Guide to the Birds of Australia* by Ken Simpson and Nicholas Day. New Zealand and overseas birdwatchers whom we consulted liked the format of having all the colour plates grouped together in a handy identification section, and also wanted distribution maps added as a new feature. There was a clear call for us to also retain the type of informative text available in the earlier Falla, Sibson and Turbott guides.

Derek Onley, a highly respected New Zealand ornithologist, was commissioned by the Ornithological Society of New Zealand to paint 74 new colour plates depicting all 328 species, and most subspecies, of birds recorded in the New Zealand region up to 1995. Since 1978, much new information on the distribution and biology of New Zealand birds had become available through publication of *The Atlas of Bird Distribution in New Zealand* in 1985, the *Checklist of the Birds of New Zealand* in 1990, early volumes of *The Handbook to the Birds of Australia, New Zealand and Antarctica*, and about 6000 pages of *Notornis*, the journal of the Ornithological Society of New Zealand, as well as scholarly articles in other scientific journals. This meant that much of the original material had become so dated that we had to write the text afresh, although we retained some of the pithy lines or gems from the previous field guide. The growth of interest in conservation since the 1970s prompted us to add a section on conservation management for appropriate species, and we added a section of more detailed information to aid the identification of ages and sexes of some particular groups of birds.

The first edition of the *Field Guide* included 20 species added to the New Zealand list between 1978 and 1995 as a result of recent records and some taxonomic changes. A revised edition, published in 2000, included an addendum with text for five new species seen in New Zealand between 1994 and 1998, and added a new section describing 12 sites where bird enthusiasts in New Zealand could expect to see a good variety of our native birds. A further revision was published in 2005, this time with much improved maps, and the addendum was expanded to include an extra six species seen up to 2004. This fourth edition includes illustrations and standard text for these 11 new species seen up to 2004 as well as a further eight species added to the New Zealand list between 2005 and 2014. Taxonomic revisions, mainly splitting one species into two or more species, have led to this edition containing 374 species – 46 extra species compared with our first edition in 1996.

SCOPE

For the purposes of this guide, the New Zealand region includes only New Zealand territory, from the Kermadec Islands at latitude 29°S to the Ross Dependency in Antarctica (see maps on page 18). Some New Zealand ornithological publications include Norfolk and/or Macquarie islands because they are part of the New

Zealand biogeographic subregion, but they are part of Australia and are covered by Simpson and Day, and other Australian bird guides. We have included all species accepted on the New Zealand list between 1900 and 2014. We have therefore excluded records of vagrants seen in the 1800s, and of native birds that became extinct before 1900. We have included two plates (Plates 84 and 85) that depict those species that have probably become extinct since 1900, in the slim hope that a few birds may survive somewhere; these plates also serve as a reminder of what richness we have recently lost from our New Zealand heritage.

LAYOUT

The first part of the book is an identification guide; on the page opposite each colour plate is a distribution map for most species breeding in New Zealand, and sufficient plumage and behavioural details that should help identify the species, sex and/or age of the bird you see in the field. Key identification features are given in italics. Sp 1 refers to the first species in the Handbook section, Sp 2 to the second, and so on.

The distribution maps show where species breeding in New Zealand may be found in suitable habitat; maps for vagrants, stragglers and non-native seabirds, and for migratory waders (which can turn up in any estuary around the coast) and extinct birds are not necessary for identification purposes, and so this information is instead given in the second part of the book. Most of the information in the maps comes from the *Atlas of Bird Distribution in New Zealand 1999–2004*, and from the *New Zealand eBird* website.

The plates are arranged approximately in the taxonomic order used in the 2010 edition of the *Checklist of the Birds of New Zealand*, but where two similar-looking species are not closely related, they are shown together on the same plate. Two main exceptions to this rule are the plates devoted to rare Australian passerine vagrants (Plates 73 and 74), and the final plates (Plates 84 and 85), which depict a variety of species believed to have become extinct since 1900.

The second part of the book gives more details on the distribution and ecology of each species, but does not attempt to present a full coverage of all that is known for each species, which the impressive seven-volume *Handbook of Australian, New Zealand and Antarctic Birds* has done. Those species that breed in New Zealand generally receive full treatment under the headings: Other name(s), Size, Geographical variation, Distribution, Population, Conservation, Breeding, Behaviour, Feeding, In the hand (optional) and Reading.

In the handbook section, we use the notation 1–**3**–4 for discrete entities (e.g. number of eggs in a clutch) to denote that the range is from 1 to 4, and 3 is the most common value. For continuous variables (e.g. time, linear measurements), 36–**39**–43 denotes that the range is from 36 to 43, and 39 is the mean or average.

The final section of the book is an introduction to 12 easily accessible birdwatching sites around New Zealand. A visit to these sites will allow you to see or hear a wide variety of native birds, often in spectacular or interesting settings. Many common native species can be seen almost anywhere and so they are not included in the lists of notable native species you are likely to see at each site.

TREATMENT

The scientific world has recently incorporated new genetic techniques to help define species and to determine relationships between different groups of birds. We have decided to follow the order and scientific names given in the 2010 edition of the *Checklist of the Birds of New Zealand*, except that we have included a few introduced species that have bred in the wild in New Zealand in the last 50 years.

Scientific names follow a standard format throughout the world and are traditionally given in italics with the genus listed first, the species name second, and the subspecific name (if required) third. For example, the full scientific name for the Red-billed Gull is *Larus novaehollandiae scopulinus*. The word *Larus* refers to the genus, a group of related species (the Black-billed Gull and Black-backed Gull also belong to this group of gulls, although not all 'gulls' around the world do). The word *novaehollandiae* distinguishes this particular species, and forms a unique combination with the word *Larus* to identify the species wherever it occurs in the world. Some species can be further divided into geographically distinct forms, called subspecies or races; these are distinguished by a third name. In this case, *scopulinus* refers to the form breeding in New Zealand, which are slightly, but consistently, different from those breeding in Australia (*novaehollandiae*) and in New Caledonia and the southwest Pacific (*forsteri*). The subspecies in Australia is called the 'nominate' subspecies, as it has the same subspecific name as the species name, which indicates that a bird of this form was used to originally describe the species as being different from other gulls.

There is an international move to standardise the popular or common names of birds, in addition to the already accepted norm of having standardised scientific names. This move is prompted partially by people who list all the species they have seen (variously known as listers, tickers or twitchers) who want to know if they can add a tick to their 'world list' if they see a Red-billed Gull in New Zealand, having seen a Silver Gull in Australia – they can't because they belong to the same species. We have resisted attempts to internationalise the common names used in New Zealand; calling our Red-billed Gulls 'Silver Gulls' would add confusion, because our endemic Black-billed Gull is more silver-coloured than the Red-billed Gull!

Some species in New Zealand are known to everyone by their Maori name, e.g. Tui, Takahe, and we resist the loss of part of our heritage by imposing artificial labels on New Zealand birds. We have given the most widely accepted Maori name(s), but not all, because some species (e.g. Stitchbird) have up to seven recorded geographical variations of their Maori names. Due to the complexity of catering for this variation, we have followed the *Checklist* and not macronised Maori names and instead refer readers to Appendix 3 of that volume. However, we have followed Maori usage by not adding 's' to plurals; so we have one Takahe and three Tui.

Again, we have generally followed the common names given in the *Checklist*, except that we have used our own personal preferences in some instances, for example, we have retained the term 'Mollymawk' for the black-backed albatrosses of the genus *Thalassarche*. Species or subspecies endemic to a particular island group often end up with the name of the main island in their name, but we have instead used the name for the island group, so we now have Chatham Islands Shag, which seems more appropriate than Chatham Island Shag given that many breed elsewhere in the Chatham Islands group. Some publications simplify this name to Chatham Shag, but this formula becomes confusing with the Auckland Islands, because people might expect the Auckland Shag to be seen somewhere near Auckland city!

Instead of just giving body length from the tip of the bill to the tip of the tail, in the 'Size' sections we have also tried to give an impression of the size of the bird by presenting the weight. Where males and females differ appreciably in size, these are given separately. The weights are only approximate, because weights of birds are highly variable, depending on such things as time of year, time of day (up to 10% difference between dawn and dusk weights of some passerines), stage in the breeding cycle (e.g. a 30% weight loss between the start and end of incubation in male kiwi, and similar declines during incubation shifts of some seabirds), and weights can be inflated when a bird is preparing for laying, moulting or migration.

We briefly review the geographical variation within each species. It is beyond the scope of this book to give all the information to allow identification to the subspecies level for all species, but location is a key guide, and specialist textbooks and papers in scientific journals will need to be consulted if in doubt.

For most landbirds breeding in New Zealand, there is no significant seasonal change in distribution, as the equable climate of New Zealand means that there is no need for major migration, although there is some evidence of altitudinal migration, local movements and some movement across Cook Strait, and the two native cuckoos migrate to the tropical Pacific. Inland breeding waders, terns and gulls show the most obvious migration within New Zealand; Banded Dotterels, Australasian Gannets, White-fronted Terns and some other seabirds visit Australia outside the breeding season. Many waders, terns and seabirds undertake major transequatorial migration, and some seabirds have a circumpolar movement pattern between breeding seasons. Much of the information on the movements of birds comes from banding (ringing) or leg-flag studies and, more recently, from radio-tracking or satellite-tracking research. If you find a dead banded bird it is important that you remove the band and send it to the address shown on the band, accompanied by details of where and when it was found. If you see, photograph or catch a live banded bird, please send band details, including colour-band combinations on each leg (the left leg is the bird's left leg), to The Banding Office, Department of Conservation, PO Box 10420, Wellington 6140, or email: bandingoffice@doc.govt.nz.

In the 'Distribution' sections, we explain in more detail the breeding distribution; historical changes since human settlement, as shown in subfossil, midden or historical evidence; discuss seasonal movements and habitat use of birds; summarise the geographical and seasonal patterns of beach-wrecked seabirds, main sites used by waterfowl and waders; and give details on the records of vagrants and stragglers from published papers in *Notornis*, from files of the Records Appraisal Committee of the Ornithological Society, and from the *Checklist*.

Many people want to know how many birds there are of a particular species. This information is now becoming available for many threatened species that are being studied or managed intensively, and for some seabird populations where it is possible to make reasonably accurate counts of birds at breeding colonies. The Ornithological Society's National Wader Census, conducted in winter and summer each year since 1983, has provided excellent information on the numbers of waders using estuaries or lake shores. For common landbird species, population estimates are not possible and so we have simply used subjective terms to describe the populations.

New Zealand is regarded as one of the world leaders in bird conservation; first, through the work of the Wildlife Service of the Department of Internal Affairs, and since 1987 through the Department of Conservation and a burgeoning number of community group projects dedicated to managing or excluding pests at a particular site. Much of this innovative management work has relied heavily on preparatory work undertaken in research sections of government departments and universities, and by amateur ornithologists, especially members of the Ornithological Society of New Zealand. Many amateurs have volunteered their time to give practical field assistance to conservation programmes, perhaps best exemplified by the Chatham Islands Taiko expeditions organised by David Crockett that led to the rediscovery of the species in 1978. Other organisations such as Ducks Unlimited, Royal Forest and Bird Protection Society and the Miranda Naturalists' Trust have helped with specific conservation programmes. The corporate sector has become increasingly active in providing financial support for bird conservation programmes, notably the Bank of New Zealand with kiwi, Genesis with Blue Ducks, Mainland Cheese with Yellow-eyed Penguin, Mitre 10 with Takahe, and Rio Tinto Alcan with Kakapo.

Almost all of our native birds are fully protected, as are migrants, vagrants, stragglers and visitors. In the 'Conservation' sections, we have given a brief outline of conservation problems for many native species and outlined the management undertaken or planned for those species. Somewhat loosely, we have also included under this heading the harvest and management of gamebirds and the impact of some bird pests.

The information on breeding has been gleaned from a variety of sources, especially the Nest Record Scheme of the Ornithological Society, which holds details of the breeding biology of about 150 species on over 30,000 cards, and from research papers and university theses. There is still much to be learnt about the basic breeding biology of even moderately common species, and for most species there are insufficient data to investigate geographical patterns of timing of breeding, clutch size, incubation and fledging periods, and productivity. Within these sections we also present what little information is known on the age at first breeding. Because a common question is: how long does Species X live?, we have given what information we could find on adult survivorship and life expectancy, and the Banding Office of the Department of Conservation has kindly provided information on the longest elapsed time between banding and recovery for a number of species; similar data have been gleaned from published material on overseas studies. In general, birds in New Zealand have relatively small clutch sizes, long incubation and fledging periods, and seem exceptionally long-lived compared with the same or similar-sized species in the Northern Hemisphere.

The 'Behaviour' sections have tended to be catch-alls for interesting snippets on whether the bird forms flocks at certain times of the year, how it relates to its mate and other birds in the breeding and non-breeding seasons, and how it relates to humans. These sections include descriptions of the main songs, calls and displays. In New Zealand, there are very few species that look so similar that calls are needed to clinch the identification, but there are many cryptic or nocturnal species that can be identified reliably from call alone.

The rapidly growing body of knowledge on the foods and feeding behaviour of New Zealand birds is summarised in the 'Feeding' sections. Many specific studies have been undertaken, but a number of incidental observations have been included in the Classified Summarised Notes section of *Notornis*.

The sections entitled 'In the hand' are intended to help identify species or subspecies of seabirds and to identify the ages and sexes of some landbirds. These accounts are aimed more at the specialist ornithologist than the general reader. The seabird-related sections are particularly aimed at Ornithological Society beach-patrollers who record the species and numbers of seabirds found dead on beaches as a means of monitoring the status of populations, searching for banded birds, and providing suitable material for museum skins for further study or display purposes. Many seabird species are similar, and beach-wrecked specimens not only smell horrible but generally do not look like the live birds depicted in the plates, and so accurate identification often relies on measurements, colours and shape of bill, wing, tail and legs.

Coverage of landbirds is aimed largely at researchers who want to determine the age and sex of birds caught so that they can distinguish different parts of the population, which may behave, breed or survive differently. Information on introduced passerines is mainly from the Central Passerine Banding Group.

At the foot of most species' accounts is a 'Reading' list of books, scientific papers or theses that contain further information about the particular species; this is in addition to the following list of more general sources and books that cover many species, particular groups of birds, or birds from specific geographical areas. The

'Reading' sections are a form of acknowledgement to those who have gathered much of the original information that we have compiled to make this book. All the references given should be available to the reader through the interloan service at any public library in New Zealand, and many are available on the internet via Google Scholar.

KEY REFERENCES

Checklist Committee (OSNZ). 2010. *Checklist of the Birds of New Zealand, Norfolk and Macquarie Islands, and the Ross Dependency, Antarctica* (4th edn). Wellington: Te Papa Press.

Handbook of Australian, New Zealand and Antarctic Birds. Melbourne: OUP. This seven-volume set, published sequentially between 1990 and 2006, with a 1–4-year interval between volumes, provides very detailed information on all that is known on New Zealand birds. This is an authoritative source of information on any species that you may wish to learn more about.

NZ Birds Online (www.nzbirdsonline.org). This website, the result of a collaboration between the Ornithological Society of New Zealand, Department of Conservation and Te Papa Tongarewa, led by Dr Colin Miskelly, is an excellent online source of information on New Zealand birds. It has photographs, sound recordings and links to further sources of information such as the third edition of this field guide.

Robertson, C. J. R., Hyvönen, P., Fraser, M. J. & Pickard, C. R. 2007. *Atlas of Bird Distribution in New Zealand 1999–2004.* Wellington: Ornithological Society of New Zealand.

STANDARD REFERENCES

The following books provide information on the birds that are found in the New Zealand region. They have been the source of much information used to compile this field guide, and all are recommended for any private or public library collection.

Bull, P. C., Gaze, P. D. & Robertson, C. J. R. 1985. *The Atlas of Bird Distribution in New Zealand.* Wellington: Ornithological Society of New Zealand.

Chambers, S. 2009. *Birds of New Zealand: Locality Guide* (3rd edn). Orewa: Arun Books.

Chandler, R. 2009. *Shorebirds of the Northern Hemisphere.* London: Christopher Helm.

Coates, B. J. 1985. *The Birds of Papua New Guinea.* Vols 1 & 2. Alderley: Dove.

Dutson, G. 2011. *Birds of Melanesia: Bismarcks, Solomons, Vanuatu and New Caledonia.* London: Christopher Helm.

Falla, R. A., Sibson, R. B. & Turbott, E. G. 1979. *The New Guide to the Birds of New Zealand and Outlying Islands.* Auckland: Collins.

Fleming, C. A. 1982. *George Edward Lodge: The Unpublished New Zealand Bird Paintings.* Wellington: Nova Pacifica and National Museum of New Zealand.

Gaze, P. D. 1994. *Rare and Endangered New Zealand Birds.* Christchurch: Canterbury University Press.

Gill, B. & Martinson, P. 1991. *New Zealand's Extinct Birds.* Auckland: Random Century.

Harrison, P. 1988. *Seabirds: An Identification Guide.* London: Christopher Helm.

Hayman, P., Marchant, J. & Prater, T. 1986. *Shorebirds: An Identification Guide to the Waders of the World.* Beckenham: Croom Helm.

Jonnson, L. 1992. *Birds of Europe, with North Africa and the Middle East.* London: Christopher Helm.

Lane, B. A. 1987. *Shorebirds in Australia.* Melbourne: Thomas Nelson.

Maclean, G. L. 1993. *Roberts' Birds of Southern Africa.* London: New Holland.

Madge, S. & Burn, H. 1988. *Wildfowl: An Identification Guide to the Ducks, Geese and Swans of the World.* London: Christopher Helm.

Morcombe, M. 2003. *Field Guide to the Birds of Australia.* Archerfield: Steve Parish Publishing.

Oliver, W. R. B. 1955. *New Zealand Birds.* Wellington: Reed.

Ombler, K. 2007. *Where to Watch Birds in New Zealand.* Auckland: New Holland.

Onley, D & Scofield, P. 2007. *Albatrosses, Petrels and Shearwaters of the World.* London: Christopher Helm.

Perrins, C. M. & Middleton, A. L. A. 1985. *The Encyclopaedia of Birds.* London: George Allen & Unwin.

Pizzey, G. & Knight, F. 2012. *The Field Guide to the Birds of Australia* (9th edn). Sydney: Harper Collins.

Pratt, H. D., Bruner, P. L. & Berrett, D. G. 1987. *A Field Guide to the Birds of Hawaii and the Tropical Pacific.* Princeton: Princeton University Press.

Pringle, J. D. 1985. *Waterbirds.* Sydney: Angus & Robertson.

Pringle, J. D. 1986. *The Shorebirds of Australia.* Sydney: Angus & Robertson.

Robertson, C. J. R. (ed.) 1985. *Reader's Digest Complete Book of New Zealand Birds.* Sydney: Reader's Digest.

Serventy, D. L., Serventy, V. & Warham, J. 1971. *The Handbook of Australian Sea-birds*. Sydney: Reed.

Simpson, K. & Day, N. 2010. *Field Guide to the Birds of Australia* (8th edn). Melbourne: Viking.

Sinclair, I., Hockey, P. & Tarboton, W. 1993. *Illustrated Guide to the Birds of Southern Africa*. London: New Holland.

Soper, M. F. 1984. *Birds of New Zealand and Outlying Islands*. Christchurch: Whitcoulls.

Svensson, L. 1992. *Identification Guide to European Passerines*. Stockholm: Lars Svensson.

Turbott, E. G. 1967. *Buller's Birds of New Zealand*. Christchurch: Whitcombe & Tombs.

Watling, D. 2001. *A Guide to the Birds of Fiji and Western Polynesia, including American Samoa, Niue, Samoa, Tokelau, Tonga, Tuvalu and Wallis & Futuna*. Suva: Environmental Consultants (Fiji) Ltd.

ACKNOWLEDGEMENTS

It would have been impossible to compile a book of this nature without considerable help from many others. We are extremely grateful for the time and efforts of the following people who have either checked texts, provided comments on earlier editions, provided unpublished data, commented constructively on artwork, or allowed free access to museum collections:

Hilary Aikman, Maida Barlow, Sandy Bartle, Kevin Bartram, Phil Battley, Brian Bell, Peter Bull, Isabel Castro-Udy, George Chance, Mick Clout, Rogan Colbourne, Rod Cossee, Les Cristidis, David Crockett, John Darby, Rose Delany, Peter Dilks, John Dowding, Graeme Elliott, Mike Fitzgerald, Ian Flux, Robin Fordham, James Fraser, John Gibb, Brian Gill, Andrew Grant, Lou Gurr, Don Hadden, Jenny Hawkins, Rod Hay, Allan Hemmings, Peter Higgins, Noel Hyde, Mike Imber, John Innes, Ian Jamieson, Paddy Latham, Linda Lawrence, John Lyall, Tim Lovegrove, Gabor Lovei, Nikki McArthur, Ian McLean, John McLennan, David Medway, Don Merton, Pat Miller, Colin Miskelly, Geoff Moon, Jim Moore, Peter Moore, Ron Moorhouse, Rory O'Brien, Colin O'Donnell, Richard Parrish, Rosemary Penwarden, Ray Pierce, Murray Potter, Mary Powlesland, Ralph Powlesland, Gwenda Pulham, Kristina Ramstad, Gretchen Rasch, Christine Reed, Adrian Riegen, Christopher Robertson, Jessica Robertson, Lea Robertson, Danny Rogers, Paul Sagar, Ed Saul, Peter Schweigman, Paul Scofield, Ken Simpson, Hamish Spencer, John Squire, Jean-Claude Stahl, Andrew Styche, Roger Sutton, Graeme Taylor, Helen Taylor, Jack Taylor, Rowley Taylor, Alan Tennyson, Phil Tisch, Geoff Tunnicliffe, Dick Veitch, Roy Weston, Murray Williams, David Wilson, Pete Wilson, Keith Woodley, Malcolm Wylie, Sandy Yong, Euan Young.

David Medway, Ray Richards, Ken Simpson and Geoff Walker helped to get the first edition off the ground, and Ian Armitage (OSNZ), Jeremy Sherlock, Catherine O'Loughlin, Andrea Davison, Kate Stockman and Anna Egan-Reid produced this edition. Chris Edkins drew the endpaper maps. Lea Robertson typed much of the new text for this edition.

To all, a big thank you!

ORNITHOLOGICAL SOCIETY OF NEW ZEALAND (OSNZ)/BIRDS NEW ZEALAND

The OSNZ, also known as Birds New Zealand, has supported the production of this field guide by commissioning Derek Onley to paint the original 74 colour plates and some black and white illustrations for the first edition, plus the addition of 11 extra plates and many new paintings in this edition. Like the authors of the earlier *Field Guide*, the authors are donating royalties from sales of this book to the Society to support further bird study in New Zealand.

The object of the OSNZ, which was founded in 1939, is to encourage, organise and carry out ornithological field work on a national scale. No special qualifications are needed for membership, except for an interest in the study of the habits and distribution of birds.

Because members are scattered throughout New Zealand, the Society operates chiefly by organising cooperative investigations, encouraging individual projects, and by issuing publications such as the quarterly scientific journal *Notornis* and accompanying newsletter, *Birds New Zealand*.

An ornithological library containing many of the world's leading ornithological journals is maintained at the Auckland War Memorial Museum. The main field activities include collection of data on storm-killed seabirds and numbers of waders in summer and winter at key estuaries and coastal lagoons, special inquiries on the status of birds common and rare, and studies of the movements of birds throughout the country.

Further information about the OSNZ can be obtained by visiting: www.osnz.org.nz.

SPECIAL THANKS

A bequest from the estate of Marjory Maud Davis (1920–2011), made available through the Canterbury branch of OSNZ, has enabled the painting of new illustrations for this revised edition. Marj was born in Tasmania, but moved to Rangiora at primary school age and later attended Hagley High School before training as a pharmacist. She was an active member of OSNZ, involved in projects on Red-capped Dotterel, Wrybill and Hutton's Shearwater, among others.

GLOSSARY

Australasia: the region including Australia, eastern Indonesia, New Guinea, the southwestern Pacific and NZ
axillaries: feathers of the 'armpit' where the underwing joins the body
banding: marking of birds with a uniquely numbered metal band (ring) on the leg, often with a combination of coloured plastic bands or flags to allow recognition of individuals or an age/sex class without the need to recapture the birds
carpal bar: a dark band at the bend of the folded wing, particularly noticeable in some immature terns
caruncles: fleshy growths on the facial skin of some shags near the nostrils
cere: waxy covering of the upper bill of certain birds, e.g. hawks, parrots, pigeons; often brightly coloured
cline: a gradual change from one end of a bird's range to the other, usually of size or colour
coverts: feathers that cover the bases of the main wing feathers and tail feathers
culmen: the ridge along the whole length or top of the upper mandible
dimorphic: species with two forms or phases, usually of plumage or size, e.g. raptors, Stewart Island Shag, Stitchbird
eclipse: dull plumage assumed by males, especially, ducks after breeding; they become very like females and immatures
endangered: likely to become extinct if not managed carefully
endemic: natural range is in a certain country and nowhere else, e.g. Kiwi and Kakapo are found in NZ only
feral: living wild after domestication
filoplumes: simple threadlike white plumes; appear in breeding plumage of some seabirds and shags
fledge: fully feathered; able to fly (fledgling)
flight feathers: the primaries, secondaries and tertials of the wings (remiges) and the main feathers of the tail (rectrices)
front: the forehead between the base of the upper bill and the crown, e.g. White-fronted Tern
frontal shield: horny shield on the forehead, taking the place of feathers, e.g. Pukeko
gape: fleshy skin at the sides of the base of the bill
gregarious: living together in flocks or in colonies
gular sac or pouch: the elastic naked skin of the throat that can be filled with food (pelicans) or air (frigatebirds)
Holarctic: includes all the Arctic region
immature: stages of plumage between the first moult and the breeding plumage (= subadult)
introduced: a bird brought to NZ by people, not by its own efforts
invertebrates: animals without a backbone, with an external skeleton, e.g. crustaceans, insects, spiders
juvenile: birds in their first plumage after replacing natal down (US = juvenal)
lamellae: fine, comb-like structure of the bill used to sieve very small prey
lobes: folds of skin on the toes, extending out for swimming and closing when feet are drawn back, e.g. grebes and coot; the equivalent of webs in ducks
maimai: duckshooting hide or blind
mandibles: the upper and lower parts of a bird's bill
mantle: the upper back
midden: the remains (often bones, shell and charcoal) of Maori feasting, showing that a species used to be locally present
migrant: a species that moves annually and seasonally between breeding and non-breeding areas, either within NZ, e.g. Wrybill, or to other countries, e.g. Bar-tailed Godwit. Includes species which reach NZ each year, even if in small numbers, e.g. Pectoral Sandpiper
mollusc: an invertebrate with a shell as a skeleton; varies from shellfish to squid in water, to snails on land
monogamous: having only one mate (cf. polygamous)
moult: the annual, or more periodic, replacement of all feathers; because feathers are soft they fray and lose their effectiveness in flight, insulation and waterproofing
mustelid: a group of mammalian predators (ferrets, stoats and weasels) introduced to NZ in the late 1800s in a misguided and vain attempt to control rabbits
nape: the back of a bird's neck
native: birds that are naturally found in a country, e.g. Tui and Fantail, or are self-introduced, e.g. the Welcome Swallow
Nearctic: belonging to the arctic zone of North America
Palaearctic: belonging to the arctic zone of Europe and Asia

pakihi: open boggy wetlands with a mix of rushes and shrubs
pelagic: of the ocean; feeding far out to sea
phase: a particular colour form of adults that persists throughout life, e.g. black Fantail
possum: the brush-tailed possum *Trichosurus vulpecula* is a browsing marsupial introduced to NZ from Australia
predator: an animal that takes birds or their eggs and chicks
protrusile tongue: can be extended to reach into flowers for nectar
rachis: the main shaft of a feather
raptor: a bird of prey
rat, ship: Rattus rattus, the 'black rat' or 'roof rat'; climbs well and so it is the most dangerous predatory rat; arrived here about 1880
rat, Pacific: R. exulans, (kiore); a predator that arrived with Maori about 1000 years ago, and takes eggs and chicks; common on many offshore islands, but now rare on the NZ mainland
rat, Norway: R. norvegicus, the 'brown rat'; climbs less readily than ship rat; arrived here about 1770.
regurgitate: bring back into the mouth food that has been swallowed and digested
scapulars: feathers that lie along upper shoulder of the wing, sometimes distinctively coloured, e.g. Black-fronted Dotterel
scrape: a shallow depression in the ground or in low vegetation to serve as a nest
species: distinct forms of birds which would not normally interbreed if they lived together
speculum: iridescent patch on the upperwing secondary feathers of ducks
straggler: a bird that follows its normal migratory path but goes too far or strays off course
subfossil: bones too young to be a true fossil, e.g. in sand dunes or caves
subspecies: a geographical race of a species that has some consistent differences from others of the species
taxon: (plural *taxa*) any taxonomic group, usually referring to species or subspecies that have not been clearly defined or where there is a mix of species and/or subspecies being discussed
taxonomy: the system of classifying birds (and other organisms) to reflect their natural relationships
threatened: species that are in low numbers or declining in number and/or range and that require management or intervention to ensure their survival
vagrant: a wanderer; a bird that has turned up unexpectedly in an unusual direction, having strayed there by mistake or that, having been caught up in a severe storm, is blown well off course, whereas a straggler is in about the right direction but has gone further than usual
vestigial: a non-functional remnant of something other birds have, e.g. tail of grebes, wings of kiwi
visitor: species which disperse from mating areas and some reach NZ every year, e.g. Thin-billed Prion
wattles: colourful fleshy drupes on either side of the gape in Saddleback, Kokako and Huia
wingbar: a band of contrast, usually white, on the upperwing in flight, often formed by the coloured tips of the wing-coverts

LIST OF PLATES

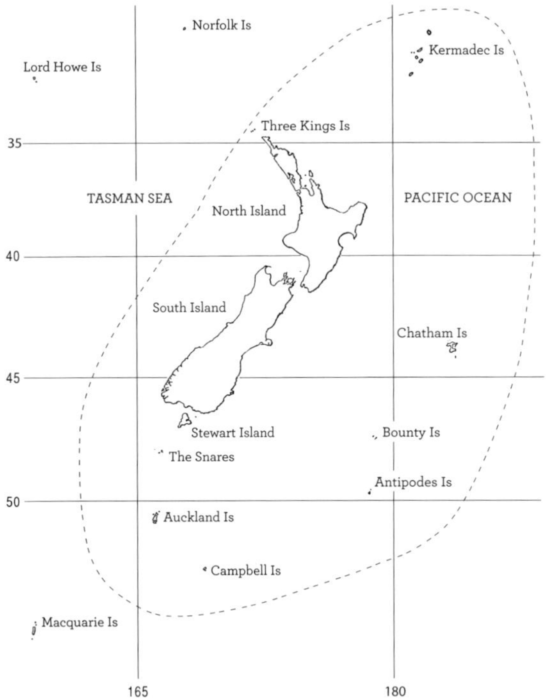

The New Zealand region

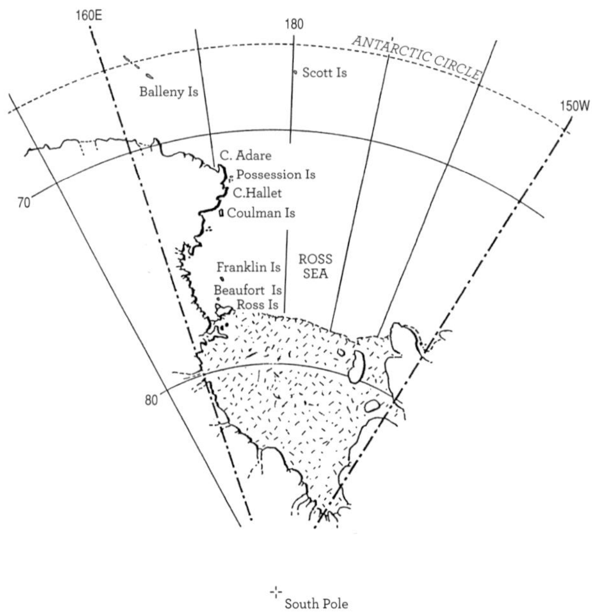

Ross Dependency

Parts of a bird

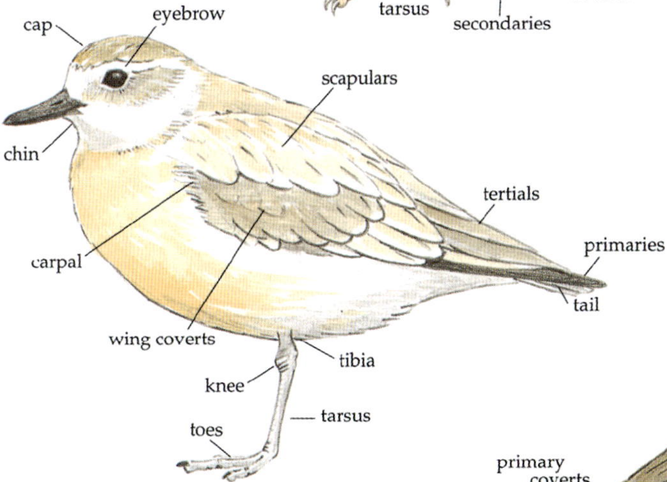

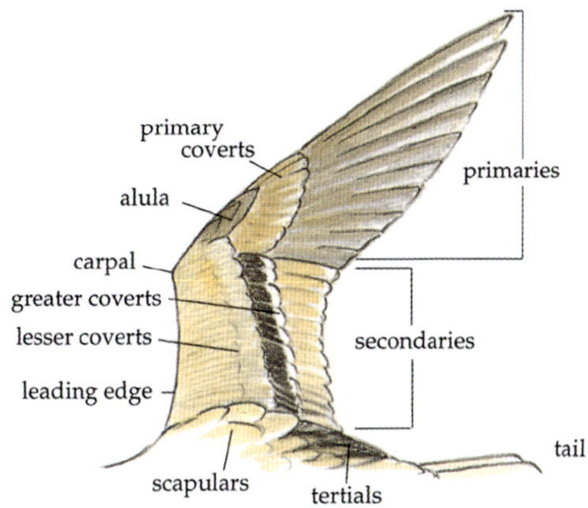

Upperwing

Key to distribution maps

- Distribution at sea
- Distribution on land
- Important distribution or breeding sites

Note: On the facing pages, Sp 1 refers to the first species in the handbook, Sp 2 to the second, and so on.

Distinctive flightless and generally nocturnal ratites. Males smaller and have loud, shrill, clear ascending whistle; females deeper hoarser cry; calls repeated 10–25 times. Long bill with nostrils uniquely near tip; minute remnant wings and no tail; coarse loose feathers; strong legs and toes with long sharp claws. Lumbering deliberate gait, but can run fast. In forest, scrub, tussock, bush patches and adjacent farmland from sea level to subalpine. Kiwi snuffle as they explore for food on ground. Feed on large invertebrates and fallen fruits, from surface or by probing up to 10cm into the soil. Lay 1–2 huge eggs in a burrow, hollow log or under dense vegetation. Very long incubation. Chicks hatch fully feathered, like miniature adults, and are mobile within a week, but return to the nest each day for weeks or months. Slow growing, taking about 4 years to reach full size.

ROWI *Apteryx rowi*

Rare endemic

40cm;♂ 1.9kg, ♀ 2.7kg. Dark greyish brown *streaked lengthways* brown, often has white patches on face; long ivory bill. Male has shrill, clear, ascending whistle; female has lower-pitched hoarse cry; calls repeated 10–25 times. **Habitat:** Native forest near Okarito; small populations have been established on Mana and Blumine islands, and Motuara Island is used as a crèche. **Breeding:** Jun–Feb. [Sp 2]

BROWN KIWI *Apteryx mantelli*

Uncommon endemic

40cm;♂ 2.2kg, ♀ 2.8kg. Dark greyish brown *streaked lengthways* reddish brown; long ivory bill. Male has shrill, clear, ascending whistle; female has lower-pitched hoarse cry; calls repeated 10–25 times. **Habitat:** Native forest, scrub, exotic forest (especially in Northland, Coromandel and eastern Bay of Plenty) and adjacent farmland. Strongholds in Northland, northern Coromandel, Te Urewera NP and inland Taranaki–Whanganui. **Breeding:** Jun–Apr. [Sp 1]

TOKOEKA *Apteryx australis*

Uncommon endemic

45cm;♂ 2.4kg, ♀ 3.1kg. Brown *streaked lengthways* reddish brown; long ivory bill. Male has shrill, clear, ascending whistle; female has lower-pitched hoarse cry; calls repeated 10–25 times. **Habitat:** Native forest, scrub, tussockland. Most common on Stewart Island and in western Fiordland. Recently Haast birds have been introduced to Rarotoka, Coal and Pomona islands, and Orokonui Ecosanctuary (Dunedin). **Breeding:** Jul–Feb. [Sp 3]

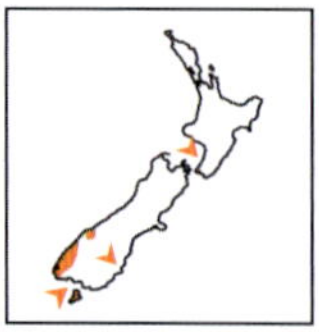

GREAT SPOTTED KIWI (Roroa) *Apteryx haastii*

Uncommon endemic

45cm;♂ 2.4kg, ♀ 3.3kg. Light brownish grey *mottled or banded horizontally* with white; long ivory bill; legs and feet dark brown. Male has shrill warbling whistle; female has lower-pitched ascending warble; calls repeated 8–20 times. **Habitat:** Native forest, scrub, tussockland. Strongholds in Kahurangi NP, Paparoa Range and Arthur's Pass NP. **Breeding:** Jul–Feb. [Sp 5]

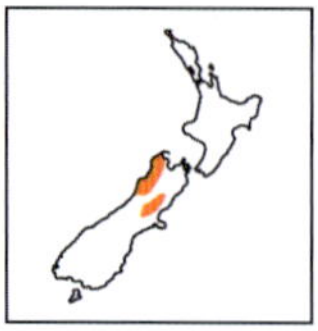

LITTLE SPOTTED KIWI (Kiwi pukupuku) *Apteryx owenii*

Rare endemic

30cm;♂ 1150g, ♀ 1325g. Light brownish grey *mottled or banded horizontally* with white; long ivory bill; legs and feet pale pink. Male has shrill ascending whistle; female lower and more tremulous warble; calls faster and higher-pitched than other kiwi; repeated 12–25 times. **Habitat:** Native forest, scrub and grassland; mainly Kapiti Island, but introduced to several offshore islands, including Tiritiri Matangi and Motuihe, and Zealandia (Wellington). **Breeding:** Aug–Jan. [Sp 4]

ROWI
BROWN KIWI
TOKOEKA
GREAT SPOTTED KIWI
LITTLE SPOTTED KIWI

All gamebirds are introduced, often with great persistence and cost. Small to large plump birds that feed on the ground. Omnivorous but mainly take plant food, scratching and digging at the ground surface with legs and strong claws, and bill. When disturbed, they crouch, run to cover, or burst from cover with whirring wings and alarm notes, flying fast and low to pitch a short distance away. Sexes usually differ: females and immatures have subdued plumage that blends with the surroundings; males are sometimes brightly coloured, but even strongly patterned males blend with their surroundings. Immatures are usually seen with adults, so identity should not be a problem.

PHEASANT (Ring-necked Pheasant) *Phasianus colchicus* — Common European introduction

♂ 80cm, 1400g; ♀ 60cm, 1200g. Long-tailed gamebird. Male colourful, mainly rich orange-reds, glossy dark green head, red facial wattles. Female smaller, pale brown heavily mottled dark brown, lacks facial wattles. Male territorial call a loud, abrupt crow: 'kok-kok', with emphasis on the second syllable. Explodes suddenly from undergrowth when disturbed, with noisy wingbeats and rapid calls, and glides back to cover. **Habitat:** Open scrubland, vegetated sand dunes, riverbanks and agricultural land with plenty of cover. **Breeding:** Jul–Mar. [Sp 14]

PEAFOWL *Pavo cristatus* — Uncommon Asian introduction

90cm (+ male's 1m tail);♂ 4.5kg, ♀ 3.5kg. Peacock distinctive and well known; peahen smaller, brown mottled black and white, and with a pointed tail. The peacock's loud wailing *trumpet-like cry* – 'kay-yaaw' – draws attention. Roosts in trees. **Habitat:** Parks and private gardens, rough agricultural land with good cover in warm, dry districts. **Breeding:** Aug–Jan. [Sp 15]

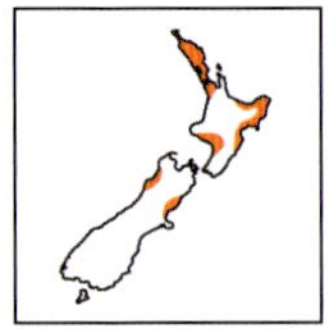

WILD TURKEY *Meleagris gallopavo* — Locally common North American introduction

♂ 120cm, 8kg; ♀ 90cm, 4kg. Large black bird with blue and red head. Male black with paler barred wings and tail; beard of long feathers hangs from upper chest; head and neck naked and wrinkled, blue and red. Female smaller and browner, and lacks beard and neck wattles. The familiar territorial gobbling is mainly by males. Seldom flies, except to roost in trees. **Habitat:** Farmland, especially where there is good cover. **Breeding:** Season unknown in NZ. [Sp 16]

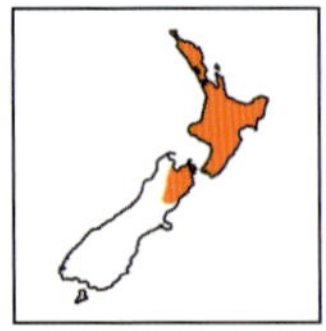

HELMETED GUINEAFOWL *Numida meleagris* — Rare African introduction

60cm, 1500g. Large rounded gamebird with a small blue-grey bare head, red wattles, and a bony horn protruding from the crown. Body slate grey thickly spotted white. Sexes alike. Roosts in trees. **Habitat:** Semi-feral at many farms and rural homesteads; a few are feral in rough agricultural land in Northland, Waikato, Rotorua and Whanganui. **Breeding:** Oct–Feb. [Sp 7]

FERAL CHICKEN *Gallus gallus* — Locally common Asian introduction

40cm;♂ 850g, ♀ 550g. Highly variable plumage forms have been bred during 8000 years of domestication. In the 'wild type' of the Red Junglefowl, the male is a vibrant mix of reds, browns and greens, with a long, erect, dark green tail curled down at the tip, red fleshy comb and wattles; female dull brown and black. **Habitat:** Semi-feral or free-range at many farms and rural homesteads; a few are feral at rest areas off highways, where their diet is supplemented with scraps from picnickers. **Breeding:** Season unknown in NZ. [Sp 13]

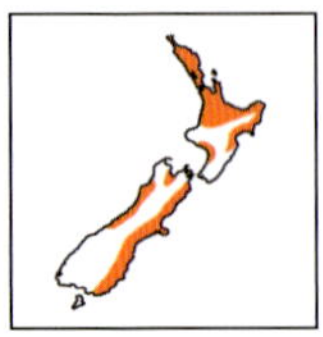

PHEASANT
♂
♀
PEAFOWL
♂
♀
WILD TURKEY
FERAL CHICKEN
HELMETED GUINEAFOWL

GREY PARTRIDGE *Perdix perdix*

Rare European introduction

30cm, 500g. Medium-sized *grey* partridge, mottled brown on back and barred chestnut on flanks. Male has *orange-brown face and throat and dark horseshoe-shaped patch on breast.* Female has paler face and less distinct patch on breast. Bill and legs blue-grey. In flight, *mottled upperparts and rusty tail.* Flight fast direct and low with rapid whirring wingbeats; when flushed, a covey usually keeps together. Voice is sharp 'kirrik', likened to rusty gate hinges. **Habitat:** Open country with dense cover. **Breeding:** Season unknown in NZ.**[Sp 10]**

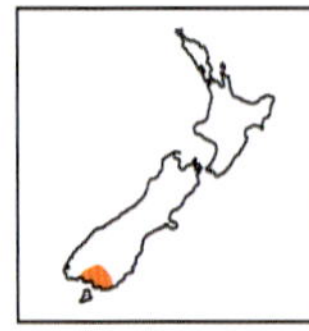

RED-LEGGED PARTRIDGE *Alectoris rufa*

Rare European introduction

31cm, 500g. Like Chukor in size, plumage, bright red bill and legs, and voice, but has *black necklace higher on throat, streaked black and white* on lower throat and sides of neck; *crown, nape and hindneck brown.* Flank bars are more chestnut than black. Sexes alike. In flight, shows *plain grey-brown back.* **Habitat:** Open country with dense cover, such as riverbeds flanked by willows and gorse. **Breeding:** Season unknown in NZ. **[Sp 9]**

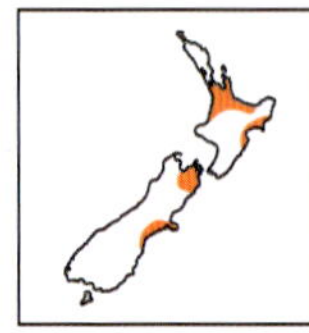

CHUKOR *Alectoris chukar*

Locally common Asian introduction

31cm;♂ 600g, ♀ 500g. Like Red-legged Partridge but has *solid clear-cut black necklace* that crosses *low on the throat*; *crown, nape and hindneck grey.* Flank bars are more black than chestnut. Sexes alike. In flight, *upperparts plain grey with rusty wash at base of wings* and rusty outer tail feathers. When flushed, a covey usually scatters. Voice a loud 'chuck-chuck-chuck-per-chuck-per-chuck-chuckar-chuckar-chuckar'. **Habitat:** South Island hill country, especially rocky hillsides with tussock and sparse scrub. **Breeding:** Sep–Feb. **[Sp 8]**

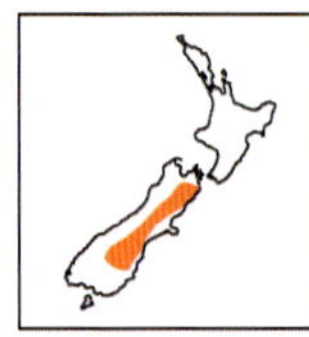

CALIFORNIA QUAIL *Callipepla californica*

Common North American introduction

25cm, 180g. Small partridge with forward-curving topknot crest plume, smaller in female. Male has a black throat bordered by a white band, blue-grey breast and scaly upperparts. Female duller. Male has a loud 3-syllable call: 'chi-ca-go' or 'where are you?', with emphasis on the second syllable. **Habitat:** Open country with patches of low scrub, riverbeds flanked by willows and gorse. **Breeding:** Sep–Mar. **[Sp 6]**

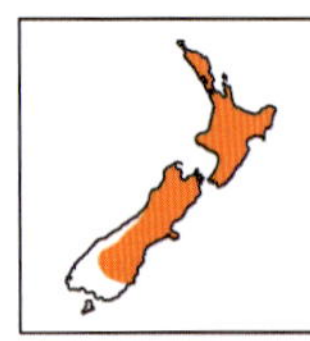

BROWN QUAIL *Coturnix ypsilophora*

Locally common Australian introduction

18cm, 100g. *Very small rounded brown quail.* Mottled black and chestnut above; fine wavy bars below. Bill dark, eye reddish, legs yellowish. Sexes alike. Call a plaintive languid 'ker-wee', the second syllable drawn out and with rising inflexion. **Habitat:** Scrub edges in rough farmland; most common in Northland, uncommon further south. **Breeding:** Sep–Feb. **[Sp 12]**

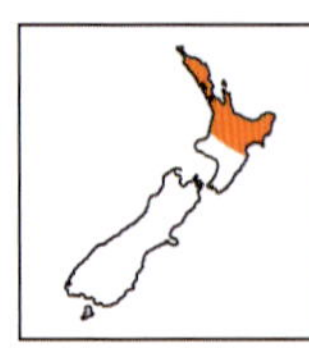

BOBWHITE QUAIL *Colinus virginianus*

Rare North American introduction

23cm, 180g. Small quail with *longitudinal pale chestnut stripes on the flanks*, dark grey bill and yellowish-brown legs. Male has *white face, black cap and line through eye* to join black necklace across throat, trailing down onto breast. Female has yellowish-buff face and brown markings. Male call a whistling 'poor-bob-white', with accent on the last note. **Habitat:** Low scrub with grassy clearings; may persist in South Auckland and northern Hawke's Bay. **Breeding:** Season unknown in NZ. **[Sp 11]**

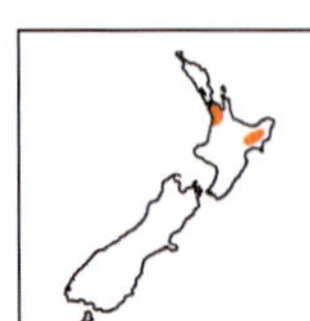

GREY PARTRIDGE
♂
♀
RED-LEGGED PARTRIDGE
CHUKOR
CALIFORNIA QUAIL
♂
♀
BROWN QUAIL
BOBWHITE QUAIL
♂
♀

Aquatic birds with a small rounded head, short flattened bill, rounded body, short legs, webbed feet and a waddling gait on land. They fly strongly with neck outstretched. Sexes alike in swans and geese, but male ducks are usually more colourful than females. Lay large clutches. Chicks leave the nest within days but are guarded for several months until they can fly.

BLACK SWAN *Cygnus atratus* — **Common Australian introduction**

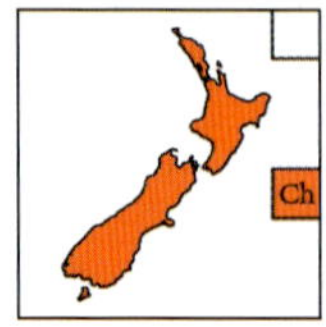

120cm;♂ 6kg, ♀ 5kg. *Very large black swan.* Bill crimson with white tip and bar near tip. Juvenile is ashy brown with a dull red bill. Takes off laboriously and noisily, running across the surface, wings striking on each downstroke. Flies with long neck extended and slow deep wingbeats, showing *prominent white wing tips.* Flocks fly in long skeins. *Voice a musical bugling.* Feeds mainly on vegetation by dabbling at the surface, upending to reach bottom plants, or grazing on nearby damp pasture. **Habitat:** Lakes, estuaries and parks; sometimes seen at sea or on pasture. **Breeding:** Jul–Feb. [Sp 19]

MUTE SWAN *Cygnus olor* — **Rare European introduction**

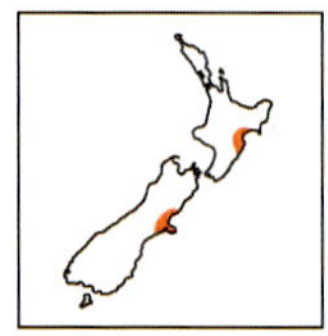

150cm;♂ 12kg, ♀ 9kg. *Very large white swan.* Bill orange with a black knob at the base, larger in breeding males. Juvenile grey-brown, paler than juvenile Black Swan; grey bill bordered with black at the base and lacking knob. Not mute but usually silent. Noisy 'swishing' flight with long neck extended. **Habitat:** Lakes, parks and private waterfowl collections. **Breeding:** Sep–Jan. [Sp 18]

CANADA GOOSE *Branta canadensis* — **Common North American introduction**

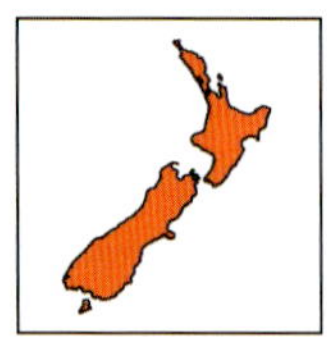

83cm;♂ 5.4kg, ♀ 4.5kg. *Large brown goose* with pale brown and white barring below; *black neck and head with conspicuous white patch on cheeks and chin.* Loud *honking* call given when alarmed and in flight. Flocks fly in V-formation. Grazes on pasture, young crops and aquatic plants. **Habitat:** High-country pasture, freshwater lakes and margins, and coastal lagoons. **Breeding:** Sep–Feb. [Sp 22]

CAPE BARREN GOOSE *Cereopsis novaehollandiae* — **Rare Australian introduction**

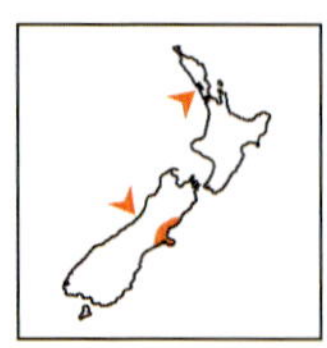

87cm, 5kg. *Large bulky pale grey goose* with dark spots on scapulars and wing coverts. *Bill short and largely covered by a greenish-yellow cere*; legs pink and feet black. In flight, uniformly grey with black tail and wingtips. Grazes on pasture plants. **Habitat:** Parks, occasionally on lakes. Vagrants may occasionally reach NZ. **Breeding:** Season unknown in NZ. [Sp 20]

FERAL GOOSE *Anser anser* — **Common European introduction**

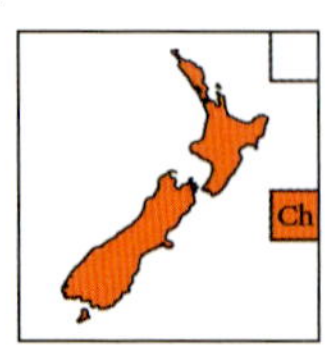

80cm, 3kg. The familiar domestic goose of farms and parks, often feral. Males are all white, females white with brown on wings and thighs. Juveniles all grey-brown. Bill, legs and feet orange-pink. Usually graze away from water. **Habitat:** Lakes, estuaries and farmland. **Breeding:** Season unknown in NZ. [Sp 21]

juv
BLACK SWAN
juv
MUTE SWAN
CANADA GOOSE
CAPE BARREN GOOSE
♂
♀
FERAL GOOSE

PARADISE SHELDUCK (Putangitangi) *Tadorna variegata* **Common endemic**

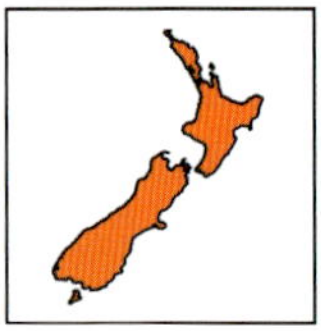

63cm;♂ 1700g, ♀ 1400g. Large goose-like duck with *orange-chestnut undertail* and tertials. Male has *black head with greenish gloss, body dark grey finely barred black.* Female has *brilliant white head, body bright orange-chestnut,* obscured by darker fine barring in eclipse plumage. Juveniles like male, but immature females develop white patches around eyes and at base of bill. In flight, prominent white patches on upperwings. Often call; male a deep 'zonk-zonk . . .', female a shrill 'zeek, zeek . . .' Mostly seen as pairs or in large flocks, especially during the moult in Dec–Mar. **Habitat:** Farmland, lakes, ponds and high-country riverbeds. **Breeding:** Aug–Dec. **[Sp 24]**

CHESTNUT-BREASTED SHELDUCK *Tadorna tadornoides* **Uncommon vagrant**

65cm;♂ 1600g, ♀ 1300g. Like male Paradise Shelduck, but *undertail black and chest and lower neck orange-chestnut, bordered above by thin white collar.* Male has upper back and breast pale orange-chestnut, thin white collar, and occasionally has a small white patch at base of bill. Female has darker orange-chestnut upper back and breast, very thin white collar and white patches at base of bill and around eye. Juvenile like female but smaller, duller and lacks collar. Often seen with Paradise Shelduck in NZ. **Habitat:** Freshwater and brackish lakes. First recorded in 1973, bred in eastern South Island in 1980s and 1990s, but not since. **Breeding:** Season unknown in NZ. **[Sp 25]**

BLUE DUCK (Whio) *Hymenolaimus malacorhynchos* **Uncommon endemic**

53cm;♂ 900g, ♀ 750g. *Blue-grey duck with a pale pink bill,* tipped with black flaps. Adult has yellow eyes, breast spotted reddish chestnut. Sexes similar. Juvenile has dull grey bill and eyes, and fewer breast spots. Uniformly grey in flight. Male call a whistling 'whio, whio' (fee-o, fee-o); female call a rattling growl; often call together in flight. Remain in territorial pairs all year. Seen standing on rocks or feeding with head and neck underwater. **Habitat:** 2000–3000 birds in fast-flowing mountain streams and rivers, mainly in native forest or tussockland, occasionally on lakes. **Breeding:** Jul–Jan. **[Sp 28]**

AUSTRALIAN WOOD DUCK *Chenonetta jubata* **Rare Australian vagrant**

48cm, 800g. *Pale grey duck with chest spotted brown,* head dark brown, and short thin bill. Male has dark brown head and neck, with a short black mane on back of head; grey flanks. Female has pale lines above and below eye; flanks broadly barred brown and white. Juvenile like female but duller. In the water, sits higher than other ducks. Spends much time out of water grazing or roosting. Upright stance. Call a rising 'mew' or 'wee-ow'. **Habitat:** Grassland near wetlands. **[Sp 27]**

PLUMED WHISTLING DUCK (Grass Whistling Duck) *Dendrocygna eytoni*

Rare Australian vagrant

50cm, 800g. Pale brown duck with goose-like profile and *stiff cream plumes curving up from the flanks* to above back. Bill flecked pink and grey. Sexes alike. Juvenile paler with small plumes. In flight, head held below the horizontal, back hunched and legs trailing. When flying, constantly twittering and whistling; the wings also whistle. **Habitat:** Grassland near wetlands. **[Sp 17]**

PARADISE SHELDUCK
♀
♂
♀ eclipse
♂
♀
♀ imm
CHESTNUT-BREASTED
SHELDUCK
♂
♀
♀
BLUE DUCK
AUSTRALIAN WOOD DUCK
♂
♀
PLUMED WHISTLING DUCK

GREY TEAL (Tete) *Anas gracilis*

Common native

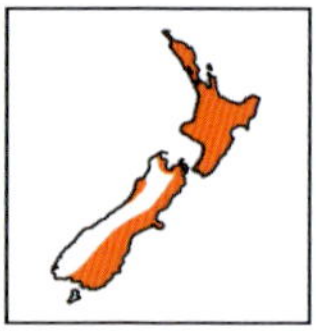

43cm;♂ 505g, ♀ 470g. *Delicate light grey-brown duck with pale grey cheeks, chin and foreneck*. Silhouette rounded, including head. Sits high and upright on the water. Bill blue-grey; *eye red*. Sexes alike. Juvenile paler, eye brown. In flight, speculum black with a green sheen, a narrow white bar behind, and a *prominent white triangle* in front; underwing white in the centre. Wingbeats very fast. Feeds by filtering on water surface or dredging bill in soft mud. **Habitat:** Lowland lakes and lagoons, and estuaries. **Breeding:** Jun–Feb. [Sp 29]

CHESTNUT TEAL *Anas castanea*

Rare Australian vagrant

♂ 45cm, 680g; ♀ 40cm, 590g. Like large dark-faced Grey Teal. Breeding male has *dark glossy green head and neck, bright chestnut underparts, a large white flank patch and a black undertail.* Female and juvenile like Grey Teal, but *pale buff rather than whitish chin and throat*, and dark crown is less distinct. Eclipse male like a dark female, but traces of colour are usually apparent. Bill blue-grey; *eye red*. In flight, wing pattern like Grey Teal. **Habitat:** Lowland lakes and estuaries. [Sp 30]

BROWN TEAL (Pateke) *Anas chlorotis*

Rare endemic

48cm;♂ 650g, ♀ 580g. Like Chestnut Teal, but *eye brown with narrow white eye-ring* in all plumages. In flight, *lacks white triangle* in front of speculum. Breeding male has a glossy green head, an *indistinct narrow white collar* and a conspicuous white flank patch. Eclipse male, female and juvenile are warm brown; breast is mottled dark brown. Bill blue-black. Gather to roost in flocks by day, and feed at dusk and at night. **Habitat:** Tidal creeks, lagoons and swamps, and adjacent wet pasture. The 2000–2500 Brown Teal are mostly on Great Barrier Island, eastern Northland and Coromandel. **Breeding:** Jul–Nov. [Sp 31]

AUCKLAND ISLANDS TEAL *Anas aucklandica*

Rare endemic

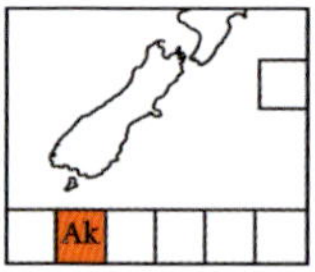

45cm;♂ 550g, ♀ 420g. Like Brown Teal, but flightless and colours more subdued. **Habitat:** Restricted to the Auckland Islands. Mainly in peaty creeks and soaks, and on wave platforms and kelp beds. **Breeding:** Dec–Feb. [Sp 32]

CAMPBELL ISLANDS TEAL *Anas nesiotis*

Rare endemic

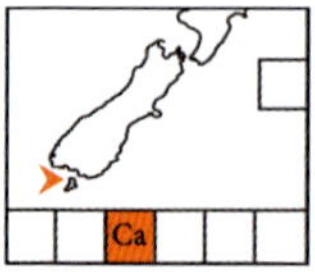

43cm;♂ 450g, ♀ 350g. Like Brown Teal, but flightless and prominent white eye-ring. **Habitat:** Restricted to the Campbell Islands, except for some introduced to Codfish Island. Mainly in peaty creeks and soaks, and on wave platforms and kelp beds. **Breeding:** Oct–Feb. [Sp 33]

GREY TEAL
CHESTNUT TEAL
♀
♂
BROWN TEAL
♀
♂ breeding
♀
♂
♂
AUCKLAND ISLANDS TEAL
CAMPBELL ISLANDS TEAL

NEW ZEALAND SCAUP (Papango) *Aythya novaeseelandiae* **Locally common endemic**

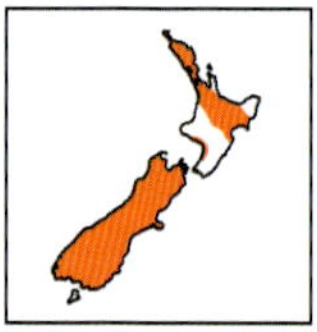

40cm,♂ 700g, ♀ 600g. Small blackish diving duck with *rounded toy 'rubber duckie' profile* and a *steep forehead*. Male *glossy black*, maroon on flanks and brown on belly. Bill blue-grey, tipped black; eye *golden-yellow*. Female *blackish brown*, usually with *vertical white band at the base of the bill*; eye *brown*. Juvenile like female but no white on face. In flight, upperwing has a broad white trailing band from wingtip, but *not reaching body*; underwing white. Patters along water when taking off and flies low to the surface. Feeds on bottom weeds and invertebrates by diving. **Habitat:** Large deep freshwater lakes, including hydro lakes; also coastal dune lakes. **Breeding:** Oct–Mar. **[Sp 40]**

AUSTRALIAN WHITE-EYED DUCK *Aythya australis* **Rare Australian vagrant**

48cm, 900g. Diving duck like NZ Scaup, but *chocolate brown with white undertail*; *forehead slopes gently*. Bill dark grey with whitish band near the end, tipped black. Male has *white eye*; female brown eye. Female and juvenile lighter brown than male, and white patch on bill is smaller. In flight, upperwing has a broad white trailing band *from wingtip to body*; underwing white. Feeds and roosts on water, rarely coming onto land. **Habitat:** Large deep freshwater lakes, occasionally estuaries. **[Sp 39]**

PINK-EARED DUCK *Malacorhynchus membranaceus* **Rare Australian vagrant**

40cm, 400g. Small duck with a large square-ended bill, black flaps at the tip. Back and wings grey-brown, distinctly *striped dark brown and white on lower neck, breast and flanks*; white flank patch extends across rump; undertail yellow-brown. *Large dark patch around eye*, contrasting white eye-ring, and small pink patch on ear coverts. In flight, *white rump contrasts with grey-brown upperwing and back, and dark brown white-tipped tail.* Constant chirruping call on the water and in flight. Feeds by filtering with bill submerged up to eyes. **Habitat:** Lakes. One NZ record: Auckland, 1990. **[Sp 23]**

NORTHERN PINTAIL *Anas acuta* **Rare Arctic vagrant**

55cm, 800g. Large slender duck with *long slim neck and long pointed tail*; *bill, legs and feet grey with black webs.* Flight swift with rapid wingbeats. Floats higher than most ducks, accentuated by a raised tail. Breeding male has chocolate brown head and neck, with a white streak down the side of the nape from eye level; *white patch on thigh*; speculum green. Long thin central pair of tail feathers project 10cm beyond rest of tail. Eclipse male, female and juvenile are brown with pale buff edges to feathers on body and finely streaked buff on neck and head; speculum brown. **Habitat:** Lowland wetlands; one NZ record: Farewell Spit, 1997. **[Sp 34]**

juv
♂
♀
NEW ZEALAND SCAUP
AUSTRALIAN WHITE-EYED DUCK
♂
♀
PINK-EARED DUCK
♀
♂
NORTHERN PINTAIL

MALLARD *Anas platyrhynchos*

Abundant European introduction

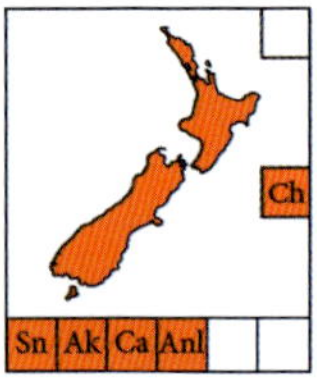

58cm;♂ 1300g, ♀ 1100g. The familiar duck of parks and farm ponds. *All have orange legs and feet, and a blue speculum bordered with thin black and broader white bands front and back.* Breeding male has dark glossy green head, chestnut breast, pale grey body, black rump and undertail; bill yellow-green. Female is streaked and spotted brown and buff on body and wings; bill brownish grey with orange at base, sides and tip. Eclipse male like female but has greyer head and neck, with remnants of green on crown and nape, and chestnut wash on breast. Juvenile similar to female. Variable plumage because of interbreeding with Grey Duck. Feeds by dabbling on water surface or by upending; also grazes and eats cereals. Rises nearly vertically from water and flies with fast shallow wingbeats. Female call the well-known 'quack, quack'; male call a soft high-pitched 'quek'. **Habitat:** Wetlands, estuaries, rivers, farm ditches, parks and cereal crops. **Breeding:** Jul–Jan. [Sp 35]

GREY DUCK (Parera) *Anas superciliosa*

Very rare native

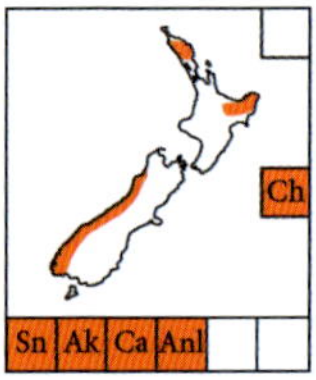

55cm;♂ 1100g, ♀ 1000g. Like female Mallard but *darker with conspicuously striped pale head, grey bill, greenish-brown legs and feet. Green speculum with black borders and thin white band on trailing edge only.* Sexes alike. In flight, looks dark with a very pale head and upper neck. Calls like Mallard. Has interbred extensively with the Mallard to produce paler birds with less distinct facial stripes and greyish bills, yellowish-brown legs and feet, and blue speculum. **Habitat:** Pure birds very rare, mainly in remote wetlands, including forest lakes and rivers. **Breeding:** Aug–Jan. [Sp 36]

AUSTRALASIAN SHOVELER (Kuruwhengi) *Anas rhynchotis*

Common native

49cm;♂ 650g, ♀ 600g. Duck with heavy spatulate bill. Sits low in the water and profile shows no apparent forehead. Breeding male has *blue-grey head with a white crescent in front of golden eye*; breast off-white with extensive dark brown mottling; flanks bright chestnut with prominent *white patch at base of tail*. Bill dark grey; legs orange. Eclipse male has head speckled blue-grey, underparts mottled bronzy chestnut, with paler (sometimes almost white) breast, and lacks white flank patch. Female streaked and spotted brown and buff on body; bill grey with some pale orange at base and sides in some birds. In flight, *upperwing has sky-blue panel on inner forewing, narrow white wingbars and dark green speculum*. Flight swift, wings noticeably narrow and pointed. Whistling wings and jinking flight as it approaches to land. Birds utter a quiet 'cuck-cuck-cuck . . .'. Feeds by sieving seeds and small aquatic animals through immersed bill. **Habitat:** Mainly shallow lowland wetlands, and muddy estuaries. **Breeding:** Oct–Feb. [Sp 37]

NORTHERN SHOVELER *Anas clypeata*

Rare Arctic vagrant

50cm, 650g. Like Australasian Shoveler, including the same profile and upperwing pattern, but male in breeding plumage has *pure dark green head, and clean white breast extends to shoulders.* Eclipse male can have crescent on face, but head greener and flanks and undertail paler than Australasian Shoveler. Female paler and greyer than Australasian Shoveler, and usually has more orange on sides of bill and more white on outer tail. **Habitat:** Lowland wetlands. [Sp 38]

MALLARD
♂
♂ eclipse
♀
GREY DUCK
♂ eclipse
♂
AUSTRALASIAN SHOVELER
♀
♂ eclipse
♂
NORTHERN SHOVELER
♀

PLATE 9 GREBES

Freshwater diving birds with a distinctive silhouette – dumpy body, low to the water, with rounded rear end because of no visible tail; bill pointed; head held erect. Sexes alike. They feed underwater, propelled by special lobed feet. As their legs are set well back, they are awkward on land and seldom venture onto it. Patter across the water when disturbed or during displays, but can fly well at night. Gather in loose flocks in autumn and winter. Silent. Nests are bulky floating structures, often attached to emergent or overhanging vegetation. Lay 2–4 chalky white eggs, staining to brown; covered whenever the adult leaves the nest. Chicks are carried on an adult's back when very small. Young have striped heads, through to the age of independence.

AUSTRALASIAN CRESTED GREBE (Puteketeke) *Podiceps cristatus* — Uncommon native

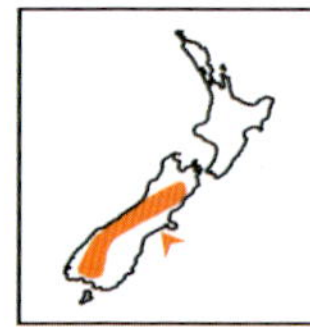

50cm, 1100g. A large long-necked grebe with a dagger-like bill and a prominent double crest and ruff. Swims with its slender white neck held erect, head horizontal. Brilliant white foreneck and chest visible when head lowered at rest. Adult plumage similar all year. Juveniles retain stripes on head until independent. Immature lacks ruff and has only a small crest, making it look like an immature Pied Shag. In flight, long thin body and prominent white panels on front and back of dark upperwing. Dives smoothly without splash. **Habitat:** *c.* 600 on large open lakes of inland South Island. Usually in pairs but gather on some Canterbury lakes in winter. Rare vagrant to North Island. **Breeding:** Sep–Mar. **[Sp 41]**

NEW ZEALAND DABCHICK (Weweia) *Poliocephalus rufopectus* — Locally common endemic

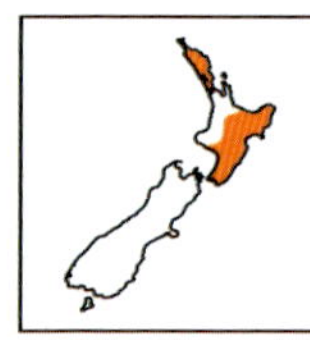

29cm, 250g. A small dark grebe with a dumpy body, slim neck, small head, short bill and tiny, fluffy white tail. *Blackish head, finely streaked with silver feathers*; *prominent yellow eye*; *rusty chestnut foreneck and breast*. After breeding, plumage paler and nondescript. After several months, juveniles look like adults. Dives frequently, often smoothly but sometimes after a leap. When alarmed, swims quietly away on or under the water, or skitters across the water, its rapidly beating wings hitting the surface. **Habitat:** Sheltered parts of lakes, farm ponds and, in winter, sewage oxidation ponds. *c.* 1700 in North Island, mainly Volcanic Plateau, Hawke's Bay, Manawatu and Wairarapa; rare in South Island. **Breeding:** Jun–Mar. **[Sp 42]**

HOARY-HEADED GREBE *Poliocephalus poliocephalus* — Rare Australian vagrant

28cm, 250g. Similar to NZ Dabchick in size and habits; *much paler and slimmer* than other small grebes. Breeding adult dark grey above, breast pale buff, *head prominently streaked silver* (hoary), eye not contrasting; bill tipped white. Non-breeding adult *pale grey with contrasting grey-brown cap to below eye* and extending as a dark stripe from the crown down the hindneck; bill pinkish. Regularly swims with thin neck held erect. **Habitat:** Lakes and farm ponds; a few bred in NZ in 1970s. **[Sp 43]**

AUSTRALASIAN LITTLE GREBE *Tachybaptus novaehollandiae* — Rare native

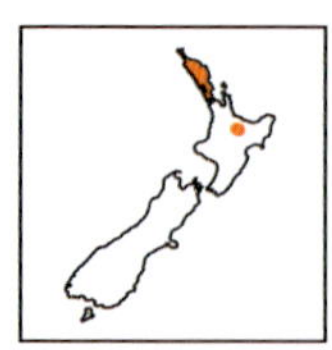

25cm, 220g. The smallest grebe in NZ. Breeding adult has black head with contrasting yellow eye, *a yellow patch of skin between eye and bill*, and broad band of rich chestnut on sides of neck. Non-breeding adult and immature lack head and neck colours, the skin patch becomes whitish and hard to see, but upperparts remain dark brown; *pale cheeks and foreneck contrast with dark brown cap to level of eye*. Dives frequently. Wary; when disturbed, dives and may lurk in vegetation, often with only its head above water. **Habitat:** Lakes and farm ponds. **Breeding:** Dec–Apr. **[Sp 44]**

AUSTRALASIAN CRESTED GREBE
juv
NEW ZEALAND DABCHICK
imm/non-breeding
HOARY-HEADED GREBE
breeding
non-breeding
AUSTRALASIAN LITTLE GREBE
breeding
non-breeding

PLATE 10 PENGUINS

Flightless stocky seabirds with dark upperparts and white underparts. Wings modified into flippers. Robust bill. Short stout legs with webbed feet. Dense short and flattened feathers in adults; thick down in chicks. Swim low in the water, with head and upper back (occasionally tail) visible; some porpoise when swimming fast. Feed at sea by diving. On land, walk upright with waddling gait or short hops with flippers used to maintain balance. Toboggan on ice and mud. Visit land to breed and to moult. During the 2–6-week moult, birds look ragged while all feathers are replaced rapidly; birds fast and are unable to swim. Breed solitarily in burrows or under vegetation, or in large dense colonies on the surface. Lay 1–2 white eggs.

KING PENGUIN *Aptenodytes patagonicus* — **Uncommon subantarctic visitor**

90cm, 13kg. Glossy black head and sides of face; golden-orange comma-shaped wedge behind eye tapering towards orange upper breast; silver-grey nape, shading to blue-grey on back and darker margin on flanks; rest of underparts white. Bill long and decurved at tip; broad tapering panel of orange-pink at base of lower mandible. Juvenile similar but much paler yellow, bill patch small and pink, and dark chin and throat. **Habitat:** Breeds circumpolar in subantarctic; nearest colony to NZ at Macquarie Island. Ranges south to pack ice; regularly seen at NZ subantarctic islands in summer and autumn, but rarely reach the mainland. [Sp 46]

EMPEROR PENGUIN *Aptenodytes forsteri* — **Uncommon native**

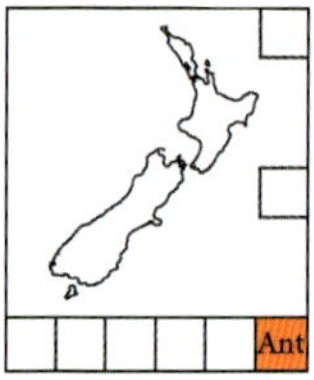

115cm, 30kg. Head, chin and throat blackish blue; orange patch extending downward from behind eye towards the back, connected to lemon-yellow upper breast; upperparts bluish grey with darker border along flanks; underparts white. Bill long and decurved towards tip; tapering panel of lilac-pink at base of lower mandible. Juvenile lacks yellow and has white chin and throat. **Habitat:** Breeds circumpolar in large colonies around Antarctica, including Ross Dependency. Two vagrants seen on NZ mainland: Oreti Beach, 1967, and Pekapeka Beach, 2011. **Breeding:** Apr–Jan. [Sp 45]

MAGELLANIC PENGUIN *Spheniscus magellanicus* — **Rare South American vagrant**

70cm, 3.5kg. Upperparts blue-black; wide white crescent from above bill, behind eye to upper breast separates crown and nape from black face and chin; two black bands cross upper breast, the narrower lower one horseshoe-shaped, turning down sides of belly to near feet. Juvenile has less clearly marked face pattern and a smudgy breast band. **Habitat:** Breeds on Juan Fernández and Falkland islands, and coast of South America. Rare vagrant to NZ. [Sp 60]

GENTOO PENGUIN *Pygoscelis papua* — **Rare subantarctic vagrant**

80cm, 5.5kg. Upperparts, chin and throat dark slate grey; white triangle above each eye, connected by thin white line over top of head; scattered white spots on head and neck; underparts white. Bill black with sides orange (male) or pinkish orange (female). Juvenile similar, but throat pale and patches over eye do not connect over crown. **Habitat:** Breeds circumpolar subantarctic and Antarctica; nearest colony to NZ at Macquarie Island. Vagrants reach NZ subantarctic islands and occasionally NZ mainland. [Sp 48]

juv
KING PENGUIN
juv
EMPEROR PENGUIN

moulting
MAGELLANIC PENGUIN
GENTOO PENGUIN

YELLOW-EYED PENGUIN (Hoiho) *Megadyptes antipodes*

Uncommon endemic

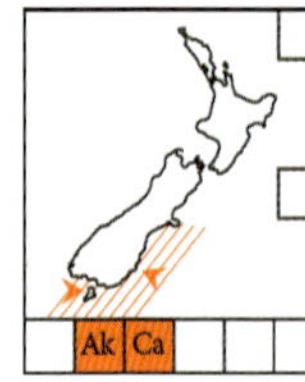

65cm; ♂ 5.5kg, ♀ 5.25kg. Upperparts slaty grey; forehead, crown and sides of face pale golden yellow with black feather shafts; eye yellow. Adult has band of yellow feathers starting at eye and encircling back of head. Juvenile has greyer head and lacks yellow band. **Habitat:** *c.* 5000 birds breed and moult around southeastern South Island, Foveaux Strait, Stewart, Codfish, Campbell and Auckland islands. Mainly sedentary, but some disperse northwards to Cook Strait, occasionally further. **Breeding:** Sep–Mar. **[Sp 58]**

ADÉLIE PENGUIN *Pygoscelis adeliae*

Locally common native

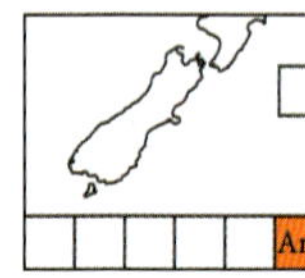

70cm, 5kg. Black head, face, chin and upperparts, except conspicuous white eye-ring; underparts white; no crest. Juvenile similar but has white chin and sides to face to just below the eye. **Habitat:** Breeds circumpolar in large colonies in Antarctica, including Ross Dependency. Rare vagrants reach NZ mainland. **Breeding:** Nov–Feb. **[Sp 47]**

CHINSTRAP PENGUIN *Pygoscelis antarctica*

Very rare native

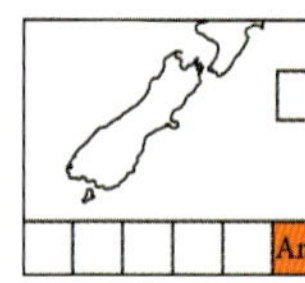

75cm, 5.5kg. Black upperparts; sides of face from above eye, chin and underparts white, except for a narrow black band extending diagonally across face from behind eye to under throat. Juvenile has dusky face above facial band. **Habitat:** Breeds Antarctica from Antarctic Peninsula eastwards to Ross Dependency, where a few pairs breed on the Balleny Islands. Rare vagrants reach NZ mainland. **Breeding:** Nov–Mar. **[Sp 49]**

BLUE PENGUIN (Korora) *Eudyptula minor*

Common native

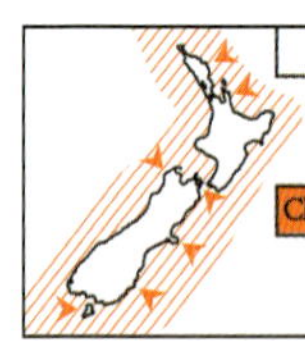

40cm, 1100g. Smallest penguin. Slate-blue upperparts and sides of face to near eye, white below; lacks crest or distinctive face markings. Juvenile has a brighter blue back. White-flippered phase of Canterbury has more white on upperside of flipper. Often noisy on land at night; utters loud screams, wails, trumpeting and deep growls. **Habitat:** Breeds on rocky coasts and islands throughout NZ, but can nest hundreds of metres inland. When breeding, comes ashore at dusk and departs at dawn. Moults in burrows, under rock piles or in dense vegetation; often surrounded by piles of moulted feathers. Often seen in coastal waters. **Breeding:** Jul–Mar. **[Sp 59]**

YELLOW-EYED PENGUIN
moulting
juv
juv
ADÉLIE PENGUIN
juv
BLUE PENGUIN
white-flippered form
CHINSTRAP PENGUIN

FIORDLAND CRESTED PENGUIN (Tawaki) *Eudyptes pachyrhynchus*

Rare endemic

60cm, 4kg. Upperparts dark bluish grey, darker on head; sides of face, chin and throat dark slaty grey; broad yellow eyebrow stripe that *splays out and droops* down neck; most have 3–6 whitish stripes on cheeks. Little black on tip of underflipper. Moderately large orange bill with *no bare skin at base*. Juvenile has thin eyebrow, and whitish chin and throat. **Habitat:** 2500–3000 pairs breed and moult in dense coastal forest or in caves on rocky shores of southern NZ, mainly South Westland, Fiordland and Codfish Island. During breeding, stays close to shore over continental shelf. Stragglers recorded around NZ coast and subantarctic islands. **Breeding:** Jul–Dec. [Sp 53]

ERECT-CRESTED PENGUIN *Eudyptes sclateri*

Locally common endemic

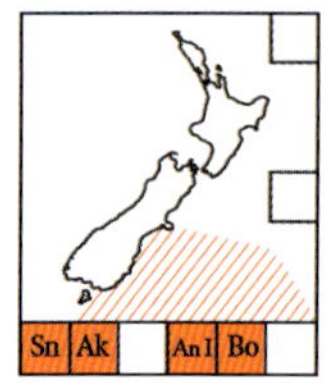

60cm, 4.5kg. Forehead, sides of face, chin and throat jet black; crown and upperparts very dark bluish black; underparts white. Broad bright yellow eyebrow stripe rises at a *steep angle over each eye to form a short brush-like erectile crest*. Whitish skin at base of slender reddish-brown bill. Solid black tip to underflipper, extending well along leading edge. Juvenile has smaller and creamy crest, and throat mottled grey and white. **Habitat:** Breeds NZ subantarctic; main colonies at Bounty and Antipodes islands. After breeding, disperses widely; a few moult each autumn on NZ mainland coast, and regularly seen off NZ mainland in winter. **Breeding:** Oct–Feb. [Sp 55]

SNARES CRESTED PENGUIN *Eudyptes robustus*

Locally common endemic

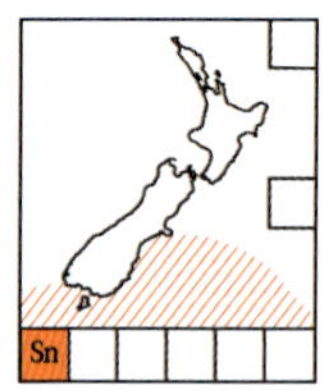

60cm, 3kg. Head, throat and upperparts dark blue-black; underparts white. Thin bright yellow eyebrow stripe forms *bushy drooping crest* behind eye. *Prominent pink skin at base of heavy* reddish-brown bill. Solid black tip to underflipper. Juvenile has smaller and creamy crest, darker bill and mottled whitish throat. **Habitat:** Breeds only at The Snares. Straggles to other subantarctic islands and mainland NZ. **Breeding:** Sep–Mar. [Sp 54]

FIORDLAND CRESTED PENGUIN
juv
ERECT-CRESTED PENGUIN
SNARES CRESTED PENGUIN

EASTERN ROCKHOPPER PENGUIN *Eudyptes filholi* **Locally common native**

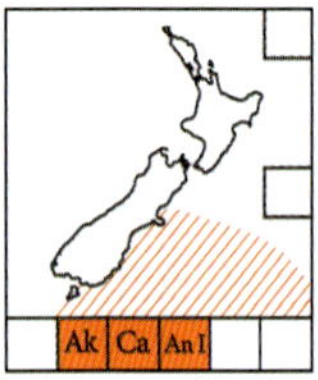

55cm, 2.8kg. Smallest crested penguin. Upperparts slate, darker on head, sides of face and chin. *Thin even-width golden-yellow eyebrow stripe from either side of forehead extending to flare at crown*; some droop towards neck, others forming a plume at edge of crest on hindcrown. *Skin at base of bill is pale pink.* Juvenile similar but shorter crest, eyebrow stripe less well developed, and chin and throat streaked with ashy white. **Habitat:** Breeds circumpolar subantarctic; in NZ region, at Antipodes, Auckland and Campbell islands. Stragglers reach The Snares, Chathams and NZ mainland. **Breeding:** Oct–Mar. [Sp 51]

MOSELEY'S ROCKHOPPER PENGUIN *Eudyptes moseleyi* **Rare subantarctic vagrant**

58cm, 2.8kg. Like Eastern Rockhopper Penguin, but drooping crest extends below the transition between black and white on the throat. *Skin at base of bill is black.* Flippers longer than in the other two Rockhopper penguins. **Habitat:** Breeds on subantarctic of South Atlantic and Indian oceans; vagrants reach NZ. **[Sp 52]**

WESTERN ROCKHOPPER PENGUIN *Eudyptes chrysocome* **Rare subantarctic vagrant**

61cm, 2.7kg. Like Eastern Rockhopper Penguin, but *larger; the eyebrow stripe broadens before flaring*, and *skin at base of bill is black.* **Habitat:** Breeds on Falkland Islands and near Cape Horn. Vagrants have reached The Snares. **[Sp 50]**

MACARONI PENGUIN *Eudyptes chrysolophus* **Rare subantarctic straggler**

70cm, 4.5kg. Large crested penguin. Upperparts black; *sides of face, chin and throat black.* Massive red-brown bill with fleshy gape; yellow, golden orange and black plumes starting from centre of forehead. Juvenile has smaller tuft-like plumes. **Habitat:** Breeds Antarctica and subantarctic of South Atlantic and Indian oceans. Occasionally reaches NZ sector of Antarctica and, rarely, NZ subantarctic islands. **[Sp 56]**

ROYAL PENGUIN *Eudyptes schlegeli* **Rare subantarctic straggler**

70cm, 5kg. Largest crested penguin. Upperparts black; *sides of face, chin and throat grey or white.* Massive red-brown bill with fleshy gape; yellow, golden orange and black plumes starting from centre of forehead. Juvenile has smaller tuft-like plumes. **Habitat:** Breeds only at Macquarie Island. Occasionally reaches NZ subantarctic islands and, rarely, the NZ mainland. **[Sp 57]**

EASTERN ROCKHOPPER PENGUIN
MOSELEY'S ROCKHOPPER PENGUIN
EASTERN ROCKHOPPER PENGUIN
WESTERN ROCKHOPPER PENGUIN
juv
MACARONI PENGUIN
ROYAL PENGUIN

SOUTHERN ROYAL ALBATROSS (Toroa) *Diomedea epomophora* **Locally common endemic**

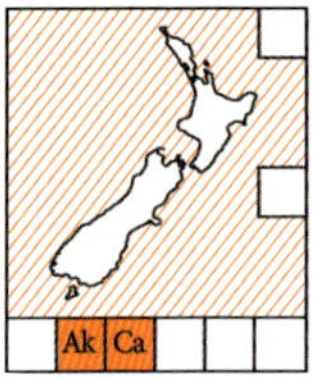

115cm, 9kg. Adult has completely white body, back and tail; upperwings *black with white patches extending backwards along the leading edge of the inner wing*; bill massive (165–190mm), light pink with creamy tip and with *black cutting edge to upper mandible.* Underwings white with black tip and thin black trailing edge. Legs and feet pinkish to bluish white. Juvenile similar, except for heavy black flecking on the back, flanks, crown and tail; upperwings black with small patches of white at base of leading edge *and in centre of inner wing*, becoming increasingly white from the leading edge backwards. **Habitat:** Breeds on Campbell and Auckland islands. Ranges widely circumpolar through the southern oceans, and most often seen in NZ coastal waters in winter. **Breeding:** All year; eggs laid Nov–Dec; young fledge *c.* 11 months later. **[Sp 63]**

NORTHERN ROYAL ALBATROSS (Toroa) *Diomedea sanfordi* **Locally common endemic**

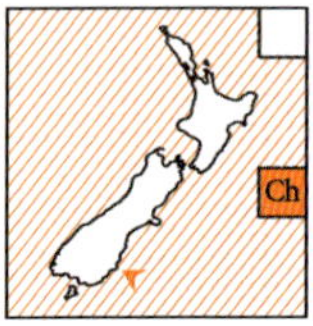

115cm, 9kg. Adults are like Southern Royal Albatross except wings are black above; bill smaller (155–175mm), light pink with creamy tip and with *black cutting edge to upper mandible.* Juvenile has heavy black flecking on the back, flanks, crown and tail; upperwings black with *small* patches of white at very base of leading edge. **Habitat:** Breeds at Taiaroa Head (Dunedin) and The Sisters and The Forty-fours (Chathams). Ranges widely circumpolar through the southern oceans, and most often seen in NZ coastal waters in winter, except seen throughout the year at Taiaroa Head, where 30–35 pairs breed. **Breeding:** All year; eggs laid Oct–Dec; young fledge *c.* 11 months later. **[Sp 64]**

ANTIPODEAN ALBATROSS *Diomedea antipodensis* **Locally common endemic**

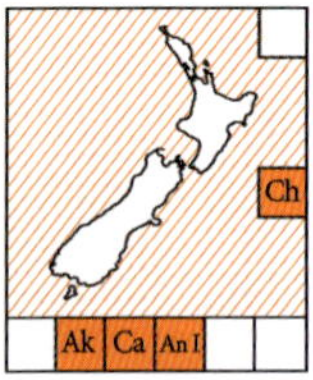

115cm, 6.5kg. Variable plumages, according to age and race. Some pale adults are like the Royal Albatrosses, but bill is smaller (135–160mm), light pink with creamy tip and with *no black on cutting edges*; breast and back often have fine black vermiculations; *leading edge of inner upperwing usually black or mottled black* in all but the whitest birds (which have much more extensive white on upperwings than the whitest Southern Royal). Often has white patches in central inner wing; *tail usually black-tipped.* Juvenile initially uniformly dark brown, except for white face and dark-tipped white underwings (A). Over the next 10–15 years, the plumage whitens, initially on the belly (B), then from the back onto the upperwings, and outwards from a central patch on the upperwing, following the progression from C to F in the whitest NZ breeding birds; however, birds breed in the NZ region in all forms from A through to F. Underwings white with black tip and thin black trailing edge. Legs and feet pinkish to brownish grey. The subspecies (*gibsoni*) of the Auckland Islands is paler (and breeds in plumages C to F) than the subspecies (*antipodensis*) of the Antipodes and Campbell islands and at the Chathams (which breed in plumages A to E). **Habitat:** Breeds at only Antipodes, Campbell and Auckland islands and, since 2003, on Chatham and Pitt islands. Ranges widely through the southern oceans and most often seen in NZ coastal waters in winter. **Breeding:** All year; eggs laid Jan–Mar, young fledge *c.* 11 months later. **[Sp 62]**

WANDERING ALBATROSS *Diomedea exulans* **Uncommon migrant**

115cm. 6.5kg. Similar plumage variation with age as in Antipodean Albatross, from which it is not possible to distinguish at sea, except that most adults have *much whiter upperwings* (G) than any other albatross in NZ region. Bill is longer than in Antipodean (155–180mm). **Habitat:** Breeds on subantarctic islands of the Atlantic and Indian oceans and at Macquarie Island. Ranges widely through the southern oceans and a few regularly visit NZ coastal waters. **[Sp 61]**

SOUTHERN ROYAL ALBATROSS
NORTHERN ROYAL ALBATROSS
juv
SOUTHERN/NORTHERN ROYAL ALBATROSS
A
juv
B
ANTIPODEAN/WANDERING ALBATROSS
C
D
E
F
G

ALBATROSSES & MOLLYMAWKS

Huge, mainly white-backed ('albatrosses') or very large, mainly black-backed ('mollymawks') seabirds with long narrow wings and short tail. Long, heavy, hooked bill covered with horny plates, nostrils in small tubes on the sides near the base. Most are dark above and mainly white below. Pattern of upperwing, underwing, head and bill are distinctive. In flight, soar gracefully on stiffly held wings, and only rarely flap. Clumsy on ground; legs and webbed feet set well back. Generally oceanic; occasionally seen near land. Many follow ships or gather around fishing boats. Silent at sea except when fighting over food. Loud bleats, croaks, whines and cackles at breeding colonies, and elaborate displays accompanied by bill-clapping and calls. Lay one large white egg in shallow bowl or on top of pedestal constructed of vegetation and mud. Long incubation period and extremely long fledging period (7–11 months for full breeding cycle). Sexes alike but males larger. Juveniles generally distinctive for several years.

INDIAN OCEAN YELLOW-NOSED MOLLYMAWK *Thalassarche carteri* **Uncommon migrant**

75cm, 2.2kg. Similar to Atlantic Yellow-nosed Mollymawk in having a *slender black bill with yellow ridge deepening to reddish orange at the tip*, except that adult has *completely white head including in front of eye*, except sometimes with grey wash on cheeks. Juvenile similar but hindneck is washed grey; leading margin of underwing is broader and less clear-cut; *bill completely black*. **Habitat:** Breeds on islands in South Indian Ocean. Ranges through warm subantarctic and subtropical waters of the Indian Ocean to Australia, and a few regularly reach the Tasman Sea, Hauraki Gulf and Bay of Plenty, mostly in winter. **[Sp 67]**

ATLANTIC YELLOW-NOSED MOLLYMAWK *Thalassarche chlororhynchos* **Very rare straggler**

75cm, 2.4kg. Small slender mollymawk. Adult has *pale grey head with a small dark triangle in front of eye*, sometimes with grey cheeks; neck, underparts and rump white; back, upperwings and tail black; underwings white with black tips and thin clear-cut black margins, wider on leading than trailing edge. *Bill slender (117mm), black with yellow ridge deepening to reddish orange at the tip*. Juvenile similar but eye patch smaller; hindneck is washed grey; leading margin of underwing is broader and less clear-cut; *bill completely black*. **Habitat:** Breeds on islands in South Atlantic Ocean. Ranges through warm subantarctic and subtropical waters of South Atlantic and Indian oceans, and two have been seen in NZ, at the Chathams. **[Sp 66]**

LAYSAN ALBATROSS *Phoebastria immutabilis* **Very rare straggler**

80cm, 2.4kg. Adult similar to Campbell Islands Mollymawk, but slightly smaller and the *bill is pink, tipped bluish*. The dark eye patch is usually larger, especially below the eye, giving a frowning appearance. Upperwings, back and *upper rump*, black; tip of tail dark grey; underwings have broad black edges and central white patch often streaked with black. **Habitat:** Breeds in the North Pacific, and winters across temperate and tropical waters of the North Pacific. A few stray to the South Pacific; seen once in NZ waters, Hawke Bay, 1995. **[Sp 65]**

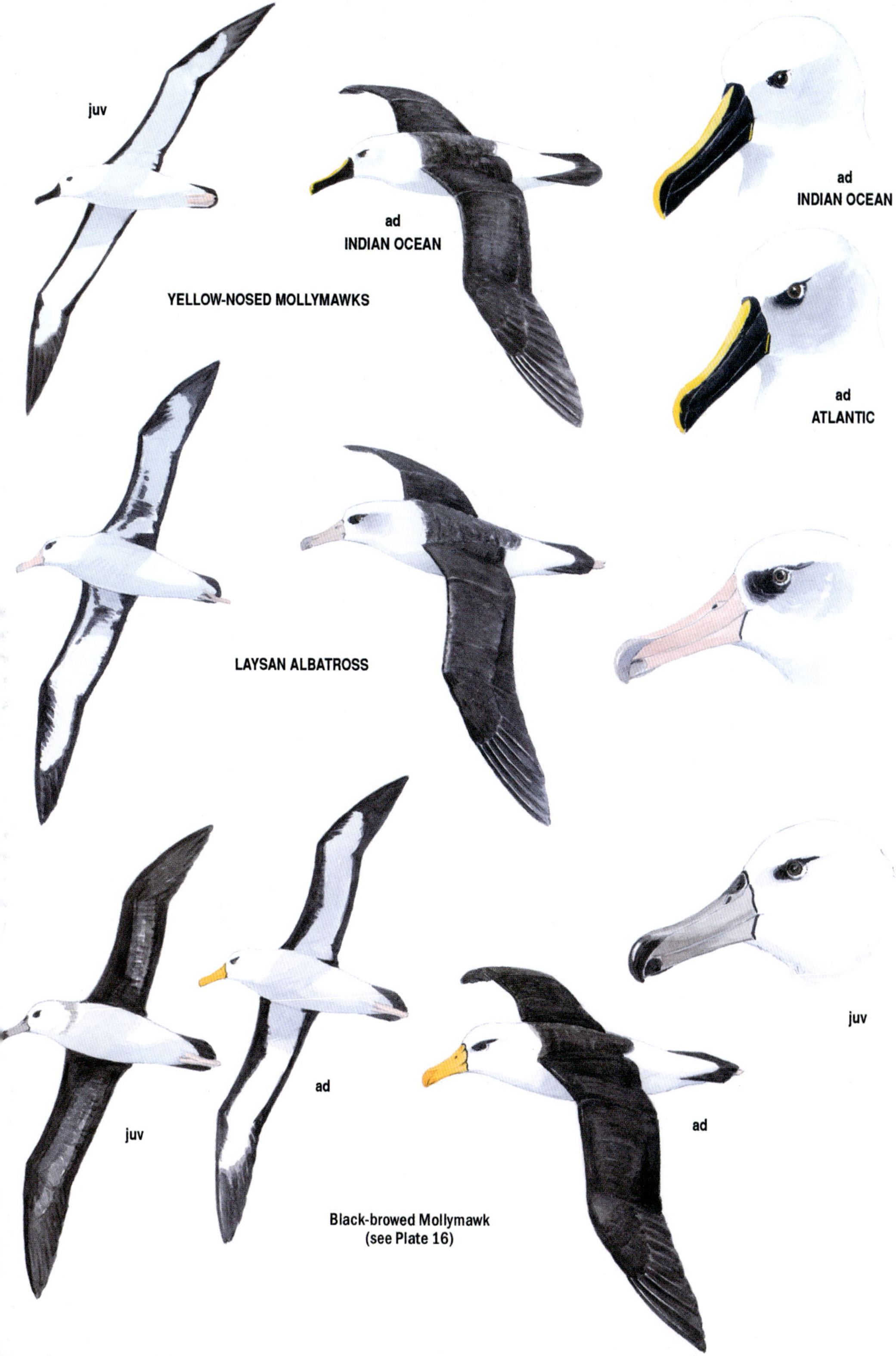
juv
ad
INDIAN OCEAN
ad
INDIAN OCEAN
YELLOW-NOSED MOLLYMAWKS
ad
ATLANTIC
LAYSAN ALBATROSS
juv
ad
juv
ad
Black-browed Mollymawk
(see Plate 16)

BLACK-BROWED MOLLYMAWK *Thalassarche melanophris* — **Rare native**

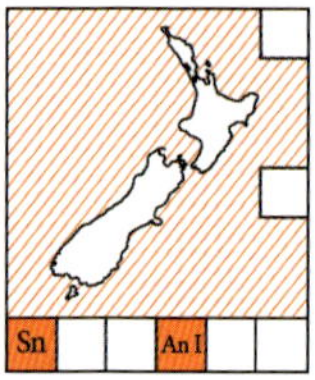

88cm, 3.5kg. Adult similar to Campbell Islands Mollymawk, but underwings white with *broad, clear-cut, black edges*, wider on the leading edge especially on the inner part of the wing; bill (114–122mm) *yellowish-orange with orange tip*; *eye brown*. Juvenile indistinguishable from juvenile Campbell Islands Mollymawk until the latter's eyes start to turn pale yellow. **Habitat:** Breeds mainly off Chile and at the Falkland Islands; fewer than 150 pairs breed in NZ, at Bollons Island, Antipodes, and on the Western Chain, The Snares. **Breeding:** Sep–Apr. **[Sp 69]**

CAMPBELL ISLANDS MOLLYMAWK *Thalassarche impavida* — **Locally common endemic**

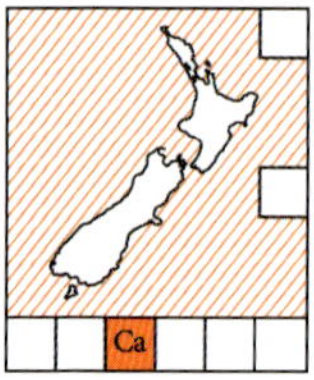

85cm, 3kg. Adult has *whole body white except for heavy black triangle around eye* giving frowning appearance, blackish-grey back connecting black upperwings, and dark grey tail; underwings white with *broad, ill-defined black edges*, wider on the leading edge especially on the inner part of the wing; some have extensive dark streaking in armpits, almost connecting front to back; bill (106–118mm) *yellowish-orange with orange tip*; *eye honey coloured*; legs and feet pale bluish white. Juvenile like adult except eyebrow smaller; greyish wash on crown and hindneck; *underwings almost completely black*; bill *greyish green with dark tip*, turning yellow with a dark tip in older birds; eye brown. **Habitat:** Breeds only at Campbell Island and adjacent Isle de Jeanette-Marie. Ranges to NZ waters and the Tasman, and after breeding, many move northwards to NZ waters, the Coral Sea and western South Pacific. Often seen behind boats, especially in winter. **Breeding:** Sep–Apr. **[Sp 70]**

BULLER'S MOLLYMAWK *Thalassarche bulleri* — **Locally common endemic**

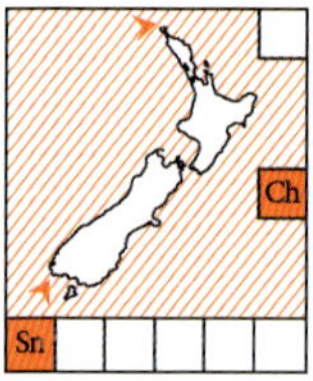

80cm, 3kg. Adult Southern Buller's has *silvery-white forehead*, black patch around and ahead of eye, small white crescent behind to below eye; face, neck and throat grey, underparts and rump white, tail grey. Upperwings and back dark grey; underwings *white with clear-cut, narrow, black leading edge and very narrow black trailing edge*. Bill (118mm) *black with golden yellow tip and ridge, widening at base*, and along bottom edge; legs and feet pale bluish grey. Northern Buller's has *silvery grey forehead and darker grey hood*. Bill (120mm) larger. Juvenile like adult except whole head dark grey and bill brownish horn with darker tip. **Habitat:** Southern Buller's breeds at The Snares and Solander Islands; Northern Buller's breeds at Three Kings and Chathams. Commonly seen off NZ coast or behind boats and trawlers during breeding. Most disperse to eastern Pacific after breeding. **Breeding:** Dec–Oct (Southern), Oct–Jun (Northern). **[Sp 71]**

GREY-HEADED MOLLYMAWK *Thalassarche chrysostoma* — **Locally common native**

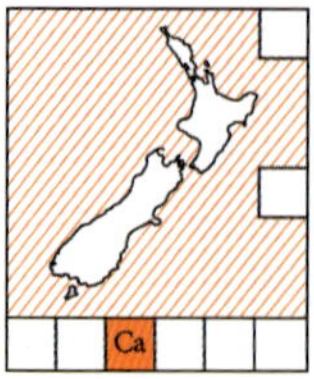

80cm, 3.25kg. Adult has *light grey head, throat and neck*, paler on forehead; dark grey patch around and ahead of eye, small white mark just behind eye; underparts and rump white; tail grey. Upperwings and back dark grey; underwings *white with broad black leading edge and narrow black trailing edge. Bill (113mm) black with rich yellow along ridge, narrowing at base, and along bottom edge*, shading to rosy at tip; legs and feet greyish white. Juvenile similar, but initial darker grey on head wears to very pale on forehead and cheeks in some birds; underwings black, with greyish or white central stripe appearing with increasing age. Bill dark grey, darker tip changing to dull yellow with age. **Habitat:** Breeds circumpolar subantarctic; in NZ region, only at Campbell Island. Ranges widely through southern oceans, and a few visit NZ coastal waters, especially juveniles in winter. **Breeding:** Sep–May. **[Sp 68]**

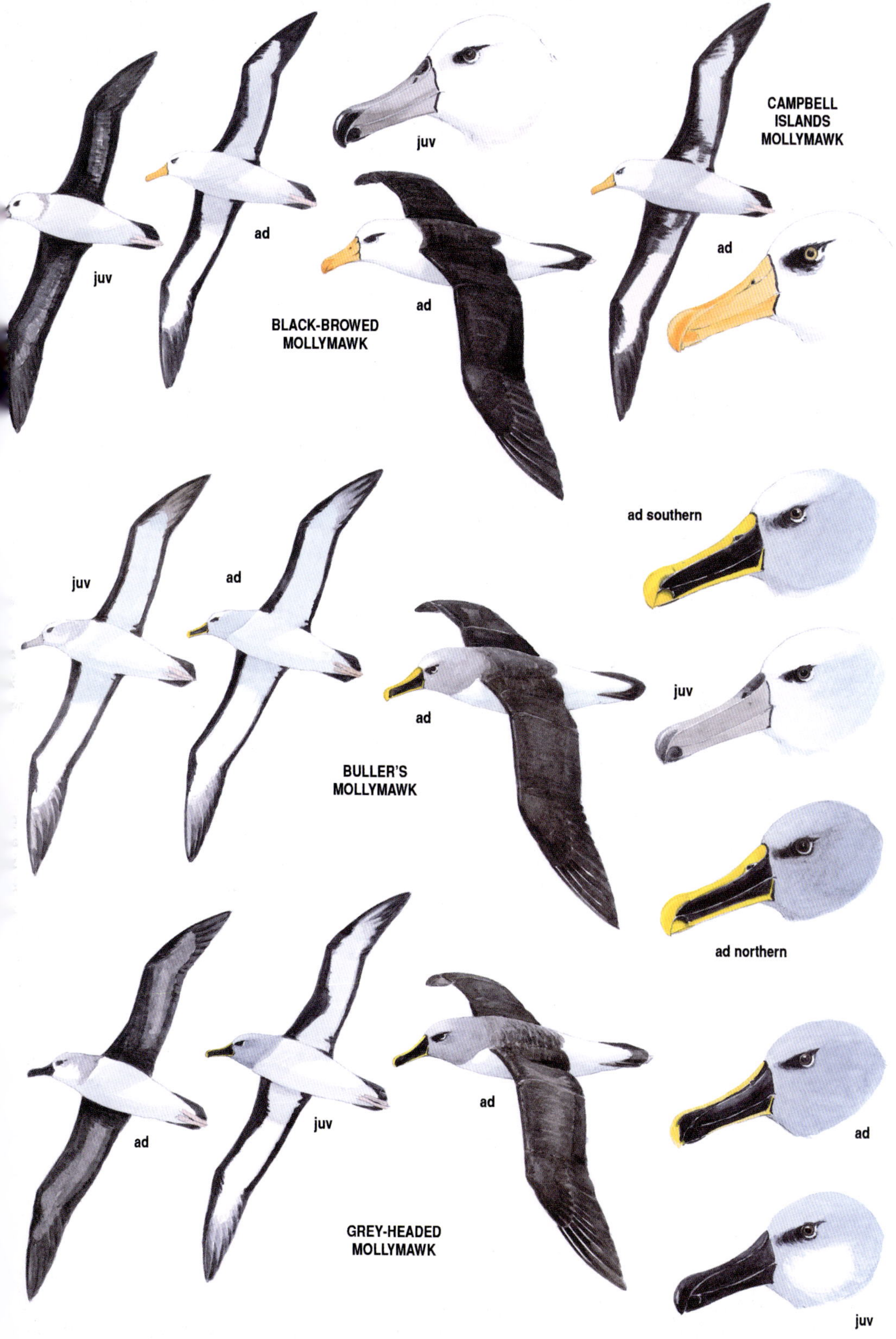

juv
ad
juv
CAMPBELL ISLANDS MOLLYMAWK
ad
ad
BLACK-BROWED MOLLYMAWK
ad southern
juv
ad
juv
ad
BULLER'S MOLLYMAWK
ad northern
ad
juv
ad
ad
GREY-HEADED MOLLYMAWK
juv

PLATE 17 ALBATROSSES & MOLLYMAWKS

WHITE-CAPPED MOLLYMAWK (Shy Mollymawk) *Thalassarche cauta* — **Common native**

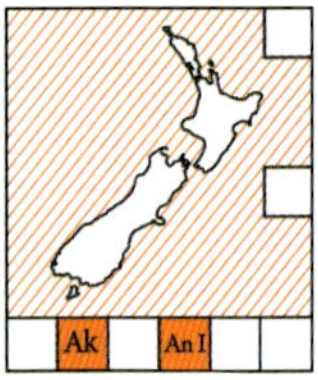

95cm, 4kg. Two subspecies in NZ region, separated in the hand by bill size and wing length. Both have *white underwing with very narrow black borders reaching a prominent black triangular tab at base of the leading edge.* Adult has *white head and neck,* small black patch from eye to bill shading to very faint grey wash on cheeks; mantle grey-brown merging into grey-black back and upperwings; rump white; tail grey-black; underparts white; underwing has thin black edges and *mainly white tip*; bill (130–135mm) pale bluish horn with yellowish top to bill, especially at base and tip; legs and feet pale blue-grey. Immatures have more extensive grey wash on cheeks; underwing patterns are similar to that in adults; *bill bluish grey with black tips to both mandibles.* **Habitat:** Breeds around Tasmania and NZ subantarctic, mainly at Disappointment Island, Auckland Islands; also Auckland and Adams islands and a few at Bollons Island, Antipodes. Ranges widely through southern oceans and often to NZ coastal waters, especially seen around fishing boats. **Breeding:** Nov–Aug. [Sp 72]

SALVIN'S MOLLYMAWK *Thalassarche salvini* — **Locally common native**

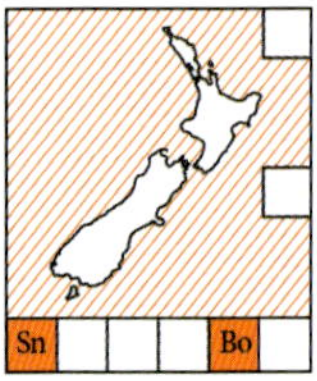

95cm, 4kg. Has *white underwing with very narrow black borders reaching a black triangular tab at base of the leading edge.* Adult has *pale grey head and neck,* paler on crown; black patch from eye to bill; mantle grey-brown merging into grey-black back and upperwings; rump white, tail grey-black, underparts white; underwing has thin black edges and *moderate black tip*; bill (125–130mm) *greyish-horn with yellowish hook and top, black tip to lower mandible*; legs and feet pale blue-grey. Bill of immature *pale grey with dark tip.* **Habitat:** Breeds mainly at the Bounty Islands, but a few at the Western Chain of The Snares and at the Crozet Islands in the South Indian Ocean. During breeding, many seen in NZ coastal waters and in the Tasman, especially around fishing boats. Winters off eastern South America. **Breeding:** Aug–Apr. [Sp 74]

CHATHAM ISLANDS MOLLYMAWK *Thalassarche eremita* — **Uncommon endemic**

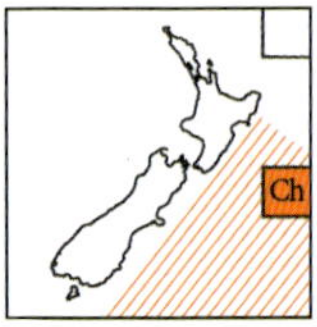

90cm, 4kg. Has *white underwing with very narrow black borders reaching a black triangular tab at base of the leading edge.* Adult has *dark grey head and neck,* paler on crown; small black patch from eye to bill; mantle grey-brown merging into grey-black back and upperwings; rump white, tail grey-black, underparts white; underwing has thin black edges and *extensive black tip*; bill (120mm) *pale yellow with black tip to lower mandible*; legs and feet pale blue-grey. Bill of immature *yellowish grey with black tips to both mandibles.* **Habitat:** Breeds only on Pyramid Rock, Chathams, and feeds mainly to the south and east of the Chathams but sometimes in the Tasman Sea and NZ coastal waters. Winters off eastern South America. **Breeding:** Aug–Mar. [Sp 73]

WHITE-CAPPED MOLLYMAWK
ad
imm
ad
imm
ad
imm
ad
imm
ad
SALVIN'S MOLLYMAWK
ad
imm
ad
CHATHAM ISLANDS MOLLYMAWK

PLATE 18 **SOOTY ALBATROSSES & GIANT PETRELS**

Sooty albatrosses are slender sooty-brown and grey birds with black bill, long narrow wings and very long, pointed tail.

LIGHT-MANTLED SOOTY ALBATROSS *Phoebetria palpebrata* — Uncommon native

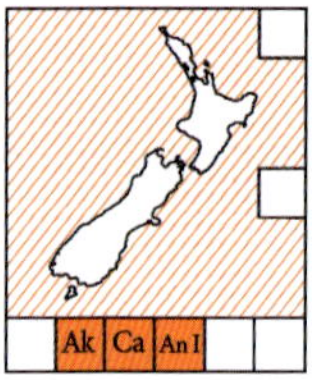

80cm, 3kg. Adult has sooty-brown head, throat and wings; *ash-grey back from nape to rump*, pale brownish-grey underparts. Bill (105mm) slender, black with blue line along lower bill; legs and feet pale grey-flesh. Juvenile similar, but brown scalloping on neck and upper back, grey eye-ring and greyish-yellow line along lower bill. **Habitat:** Breeds circumpolar subantarctic; in NZ region, at Antipodes, Auckland and Campbell islands. Ranges widely at sea, and a few reach mainland NZ waters or are beach-wrecked, mainly in winter. **Breeding:** Oct–Jun. [Sp 76]

SOOTY ALBATROSS *Phoebetria fusca* — Very rare vagrant

80cm, 2.5kg. Adult is *sooty brown* except slightly darker on head and wings, white eye-ring, and pale shafts to primaries and tail. Bill (112mm) slender, black with yellow line along lower bill; legs and feet pale grey-flesh. Juvenile similar but buff scalloping on collar and sides of neck; ash-grey nape, grey eye-ring and grey line along lower bill. **Habitat:** Breeds subantarctic and subtropical Atlantic and Indian oceans. Recorded a few times in NZ waters. [Sp 75]

The two giant petrels are very similar robust brown-to-white (rare) fulmarine petrels with short wings and tail. Massive pale bill with prominent nasal tubes. Flight laboured with burst of flapping interspersed with long glides and wheeling, not soaring. On land, mobile and can stand upright. Oceanic and coastal. Frequently follow ships and trawlers. Silent at sea except when fighting for food. Loud calls at colonies. Lay one large white egg in low cup-shaped bowl. Long incubation and fledging periods. Sexes alike but male larger; juveniles darker.

NORTHERN GIANT PETREL (Nelly) *Macronectes halli* — Common native

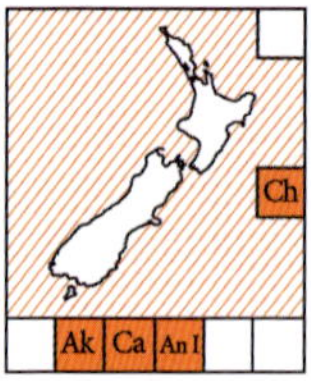

90cm, 4.5kg. Similar to dark phase Southern Giant Petrel, but *bill pinkish-yellow horn, tipped brownish*, and face darker. Adult has greyish-brown body with paler forehead, sides of face and chin, sometimes white on chin and around base of bill. Bill robust (90–105mm); eye grey to off-white. No white plumage phase. Juvenile all dark sooty brown, fading to grey-brown with age; eye usually grey. **Habitat:** Breeds circumpolar subantarctic; in NZ region, at Chathams, Port Pegasus (Stewart Island), Antipodes, Auckland and Campbell islands. Ranges widely through southern oceans and often seen in NZ waters, especially Cook Strait. **Breeding:** Aug–Feb. [Sp 78]

SOUTHERN GIANT PETREL (Nelly) *Macronectes giganteus* — Common visitor

90cm, 4.5kg. Variable plumages; dark adults and juveniles are almost identical to Northern Giant Petrel except *bill yellowish horn, tipped green*, and face paler. Adult (dark phase) has white head, flecked brown, merging into greyish-brown body, wings and tail; often shows thin white leading edge to innerwings. Bill robust (90–105mm); eye brown to grey, usually brown. Juvenile all dark sooty brown, fading to grey-brown with age; eye generally brown. Adult and juvenile (white phase) completely white except for scattered flecks of brown. **Habitat:** Breeds circumpolar subantarctic and around Antarctic coast; in NZ region, recorded breeding once at Cape Crozier, Antarctica. Ranges widely through southern oceans, and juveniles common in NZ waters, especially in winter and spring; a few adults reach NZ. [Sp 77]

LIGHT-MANTLED
SOOTY ALBATROSS
juv
SOOTY ALBATROSS
worn
plumage
juv
NORTHERN
GIANT PETREL
SOUTHERN
GIANT PETREL
juv

PLATE 19 FULMARINE PETRELS & Blue Petrel

The fulmarine petrels are a diverse group of distinctive medium to large seabirds, with which the Blue Petrel is sometimes placed. Sexes alike. Most breed at high latitudes and lay one white egg, mostly in a scrape on ledges, in crevices or rockfalls; the exceptions being giant petrels (Plate 18), which lay in a cupped mound, and Kerguelen Petrels (Plate 20), which nest in a burrow.

ANTARCTIC PETREL *Thalassoica antarctica* — **Locally common native**

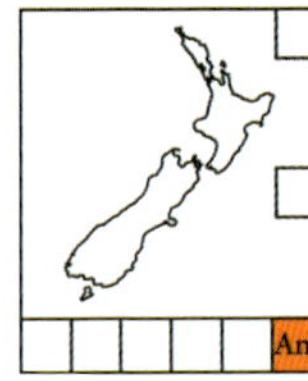

45cm, 650g. Head, neck, back and rump dark brown; *upperwings dark brown with broad white trailing edge and inner part of primaries*; *tail white, tipped brown*; underparts white; underwing white with black leading edge and thin border. Bill dark olive brown (black in juvenile); legs and feet greyish flesh. **Habitat:** Breeds circumpolar Antarctica, sometimes well inland; in NZ region, at Rockefeller Mountains, Scott Island and possibly Balleny Islands. Ranges through Antarctic waters; especially common in Ross Sea sector. In most winters, few, if any, reach NZ mainland waters. **Breeding:** Nov–Mar. [Sp 80]

ANTARCTIC FULMAR *Fulmarus glacialoides* — **Locally common native**

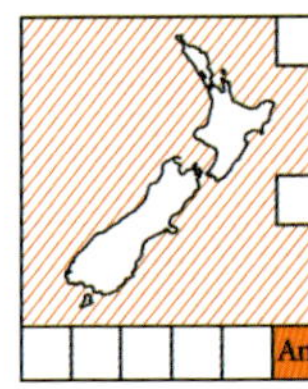

50cm, 800g. Head, neck and underparts white; mantle, back, rump and tail pearly grey; *upperwings pearly grey with darker grey trailing edge*, and *primaries black with large white patch near wingtip*. Bill strong (45mm), pinkish horn with blue tinge on nasal tubes, and black tip; legs and feet pinkish blue. Appears large-headed; glides on stiff wings. **Habitat:** Breeds circumpolar on coast of Antarctica and subantarctic islands of Atlantic Ocean; in NZ region, at Balleny Islands. Ranges widely in southern oceans, and a few visit NZ waters in winter and spring, but sometimes many are beach-wrecked in spring. **Breeding:** Dec–Mar. [Sp 79]

CAPE PIGEON *Daption capense* — **Common native**

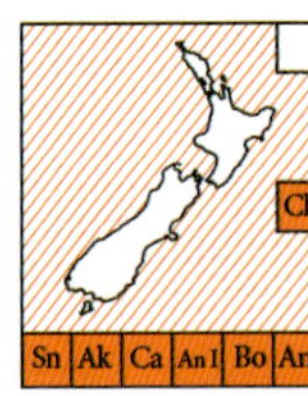

40cm, 450g. Head, neck and mantle black; lower back, base of upperwing and rump white, *heavily chequered* with black; outer upperwing black with broad white patches near body and past bend of wing; white tail is flecked black and broadly tipped black; underparts white; underwings white with black leading edge and thin borders. Bill stout (30 x 15mm), black; legs and feet black. Snares Cape Pigeon (*australe*) has less white on upperparts than Southern Cape Pigeon (*capense*). Often gathers at fishing boats. **Habitat:** Breeds coastal Antarctica and circumpolar subantarctic; in NZ region, as far north as The Snares and Chathams. Ranges widely in southern oceans and common off NZ mainland in winter. **Breeding:** Nov–Mar. [Sp 81]

BLUE PETREL *Halobaena caerulea* — **Uncommon subantarctic visitor**

29cm, 200g. Head bluish black; upperparts and side of neck pale blue, with dark M-shaped mark from wingtip to wingtip, broken only on lower back; *tail distinctively tipped white*. Bill narrow (27 x 11mm), bluish black; legs and feet blue with flesh webs. At sea, looks like a prion (see Plate 24), but tail distinctive and flight faster and wheeling. Rarely follows ships. **Habitat:** Breeds circumpolar subantarctic; nearest colony to NZ is on Macquarie Island. Uncommon winter and spring visitor to waters around NZ mainland but sometimes beach-wrecked in moderate numbers. [Sp 100]

SNOW PETREL *Pagodroma nivea* — **Locally common native**

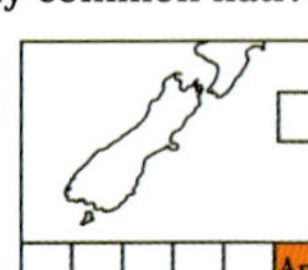

35cm, 325g. *All white*. Bill narrow (22 x 11mm), black; legs and feet black. Flight erratic with short, rapid wingbeats. **Habitat:** Breeds circumpolar coast of Antarctica; in NZ region, at Balleny Islands (Greater Snow Petrel *nivea*) and around Ross Sea (Lesser Snow Petrel *minor*). Ranges through southern oceans but never confirmed as far north as NZ mainland. **Breeding:** Nov–Mar. [Sp 82]

ANTARCTIC PETREL
ANTARCTIC FULMAR
CAPE PIGEON
Snares
Southern
BLUE PETREL
SNOW PETREL

PLATE 20 GADFLY PETRELS

Medium to large seabirds with mostly short, deep and heavily hooked bill, nostrils encased in a tube at base of bill. Most are dark above and mainly white below. Sexes and ages alike; males slightly larger. Underwing patterns are often distinctive. In flight, long narrow wings held stiffly, and gracefully glide and wheel in huge arcs. Generally oceanic; rarely seen near land. Many species highly migratory. Many give high-pitched repetitive calls over breeding grounds at night. Lay one large egg, usually deep in a burrow. Long incubation and fledging periods.

WHITE-HEADED PETREL *Pterodroma lessonii* — **Locally common native**

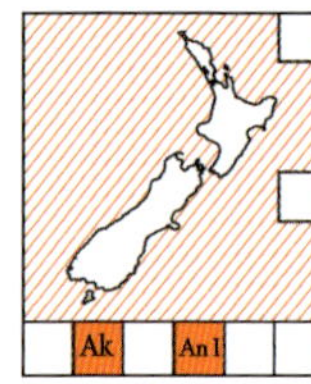

43cm, 600g. *Head mainly white with dark eye patch* and very faintly grey on crown and hindneck; pale grey on back and tail; upperwings greyish brown with indistinct M joining across lower back; underwings dark grey, undertail white. Bill stout (37 x 15mm), black; legs and feet fleshy pink with brown on outer toe, joints of toes and ends of webs. Flight strong and rapid, wheeling and swooping in high arcs. Rarely follows ships. **Habitat:** Breeds subantarctic in Indian Ocean and at Macquarie Island; in NZ region, at Antipodes and Auckland islands. Ranges through southern oceans between pack ice and about 34° S in winter. Regularly recorded beach-wrecked on west coast of North Island. **Breeding:** Nov–May. **[Sp 85]**

KERGUELEN PETREL *Lugensa brevirostris* — **Uncommon subantarctic visitor**

33cm, 350g. Almost uniformly *dark frosty grey*, with slight mottling on forehead, chin and sometimes flanks; underwings silvery grey. Bill short and narrow (26 x 10mm), black; looks small compared to large head. Legs and feet purplish flesh, darker on outsides. *Flight extremely fast.* **Habitat:** Breeds subantarctic in Atlantic and Indian oceans. Ranges eastwards and can be quite common in the Tasman Sea some years in winter and early spring, when sometimes wrecked on west coast NZ beaches. **[Sp 83]**

PROVIDENCE PETREL *Pterodroma solandri* — **Very rare subtropical vagrant**

40cm, 500g. Brown head, mottled white on face and forehead and dark patch in front of eye; upperparts steely grey, contrasting with browner wings and tail; underparts greyish brown; underwings dark grey with *distinctive white patch at the base of dark primaries.* Bill stout (35 x 15mm), black; legs and feet dark grey. **Habitat:** Breeds in winter at Lord Howe and Philip islands; formerly also at Norfolk Island. Migrates to North Pacific. A few records from northern NZ. **[Sp 86]**

GREY-FACED PETREL (Oi) *Pterodroma macroptera* — **Common native**

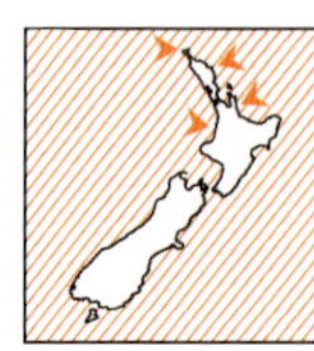

41cm, 550g. *Entire plumage blackish brown except pale grey forehead, sides of face, chin and throat.* Bill stout (36 x 14mm), black; legs and feet black. Long narrow wings. Flight strong and rapid, wheeling and swooping in big arcs. Aerial chases at dusk or after dark over breeding colonies often accompanied by *'o-hi' or 'o-hoe' calls.* Many calls also from birds on ground or in burrows, especially a loud 'or-wik' and 'si-si-si'. **Habitat:** Breeds circumpolar subantarctic and southern temperate; in NZ, on many northern offshore islands and some mainland cliffs and headlands, within the triangle Cape Egmont to Three Kings Islands to Gisborne. **Breeding:** Jun–Jan. **[Sp 84]**

KERMADEC PETREL *Pterodroma neglecta* — **Locally common native**

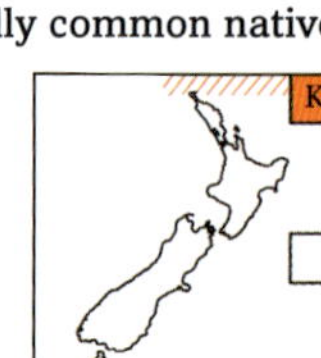

38cm, 500g. Variable plumages. Dark phase is uniformly brownish black except for *obvious white bases to the primaries on underwing,* and white inner webs and shafts of primaries sometimes visible on upperwing. Bill (30 x 13mm) black; feet and legs variable from black to pale flesh with dark tips to webs. See Plate 21 for other phases. **Habitat:** Breeds subtropical South Pacific, including the Kermadecs. Migrates to tropical Pacific. Vagrants occasionally reach NZ mainland. **Breeding:** Oct–May. **[Sp 88]**

WHITE-HEADED PETREL
KERGUELEN PETREL
PROVIDENCE PETREL
GREY-FACED PETREL
KERMADEC PETREL
dark phase

SOFT-PLUMAGED PETREL *Pterodroma mollis* — **Uncommon native**

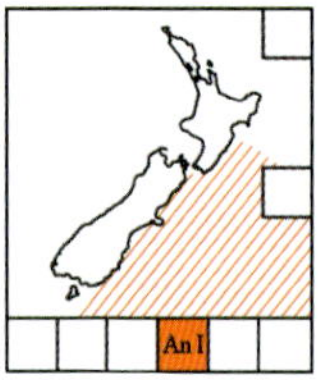

34cm, 300g. Head including patch below and behind eye greyish brown; forehead scaled white; eyebrow, chin, sides of neck and throat white. Upperparts slate grey with a broad blackish band across wing coverts; underparts white except for a *narrow grey band completely or partially across the chest*; *underwing grey*. Bill stout (35 x 12mm), black; feet and legs pinkish with dark outer toe and tips to webs. **Habitat:** Breeds subantarctic in Atlantic and Indian oceans, and at Antipodes Islands. Ranges through southern oceans but not common in South Pacific, although increasing numbers seen off southern and eastern coasts of NZ since 1970s. **Breeding:** Dec–May. **[Sp 90]**

CHATHAM ISLANDS TAIKO (Magenta Petrel) *Pterodroma magentae* — **Very rare endemic**

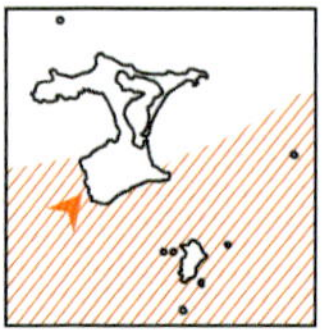

38cm, 475g. Head, neck, upper breast and upperparts uniformly dark sooty grey except for *variable greyish scalloping on forehead and grey chin*; lower breast, underparts and undertail white; underwing sooty grey. Bill robust (32 x 16mm), black; legs and feet pink with dark outer toe and tips to webs. **Habitat:** Believed extinct until rediscovered in Tukuatamatea Valley, Chatham Island, in 1978. Fewer than 200 birds breed in forests of southwestern Chatham Island; feeds mainly to the south and east of the Chathams, but after breeding some visit the Tasman and most migrate to the tropics of South Pacific and the west coast of South America. **Breeding:** Nov–May. **[Sp 87]**

PHOENIX PETREL *Pterodroma alba* — **Very rare tropical vagrant**

35cm, 275g. Head, upperparts and upper breast uniform sooty brown; chin and upper throat white; breast, belly and undertail white except for narrow dark rim around tip of long tail; underwings sooty brown except for *thin white band just back from leading edge from body to bend of wing*. Bill slight (28 x 11mm), black; legs and feet pink with dark outer toe and tips to webs. **Habitat:** Breeds tropical and subtropical Pacific; possibly formerly on the Kermadecs, where twice recorded. **[Sp 89]**

TAHITI PETREL *Pseudobulweria rostrata* — **Very rare tropical vagrant**

38cm, 400g. Head, upperparts, chin, throat and upper breast uniform sooty brown; lower breast, belly and undertail white; *underwings uniformly sooty brown*; long pointed tail. Bill massive (37 x 17mm), black; legs mainly pink, feet mainly dark. **Habitat:** Breeds tropical and subtropical Pacific. One NZ specimen: Dargaville Beach, 1988; but others seen east of Northland and in Bay of Plenty in winter 1988. **[Sp 112]**

KERMADEC PETREL *Pterodroma neglecta* — **Locally common native**

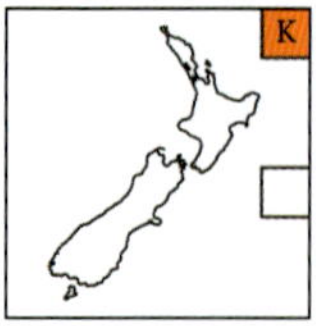

38cm, 500g. Variable plumages. Pale phase has head, neck and body white to pale ashy grey with flecks of grey or brown; upperwing brownish black except white inner webs and shaft of primaries sometimes visible; underwing dark greyish brown with *obvious white bases to the primaries*. Intermediate phase similar but has variable amounts of brown on head, upperparts, upper breast and undertail. See Plate 20 for dark phase. Bill (30 x 13mm) black; feet and legs variable from black to pale flesh with dark tips to webs. **Habitat:** Breeds subtropical South Pacific, including the Kermadecs. Migrates to tropical Pacific. Vagrants occasionally reach NZ mainland. **Breeding:** Oct–May. **[Sp 88]**

SOFT-PLUMAGED PETREL
CHATHAM ISLANDS TAIKO
KERMADEC PETREL light phase
OENIX PETREL
KERMADEC PETREL intermediate phase
TAHITI PETREL

WHITE-NAPED PETREL *Pterodroma cervicalis* — **Uncommon native**

43cm, 450g. Forehead white; blackish cap on crown, nape and sides of face to below eye; *broad white collar across hindneck*; upperparts frosty grey with broad black M across wings; small grey tab in front of wings. Underparts and underwing white except for black patch at bend of wing extending towards tip and diagonally towards body. Bill sturdy (37 x 16mm), black; feet and legs fleshy pink with black toes and ends of webs. **Habitat:** Breeds Macauley Island, Kermadecs, and recently colonised Philip Island, off Norfolk Island. Migrates to subtropical North Pacific, mainly in the west. A few vagrants reach waters off mainland NZ. **Breeding:** Dec–Jun. [Sp 93]

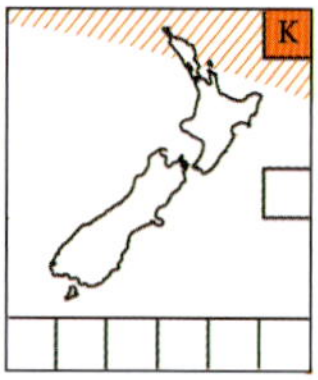

JUAN FERNÁNDEZ PETREL *Pterodroma externa* — **Very rare subtropical vagrant**

43cm, 500g. Like White-naped Petrel except hindneck grey, cap is paler and underwings have only a *short black tab* extending from bend of wing towards body. **Habitat:** Breeds Alejandro Selkirk Island (formerly Más Afuera), Juan Fernández Islands, off Chile. Migrates to subtropical North Pacific. A few vagrants reach NZ waters. [Sp 92]

MOTTLED PETREL (Korure) *Pterodroma inexpectata* — **Common endemic**

34cm, 325g. *Face white, heavily mottled grey*; upperparts dark frosty grey, with darker M across wings; dark eye patch; underparts white except *grey patch on the lower breast and belly*. Underwing white with broad black diagonal band from bend of wing to near body. Bill small (27 x 12mm), black; legs and feet fleshy pink with black toes and ends of webs. **Habitat:** Breeds Fiordland, Codfish Island and other islands off Stewart Island, and at The Snares. Ranges to pack ice, around NZ mainland and to Chathams in breeding season. Migrates to North Pacific. **Breeding:** Dec–Jun. [Sp 91]

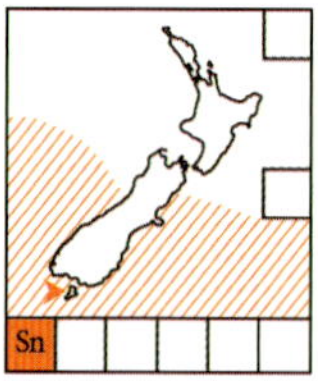

BLACK-WINGED PETREL *Pterodroma nigripennis* — **Common native**

30cm, 175g. Forehead white, mottled on forecrown; dark patch below eye; crown, sides of neck and upperparts pale grey; upperwings grey with darker M across wings. Underparts and underwings white except for dark outer half to primaries, dark trailing edge and *black diagonal band from bend of wing to short of body*. Bill short and stubby (24 x 11mm), black; legs and feet fleshy pink with dark toes and ends to webs. **Habitat:** Breeds subtropical South Pacific, including Kermadecs, Three Kings, East, Portland and Chatham islands. Seen prospecting over headlands on northern NZ coast. Migrates to North Pacific. **Breeding:** Dec–Jun. [Sp 94]

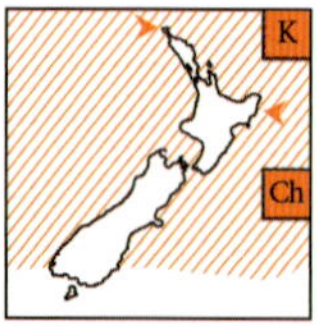

CHATHAM ISLANDS PETREL *Pterodroma axillaris* — **Very rare endemic**

30cm, 200g. Like Black-winged Petrel, but underwing has only tips of primaries dark, narrow dark trailing edge, but *black diagonal bar reaches to black base of underwing*. **Habitat:** *c.* 250 pairs breed at South East Island, and also breeding in predator-free enclosures on Pitt Island and southern Chatham Island following successful translocations of chicks in 2002–11. Feeds mainly south and southeast of the Chathams, and winters off western South America. **Breeding:** Dec–Jul. [Sp 95]

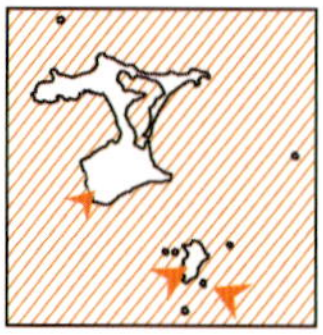

WHITE-NAPED PETREL
JUAN FERNÁNDEZ PETREL
MOTTLED PETREL
BLACK-WINGED PETREL
CHATHAM ISLANDS PETREL

COOK'S PETREL (Titi) *Pterodroma cookii*

Locally common endemic

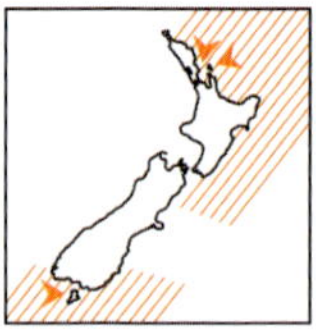

29cm, 190g. Forehead white, scaled grey on forecrown; dark eye patch; crown and *upperparts pale grey* with dark M across wings. Underparts and underwings white except mottled black patch at bend of wing extending towards tip and as short diagonal line a short way towards body. Bill long and fine (28 x 10mm), black; legs and feet bluish with yellowish base of webs, dark toes and ends to webs. **Habitat:** Breeds Little Barrier, Great Barrier and Codfish islands. Migrates to eastern Pacific, from California to Chile. **Breeding:** Oct–May. **[Sp 96]**

PYCROFT'S PETREL *Pterodroma pycrofti*

Locally common endemic

28cm, 160g. Forehead and forecrown white scaled with grey; crown, hindneck and sides of face to under eye and upperparts medium grey (*paler than Stejneger's Petrel but darker than Cook's Petrel*) with dark M across wings. Underparts and underwings white except for mottled black patch at bend of wing extending towards tip and as short diagonal line a short way towards body. Bill short and fine (24 x 9mm), black; legs and feet bluish with darker toes and ends to webs. **Habitat:** Breeds northeastern NZ; main colonies at Mercury, Hen and Chickens, and Poor Knights islands. Occasionally beach-wrecked, mainly in northern NZ in summer and autumn. Migrates to central North Pacific. **Breeding:** Nov–Apr. **[Sp 98]**

GOULD'S PETREL *Pterodroma leucoptera*

Uncommon subtropical visitor

29cm, 175g. Forehead white; *black crown, sides of face, nape and sides of neck to wing*; rest of upperparts grey with darker M across wings. Underparts and underwings white except for black patch at bend of wing extending towards tip and as thick diagonal bar well towards body. Bill short and fine (24 x 10mm), black; legs and feet bluish with dark toes and ends to webs. **Habitat:** Breeds Cabbage Tree and Boondelbah islands (NSW) and mountains of New Caledonia. Non-breeders range through Tasman Sea and to NZ waters in Nov–May. Migrates to eastern tropical Pacific for winter. **[Sp 99]**

STEJNEGER'S PETREL *Pterodroma longirostris*

Rare subtropical vagrant

28cm, 160g. Like Gould's Petrel except smaller and *black cap is reduced with white on forecrown*; *grey neck and sides of neck*; diagonal bar on underwing less prominent. **Habitat:** Breeds at Alejandro Selkirk Island (formerly Más Afuera), Juan Fernández Islands, off Chile. Migrates to subtropical North Pacific. Vagrants occasionally reach NZ in summer. **[Sp 97]**

COOK'S PETREL
PYCROFT'S PETREL
GOULD'S PETREL
STEJNEGER'S PETREL
Black-winged Petrel (see Plate 22)

Small seabirds with blue-grey upperparts with black M across upperwings and lower back, white underparts, black-tipped tail, and blue legs and feet. Bill has comb-like lamellae on inside. Sexes and ages alike. Species separated by size, bill structure, face colours and extent of black on tail. Flight fast, buoyant and erratic; usually stay close to the surface. Feed near surface by plunging or dipping. Generally oceanic. Do not follow ships or fishing boats. Noisy at night at breeding colonies, with harsh cooing and cackling calls in air or on ground. Occasionally wrecked in huge numbers on NZ beaches.

FAIRY PRION (Titi Wainui) *Pachyptila turtur* — **Abundant native**

25cm, 125g. Upperparts blue-grey; faint white eyebrow; bold black M across wings; *tail broadly tipped black, including tips of uppertail coverts.* Bill (22 x 11mm) blue with large nail. **Habitat:** Breeds circumpolar subantarctic, including many islands around NZ, especially Poor Knights, Cook Strait, Motunau Island, Foveaux Strait, The Snares and Chathams. Abundant in coastal waters near breeding colonies, and the most common beach-wrecked bird. Ranges through Tasman Sea and east of NZ. **Breeding:** Oct–Mar. [Sp 105]

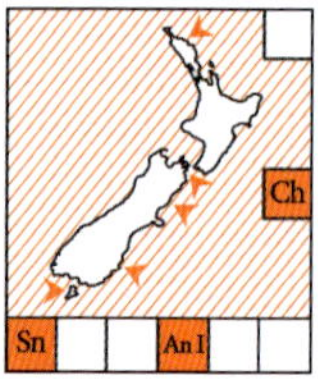

FULMAR PRION *Pachyptila crassirostris* — **Locally common native**

26cm, 140g. Like Fairy Prion but slightly larger and paler. Bill (23 x 11mm) deeper and with *very large nail.* **Habitat:** Breeds subantarctic at Heard Island (South Indian Ocean), Chathams (Pyramid, The Forty-fours), Bounty, The Snares and Auckland islands. Probably mainly sedentary but occasionally reaches NZ coast. **Breeding:** Oct–Feb. [Sp 106]

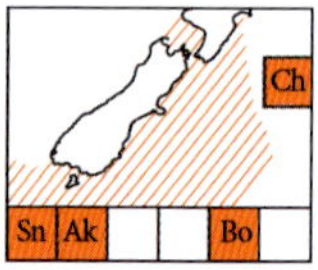

BROAD-BILLED PRION (Parara) *Pachyptila vittata* — **Common native**

28cm, 200g. Upperparts blue-grey; black M across wings; dark face with clear white eyebrow; *very narrow black tip to tail. Bill very broad* (34 x 20mm), iron-grey. **Habitat:** Breeds South Atlantic and around southern NZ; main colonies are in Fiordland, Foveaux Strait, off Stewart Island, The Snares and Chathams. Ranges around NZ coast and rarely to Australia. **Breeding:** Aug–Jan. [Sp 101]

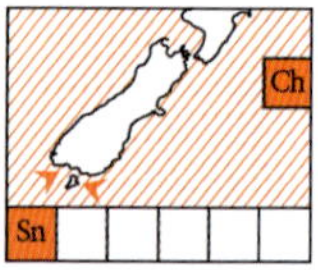

THIN-BILLED PRION *Pachyptila belcheri* — **Common subantarctic visitor**

26cm, 145g. Upperparts pale blue-grey; indistinct blackish M across wings; very pale face with prominent white eyebrow; *very narrow black tip to tail.* Bill slender (25 x 11mm) with weak hook. **Habitat:** Breeds subantarctic South America, Falklands and Indian Ocean. Ranges through southern oceans in winter and spring, regularly reaching NZ. [Sp 104]

SALVIN'S PRION *Pachyptila salvini* — **Common subantarctic visitor**

27cm, 170g. Upperparts blue-grey, slightly darker on the head; blackish M across wings; *narrow black tip to tail.* Bill stout (30 x 16mm), bluish. Like Antarctic Prion, but in the hand, bill larger and *lamellae visible at base of closed bill.* **Habitat:** Breeds in subantarctic Indian Ocean. Regular visitor to NZ seas in winter and spring. [Sp 102]

ANTARCTIC PRION *Pachyptila desolata* — **Locally common native**

26cm, 150g. Like Salvin's Prion, but in the hand, bill smaller (27 x 14mm) and *lamellae not visible at the base of the closed bill.* **Habitat:** Breeds widely in subantarctic and Antarctic zones; in NZ region, many breed at Auckland Islands and a few nest at Scott Island, Ross Sea. Regular visitor to seas off NZ mainland, mainly in winter and spring. **Breeding:** Dec–Mar. [Sp 103]

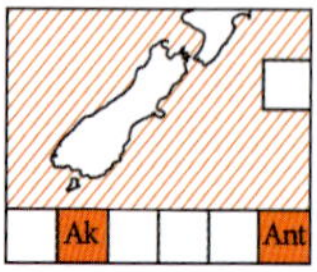

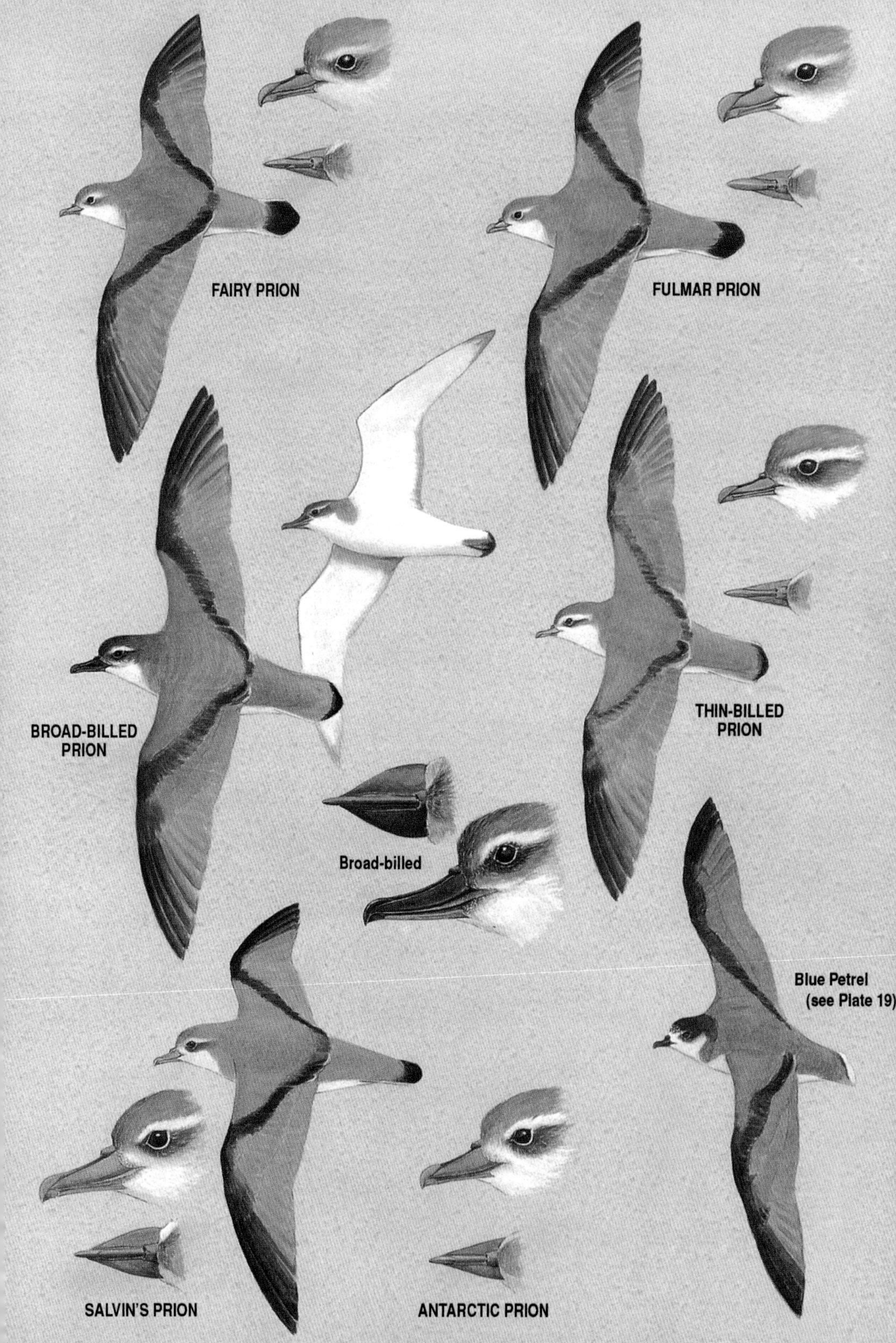
FAIRY PRION
FULMAR PRION
BROAD-BILLED PRION
THIN-BILLED PRION
Broad-billed
Blue Petrel
(see Plate 19)
SALVIN'S PRION
ANTARCTIC PRION

Large, heavy-bodied seabirds with robust, pale and well-hooked bill; prominent nostrils encased in a tube. Sexes and ages alike. In flight, long glides on stiffly held wings with occasional wingbeats. When windy, soar and wheel in huge arcs. Dive into sea and swim underwater with wings. Generally oceanic; rarely seen near land. Most follow ships and fishing boats. Clumsy on ground; legs and webbed feet set well back. Generally silent over breeding grounds at night, but loud calls and clacks from ground and burrows. Lay one large white egg, usually deep in a burrow. Long incubation and fledging periods.

WHITE-CHINNED PETREL (Shoemaker) *Procellaria aequinoctialis*

Uncommon native

55cm, 1250g. Entirely dark blackish brown except for a variable amount of *white feathering on chin*. Bill (52 x 21mm) yellowish horn, *without dark tip*, but dark nostrils and lines between plates; legs and feet black. Sometimes follows ships and fishing boats. **Habitat:** Breeds circumpolar subantarctic, including Antipodes, Auckland and Campbell islands. Occasionally seen near mainland NZ but mainly ranges to the south and east. **Breeding:** Nov–May. **[Sp 108]**

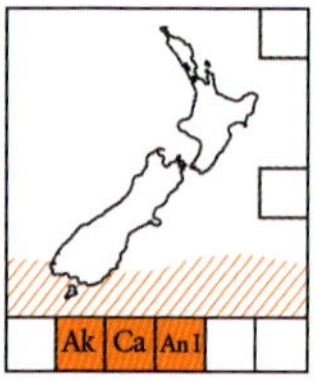

WESTLAND PETREL *Procellaria westlandica*

Uncommon endemic

48cm, 1100g. Entirely dark blackish brown. Bill (49 x 20mm) yellowish horn *with dark tip* and black between the plates; legs and feet black. Like Black Petrel but larger. Often follows ships and fishing boats. **Habitat:** *c.* 4000 pairs breed only in the forested coastal foothills of the Paparoa Range between Barrytown and Punakaiki, West Coast. In breeding season, seen mainly off east coast from East Cape to Banks Peninsula, Cook Strait and off west coast from Fiordland to Taranaki, but ranges west to Australia. Migrates to central or eastern South Pacific, Dec–Mar. **Breeding:** May–Dec. **[Sp 109]**

BLACK PETREL (Taiko) *Procellaria parkinsoni*

Uncommon endemic

46cm, 700g. Entirely dark blackish brown. Bill (41 x 15mm) bluish yellow *with dark tip* and black between the plates; legs and feet black. Like Westland Petrel but smaller. Often follows ships and fishing boats. **Habitat:** *c.* 1750 pairs breed only on Great Barrier and Little Barrier islands; formerly on inland ranges of the mainland. In breeding season, seen mainly around North Island and west to Australia. Migrates to eastern tropical Pacific, Jul–Oct. **Breeding:** Nov–Jul. **[Sp 110]**

GREY PETREL (Pediunker) *Procellaria cinerea*

Uncommon native

48cm, 1000g. Head and sides of face to below eye dark grey; upperparts ashy grey, darker on tail and wings, merging into white underparts without any strongly defined line; *dark grey underwings and undertail* separate it from large grey and white shearwaters (see Plate 26). Bill stout (47 x 17mm), greenish flesh with black between plates and on nostrils; legs and feet greyish flesh, darker on outside, yellowish webs. Distinctive albatross-like gliding with rapid duck-like wingbeats. Regularly follows ships and fishing boats. **Habitat:** Breeds circumpolar subantarctic; in NZ region, at Antipodes and Campbell islands. Rarely seen near NZ mainland. **Breeding:** Apr–Dec. **[Sp 111]**

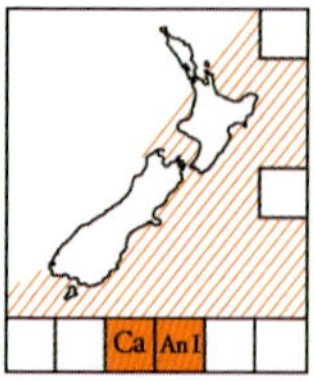

Flesh-footed
Shearwater
(see Plate 28)
WHITE-CHINNED PETREL
WESTLAND PETREL
BLACK PETREL
GREY PETREL

Medium to large seabirds with long slender bill and nostrils encased in a short flattened tube. Sexes and ages alike; most are dark above and mainly white below, but some are all dark. Many species form large feeding flocks. Usually fly close to the surface, often with a series of rapid wingbeats followed by a glide, but in windy conditions can wheel high on stiffly held wings. Clumsy on ground; legs and webbed feet set well back. Range from coastal to oceanic. Some species are highly migratory. Most species very vocal at breeding colonies at night. Lay one large white egg, usually deep in a burrow. Long incubation and fledging periods.

BULLER'S SHEARWATER *Puffinus bulleri*

Common endemic

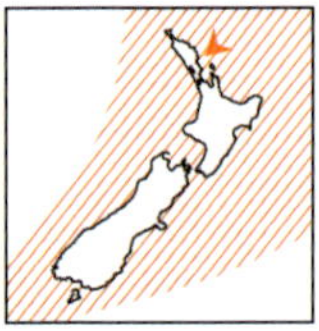

46cm, 425g. Head and hindneck blackish brown; *back and upperwings frosty grey with bold dark M across wings, lower back and rump*; uppertail light grey with broad black tip to long wedge-shaped tail; sharp line of demarcation from white underparts and underwing. Bill long and slender (41 x 12mm), bluish grey with darker tip; legs and feet pink with dark outer toes and outer edge of tarsus. **Habitat:** Breeds only at Poor Knights Islands. Ranges widely around NZ coast and migrates to northern and eastern Pacific. **Breeding:** Nov–May. [Sp 116]

WEDGE-TAILED SHEARWATER *Puffinus pacificus*

Locally common native

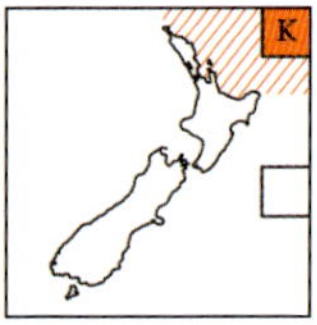

46cm, 450g. Variable plumages but always with *broad wings and long wedge-shaped tail.* Rare pale phase has head, hindneck and upperparts dark brown with a sharp line of demarcation from white chin and throat; underparts mainly white but variably mottled brown on sides of breast, flanks and undertail; underwing white with dark borders and tip, mottled brownish grey on underwing coverts. Bill compressed (38 x 13mm), slate grey; legs and feet pale flesh. Main ground call a wailing 'ka-whoo-ahh'. **Habitat:** Subtropical and tropical Pacific and Indian oceans. Breeds on Kermadec Islands and rarely reaches NZ mainland. **Breeding:** Dec–Jun. [Sp 115]

BULLER'S
SHEARWATER
Grey Petrel
(see Plate 25)
pale phase
dark phase
WEDGE-TAILED
SHEARWATER

GREAT SHEARWATER *Puffinus gravis* **Very rare South Atlantic vagrant**

48cm, 800g. Distinctive black *cap to below eyes and contrasting pale collar*, back and rump greyish brown; chin, throat and underparts white, but with a *greyish-brown belly patch and undertail coverts*; underwings white with black tips and broad trailing edge, and *two parallel diagonal black lines on the innerwing. Bill black*; legs and feet greyish pink. **Habitat:** Breeds on islands in the South Atlantic Ocean and mainly winters in the North Atlantic, but a few winter in the eastern Pacific. Seven NZ records, all since 2006 and off eastern coast or Chathams. **[Sp 119]**

STREAKED SHEARWATER *Calonectris leucomelas* **Very rare North Pacific straggler**

48cm, 500g. *Small sleek head and hindneck white, heavily streaked with dark brown*, especially on the hindcrown and neck; upperparts greyish brown with white edges to feathers giving a scaly appearance; chin, throat and underparts white; underwings white with broad dark trailing edge and brown splashes on coverts. *Bill horn coloured with a dark tip*; legs and feet greyish pink. **Habitat:** Breeds on islands in the northwest Pacific in northern winter, migrates to tropical west Pacific, Arafura Sea and Coral Sea in Oct–Apr. One NZ record: Kawhia Beach, Waikato, 2006. **[Sp 114]**

CORY'S SHEARWATER *Calonectris borealis* **Very rare Atlantic vagrant**

46cm, 900g. Head, hindneck and upperparts greyish brown; chin, throat and underparts white, without clear line of demarcation. Underwing white, with narrow dark margins and tips. *Bill large* (57 x 21mm), *dull yellow with darker tip*; legs and feet fleshy pink, stained brown on outer toe and outer surface of tarsus. **Habitat:** Breeds North Atlantic and Mediterranean. Migrates to South Atlantic and South Indian oceans. One NZ record: Foxton Beach, 1934. **[Sp 113]**

PINK-FOOTED SHEARWATER *Puffinus creatopus* **Very rare subtropical vagrant**

48cm, 900g. Head, hindneck and upperparts greyish brown; chin, throat and underparts mainly white, but some have greyish brown on chin, throat and flanks; underwings whitish with varying grey and white mottling. Bill heavy (42mm), *pinkish with a dark tip*; legs and feet pink. **Habitat:** Breeds off Chile. Migrates to eastern North Pacific. A few have reached NZ waters, off east coast South Island. **[Sp 118]**

GREAT SHEARWATER
STREAKED SHEARWATER
CORY'S SHEARWATER
PINK-FOOTED SHEARWATER

SOOTY SHEARWATER (Titi, Muttonbird) *Puffinus griseus*

Abundant native

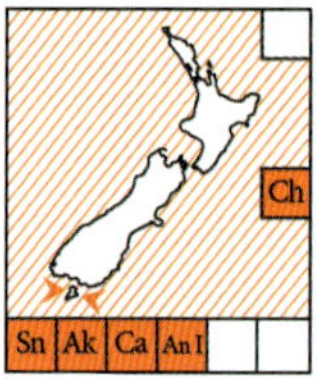

44cm, 800g. Sooty-brown upperparts, slightly greyer underparts with *silvery-grey flash on underwings.* Wings long and narrow, tail short and rounded. Bill long and slender (42 x 13mm), dark grey; feet dark lilac with brown markings on the outer side. Main call a series of hoarse moans: 'oo-oo-ah', getting louder and faster each time. **Habitat:** Breeds mainly around NZ, on islands and mainland headlands from the Three Kings to Campbell Island, but also southern Australia, Macquarie Island and southern South America. Main NZ colonies are at The Snares, islands off Stewart Island and in Foveaux Strait, and the Chathams. NZ birds migrate to North Pacific, many becoming beach-wrecked in NZ in Apr–May and Oct–Dec. **Breeding:** Nov–May. [Sp 120]

SHORT-TAILED SHEARWATER *Puffinus tenuirostris*

Common Australian migrant

42cm, 550g. Like small Sooty Shearwater but shorter-billed (32 x 11mm) and *underwings are normally dull grey and do not flash prominently.* Feet dark lilac with brown markings on the outer side. **Habitat:** Breeds southern Australia, especially on islands in Bass Strait. Migrates to North Pacific, but some pass through NZ waters on the outward and return journeys, and are often beach-wrecked around May and October. [Sp 121]

WEDGE-TAILED SHEARWATER *Puffinus pacificus*

Locally common native

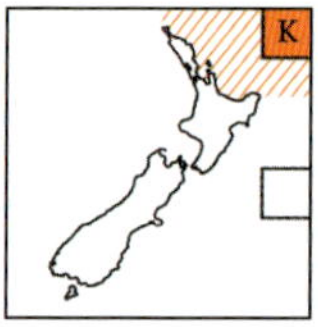

46cm, 450g. Variable plumages but always with *broad wings and long wedge-shaped tail.* Common dark phase all blackish brown except for slightly paler but nonreflective centres to underwing. Bill compressed (38 x 13mm), slate grey; legs and feet pale flesh. See Plate 26 for pale phase. Main ground call a wailing moan: 'ka-whooo-ahh'. **Habitat:** Subtropical and tropical Pacific and Indian oceans. Breeds on the Kermadecs and rarely reaches NZ mainland. **Breeding:** Dec–Jun. [Sp 115]

CHRISTMAS ISLAND SHEARWATER *Puffinus nativitatis*

Very rare tropical vagrant

37cm, 350g. *Completely sooty brown.* Like Sooty Shearwater and Short-tailed Shearwater but much smaller; *dark brown underwing and longer slightly wedge-shaped tail.* Bill long and slender (40 x 10mm), black; feet dark brown. **Habitat:** Breeds tropical and subtropical mid-Pacific Ocean. Two NZ records: Dargaville Beach, 1976 and Curtis Island (Kermadecs), 1989. [Sp 122]

FLESH-FOOTED SHEARWATER (Toanui) *Puffinus carneipes*

Common native

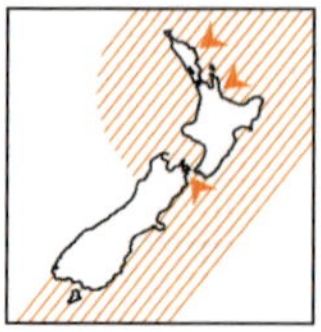

44cm, 600g. Large, bulky, chocolate-brown shearwater with *pale bill* (42 x 13mm), *darker at tip,* and *flesh-pink legs and feet.* Main call a series of high-pitched moans, resembling sound of cats fighting. **Habitat:** Breeds in western Indian Ocean, southern Australia, Lord Howe Island, northern NZ and in Cook Strait. Main NZ colonies at Hen and Chickens, Mercury group, Karewa Island, Saddleback Island (near New Plymouth), and Trio and Titi islands (Cook Strait). Ranges through coastal waters of North Island, occasionally south to Foveaux Strait in the west and Banks Peninsula to the Chathams in the east. Migrates to North Pacific. **Breeding:** Nov–May. [Sp 117]

SOOTY SHEARWATER
SHORT-TAILED SHEARWATER
WEDGE-TAILED
SHEARWATER
dark phase
FLESH-FOOTED
SHEARWATER
CHRISTMAS ISLAND
SHEARWATER

FLUTTERING SHEARWATER (Pakaha) *Puffinus gavia* — **Abundant endemic**

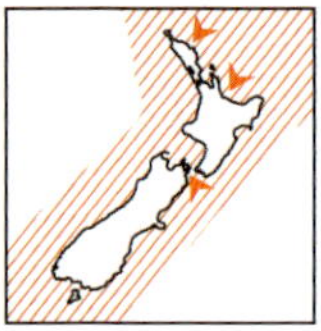

33cm, 300g. Head to below eye, upperparts and thigh patch dark greyish brown *merging into* white underparts and flank patch; faintly mottled partial collar; *underwings white* with brownish borders and dusky-grey armpits. Bill fine (33 x 9mm). Like Hutton's Shearwater at sea but smaller; paler underwings. In hand, *sides of undertail coverts white.* Main call at colony a rapid staccato 'ka-how ka-how ka-how ka-how kehek kehek kehek kehek-errr'. **Habitat:** Breeds on many islands around North Island and Cook Strait. Flocks common in coastal waters and harbours; some, especially juveniles, visit Australian waters in non-breeding season. **Breeding:** Sep–Feb. [Sp 125]

HUTTON'S SHEARWATER *Puffinus huttoni* — **Locally common endemic**

36cm, 350g. Head to below eye, upperparts and thigh patch blackish brown merging into white underparts and flank patch; faintly mottled broad collar; *underwings centred off-white with indistinct broad brownish borders and extensive dusky-grey armpits.* Bill fine (37 x 9mm). Like Fluttering Shearwater at sea but larger; darker underwings. In hand, *sides of undertail coverts brown.* Main colony call 'ko-uw ko-uw ko-uw ko-uw, kee kee kee kee – aaah'. **Habitat:** Breeds only in Seaward Kaikoura Range. In NZ waters, mainly off east coast South Island and in Cook Strait but migrates to Australian waters in winter. **Breeding:** Oct–Apr. [Sp 126]

MANX SHEARWATER *Puffinus puffinus* — **Very rare North Atlantic vagrant**

36cm, 450g. Head to below eye, and upperparts dark brownish black, *sharply demarcated* from white underparts; notch of white on upper neck. *Underwings, including armpits, white* with sharply defined black edges and tips. Bill slender (35 x 8mm). **Habitat:** Breeds North Atlantic. Three NZ records: Pukerua Bay, 1972, Waikanae, 1985 and Otaki, 2002. [Sp 124]

NEWELL'S SHEARWATER *Puffinus newelli* — **Very rare North Pacific straggler**

33cm, 390g. A small black and white shearwater in the Fluttering/Hutton's shearwater group, but separable from these species by its *black upperparts,* white underwings, and *extensive black feathering on the undertail coverts.* **Habitat:** Breeds in Hawai'i and a few on Rapa Island, French Polynesia; winters in eastern tropical Pacific. One NZ record: Dargaville Beach, 1994. [Sp 123]

SUBANTARCTIC LITTLE SHEARWATER *Puffinus elegans* — **Locally common native**

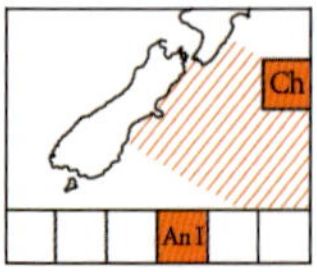

28cm, 250g. Similar to Little Shearwater, except that *slate-black on head extends below eye* and has a clear-cut margin; feathers on upperwing coverts and lower back often have white tips, underwings darker; and bill more robust (25 x 9mm), **Habitat:** Breeds in South Atlantic and NZ subantarctic. Main NZ colonies at the Chathams and Antipodes, especially Bollons Island. Mostly sedentary but occasionally seen off eastern South Island and lower North Island. **Breeding:** Aug–Feb. [Sp 128]

LITTLE SHEARWATER *Puffinus assimilis* — **Common native**

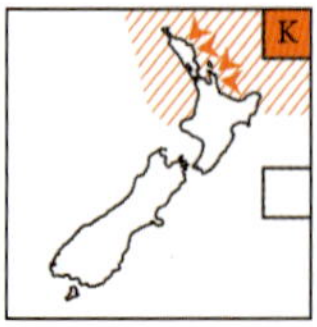

28cm, 240g. Head *to above eye,* and upperparts slate-black; eyebrow, face and underparts white; underwing white except for thin black border on trailing edge. Bill slender (23–26 x 8mm), dull lead blue with black ridge and tip; legs and feet pale blue with fleshy webs. **Habitat:** Breeds in the South Indian Ocean, in the Tasman and around NZ. Main NZ colonies at Kermadecs, off eastern Northland, Mokohinau, Mercury and Aldermen islands. Mostly sedentary but usually feeds well offshore and so rarely seen in coastal waters. **Breeding:** Jun–Dec. [Sp 127]

FLUTTERING
SHEARWATER
HUTTON'S
SHEARWATER
MANX
HEARWATER
NEWELL'S
SHEARWATER
SUBANTARCTIC
LITTLE SHEARWATER
LITTLE
SHEARWATER

PLATE 30

Bulwer's Petrel, STORM PETRELS & DIVING PETRELS

BULWER'S PETREL *Bulweria bulwerii* **Very rare North Pacific straggler**

27cm, 100g. Dainty, prion-sized, dark sooty brown petrel, except for a slightly paler chin and face, and grey diagonal bar across coverts on inner part of the upper wing, with *very long wings, exceptionally long tail* and small head. The tail is wedge-shaped, but usually appears pointed. Bill black with large nail at tip. Legs pink with grey and pink feet. *Flight erratic and often zigzagging with rapid flapping interspersed with long glides*; appears buoyant like a tern or noddy, although rarely rises more than 5m from the surface. **Habitat:** Breeds North Pacific and North Atlantic oceans, winters in tropical waters, including some movement from Pacific to Indian oceans. Two NZ records: Te Horo Beach, 1988 and New Brighton Beach, 2014. [Sp 107]

Storm petrels are very small dainty seabirds with broad rounded wings, short bill with a prominent nostril with a single opening, and very long legs. Sexes and ages alike. Fly close to the surface, erratically with short glides or hops. Pick up food while hovering or pattering on the water. Oceanic; rarely follow boats. Most silent at night over colonies, but give coos, churrs or whistles from burrows or the ground.

WHITE-FACED STORM PETREL (Takahikare-moana) *Pelagodroma marina* **Common native**

20cm, 45g. *Forehead, eyebrow and underparts white*; crown, nape and patch through eye dark grey brown; back and upperwing brownish grey, contrasting with *pale grey rump*; forked (5–15mm) black tail. **Habitat:** Breeds temperate and subtropical Atlantic and around Australia and NZ; main NZ colonies in Hauraki Gulf, Bay of Plenty, Motunau Island, around Stewart and Auckland islands and Chathams. Disperses widely after breeding and rarely seen in NZ coastal waters. **Breeding:** Oct–Mar. [Sp 131]

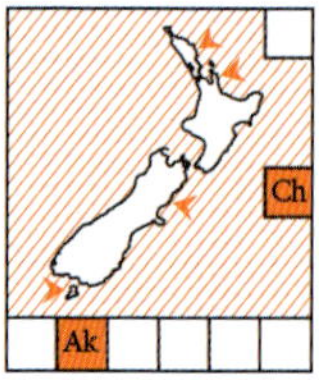

KERMADEC STORM PETREL *Pelagodroma albiclunis* **Very rare endemic**

20cm, 50g. Like White-faced Storm Petrel, except with a distinctive *white rump*, and an *only slightly forked tail* (1.5–6mm). **Habitat:** 100–300 pairs breed only on Haszard Island, and possibly Macauley Island, in the southern Kermadecs. Seen at sea between NZ and Kermadecs, and also off Lord Howe Island. **Breeding:** Aug–Jan. [Sp 132]

Diving petrels are small, stocky seabirds with short, broad wings, short, wide bill and paired nostrils opening upwards; blue legs. Sexes alike. Fast whirring flight close to the surface. Generally coastal. Do not follow ships or trawlers. Noisy at night over and at breeding colonies.

COMMON DIVING PETREL (Kuaka) *Pelecanoides urinatrix* **Abundant native**

20cm, 130g. Upperparts black; sides of face, neck and throat mottled grey; underparts white *but underwings smoky grey*. Bill stubby (16 x 8mm), black; blue legs and feet. Like South Georgian Diving Petrel at sea but underwing darker. In hand, underwing coverts greyish brown, *inner webs of three outer primaries dusky brown, and septal process near base of nostril*. **Habitat:** Breeds circumpolar subantarctic. Main NZ sites off eastern North Island, Cook and Foveaux straits, Chatham Islands, The Snares, Antipodes and Auckland islands. **Breeding:** Aug–Feb. [Sp 137]

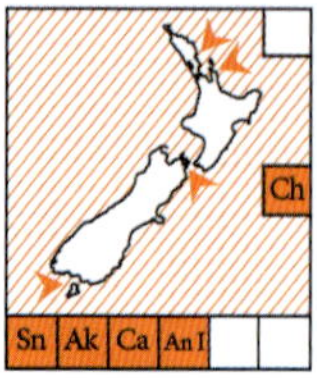

SOUTH GEORGIAN DIVING PETREL *Pelecanoides georgicus* **Very rare native**

18cm, 120g. Like Common Diving Petrel at sea, but *underwing usually paler*. In hand, underwing coverts white, *inner webs of three outer primaries white or pale grey, septal process in bill near centre of nostril*. **Habitat:** Breeds circumpolar subantarctic; in NZ region, only on Codfish Island. **Breeding:** Nov–Mar. [Sp 138]

WHITE-FACED
STORM PETREL
KERMADEC
STORM PETREL
BULWER'S
PETREL
White-faced
Storm Petrel
COMMON
DIVING PETREL
SOUTH GEORGIAN
DIVING PETREL

WILSON'S STORM PETREL *Oceanites oceanicus*

Uncommon native

18cm, 35g. *Brownish black* with faint diagonal grey-brown bar on upperwing from bend of wing to body; prominent *unmarked white rump*; *square tail.* Yellow-webbed feet project beyond tail. **Habitat:** Breeds subantarctic and Antarctica, including several colonies in the Ross Sea sector. Migrates to Northern Hemisphere but occasionally seen in NZ waters, mainly Nov–Dec and Mar–May. **Breeding:** Dec–Apr.

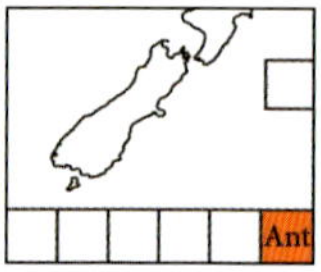

[Sp 129]

LEACH'S STORM PETREL *Oceanodroma leucorhoa*

Rare straggler

20cm, 45g. *All blackish brown* except head darker, clear diagonal grey-brown bar on upperwing from bend of wing to body, *white rump with a dark central line*; *forked tail.* **Habitat:** Breeds North Pacific and North Atlantic oceans. Migrates to tropics, but a few reach NZ waters. **[Sp 136]**

GREY-BACKED STORM PETREL *Garrodia nereis*

Locally common native

18cm, 35g. Head, neck, throat and upper breast greyish black, rest of underparts white; back, upperwings and tail ashy grey, with black tips to wings and square tail. **Habitat:** Breeds circumpolar subantarctic; in NZ region, at Chathams, Antipodes, Auckland and Campbell islands. Mainly sedentary but ranges to 30° S in NZ seas, though rarely seen near mainland coast. **Breeding:** Sep–Mar. **[Sp 130]**

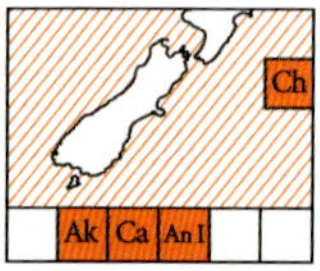

NEW ZEALAND STORM PETREL *Pealeornis maoriana*

Very rare endemic

18cm, 33g. Sooty-black upperparts except broad white rump, and slightly paler wingbar. Sooty-black chin, neck and chest; white belly with a variable amount of *dark streaks bleeding from chest onto belly, especially on flanks*, and even onto the undertail in some birds; undertail mottled dark brown; square tail; underwings have pale central panel; *feet extend well beyond tail.* **Habitat:** Three specimens collected off eastern NZ in the 1800s, but then believed extinct until rediscovered in January 2003. Breeding only on Little Barrier Island, and feeds off northeastern NZ from the Three Kings Islands to the northern Bay of Plenty; after breeding some move to the western Tasman Sea and Coral Sea. **Breeding:** Feb–Jun.

[Sp 133]

BLACK-BELLIED STORM PETREL *Fregetta tropica*

Locally common native

20cm, 55g. Variable; some almost identical to White-bellied Storm Petrel, but *feet project well beyond tail.* Typically has sooty-black upperparts except broad white rump, grey chin and *variable black line down centre of white belly* connecting black breast and dark undertail. A few have all-white belly. **Habitat:** Breeds circumpolar subantarctic, including Antipodes and Auckland islands. Ranges widely and migrates to tropics in winter. **Breeding:** Dec–May. **[Sp 134]**

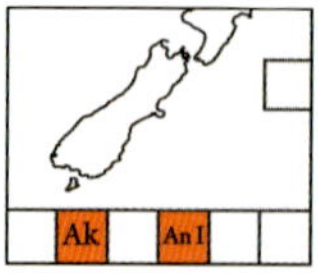

WHITE-BELLIED STORM PETREL *Fregetta grallaria*

Rare native

20cm, 50g. Variable plumages; some like a few Black-bellied Storm Petrels, but *feet level with or just past tip of tail.* Typically has sooty-black upperparts, mantle feathers often white-tipped; rump white; black chin, throat and breast contrasts with *white belly*; black undertail. Some have smudgy, not white, underwings. **Habitat:** Breeds subtropics, including Kermadecs. Ranges widely at sea but rarely seen off NZ coast. **Breeding:** Mar–Aug. **[Sp 135]**

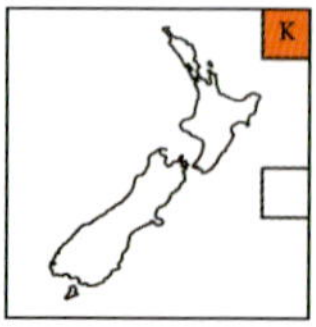

WILSON'S
STORM PETREL
LEACH'S
STORM PETREL
GREY-BACKED
STORM PETREL
NEW ZEALAND
STORM PETREL
BLACK-BELLIED STORM PETREL
WHITE-BELLIED STORM PETREL

Tropicbirds are medium-sized, white, rather tern-like seabirds mostly confined to the tropics. Distinguished from terns by their wedge-shaped tail. Sexes alike. Adults have two long central tail-streamers. Juveniles have black barring above and lack tail streamers. Their flight is distinctive; direct with strong steady wingbeats about 30m above the sea. Over land, they ride the updraughts along cliffs and hills. At sea, they plunge-dive for fish and squid.

RED-TAILED TROPICBIRD (Amokura) *Phaethon rubricauda* — Rare tropical native

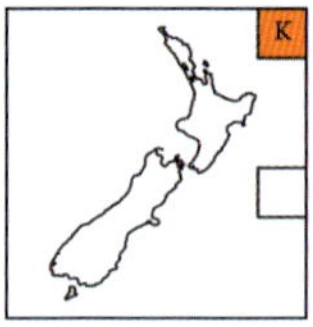

46cm, (+ up to 40cm for tail streamers), 800g. Adult white with *black feather-shafts* on primaries, tertials and tail; black mark through eye. Tern-like *bright red bill*; *tail streamers red* but often difficult to see. Juvenile lacks tail streamers, is barred black above and has *black or dull red bill*. **Habitat:** Tropical seas; in NZ region, breeds at Kermadecs. Rare annual vagrant to northern NZ mainland, mainly driven south by tropical storms. **Breeding:** Dec–Aug. [Sp 139]

WHITE-TAILED TROPICBIRD *Phaethon lepturus* — Rare tropical vagrant

38cm, (+ up to 40cm for tail streamers), 300g. Smaller and more graceful in flight than Red-tailed Tropicbird. Adult white with prominent *diagonal black band on inner wing and solid black patch near the tip of the upperwing*; tail streamers *white*; *bill yellow to orange*. Juvenile like that of Red-tailed Tropicbird but has black patch on the outer upperwing and *pale yellow bill*. **Habitat:** Breeds widely through the tropics and ranges throughout tropical seas. About 20 vagrants recorded in NZ, mainly immature birds driven south by tropical storms. [Sp 140]

Frigatebirds are large, dark seabirds with very long, thin, pointed wings, long, deeply forked tail and long hooked bill. The sexes differ in the amount of white on their underparts; males are mostly black and have a dark bill, whereas females have a prominent white chest and a pale bill. Immatures are hard to separate, as they have gingery heads and white chests like females. Usually seen soaring high over tropical seas or pursuing other birds, particularly boobies and terns, forcing them to drop their food, which they catch in mid-air. In NZ, often seen drifting effortlessly high above the shore facing into the prevailing wind. They feed entirely on the wing, snatching flying fish and picking fish and squid from the surface of the sea.

LESSER FRIGATEBIRD *Fregata ariel* — Rare tropical vagrant

76cm, 1000g. Diagnostic *thin white tab extends from the chest onto the armpits and base of the underwing*. Adult male is *otherwise all dark*. Adult female has white of chest and flanks extending to hindneck as *a white collar* contrasting with the *dark hood, chin and throat*. Juvenile has a white chest and gingery head, blotched white when worn. **Habitat:** Breeds widely through the tropics and ranges throughout tropical seas. About 40 vagrants recorded in NZ, mainly driven south by tropical storms. [Sp 160]

GREAT FRIGATEBIRD *Fregata minor* — Rare tropical vagrant

95cm, 1450g. Largest frigatebird. Adult male *all dark*. Adult female and juveniles have white of chest and flanks *extending up to chin and throat but not onto underwing*. Juveniles have a gingery head, blotched white when worn. **Habitat:** Breeds widely through the tropics and ranges throughout tropical seas. About 15 vagrants recorded in NZ, mainly driven south by tropical storms. [Sp 159]

RED-TAILED TROPICBIRD
WHITE-TAILED TROPICBIRD
juv
juv
juv
♂
♀
LESSER FRIGATEBIRD
♂
♀
juv
GREAT FRIGATEBIRD

Large, mainly black and white or brown and white seabirds. Streamlined body with long narrow wings and a long tapering tail. Conical bill, bare facial skin; fully webbed feet. Sexes alike. Juveniles and immatures darker than adults, taking several years to attain full adult plumage. Flight steady and direct; short periods of deliberate flapping and long glides. Feed on fish and squid caught by spectacularly diving into the sea, often from a considerable height. Often sit on the surface between feeding bouts. Gannets favour temperate and subtropical seas, whereas boobies favour tropical and subtropical seas. Gannets nest on the ground in large dense colonies; boobies nest on the ground or in trees singly or in loose colonies. Lay 1–4 plain pale eggs.

AUSTRALASIAN GANNET (Takapu) *Morus serrator*

Common native

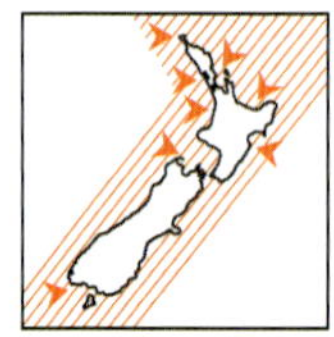

89cm, 2.3kg. *White with buff-yellow head and most flight feathers black* (but not the three innermost secondaries or tertials as in Masked Booby); amount of black in the tail varies with age and moult, adults typically have only four central feathers black. Gular (throat) stripe runs from base of bill to chin. Bill pale bluish grey; feet slate grey with blue-yellow lines on legs and toes. Juvenile is grey-brown spotted above, white with brown streaks below, and a dark bill. Adult plumage is attained over 3–5 years, head and underparts whitening first, whereas the rump and tail often remain blotched. **Habitat:** Breeds on many islands and some headlands around the NZ coast. Feeds mostly in coastal waters over the continental shelf. Most juveniles move to the seas off eastern and southern Australia and return when 3–7 years old. **Breeding:** Jul–Jan. [Sp 143]

CAPE GANNET *Morus capensis*

Very rare vagrant

90cm, 2.6kg. Similar to Australasian Gannet, but its gular (throat) stripe is 3–4 times as long, running from the *base of the bill to the foreneck* rather than to the chin, the eye is a paler pearly white, and the black face mask is slightly larger. At sea, the *tail is usually completely black*, but about 10% have white outer tail feathers, like Australasian Gannet. Juveniles and immatures have a great variety of black, brown and white mottled plumages and are indistinguishable from Australasian Gannets at sea. **Habitat:** Breeds southern Africa and usually quite sedentary, but vagrants have reached Australia and Cape Kidnappers, where one bred with an Australasian Gannet in 1999–2000, and the resulting hybrid bred in 2005. [Sp 142]

MASKED BOOBY *Sula dactylatra*

Locally uncommon native

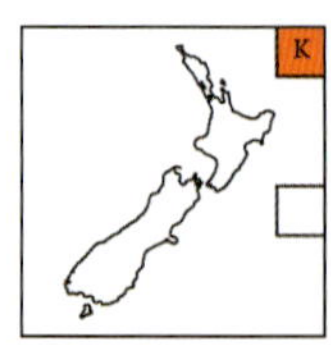

80cm, 2.1kg. Adult resembles adult Australasian Gannet but has *white head, orange-yellow or pink bill, black face mask* with dark brown eye. *Black trailing edge of upperwing includes tertials and so extends to body*; tail all dark. Feet greyish-yellow. Juvenile has mottled brown upperwings, paler back, heavily streaked (almost brown) head and neck grading to white on the collar and lower neck, and a pale yellowish bill. **Habitat:** Tropical and subtropical seas; in NZ region, 200+ pairs breed at the Kermadecs; only seven vagrants recorded from NZ mainland. **Breeding:** Jul–Apr. [Sp 145]

BROWN BOOBY *Sula leucogaster*

Rare tropical vagrant

70cm, 1300g. *Dark chocolate brown, sharply cut off at mid-breast from white undersurface of body*; centre of underwing white. Legs yellow or greenish yellow. Male has blue facial skin and yellowish-grey bill; female has yellow facial skin and base of bill. Juvenile like adult, but brown parts paler, white parts mottled grey-brown, and less white on underwing. Bill and facial skin blue-grey; legs flesh-grey. **Habitat:** Breeds widely through the tropics and ranges throughout tropical seas. Vagrants are often seen at the Kermadecs, and almost annually in northern NZ. [Sp 144]

AUSTRALASIAN GANNET
juv
juv
imm
APE GANNET
MASKED BOOBY
juv
juv
BROWN BOOBY
juv
juv

Shags are medium to large aquatic birds. Most are all black, or black above and white below. Bill long, strongly hooked at the tip. Upright posture when perched. Short legs; feet are fully webbed. Many have brightly coloured facial skin when breeding. Sexes alike. In flight, wings short and broad, and neck is extended. Swim with head held uptilted and body low in the water.

BLACK SHAG (Kawau, Great Cormorant) *Phalacrocorax carbo*

Common native

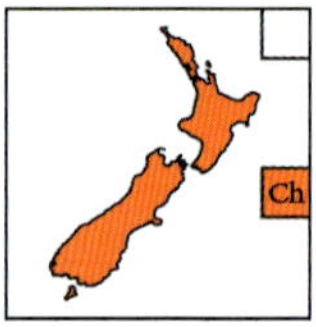

88cm;♂ 2.5kg, ♀ 1.9kg. Black with browner wings and tail, and white patch on cheeks and throat. Facial skin yellow, but orange-red below eye when breeding. Breeding adult also has a white thigh patch, a small black crest on nape, and thin white streaks (filoplumes) on the crown and upper neck. Bill grey; eye green; feet black. Juvenile dull brown above, brown mottled white below, and no throat patch. **Habitat:** Rivers, streams and lakes, also estuaries, harbours and sheltered coastal waters. **Breeding:** Apr–Jan. **[Sp 147]**

PIED SHAG (Karuhiruhi, Pied Cormorant) *Phalacrocorax varius*

Locally common native

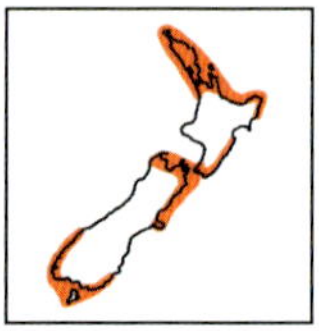

81cm;♂ 2.2kg, ♀ 1.7kg. Glossy black above, face from above eye and all underparts white, except for black thighs. Long grey bill; bare skin buff in front of green eye, pink below bill; eye-ring blue; feet black. Juvenile similar but brownish above, white underparts streaked and mottled brown. **Habitat:** Coastal, ranging inland only to coastal lagoons and lakes. **Breeding:** All year. **[Sp 148]**

LITTLE BLACK SHAG (Little Black Cormorant) *Phalacrocorax sulcirostris*

Locally common native

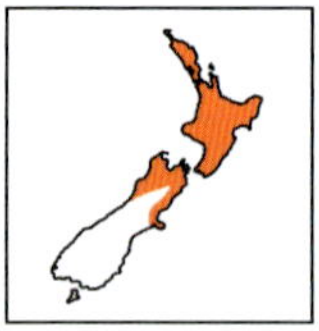

61cm, 800g. Small elegant shag. Wholly black with green gloss, *dark-edged feathers give a scalloped effect* on back. *Long, slender lead-grey bill*; dark facial skin; eye green; feet black. Juvenile similar but brownish. *Tail short* compared with that of Little Shag. Gregarious, *often feeding as a coordinated pack* and flying in V-formation low to the water. **Habitat:** Lakes, estuaries and harbours. Common in North Island but rare in South Island. **Breeding:** Nov–Apr. **[Sp 149]**

LITTLE SHAG (Kawaupaka, Little Pied Cormorant) *Phalacrocorax melanoleucos*

Common native

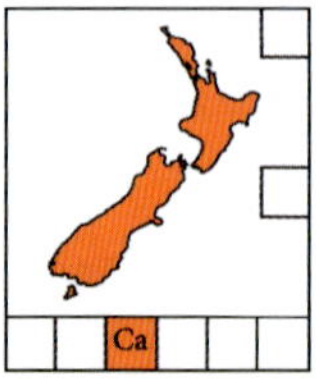

56cm, 700g. Smallest shag. Highly variable plumages from all black to pied, but *all have short stubby bills*, yellow in adults, dark in juveniles; eye brown; feet black. Adults have yellow facial skin and small black crest on forehead. *Tail long* compared with that of Little Black Shag. Usually feed solitarily or in small loose groups, but gregarious when roosting and nesting. **Habitat:** Lakes, farm ponds, rivers and streams, also estuaries, harbours and sheltered coastal waters. **Breeding:** Aug–May. **[Sp 146]**

Darters are rather like slim, long-necked shags. When swimming, only their head and neck are visible. They spend long periods perched, mostly in trees, with wings and tail spread.

DARTER *Anhinga melanogaster*

Very rare Australian vagrant

90cm, 1750g. Large but slim, *very long thin kinked neck, straight dagger-like yellow bill and very long tail.* A white flash runs from eye onto neck; prominent *cream streaks on upper wings and long scapular feathers.* Male otherwise all brownish black except for red patch on foreneck. Female and immatures paler with upperparts grey-brown and underparts white or pale buff. In flight, *long broad wings and long flared tail*; rapid shallow wingbeats interspersed with glides. **Habitat:** Lakes, coastal lagoons and estuaries. Four NZ records. **[Sp 158]**

BLACK SHAG
juv
breeding
PIED SHAG
juv
♂
♀
DARTER
LITTLE BLACK SHAG
juv
white-throated phase
pied phase
intermediate phase
juv
LITTLE SHAG

SPOTTED SHAG (Parekareka, Blue Shag) *Stictocarbo punctatus* **Locally common endemic**

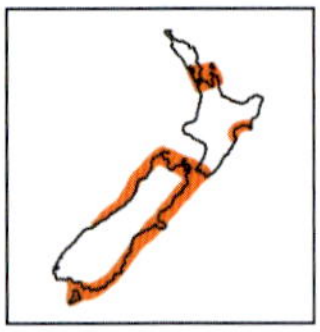

70cm, 1200g. Slender grey shag with *yellow feet* and long slender brown bill. Breeding adult has small black spots on back and wings; rump, tail and thighs black; underparts grey; a *broad white stripe from above eye down sides of the neck*, and sparse white streaks (filoplumes) on neck and thighs; conspicuous double crest, curled forward; green facial skin. Non-breeding adult lacks crests and has obscure white stripe on neck, yellow facial skin, and paler underparts. Immature is paler and browner, lacks distinct head or neck markings. In flight, looks very slender and pale with darker rump and tail. Flies low to the water, often in strings, with rapid wingbeats. **Habitat:** Estuaries, harbours and coastal waters around mainland NZ. **Breeding:** All year. **[Sp 156]**

PITT ISLAND SHAG *Stictocarbo featherstoni* **Locally common endemic**

63cm, 1200g. Like Spotted Shag but darker, no white neck stripe and facial skin apple green in breeding season. **Habitat:** *c.* 450 pairs in coastal waters around Chatham Islands only. **Breeding:** Aug–Mar. **[Sp 157]**

KING SHAG *Leucocarbo carunculatus* **Rare endemic**

76cm, 2.5kg. Large black and white shag with *pink feet*. White patches on wings appear as a *white bar on the folded wing*; yellow-orange fleshy swellings (caruncles) above base of bill; other facial skin and throat (gular) pouch reddish in breeding season, otherwise grey-blue; eye-ring blue. **Habitat:** *c.* 125 pairs in coastal waters of Marlborough Sounds only. **Breeding:** May–Nov. **[Sp 150]**

STEWART ISLAND SHAG *Leucocarbo chalconotus* **Locally common endemic**

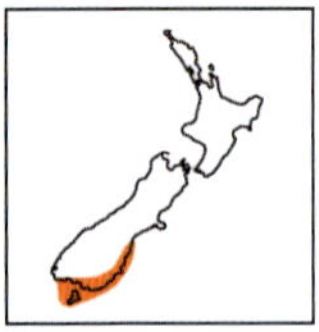

68cm, 2.5kg. Large *pink-footed* shag with pied and bronze phases and some intermediates. Pied phase is like King Shag, but caruncles orange and facial skin purplish; juvenile is brown above and white below, and usually lacks white on wings and back. Bronze phase is brownish black with green and blue sheen, orange caruncles and purplish facial skin; juvenile is brown except for some white streaks on breast. Breeding birds develop black crest on forehead and scattered faint white streaks (filoplumes) on head. **Habitat:** Coastal waters off southeastern South Island and Stewart Island. **Breeding:** Sep–Mar. **[Sp 151]**

CAMPBELL ISLANDS SHAG *Leucocarbo campbelli* **Locally common endemic**

63cm, 2kg. Like King Shag, but caruncles absent and entire head and neck black, apart from a white chin. **Habitat:** *c.* 2000 pairs in coastal and offshore waters around Campbell Islands only. **Breeding:** Nov–May. **[Sp 155]**

AUCKLAND ISLANDS SHAG *Leucocarbo colensoi* **Locally common endemic**

63cm, 2kg. Like King Shag, but caruncles absent. **Habitat:** *c.* 2000 pairs in coastal and offshore waters around Auckland Islands only. **Breeding:** Nov–May. **[Sp 154]**

BOUNTY ISLANDS SHAG *Leucocarbo ranfurlyi* **Locally common endemic**

71cm, 2.5kg. Like King Shag, but caruncles absent. **Habitat:** *c.* 300 pairs in coastal and offshore waters around Bounty Islands only. **Breeding:** Oct–Mar. **[Sp 153]**

CHATHAM ISLANDS SHAG *Leucocarbo onslowi* **Locally common endemic**

63cm, 2.25kg. Like King Shag, but orange caruncles are large and prominent. **Habitat:** *c.* 350 pairs in coastal and offshore waters around the Chatham Islands only. **Breeding:** Aug–Mar. **[Sp 152]**

SPOTTED SHAG
imm
breeding
non-breeding
PITT ISLAND SHAG
non-breeding
KING SHAG
juv
STEWART ISLAND SHAG
bronze phase
pied phase
juv pied phase
CHATHAM ISLANDS SHAG
CAMPBELL ISLANDS SHAG
AUCKLAND ISLANDS SHAG
BOUNTY ISLANDS SHAG

Medium to large elegant wading birds with long neck and legs, straight dagger-like bill and long unwebbed toes. Flight strong, typically with heavy languid wingbeats on broad wings, neck folded back and head tucked in, and legs trailing. Sexes alike. Immatures generally duller. Many have ornamental plumes on the head, back and chest. The colours of bill, facial skin, legs and feet brighten or change in breeding season. They feed in shallow water or on damp pasture, walking slowly or standing motionless and lunging at prey. Diet is mainly aquatic animals. All make a harsh grating call in flight; otherwise silent except at breeding colonies. Many species breed and roost communally, others are solitary. Lay 2–5 blue-green eggs on a platform of sticks built in trees or on cliffs.

REEF HERON *Egretta sacra* **Very rare Pacific vagrant**

66cm, 400g. White phase is stocky with *short legs and long heavy brownish-yellow bill.* Feeding stance typically hunched and horizontal. **Habitat:** Coasts. All *c.* 500 NZ resident birds are dark (see Plate 37), but a vagrant or white colour variant has been seen once in NZ: Canterbury, 1987. **Breeding:** Sep–Mar. **[Sp 167]**

PLUMED EGRET *Ardea intermedia* **Rare Australian vagrant**

64cm, 450g. All-white stocky heron, smaller than White Heron, larger than Little Egret. Fully stretched neck about same length as body and thicker than White Heron's. *Black line of gape ends level with eye.* In breeding plumage, extensive filamentous plumes on back and chest; legs and bill reddish; facial skin green. In non-breeding, bill and facial skin yellow; legs black, paler grey above 'knees'. **Habitat:** Freshwater and coastal wetlands, occasionally pasture. **[Sp 164]**

WHITE HERON (Kotuku, Eastern Great Egret) *Ardea modesta* **Very rare native**

92cm, 900g. Clearly the largest all-white heron. Long thin S-shaped neck with a distinct kink one-third back from the head; *fully stretched neck is longer than the body; black line of gape extends past the eye.* In breeding plumage, elegant filamentous plumes on back extend beyond the folded wings and the tail; *bill black*; facial skin green; legs black, yellowish above 'knees'. In non-breeding, plumes absent, *bill yellow*, facial skin greenish yellow and legs black. Usually solitary, standing or walking sedately in shallow water. **Habitat:** Freshwater wetlands and estuaries, occasionally wet pasture. In NZ, *c.* 50 pairs breed only at Okarito, West Coast, but disperse throughout mainland. **Breeding**: Sep–Jan. **[Sp 162]**

LITTLE EGRET *Egretta garzetta* **Rare Australian visitor**

60cm, 400g. Small *dainty* all-white heron with *long slender black bill*; facial skin yellow; legs and feet black except for *yellow soles. Black line of gape ends level with eye.* In breeding season, plumes on nape, chest and back; the two nape plumes are strap-like, whereas chest and back plumes are filamentous. *Very active when feeding,* dashing about in pursuit of fish, often with wings raised and with a high-stepping gait. Often solitary but may associate with White Herons. **Habitat:** Coastal lakes and estuaries. **[Sp 166]**

CATTLE EGRET *Ardea ibis* **Uncommon Australian migrant**

50cm; ♂ 390g, ♀ 340g. *Small stocky and short-necked* (shorter than body) heron with *yellow bill,* grey legs and feet, and a *heavy jowl* of feathers under the bill. In breeding plumage, orange-buff plumes on head, neck and breast. Transitional stages from all white to buff common from September onwards. Non-breeding and immature birds all white but can have a faint buff wash on the crown. **Habitat:** *Usually associate with livestock,* especially cattle, in damp pasture. May return to the same farms for autumn and winter year after year. **[Sp 163]**

REEF HERON
white phase
breeding
non-breeding
PLUMED EGRET
WHITE HERON
breeding
LITTLE EGRET
breeding
CATTLE EGRET

WHITE-FACED HERON *Egretta novaehollandiae*

Abundant native

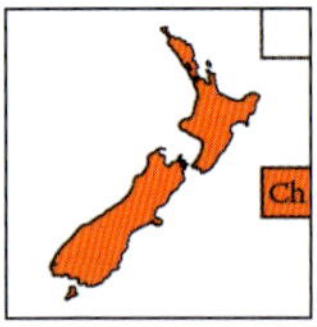

67cm, 550g. Slim *bluish-grey heron with white face, chin and upper throat, black bill* and greenish yellow legs. Strap-shaped plumes, more prominent in the breeding season, are long and pale grey on the back and short and pinkish brown on the chest. Juvenile lacks plumes and the white face is reduced, often white chin only. Flight slow, often high, with steady beats of two-toned wings. **Habitat:** Uses a wide variety of habitats from coastal estuaries and lagoons to rivers, lakes and farmland. Nests in solitary pairs high in trees, especially eucalypts and shelterbelt pines on farmland. **Breeding:** Jun–Feb. **[Sp 165]**

REEF HERON (Matuku moana) *Egretta sacra*

Uncommon native

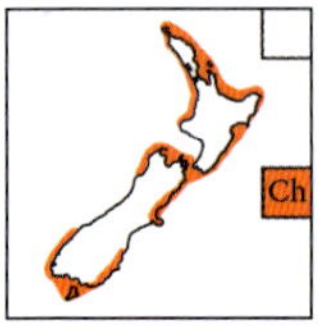

66cm, 400g. Dark phase uniformly *slate-grey* heron with a long heavy *horn-coloured-to-yellowish bill; legs relatively short*, yellow-green. Early in breeding season, long strap-like plumes form on back and short ones form on nape and foreneck. Juvenile browner and lacks plumes. *Feeding stance hunched and almost horizontal*; flight slow just above the water surface. Usually solitary or in pairs. **Habitat:** *c.* 500 birds in mangrove-filled inlets, rocky shores, wave platforms and sometimes on intertidal mudflats. Commonest in Northland, density decreasing southward, and uncommon in the South, Stewart and Chatham islands except Marlborough Sounds and Fiordland. **Breeding:** Sep–Mar. **[Sp 167]**

NANKEEN NIGHT HERON *Nycticorax caledonicus*

Very rare native

60cm, 800g. Stocky rounded short-necked heron, rufous brown or heavily streaked and spotted brown. Thick black bill; short yellow legs. Adult has rufous-brown (nankeen) upperparts, paler underparts, black cap. When breeding, two long slender white plumes hang from the nape. Juvenile dark brown, heavily spotted and streaked pale buff. In flight, looks heavy-headed, round-winged and short-tailed, and has shallower and faster wingbeats than other herons. Usually feeds at dusk or night and roosts in trees by day. **Habitat:** Margins of freshwater wetlands or tidal lagoons. Vagrant until it started breeding on Whanganui River in 1990s. **Breeding:** Oct–Mar. **[Sp 168]**

Bitterns are specialised for living in swamps; typically short-necked and camouflaged brown with dark and pale streaks, especially on underparts. Sexes alike. When disturbed, they 'freeze', with body and bill pointing skywards, sometimes swaying with raupo or reeds moving in the breeze.

AUSTRALASIAN BITTERN (Matuku) *Botaurus poiciloptilus*

Uncommon native

71cm; ♂ 1400g, ♀ 1000g. *Large bulky thick-necked bittern, mottled brown and buff.* Secretive, partially nocturnal, generally keeping within dense cover where its plumage blends with the vegetation. When flushed, rises with broad rounded wings labouring. Flight direct, neck withdrawn, legs trailing and with slow steady wingbeats. Usually solitary. During breeding, *distinctive deep booming calls, like air being blown over an open bottle.* **Habitat:** Mainly freshwater wetlands, especially with dense cover of raupo or reeds. Some movement to coastal wetlands in autumn and winter. **Breeding:** Aug–Mar. **[Sp 169]**

LITTLE BITTERN *Ixobrychus minutus*

Very rare Australian vagrant

30cm, 150g. *Very small bittern.* Adult male has *large buff wing patches* contrasting with *black flight feathers, back and tail*; ginger sides to face and neck. Adult female like male, but black replaced with brown. Juvenile yellowish buff, heavily streaked dark brown. Flight as in Australasian Bittern; *adults show prominent pale patches on dark upperwings.* **Habitat:** Freshwater wetlands. One NZ record: Westport, 1987. **[Sp 170]**

WHITE-FACED HERON
juv
REEF HERON
juv
AUSTRALASIAN BITTERN
NANKEEN NIGHT HERON
LITTLE BITTERN
uv
♀
♂
juv

SPOONBILLS & Australian Pelican

Spoonbills are large heron-like waterbirds with flat spoon-shaped bill. Sexes alike. They fly with neck outstretched, rapid wingbeats alternating with long glides. Roost in trees; breed in colonies with platform nests made from twigs and tidal debris. Disperse widely after breeding. Silent away from colonies. Diet is fish, crustaceans and other aquatic invertebrates.

ROYAL SPOONBILL *Platalea regia*

Common native

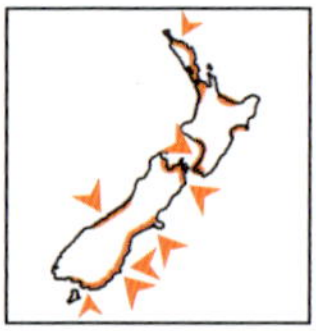

77cm, 1700g. Large *brilliantly white bird with long black spoon-shaped bill and black legs.* Adult has black facial skin marked with a yellow patch above each eye and a red spot in the centre of the forehead, and the surface of the bill is wrinkled. In breeding plumage, large white drooping plumes on the rear of the head and a yellowish wash across breast. Juvenile has plain black facial skin, smooth bill and small black tips to wings. Feeds by walking slowly forwards in shallow water, *sweeping partly open bill from side to side.* **Habitat:** Tidal mudflats, occasionally on margins of freshwater lakes. Main breeding colonies at Parengarenga Harbour, Kapiti Island, Okarito, Vernon Lagoons (Marlborough), and islands off Otago and Southland coasts. **Breeding:** Sep–Mar. **[Sp 174]**

YELLOW-BILLED SPOONBILL *Platalea flavipes*

Very rare Australian vagrant

88cm, 1900g. Like Royal Spoonbill, but plumage off-white and *bill and legs pale yellow.* Facial skin pale grey, bordered by a black line. In breeding plumage, medium-length stiff white plumes on lower neck, thin black lace-like plumes on wings, and red patches in front of eye. Feeds by *sweeping partly open bill from side to side* in shallow water. **Habitat:** Mainly inland wetlands and wet pasture. Two NZ records: Kaitaia area, 1976–81 and Wairarapa, 1981. **[Sp 175]**

Pelicans are large bulky birds with an enormous bill and gular (throat) pouch. Short legs make them ungainly on land, but they swim gracefully. Fly strongly with head tucked in, often in a flock in V-formation, or soar high on thermals. They feed mainly on fish scooped from the water, often feeding in a group to surround a shoal of fish. Favour large open waterbodies.

AUSTRALIAN PELICAN *Pelecanus conspicillatus*

Rare Australian vagrant

170cm, 5kg. *Enormous white bird with huge pink bill and pouch*; upperwing black with a large white panel; underwing white with black primaries. Juvenile brown where adult black. **Habitat:** Occasionally recorded in freshwater and tidal wetlands in NZ; irruption of *c.* 20 birds into northern NZ in 2012. **[Sp 141]**

non-breeding
breeding
juv
ROYAL SPOONBILL
YELLOW-BILLED SPOONBILL
Australian White Ibis (see Plate 39)
AUSTRALIAN PELICAN

IBISES & Pacific Heron

Ibises are large, heron-like, mainly wetland birds with strongly downcurved bill. Sexes alike. They fly with neck outstretched, rapid wingbeats alternating with long glides. Roost in trees. Diet is large invertebrates, worms, fish and crustaceans.

GLOSSY IBIS *Plegadis falcinellus* — Rare Australian vagrant

60cm, 500g. Slender *glossy dark brown ibis with long downcurved bill.* At a distance, stance like a feeding Pukeko. In breeding plumage, head, neck and upperparts deep glossy reddish brown, wings iridescent green; bill and facial skin grey, bordered at the base with a conspicuous white line. Non-breeding and juvenile dull brown with variable white mottling on head and neck. Flies with head and neck outstretched like a shag, but alternates rapid wingbeats with short glides. Feeds mainly by *probing* in soft mud. **Habitat:** Margins of freshwater lakes and swamps, and damp pasture. Occasional irruptions into NZ. A pair bred at Wainono Lagoon, South Canterbury, in 2014/15. [Sp 171]

AUSTRALIAN WHITE IBIS *Threskiornis molucca* — Rare Australian vagrant

70cm, 2kg. Large scruffy *white ibis with long heavy downcurved bill and unfeathered black head.* In breeding plumage, short yellowish plumes on foreneck, and long frilly black tertials droop over tail and folded wing. Non-breeding lacks neck plumes, and tertials shorter and greyer. Juvenile has head and neck fully feathered dark grey and white. In flight, head and neck outstretched, wings tipped black, and in adults a line of red bare skin shows on the underwing. Walks slowly, *probing* in mud. **Habitat:** Freshwater or brackish wetlands and wet pasture. Occasional small irruptions into NZ. [Sp 172]

STRAW-NECKED IBIS *Threskiornis spinicollis* — Very rare Australian vagrant

65cm, 1400g. Large *pied ibis with long downcurved bill.* Bare black head. Hind neck, back, upperwings and outer underwings black with glossy green and violet sheen. *Sides of neck and underparts and inner triangle on underwings white.* Adults have yellow straw-like plumes on the lower neck and red legs, whereas juveniles lack plumes and have black legs. Flies with head and neck outstretched, and alternates deep steady wingbeats with short glides. The *black and white underwings* are distinctive. Often croaks when alarmed or when taking flight. Walks slowly, *probing* in mud. **Habitat:** Pasture and shallow freshwater wetlands, rarely on intertidal flats. One NZ record: Tarras, Central Otago, 2009. [Sp 173]

PACIFIC HERON (White-necked Heron) *Ardea pacifica* — Very rare Australian vagrant

90cm, 900g. Robust *dark grey heron with a white head, neck and upper breast*; variable line of dark spots down the front of the neck. Greenish sheen and maroon plumes on back in the breeding season. Juvenile lacks plumes and is more heavily spotted and barred brown on neck and breast. In flight, upperparts dark with a striking *white patch at the bend of the wing.* **Habitat:** Margins of swamps and ponds, and damp pasture. [Sp 161]

GLOSSY IBIS
breeding
non-breeding
AUSTRALIAN WHITE IBIS
STRAW-NECKED IBIS
PACIFIC HERON

Diurnal birds of prey with long fingered or pointed wings; long tail; short hooked bill with coloured facial skin at the base of the bill (cere); powerful, largely unfeathered legs with long sharp talons for grasping prey or gripping carrion. Sexes usually alike, but females larger. Juveniles darker than adults.

SWAMP HARRIER (Kahu, Australasian Harrier) *Circus approximans* — **Abundant native**

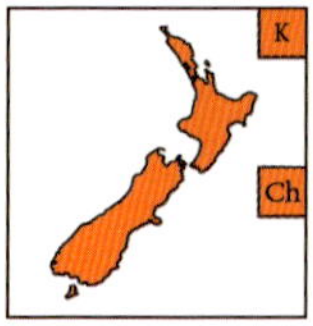

♂ 55cm, 650g; ♀ 60cm, 850g. *Large brown hawk with long fingered wings held in shallow V*, and a long slightly rounded tail. In adult, head and upperparts dark brown, face paler; rump white, tail light brown barred dark brown; underparts reddish brown streaked dark brown, underwings barred at tips and on trailing half. Becomes paler with age; some very old males are frosty grey above, pale buff underparts and white underwings. Eye yellow in males, very pale yellow in females. Juvenile very dark brown with a prominent *white patch on back of head*; brown rump and brown eye. *Commonly soars and glides* in search of prey or carrion; *often feeds on road-killed animals*. **Habitat:** Farmland, tussockland and swamps, also forest edges. **Breeding:** Sep–Feb. [Sp 177]

NEW ZEALAND FALCON (Karearea) *Falco novaeseelandiae* — **Uncommon endemic**

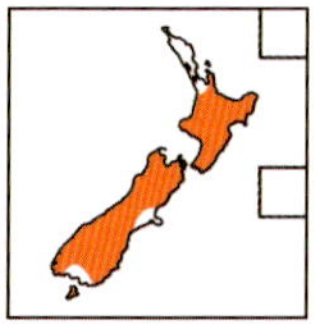

♂ 43cm, 300g; ♀ 47cm, 500g. *Fast-flying raptor with rapid beats of long pointed wings*; also soars and glides. Adult has head, sides of face and vertical patch (like drooping moustache) below eye dark brownish black, faint rufous eyebrow; nape, back, wings and tail bluish black, faintly barred buff. Chin white, throat and sides of neck buff streaked dark brown; breast and belly dark brown narrowly barred white; thigh and undertail rufous. Bill black; cere, legs and feet yellow; eye dark brown. Juvenile distinctly darker brown and less boldly marked. Bush Falcon form (North and northwestern South islands) as above; eastern form (eastern South Island) larger and paler; southern form (southwestern South, Stewart and Auckland islands) intermediate, more rufous on Auckland Islands. Often perches high in trees or on a rock, swoops to catch prey. *Call a loud rapid 'kek-kek-kek'*. **Habitat:** Forests and bush patches, open tussockland of South Island. Juveniles wander to cities, orchards, and offshore islands. **Breeding:** Aug–Mar. [Sp 180]

BLACK KITE *Milvus migrans* — **Very rare Australian vagrant**

♂ 50cm, 550g; ♀ 55cm, 600g. Large *dark-brown* raptor with paler head and shoulder patches. Soars or glides on long fingered *wings held flat*, and frequently twists its *long forked tail*. Adult has forehead and chin grey merging into brown on the crown, cheeks and throat; rest of body dark brown with some darker streaks. Pale shoulder patch when bird is at rest. Bill black, cere yellow, legs and feet yellow. Juvenile paler, and head, neck and breast heavily streaked buff; upperwing mottled buff; bill black, cere grey, legs and feet yellow. **Habitat:** Open country; seven NZ records. [Sp 176]

BLACK FALCON *Falco subniger* — **Very rare Australian vagrant**

♂ 50cm, 600g; ♀ 54cm, 800g. Like *large* NZ Falcon but *uniformly sooty brown* except for pale streaked chin and face, and dark grey glossy wash on underwing and undertail. Juvenile darker with pale feather edges and faint barring under tail and wings. **Habitat:** Open country and scattered forest. One NZ record: Gisborne, 1983. [Sp 179]

NANKEEN KESTREL *Falco cenchroides* — **Uncommon Australian vagrant**

♂ 32cm, 160g; ♀ 34cm, 180g. Small long-winged and long-tailed raptor with *habit of hovering*, poised in mid-air facing into the wind with tail fanned. In flight, *back and upperwings cinnamon brown* with black wingtips; underparts white with buff wash on breast and variable fine dark streaks. Male has *blue-grey head* streaked black, and *tail blue-grey* with black band near tip and narrow white tip. Female and juvenile have pale rufous head, finely streaked black; *tail pale rufous* with black band near tip and narrow white tip. **Habitat:** Open country. Occasional small irruptions into NZ. [Sp 178]

SWAMP HARRIER
juv
ad
juv
ad ♀
ad ♂
imm
NEW ZEALAND FALCON
ad
juv
BLACK KITE
BLACK FALCON
NANKEEN KESTREL
♂
♀
♂

Most rails and crakes are secretive birds of wetlands and are rarely seen except when attracted by recorded calls. Plumage is usually a pattern of black, white, brown and chestnut. Immatures are duller. Sexes alike. Body is narrow, for slipping through dense vegetation. Long unwebbed toes spread their weight. The short tail flicks as they walk. Bill stout and dagger-like in rails, shorter in crakes. Fly reluctantly when disturbed but are capable of sustained flight, mainly at night.

WEKA *Gallirallus australis* — Locally common endemic

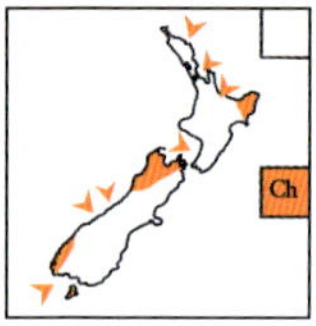

53cm;♂ 1000g, ♀ 700g. *Flightless. Brown, streaked black.* Sturdy short bill and legs. The four subspecies are separated by plumage colour. Rare North Island Weka is greyer below and has brown legs; Buff Weka, introduced to Chatham Islands, is the palest; Western Weka (Nelson to Fiordland) is noticeably chestnut, except in Fiordland, where a dark form is common; Stewart Island Weka is the smallest and also has a dark form, but paler than Western Weka. Sometimes very inquisitive. Walks quietly, flicking leaves aside with bill in search of food. Runs fast, neck outstretched. *Territorial call a loud repeated 'coo-eet', rising in pitch.* **Habitat:** Forests, scrub and open country with good cover. **Breeding:** Aug–Feb. **[Sp 183]**

BANDED RAIL (Moho pereru) *Gallirallus philippensis* — Uncommon native

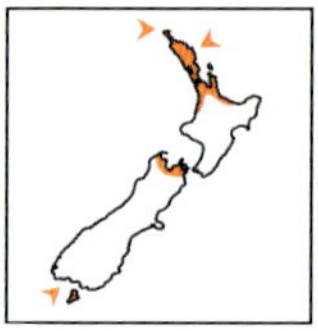

30cm, 170g. Strikingly marked but secretive. *Upperparts olive brown and black with white spots, and underparts barred black and white.* A chestnut band crosses chest, and a narrower one passes through eye to hindneck; whitish eye stripe, grey chin and throat. Long stout bill, brown. Juvenile less distinctly marked. Can fly well but, when flushed, flies for a short distance with legs dangling. Call a creaky 'swit', heard mostly at dusk and dawn. **Habitat:** Salt marshes, mangroves and, less often, freshwater swamps; also some offshore islands. **Breeding:** Sep–Mar. **[Sp 182]**

AUCKLAND ISLANDS RAIL *Lewinia muelleri* — Locally common endemic

21cm, 90g. Smaller and darker than Banded Rail. Back, wings and uppertail olive brown streaked black. Crown, sides of head and neck rufous to gingery brown. Throat and bill grey. Flanks and undertail finely barred black and white. Long slim bill, reddish. Legs pale brown. **Habitat:** Dense scrub cover, tussock and herb fields on Adams and Disappointment islands of the Auckland Islands only. **Breeding:** Oct–Dec. **[Sp 181]**

SPOTLESS CRAKE (Puweto, Putoto) *Porzana tabuensis* — Uncommon native

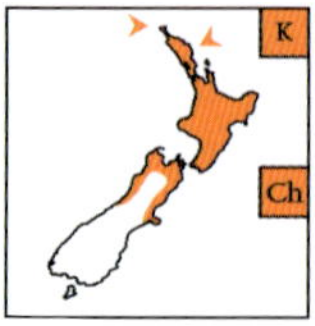

20cm, 45g. Small dark rail, secretive but responds to taped calls. Head and underparts leaden grey with a bluish sheen, *upperparts plain dark chocolate brown*, undertail black barred white. Bill short, black; eye and eye-ring red; legs reddish. Juvenile lacks sheen, and chin and throat dull white. Varied calls; usually sharp 'pit-pit', a repeated 'book' and a distinctive *rolling 'purrrrrrrr'*, like an alarm clock going off and gradually running down. **Habitat:** Freshwater wetlands with raupo or sedge, especially in the North Island; forest on some offshore islands. **Breeding:** Aug–Feb. **[Sp 184]**

MARSH CRAKE (Koitareke, Baillon's Rail) *Porzana pusilla* — Uncommon native

17cm, 35g. Tiny slim secretive rail. Like a miniature Banded Rail, but upperparts cinnamon brown streaked black and white. Sides of head and underparts blue-grey; flanks, abdomen and undertail are black, barred white. Bill, legs and feet greenish; eye red. Juvenile barred brown and buff on underparts, pale buff on cheeks and throat. Readily walks on duckweed and other floating vegetation. *Call a harsh 'krek'*, like a fingernail being drawn along a comb. **Habitat:** Dense beds of reeds and rushes in freshwater and estuarine wetlands. **Breeding:** Sep–Jan. **[Sp 185]**

Western
dark form
WEKA
Buff
Western
BANDED RAIL
AUCKLAND ISLANDS RAIL
juv
juv
MARSH CRAKE
SPOTLESS CRAKE

Birds of marsh and open water. Most are black, brown and purple-blue. Sexes alike. Wings short and broad. The bill extends onto their forehead as a shield, usually with diagnostic colour. Their strong legs and long toes aid walking on floating vegetation. Toes may be lobed (coots) for specialised swimming. They run well, walk with flicking tail, exposing a white undertail, and swim with bobbing head.

TAKAHE (Notornis) *Porphyrio hochstetteri* — **Very rare endemic**

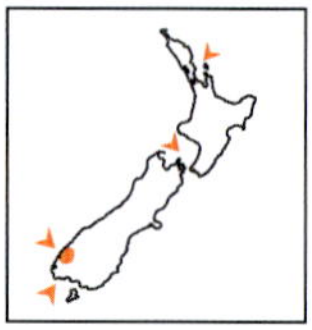

63cm, 3kg. *Like an enormous Pukeko. Flightless.* Colour ranges from iridescent dark blue head, neck and breast and peacock-blue shoulders to olive-green and blue back and wings. *Bill and shield massive*, scarlet, paler toward the tip; legs and feet red; eye brown. Immature duller; bill and shield dark grey. Mainly vegetarian; leaving behind *chewed and abandoned stems of tussock or other grasses* and 8cm-long *sausage-shaped fibrous droppings*. Male and female duet with a loud Weka-like, but *slow and deep, 'coo-eet'*; alarm note a *deep resonant 'oomf'*. **Habitat:** Natural range is now tussockland and beech forest in mountains west of Lake Te Anau. Introduced to rank grassland on Tiritiri Matangi, Motutapu, Kapiti, Mana, Maud, Secretary and Rarotoka islands. **Breeding:** Oct–Feb. **[Sp 189]**

PUKEKO (Purple Gallinule, Purple Swamphen) *Porphyrio melanotus* — **Abundant native**

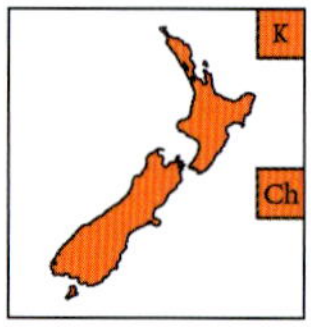

51cm; ♂ 1050g, ♀ 850g. Deep blue with black head and upperparts. *Undertail white, flirted with every step. Bill and shield scarlet*; eye red; legs and feet orange-red. Sexes alike. Immature has much brown and buff in the plumage and on bill and legs. Voice a loud unmusical screech. Runs well and swims with tail held high. Clambers about and may perch in scrub and trees. When disturbed in the open, runs to cover or flies, legs dangling, for a short distance. Flies high at night, calling – a loud harsh screech. **Habitat:** Wetlands, estuaries, short damp pasture and parks. Often in extended family groups. **Breeding:** Aug–Mar. **[Sp 188]**

AUSTRALIAN COOT *Fulica atra* — **Locally common native**

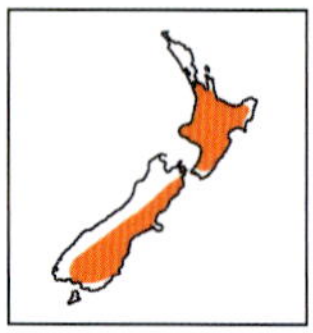

38cm; ♂ 570g, ♀ 520g. *Black with white bill and shield. No white under tail.* Eye red; legs dark grey, *feet lobed*. Immature dark brown-grey, shield small and pinkish grey. Mainly aquatic; swims with head jerking back and forth, *dives* with a short forward jump to pluck submerged aquatic plants, patters across the surface as it labours to take off. Sometimes comes ashore to graze on short grass. Often in flocks. Main call a loud harsh 'krark'. **Habitat:** Small freshwater lakes and shallow bays of larger lakes. **Breeding:** Aug–Mar. **[Sp 190]**

DUSKY MOORHEN *Gallinula tenebrosa* — **Very rare Australian vagrant**

37cm, 500g. Like a coot but wings olive brown, *shield orange-red, bill red with a yellow tip, and undertail dark with white sides*; legs green with red at 'knee' joint. Immature browner; bill varying from greenish yellow to brown. Wings project high above tail when swimming. Common call a loud explosive 'prurk'. **Habitat:** Weedy shallows or edge of reedbeds of freshwater wetlands, sometimes on nearby pasture. Two NZ records: Lake Hayes, Arrowtown, 1968 and Lake Ellesmere, 2005. **[Sp 187]**

BLACK-TAILED NATIVE-HEN *Gallinula ventralis* — **Very rare Australian vagrant**

35cm, 400g. Similar in size and shape to Dusky Moorhen but more upright stance with tail held cocked. *Shield, upper bill and bill tip green, lower bill orange*; eye yellow; legs brick red. Olive brown above, slate grey below, with prominent *white pear-shaped spots on the flanks*. Tail and undertail black; tail flicked constantly. **Habitat:** Feeds on dry land near freshwater wetlands. Six NZ records. **[Sp 186]**

TAKAHE
PUKEKO
imm
AUSTRALIAN COOT
imm
imm
DUSKY MOORHEN
BLACK-TAILED NATIVE-HEN

A large diverse group of birds of estuaries, coasts, riverbeds and farmland. Most are long-legged and feed in or near shallow water. Bill shape is varied; short and stubby in those (e.g. dotterels) that peck from the surface, but longer in those that feed in shallow water (e.g. stilts), or probe deeply (e.g. godwits). Flight strong and direct. Often form flocks while roosting or flying, but disperse to feed. Many species seen in NZ breed in the Arctic and arrive in September, with remnants of breeding plumage, and depart in March, often in breeding plumage. Most subadults and a few adults spend the southern winter here.

PAINTED SNIPE *Rostratula benghalensis* — Very rare Australian vagrant

25cm, 120g. Distinctive large-bodied chestnut, olive and white wader with short greenish legs and long (5cm) slightly decurved bill. Buff stripe over centre of head from bill to nape; white band sweeps up in front of wings from breast to back; broad olive or buff and black patterned wings. Adult male has brown head with pale buff eye patch; nape, throat and breast streaked greyish brown; wings, back and uppertail spangled buff and grey; belly white. Adult female has maroon-brown head with white eye patch; reddish-brown nape, throat and breast; dark olive-grey wings, back and uppertail; white belly. *When flushed, flies with slow wingbeats, legs dangle* like in Pukeko, and gives repeated 'kuk' call. **Habitat:** Breeds Africa and Australasia; usually in long grass near freshwater wetlands. One NZ record: Lake Ellesmere, 1986. [Sp 235]

JAPANESE SNIPE *Gallinago hardwickii* — Rare Arctic migrant

24cm, 160g. Richly variegated rotund brown wader with *very long (7cm) straight bill*, short grey legs, heavily streaked head with large eyes set high on the head. *Fast zigzagging flight when flushed* from thick cover near wetland margins; gives harsh call: 'kok'. Head streaked dark brown and buff; upperparts heavily streaked brown, buff and black; breast buff, speckled dark brown; flanks barred; belly and undertail creamy white. **Habitat:** Breeds Japan and eastern Russia. Migrates to Australasia. Only a few reach NZ, mainly in long grass near freshwater wetlands. [Sp 195]

CHATHAM ISLANDS SNIPE *Coenocorypha pusilla* — Locally common endemic

20cm, 80g. Like Subantarctic Snipe but smaller, shorter (4.5cm) bill, and pale unmarked lower breast and belly. **Habitat:** Forest and thick vegetation on offshore islands in Chathams group, mainly South East and Mangere islands. **Breeding:** Sep–Feb. [Sp 192]

SNARES SNIPE (Tutukiwi) *Coenocorypha huegeli* — Locally common endemic

22cm, 110g. Like Subantarctic Snipe but darker and stockier, and with finer barred markings on lower breast and belly. **Habitat:** Areas of dense groundcover under forest and scrub on The Snares; introduced to Putauhina Island (2005) and Codfish Island (2012). **Breeding:** Nov–May. [Sp 193]

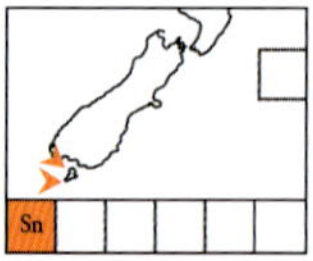

SUBANTARCTIC SNIPE (Hakawai) *Coenocorypha aucklandica* — Locally common endemic

23cm, 110g. Small rotund richly variegated brown wader with *long (6cm) slightly drooping brown bill* and short yellowish legs (grey on Antipodes). Head marked boldly with buff central stripe over head from forehead to nape, long buff eyebrows and brown line through eye; pale buff cheek patch, streaked darker. Upperparts heavily mottled with black feather centres and chestnut brown or buff edges. Throat, neck and breast buff, streaked brown. Female larger than male. Male calls a low 'trerk trerk trerk' and 'queeyoo, queeyoo', but sometimes a *ghostly whistle at night* caused by vibrating tail feathers as air passes through the spread tail during aerial display. Confined to Antipodes, Auckland and Campbell islands. **Habitat:** Areas of dense groundcover under forest and scrub. **Breeding:** Aug–Apr. [Sp 194]

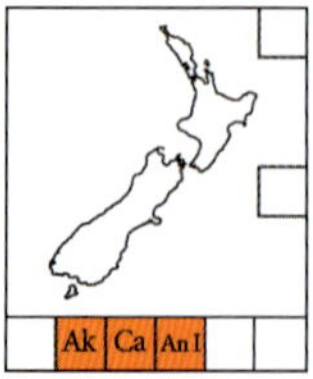

PAINTED SNIPE
♂
♀
♀
JAPANESE SNIPE
Japanese Snipe
SUBANTARCTIC SNIPE
SNARES SNIPE
CHATHAM ISLANDS SNIPE

RED KNOT (Huahou, Lesser Knot) *Calidris canutus* **Abundant Arctic migrant**

24cm, 120g. A *rather nondescript stocky wader* with a heavy (3cm) straight black bill and short dull green legs, but distinctive rusty red head and underparts in breeding plumage. Head and upperparts of non-breeding adult plain grey with paler feather edges, whitish eyebrow; underparts pale grey to off-white, with lightly speckled grey on neck, breast and flanks. Head, neck and breast of breeding adult become *rusty red*, and back black with rust and white speckling; females less richly coloured. Juvenile like non-breeding, but back more scaly with white feather tips and subterminal black lines. In flight, indistinct white wingbar, *pale rump barred white and grey*. Often seen in flocks and with Bar-tailed Godwits. **Habitat:** Breeds Holarctic; migrates to tropics and Southern Hemisphere. Second most common migrant wader visiting NZ estuaries each summer (*c.* 30,000 birds); 4–10% overwinter. Favours northern and western estuaries, especially Kaipara, Manukau, Firth of Thames and Farewell Spit; only occasionally on margins of freshwater lakes. **[Sp 196]**

GREAT KNOT *Calidris tenuirostris* **Rare Arctic migrant**

27cm, 160g. Like Red Knot but larger, with a *heavier longer (4cm) black bill and white rump*. Head and upperparts of non-breeding adult plain grey with paler feather edges, finely streaked dark grey on crown, neck and breast; indistinct eyebrow; flanks usually marked with *dark arrowhead-shaped spots*. Breeding adult has head and neck heavily streaked black; breast very heavily blotched blackish brown, extending onto flanks as bold arrowhead-shaped spots; rusty-red feathers on base of upperwing only. Juvenile like non-breeding, but back and wing feathers have darker centres with buff fringes; brownish-buff wash on breast. **Habitat:** Breeds Siberia; migrates to Australasia, especially northwest Australia. Only a few reach NZ, normally with Red Knots at northern or western estuaries. **[Sp 197]**

BROAD-BILLED SANDPIPER *Limicola falcinellus* **Rare Arctic migrant**

17cm, 35g. Small wader with short olive-green legs, *very long (3cm) heavy black bill slightly drooped at tip, and double eyebrow; a broad white eyebrow joining a thinner, higher stripe in front of each eye*. Non-breeding adult has crown, neck and upperparts pale brown-grey with dark feather shafts and pale edges giving a scaly appearance; underparts white, lightly streaked grey on sides of neck and breast. Breeding adult has head, neck and breast streaked black; upperparts very dark with thinly edged buff or rufous feathers. Juvenile has prominent V on mantle, rufous edges to mantle and inner scapulars, buff and white edges to rest of upperparts. In flight, dark grey leading edges to upperwing and narrow white wingbar; white sides to rump contrast with broad dark grey stripe down centre of tail. **Habitat:** Breeds Arctic Eurasia; migrates to Southeast Asia. Scarce visitor to NZ estuaries. **[Sp 212]**

DUNLIN *Calidris alpina* **Very rare Arctic vagrant**

18cm, 50g. Like Curlew Sandpiper (see Plate 46) but shorter legs, *a shorter only slightly downcurved bill, and black central stripe down white rump*. Non-breeding adult browner with streaked buff-washed upper breast, and less distinct eyebrow. Breeding adult has rusty red on crown and edges of dark-centred back feathers, breast and flanks streaked black, belly black, and undertail white. **Habitat:** Breeds Holarctic; migrates to estuaries of the northern tropics. Four recorded from northern NZ estuaries in summer. **[Sp 199]**

STILT SANDPIPER *Calidris himantopus* **Very rare Arctic vagrant**

21cm, 50g. Non-breeding birds are similar to Curlew Sandpiper (see Plate 46) but *longer neck and much longer legs* make it look larger, and reminiscent of a small Marsh Sandpiper (see Plate 50). Similar in flight to Curlew Sandpiper with a bold *white rump*, but there is *no clear wingbar*. The bill is heavier, slightly longer and straighter than that of a Curlew Sandpiper, and the legs are *greenish* or *yellowish*. Often feeds in belly-deep water by probing vertically. **Habitat:** Breeds North American Arctic; migrates to southern South America estuaries and coasts. Two NZ records: Lake Ellesmere 1998 and 2000. **[Sp 201]**

breeding
non-breeding
juv
RED KNOT
breeding
non-breeding
GREAT KNOT
breeding
BROAD-BILLED
SANDPIPER
non-breeding
breeding
DUNLIN
non-breeding
juv
non-breeding
STILT SANDPIPER

SHARP-TAILED SANDPIPER *Calidris acuminata* — **Uncommon Arctic migrant**

21cm;♂ 75g, ♀ 60g. A medium-small richly speckled brown wader with *rufous crown*, finely streaked black, and white eyebrow. Bill (2.5cm) slightly downcurved, *grey-brown with greenish base. Legs yellowish green.* Non-breeding has upperparts dull brown with pale feather edges; neck and breast mottled grey or buffish with irregular streaks, fading to white on lower breast and belly. In breeding plumage, upperparts richly coloured with chestnut and buff edges to feathers; breast heavily streaked and marked with *small boomerang-shaped streaks on lower breast and along flanks.* Juvenile like non-breeding adult but more rufous, especially on crown, neck and *edges of tertials.* In flight, faint white wingbar and white sides to black rump and uppertail. **Habitat:** Breeds Siberia. Migrates to Australasia. In NZ, favours low-growing salt marsh of estuaries and open marsh-turf flats of coastal lakes, mainly at Kaimaumau, Firth of Thames, Ahuriri and Manawatu estuaries, Lakes Wairarapa and Ellesmere, and Awarua Bay. **[Sp 202]**

PECTORAL SANDPIPER *Calidris melanotos* — **Rare Arctic migrant**

22cm;♂ 80g, ♀ 70g. Non-breeding like Sharp-tailed Sandpiper, but darker, crown streaked brown and buff, neck and *breast heavily streaked dark brown that ends abruptly* and contrasts with white underparts. Bill (2.5cm) slightly downcurved, *brown with yellowish base; legs yellow.* In breeding plumage, upperparts become darker, with chestnut and buff feather edges; breast heavily streaked in male, blackish brown flecked white in female. Juvenile like non-breeding adult but more rufous on head and back. In flight, faint white wingbar and white sides to black rump and uppertail. **Habitat:** Breeds Arctic North America. Migrates to South America. A few reach NZ each summer, often with Sharp-tailed Sandpipers on open marsh-turf flats of coastal lakes, especially Lakes Wairarapa and Ellesmere, or in low-growing salt marsh of estuaries. **[Sp 203]**

BUFF-BREASTED SANDPIPER *Tryngites subruficollis* — **Very rare Arctic vagrant**

20cm, 60g. A distinctive *buffish* wader with a long neck and a *small rounded head.* Crown and upper back finely streaked with black; back dark brown scalloped with buff feather edges; juvenile has almost white feather edges. Face, sides of neck and underparts uniformly buffish, except for a few dark flecks on the upper breast. Short straight black bill; prominent dark eye, *long yellow legs.* Erect stance when alert, but hunched posture when feeding. In flight, uniformly dark above, but *white underwings.* **Habitat:** Breeds high Arctic tundra of North America and a few in Siberia; migrates to inland southern South America. One NZ record, South Kaipara Harbour, March 2014. **[Sp 213]**

RUFF (Reeve – female) *Philomachus pugnax* — **Very rare Arctic vagrant**

♂ 29cm, 170g; ♀ 22cm, 110g. Non-breeding like large upright Sharp-tailed Sandpiper, but lacks rufous crown and has small head, short fine bill, long neck and legs. Head and upperparts scaly grey-brown with grey feather edges, wings darker; throat and sides of face white; breast buff, washed grey brown; belly, undertail and underwings white. Bill (3.5cm) slightly downcurved, brown with paler base. Legs from orange to green. Breeding plumage (not recorded in NZ) is highly variable, especially in males, which have many colours and large neck ruffs and head tufts; female like non-breeding but dark barring on upperparts and black blotches on breast. Juvenile like non-breeding but upperparts have buff feather edges and neck and breast washed buff. In flight, looks long-winged with narrow white wingbar; prominent white oval patches on sides of rump. **Habitat:** Breeds Eurasian Arctic; migrates to Africa and Southeast Asia; straggles to Australasia, including *c.* 20 NZ records, mainly at margins of freshwater or brackish lakes. **[Sp 214]**

SHARP-TAILED
SANDPIPER
non-breeding
juv
breeding
ECTORAL
ANDPIPER
non-breeding
juv
BUFF-BREASTED
SANDPIPER
RUFF
♀ moulting
juv
♂ non-breeding

CURLEW SANDPIPER *Calidris ferruginea* **Uncommon Arctic migrant**

19cm, 60g. A small slender wader with *long thin downcurved bill*, black legs, *white rump* and white wingbar. Non-breeding adult has *pale plain grey-brown head and upperparts*; white eyebrow; underparts white with pale grey wash and streaks on breast. Legs grey. Breeding adult has distinctive rusty-red head and underparts, with feathers initially edged white; back feathers black, notched grey and rust red. Juvenile like non-breeding, but back feathers darker, edged white, and lightly streaked neck and breast washed buff. **Habitat:** Breeds Arctic Asia. Regular summer visitor to NZ, and some overwinter. Favours tidal flats, brackish pools and margins to coastal lakes, mainly at Firth of Thames, Lake Ellesmere and Awarua Bay. **[Sp 200]**

WHITE-RUMPED SANDPIPER *Calidris fuscicollis* **Very rare Arctic vagrant**

17cm, 35g. Small slender wader with a *slightly drooping black bill, usually pale at base of lower mandible*; *white rump*; black legs. Folded wings project well beyond tail to give elongated appearance. Non-breeding adult has drab grey head and upperparts with paler feather edges; neck, breast and *flanks streaked and washed grey*; belly off-white. Breeding adult has pale rufous wash on crown and ear coverts, streaked dark; rufous fringes to feathers of back and inner wing; breast heavily streaked brown, often extending onto flanks as chevrons. In flight, *narrow white wingbar*. **Habitat:** Breeds Arctic North America; migrates to South America. Two NZ records. **[Sp 205]**

BAIRD'S SANDPIPER *Calidris bairdii* **Rare Arctic vagrant**

16cm, 40g. Small buff-brown wader with *straight fine black bill*, short black legs, *broad black centre to white rump and tail*, and *long wings that project well beyond tail*, giving it an elongated look. Complete finely streaked buff breast band. Non-breeding adult has head and upperparts uniformly scaly brown, with buff feather edges. In breeding plumage, crown and breast become strongly streaked dark brown, upperparts dark brown and black with white feather edges, and some rufous on the back. Juvenile has rusty brown upperparts and chest; pale edges to feathers give a scaly effect on the back and wings. In flight, a very narrow short wingbar. **Habitat:** Breeds Arctic North America; migrates to South America. Seven NZ records. **[Sp 204]**

SEMIPALMATED SANDPIPER *Calidris pusilla* **Very rare Arctic vagrant**

14cm, 25g. Small slender grey wader with a *stout straight black bill with a blunt tip*; black or dark olive legs. Folded wings just project beyond tail and tertials. In flight, *narrow white wingbar, and broad black centre through white rump*. Non-breeding adult has brownish-grey head and upperparts with paler feather edges; underparts white with streaks on sides of breast, and sometimes across it. Breeding adult relatively dull, lacking the rufous of many congeners, but feathers on upperparts have dark centres and grey or buff fringes; breast and upper flanks heavily streaked brown. **Habitat:** Breeds Arctic North America; migrates to South America. One NZ record, Ahuriri Estuary, Hawke's Bay, 1966. **[Sp 210]**

breeding
non-breeding
CURLEW SANDPIPER
breeding
non-breeding
WHITE-RUMPED SANDPIPER
juv
ad non-breeding
BAIRD'S SANDPIPER
SEMIPALMATED SANDPIPER
juv
non-breeding

RED-NECKED STINT *Calidris ruficollis* **Common Arctic migrant**

15cm, 30g. Tiny wader with short straight black bill and short black legs. Non-breeding adult has white forehead and eyebrow; crown, neck and upperparts *pale brownish-grey*, paler feather edges. Breeding adult has crown and back blackish brown with rufous feather edges, *contrasting* with grey-brown feathers on wing coverts; *sides of face, throat and neck brick red*; underparts white. Juvenile like non-breeding, but crown and sides of breast washed pale rufous; back feathers dark rufous-edged but greyer wing coverts. In flight, white wingbar reaches base of primaries; black central stripe down white rump. Pecks with rapid sewing-machine action. **Habitat:** Breeds Siberia and Alaska; migrates to Australasia. Several hundred reach NZ in summer, and some overwinter. Mainly at estuaries and coastal lakes, especially at Parengarenga, Manukau, Porangahau, Farewell Spit, Lake Ellesmere and Awarua Bay. [Sp 207]

LITTLE STINT *Calidris minuta* **Very rare Arctic vagrant**

14cm, 25g. Like Red-necked Stint, but even smaller, slightly longer black legs, and slightly longer bill, decurved at the tip; shorter wings give less attenuated rear end; non-breeding adult slightly browner. Breeding adult paler *orange-rufous, throat white*; creamy-white V-shaped line on back, broad orange-rufous feather edges *without a contrast* between back and wing coverts. Juvenile has a *prominent white V on the back* and a double eyebrow. In flight, white wingbar does not reach primaries; black central stripe down white rump. **Habitat:** Breeds Arctic Eurasia; migrates to Europe, Africa and Asia. Three NZ records, all at Lake Ellesmere.

[Sp 206]

LEAST SANDPIPER *Calidris minutilla* **Very rare Arctic vagrant**

14cm, 25g. Like Red-necked Stint but browner and with *dull yellow legs*, and more crouched bent-legged feeding posture. The mantle is *scalloped* with black and rufous, whereas in the Long-toed Stint it is streaked. *Shrill 'kreep' call and thicker all black bill* are best field features of Least Sandpiper. In flight, narrow white wingbar, and thin black centre line down white rump. **Habitat:** Breeds Arctic North America; migrates to South America. One record in NZ (Wairoa, 1952), but several other yellow-legged stints have been recorded.

[Sp 209]

LONG-TOED STINT *Calidris subminuta* **Very rare Arctic straggler**

14cm, 25g. Like Red-necked Stint, but slightly smaller; finer head and longer neck, a short rear-end, longer *pale greenish yellow legs*; black bill with paler base to lower mandible. Upright stance and bold rufous markings on cap, mantle and back in juvenile and breeding plumage is reminiscent of a Sharp-tailed Sandpiper (see Plate 45). *Call a liquid 'chee' or 'chee-che'*. Compared with other yellow-legged stints, it is very grey in non-breeding plumage and has long toes, especially the middle one, *giving the foot a gangly appearance*. The mantle is *streaked* with black and rufous, whereas in the Least Stint it is scalloped. **Habitat:** Breeds subarctic Asia; migrates to Southeast Asia and Australia. Two NZ records, both at Lake Ellesmere. [Sp 208]

WESTERN SANDPIPER *Calidris mauri* **Rare Arctic vagrant**

16cm, 30g. Like Red-necked Stint but with *distinctly longer (2.5cm) slightly drooping black bill*. Non-breeding adult has pale grey upperparts with paler feather edges, white eyebrow, breast finely streaked grey, underparts white. Breeding adult has rufous crown, nape and patch behind eye, prominent white eyebrow; back grey-brown, mottled rufous and black on scapulars; breast and flanks marked with black streaks and chevrons. Juvenile like breeding adult but paler rufous on head; breast washed buff and lightly streaked black at sides. In flight, narrow white wingbar, white sides to black rump. **Habitat:** Breeds Arctic North America and eastern Siberia; migrates to Central America. A few reach NZ estuaries. [Sp 211]

ED-NECKED STINT
breeding
non-breeding
juv
LITTLE STINT
breeding
non-breeding
juv
LEAST SANDPIPER
non-breeding
Little
Stint
NG-TOED
STINT
non-breeding
juv
WESTERN
SANDPIPER
breeding
non-breeding

FAR-EASTERN CURLEW (Eastern Curlew) *Numenius madagascariensis*
Uncommon Arctic migrant

63cm, 900g. *Largest wader in NZ. Distinctive very long (19cm) downcurved bill.* Body streaked greyish brown and buff, paler on underparts, with indistinct white eyebrow and brown rump. Bill dark brown with pink base to lower bill. *Flight call a distinctive carrying 'croo-lee'.* **Habitat:** Breeds northeastern Asia; migrates to Southeast Asia and Australasia. Each summer, *c.* 10 visit NZ, mainly at Manukau Harbour, Firth of Thames, Farewell Spit and Southland lagoons. **[Sp 216]**

WHIMBREL *Numenius phaeopus* **Uncommon Arctic migrant**

43cm, 450g. Medium-sized curlew with *long (9cm) downcurved bill*, head marked boldly with white eyebrows and centre stripe over top of dark brown head. Asiatic subspecies (*variegata*) has *off-white rump*. American subspecies (*hudsonicus*) has *speckled brown rump*. Body completely streaked greyish brown and buff. Bill black, legs bluish grey. *Flight call a rippling whistle of about 7 notes: 'ti-ti-ti-ti-ti-ti-ti'.* Often very wary and stands alert near roosting flocks of waders. **Habitat:** Breeds Arctic; migrates to tropics and temperate Southern Hemisphere. About 30–50 visit NZ each summer (mainly Asiatic), especially at Parengarenga, Firth of Thames and Farewell Spit. **[Sp 217]**

BRISTLE-THIGHED CURLEW *Numenius tahitiensis* **Very rare Arctic straggler**

42cm, 400g. Medium-sized *buff and brown* curlew with *long (9cm) downcurved bill and very boldly marked head.* Dark eye stripe, pale buff eyebrow and central stripe over top of dark brown head. Body streaked brown and buff; *rump smooth cinnamon*; tail rusty buff, barred black; belly whitish, and upper legs have a few long loose white feathers. *Flight call a clear 'kee-vee'*, unlike trilling call of other curlews. **Habitat:** Breeds western Alaska; migrates to islands and atolls of the central Pacific. All three NZ records from the Kermadecs. **[Sp 219]**

LITTLE WHIMBREL *Numenius minutus* **Rare Arctic migrant**

30cm, 160g. *Small curlew with long (5cm) downcurved bill* and boldly marked head. Dark eye stripe, buff eyebrow and thin central stripe over top of brown head. Body streaked brown and warm buff, brown rump, and upperwing in flight looks uniformly dark. Bill dark brown, pink base to lower bill; legs bluish grey. *Flight call a three-note 'te-te-te'.* **Habitat:** Breeds Siberia; migrates to Australasia. A rare visitor to NZ, mostly in short pasture or ploughed ground, often with Banded Dotterels or rather similar-looking Golden Plovers. **[Sp 218]**

FAR-EASTERN CURLEW
American
Asiatic
WHIMBREL
BRISTLE-THIGHED CURLEW
LITTLE WHIMBREL

BAR-TAILED GODWIT (Kuaka) *Limosa lapponica* **Abundant Arctic migrant**

♂ 39cm, 300g; ♀ 41cm, 350g. Commonest migrant wader in NZ. Long (♂ 8.5cm, ♀ 10.5cm) *slightly upturned black bill with a pink base.* Legs and feet black. Non-breeding has head, upperparts and upperwings streaked grey-brown; lower back, *rump and tail barred brown and white*; underparts dirty white, washed grey on breast; underwings extensively flecked dark brown. Breeding adult, seen from February onwards, has black and buff upperparts; brick-red head, neck, breast and underparts in males; buffy red with fine barring in females. Juvenile like non-breeding but buffer and with more heavily marked upperparts, but unmarked breast. In flight, wingbar indistinct, pale rump and barred tail. Flies fast with twisting and turning, or direct in long lines or chevrons. **Habitat:** Breeds Arctic in Eurasia and Alaska. Eastern race *baueri* migrates to Australasia, especially NZ estuaries, sandy beaches and shores of coastal lakes, which they reach with a direct 8–9-day flight of 11,700km. Each summer, *c.* 90,000 visit NZ, and about 10% remain through our winter. Main sites, where 10,000+ spend the southern summer, are Kaipara and Manukau harbours, and Farewell Spit, but seen at many estuaries and coastal lakes and lagoons. **[Sp 220]**

HUDSONIAN GODWIT *Limosa haemastica* **Rare Arctic migrant**

39cm, 300g. In non-breeding plumage like Bar-tailed Godwit, but smooth grey upperparts and grey wash on breast. *Conspicuous white rump contrasts with broad black tip to the tail; narrow white wingbar. Black armpits and extensive black on underwing* separate from non-breeding Black-tailed Godwit. Breeding adult male has head and neck finely barred black and white, upperparts dark brown spotted buff, breast and belly chestnut; female paler on breast and belly. **Habitat:** Breeds North America; migrates to South America. A few reach NZ most summers, usually with Bar-tailed Godwits at estuaries or coastal lakes and lagoons. **[Sp 222]**

BLACK-TAILED GODWIT *Limosa limosa* **Rare Arctic migrant**

39cm, 350g. In non-breeding plumage like Bar-tailed Godwit, but more elegant with smooth grey plumage and *long straight bill.* In flight, *conspicuous white wingbars*, and *white rump contrasts with broad black tip to the tail. White underwings and armpits with thin black margins* separate from non-breeding Hudsonian Godwit. Breeding adult has head, neck and breast brick red; belly barred black and white; upperparts mottled rusty and black. **Habitat:** Breeds temperate Eurasia. Race *melanuroides* migrates to Asia and Australasia. Only a few reach NZ each summer, usually with Bar-tailed Godwits at estuaries or with Pied Stilts on lake margins. **[Sp 221]**

ASIATIC DOWITCHER *Limnodromus semipalmatus* **Very rare Asian straggler**

35cm, 180g. Like a small godwit but with *short legs and a long (8cm), straight stout black bill.* In non-breeding plumage, face clearly marked with white eyebrow and dark line from bill to eye. Upperparts dark grey-brown, streaked paler; back, rump and tail barred brown and off-white; underparts flecked grey on breast and along flanks, belly white and *underwings mainly white.* Feeds with sewing-machine action of rapid probes with bill pointed straight down. **Habitat:** Breeds Central Asia; migrates to South Asia and Australasia. Five records at NZ estuaries. **[Sp 215]**

juv
♂ breeding
♀ non-breeding
BAR-TAILED GODWIT
♂ breeding
non-breeding
HUDSONIAN GODWIT
ACK-TAILED GODWIT
juv
♂ breeding
non-breeding
ASIATIC DOWITCHER
non-breeding

MARSH SANDPIPER *Tringa stagnatilis* **Uncommon Arctic migrant**

22cm, 70g. Elegant *pale grey* wader, like small Greenshank but *very long greenish legs and needle-like (4cm) black bill.* Non-breeding has crown and eye stripe streaked grey, eyebrow white, upperparts ash grey, darker at shoulder. Underparts white. Breeding adult has head and neck flecked dark grey, upperparts brownish grey heavily barred and spotted dark brown, breast spotted dark brown and black; legs can turn yellowish. In flight, lacks wingbar, *white rump extends as a V well up back*; tail white, lightly barred grey in centre. Wades in shallow water and feeds with *head-down, tail-up, triangular stance.* **Habitat:** Breeds Central Asia; migrates to Africa, Asia and Australasia. A few reach NZ estuaries and lake margins each summer, often with Pied Stilts. **[Sp 228]**

GREENSHANK *Tringa nebularia* **Uncommon Arctic migrant**

32cm, 170g. Large elegant grey wader with long (5.5cm) heavy *slightly upturned bill, blue-grey at base*; *long green legs.* Non-breeding has head and neck finely streaked grey, indistinct white eyebrow, upperparts dark grey, lightly flecked white and black; underparts white. Breeding adult has head, neck and upperbreast heavily flecked blackish brown; irregular dark mottling on upperparts. In flight, lacks wingbar, *white rump extends as a V well up back*; tail white, broadly barred dark grey. Wades in shallow water with horizontal stance. *Distinctive voice, a loud ringing 'tew-tew-tew'.* **Habitat:** Breeds Eurasia; migrates to Africa, Asia and Australasia. A few reach NZ most summers, often associated with Pied Stilts in muddy estuarine creeks and on lake margins. **[Sp 227]**

LESSER YELLOWLEGS *Tringa flavipes* **Rare Arctic vagrant**

24cm, 75g. Elegant grey wader, like Marsh Sandpiper but *long slender yellow legs*, and *lower back greyish brown.* Bill (4cm) fine and straight, slightly longer than head. Non-breeding has upperparts brownish grey, *white eyebrow only in front of eye*; wing feathers pale-edged giving a spotted look; underparts white except upper breast streaked brownish grey. Juvenile like non-breeding, but upperparts browner, strongly spotted white; neck and breast spotted and streaked brown. In flight, lacks wingbar, *square white rump not extending up back.* **Habitat:** Breeds North America; migrates to South America. About 20 records at NZ estuaries and muddy lake margins. **[Sp 229]**

WANDERING TATTLER *Tringa incana* **Uncommon Arctic migrant**

27cm, 120g. Medium-sized wader with smooth slate-grey back and *short yellow legs.* Like Grey-tailed Tattler but *call a clear rippling trill of 6–10 notes.* Bill grey, *nasal groove extends 70% of length.* Non-breeding has head, upperparts and upperbreast slate grey, *white eyebrow only in front of eye*, underparts white. Breeding adult has all underparts, including flanks and undertail, heavily barred dark grey. In flight, smooth grey upperparts; flies on stiffly held wings. When alert, *bobs head and tips tail.* **Habitat:** Breeds western North America; migrates to Central America and Pacific Islands. A few reach NZ estuaries and especially rocky shores each summer. **[Sp 224]**

GREY-TAILED TATTLER (Siberian Tattler) *Tringa brevipes* **Uncommon Arctic migrant**

25cm, 100g. Like Wandering Tattler, but *call a sharp high-pitched two-note 'too-weet'.* Usually slightly paler and browner, and *white eyebrow extends behind eye* and as a thin line over the base of the bill. Bill grey, *nasal groove extends 50% of length.* In breeding plumage, underparts heavily barred dark grey, but flanks and undertail remain white. In flight, smooth grey-brown upperparts; flies on stiffly held wings. When alert, *bobs head and tips tail.* **Habitat:** Breeds Siberia; migrates to southern Asia, Australasia and Southwest Pacific. A few reach NZ estuaries and sometimes rocky shores each summer. **[Sp 225]**

Pied Stilt juv
Marsh Sandpiper
MARSH SANDPIPER
breeding
non-breeding
non-breeding
GREENSHANK
breeding
non-breeding
juv
LESSER YELLOWLEGS
WANDERING TATTLER
non-breeding
breeding
non-breeding
breeding
GREY-TAILED TATTLER

RED-NECKED PHALAROPE *Phalaropus lobatus* **Rare Arctic straggler**

19cm;♂ 35g, ♀ 40g. Unusual small slim and graceful wader. *Feeds by swimming jerkily or in circles, pecking from the water surface. Short very fine black bill*; very short dark grey legs with lobed feet; white wingbar; large white patches at sides of rump contrast with black stripe down grey-tipped tail. Non-breeding adult like Grey Phalarope, but bill finer, back feathers have dark centres and broad white edges, giving a scaly appearance. Breeding adult unmistakable: mainly grey above, with rufous patch sweeping from behind eye down sides of neck to throat; male duller. Juvenile has grey patch behind and below eye, and grey on crown extends down hindneck to back. **Habitat:** Breeds Arctic; migrates to pelagic waters off western North America, Arabia, Micronesia and Namibia. About 12 have been recorded at NZ estuaries or coastal lakes. [Sp 233]

GREY PHALAROPE (Red Phalarope) *Phalaropus fulicaria* **Rare Arctic vagrant**

20cm;♂ 50g, ♀ 60g. Unusual dainty wader. Feeds *by swimming jerkily or in circles, pecking from the water surface. Short thick black bill (yellow with black tip in breeding adult)*; short brownish-grey legs with yellow lobes on feet; white wingbar; small white patches at sides to grey tail. Non-breeding adult like non-breeding Red-necked Phalarope but bill stouter, back feathers have very thin white edges giving a smooth appearance. Breeding adult unmistakable: neck and underparts mainly brick red, back black and buff, and white patch around back of head behind eye; male duller. Juvenile initially a warm pinkish buff but quickly becomes like non-breeding adult; however, retains buff edges to wing feathers. **Habitat:** Breeds Arctic; migrates to pelagic areas off Senegal and Sierra Leone, off Namibia and South Africa, and off western South America. About 10 vagrants have reached NZ estuaries and coastal lakes, almost all in June–July in full or partial breeding plumage. [Sp 232]

WILSON'S PHALAROPE *Phalaropus tricolor* **Very rare American vagrant**

22cm;♂ 50g, ♀ 65g. Unusual slim and graceful wader. *Feeds by swimming jerkily or in circles pecking at the water surface, or by wading, or running actively with waddling gait on dry land.* Short yellow legs in immature and non-breeding adult, darkening to black in breeding adult. *Long needle-like black bill, no wingbar*, and *white rump* distinguish from other phalaropes. Non-breeding adult resembles small very short-legged Marsh Sandpiper (see Plate 50), with very pale grey head and upperparts, darker on wings and back; white eyebrow and underparts. Breeding adult unmistakable: silver-grey and chestnut head, neck and upperparts on female; male duller and lacks grey areas. **Habitat:** Breeds North America; migrates to wetlands of South America. Three NZ records at estuaries and coastal lakes. [Sp 234]

ORIENTAL PRATINCOLE *Glareola maldivarum* **Rare Asian migrant**

23cm, 75g. Distinctive atypical wader with *graceful buoyant tern-like flight while feeding by hawking*, swooping and soaring; sometimes feeds on ground with rapid tip-toeing run. Non-breeding adult has dull olive-brown crown, back and upperwings; throat buff, enclosed by a streaked black necklace; neck and upper breast pale olive-grey-brown, lower breast and belly white. Breeding adult has brighter olive-brown on head and upperparts; throat enclosed by bold black necklace; lower breast becomes buff. Juvenile has flecked appearance from back and upper breast feathers being tipped dark and edged buff. In flight, *underwing chestnut with dark grey trailing edge and tip, deeply forked white tail with olive brown tip.* **Habitat:** Breeds Southeast Asia; migrates to Australasia, occasionally in huge numbers (*c.* 3 million in northwest Australia in February 2004). Occasionally reaches NZ estuaries, coastal lakes and over open grassland. [Sp 257]

RED-NECKED PHALAROPE
juv
♂ breeding
♀ breeding
non-breeding
♂ breeding
GREY PHALAROPE
♀ breeding
non-breeding
juv
♂ breeding
♀ breeding
WILSON'S PHALAROPE
non-breeding
imm
ORIENTAL PRATINCOLE
non-breeding
breeding

WRYBILL (Ngutuparore) *Anarhynchus frontalis* **Locally common endemic**

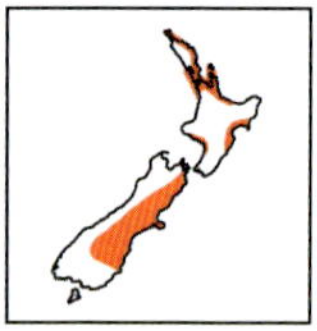

20cm, 55g. *Very pale grey, stocky, confiding wader* with short thick neck and black bill with *tip curved to the right*. Legs grey-green. Breeding adult has white forehead edged above with thin black frontal band in male; crown, nape and upperparts plain ashy grey. Underparts white except *black band across upper breast*, narrower in female. Non-breeding lacks frontal band, and breast band is indistinct or absent. Juvenile has back feathers edged white, and breast band absent. In flight, small white wingbar. Forms dense flocks at roosts, usually apart from most Arctic waders. **Habitat:** Breeds shingle riverbeds of Canterbury and Otago. Almost all of the *c.* 5300 birds migrate to spend Jan–Aug at estuaries of North Island, especially Firth of Thames, Manukau and Kaipara. Feeds on wet mudflats. **Breeding:** Aug–Feb. **[Sp 252]**

TURNSTONE (Ruddy Turnstone) *Arenaria interpres* **Common Arctic migrant**

23cm, 120g. Very striking *stout* wader with *variegated white, black, brown and tortoise-shell plumage*, short black bill and *short orange legs*. Horizontal stance and habit of *busily fossicking along the tideline*, probing under debris and bulldozing or flicking over tide-wrack. Non-breeding has head and upperparts dark brown, mottled black and chestnut; face variegated black, white and brown; upperbreast black, underparts white. In breeding plumage, male more boldly marked with white cap, finely streaked black; female has brown cap, streaked black and white. *In flight, striking complex pattern of black, white and chestnut.* **Habitat:** Breeds high Arctic; migrates to tropical and temperate coasts of both hemispheres. Third most common Arctic wader to visit NZ; about 1000–2000 visit each year and favour wave platforms, coastal lagoons and some estuaries, especially Parengarenga, Kaipara, Farewell Spit, Motueka, Lake Grassmere, Kaikoura Peninsula, Awarua Bay and Te Whanga Lagoon (Chathams). **[Sp 231]**

TEREK SANDPIPER *Tringa cinerea* **Uncommon Arctic migrant**

23cm, 70g. Plain pale grey-brown wader with *long thin upcurved black bill with orange base, short orange-yellow legs*, and dark patch at bend of wing. Moves actively with crouched run and bobs head and tail. Non-breeding has head and upperparts pale brownish grey with faint white eyebrow; throat and breast variably streaked grey; underparts white. Breeding has browner back, finely flecked grey, and black streak at base of upperwing appears as a black line along back. In flight, broad white trailing edge to upperwing near body, pale sides to rump and tail. **Habitat:** Breeds Eurasia; migrates to coasts of Africa, Asia and Australasia. A few reach NZ estuaries each summer, often roosting with Wrybills. **[Sp 230]**

SANDERLING *Calidris alba* **Rare Arctic migrant**

20cm, 50g. *Very pale wader with black patch at bend of wing*, short stout black bill and short black legs. *Feeds actively; runs along water edge on sandy beaches.* Non-breeding has head and back pearly grey; sides of face white with grey wash through eye; underparts white. Breeding has head, breast and upper back pale rusty red, speckled black. Juvenile like non-breeding, but back scalloped black and grey, and head and sides of lower neck streaked black. In flight, *prominent white wingbar*, enhanced by dark grey leading edge and tips to wing; black stripe down centre of white rump and grey tail. **Habitat:** Breeds Arctic; migrates to tropical and temperate coasts of both hemispheres. A few reach NZ each summer, on sandy beaches and estuaries. **[Sp 198]**

COMMON SANDPIPER *Tringa hypoleucos* **Rare Arctic migrant**

20cm, 50g. Small dark solitary sandpiper with *white tab in front of folded wing*. Often perches on rocks or logs and *bobs head and tips tail. Jerky, flickering flight interspersed with glides on stiffly held wings.* Head and upperparts olive brown except white eye-ring and eyebrow, boldest in front of eye; underparts white. Tail long, extending well beyond folded wings. Short straight dark brown bill; short greenish-grey legs. In flight, white wingbar and white sides to brown rump and tail. *Flight call a distinctive clear 'hee-dee-dee'.* **Habitat:** Breeds Eurasia; migrates to coasts of Africa, Asia and Australasia. A few reach NZ, usually in small muddy estuaries. **[Sp 226]**

WRYBILL
non-breeding
♀ breeding
♂ breeding
TURNSTONE
♂ breeding
non-breeding
♀ breeding
TEREK SANDPIPER
breeding
non-breeding
SANDERLING
breeding
juv
non-breeding
Sanderling
COMMON SANDPIPER

SOUTH ISLAND PIED OYSTERCATCHER (Torea, SIPO) *Haematopus finschi*

Abundant endemic

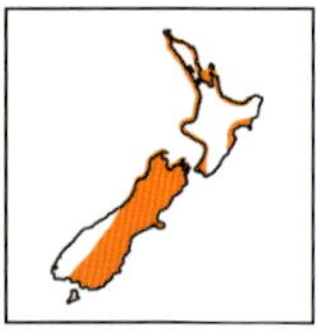

46cm, 550g. Striking black and white wader with long stout red bill and short stubby pink legs. *Sharp border on lower chest between black upperparts and white underparts, a white tab extends upwards in front of folded wing.* In flight, *white wingbar, rump and lower back.* Orange eye-ring. Sexes alike. Immature has browner plumage, dusky-red bill and dull legs. Forms large roosting and feeding flocks. Flight call a loud shrill 'kleep'. **Habitat:** Breeds inland on riverbeds and farmland, mainly in South Island. Most of the *c.* 80,000 birds migrate to spend Jan–Jul at estuaries of the North Island and northern South Island, especially Kaipara, Whangarei, Manukau and Kawhia harbours, Firth of Thames, and the coast between Nelson and Farewell Spit; though 1000+ winter at Avon–Heathcote Estuary and in coastal Southland. **Breeding:** Aug–Jan. [Sp 237]

CHATHAM ISLANDS OYSTERCATCHER *Haematopus chathamensis*

Rare endemic

48cm, 600g. Like pied phase Variable Oystercatcher in having a *slightly smudgy border on chest,* but *shorter bill and thicker legs and feet.* **Habitat:** Breeds on rocky and sandy coasts of Chatham Islands, especially northern beaches of Chatham Island, where about 70% of the 110 breeding pairs live. **Breeding:** Oct–Mar. [Sp 238]

VARIABLE OYSTERCATCHER (Torea, Torea Pango) *Haematopus unicolor*

Uncommon endemic

48cm, 725g. *Variable plumage, from black to pied,* with continuous gradient between. Long robust red bill and short stubby pink legs. Pied phase like Pied Oystercatcher but *larger, bill heavier, and smudgy border on chest; most lack tab in front of folded wing.* In flight, white wingbar and rump have smudgy edges, and lower back is black or smudgy. Black phase, commonest south of Taranaki and Gisborne, is pure black. Immature has browner plumage, dusky-red bill and dull legs. Flight call a loud shrill 'kleep'. **Habitat:** Breeds on rocky and sandy coasts, occasionally on shores of coastal lakes. About 20% of the *c.* 6000 birds gather on estuaries in autumn and winter. **Breeding:** Sep–Mar. [Sp 236]

SPUR-WINGED PLOVER *Vanellus miles*

Abundant native

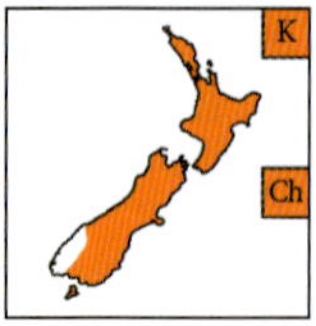

38cm; ♂ 370g, ♀ 350g. Conspicuous *noisy* large plover. Black crown, hindneck and shoulders in front of bend of wing; smooth brown back and wings; white rump and tail tipped black. White underparts; wings have dark trailing edge. *Yellow facial patch, wattles and bill*; legs and feet reddish. Spur on bend of wing usually hidden. Juvenile has small wattles, and feathers on upperparts are narrowly edged black and buff. *Flies with slow deliberate beats of rounded wings. Call a loud staccato rattle*: 'kerr-kick-ki-ki-ki'. **Habitat:** Colonised NZ from Australia in the 1930s and after a slow start, spread rapidly after 1960 to the whole country. Favours farmland, rough grassland, wetland margins and estuaries. **Breeding:** Jun–Dec. [Sp 256]

SOUTH ISLAND PIED OYSTERCATCHER
CHATHAM ISLANDS OYSTERCATCHER
pied phase
VARIABLE OYSTERCATCHER
black phase
intermediate phase
SPUR-WINGED PLOVER
juv

PIED STILT (Poaka, Black-winged Stilt) *Himantopus himantopus*

Abundant native

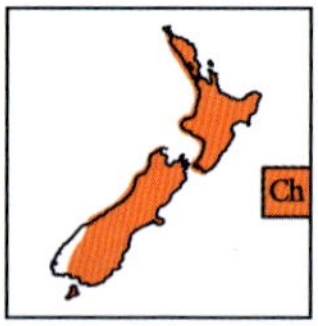

35cm, 190g. Distinctive *black and white wader with extremely long pinkish-red legs and long fine black bill.* Variable black on crown, nape, hindneck and collar on the lower neck; black wings and back; grey wash at end of tail. Face, throat and underparts white. Eye red. Juvenile has grey wash on head and neck, dull pink legs, dark brown back and wings. Distinctive *yapping calls*, often heard at night or when breeding birds are disturbed. Some have hybridised with Black Stilt, and so darker intermediate forms are seen. **Habitat:** Breeds on riverbeds, lake margins and damp pasture. Most of the *c.* 30,000 birds in NZ form flocks at estuaries and lakes outside breeding season. Many South Island and southern North Island birds migrate to northern North Island after breeding season. **Breeding:** Jul–Dec. [Sp 239]

BLACK STILT (Kaki) *Himantopus novaezelandiae*

Very rare endemic

40cm, 220g. Pure adults *entirely black* with a greenish gloss on upper surface. *Very long pinkish-red legs, very long fine black bill,* red eye. Juvenile has white on head, neck and breast, with black patch around eye and grey wash on back of neck. Wings, belly, flanks and undertail black. Full black plumage acquired over the first year, but throughout the bill is longer than in Pied Stilt and the legs slightly shorter. A few have hybridised with Pied Stilt; adult hybrids are very variable, but longer bill and shorter legs are apparent in darker birds. Unlike juvenile Black Stilt, hybrid adults have some solid black on the breast. **Habitat:** Breeds on riverbeds, lake margins and ponds of Mackenzie Basin, inland South Canterbury. After breeding, most of the *c.* 70 adult birds move to river deltas of major lakes in the Mackenzie Basin, but some, especially hybrids, move to estuaries of eastern South Island and western North Island. **Breeding:** Sep–Jan. [Sp 240]

RED-NECKED AVOCET *Recurvirostra novaehollandiae*

Very rare Australian vagrant

44cm, 300g. Distinctive *black and white wader with chestnut head and neck, and fine upcurved bill* (more steeply in male) and long pale blue-grey legs. White body; black and white pattern on wings and back especially noticeable in flight. Juvenile has paler chestnut head and neck, and brown and white wing markings. Feeds in lakes and estuaries *with scythe-like sweep of the bill.* **Habitat:** Bred on South Island riverbeds to 1892; only two NZ records since then. [Sp 241]

imm
juv
PIED STILT
BLACK STILT
imm
juv
ybrid Black/Pied Stilts
RED-NECKED AVOCET

PACIFIC GOLDEN PLOVER *Pluvialis fulva* — **Common Arctic migrant**

25cm, 130g. Medium-sized *speckled leggy wader*. Wary in NZ; when alert stands tall, looking slim with long neck and large head. Breeding adult has brown upperparts heavily speckled golden yellow and white; black face and underparts (*mottled on flanks*) separated by broad white stripe from bill, above eye and down neck to flanks. Non-breeding has head and upperparts pale brown with golden-buff or cream spots; tail barred brown and buff; pale buff eye stripe; throat and chest buff, speckled brown and yellow, grading into pale buff flanks, belly and undertail. Juvenile has more heavily speckled upperparts and yellower head and underparts; more dark markings on breast and flanks. In flight, dark brown upperwing with an indistinct pale wingbar, and uniform brownish-grey underwing and armpits. At rest, tip of tertials level with tip of tail, and wings just longer than tail. Short black bill. Long dark grey legs give leggy appearance. Flight fast and direct, often in small flocks. *Flight call a musical 'too-weet'.* **Habitat:** Breeds Arctic tundra of Siberia and West Alaska; migrates to southern Asia, Australasia and Pacific Islands. About 150–200 visit NZ each summer, mainly at estuaries with extensive *Zostera* and *Sarcocornia/Samolus* beds (especially Parengarenga, Manawatu, Farewell Spit, Awarua Bay) or freshwater wetlands with marsh-turf on fringes (Kaimaumau, Lakes Wairarapa and Ellesmere); rarely on short grassland in NZ. Very few overwinter. **[Sp 242]**

AMERICAN GOLDEN PLOVER *Pluvialis dominicus* — **Very rare Arctic vagrant**

26cm, 165g. Like Pacific Golden Plover but slightly larger, deeper chested with stouter bill and shorter legs (especially tibia). *Tip of tertials falls well short of tip of tail*, and wing usually much longer than tail. Breeding plumage male has *completely black flanks*; non-breeding adults and juveniles are greyer than Pacific Golden Plover, golden tones restricted to the back and scapulars. Juvenile has more mottling and barring on underparts, and ear coverts and cap are darker, making white eyebrow more prominent. **Habitat:** Breeds Arctic America; migrates to inland South America. Two NZ records: Karikari Peninsula, 1991; Bay of Plenty, 2011. **[Sp 243]**

GREY PLOVER *Pluvialis squatarola* — **Uncommon Arctic migrant**

29cm, 250g. Much *larger, heavier-billed and greyer than Pacific Golden Plover*. Has spangled appearance, and black face, throat and underparts in breeding plumage. Non-breeding is very pale, speckled grey and white head, upperparts and breast; white underparts. In flight, *white underwings have diagnostic black armpits*, thin white wingbar, *white rump*, and barred tail. Sexes alike. Juvenile grey-brown above with white and a few yellow spots. Large black eye, stout black bill and long ash-grey legs. Flight call a three-note 'hee-oo-ee'. **Habitat:** Breeds high Holarctic; migrates to tropics and temperate areas of both hemispheres. A few visit NZ estuaries each summer, especially Parengarenga, Firth of Thames and Farewell Spit. **[Sp 244]**

UPLAND SANDPIPER *Bartramia longicauda* — **Very rare American vagrant**

28cm, 140g. A brown-streaked wader with *large body, long slender neck, long tail, small head*, large black eye and short thin straight bill. Head, throat and upperparts olive-buff, streaked dark brown; flanks white with dark brown chevrons, abdomen white. In flight, rump and tail have dark centre and thin white or creamy margins, dark upperwing with black primaries. *Wings held upright on landing* show pied barring on underwings. **Habitat:** Breeds North America; migrates to South America. One NZ record: Manukau Harbour, 1967. **[Sp 223]**

ORIENTAL DOTTEREL *Charadrius veredus* — **Rare Asian migrant**

24cm, 95g. Medium-sized plover with a *slim elegant build, long legs and an erect stance*. Breeding adult has broad chestnut breast band with black lower margin. Non-breeding has plain grey-brown upperparts, but some have narrow buff margins to feathers; pale buff eyebrow, face and throat, broad grey-buff breast band contrasts with off-white abdomen. Juvenile like non-breeding but broad pale margins to feathers on upperparts. In flight, no clear wingbar, underwing grey. Fine black bill; *proportionately long dull yellow legs*. **Habitat:** Breeds North China; winters mainly in Indonesia and Australasia. About 20 NZ records, mainly at estuaries, in areas of dried mud or short pasture, often with Banded Dotterels or Pacific Golden Plovers. **[Sp 251]**

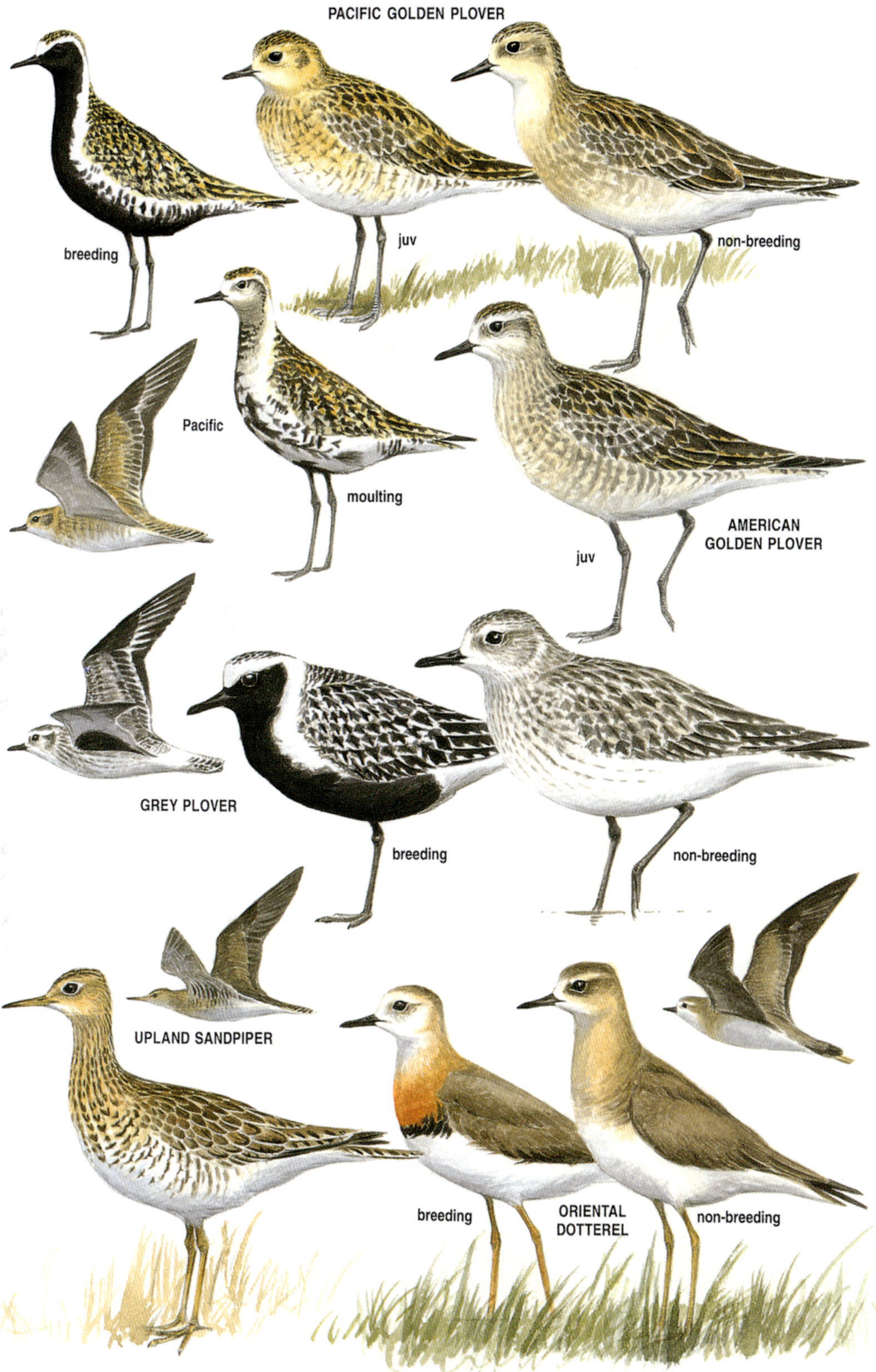
PACIFIC GOLDEN PLOVER
breeding
juv
non-breeding
Pacific
moulting
AMERICAN
GOLDEN PLOVER
juv
GREY PLOVER
breeding
non-breeding
UPLAND SANDPIPER
breeding
ORIENTAL
DOTTEREL
non-breeding

BANDED DOTTEREL (Tuturiwhatu) *Charadrius bicinctus* — **Abundant endemic**

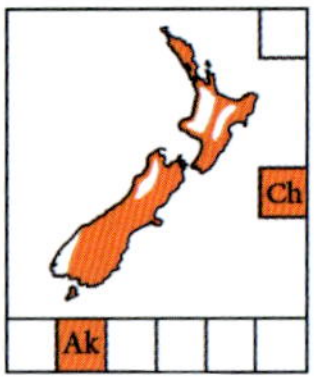

20cm, 60g. Medium-sized dotterel with a confusing range of plumages according to age, sex and time of year. Breeding adult has white underparts except for *two bands, a thin black band on the lower neck and a broad chestnut band on the breast.* Male has bolder and darker bands, and also has a thin black band above white forehead, and a dark line through eye. Non-breeding adults of both sexes are highly variable: black facial markings are lost; breast bands fade and often lost except as yellow to grey-brown tabs at the shoulders; upper band usually shows as a faint incomplete necklace of spots, but some retain a distinct upper band. Juvenile like non-breeding, but *whole head washed yellowish buff*, brown mottling on breast usually forms dark shoulder tabs, and upperparts grey-brown with fawn or off-white edges to the feathers. All have short dark grey bill, black eye, variable yellowish-grey-green legs. Main calls a loud 'pit' and a fast rolling 'che-ree-a-ree'. **Habitat:** Breeds on sandy beaches, shellbanks and especially braided riverbeds. After breeding, forms flocks at estuaries, lake margins and sometimes short grassland. Many, especially those breeding in high-country South Island, migrate to Australia. **Breeding:** Jul–Jan. **[Sp 248]**

NEW ZEALAND DOTTEREL (Tuturiwhatu) *Charadrius obscurus* — **Locally common endemic**

25cm; northern subspecies (*aquilonius*) 145g , southern subspecies (*obscurus*) 160g. *Large, squat, tame dotterel with large head and robust bill.* Breeding adult has *pale orange-buff to rich rufous underparts*; darker red in males and in southern subspecies. Non-breeding adult is nondescript but distinctly pale; grey-brown upperparts have broad whitish feather edges; underparts white with obscure pale grey-brown breast band, often restricted to just the shoulders. Juvenile like a pale breeding adult but with buff feather edges and pale orange-buff wash on breast and belly, flecked dark brown on breast and flanks. In flight, white wingbar and white edges to rump and tail. Heavy black bill, tip slightly upturned; proportionately short olive-grey legs. Usual call a penetrating 'chip'. **Habitat:** The *c.* 2200 birds of the northern subspecies breed on beaches and sandspits of northern and eastern North Island, and many visit local estuaries after breeding. The *c.* 250 birds of the southern subspecies breed on mountain tops of Stewart Island, moving to estuaries of Stewart Island and Southland after breeding, but some seen as far away as Farewell Spit. **Breeding:** Aug–Feb. **[Sp 245]**

LESSER SAND PLOVER (Mongolian Dotterel) *Charadrius mongolus* — **Rare Asian migrant**

20cm, 60g. *Medium-sized leggy grey dotterel with heavy short black bill with bulbous tip.* Breeding adult has broad brick-red breast band with thin black line on upper margin, red extends onto nape and upper forehead; black facial mask sometimes with two white patches separated by thin line down centre of forehead. Non-breeding like non-breeding Banded Dotterel and Greater Sand Plover, separated only with care. *Forehead and eyebrow clean white*; *upperparts plain grey-brown*, greyer than Banded Dotterel; *conspicuous dark eye patch*; underparts white, with *broad grey shoulder tabs*, sometimes meeting to form a band on lower neck. In flight, distinct *straightish wingbar* just onto primaries and *feet do not project beyond tail.* Usual call 'chirrip' with rolled 'r'. **Habitat:** Breeds Asia; migrates to Africa, Asia and Australasia. Only a few reach NZ estuaries each year, most regularly at Manukau, Firth of Thames and Farewell Spit. **[Sp 249]**

GREATER SAND PLOVER (Large Sand Dotterel) *Charadrius leschenaultii* — **Rare Asian migrant**

24cm, 90g. *Large leggy grey dotterel with long heavy black bill without bulbous tip.* Like Lesser Sand Plover but larger, much longer legs and body held more horizontal, and bill more robust but tapering. Breeding adult has a narrow pale reddish-orange breast band, extending upwards on sides of neck to behind eye; black line through eye to bill and across top of forehead. Non-breeding has white forehead and eyebrow, *plain grey-brown upperparts* and white underparts except for grey-brown shoulder tabs, which may meet to form a thin breast band. Legs long, yellowish grey to green. In flight, distinct *wingbar bulges* well onto primaries, and *feet project beyond the tail.* Usual call is a soft *churring trill.* **Habitat:** Breeds Central Asia; migrates to Africa, Asia and Australasia. Only a few reach NZ estuaries each year, mostly at Kaipara, Manukau, Firth of Thames and Farewell Spit. **[Sp 250]**

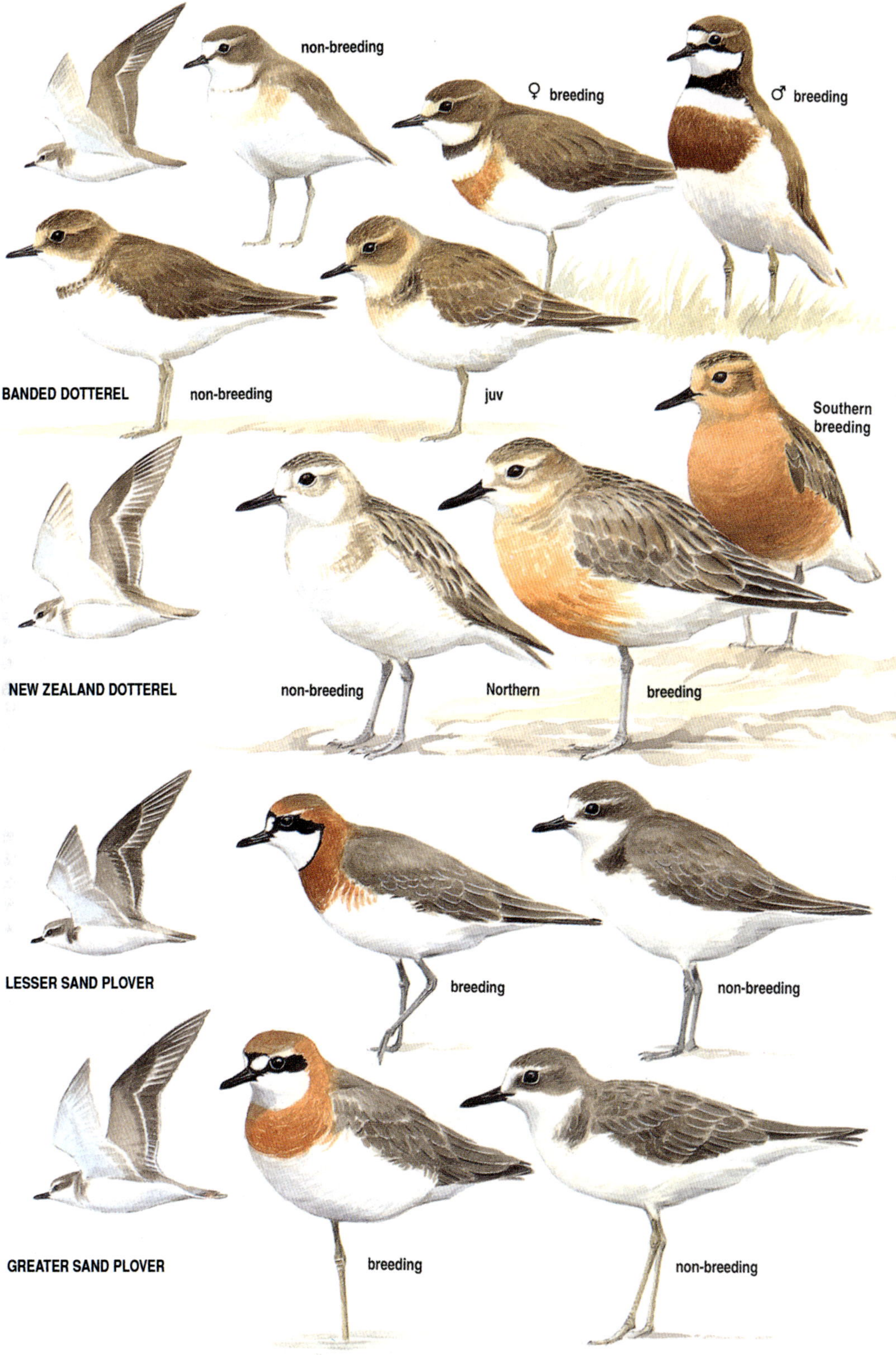
non-breeding
♀ breeding
♂ breeding
BANDED DOTTEREL
non-breeding
juv
Southern
breeding
NEW ZEALAND DOTTEREL
non-breeding
Northern
breeding
LESSER SAND PLOVER
breeding
non-breeding
GREATER SAND PLOVER
breeding
non-breeding

BLACK-FRONTED DOTTEREL *Elseyornis melanops*

Locally common native

17cm, 33g. Distinctive small dotterel with *slow jerky flight, black wingtips and metallic 'pit' flight call.* Upperparts mottled light brown with chestnut shoulder patch; black forehead, vertical patch onto crown, eyeline and V-shaped breast band; white eyebrow, side of neck and underparts. *Bill bright red, tipped black*; legs dull pink. Sexes alike. Juvenile lacks breast band, black forehead and shoulder patch. **Habitat:** Colonised from Australia in the late 1950s. Breeds on riverbeds (especially near backwaters), gravel pits and bare ground. Forms flocks after breeding, especially on lake margins and damp paddocks. **Breeding:** Aug–Mar. [Sp 253]

SHORE PLOVER (Tuturuatu) *Thinornis novaeseelandiae*

Very rare endemic

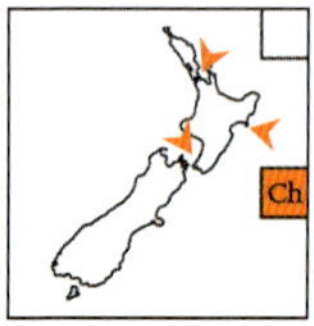

20cm, 60g. Distinctive *small stocky dotterel* with a total population of *c.* 200 birds. Crown, neck and upperparts greyish brown; *white halo around head above eyes*; black forehead, sides of face and throat in males, dirty brown in females; underparts white. Bill red, tipped black; legs orange. Juvenile has white head and neck with brown-grey cap and eye patch; bill brown with orange base. Usual call a quiet 'kleet', but loud ringing aggressive calls sound like oystercatcher piping calls. **Habitat:** Natural range is now only South East Island, Chathams, but introduced to Mangere Island, and to islands off mainland NZ, including Motutapu, Portland and Mana, and seen on nearby estuaries. Feeds on wave platforms, marsh-turf and at estuaries. **Breeding:** Oct–Feb. [Sp 254]

RED-KNEED DOTTEREL *Erythrogonys cinctus*

Very rare Australian vagrant

18cm, 50g. Distinctive dotterel with *broad white trailing edge to chocolate brown wings* and white tail with dark central stripe. *Black head and breast band boldly contrasts with white chin and sides of neck.* Back brown, underparts white with chestnut patch under bend of wing. Bill red, tipped black; *long legs, pink above 'knee', grey below.* Sexes alike. Immature has head grey-brown, breast band absent or smudgy grey-brown. **Habitat:** In Australia, usually feeds in freshwater or brackish wetlands. One NZ record: Manawatu Estuary, 1976. [Sp 255]

RED-CAPPED PLOVER (Red-capped Dotterel) *Charadrius ruficapillus*

Rare Australian vagrant

15cm, 38g. Small active *pale greyish-brown dotterel with bright white underparts and black legs,* rufous head and nape, black bill and thin white wingbar. Bill and legs black. Male has white forehead edged black above, black line through eye edging rufous neck. Female has much less extensive rufous and lacks black markings. Juvenile duller and mottled above. **Habitat:** Bred on shingle riverbeds of North Canterbury in 1960s and 1970s, but not seen since 1980s. [Sp 247]

SEMIPALMATED PLOVER *Charadrius semipalmatus*

Very rare North American vagrant

18cm, 55g. Small dotterel with short neck and *very short bi-coloured bill with bulbous tip, thin yellow orbital ring, and orange-yellow legs.* Breeding adult has black-tipped orange bill; black face and forecrown, contrasting white forehead; white chin, throat and collar. Narrow breast band extends around back of neck; black in males, brown in females. Small eyebrow in females, only trace in males. Non-breeding has small yellow–orange base to black bill, face and breast band brown, white supercilium. In flight, has white wingbar, and white-tipped black tail. *Call a distinctive 'cheee-wit'.* **Habitat:** Breeds in northern Canada and Alaska; migrates to southern USA, Central America and South America. Vagrant to Europe, Australia, and NZ. Three NZ records: Firth of Thames (1970–71, 2010) and Manukau Harbour (2009–10). [Sp 246]

BLACK-FRONTED DOTTEREL
juv
juv
♀
♂
SHORE PLOVER
imm
RED-KNEED DOTTEREL
imm
♀
♂
RED-CAPPED DOTTEREL
non-breeding
breeding
SEMIPALMATED PLOVER

A small group of widespread and highly mobile coastal or marine birds, medium to large. Plumages are highly variable but mainly brown and white, with white flashes in the outer wing. The small skuas are difficult to separate during moult from juvenile to immature, or immature to adult plumages, or between breeding and non-breeding plumages. Sexes alike. Flight is fast and direct, or twisting and turning in pursuit while relentlessly chasing terns and gulls to force them to drop or disgorge food. Strongly territorial when breeding, and aggressively defend their territory from intruders. Usually lay two brown eggs in a shallow scrape or cup of vegetation.

ARCTIC SKUA *Stercorarius parasiticus* — **Common Arctic migrant**

43cm (+ projecting tail feathers), 400g. Small elegant skua with highly variable plumages: two main phases (about 80% dark in NZ), intermediates and a wide range of juvenile and immature plumages. Difficult to distinguish from larger Pomarine Skua unless in mixed groups 'working' a flock of terns. Bill black; *legs and feet black in adults*, or *grey-blue tipped black in juveniles*. Dark phase breeding adult is blackish brown with slightly paler yellowish nape and ear coverts; pale phase has black cap, white cheeks, yellowish nape and ear coverts; brown back, wings and tail, white underparts with variable dark breast band and dark undertail. Continuous variation between; all adults have dark underwing with *single pale patch at base of primaries*, upperparts uniformly dark except for *3–4 pale shafts at base of primaries*, and *pointed central tail feathers project 10cm beyond rest of tail*. Non-breeding similar but lacks tail projection; dark phase can have white flecks on rump; pale phase has less distinct cap, underparts and flanks barred and washed brown, undertail streaked, pale flecks on rump and uppertail. Juvenile highly variable, but all have barred underwings with single pale patch and upperwings as in adults; most have rusty-brown body, mottled and barred darker, and paler streaked neck. Immatures acquire adult plumage over several years; mostly like non-breeding adult, but pale phase more heavily barred and washed brown on underparts and face, and rump and undertail lightly barred; *rump is darker than the neck*. **Habitat:** Breeds Arctic and subarctic; migrates to southern oceans. Commonest skua seen off NZ coast and in harbours, especially Jan–Apr, when often seen harrying slightly smaller White-fronted Terns or Red-billed Gulls. Sometimes roosts on beaches. **[Sp 261]**

POMARINE SKUA *Coprotheres pomarinus* — **Uncommon Arctic migrant**

48cm (+ projecting tail feathers), 600g. Similar range of plumages and pattern of plumage changes with age as Arctic Skua, but larger, more *heavily built and broader-winged*; underwing dark with *two pale patches at base of primaries*; upperwing shows 3–4 pale shafts on primaries. Breeding adult has *twisted pair of tail feathers with broad blunt ends projecting 10cm beyond rest of tail*. Juvenile and immature have *rump paler than the neck*. Flight similar to Arctic Skua but less dashing as it twists and turns after distinctly smaller White-fronted Terns and Red-billed Gulls; direct flight with slower steadier wingbeats. **Habitat:** Breeds Arctic; winters in tropics and southern oceans, especially off West Africa and eastern Australia. Regular summer and autumn visitor to NZ coast, especially open coasts, e.g. Manawatu coast, Farewell Spit; rarely in harbours. **[Sp 260]**

LONG-TAILED SKUA *Stercorarius longicaudus* — **Rare Arctic migrant**

36cm (+ projecting tail feathers), 300g. Smallest skua. Like small slender Arctic Skua but more *buoyant tern-like flight*; *greyer upperparts with darker primaries*, which have only *1–2 pale shafts*; *short blue legs*. Similar variety of plumages and changes with age as in Arctic Skua. Pale phase usual in NZ, dark phase rare, and intermediates very rare. Breeding adult has greyish-brown upperparts contrasting with dark brown primaries and trailing edge to secondaries; very long and *thin central tail streamers project 20cm beyond rest of tail*. Non-breeding adult lacks or has short pointed tail projection, and undertail is barred brown and white. Juvenile and immature have short tail projection, heavily barred underwing and undertail, and often a barred rump. **Habitat:** Breeds Arctic and subarctic; winters in tropical and southern temperate oceans. A few are seen in NZ waters, mainly off the North Island, but sometimes appears in moderate numbers. **[Sp 262]**

ad light phase
non-breeding
ad dark phase
ad light phase
ARCTIC SKUA
ad dark phase
moulting
juv
juv
ad ♂ breeding
imm
imm
POMARINE SKUA
juv
juv
ad
LONG-TAILED SKUA
imm moulting
juv
ad
non-breeding
ad breeding

SOUTHERN SKUA (Hakoakoa, Brown Skua) *Catharacta antarctica* **Locally common native**

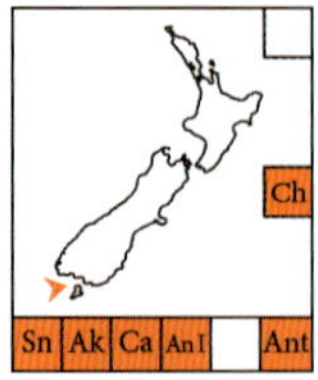

63cm;♂ 1675g, ♀ 1950g. Very large stocky skua, like a large juvenile Black-backed Gull but *chocolate brown* except for some bronzy-yellow flecking on hindneck and *conspicuous white flashes on wings*. Wings broad and rounded; large hooked black bill; legs and feet black. Juvenile lacks yellow, upperparts often more mottled and rusty. Slow powerful wingbeats and short glides. Defends breeding territory with raucous calls and low dives. **Habitat:** Breeds circumpolar subantarctic; in NZ region, on Chathams, Fiordland coast, islands around Stewart Island, Solanders, and all subantarctic islands, especially near seabird colonies. Disperse through southern oceans; occasionally seen on NZ mainland coasts in winter, often at beach-washed offal. **Breeding:** Sep–Mar. [Sp 258]

SOUTH POLAR SKUA *Catharacta maccormicki* **Locally common native**

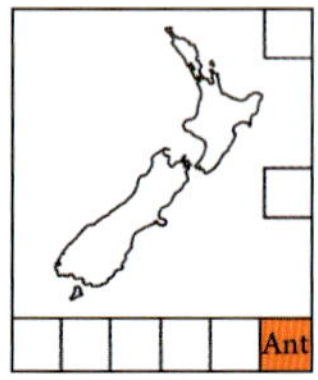

59cm;♂ 1275g, ♀ 1425g. Large stocky skua. *Like small Southern Skua but shorter stockier bill* and more yellow on hindneck. Variable plumages from pale to all dark, but all have *prominent white wing flashes*. Wings broad and rounded; tail short; legs and feet black. Pale phase has head and underparts pale ashy grey-brown with yellowish collar and brown back, wings and tail. Dark phase has body brown; back, wings and tail paler brown; white flecks at base of bill; buff collar. Juvenile lacks collar and has pale feather edges on upperparts. **Habitat:** Breeds Antarctica, including Ross Sea, usually near seabird colonies. Occasionally beach-wrecked or seen off NZ mainland while on passage to North Pacific, usually Jan–Apr. **Breeding:** Nov–Mar. [Sp 259]

> Gulls, terns and noddies are a large cosmopolitan group of mainly coastal birds. Most have short straight bills and short legs. Sexes alike. Usually grey, black or brown above, and white below in adults; juveniles usually have brown barring on back and wings. Bill and legs are often brightly coloured but usually change with age and/or season.

PACIFIC GULL *Larus pacificus* **Very rare Australian vagrant**

63cm, 1300g. *Distinctly larger than Black-backed Gull, with a massive bill.* Juvenile and immature plumages similar to Black-backed Gull, but generally darker. Adult also similar but with *wingtips entirely black*, and a subterminal black band across entire tail except for outermost feathers (but note that third-year Black-backed Gulls have black-tipped tail). *Bill yellow with red tip to both mandibles.* **Habitat:** Breeds in southern Australia. Adults sedentary but immatures disperse. One NZ record: an immature at Dargaville Beach, 2010. [Sp 263]

BLACK-BACKED GULL (Karoro, Kelp Gull) *Larus dominicanus* **Abundant native**

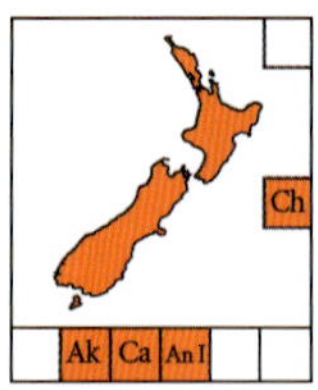

60cm;♂ 1050g, ♀ 850g. The *common large gull* in NZ. Juvenile dull brown, pale feather edges give a mottled appearance; bill and eye dark brown; legs pinkish brown. In flight, looks dark brown with a paler rump. Second-year has head, neck and underparts white, mottled and flecked brown; back and upperwings scruffy brown and black; bill dull yellowish or greenish, darker at tip; legs pinkish brown to greyish green. In flight, rump white, mottled brown, tail usually barred brown and white. Third-year has head and underparts white; neck lightly flecked brown; back and upperwings brown and black, the extent of black depending on the stage of moult; rump and tail white, with black band across tip. Bill dull yellow, darker at tip; legs yellowish green. Adult white apart from black back and upperwings except for narrow white trailing edge and white window in outer primary which, together with white-tipped inner primaries, shows as *black and white bars on the closed wing*; *bill yellow with red spot at tip of lower bill*; eye pale yellow; legs greenish yellow. **Habitat:** Breeds circumpolar subantarctic; in NZ region, breeds on mainland coast, offshore and most outlying islands; also breeds far inland on riverbeds, near lakes and alpine tarns. Ranges widely, feeds at rubbish tips, farmland, ploughed fields, beaches, harbours and behind boats, but rarely ventures far out to sea. **Breeding:** Oct–Feb. [Sp 264]

SOUTHERN SKUA
dark phase
SOUTH POLAR SKUA
pale phase
Pacific Gull
imm
Pacific Gull ad
PACIFIC GULL
ad
Black-backed Gull
juv
ad
juv
3rd year
2nd year
BLACK-BACKED GULL
ad

RED-BILLED GULL (Tarapunga) *Larus novaehollandiae*

Abundant native

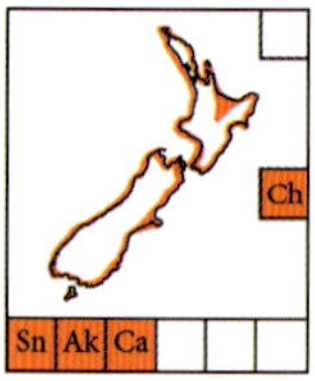

37cm;♂ 300g, ♀ 260g. Grey and white gull, mainly of the coast. Like Black-billed Gull but *shorter deeper bill and boldly patterned wingtips*. Adult has head, underparts and tail white, sometimes pinkish on breast; back and wings pearly grey, except *wingtips black with small white window. Short deep bright red bill*; legs and feet red; eye white. Juvenile and first-year have larger dark patch at wingtip and very small, if any, white window. *Bill dark with pink near base*; legs pale flesh to reddish black; eye brown. **Habitat:** Breeds subantarctic from Africa to Chathams; in NZ region, on coast from the Three Kings to Campbell Islands; inland colony at Lake Rotorua. Common in coastal waters, beaches and estuaries; only occasionally (but sometimes in large flocks) inland to wet paddocks, playing fields and lakes. **Breeding:** Oct–Feb. [Sp 266]

BLACK-BILLED GULL *Larus bulleri*

Locally common endemic

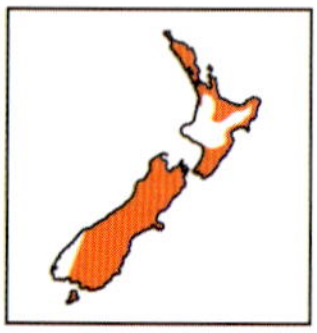

37cm;♂ 300g, ♀ 250g. Very pale gull of inland South Island and coasts. Like Red-billed Gull *but longer thinner bill and very pale wingtips*. Adult has back and wings pale silvery grey, wingtips only thinly bordered black. *Long thin black bill*; legs and feet black or reddish black; eye white. Juvenile quickly loses small grey patch behind eye; has more extensive black on wingtips; *bill pale flesh with dark tip*; legs from pinkish to reddish black; eye brown. **Habitat:** Breeds on riverbeds and lake margins of South Island, some also in southern North Island and at Lake Rotorua; a few coastal colonies in both islands. Feeds inland in wet paddocks, ploughed fields and over lakes; also coastal waters, beaches and estuaries. **Breeding:** Sep–Feb. [Sp 267]

FRANKLIN'S GULL *Larus pipixcan*

Very rare North American vagrant

35cm, 280g. Like a very dark grey Black-billed Gull or Red-billed Gull with extensive *black on the head, especially from the eye to the hindcrown* in all plumages, and contrasting white crescent around the back of the eye. Back, scapulars and wing coverts slate grey, separated from the black hood, hindcrown and upper neck by a white lower neck. Bill black, turning red in breeding plumage. *Flight graceful, almost tern-like*, the wings appearing long and narrow. In flight, the upperwing is grey with a *broad white trailing edge, tipped with bands of white, black, then white*. Immatures have *a black subterminal bar across the entire tail* and less distinct wing markings except for the broad white trailing edge. **Habitat:** Breeds in inland North America; migrates to central America and the Pacific coast of South America. Vagrants occasionally appear on Pacific Islands and Australia; four NZ records: Kermadecs, 1988, Dunedin, 2002, Manukau Harbour, 2009, and Marlborough, 2013. [Sp 265]

GULL-BILLED TERN *Gelochelidon nilotica*

Rare Australian vagrant

43cm, 230g. Robust pale tern with long broad wings, *short slightly forked tail, short thick gull-like black bill and long black legs*. Breeding adult has black cap; back and wings very pale grey; neck and underparts white. Non-breeding adult has a *black patch from eye to ear coverts*, and grey flecking on nape. Hawks and skims over water or land, picking up prey in flight; rarely dives into water. **Habitat:** Breeds tropics and subtropics, including Australia. A few reach NZ estuaries and coastal marshes; major influx in 2011. [Sp 277]

RED-BILLED GULL
juv
juv
ACK-BILLED GULL
juv
juv
FRANKLIN'S GULL
non-breeding
breeding
non-breeding
breeding
GULL-BILLED TERN

CASPIAN TERN (Taranui) *Hydroprogne caspia*

Uncommon native

51cm, 700g. *Very large silver-grey tern with massive red bill tipped black and yellow*; short white, slightly forked tail; underparts white with dark tips to underwing. Adult has black cap when breeding, heavily flecked white in non-breeding plumage; legs black. Juvenile has browner cap; back feathers sparsely edged buff and white; bill orange-red; legs dull orange. Flight direct, with steady shallow beats of broad wings; head and bill pointing downward when hunting. Dives into water. Adult call a loud harsh 'kaaa'; *juveniles beg with a persistent high-pitched mewing.* **Habitat:** Breeds widely, including *c.* 4000 birds in NZ. Colonies in NZ found on isolated sandspits and shellbanks of coast and harbours; some pairs on riverbeds or lake shores. Feeds in inshore waters, up rivers and over coastal lakes. Rare vagrant to Kermadecs and Chathams. **Breeding:** Sep–Feb. [Sp 278]

CRESTED TERN *Sterna bergii*

Rare tropical vagrant

47cm, 350g. *Large tern with long slender greenish-yellow bill.* Breeding adult has white forehead, black cap and a *straggly crest*; upperparts slate grey, paler on rump and tail; underparts white; legs black. Non-breeding adult has crown white or streaked black. Juvenile similar, but cap browner and extends around eye, wings brownish grey and mottled. Looks rakish yet graceful in flight. Plunge-dives. Noisy; call a rasping 'kerrcrik'. **Habitat:** Breeds eastern Asia, South Pacific and Australia. About 15 birds have been seen around the NZ coast, sometimes staying for years. [Sp 286]

BROWN NODDY (Common Noddy) *Anous stolidus*

Rare native

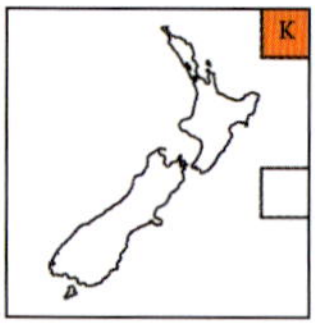

39cm, 200g. Medium-sized dark tropical tern with *very long broad tail* with shallow central notch. Like large Black Noddy but *browner*, and in flight, *underwing has pale central panel.* Adult has *whitish-grey forehead and cap*, merging into brown on sides of face and nape; black line from bill to eye; body, upperwing and tail dark brown; underwing grey-brown, edged dark brown. Thin straight (4.5cm) black bill; legs and feet black. Juvenile similar but duller, cap less clearly defined, and back and wing feathers edged pale. Flight buoyant. Feeds mainly from sea surface and sometimes settles on the water. **Habitat:** Breeds tropics and subtropics; about 25 pairs breed on Curtis Island, southern Kermadecs. After breeding, they disperse to feed in flocks over deep warm waters. Two records from the NZ mainland: Muriwai, 1992 and Waitara, 2002. **Breeding:** Sep–Jan. [Sp 268]

BLACK NODDY (White-capped Noddy, Lesser Noddy) *Anous minutus*

Locally common native

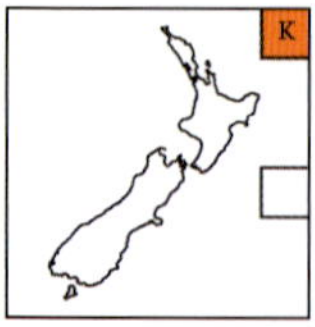

37cm, 120g. Medium-sized dark tropical tern with long broad tail, square or slightly notched. Like small Brown Noddy but *blacker*, and in flight has *completely dark underwings.* Adult has *silvery-white forehead, cap to level of eyes, and hindcrown*; black line from bill to eye; sooty black neck, body and wings; tail brownish black, underwings black. Fine slightly decurved (4cm) black bill; legs and feet dark brown. Juvenile similar but less white on hindcrown, sharper separation of pale crown from dark neck, and feathers on back and wings edged pale. Flight buoyant; feeds mainly from sea surface but sometimes dives; occasionally settles on the water. **Habitat:** Breeds tropics and subtropics, including *c.* 1100 pairs in the Kermadecs. After breeding, remains close to breeding sites, but vagrants occasionally reach NZ mainland, mostly in autumn after northerly gales. **Breeding:** Aug–Apr. [Sp 269]

juv
CASPIAN TERN
breeding
non-breeding
CRESTED TERN
juv
non-breeding
breeding
Crested Tern
juv
BROWN NODDY
BLACK NODDY

LITTLE TERN *Sternula albifrons*

Uncommon Asian migrant

25cm, 50g. Very small vocal tern like a dark Fairy Tern, but *dark primaries contrast with rest of upperwing.* Flight erratic with rapid deep wingbeats, often hovers. Breeding adult has *white sloping forehead and sharp recess to just behind eye*; black crown, nape and *line through eye to yellow bill with black tip*; upperparts pale grey, darker on wingtips with outermost 2–3 primaries black; deeply forked white tail; underparts white; legs orange-yellow. In non-breeding plumage (seen in NZ summer), cap recedes to band from eye to eye around back of head and down nape; bill dull yellow, dusky at tip; legs dull yellow. Immature similar, but bill black and *dark leading edge to wing* prominent as dark shoulder (carpal) bar at rest; some retain brown feather tips on upperparts; legs blackish brown. Flight call a sharp chattering 'kik, kik, kik . . .' and a rasping 'kree-ik'. **Habitat:** Breeds widely in Northern Hemisphere and Australia. Most in NZ are in non-breeding plumage in Oct–Mar, probably migrants from eastern Asia. Single birds and small flocks regularly seen at NZ estuaries or coastal lakes, mainly at North Island harbours, especially Firth of Thames. **[Sp 275]**

FAIRY TERN (Tara-iti) *Sternula nereis*

Very rare native

25cm, 70g. Very small tern, very like pale Little Tern but *upperwing almost uniform pale grey.* Flight erratic with rapid deep wingbeats; often hovers. Breeding adult (Oct–Mar) has *white steep forehead and rounded recess to above eye*; black crown, nape and line to eye; *white feathering between eye and completely yellow-orange bill*; upperparts uniform pale grey; deeply forked white tail; underparts white; legs orange-yellow. In non-breeding plumage, cap recedes to above eye and down nape; bill orange-brown, dusky at tip and base; legs dull orange. Immature similar, but bill black with dusky-yellow base, thin *dark leading edge to wing* faintly visible as dark shoulder (carpal) bar at rest; legs brown. Flight call a high-pitched 'zwit'. **Habitat:** Breeds Australia, New Caledonia and NZ. The NZ subspecies, limited to *c.* 35 birds, breeds at Waipu, Mangawhai, Te Arai and Pakiri on the east coast of southern Northland and at Papakanui Spit on the south side of Kaipara Harbour, and feeds on nearby estuaries. Most winter at the Kaipara Harbour, especially near Tapora. **Breeding:** Nov–Feb. **[Sp 276]**

GREY TERNLET (Blue-grey Noddy) *Procelsterna cerulea*

Locally common native

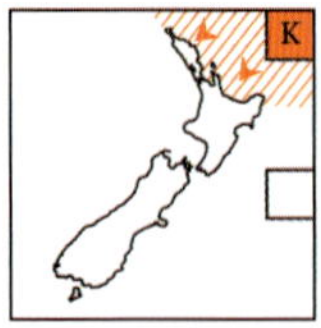

28cm, 70g. Distinctive small delicate *blue-grey tern. Wings darker grey, especially at tips, and with a thin white trailing edge.* Prominent eye owing to small black patch in front of eye; long forked tail; bill black; long black legs, feet black with yellow to pink webs. Juvenile has head streaked and upperparts and wings washed brownish. Flight graceful. Feeds by hovering, fluttering and paddling on sea surface like a huge Storm Petrel; sometimes settles on the surface. **Habitat:** Tropical and subtropical Pacific; in NZ region, *c.* 20,000 pairs breed at Kermadecs, in some years also at Three Kings Islands and rock stacks off eastern coast of Northland and in Bay of Plenty. Occasionally seen in northern NZ coastal waters; straggles as far south as Canterbury. **Breeding:** Aug–Jan. **[Sp 270]**

WHITE TERN *Gygis alba*

Very rare native

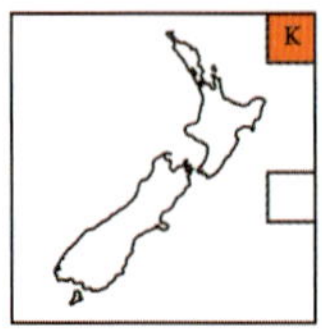

31cm, 110g. *Delicate pure white tern* with almost translucent wings and short forked tail; prominent eye because of narrow black ring of feathers around eye; long straight bill, black with bluish base; legs and feet blue-grey with yellowish webs. Juvenile has smudgy brown patch behind eye and across back of head, and rusty brown flecks on back and upperwings. Flight swift and graceful; often circles over breeding areas by day. **Habitat:** Tropical seas; in NZ, fewer than 10 pairs breed at Raoul Island, Kermadecs; vagrants occasionally reach NZ mainland in autumn and winter. **Breeding:** Oct–Mar. **[Sp 271]**

breeding
LITTLE TERN
non-breeding
imm
imm
breeding
FAIRY TERN
non-breeding
imm
imm
GREY TERNLET
WHITE TERN

SOOTY TERN *Onychoprion fuscatus* **Locally common native**

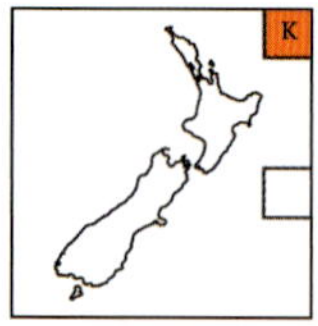

43cm, 210g. Large tropical tern. Adult has white forehead and *eyebrow to just above eye*; cap, line through eye to bill, nape and *upperparts dark brownish black*; sides of neck and underparts white, washed pale grey towards long deeply forked tail. Bill and legs black. Juvenile dark brown except feathers on back and upperwings edged white or buff, underwings pale grey, and underparts white towards tail. Distinctive harsh 'wideawake' call. **Habitat:** Breeds tropics and subtropics, including *c.* 24,000 pairs throughout the Kermadecs. After breeding, ranges widely over deep water and a few reach northern NZ most years, especially after autumn and winter gales. **Breeding**: Oct–Feb. [Sp 272]

BRIDLED TERN *Onychoprion anaethetus* **Very rare tropical vagrant**

38cm, 120g. Like small pale Sooty Tern. Adult has white forehead and *eyebrow clearly extending behind eye*; black cap, line through eye to bill, and nape contrasts with *dark greyish-brown upperparts*; sides of neck and underparts white, long deeply forked tail. Bill and legs black. Juvenile similar, but crown streaked white, incomplete black line between eye and bill, and feathers on back and upperwings edged white or buff. **Habitat:** Breeds tropics, including northern Australia. One NZ record: Canterbury, 1987. [Sp 274]

GREY-BACKED TERN (Spectacled Tern) *Onychoprion lunatus* **Very rare tropical vagrant**

38cm, 150g. Like Bridled Tern but with bluish-grey upperparts. Breeding adult has white forehead and *eyebrow extending well behind eye*; black cap, line through eye, and nape contrasts with *pale bluish-grey upper back and darker grey lower back, tail and wings*; sides of neck and underparts white, long deeply forked tail. Bill and legs black. Non-breeding and juvenile similar, but crown heavily streaked white, incomplete black line between eye and bill, and feathers on back and upperwings faintly edged white. **Habitat:** Breeds central tropical Pacific; nearest colonies in Tonga. Two NZ records: South Kaipara Heads, 1999 and Pungaereere Estuary, Taranaki, 2002. [Sp 273]

juv
SOOTY TERN
juv
BRIDLED TERN
juv
breeding
non-breeding
GREY-BACKED TERN

BLACK-FRONTED TERN (Tarapiroe) *Chlidonias albostriatus* **Locally common endemic**

29cm, 90g. The common inland tern of the South Island. Smaller and greyer than White-fronted Tern (see Plate 65). *Bluish-grey body, wings and short shallow-forked tail* contrast with *white rump* in flight; undertail white. Breeding adult has black cap down to bill; thin white streak across cheeks; *bill and legs bright orange.* Non-breeding adult similar, but cap recedes to arc from eye to eye around back of head, except crown flecked grey; *bill and legs dull orange.* Immature has crown flecked black; dark patches around eye; chin white; breast very pale grey; bill dusky brown, becoming yellow with age; *legs dull orange.* Feeds mainly by hawking insects over riverbeds and dropping to pick prey from the surface of lakes, swamps and farmland. **Habitat:** *c.* 8000 birds breed in small colonies on gravel riverbeds of South Island, mainly east of Southern Alps. Migrates to coast to feed at sea, especially in Cook Strait and off eastern coast of North and South islands, as far north as Bay of Plenty. **Breeding:** Oct–Feb. **[Sp 281]**

WHITE-WINGED BLACK TERN *Chlidonias leucopterus* **Uncommon Asian migrant**

23cm, 65g. Distinctive very small tern with slow buoyant flight. Black and white in breeding plumage; grey and white in non-breeding, but with distinctive *black 'ear-muffs' and club-shaped patch on nape.* Breeding adult has black head, neck, back and underparts: white rump and only barely forked tail; upperwing very pale grey, darker at tips; underwing black at base, white at tips; bill and legs red. Non-breeding adult has white head except crown streaked black, and black club-shaped band extends over top of head from behind eyes and also down nape; grey back; upperwing grey, darker at tips and along trailing edge of secondaries; shows dark carpal bar at rest; rump, tail and underparts white; bill and legs black, some with reddish tinge. Immature similar, but upperwings darker grey, rump very pale grey and tail grey. Hawks insects over water or land; flies persistently back and forth, dropping down to pick insects from water surface; rarely plunges. **Habitat:** Breeds Eurasia; migrates to tropics and subtropics. A few reach NZ coastal lakes, swamps and estuaries each year, and several pairs have bred in New Zealand. **[Sp 279]**

WHISKERED TERN *Chlidonias hybridus* **Rare Australian vagrant**

26cm, 90g. Small tern with slow buoyant flight, long legs and gull-like stance; *even grey on rump and slightly forked tail.* Breeding adult has black cap down to red bill; white cheeks; dark grey underparts and sooty belly contrast with white undertail; red legs. Non-breeding is pale grey above and dull white below with black arc from eye to eye around back of head, solid on ears but flecked on nape; wingtips darker than rest of wings; bill and legs dull red-brown. Immature similar but narrow dark borders to upperwing, and rump slightly paler than rest of upperparts. Feeds by hawking insects, picking prey from the water surface or by taking shallow plunges into water. **Habitat:** Breeds Africa to Australia; nomadic or migratory. A few reach NZ, mainly at coastal lakes or sewage ponds. **[Sp 280]**

breeding
non-breeding
imm
juv
BLACK-FRONTED TERN
non-breeding
breeding
WHITE-WINGED BLACK TERN
imm
moulting
imm
imm
breeding
breeding
WHISKERED TERN
imm

WHITE-FRONTED TERN (Tara) *Sterna striata*

Abundant native

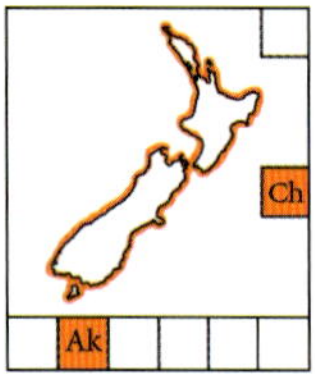

42cm, 160g. Commonest tern on NZ coast, often in large flocks. *Long black bill*; short legs, black or reddish black. Breeding adult is very pale pearly grey and white; *black cap separated from bill by steep white forehead*; neck and underparts white, sometimes pinkish on breast. In flight, *upperwing entirely pale grey* except for black outer web to outer primary; *underwing white to tips*. At rest, deeply forked tail extends well beyond wings. Non-breeding adult similar, but cap recedes to above eyes; at rest, tail level with wings. Juvenile heavily marked brown and white on upperparts; dark mottling on upperwing (carpal bar), prominent at rest, and in flight forms a dark triangle on inner forewing; primaries mid-grey; tail even with or shorter than wings. Immature similar, but mottling on inner forewing shows as black line at shoulder. Feeds by plunge-diving. Call a high-pitched 'siet'. **Habitat:** Apart from a small number breeding in Bass Strait, Australia, the rest of the 15,000–20,000 pairs breed on the coast of NZ mainland, Chatham and Auckland islands; visitor to other subantarctic islands. Favours coastal waters and harbours. Large flocks form over shoaling fish, especially in summer and autumn. Roosts on shellbanks or sandspits. Rare inland. Many, including most juveniles, winter in Australian waters. **Breeding:** Oct–Mar. [Sp 282]

COMMON TERN *Sterna hirundo*

Rare Arctic migrant

36cm, 120g. Like small dark White-fronted Tern, but bill shorter and finer; legs rather long. At rest, *deeply forked tail even with or slightly shorter than wings*. Breeding adult has black cap *sloping* down to black bill with dull red base; pearl-grey underparts. In flight, *outermost 3–4 dark grey primaries contrast with paler grey inner primaries*, which appear as a *translucent patch* against the light, diffuse trailing edge to tip of underwings; dark outer edge to tail; reddish-black legs. In non-breeding plumage, black cap recedes to level of eye; underparts white; many have *prominent carpal bar at rest*; bill black; legs reddish black. Immature similar, but primaries darker, and tertials often have brownish tips. Flight more buoyant than White-fronted Tern, wingbeats faster and deeper. Feeds by plunge-diving; frequently hovers. Calls a short 'kik' and a raspy 'kreer'. **Habitat:** Breeds subarctic; migrates to temperate oceans. A few identified in NZ each year, mainly from North Island coasts or coastal lakes. [Sp 285]

ARCTIC TERN *Sterna paradisaea*

Rare Arctic migrant

34cm, 110g. Like small dark White-fronted Tern and similar to Common Tern, but paler, smaller-bodied and longer-winged. Head rounded except *steep forehead*; bill rather short; *legs very short, brilliant red to reddish black*. Breeding adult has black cap down to blood-red bill; underparts darker grey than upperparts; small amount of black on tips of outer 3–4 primaries; *all of outerwing appears translucent* against the light except for *a thin well-defined dark trailing edge to tip of underwing*; thin dark outer edge to tail; at rest, deeply forked tail even with or longer than wings. In non-breeding plumage, *cap recedes to well behind eye*; underparts white; some develop a faint carpal bar; bill black. Immature has thin carpal bar and darker primaries. In flight, looks slim, long-winged and long-tailed. Flight buoyant, with deeper, faster wingbeats than White-fronted Tern. Calls like Common Tern. **Habitat:** Breeds Arctic; migrates to southern oceans. A few seen each summer at NZ estuaries or coastal lakes. [Sp 284]

ANTARCTIC TERN *Sterna vittata*

Locally common native

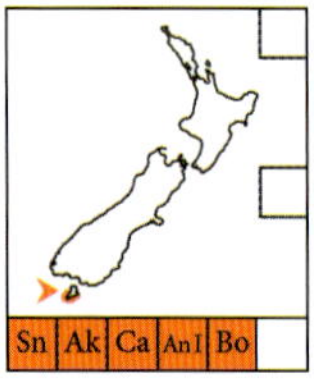

36cm, 140g. Medium-sized tern with white rump and forked tail. Breeding adult has *black cap down steep forehead to red bill*; white cheeks; even grey body; wings grey with black only on the outer web of the outer primary; *legs red*. Non-breeding adult similar, but *cap recedes to just behind eye*; underparts white; *bill dull pinkish red*. Juvenile initially marked brown and white on back; bill dark brown, *legs dull reddish*. In flight, thinner-winged and more delicate than White-fronted Tern. Feeds by dipping and plunge-diving. **Habitat:** Breeds circumpolar subantarctic, including *c.* 1000 pairs in NZ subantarctic south of Stewart Island. Stays close to breeding sites; not recorded off mainland NZ. **Breeding:** Sep–Apr. [Sp 283]

WHITE-FRONTED TERN
imm
non-breeding
ad
imm
breeding
juv
imm
breeding
non-breeding
ad Common
COMMON TERN
imm Common
imm
breeding
non-breeding
imm Arctic
ad Arctic
ARCTIC TERN
imm
non-breeding
ad
ANTARCTIC TERN
breeding
juv

Medium to large birds with short bill, small head, rounded wings and short feathered legs. Sexes alike. Calls simple and often repetitive variations of 'coo'. Flight strong, direct and often noisy. Aerial displays of stall dives are part of breeding displays. Can breed at any time of year if food supplies are suitable. Lay 1–2 white eggs on a flimsy platform of sticks. Short incubation and nestling periods; young fed 'crop milk' and, later, regurgitated food. They often fledge well below adult weight, with short wings and tail, and dull bill and feet. All are herbivorous; the NZ endemic species feed on fruit and foliage, the three introduced species feed on seeds, especially grain.

CHATHAM ISLANDS PIGEON (Parea) *Hemiphaga chathamensis* — Locally common endemic

55cm, 800g. Like NZ Pigeon, except larger and coloured plumage has an *ashy-grey wash*; *bill red with yellow tip*. **Habitat:** Mainly in forests and adjacent pasture of southwest Chatham Island, but some also on Pitt and South East islands. **Breeding:** Jun–Mar. [Sp 291]

NEW ZEALAND PIGEON (Kereru, Kukupa) *Hemiphaga novaeseelandiae* — Common endemic

51cm, 650g. Head, throat, upper breast and upperparts metallic green with purplish sheen and bronze reflections, especially around neck; sharp line separates upper breast from white lower breast, belly and legs. Eye crimson; bill red with orangish tip; feet crimson. Juvenile has duller upperparts, bill and feet, smudgy breast, and often the tail is shorter. Strong steady wingbeats on broad rounded wings and long broad tail; *noisy swish of wings* is distinctive. Call a single soft penetrating 'kuu'. **Habitat:** Native forests, especially in lowland areas, scrub, forest patches among farmland, rural and city gardens and parks. **Breeding:** Variable, depending on availability of ripe fruit; usually Sep–May. [Sp 290]

ROCK PIGEON (Feral Pigeon) *Columba livia* — Common European introduction

33cm, 400g. Highly variable plumages seen in descendants of domestic and racing pigeons. In the wild form, the plumage is mainly blue-grey, with sides of neck glossy green and purple; rump whitish; two prominent black bars across the wings; dark tip to the tail. Bill leaden; feet pinkish. Flight fast and direct, with flicking wingbeats; pointed angled wings, and short tail. **Habitat:** City parks and streets; grain stores, wharfs and railway stations. In rural areas, favours drier arable farmland. Often nests on cliffs and caves in river gorges and on sea coast. **Breeding:** All year, peak Sep–Feb. [Sp 287]

BARBARY DOVE *Streptopelia risoria* — Locally common African introduction

28cm, 140g. *Pale creamy buff*, shading to white on chin, belly and undertail coverts; distinctive *black half-collar around back of neck*. Eye red; bill horn-black; feet crimson. Juvenile similar but lacks black half-collar and has pale bill. Distinctive *call: a persistent 'coo-crroo'*. **Habitat:** Parks, gardens and orchards in Bay of Islands, Whangarei, Auckland, Waikato, Hawke's Bay, and coastal Horowhenua. **Breeding:** Sep–Mar. [Sp 288]

SPOTTED DOVE *Streptopelia chinensis* — Locally common Asian introduction

30cm, 130g. Head grey, tinged pink; *nape and back of neck black, finely spotted with white*; back, wings and rump mottled brown; tail long, with darker outer feathers, broadly tipped with white. Eye red; bill black; feet pink. Juvenile similar but lacks patterning on nape. Calls mellow, varying from one to four notes: 'coo', 'croo-croo', 'coo-coo-croo', 'cu-cu-croo-crook'. **Habitat:** Suburban parks, gardens, farmland and orchards of Auckland, South Auckland, and near Te Puke and Opotiki. **Breeding:** Sep–Mar. [Sp 289]

CHATHAM ISLANDS PIGEON
NEW ZEALAND PIGEON
ROCK PIGEON
BARBARY DOVE
juv
SPOTTED DOVE

A large cosmopolitan family of often very colourful birds, but the NZ species are relatively drab, mainly green. All have a short bill with a horn covering (cere) enclosing the nostrils. The upper mandible is strongly curved, fitting neatly over the lower mandible. Their legs are short, and their feet have two toes pointing forward and two back.

KAKAPO *Strigops habroptilus* **Very rare endemic**

63cm;♂ 2.1kg, ♀ 1.5kg. Large flightless nocturnal parrot. *Moss green above, greenish yellow below*; feathers mottled with fine brown and yellow bars. Owl-like facial disc. Male has broader head and larger bill. Feeds on ground or by clambering into shrubs. *Male call a loud repetitive low-pitched booming* for hours, from cleared track-and-bowl system on ridge of prominent hill. **Habitat:** Formerly in forests of all three main islands, but after transfers, the total population of *c.* 125 birds is now confined to Codfish, Little Barrier, Chalky and Anchor islands. **Breeding:** Usually every 3–5 years following mast fruiting or seeding, Jan–Jul. [Sp 292]

KEA *Nestor notabilis* **Locally common endemic**

46cm;♂ 950g, ♀ 775g. A large, often bold parrot, olive green with scarlet underwings and rump. Dark-edged feathers make it look sculpted. Bill, cere, eye and legs dark brown; upper mandible longer in the male. Juvenile has pale crown, yellow cere, eye-ring and on bill; yellow fades in a couple of years to bill only. *Call a loud ringing 'keee-aa'*, mainly in flight. Delights in aerobatics and playful but sometimes destructive behaviour. **Habitat:** Mainly in alpine zone, but also in forest and descends to lowland riverflats. **Breeding:** Jul–Apr. [Sp 294]

KAKA *Nestor meridionalis* **Locally common endemic**

45cm;♂ 475g, ♀ 425g (North Island);♂ 575g, ♀ 500g (South Island). A large, sometimes inquisitive, forest parrot with crimson underwings and rump. North Island birds are mainly olive brown with darker feather edges; crown paler and greyer; golden wash on cheeks; dark crimson collar, undertail and lower belly. Bill longer and more arched in the male. Juvenile has yellow base of lower mandible. South and Stewart islands birds (illustrated) brighter, and crown almost white. Noisy; *many varied calls from liquid whistling notes to harsh grating calls.* **Habitat:** Favours native forest and predator- and possum-free offshore islands and mainland sanctuaries, but some visit city and rural gardens and orchards. **Breeding:** Oct–Jun. [Sp 293]

KAKAPO
KEA
KAKA

CRIMSON ROSELLA *Platycercus elegans*

Very rare Australian introduction

35cm, 130g. Distinctive medium-sized parrot with a long tail. Adult *rich crimson with blue cheeks*, wings and tail, mottled black on the back. Immature green but with crimson on forehead, breast and undertail, blue on chin, wings and tail. **Habitat:** Parks and gardens, mainly in central Wellington. **Breeding:** Aug–Feb. **[Sp 298]**

RAINBOW LORIKEET *Trichoglossus haematodus*

Very rare Australian introduction

28cm, 150g. A *richly coloured and raucous small parrot*. Bill short, red. Head, face and belly dark blue; hindneck pale green; upperparts green. Chest reddish orange with yellow sides; underwings red with yellow bar across primaries. Long thin pointed tail. Swift direct flight, or flocks twist and wheel among trees. Loud raucous screeches in flight, chatters while feeding. **Habitat:** Parks and gardens, mainly in Auckland. **Breeding**: Jul–Feb. **[Sp 297]**

EASTERN ROSELLA *Platycercus eximius*

Locally common Australian introduction

32cm, 110g. Distinctive long-tailed parrot with a bell-like *'kwink, kwink' flight call*. Head, upper breast and undertail crimson; *cheeks white*; lower breast yellow; back, rump, flanks and belly yellowish green, mottled black on back; leading edge of inner wing black, contrasts with pale blue on the central wing and dark blue on the wingtips; tail dark bluish green, edged pale blue. Female and immature more heavily mottled black on back, and red areas duller and patchy. Loud ringing calls and chattering notes. **Habitat:** Favours lightly wooded country (e.g. scattered totara) but uses forest and urban parks and gardens. **Breeding:** Oct–Apr. **[Sp 299]**

SULPHUR-CRESTED COCKATOO *Cacatua galerita*

Uncommon Australian introduction

50cm, 900g. A large *white parrot with a bright yellow crest*; a yellow tinge on underwing and undertail; bill and legs grey-black. Female slightly larger. Flies strongly on broad rounded wings, *screeching raucously*. Often feeds on the ground. **Habitat:** Forest patches in open country, especially western Waikato, Turakina Valley and Pohangina Valley. **Breeding:** Aug–Feb. **[Sp 295]**

GALAH *Eolophus roseicapillus*

Rare Australian introduction

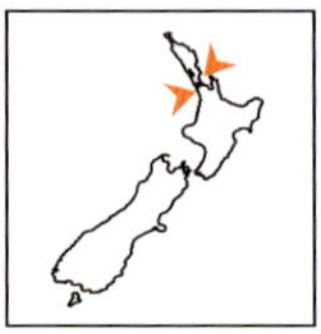

36cm, 325g. A noisy *pink and grey parrot* with paler crown and crest. Immature duller than adult, with grey about the face. **Habitat:** Forest patches in open country; recently established in South Auckland, especially near Hunua Ranges, Pukekohe, and Pakihi and Ponui islands. **Breeding:** Season unknown in NZ. **[Sp 296]**

CRIMSON ROSELLA
juv
RAINBOW LORIKEET
♂
EASTERN ROSELLA
GALAH
SULPHUR-CRESTED COCKATOO

ORANGE-FRONTED PARAKEET (Kakariki) *Cyanoramphus malherbi* — Very rare endemic

♂ 22cm, 45g; ♀ 20cm, 35g. Like Yellow-crowned Parakeet, but *plainer and duller green with orange forehead and band from bill to eye*. **Habitat:** Now naturally restricted to three valleys in inland Canterbury, but transferred to Mayor, Maud, Blumine and Chalky islands. Usually *feeds at mid-level in the forest* rather than the canopy. **Breeding:** Dec–Jun.

[Sp 302]

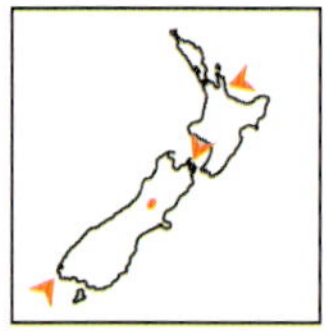

FORBES' PARAKEET *Cyanoramphus forbesi* — Locally common endemic

♂ 28cm, 80g; ♀ 26cm, 70g. Like Yellow-crowned Parakeet, but larger. **Habitat:** Mature and older seral forests, mainly of Mangere and Little Mangere islands, Chathams. **Breeding:** Oct–May.

[Sp 303]

REISCHEK'S PARAKEET *Cyanoramphus hochstetteri* — Locally common endemic

♂ 28cm, 125g; ♀ 26cm, 95g. Like Red-crowned Parakeet, but larger. **Habitat:** Tussock and scrub of Antipodes Islands only. **Breeding:** Nov–Mar.

[Sp 305]

YELLOW-CROWNED PARAKEET (Kakariki) *Cyanoramphus auriceps*

Locally common endemic

♂ 25cm, 50g; ♀ 23cm, 40g. Long-tailed bright yellow-green parrot of native forest. *Golden yellow crown; red forehead and band from bill to eye*, and small crimson patch on sides of rump; violet-blue on wing coverts and some outer flight feathers. Flight fast and direct, with rapid wingbeats. *Flight call a rapid high-pitched chatter*. **Habitat:** Native forests of the mainland of NZ and Auckland Islands; often *feeds in the canopy*. **Breeding:** Oct–Mar.

[Sp 301]

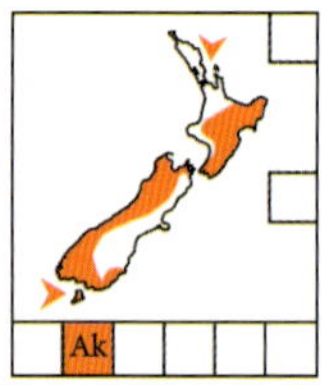

RED-CROWNED PARAKEET (Kakariki) *Cyanoramphus novaezelandiae*

Locally common endemic

♂ 28cm, 80g; ♀ 25cm, 70g. Very like the Yellow-crowned Parakeet but larger and with *red crown, forehead and band from bill to behind eye*; crimson rump patches. Flight direct and rapid, often above the canopy, or side-slipping through the trees. *Flight call a rapid loud chatter, lower-pitched than Yellow-crowned Parakeet*. **Habitat:** Rare in native forests on the two main islands but common in forest and scrub on Stewart Island and many predator-free offshore and outlying islands. Often *feeds low in the forest or on the ground*. **Breeding:** Oct–Mar.

[Sp 300]

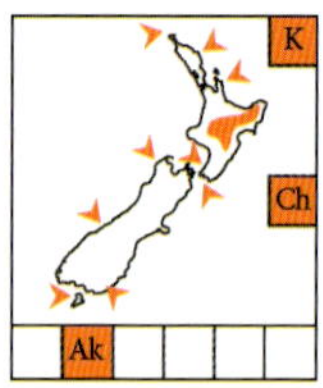

ANTIPODES ISLANDS PARAKEET *Cyanoramphus unicolor* — Locally common endemic

♂ 32cm, 160g; ♀ 29cm; 130g. *Entirely green head and body*, except for blue on wing coverts and some flight feathers; underparts tinged yellow. **Habitat:** Tussock and scrub of Antipodes Islands only. **Breeding:** Oct–Mar.

[Sp 304]

ORANGE-FRONTED PARAKEET
FORBES' PARAKEET
REISCHEK'S PARAKEET
RED-CROWNED PARAKEET
YELLOW-CROWNED PARAKEET
ANTIPODES ISLANDS PARAKEET

A diverse group ranging in size from the Shining Cuckoo to the Channel-billed Cuckoo. Generally grey or brown, often with conspicuous barring, especially on the underparts; long tail with transverse bars and white notches; short bill and short legs. Sexes alike. Most lay one egg in nests of other insectivorous species. Young cuckoos make insistent penetrating begging calls. The adults are vocal when breeding and are more often heard than seen.

SHINING CUCKOO (Pipiwharauroa) *Chrysococcyx lucidus* — Common native

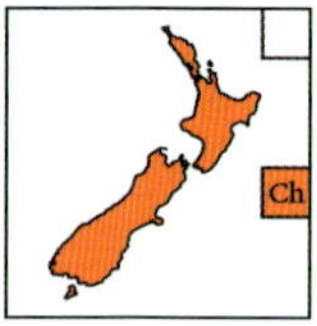

16cm, 25g. Short-tailed *metallic bronze-green cuckoo, barred dark green on white face and underparts.* Juvenile duller and less distinctly barred. *Song a distinctive series of high-pitched upward-slurring whistles: 'coo-ee, coo-ee, . . .' followed by 1–2 downward-slurring notes: 'tsee-ew'*; the latter often given when flying at night. Usual hosts are Grey Warbler and Chatham Islands Warbler. **Habitat:** Native forest, scrub, parks and gardens from Sep–Apr. Migrates to Solomon Islands and Bismarck Archipelago for NZ winter. **Breeding:** Oct–Feb. **[Sp 309]**

LONG-TAILED CUCKOO (Koekoea) *Eudynamys taitensis* — Locally common endemic

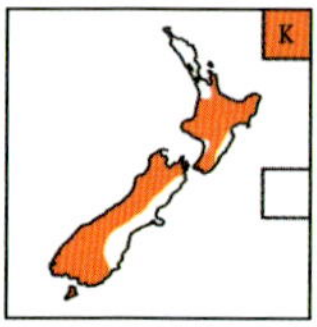

40cm, 125g. *Large brown cuckoo with very long tail.* Adult has upperparts rich brown, barred black; face and underparts pale buff, boldly streaked brown and black. Juvenile has upperparts dull brown, spotted white; face and underparts buff, lightly streaked. *Main call a loud harsh shriek – 'zzwheesht'* – from a high perch or in flight, any time of day. In flight, tail as long as body. Usual hosts are Whitehead, Brown Creeper and Yellowhead. **Habitat:** Mainly native and exotic forest, Oct–Mar, but almost anywhere on migration. Overwinters on Pacific islands from Micronesia to French Polynesia. **Breeding:** Nov–Jan. **[Sp 310]**

CHANNEL-BILLED CUCKOO *Scythrops novaehollandiae* — Very rare Australian vagrant

61cm, 700g. *Huge grey cuckoo* with a long black and white-tipped tail, and *large powerful yellow bill.* Red skin round the red eye. **Habitat:** Breeds Australian forests; winters in Indonesia. Seven NZ records, spring and summer. **[Sp 311]**

PALLID CUCKOO *Cuculus pallidus* — Rare Australian vagrant

32cm, 85g. Medium-sized cuckoo with long wings and tail and falcon-like profile in flight. Adult *plain grey, barred only on undertail*; a dark grey line passes through the eye; pale eyebrow and patch on the nape. Immature boldly marked brown and buff on head and upperparts; pale buff underparts. Feeds by swooping to ground from a perch. *Male song a series of slowly rising and accelerating melancholy notes: 'too, too . . . too, too'.* **Habitat:** Breeds Australia; winters northern Australia, New Guinea and Indonesia. Seven NZ records, mainly in lightly forested open country. **[Sp 307]**

ORIENTAL CUCKOO *Cuculus optatus* — Rare Asian straggler

33cm, 100g. Like Pallid Cuckoo but darker grey, and *lower chest, belly and undertail boldly barred black on white.* Brown phase rich brown above, paler below and heavily barred black all over. Feeds by swooping to ground from a perch. Usually silent in NZ. **Habitat:** Breeds Asia; migrates to Indonesia and Australia. A few reach NZ most years, mainly in lightly forested open country, Oct–Apr. **[Sp 306]**

FAN-TAILED CUCKOO *Cacomantis flabelliformis* — Rare Australian vagrant

26cm, 60g. Slim cuckoo with habit of cocking and fanning tail on alighting on a perch. Adult *blue-grey above, mostly rust red below, but with tail notched black on white.* Immature speckled rufous and brown with pale brown belly and undertail coverts, dark bars on chest and undertail. Feeds by swooping to ground from a perch. *Call a repeated rapid descending trill.* **Habitat:** Breeds Australia and southwest Pacific. Six NZ records, mainly in open country, Sep–Dec. **[Sp 308]**

CHANNEL-BILLED CUCKOO
SHINING CUCKOO
juv
LONG-TAILED CUCKOO
FAN-TAILED CUCKOO
PALLID CUCKOO
ORIENTAL CUCKOO
juv
brown phase

OWLS & KINGFISHERS

Owls are mainly nocturnal. Usually streaked brown and buff and spotted white. Large head and flat-faced with large eyes in a paler facial disc. Bill short and hooked. Powerful feet and talons. Sexes alike; females slightly larger. Plumage is soft, and flight is silent. Voice ranges from plaintive calls to harsh screeches.

LITTLE OWL *Athene noctua* — Uncommon European introduction

23cm, 180g. *Small grey-brown owl, heavily streaked and spotted white.* Flatter head and shorter tail than Morepork. Often seen by day perching on posts and farm sheds. Flight undulating. *Call a clear high-pitched 'kiew'.* **Habitat:** Farmland of South Island only, especially near east coast. **Breeding:** Oct–Jan. [Sp 314]

MOREPORK (Ruru) *Ninox novaeseelandiae* — Abundant native

29cm, 175g. *Dark brown owl,* obscurely spotted and barred buff. Yellow eyes set in dark facial mask. Larger rounder head and longer tail than Little Owl. Nocturnal; roosts by day in thick vegetation, especially in tree ferns. *Main call a loud double hoot – 'more-pork'* – also repeated monotonous 'more' and rising vibrating 'cree'. **Habitat:** Forest, scrub, lightly forested open country, parks and gardens. **Breeding:** Sep–Apr. [Sp 312]

BARN OWL *Tyto alba* — Very rare native

♂ 30cm, 300g; ♀ 35cm, 400g. *Large pale buff and white owl*; looks ghostly white when seen at dusk or in headlights. Heart-shaped white facial disc. Call a rasping screech: 'skiirrr'. **Habitat:** Almost worldwide in open country; vagrant to NZ until they bred successfully near Kaitaia since 2007. **Breeding:** Sep–Apr. [Sp 315]

Kingfishers have a dumpy body, short legs, large head, and a bill that looks too large and heavy. Sexes alike. Often associated with water. They sit patiently on a branch, powerline or other prominent perch and dart or glide to snatch prey from the ground, or to plunge into shallow water. Calls are harsh.

LAUGHING KOOKABURRA *Dacelo novaeguineae* — Rare Australian introduction

45cm, 350g. *Very large bird with heavy black and yellow bill*; pale head and underparts, brownish back; tail rufous, barred black. Perches prominently on bare branch or powerline. In flight, clear white wing flashes. *Call a raucous laughing cackle*, mainly at dawn and dusk. **Habitat:** Lightly forested open country, mainly from Orewa and Kaukapakapa to Whangarei, especially south of Wellsford. **Breeding:** Nov–Apr. [Sp 318]

KINGFISHER (Kotare, Sacred Kingfisher) *Todiramphus sanctus* — Abundant native

24cm, 65g. *Small deep green-blue and buff bird*; green grading to blue on the head and upperparts. Pale yellowish-buff to off-white underparts and collar round back of neck. Immature duller with buff feather edges on upperparts and brownish mottling on chest. *Often seen perched on powerlines, or on branches and rocks near water.* Flight direct. *Call a loud penetrating 'kek-kek-kek-kek'.* **Habitat:** Forest, river margins, farmland, lakes, estuaries and rocky coastlines; movement towards the coast in winter. **Breeding:** Oct–Feb. [Sp 319]

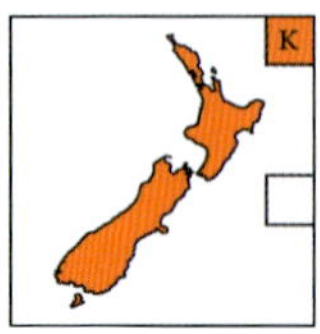

MOREPORK
LITTLE OWL
BARN OWL
LAUGHING
KOOKABURRA
imm
KINGFISHER

Swifts are reminiscent of swallows but are designed for aerial feeding and speed, with wide flattened bill and very long thin swept-back wings. Generally black, with white patches and distinctive tail shape. Sexes alike. They fly high, with bursts of rapid wingbeats alternating with long swift glides, dives and banking turns; at dusk and in bad weather, they fly low over water or circle headlands, hilltops and stands of tall trees. Rarely land (clinging to side of tree or building) except when breeding. Voice an excited twittering.

SPINE-TAILED SWIFT (White-throated Needletail) *Hirundapus caudacutus*

Rare tropical straggler

20cm, 100g. Large swift with *short square tail.* All dark except for *white patches on throat and undertail.* In the hand, each tail feather has a short projecting spine. **Habitat:** Breeds eastern Asia; migrates to Australia. Most stragglers to NZ seen over open country, mainly Nov–Mar; once 60+ birds together. **[Sp 316]**

FORK-TAILED SWIFT *Apus pacificus*

Rare tropical straggler

18cm, 45g. Slightly smaller and much slimmer than Spine-tailed Swift, with *long deeply-forked tail.* All dark except for *white rump and pale throat and lightly barred upperbreast.* **Habitat:** Breeds eastern Asia; migrates to Australia. Stragglers to NZ seen over open country, mainly Oct–Feb, but some in winter. **[Sp 317]**

Swallows and martins are small birds with rapid erratic darting and gliding flight in pursuit of flying insects or snatching them from the surface of water or the ground. NZ species mostly blue above, pale below; each species has distinctive combination of pattern of red on head, colour of rump, and shape of tail. Sexes alike. Juveniles duller. Perch and come to ground readily; often seen gathered on powerlines, fences, shed roofs and riverbed shingle. Build distinctive mud nests under bridges, in caves or rock outcrops, trees or around buildings. Lay 3–5 pale pink eggs, speckled brown.

WELCOME SWALLOW *Hirundo neoxena*

Abundant native

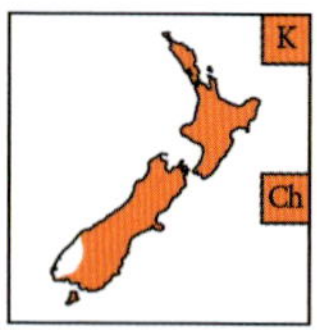

15cm, 14g. Adult has head and back blue-black; forehead, throat and chest rufous; underparts dull white; *deeply forked tail* with a row of white spots near the tip. Juvenile duller on upperparts, paler rufous markings, and tail less deeply forked. Often in swirling groups low over open water or crops, or sit on wires like clothes pegs. **Habitat:** Open country, especially near water. Builds cup-shaped mud nest, often under bridges or under eaves of buildings. **Breeding:** Aug–Mar. **[Sp 359]**

TREE MARTIN *Petrochelidon nigricans*

Rare Australian vagrant

13cm, 15g. Smaller and stockier than Welcome Swallow. Head and back blue-black; forehead of adult rufous, juvenile pale rufous; underparts and *rump dull white*; *tail short, almost square.* **Habitat:** Breeds throughout Australia; southern birds migrate north in autumn and south in spring. Vagrants reach NZ most years, usually in autumn and spring, with sometimes as many as 30–35 together. Mainly in open country in company with Welcome Swallows. **[Sp 361]**

FAIRY MARTIN *Petrochelidon ariel*

Rare Australian vagrant

12cm, 11g. Much smaller than Welcome Swallow. *Whole head pale chestnut*; back blue-black; *rump bright white*; underparts dull white; *tail short, almost square.* **Habitat:** Breeds throughout Australia; southern birds migrate north in autumn and south in spring. About 12 records in NZ, mainly in Nov–Mar, in open country. Distinctive bottle-shaped nest found in pumping shed near Lake Wairarapa in 1970s. **[Sp 360]**

SPINE-TAILED SWIFT
FORK-TAILED SWIFT
juv
FAIRY MARTIN
WELCOME SWALLOW
juv
TREE MARTIN

AUSTRALIAN PASSERINES & Dollarbird

Passerines are the largest group of birds. They are small- to medium-sized land birds found worldwide, except on Antarctica. All species have four toes, three pointing forward and one back, well adapted for perching. Most species are songbirds, with complex musical calls, but there are exceptions (e.g. crows). They show great diversity of form, behaviour and breeding biology.

BLACK-FACED CUCKOO-SHRIKE *Coracina novaehollandiae* — **Rare Australian vagrant**

33cm, 120g. *Large pale grey bird with a long tail, and habit of folding and refolding its wings on alighting.* Adult has black face and throat. Immature has black patch from bill to ear coverts, and pale faintly barred throat and upper breast. Sexes alike. Flight undulating. Feeds mainly on insects taken in foliage or by swooping to the ground from a perch. *Call a short soft croaky 'prurr'.* **Habitat:** Birds from southern Australia migrate north for winter; *c.* 20 NZ records, mostly immatures seen in autumn, sometimes in spring. **[Sp 337]**

DOLLARBIRD *Eurystomus orientalis* — **Rare Australasian straggler**

29cm, 130g. *Stout short-tailed greenish bird* with a large brownish head and glossy blue throat. *Short broad red bill; red legs.* In flight, *prominent pale 'silver dollar' patches on wings.* Immature has brown-grey body, dark bill and brown legs. Sexes alike. Perches high on dead branches, in an upright posture, before swooping out to catch large insects. *Call a loud raspy cackle.* **Habitat:** Birds from southern Australia migrate north to winter in Asia. Most NZ records are of adults in Nov–Dec, or immatures in Mar–May. **[Sp 320]**

WHITE-BROWED WOODSWALLOW *Artamus superciliosus* — **Very rare Australian vagrant**

19cm, 35g. Like a small, slim young Starling (see Plate 79), but *soars and glides gracefully.* Head, throat and upperparts dark blue-grey; *chestnut underparts*; a prominent broad white eyebrow in males, less distinct in females. Feeds on insects taken in the air and on the ground; also nectar. **Habitat:** Open woodland and open country; two NZ records: Naseby, Central Otago, 1971–73 and Miranda, Firth of Thames, 1991. **[Sp 345]**

MASKED WOODSWALLOW *Artamus personatus* — **Very rare Australian vagrant**

19cm, 35g. Like a small slim young Starling (see Plate 79), but *soars and glides gracefully.* Males two-tone grey, darker above; *black face and throat mask*, bordered white. Females duller with less distinct mask. Feeds on insects taken in the air and on the ground; also nectar. **Habitat:** Open woodland and open country; only NZ record was a pair that bred at Naseby, Central Otago, 1972–73. **[Sp 344]**

BLACK-FACED CUCKOO-SHRIKE
imm
DOLLARBIRD
WHITE-BROWED WOODSWALLOW
♀
♂
♂
♀
MASKED WOODSWALLOW

WHITE-WINGED TRILLER *Lalage tricolor* **Very rare Australian vagrant**

18cm, 25g. Breeding male *black and white* with a grey rump. Female and immature brown with buff feather edges. Non-breeding male like female, but wings black and white. Feeds mainly on insects taken in foliage or by swooping to ground from a perch. Male song, uttered while perched and in flight, is Chaffinch-like in form, a *descending 'chiff-chiff-chiff-joey-joey-joey'*, ending with a Canary-like trill. **Habitat:** One NZ record: in a Dunedin garden, 1969. **[Sp 338]**

SATIN FLYCATCHER *Myiagra cyanoleuca* **Very rare Australian vagrant**

16cm, 17g. *Male dark glossy blue-black except lower chest and belly white*; small crest gives a peaked back of head. *Female slate grey with bluish gloss on upperparts; throat and upperbreast reddish buff*, contrasts sharply with white lower breast and belly. Feeds on insects by darting out from a perch to snatch them in mid-air. On realighting, quivers tail. **Habitat:** Of three NZ records, two seen in gardens. **[Sp 349]**

WILLIE WAGTAIL *Rhipidura leucophrys* **Very rare Australian vagrant**

20cm, 20g. *Striking black and white flycatcher with a very long tail, wagged from side to side.* Feeds with short flights from a perch like a Fantail, but also hops on the ground. The call is a scolding 'chick-a-chick-a-chick' **Habitat:** One NZ record: Mangere Island, Chathams, 1999. **[Sp 347]**

BLACK-FACED MONARCH *Monarcha melanopsis* **Very rare Australian vagrant**

17cm, 25g. *Pale grey with rufous underparts and undertail.* Adults have a large black patch on forehead, throat, and upper breast, but not to the eye. Immature has completely grey head. Often sallies into the air in pursuit of insects. Calls varied, but mainly variations on *a loud clear 'why-you, wichye-oo'*, or a *mellow descending 'why you'*. **Habitat:** Mainly forests. One NZ record: Stratford, 1996. **[Sp 350]**

AUSTRALIAN REED-WARBLER *Acrocephalus australis* **Very rare Australian vagrant**

16cm, 20g. Upperparts *plain unstreaked* warm brown, thin eyebrow and throat white, darker line through the eye. Underparts buff-cream. Tail moderately long with a rounded tip. Bill slender, dark above and pale below. Eye dark brown. *Full song a powerful clear series of varied but repeated calls* 'crut-crut-crut, deet-deet-deet, crotchy-crotchy-crotchy'. **Habitat:** Mainly dense wetland vegetation; one NZ record: St Anne's Lagoon, Cheviot, 2004. **[Sp 356]**

♂
♀
♀
♂
ding
SATIN FLYCATCHER
WHITE-WINGED TRILLER
WILLIE WAGTAIL
juv
BLACK-FACED
MONARCH
AUSTRALIAN
REED WARBLER

RIFLEMAN (Titipounamu) *Acanthisitta chloris* **Locally common endemic**

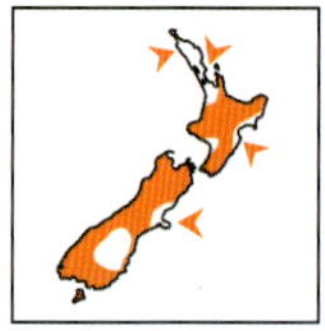

8cm; ♂ 6g, ♀ 7g. *Tiny bird with a very short stumpy tail*; bill fine and slightly upturned. Male bright yellow-green above, green rump; female streaked dark and light brown above, brownish-yellow rump. Both whitish below, bold white eyebrow stripe. Immature like female but streaked on breast. Feeds by working its way up trees and shrubs, flicking wings, and exploring trunks, branches and leaves. Call a very high-pitched sharp repeated 'zipt', out of hearing range for some. **Habitat:** Native forest and scrub; favours beech and tawa forest. In South Island, also exotic forest, gorse and willows. **Breeding:** Sep–Feb. **[Sp 321]**

ROCK WREN *Xenicus gilviventris* **Uncommon endemic**

10cm; ♂ 16g, ♀ 20g. *Small alpine bird with short tail*, rounded wings, long legs and toes, fine black bill, cream eyebrow. Male dull green above, grey-brown below, flanks yellow; brighter green and yellow in Fiordland. Female plainer olive brown. *Bobs vigorously up and down.* Usually hops and runs, flying only short distances. **Habitat:** Alpine regions of South Island only, among rockfalls, screes and subalpine scrub. **Breeding:** Oct–Feb. **[Sp 323]**

SILVEREYE (Tauhou) *Zosterops lateralis* **Abundant native**

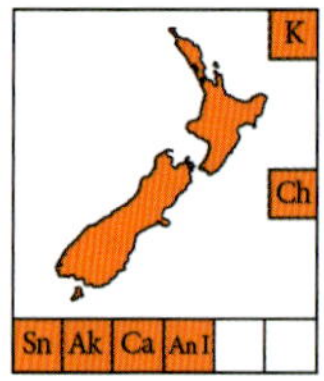

12cm, 13g. *Small green bird with conspicuous white eye-ring.* Head and upperparts olive green with grey back and wash on lower neck and onto breast; underparts creamy white with pinkish-brown flanks and white undertail. Sexes alike. Juvenile lacks eye-ring. Usually in small flocks, except when breeding. Readily attracted to bird tables in cold winters. Flight call from flocks an excited 'cli-cli-cli'; single birds give a plaintive 'cree'. Song a melodious mix of warbles, trills and slurs. **Habitat:** Forests, scrub, orchards, parks and gardens. **Breeding:** Sep–Mar. **[Sp 358]**

GREY WARBLER (Riroriro) *Gerygone igata* **Abundant endemic**

10cm, 6.5g. *Small grey bird with a darker tail, tipped white; hovers to pick insects and spiders from plants.* Adult is grey-brown above, pale grey on face, throat and breast; off-white belly and undertail, red eye. Sexes alike. Juvenile similar but yellowish on face and underparts, brown eye. Flits and hovers among outer foliage and twigs to catch invertebrates. *Song a distinctive long musical wavering trill.* **Habitat:** Scrub (especially manuka and kanuka), forest, parks and gardens. Builds a distinctive *domed hanging nest, with small side entrance hole.* **Breeding:** Aug–Jan. **[Sp 332]**

CHATHAM ISLANDS WARBLER *Gerygone albofrontata* **Locally abundant endemic**

12cm; ♂ 10g, ♀ 8.5g. Like a large Grey Warbler but browner and bill much larger. Male has olive-brown head and upperparts, darker on wings and tail; *prominent white forehead, eyebrow and underparts*; flanks and undertail pale yellow; red eye. Female lacks white forehead and has duller greyish-white underparts and yellowish eyebrow, face and throat. Juvenile like female, but upperparts olive grey; underparts yellower; eye brown. Gleans invertebrates from leaves and crevices in trunks and branches; rarely hovers. **Habitat:** Forest and scrub, especially South East and Mangere islands. **Breeding:** Sep–Jan. **[Sp 333]**

♂
RIFLEMAN
♀
ROCK WREN
♂
♀
SILVEREYE
juv
GREY WARBLER
♂
CHATHAM ISLANDS WARBLER

NORTH ISLAND KOKAKO *Callaeas wilsoni*

Rare endemic

38cm;♂ 230g, ♀ 220g. *Large dark bluish-grey bird with black face mask* and *blue wattles*, short strongly arched black bill, long legs, long tail and rounded wings. Juvenile has smaller pinkish wattles, smaller facial mask, and dull brown wash in plumage. Leaps around in trees and takes short flights, never sustained for long. More often heard than seen. Calls mostly at dawn; *song is a slow string of very loud rich mournful organ-like notes*. **Habitat:** Most of *c.* 1600 birds are in tall podocarp hardwood forest in central North Island, and Little Barrier, Tiritiri Matangi and Kapiti islands. **Breeding:** Oct–Mar. **[Sp 324]**

SOUTH ISLAND KOKAKO *Callaeas cinerea*

Possibly extinct endemic

38cm, 230g. Like North Island Kokako, but *wattles orange*. **Habitat:** Possibly extinct; last accepted sighting near Reefton, 2007. Most records from beech and mixed podocarp forests. **Breeding:** Nov–Mar. **[Sp 325]**

SOUTH ISLAND SADDLEBACK (Tieke, Jackbird) *Philesturnus carunculatus*

Locally common endemic

25cm;♂ 85g, ♀ 75g. Like North Island Saddleback, but no buff line at top of saddle. Juvenile (Jackbird) *chocolate brown*, paler below, with reddish-brown tail coverts, and small wattles. **Habitat:** Forest and scrub on several pest-free offshore islands and Orokonui Ecosanctuary, Dunedin. **Breeding:** Oct–Mar. **[Sp 327]**

NORTH ISLAND SADDLEBACK (Tieke) *Philesturnus rufusater*

Locally abundant endemic

25cm;♂ 80g, ♀ 70g. Head and body glossy black with bright chestnut saddle, rump and tail coverts; *orange-red wattles at base of black bill*. Thin buff line at top edge of saddle. Juvenile has smaller wattles and lacks buff line. Often feeds on the forest floor, and bounds from branch to branch rather than flies. *Main call is a strident ringing 'cheet, te-te-te-te' like an engine turning over*; often duet. **Habitat:** Forest and scrub on many pest-free offshore islands, and some mainland sanctuaries. **Breeding:** Aug–May. **[Sp 326]**

juv
SOUTH ISLAND KOKAKO
NORTH ISLAND KOKAKO
SOUTH ISLAND SADDLEBACK
South Island juv
NORTH ISLAND SADDLEBACK

TUI *Prosthemadera novaeseelandiae* **Abundant endemic**

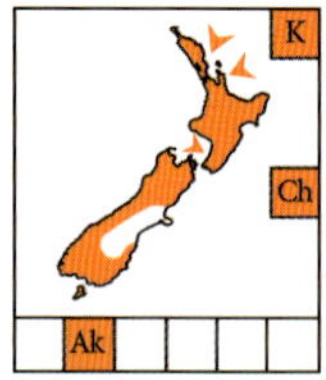

30cm;♂ 120g, ♀ 90g. Dark with two *white throat tufts*, or poi. Looks black, but has *green, bluish-purple and bronze iridescent sheen*, back and flanks dark reddish brown; a lacy collar of filamentous white feathers on neck; white wingbar; slightly decurved black bill. Sexes alike. Juvenile duller, greyish-white throat, lacks tufts. Energetic and acrobatic while feeding in trees on nectar and fruit. In flight, round wings with white shoulder patches; long broad tail; *noisy whirring flight* between short glides. Diving display. Song has rich fluid melodic notes (often repeated) mixed with coughs, clicks, grunts and wheezes; varies regionally. Occasional mimic. **Habitat:** Native forest and scrub, farmland with kowhai, gums and flax, parks and gardens. **Breeding:** Sep–Feb. **[Sp 336]**

STITCHBIRD (Hihi) *Notiomystis cincta* **Rare endemic**

18cm;♂ 37g, ♀ 30g. Male has white erectile tufts behind eyes; velvety black head, upper breast and back, bordered golden yellow across breast and folded wings; rest of underparts pale brown. Female greyish brown with white wingbar; lacks ear tufts. *Often cocks tail. Call a loud explosive whistle: 'see-si-ip'.* **Habitat:** Forest on a few predator-free islands, especially Little Barrier, Tiritiri Matangi and Kapiti islands; also Maungatautari (Waikato) and Zealandia (Wellington). **Breeding:** Sep–Apr. **[Sp 329]**

BELLBIRD (Korimako, Makomako) *Anthornis melanura* **Locally abundant endemic**

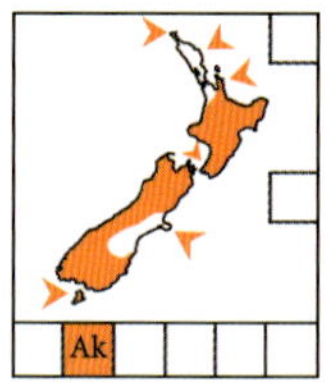

20cm;♂ 34g, ♀ 26g. Adult male olive green, paler on underparts, head tinted with purple gloss; wings and tail dark bluish black, except for yellow patch at bend of folded wing; eye red. Female browner with bluish gloss on head and *narrow white cheek stripe*. Juvenile like female, but with brown eye and *yellowish cheek stripe. Noisy whirring fast and direct flight.* Song varies regionally but always loud clear liquid ringing notes, without harsh grunts and wheezes. Alarm call a rapidly repeated harsh 'yeng, yeng, yeng'. **Habitat:** Native and exotic forest, scrub, farm shelterbelts, parks and gardens. **Breeding:** Sep–Feb. **[Sp 334]**

juv
TUI
♂
STITCHBIRD
♀
♂
♀
juv ♂
BELLBIRD

FERNBIRD (Matata) *Bowdleria punctata* **Locally common endemic**

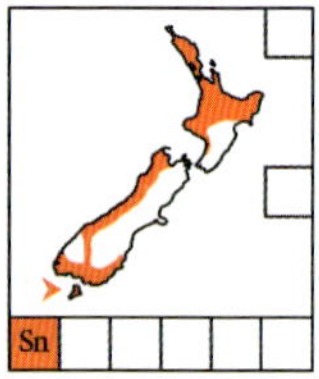

18cm, 35g. Warm brown above, paler below, heavily streaked and spotted dark brown; *forehead and crown chestnut*; whitish eyebrow stripe. *Distinctive long frayed tail.* Sexes and juveniles alike. Secretive, often remaining hidden in thick vegetation or moving mouse-like through the rushes, appearing inquisitively in the scrub canopy. Reluctant to fly. Flight weak and whirring, tail drooping. Often detected by sound alone. Common call a short sharp 'tchip', and *metallic double-note 'uu-tick'* often produced by pair in duet. **Habitat:** Freshwater and tidal wetlands, especially reedbeds or pakihi with emergent scrub; also drier sparse scrub and bracken. **Breeding:** Aug–Mar. **[Sp 357]**

BROWN CREEPER (Pipipi) *Mohoua novaeseelandiae* **Locally common endemic**

13cm; ♂ 13.5g, ♀ 11g. Crown, back, rump and tail reddish brown; ash grey on face and neck; small white stripe behind eye; light buff underparts; dark bar near tip of tail. Sexes and juveniles alike. Usually in *small fast-moving noisy flocks high in canopy*, uttering nasal notes and rapid slurred trills. Male song includes slurs, musical whistles and harsh notes: 'chi-roh-ree-roh-ree-ree', the second note being lower than the first. Females sing a rapid sequence of brief notes, the last being higher and prolonged. **Habitat:** Forest and scrub of South and Stewart islands. **Breeding:** Sep–Mar. **[Sp 342]**

WHITEHEAD (Popokatea) *Mohoua albicilla* **Locally common endemic**

15cm; ♂ 18.5g, ♀ 14.5g. Male has *white head and underparts*, with contrasting black bill, eye and legs; upperparts pale brown. Female and immature similar, but *crown and nape shaded brown*. Usually in small fast-moving *noisy feeding flocks or family groups, high in canopy*, uttering harsh chattering calls, trills and slurs. Male song can be clear and Canary-like: 'peek-o, peek-o, peek-o'. **Habitat:** Native and exotic forest, and scrub of North Island. **Breeding:** Sep–Jan. **[Sp 340]**

YELLOWHEAD (Mohua) *Mohoua ochrocephala* **Rare endemic**

15cm; ♂ 30g, ♀ 25g. Male has *bright yellow head and underparts* with contrasting black bill, eye and legs; upperparts yellowish brown. Female and immature similar, but *crown and nape shaded brown*. Tip of tail often worn to spine-like shafts. Usually in *small noisy feeding flocks or family groups, high in canopy*, uttering loud staccato chattering calls and trills and slurs. Male song clear and Canary-like. **Habitat:** Tall native forest, especially red beech of southern South Island. **Breeding:** Oct–Mar. **[Sp 341]**

FANTAIL (Piwakawaka) *Rhipidura fuliginosa* **Abundant native**

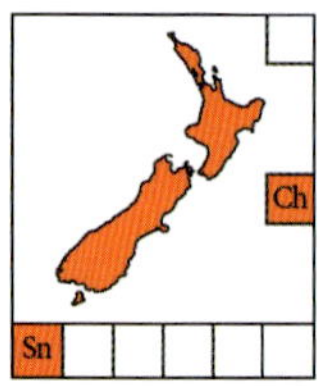

16cm (including 8cm tail), 8g. Small bird with small head and bill; *long tail, often fanned*. Pied phase has grey head, white eyebrow, brown back; yellow underparts, with white and black bands across chest; black and white tail. Juvenile similar, but browner body, rusty-brown wing coverts, and indistinct chest markings. Island subspecies have variable white in tail, most in Chathams. Black phase, mainly in South Island, all sooty black except white spot behind eye. Restless movements; twists and jerks on a perch, tail fanned, flies out to seize flying insects. *Erratic flight as it hawks over forest or scrub canopy* into an insect swarm over a clearing, paddock, pond or garden. Call a penetrating 'cheet'; song a harsh rhythmical 'saw-like' 'tweet-a-tweet-a-tweet-a-tweet . . .' **Habitat:** Forest, scrub, farmland with hedges and shelterbelts, river margins, parks and gardens. **Breeding:** Aug–Mar. **[Sp 346]**

FERNBIRD
BROWN CREEPER
WHITEHEAD
YELLOWHEAD
juv pied
FANTAIL
black phase
pied phase

STARLING *Sturnus vulgaris*

Abundant European introduction

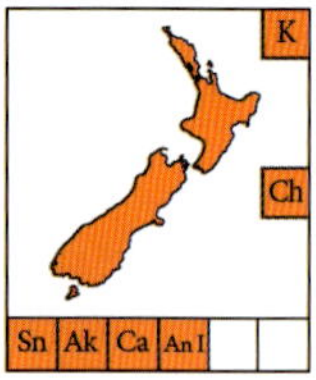

21cm, 85g. Short-tailed dark bird with waddling jerky walk. Breeding adult glossy black with purple sheen on head and breast; dark green sheen and buff spangling on wings and abdomen; pointed yellow bill, bluish base in male, pinkish in female. Non-breeding head and body spotted buff and white; bill dark. Juvenile smooth grey-brown, throat paler; bill dark. Flight fast and direct, often in large coordinated flocks. Distinctly pointed triangular wings. Large winter roosts; flocks converge at dusk and disperse at dawn. Feeds on ground by jabbing bill into soil. Noisy; call a descending whistle: 'cheeoo'; song, a rambling collection of clicks, rattles, warbles and gargles, interspersed with musical whistles. A good mimic. **Habitat:** Farmland, orchards, parks, gardens, city streets, forest margins and beaches. **Breeding:** Oct–Jan. [Sp 364]

RED-VENTED BULBUL *Pycnonotus cafer*

Rare Asian introduction

20cm, 40g. Slim dark bird with *long white-tipped tail and red patch on undertail.* Head, upperparts and breast blackish, fading to grey on belly; rump white. Feathers on back of head can be raised into triangular crest. A popular cage bird because of cheerful attractive call: 'pee pee-plo' or 'be-care-ful'. **Habitat:** Parks and gardens of Auckland; established briefly in 1950s, then exterminated; several subsequent illegal releases. [Sp 339]

MYNA *Acridotheres tristis*

Locally abundant Asian introduction

24cm, 125g. *Cheeky brown bird with jaunty walk.* Adult cinnamon brown with glossy black head and neck, white undertail and underwing; yellow legs, bill and bare patch of skin near eye. Sexes alike. Juvenile has dark brown head, paler bill and facial skin. In flight, *prominent white patches on wings*, and white-tipped tail. Roosts communally all year, largest in winter; small flocks converge at dusk and depart at dawn. Feeds mainly on the ground, often at roadsides. Voice jangling; song a rapid medley of raucous gurgling, chattering and bell-like notes. **Habitat:** Parks, gardens, orchards and farmland, sometimes on forest margins. **Breeding:** Oct–Mar. [Sp 365]

AUSTRALIAN MAGPIE *Gymnorhina tibicen*

Abundant Australian introduction

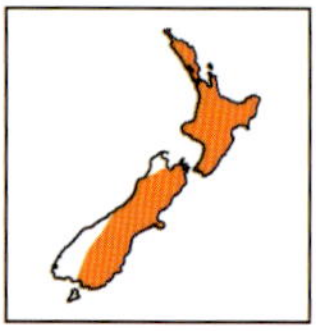

41cm, 350g. *Large black and white bird with pale blue black-tipped bill.* White-backed form has hind neck and back white in male, finely barred grey in female. Black-backed form (mostly in Hawke's Bay) has black back; hind neck white in male, finely barred grey in female. Juvenile like female, but underparts brownish grey and bill dark. Hybrids have variable black on back. Flight direct, with pointed wings and rapid shallow wingbeats. Feeds on the ground, sometimes in loose flocks. *Song distinctive flute-like carolling*, especially at dawn and dusk, rendered 'quardle oodle ardle wardle doodle'. **Habitat:** Open farmland with tall shelterbelts and scattered trees or forest, parks and gardens. **Breeding:** Jul–Jan. [Sp 343]

ROOK *Corvus frugilegus*

Locally common European introduction

45cm; ♂ 425g, ♀ 375g. *Large glossy black crow* with shaggy feathered thighs. Adult has bare whitish face. Juvenile and immature have faces feathered black. In flight, long broad 'fingered' wings, broad roundish tail. *Flight strong and direct, but languid.* Feeds mainly on ground; walks sedately with occasional hops. Feeds, roosts and nests in flocks. Often wary and gives *coarse 'caw' or 'kaah' calls* if disturbed or in flight. **Habitat:** Pasture and cultivated paddocks, farm shelterbelts, especially tall gums and pines. **Breeding:** Aug–Jan. [Sp 348]

juv
breeding
STARLING
RED-VENTED
BULBUL
non-breeding
MYNA
juv
juv
white-backed
♀
imm
white-backed
ROOK
ack-backed
AUSTRALIAN
MAGPIE
♂

TOMTIT (Miromiro – North Island, Ngirungiru – South Island) *Petroica macrocephala*

Common endemic

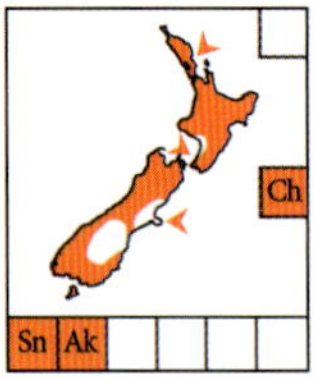

13cm, 11g. Small forest bird with a large head and short tail. Five subspecies vary slightly in size and colour; the most distinctive is the Snares subspecies, which is larger (20g) and wholly black; glossier in the male. Adult male (North Island) has black head with small white spot above bill; glossy black upperparts and upper breast; white underparts, sharply divided at breast; white wingbar and sides to tail. South, Chatham and Auckland islands subspecies similar, but have underparts yellowish, brighter or orange on upper breast near dividing line. Juvenile males similar, but have white shaft streaks to black feathers and always have white underparts. Adult females (North and South Island) have brown head and upperparts; grey-brown chin and upper breast fading to white on underparts; wingbar and sides of tail pale buff. Chatham Islands female similar but darker brown above. Auckland Islands female like male but dull black upperparts and upper breast. Feeds in the understorey by perching on branch or trunk, scanning, then flying to ground or tree to catch invertebrates. *Male song a loud jingling burst: 'ti oly oly oly oh'*, varies regionally. Male call a short high-pitched 'swee'; female call a reedy 'seet'. **Habitat:** Scrub, native and exotic forest and scrub. **Breeding:** Sep–Feb. [Sp 351]

BLACK ROBIN *Petroica traversi*

Very rare endemic

15cm;♂ 25g, ♀ 22g. Small *completely black forest bird* with short, fine black bill, long thin legs and an upright stance. Feeds mostly on the forest floor or in low branches. Male song a clear simple phrase of 5–7 notes. Call a high-pitched single note. Formerly extremely rare; in 1979 there were just five birds, including just one productive female, 'Old Blue' (depicted), but with intensive management the population has recovered to nearly 300 birds. **Habitat:** Forest and scrub of Mangere and South East islands in the Chathams. **Breeding:** Oct–Jan. [Sp 354]

NORTH ISLAND ROBIN (Toutouwai) *Petroica longipes*

Uncommon endemic

18cm, 35g. Inquisitive and *confiding dark slate-grey forest bird with long thin legs and an upright stance.* Male is dark, almost black, except for white spot above bill, *pale greyish-white lower breast and belly*; black feathers have pale shaft streaks, and so very faintly streaked upperparts; wings dark brownish black. Female and juvenile similar, but greyer with variable paler patches on breast and throat. Perches on a low trunk or branch and flies to feed on the forest floor; hops about and sometimes trembles one leg to induce prey to surface. *Male song loud clear and sustained string of phrases, usually descending* and including 'pwee-pwee-pwee' phrases; varies regionally. Call a soft 'chirp'. **Habitat:** Native and exotic forest, sometimes tall scrub of central North Island; introduced to many pest-free islands and mainland sanctuaries. **Breeding:** Sep–Feb. [Sp 352]

SOUTH ISLAND ROBIN (Toutouwai) *Petroica australis*

Uncommon endemic

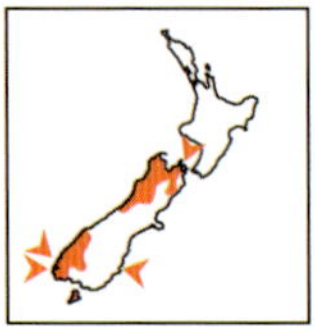

18cm, 35g. Inquisitive and *confiding dark slate-grey forest bird with long thin legs and an upright stance.* Male has dark grey upperparts and upper chest, distinctly divided *from yellowish-white lower chest and belly*; flanks variably greyish; white spot above bill; wings dark brownish black. Female and juvenile similar, usually greyer on breast with variable whitish patches. Stewart Island birds have similar patterns to North Island Robin. Perches on a low trunk or branch and flies to feed on the forest floor; hops about and sometimes trembles one leg to induce prey to surface. *Male song loud clear and sustained string of phrases, usually descending* and including 'pwee-pwee-pwee' phrases; varies regionally. Call a soft 'chirp'. **Habitat:** Native and exotic forest, sometimes tall scrub; most common north of Arthur's Pass and on Stewart Island. Introduced to pest-free islands and mainland sanctuaries. **Breeding:** Jul–Feb. [Sp 353]

TOMTIT
North Island
♂
♀
South Island
juv ♂
♂
Snares
BLACK ROBIN
♀
♂
♂
♀
juv
NORTH ISLAND ROBIN
SOUTH ISLAND ROBIN

BLACKBIRD *Turdus merula*

Abundant European introduction

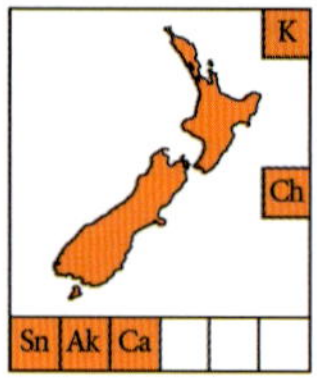

25cm, 90g. Adult male *black with a bright orange bill.* Adult female *dark brown* with paler throat and smudgy mottled breast; bill brown and dull orange. Juvenile *rusty brown,* especially on head; pale streaks on back and wing coverts; brown barring on underparts; bill dark brown. Immature male (Apr–Jan) has brown wings contrasting with black body. Long tail. Feeds mainly on the ground; *hops* rather than walks. *Song a loud clear tuneful warble, mellower than Song Thrush and not repetitive.* Alarm call a persistent sharp 'tchink-tchink'. **Habitat:** Forest, scrub, farmland with scattered trees or hedges, orchards, parks and gardens. **Breeding:** Aug–Jan. **[Sp 362]**

SONG THRUSH *Turdus philomelos*

Common European introduction

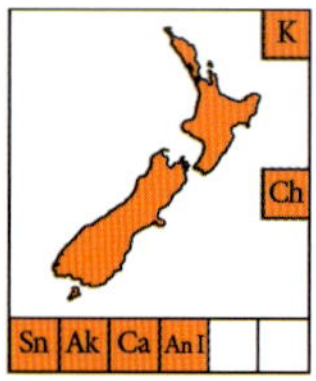

23cm, 70g. Warm brown above, buff-white below, with *breast boldly spotted dark brown.* Bill yellowish brown with yellow gape; legs pinkish brown. Sexes alike. Juvenile similar but more yellowish buff, spotted and streaked paler above and smaller spots below; bill dark brown with prominent yellow gape. Feeds mostly on the ground, where it hops and runs. Hammers snails open on a regular 'anvil'. *Song a loud string of twice repeated clear-cut musical phrases, each separated by a brief pause*: 'chitty-choo chitty-choo, oo-eee oo-eee . . .'. Song perch usually high and conspicuous. **Habitat:** Forest, scrub, farmland with scattered trees or hedges, orchards, parks and gardens. **Breeding:** Aug–Jan. **[Sp 363]**

DUNNOCK (Hedge Sparrow) *Prunella modularis*

Common European introduction

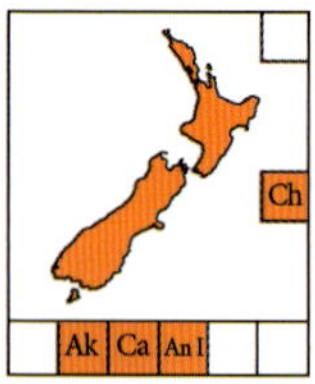

14cm, 21g. *Nondescript, dark and unobtrusive bird,* rather like a female House Sparrow (see Plate 82) but has *slim body, fine black bill.* Upperparts brown streaked darker; face, collar and breast washed grey; flanks streaked brown; red eye; *orange-brown legs.* Sexes similar but male greyer. Juvenile similar but has brown eye. Usually *feeds alone on the ground, keeping close to cover*; shuffles along in a crouched posture, delicately picking at the surface. *Sings from the top of a bush or hedge, a thin hurried warble.* Call a high-pitched insistent 'tseep'. **Habitat:** Forest, scrub, farmland with hedges, orchards, parks and gardens. **Breeding:** Aug–Feb. **[Sp 368]**

SKYLARK *Alauda arvensis*

Common European introduction

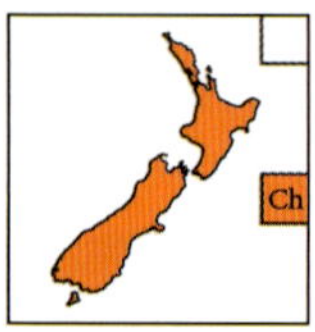

18cm, 38g. Dull yellow-buff bird, streaked and spotted brown on upperparts and breast. Adult has a small crest, raised when alert. Juvenile yellower and spottier, and lacks crest. In flight, *white outer tail feathers and white trailing edge to broad wings.* Male in territorial flight display (Aug–Jan) *soars with whirring wings* up to 100m high, and slowly descends, *all the time singing a sustained and enthusiastic torrent of varied trills and runs.* Call, usually in flight, a liquid 'chirrup'. **Habitat:** Open country, from coast to subalpine. **Breeding:** Sep–Feb. **[Sp 355]**

NEW ZEALAND PIPIT (Pihoihoi) *Anthus novaeseelandiae*

Uncommon endemic

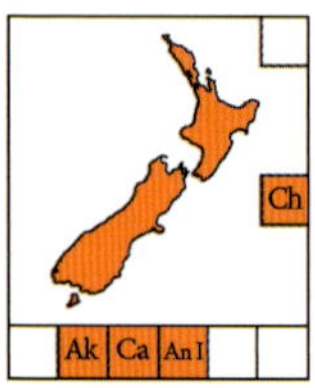

19cm, 40g. Like Skylark, including white outer tail feathers, but more slender and has the distinctive *habit of frequently wagging its long tail up and down.* Head and upperparts brown, streaked darker; prominent white eyebrow; underparts whitish, streaked brown on breast. Runs and walks jerkily on long legs; often flies a short distance ahead, calling a shrill 'scree' or drawn-out 'zwee'. **Habitat:** Open habitats from coast to alpine tops, but avoids intensively farmed areas; mainly near coast, on shingle riverbeds, gravel roads, and scree slopes. **Breeding:** Aug–Mar. **[Sp 367]**

BLACKBIRD
♂
juv
♀
juv
SONG THRUSH
Starling juv (see Plate 79)
SKYLARK
DUNNOCK
NEW ZEALAND PIPIT

HOUSE SPARROW *Passer domesticus*

Abundant European introduction

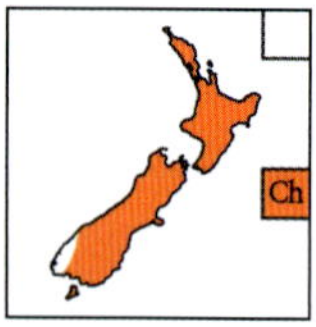

14cm, 30g. A gregarious, garrulous and quarrelsome associate of humans. Conical bill. Adult male chestnut brown above, streaked black on back; *crown dark grey*; rump greyish brown; underparts greyish white. *Black bib* and bill in breeding season, bib smaller and bill greyish pink rest of year. Female and juvenile drab sandy brown above, streaked darker on back; greyish white below; pale buffy eyebrow and sides to neck. Young juvenile often shows fleshy yellow gape. Flight fast and direct, showing small white wingbar. *Voice a variety of monotonous unmusical cheeps and chirps.* **Habitat:** Towns, arable farmland and farm shelterbelts, orchards; sometimes edges of native forest well away from human habitation. **Breeding:** Sep–Feb. **[Sp 366]**

CHAFFINCH *Fringilla coelebs*

Abundant European introduction

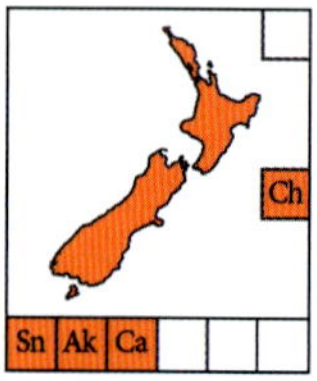

15cm; ♂ 22g, ♀ 21g. Sparrow-sized finch with *conspicuous white shoulder, wingbar and outer tail feathers.* Adult male has black forehead, blue-grey crown and nape; *rich pinkish-brown face and underparts*, fading to white on belly; reddish-brown back; olive rump. Female and juvenile lack male colours; mainly soft brownish grey, except greenish rump and prominent white wingbars on darker wing. Flight undulating; flight call a soft single 'tsip'. *Male song a series of short loud notes, ending in a flourish: 'chip chip chip tell tell tell cherry-erry-erry tissi cheweeo'*, usually given from a high perch. Usual calls a metallic 'pink' or 'chwink-chwink', and a whistling 'huit'. **Habitat:** Native and exotic forest, scrub, farmland, tussockland, parks and gardens. **Breeding:** Sep–Feb. **[Sp 369]**

REDPOLL *Carduelis flammea*

Common European introduction

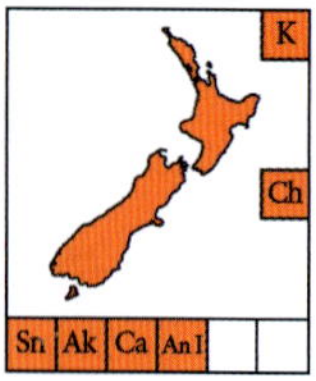

12cm, 12g. *Small dull brown-streaked finch*, but seen closely *forehead crimson* and chin black. Male in breeding season develops *a pink to crimson flush on its breast*, varying in intensity with individual and region. Juvenile lacks the crimson and black on the head and can look pale-headed. Often seen feeding or flying in large flocks, especially near weed-infested crops. Flight erratic and undulating; *flight call a fast harsh rattling metallic 'chich-chich-chich'*, sometimes followed by a 'bizzzz'. *Main call a plaintive, questioning 'tsooeet?'.* **Habitat:** Farmland, orchards, tussockland, forest and scrub margins, parks and gardens. **Breeding:** Oct–Feb. **[Sp 372]**

GOLDFINCH *Carduelis carduelis*

Common European introduction

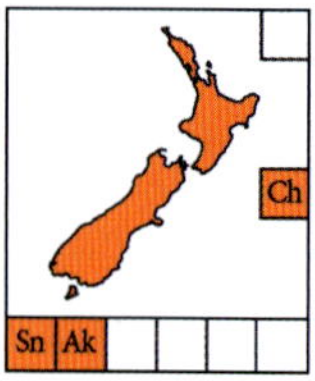

13cm; ♂ 16g, ♀ 15g. *Small finch with striking gold bars on black wings.* Adults have *brilliant red face*, slightly more extensive on the male, especially above and behind the eye; white ear coverts and sides to neck; black crown and half-collar; upperparts and breast soft brown; rest of underparts and rump white; tail black, spotted white near tip. Juvenile pale buff, streaked and spotted darker; wings and tail as in adult. Outside breeding season, usually in flocks, often feeding on seeds of thistles or other weeds. Flight undulating. *Male song a pleasant liquid twittering 'tsitt-witt-witt'.* **Habitat:** Farmland, orchards, parks and gardens. **Breeding:** Oct–Mar. **[Sp 371]**

♂ breeding
♂ non-breeding
♀
HOUSE SPARROW
♀
♂
CHAFFINCH
♀
REDPOLL
juv
♂ breeding
juv
GOLDFINCH

GREENFINCH *Carduelis chloris* **Common European introduction**

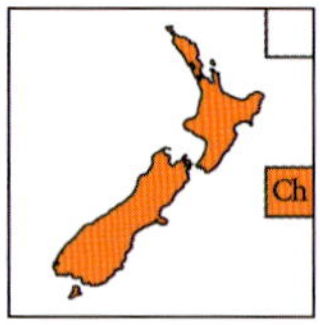

15cm, 28g. *A robust olive-green finch with a pale heavy bill and prominent yellow on the sides of the tail and the edges of the closed wing.* Males olive green, the brightest have a conspicuous yellow eyebrow and yellowish belly. Females browner, dull olive green, the dullest a washed-out greenish brown. Juvenile and many immatures duller again, mainly brown, streaked darker with yellowish-green wash on rump and upper tail coverts. Flight undulating, looking heavy-bodied and short-tailed, and showing yellow wing flashes. Out of breeding season, often form large flocks in weed-infested crops. In breeding season, *male repeatedly calls a harsh drawn-out 'dzwee'*. Other common calls are a pleasant twittering 'chichichichichit-teu-teu-teu-teu', sometimes just the 'teu' notes; and a sweet rising 'tsooeet'. **Habitat:** Farmland, pine plantations, native bush and scrub fringes, pine and macrocarpa shelterbelts, parks and gardens. **Breeding:** Oct–Mar. [Sp 370]

YELLOWHAMMER *Emberiza citrinella* **Common European introduction**

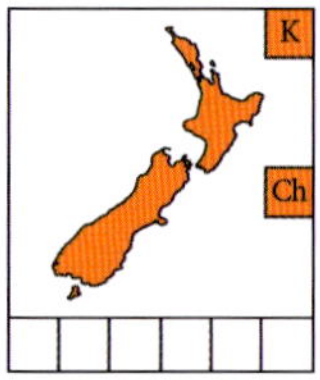

16cm, 27g. Sparrow-sized *mainly yellow bird of open country* with reddish-brown upperparts, streaked darker; *rufous rump* and white outer tail feathers. Adult male has *bright yellow head and underparts*, head lightly marked brown on crown and on sides of face; *cinnamon wash across breast*, and pale yellow flanks. Adult female duller and paler yellow, more heavily marked brown on head, and *breast band greyish green*. Juvenile and immature even paler yellow or pale buff, heavily streaked, but still with rufous rump. Hops on ground when feeding, often with crouched posture. Outside breeding season, often form flocks on weed-infested crops and where hay has been scattered. *Male song is rendered 'little bit of bread and no cheese'*. Call a ringing metallic 'tink', or 'twick'. **Habitat:** Open country from sea level to subalpine, especially arable farmland or rough pasture with scattered scrub. **Breeding:** Oct–Mar. [Sp 373]

CIRL BUNTING *Emberiza cirlus* **Uncommon European introduction**

16cm, 25g. Sparrow-sized bird of open country, similar to Yellowhammer in size and shape and also with white outer tail feathers, but much less yellow *and rump greyish olive*. Adult male distinctive with *black throat, head boldly striped black and yellow*, crown and nape dark grey, fading to pale grey wash across breast; upperparts brown, streaked darker; cinnamon patches on wings and sides of lower breast, rest of underparts pale yellow streaked darker. Adult female and juvenile nondescript mix of buff, yellow and brown, heavily streaked on crown and finely streaked on breast and flanks. Hops on ground when feeding, often with crouched posture. Outside breeding season, often form small flocks on waste ground. *Male song a monotonous metallic cricket-like rattling buzz*. Calls include a thin 'zit' or 'see', and a soft brief 'tyu'. **Habitat:** Dry pastoral or arable farmland with scattered scrub, and pine and macrocarpa shelterbelts, mainly in Nelson and eastern South Island, especially Marlborough and Central Otago. Some move to coastal wasteland and salt marsh in winter. **Breeding:** Oct–Feb. [Sp 374]

GREENFINCH
♀
♂
juv
YELLOWHAMMER
♀
♂
juv
CIRL BUNTING
♀
juv
♂
♀ House Sparrow
(see Plate 82)

SPECIES EXTINCT SINCE 1900

New Zealand, like many other isolated island groups, has a high rate of bird extinctions. About 37 species died out in the 800 years between the arrival of Polynesians and the arrival of Europeans around 1800, most notably all 10 moa species. In the *c.* 215 years since European contact, 19 further species have become extinct, eight of which have died out since 1900. Introduced mammalian predators, habitat loss and hunting were the main factors causing these extinctions.

LAUGHING OWL (Whekau) *Sceloglaux albifacies* — Extinct endemic

38cm, 600g. A large owl with *yellowish-brown plumage heavily streaked with brown. Face white around dark reddish-brown eye,* chin greyish; white splashes on scapulars, sometimes also on hindneck and mantle; wings and tail brown with brownish-white bars; long well-feathered yellowish to reddish-buff legs. *Calls, 'a loud cry made up of a series of dismal shrieks frequently repeated'*, and *'a peculiar barking noise'*. **Habitat:** Forest, scrub and open country with rock outcrops for cover. Last confirmed record: South Canterbury, 1914. **[Sp 313]**

HUIA *Heteralocha acutirostris* — Extinct endemic

♂ 45cm, ♀ 48cm; 350g. Glossy black with bluish iridescence, *last 3cm of long tail white*; rounded *orange wattles* at base of *ivory-white bill* with greyish base: *male had stout straight 60mm bill, female had slender curved 104mm bill*; legs bluish grey. Immature had duller plumage, white tip of tail tinged reddish buff, wattles small and pale. Call a soft clear whistle; also a whistling note of higher pitch. **Habitat:** Native forest of southern North Island since 1840. Last accepted record 1907. **[Sp 328]**

NEW ZEALAND MERGANSER *Mergus australis* — Extinct endemic

58cm;♂ 650g, ♀ 550g. Distinctive *slim shag-like bird. Dark red-brown head* with long feathers on back of head forming a wispy crest; upperparts dark greyish brown; underparts grey with white mottling. *Long slender orange-yellow bill,* browner above and serrated along cutting edges; legs orange. In flight, white wing-patch and underwing white mottled grey. Sexes alike. **Habitat:** Restricted to coastal waters and streams of Auckland Islands since European settlement. Last recorded 1902. **[Sp 26]**

LAUGHING OWL
HUIA
♀
NEW ZEALAND
MERGANSER

SPECIES EXTINCT SINCE 1900

NORTH ISLAND PIOPIO *Turnagra tanagra* — Extinct endemic

26cm, 130g. Upperparts olive brown; upper tail coverts and tail rust red, except olive-brown central tail feathers; *white throat; olive-grey breast and belly*; undertail coverts washed yellow; short robust dark brown bill; legs dark brown. Song varied and sustained with five distinct bars, each repeated 6–7 times. Common call a short, sharp, whistling cry, quickly repeated. **Habitat:** Native forest and scrub; last confirmed record King Country, 1902, but reports up to 1970s from inland Taranaki and Urewera. **[Sp 330]**

SOUTH ISLAND PIOPIO *Turnagra capensis* — Extinct endemic

26cm, 130g. Like North Island Piopio, but *boldly streaked brown and white below*, throat and sides of neck tinged reddish brown, and feathers of forehead, crown and face tipped rust red. **Habitat:** Native forest and scrub; last unconfirmed records in northwest Nelson and Fiordland in the 1960s. **[Sp 331]**

CHATHAM ISLANDS BELLBIRD (Komako) *Anthornis melanocephala* — Extinct endemic

22cm, 40g. Like Bellbird, but *larger and with yellow eyes*; males had darker purple on the head and neck. **Habitat:** Forest and scrub of most islands in the Chathams. Last record: Little Mangere Island, 1906. **[Sp 335]**

BUSH WREN (Matuhi) *Xenicus longipes* — Extinct endemic

9cm, 16g. Larger and darker than Rifleman but easily missed in the gloom of the forest. *Head dark olive brown with clear white eyebrow-stripe*; upperparts dark yellowish green, dark green tail; chin greyish white, *ash-grey underparts* except yellow flanks; long feet and toes. Female and Stewart Island subspecies browner. Like the Rock Wren, *bobs on alighting on the ground*. **Habitat:** Forest and scrub. Last records: Urewera, 1955, Nelson Lakes NP, 1968, Kaimohu Island, off Stewart Island, 1972. **[Sp 322]**

SOUTH ISLAND SNIPE (Tutukiwi) *Coenocorypha iredalei* — Extinct endemic

22cm, 95g. Like Snares Snipe (see Plate 43) but *richer rufous and cinnamon markings on the back* and a wide gorget of blackish crescents across the chest, and a plain belly. **Habitat:** Once throughout South and Stewart islands; became confined to forest and heathland of Big South Cape Island, but exterminated by ship rats in 1964. **[Sp 191]**

SOUTH ISLAND
PIOPIO
NORTH ISLAND
PIOPIO
CHATHAM ISLANDS
BELLBIRD
♂
♀
BUSH WREN
SOUTH ISLAND
SNIPE

Note

In the handbook section, we use the notation 1–**3**–4 for discrete entities (e.g. number of eggs in a clutch) to denote that the range is from 1 to 4, and 3 is the most common value. For continuous variables (e.g. time, linear measurements), 36–**39**–43 denotes that the range is from 36 to 43, and 39 is the mean or average.

KIWI *Apterygidae*

5 species: family endemic to New Zealand.

Kiwi are flightless birds standing up to 45cm high. They are an early offshoot from the evolutionary line of primitive flightless ratites (moa, emu, cassowary, ostrich and rhea). Kiwi are more closely related to emus than to moa. They are one of the oldest members of the New Zealand avifauna; their ancestors are believed to have been in New Zealand when it broke away from Gondwana about 65 million years ago.

Kiwi are usually nocturnal, but some Stewart Island birds and chicks forage by day. They have small eyes but apparently good night vision. Large ears enable good hearing. Kiwi have sensory pits in the bone at the tip of their bill for detecting movement of prey underground. They also have a well-developed sense of smell; the nostrils are uniquely placed near the tip of the long bill. They can be heard breathing through their nostrils as they explore the ground for food, producing a snuffling sound like that of a hedgehog.

Long, tactile facial bristles surround the base of the bill. The feathers have a simple structure with a single rachis and unlinked barbs, and they hang loose like hair. The wings are minute and largely unfeathered, but they have a soft claw at the tip. Kiwi have no tail, and thus look distinctively rounded or pear-shaped. The legs are short and powerful; the three forward-pointing toes and small hind toe have long sharp claws, used for fighting and digging. Other unusual physical features of kiwi are that females have a pair of functional ovaries rather than just one, and that the body temperature and metabolic rate are lower than in most other birds.

Kiwi live from sea level to alpine tussockland and herb fields at about 1500m asl. They are mostly found in native forest but are also found in scrubland, rough farmland, swamps and pine forests, especially where native vegetation remains in gullies. Diet is mainly invertebrates, particularly insect larvae, worms and spiders, taken from the litter layer, or from deep in the soil, obtained by plunging their bill right up to the 'hilt'. Kiwi also eat fallen fruits.

Females are larger and heavier than males. In proportion to the size of the female, the egg is very large at about 15–20% of body weight. It is also very rich in nutrients and energy. She lays 1–2 white or pale greenish eggs in a burrow, hollow log, or under dense vegetation. The eggs are laid 3–4 weeks apart. The very long incubation of 65–85 days is by the male only in Little Spotted Kiwi and Brown Kiwi, by the male and female in Great Spotted Kiwi, Rowi and Tokoeka in the South Island, and by the pair plus helpers in Tokoeka on Stewart Island. Brood patches develop on incubating birds. Each chick hatches fully feathered and first leaves the nest at about a week old. It feeds unaccompanied and returns to the nest for several weeks or months depending on the species. The young usually stay in or close to the natal territory for several months, but then disperse as the next breeding season approaches, except young of several taxa remain in loose or tight family groups for several years.

Although seldom seen, kiwi indicate their presence by their penetrating calls. Call rates are high in the two hours after dusk and before dawn. Males and females often duet, with the male call being a drawn-out, ascending, shrill whistle, repeated 15–25 times, whereas the female call is a deeper and more guttural note repeated 10–20 times.

The range and numbers of all kiwi species have been greatly reduced since humans arrived in New Zealand, but especially over the last 150 years. Forest clearance reduced available habitat and fragmented populations, but the main threat now is from introduced mammalian predators: possums can damage eggs; stoats and cats kill most young chicks; and adults are killed by dogs, ferrets and ground-set possum traps. Translocations, and extensive predator trapping and/or the use of aerial 1080 toxin have proven effective at boosting wild kiwi populations. Bank of New Zealand Operation Nest Egg, the collection of eggs from the wild, captive incubation, and rearing young in captivity or at predator-free crèches until big enough to avoid stoat predation, have been very useful in restoring the most threatened taxa, and re-establishing wild populations.

Brown Kiwi are bred in captivity and are on display at facilities in New Zealand and overseas.

Reading: www.kiwisforkiwi.org.nz. Fuller, E. (ed.) 1990. *Kiwis*. Auckland: SeTo Publishing. Holzapfel A. et al. 2008. *Kiwi Recovery Plan 2008–2018*. Wellington: DOC. Peat, N. 1999. *Kiwi: New Zealand's Remarkable Bird*. Auckland: Godwit.

1. BROWN KIWI *Apteryx mantelli* PLATE 1

Other name: North Island Brown Kiwi
Size: 40cm; male 2.2kg, female 2.8kg
Geographical variation: Genetic research has shown that there are four distinct geographical forms of Brown Kiwi: 'Northland'; 'Coromandel'; 'Eastern' in the Bay of Plenty, Gisborne and Hawke's Bay; and 'Western' in Whanganui–Taranaki and Mt Ruapehu, and introduced to Little Barrier Island.
Distribution: Subfossil and Maori midden remains indicate that Brown Kiwi were widespread through the North Island north of a line between Hawke's Bay and Whanganui in pre-European times. Since 1900, their range has contracted markedly and many populations have become fragmented and isolated, while others have become locally extinct. Still locally common between Kaitaia and Whangarei, and well established on Motukawanui, Little Barrier, Kawau, Motuora and Ponui islands, as well as on several small islands in the Bay of Islands. Sparsely distributed, but sometimes locally common, on the Coromandel Peninsula, in the Bay of Plenty from the Kaimai Range to northern Te Urewera, throughout the Ureweras and south through the Kaweka Range to the northern Ruahine Range, and from southern King Country to Whanganui, on Mt Taranaki, and east to Mt Ruapehu. Recently liberated in North Auckland at Tawharanui, near Warkworth; Marunui, Brynderwyn Hills; and at Mataia, eastern Kaipara Harbour. Also released on Motutapu Island, Hauraki Gulf; Maungatautari in the Waikato; Lake Rotokare in Taranaki; Cape Kidnappers in Hawke's Bay; Pukaha Mount Bruce in the northern Wairarapa; and in the Rimutaka Range near Wellington.
Population: North Island, widespread and locally common. In 2008, *c.* 26,000 birds; 8000 in Northland, 1000 on Little Barrier Island, 1000 on the Coromandel Peninsula, 8000 in the eastern North Island, and 8000 in Whanganui–Taranaki.
Conservation: Protected vulnerable endemic. The fragmentation and decline of populations has been alarming and continues even though clearance of native forest has almost ceased. Since the 1970s, the disappearance of Brown Kiwi from apparently suitable habitat has been noted in Northland, King Country, Kaimanawa Range and Hawke's Bay. Many populations are not self-sustaining because adult mortality (especially from dogs, ferrets, possum traps and natural causes) exceeds recruitment, which is low because possums, mustelids (especially stoats) and cats eat eggs and/or young chicks. Since 1991, much effort has been directed at identifying the main threats to kiwi and trying to manage key mainland populations in the wild by controlling predators. Intensive trapping and poisoning of introduced pest mammals has proven effective at restoring populations. The collection of eggs and chicks from the wild, raising them in captivity and in predator-free environments and then returning them to the wild as subadults has proven very effective at restoring populations and establishing new ones. The self-sustaining population of *c.* 150 Brown Kiwi in captivity at nocturnal houses in New Zealand and overseas has provided opportunities for research and education, and the New Zealand stock is being managed in a way to concentrate effort into establishing a genetically robust population of the 'Eastern' taxon.
Breeding: Most eggs are laid in June–December, in a burrow, hollow log or sometimes under dense vegetation. They lay 1–**2**–3 clutches of 1–2 white eggs (124 x 80mm; 440g). The eggs are laid about 23 days apart, and only the male incubates, for 75–90 days. Chicks hatch fully feathered 0–**12**–15 days apart, and each remains in the nest for about a week before first venturing out unaccompanied. Chicks return to the nest by day for 10–60 days, but then become independent and disperse from the natal territory. Bill and weight grow for up to 3.5 years in males and 5 years in females. First breeding is at 1–**4**–8 years old. Adult survival around the North Island is highly variable, depending on the presence of dogs and/or ferrets; in predator-free sites life expectancy is around 40–50 years.
Behaviour: Most vocal in winter and spring. The male call (higher-pitched and clearer) is often answered immediately by its mate. The male and female of a pair usually feed separately at night, but spend about 20% of days together. During courtship, a pair often remains together for hours, with the birds making loud grunts and snuffling sounds.
Feeding: Diet is mostly invertebrates but includes some fallen fruits and occasional leaves. Main prey are earthworms; larvae of beetles, cicadas and moths; spiders; orthopterans (weta and crickets) and centipedes, with the proportions varying from place to place and with season. Most are taken from the soil, rotting logs or the surface. When feeding, the bird walks slowly along, tapping the ground and sniffing loudly; it often plunges its bill deep into the earth, right up to the 'hilt'. Sometimes the bird digs a small crater up to 15cm deep and 10cm wide when it is struggling to extract a large earthworm.

In the hand: Young females pass through a stage when they cannot be distinguished from adult males. Sexes of adults are distinguished by bill length, with little or no overlap within populations, however, there is a marked clinal decrease in size from north to south, and some regional variation within taxa. In Northland, males 86–**101**–119mm, females 120–**136**–157mm, but at Tongariro, males 86–**94**–102mm, females 109–**124**–132mm. Females are heavier (2090–**2750**–4010g for non-gravid birds) than males (1720–**2250**–3060g).

Reading: Baker, A. J. et al. 1995. *Proc Natl Acad Sci USA* 92: 8254–8258. Burbidge, M. L. et al. 2003, *Cons Genetics* 4: 167–177. Colbourne, R. & Kleinpaste, R. 1984. *Notornis* 31: 191–201. McLennan, J. A. 1988. *NZ J Ecol* 11: 89–97. McLennan, J. A. et al. 1996. *NZ J Ecol* 20: 27–35. Potter, M. A. 1990. *NZ J Ecol* 14: 17–24. Robertson, H. A. *et al.* 2011. *Bird Cons Intl* 21: 207–220. Robertson, H. A. & de Monchy, P. J. M. 2012. *Bird Cons Intl* 22: 429–444. Taborsky, B. & Taborsky, M. 1992. *Ibis* 134: 1–10.

2. ROWI *Apteryx rowi* — PLATE 1

Other name: Okarito Brown Kiwi
Size: 40cm; male 1.9kg, female 2.7kg
Distribution: Subfossil and Maori midden remains indicate that Rowi occupied the southern North Island and the northwestern and western part of the South Island in pre-European times. Confined to forests around Okarito since the mid-1800s, where the population is increasing rapidly due to conservation management. Small populations have been put on Blumine and Mana islands. Motuara Island, Marlborough Sounds, is used as a crèche site for juveniles before they are returned to Okarito or transferred to other sites at about 8–11 months old.
Population: Okarito *c.* 375 in 2013; Blumine Island 10 in 2013; Mana Island 20 in 2013.
Conservation: Protected critically threatened endemic. The reason for the huge range contraction to just Okarito is unknown. In 1991, the population was estimated to be 160 birds, occupying about 10,000ha of South Okarito Forest in Westland National Park. A Bank of New Zealand Operation Nest Egg programme of egg and chick collection from the wild, captive rearing and crèching of juveniles, and subsequent return of subadult birds to Okarito resulted in an increase to *c.* 200 birds in 2000. An attempt to trap stoats in Okarito Forest from 2001–05 failed to protect sufficient wild-hatched chicks, and so the conservation programme has reverted to BNZ Operation Nest Egg, interspersed with periodic aerial 1080 toxin applications.
Breeding: Most eggs are laid in June–December, in a burrow or hollow log. Birds lay 1–3 clutches of 1 pale green egg (122 x 77mm; 410g), though overlapping clutches can give the impression of a two-egg clutch. Male and female share incubation for 65–75 days. The chick hatches fully feathered and remains in the nest about a week before venturing out unaccompanied. The chick returns to the nest by day and can remain in the nest while the next clutch is incubated. Juveniles often remain with their parents for 3–4 years, before dispersing. First breeding is at 3–7 years old. The oldest banded bird lived over 32 years, but some probably live at least 60 years.
Behaviour: Most vocal in winter and spring. The male call (higher-pitched and clearer) is often answered immediately by its mate; sometimes they call simultaneously. The male and female of a pair usually feed separately at night, but spend most days together in a few well-used burrows. During courtship, a pair often remains together for hours, with the birds making loud grunts and snuffling sounds.
Feeding: Diet has not been specifically studied, but likely to be mostly invertebrates and also some fallen fruits. Main prey are earthworms; larvae of beetles, cicadas and moths; spiders; orthopterans (weta and crickets); and centipedes, with the proportions varying with season. Most are taken from the soil, rotting logs or the surface. When feeding, the bird walks slowly along, tapping the ground and sniffing loudly; it often plunges its bill deep into the earth, right up to the 'hilt'. Sometimes the bird digs a small crater up to 15cm deep and 10cm wide when it is struggling to extract a large earthworm.
In the hand: Young females pass through a stage when they cannot be distinguished from adult males. Sexes of adults are distinguished by bill length: males 84–**95**–104mm, females 110–**126**–140mm, and weight: males 1575–**1925**–2250g, females 1950–**2650**–3570g. The bill continues to grow and weight increases for at least the first 4 years.
Reading: Baker, A. J. et al. 1995. *Proc Natl Acad Sci USA* 92: 8254–8258. Burbidge, M. L. et al. 2003, *Cons Genetics* 4: 167–177. Robertson, H. A. & de Monchy, P. J. M. 2012. *Bird Cons Intl* 22: 429–444. Tennyson, A. J. D. et al. 2003. *Rec Auck Mus* 40: 55–64.

3. TOKOEKA *Apteryx australis* PLATE 1

Other names: South Island Brown Kiwi (Haast and Fiordland), Stewart Island Brown Kiwi (Stewart Island)
Size: 45cm; male 2.4kg, female 3.1kg
Geographical variation: Genetic research has shown that there are three distinct geographical forms of Tokoeka: 'Haast' in the mountains near Haast, 'Fiordland' from near Milford Sound to southern Fiordland, and 'Rakiura' on Stewart Island.
Distribution: Subfossil and Maori midden remains indicate that Tokoeka were widespread through the southern and eastern South Island in pre-European times. Their range contracted markedly from the north and east, and on the South Island mainland they are now confined to Fiordland. The Haast Tokoeka is confined to an isolated population in the Haast Range, the western side of the mid-Arawhata River, and a few birds in the Selbourne Range; introduced to Rarotoka (Centre) Island, Foveaux Strait (2008), Coal Island, Preservation Inlet (2009–13), Orokonui Ecosanctuary, Dunedin (2010–11), and Pomona Island, Lake Manapouri (2011–13). Fiordland Tokoeka are in the mountains of Fiordland south of about Milford Sound, and established on many offshore islands, including Secretary, Resolution, Long, Cooper and Indian; introduced to Kapiti Island (1907). Rakiura Tokoeka are throughout Stewart Island, but more numerous south of Paterson Inlet; introduced to Ulva Island (1950s; supplemented 1980s and 2013).
Population: Haast *c.* 350 in 2013, mainly in the Haast Range north of Music Creek, and on the true left of the Arawhata around McArthur Creek; Fiordland *c.* 9000, widespread and locally common between Milford Sound, Lake Te Anau and Dusky Sound, scarce further south; Rakiura *c.* 12,000, mainly south of Paterson Inlet and the Ruggedy Mountains.
Conservation: Protected vulnerable endemic. The decline of populations since human arrival was dramatic and the decline continues at a slower rate even though most birds now live within national parks. Many populations are not self-sustaining because of low recruitment caused by possum, mustelid and kea predation of eggs, and stoat and cat predation of chicks. Since 1991, much effort has been directed at identifying the main threats to Tokoeka and trying to manage key mainland populations in the wild by controlling predators. Intensive trapping and poisoning of introduced pest mammals has proven effective at restoring populations. The collection of eggs from the wild, raising them in captivity and in predator-free environments, and then returning resultant subadults to the wild has proven very effective at restoring key populations and establishing new ones.
Breeding: Most eggs are laid in July–December, in a burrow, hollow log or sometimes under dense vegetation. They lay 1–2 clutches of 1 very pale green egg (131 x 81mm; 480g). Male and female share incubation for 75–80 days. Chicks hatch fully feathered, and remain in the nest for about a week before first venturing out unaccompanied. Haast Tokoeka chicks return to the nest by day for 10–60 days then become completely independent, but Fiordland and Rakiura Tokoeka chicks remain to form family groups in their natal territory. On Stewart Island, they have been recorded staying for at least 7 years, and assisting with incubation of subsequent clutches. Bill and weight grow for up to 3.5 years in males and 5 years in females. First breeding is at 4–8 years old. Adult survival is extremely high in the largely dog-free and ferret-free sites still occupied; mean life expectancy is *c.* 40–50 years.
Behaviour: Most vocal in winter and spring. The male call (higher-pitched and clearer) is often answered immediately by its mate; sometimes they call simultaneously. The male and female pair usually feed separately at night, but spend about 20% of days together. During courtship, a pair often remains together for hours, with the birds making loud grunts and snuffling sounds.
Feeding: Diet is mostly invertebrates but includes some fallen fruits and occasional leaves. Main prey are earthworms; larvae of beetles, cicadas and moths; spiders; weta and centipedes, with the proportions varying from place to place and with season. Most are taken from the soil, rotting logs or the surface. When feeding, the bird walks slowly along, tapping the ground and sniffing loudly; it often plunges its bill deep into the earth, right up to the 'hilt'. Sometimes the bird digs a small crater up to 15cm deep and 10cm wide when it is struggling to extract a large earthworm.
In the hand: Young females pass through a stage when they cannot be distinguished from adult males. Sexes of adults are distinguished by bill length, with no overlap within populations, however, there is a marked clinal increase in size from north to south, and some regional variation within taxa. Haast Tokoeka males 85–**92**–103mm and 1900–**2350**–2830g, females 109–**122**–136mm and 2200–**3000**–3500g; Fiordland Tokoeka males 90–**99**–112mm and 1900–**2400**–3100g, females 110–**132**–148mm and 2200–**3200**–4200g; Rakiura Tokoeka males 94–**106**–118mm and 2300–**2700**–3100g, females 133–**146**–168mm and 2600–**3300**–3900g.

Reading: Baker, A. J. et al. 1995. *Proc Natl Acad Sci USA* 92: 8254–8258. Burbidge, M. L. et al. 2003. *Cons Genetics* 4: 167–177. Colbourne, R. 1991. *Notornis* 38: 248–249. Colbourne, R. M. & Powlesland, R. G. 1988. *NZ J Ecol* 11: 99–104. Taborsky, B. & Taborsky, M. 1992. *Ibis* 134: 1–10.

4. LITTLE SPOTTED KIWI *Apteryx owenii* PLATE 1

Other name: Kiwi pukupuku
Size: 30cm; male 1150g, female 1325g
Distribution: Subfossil and Maori midden remains indicate that Little Spotted Kiwi were widespread throughout mainland New Zealand in pre-European times. Genetic research shows that birds in northern North Island were likely a distinct species. A report from near Pirongia in 1882 and a specimen collected in the Tararua Ranges in 1875 are the only historical records in the North Island. Many specimens were collected in the South Island and they were still common at the start of the twentieth century. They declined rapidly in the early 1900s, and are now probably extinct on the mainland. A few survived on D'Urville Island until the 1980s, when two were shifted to nearby predator-free Long Island, but they did not breed. The main population is on Kapiti Island, apparently derived from five birds introduced in 1912. Successfully transferred from Kapiti Island to Hen Island; Tiritiri Matangi Island; Motuihe; Red Mercury Island; Zealandia, Wellington; Long Island, Marlborough Sounds; and Chalky Island, Fiordland.
Population: *c.* 1700 in 2013: Kapiti Island *c.* 1200, Hen Island 60, Tiritiri Matangi Island 100, Motuihe 40, Red Mercury Island 80, Zealandia 120, Long Island 50, and Chalky Island 40.
Conservation: Protected endemic. The main population, on Kapiti Island, is apparently stable, has many juveniles and may have benefited from the eradication of possums in the 1980s and rats in the 1990s, but the arrival of a stoat in 2009 highlights their vulnerability there. The population is near carrying capacity because gaps created by transfers to other sites are filled quickly. In 1983, 12 birds were transferred to Red Mercury Island, and by 2011 there were *c.* 75 birds. In 1988–89, 38 birds were transferred to Hen Island, and by 1995 there were 50+ birds. Two birds from D'Urville Island and three from Kapiti Island were introduced to Long Island between 1982 and 1989, and by 2013 there were *c.* 50 birds on the island, all apparently derived from two of the Kapiti birds. In 1993, five pairs were transferred from Kapiti to Tiritiri Matangi Island, and a further six birds were added in 1995; by 2012 the population was *c.* 90 birds. In 2000–01, 40 birds were transferred to Zealandia in Wellington, and the population had grown to *c.* 100 birds by 2010. In 2008–10, 39 birds were transferred to Chalky Island, Fiordland, and in 2009–10, 40 birds to Motuihe, Hauraki Gulf.
Breeding: Most eggs are laid in August–December, occasionally as early as July. They lay **1**–2 clutches of **1**–2 white eggs (110 x 70mm; 300g) in a burrow, hollow log or under dense vegetation. In two-egg clutches, the eggs are laid 2–3 weeks apart. Incubation is by the male only and takes 65–75 days. The chick hatches fully feathered and remains in the nest 4–5 days before venturing out unaccompanied. It returns to the nest for several weeks but stays away for the odd day. Chicks seem to remain close to their natal territory for at least 6–9 months before dispersing to find a vacant territory. Growth continues for at least 30 months, but sometimes they form pairs before fully grown. Pairs are monogamous and persist all year and between years. The oldest bird recorded in the wild was at least 35 years old in 2013, but calculated mean life expectancy on Kapiti Island is *c.* 45 years.
Behaviour: Most vocal in spring and summer. The male call (higher-pitched and clearer) is often answered immediately by its mate. The male and female pair usually feed separately at night but spend about 25% of days together. During courtship, pairs often remain together for hours and make loud grunts and snuffling sounds.
Feeding: Diet is mostly small invertebrates but includes some fallen fruits and occasional leaves. Main prey are earthworms; larvae of beetles, cicadas, flies and moths; spiders; and adult beetles, with the proportions varying from place to place and with season. Most are taken from the upper layer of the soil, leaf litter or rotting logs. When feeding, the bird walks slowly along, tapping the ground and sniffing loudly; it sometimes plunges its bill into the earth, but rarely right up to the 'hilt'.
In the hand: The adult male develops a brood patch in summer. Sexes can be distinguished by size, with no overlap in adult bill measurements: males 62–**68**–73mm, females 75–**84**–94mm. Adult females are heavier (1010–**1350**–2010g for non-gravid birds) than adult males (880–**1125**–1450g). Birds in good condition under 1000g are considered juveniles, but males in poor condition (e.g. after incubation) can be as light as 880g. The bill of juveniles continues growing for

at least the first 30 months. Adults have greyer backs and smaller, paler legs and toenails than the otherwise similar juvenile Great Spotted Kiwi.

Reading: Colbourne, R. 1992. *J Roy Soc NZ* 22: 321–328. Colbourne, R. et al. 1990 *NZ J Zool* 17: 533–542. Colbourne, R. M. & Robertson, H. A. 1997. *Notornis* 44: 253–258. Colbourne, R. M. & Robertson H. A. 2004. Pp. 53–59 in Brown, K. (ed.) *Restoring Kapiti: Nature's Second Chance*. Dunedin: Otago Uni Press. Jolly, J. N. 1989. *J Roy Soc NZ* 19: 433–448. Jolly, J. N. 1990. Pp. 87–96 in Fuller, E. (ed.) *Kiwis*. Auckland: SeTo Publishing. Ramstad, K. M. et al. 2013. *Proc Roy Soc B* 280: doi: 10.1098/rspb.2013.0576. Robertson, H. A. et al. 1993. *Notornis* 40: 253–262. Shepherd, L. D. et al. 2012. *PLOS ONE* 7(8): doi: 10.1371/journal.pone.0042384.

5. GREAT SPOTTED KIWI *Apteryx haastii* PLATE 1

Other names: Roroa, Roa

Size: 45cm; male 2.4kg, female 3.3kg

Distribution: Subfossil and Maori midden remains indicate that Great Spotted Kiwi have always been restricted to the South Island. In the 1800s, they were recorded in Westland, western Canterbury and north-western Nelson, but specimens from South Westland appear to be hybrids between Rowi and Little Spotted Kiwi. Great Spotted Kiwi remain locally common in all three recently isolated populations: from northwestern Nelson (e.g. Heaphy Track) to the Buller River and east to the Arthur and Matiri ranges; in the Paparoa Range; and, in the Southern Alps from about the Nina Valley near Lewis Pass to the Taipo River south of Arthur's Pass. Successful translocations to Lake Rotoiti, Nelson Lakes National Park (2004–12), and the Flora Valley, Arthur Range (2010–13).

Population: *c.* 17,000 birds in 2008. Northwestern Nelson to Buller River, widespread and locally common; Paparoa Range, widespread and common in higher areas; Hurunui River to Arthur's Pass, widespread and locally common in higher, wetter forests.

Conservation: Protected vulnerable endemic. Since 1900, the disappearance of local populations from apparently suitable habitat has been noted in parts of the Grey Valley and northern Westland, but the fragmentation and decline of populations has been much slower than for the Brown Kiwi. Apparently stable or only gradually declining populations remain in remote wet country in all three populations. Some populations are probably not self-sustaining because adult mortality (from dogs and natural causes) exceeds recruitment, which is low because possums, mustelids and cats eat eggs or young chicks.

None are established on a predator-free island; 19 birds transferred from the Gouland Downs to Little Barrier Island in 1915 failed to establish. Since the 1980s, effort has been directed at studying the ecology of Great Spotted Kiwi, identifying their distribution, monitoring the three main populations, and limited captive-raising of eggs or chicks collected from the wild.

Breeding: Most eggs are laid in July–December. They lay 1 pale green egg (124 x 77mm; 435g) in a hole among roots of a tree, in hollow log, in a burrow or sometimes under a fallen log or in dense vegetation. The male incubates during the day and for about half the night, but the female incubates for half the night while the male feeds. The incubation period is *c.* 70 days. Little is known of chick development, but like other kiwi the chick hatches fully feathered and remains in the nest for about a week before venturing out. Young birds remain in or close to the natal territory and are sometimes still with their parents when two years old. They reach adult size at *c.* 5 years old. Pairs are monogamous and persist all year and between years.

Behaviour: Call rate is fairly even throughout the night, with a peak just after dusk and again before dawn, and they are most vocal in summer. Pairs often duet, with the male call (higher-pitched and clearer) sometimes alternating synchronously with the female call several times in a short burst of calling. The male and female of a pair usually feed separately at night, but spend 10–30% of days together. Great Spotted Kiwi are much warier of humans than are other kiwi, and often slip away from their daytime shelters well before they are seen.

Feeding: Diet is mostly invertebrates and fallen fruits, along with occasional leaves. Main prey are earthworms, beetles, spiders, centipedes and fruit, but weta, fresh-water crayfish and *Powelliphanta* snails have also been recorded. Most food is taken from the soil, leaf litter or rotting logs. When feeding, the bird walks along slowly, tapping the ground and sniffing loudly; it sometimes plunges its bill deep into the earth, right up to the 'hilt'. Sometimes the bird digs a distinctive small crater up to 15cm deep and 10cm wide when it is struggling to extract a large earthworm.

In the hand: Sexes are distinguished by size, with no overlap in adult bill measurements within a population, but there is a clinal decrease in size from north to south: males 85–**96**–105mm, females 103–**123**–140mm in northwest Nelson, but males 85–**93**–103mm, females 105–**118**–127mm in the Southern Alps. Females are significantly heavier than males: 2250–**2950**–4300g, cf. 1750–**2250**–3000g). Young females pass through a stage when they cannot be distinguished from adult males. Juvenile Great Spotted Kiwi can look like adult Little Spotted Kiwi, but have a browner back and legs, and have brown (not ivory or pale pink) claws.

Reading: Jahn, P. et al. 2013. *Notornis* 60: 201–209. McLennan, J. A. 1990. Pp. 73–85 in Fuller, E. (ed.) *Kiwis*. Auckland: SeTo Publishing. McLennan, J. A. & McCann, A. J. 1991. *NZ J Ecol* 15: 163–166. McLennan, J. A. & Potter, M. A. 1993. *Notornis* 40: 294–297. McLennan, J. A. et al. 1996. *NZ J Ecol.* 20: 27–35. Robertson, H. A. et al. 2005. *Notornis* 52: 27–35.

GAMEBIRDS *Phasianidae*

About 213 species worldwide. The only native member of this family, the endemic New Zealand Quail *Coturnix novaezelandiae*, became extinct *c.* 1875.

Some 28 species of gamebirds have been introduced to New Zealand, but over half have failed to establish. All were introduced for domestic or hunting purposes, often with great persistence and at great cost. Some are still supplemented annually by captive-reared stock raised by Fish and Game councils (formerly Acclimatisation societies), paid for from hunters' licence fees.

Most species favour farmland, swamp margins and open ground with plenty of coarse grass or scrub for cover. They feed on the ground and are omnivorous – grain, other seeds, berries, roots, together with whatever invertebrates are revealed as they scratch and dig at the ground surface with stout legs and strong claws and bill. Most roost in trees.

The sexes often have quite different plumage: females and immatures have subdued plumage that blends with the surroundings; males are often brightly coloured in the larger species or strongly patterned but cryptic in the smaller ones. Many species are polygamous, the male having a harem of females in the breeding season. Their nest is a shallow hollow scraped in the ground with little or no lining. Clutches are large, but, although most eggs hatch, few chicks reach independence. The chicks leave the nest soon after hatching and feed themselves, attended by the adults. Most young can fly within two or three weeks of hatching.

Reading: Delacour, J. 1977. *The Pheasants of the World*. Hindhead: Spur Publications. Johnsgard, P. A. 1988. *The Quails, Partridges and Francolins of the World*. Oxford: OUP.

6. CALIFORNIA QUAIL *Callipepla californica* PLATE 3

Size: 25cm, 180g

Geographical variation: Of the seven subspecies in western North America, *brunnescens* from southwestern Oregon and California was introduced to New Zealand.

Distribution: The natural range is western North America from southern British Columbia to Baja California. They have been introduced to Hawai'i, Chile, Australia and New Zealand. They were introduced to both main islands of New Zealand in the 1860s and 1870s, with later supplementary releases of New Zealand-bred stock. Now widely distributed in both main islands, but rare around East Cape, on the West Coast and in Southland; a few are on the Chatham Islands. California Quail are found mainly in areas with a mix of open country and low scrub, particularly tussockland or rough pasture associated with manuka scrub and, in the South Island, with such dry-country plants as wild Irishman, gorse, bracken, broom and briar. They also frequent lupin-covered riverbeds and riverbed margins.

Population: Common in certain less intensively developed districts of both main islands.

Breeding: Coveys break up in late winter and pairing begins in late August. Eggs are laid from late September to February, with a peak in early November in Otago but in early December in the central North Island. The nest is commonly in long grass near thick cover of blackberry, gorse or bracken. The female lays 8–**13**–24 creamy-white eggs (31 x 24mm), spotted dark and yellowish brown.

Eggs are laid daily. The female incubates for 22–**23** days. The young leave the nest shortly after hatching and can fly by 10 days old, when only about one-quarter grown. They first breed at 1 year old. The oldest California Quail recorded in New Zealand lived over 11 years.
Behaviour: In autumn and winter, family groups combine to form large roosting coveys. By day they break into smaller coveys that disperse to their preferred feeding grounds nearby.
Feeding: In their first weeks, chicks eat mainly small insects, but they soon adopt the adult diet of fallen seeds of a wide variety of plants, supplemented with leaves of clover and grasses and a few small insects. In late winter and spring, however, vegetation becomes the dominant food. They feed mostly in the early morning and in the last couple of hours before dusk.
Reading: Gurr, L. 1951. *Notornis* 4: 144–145. Leopold, A. S. 1977. *The California Quail.* Berkeley: Uni California Press. Williams, G. R. 1952. *J Wildl Mgmt* 16: 460–483. Williams, G. R. 1967. *Proc NZ Ecol Soc* 14: 88–99.

7. HELMETED GUINEAFOWL *Numida meleagris* PLATE 2

Other name: Tufted Guineafowl
Size: 60cm, 1500g
Distribution: Natural range is Africa south of the Sahara Desert. They have been widely introduced to farms and aviaries since the 1860s, and escapees have become feral in rough farmland in parts of Northland, Kaipara district, the outskirts of the Hunua Ranges, coastal Waikato and Taranaki, and Canterbury.
Breeding: They lay 6–12 eggs between October and January, which the female incubates for about 4 weeks. Chicks soon leave the nest and can fly well at 4 weeks old.
Behaviour: Noisy and gregarious, but wary.

8. CHUKOR *Alectoris chukar* PLATE 3

Other name: Chukar
Size: 31cm; male 600g, female 500g
Geographical variation: The many subspecies described may be only clinal. Two forms were introduced to New Zealand in the 1920s and 1930s, mostly *chukar* of India, but once (into Marlborough) *koroviakovi* of Iran. Although the resulting birds are presumably hybrids, they look most like *chukar*.
Distribution: Natural range is from southeastern Europe and Turkey east through central Asia, including the Himalayas, to Mongolia and China. They are well established on the dry, rocky country east of the Southern Alps from Marlborough (Nelson Lakes National Park, Wairau River, Seaward Kaikoura Range) to Central Otago (especially in the hills surrounding the Mackenzie Basin). North Island liberations, as recently as 1987, have been unsuccessful.
Breeding: Eggs are laid in September–January. The nest is a scrape on the rocky ground under a sheltering tussock. The female lays 8–**13**–18 cream eggs (43 x 31mm), flecked reddish brown. Eggs are laid daily. The female incubates for *c.* 24 days. The oldest Chukor recorded in New Zealand lived over 12 years.
Behaviour: After breeding, the family group remains together as a covey of 5–10 birds, but in winter these groups coalesce to form large coveys of 50–150 birds.
Feeding: Diet is mainly seeds, shoots and leaves of grasses and other ground plants such as thistles, clovers and briars; also some insects, found by scratching at and gleaning from the ground.
Reading: Marples, B. J. & Gurr, L. 1953. *Emu* 53: 283–291. Williams, G. R. 1951. *Notornis* 4: 151–157.

9. RED-LEGGED PARTRIDGE *Alectoris rufa* PLATE 3

Size: 31cm, 500g
Distribution: Natural range is Western Europe, Corsica and the Canary Islands. Despite failed introductions into New Zealand in the 1890s, a programme to establish them has been in progress since 1984, using eggs imported from Britain from 1980 onwards. Birds have been released between the Kaipara Harbour and Taumarunui, in the Bay of Plenty, Gisborne, Hawke's Bay, Manawatu, in the Upper Moutere valley near Nelson, and in Marlborough and Canterbury. It seems that most releases have been unsuccessful, but in some districts it is too early to know whether they will become permanently established.

10. GREY PARTRIDGE *Perdix perdix* PLATE 3

Size: 30cm, 500g
Distribution: Natural range is Britain and Europe from southern Sweden to France, Italy, Macedonia and eastern Russia. They were widely liberated in New Zealand with little success from the 1860s to 1909. More recently (1959–70), a further 28,000 birds, from Danish stock, were liberated in both North and South islands, including 11,000 in North Canterbury alone. Again, this was apparently also with limited success, although a few birds persisted in Southland until at least the 1980s.
Breeding: The nest is a shallow scrape on the ground in thick short cover, such as on fallow land and hay crops. The female lays 10–**16**–20 olive-brown eggs and incubates alone for *c.* 24 days. The oldest Grey Partridge recorded in New Zealand lived over 10 years.
Reading: Westerskov, K. E. 1990. Pp. 47–62 in *Proc Perdix V: Grey Partridge and Ring-necked Pheasant Workshop*.

11. BOBWHITE QUAIL *Colinus virginianus* PLATE 3

Other name: Virginian Quail
Size: 23cm, 180g
Distribution: Natural range is eastern North America, Mexico, Central America and Cuba. Introductions of 1000+ birds to New Zealand from 1898 to 1902 were mostly unsuccessful, as were liberations in Otago in 1947–48. They bred but did not thrive, and few pockets, if any, survive. They were most recently recorded in South Auckland and near Wairoa in the 1950s, and at Lake Waikaremoana in the early 1970s.
Breeding: Little is known in New Zealand. The nest is a shallow hollow hidden in thick vegetation. The female lays 7–28 white eggs and the incubation period is *c.* 23 days.
Reading: Gurr, L. 1953. *Notornis* 5: 164. Westerskov, K. 1957. *Notornis* 7: 95–98.

12. BROWN QUAIL *Coturnix ypsilophora* PLATE 3

Size: 18cm, 100g
Geographical variation: About 10 subspecies have been described, two of which, *australis* from mainland Australia and *ypsilophora* from Tasmania, were introduced to New Zealand, but current birds look most like *australis*.
Distribution: Natural range is southern Indonesia, New Guinea, and Australia, including Tasmania. They were introduced widely in the North and South islands in the 1860s and 1870s, but now survive only in the North Island. They are common in Northland and many of its offshore islands, and also on some of the developed islands in the Bay of Plenty. Moderately common in the Bay of Plenty and around East Cape, but scarce and widely scattered elsewhere north of a line from Kawhia to Lake Taupo to Gisborne. They are mainly seen along the dusty edges of country roads, on rough swamp margins and along the edges of salt marshes, as well as in the usual scrub and open rough grassland well supplied with cover.
Population: Common only in Northland and on some predator-free sanctuaries in North Auckland (Tawharanui and Shakespear) and on predator-free islands off the eastern North Island, including Motuora, Tiritiri Matangi, Motutapu, Rangitoto, and Moutohora (Whale) islands.
Breeding: Eggs are laid in September–January. The nest is a slight depression lined with grass and leaves, under thick vegetation such as roadside verges and bracken. The female lays 7–12 white eggs (28 x 23mm), freckled all over with brown. The female alone incubates for *c.* 21 days. Chicks soon leave the nest and travel as a family group.
Behaviour: Brown Quail form small coveys of 5–10 birds when not breeding. They are reluctant to fly and usually scuttle for cover into the undergrowth, but when they are flushed, they have a fast direct whirring flight.
Feeding: Diet is mainly fallen seeds from a wide variety of grasses, weeds and shrubs, but supplemented with vegetation, flowers and insects.

13. FERAL CHICKEN *Gallus gallus* PLATE 2

Other name: Red Junglefowl
Size: 40cm; male 850g, female 550g
Geographical variation: Five subspecies of Red Junglefowl, most of which are believed to have contributed to the domesticated breeds of chickens around the world.
Distribution: Natural range is Asia, from northeast India to central China and southeast to Bali. First domesticated over 8000 years ago, and they have been subsequently introduced to many parts of the world, including prehistoric introductions to many islands in the Pacific, including Hawai'i. There is no evidence that Maori brought them to New Zealand, but they were introduced here as early as 1773 by James Cook. There have been many releases in both North and South islands, especially around picnic areas off highways, and many run free-range on farms and lifestyle blocks, but none has established as a viable wild population. Although some successful breeding has been recorded in the wild, the populations seem to be maintained through ongoing releases and supplementary feeding.
Population: Small groups of birds are found in many rural localities throughout New Zealand.
Breeding: No information from feral populations in New Zealand.
Behaviour: Red Junglefowl live in forested habitats. Many are solitary, but dominant males establish small coveys with several hens.
Feeding: Diet is mainly invertebrates, fallen seeds from a wide variety of grasses, weeds and shrubs, and food scraps.
Reading: Liu, Y. -P. et al. 2006. *Molecular Phylogen & Evoln* 38: 12–19.

14. PHEASANT *Phasianus colchicus* PLATE 2

Other names: Common Pheasant, Ring-necked Pheasant
Size: Male 80cm, 1400g; female 60cm, 1200g
Geographical variation: New Zealand stock is derived from several subspecies, although most birds resemble the Ring-necked Pheasant from China, *torquatus*, especially in having a broad white neck-ring.
Distribution: Natural range is from Turkey east through central Asia to China. They have been repeatedly introduced to New Zealand from 1842 onwards, and local birds are still reinforced by releases of New Zealand-bred stock. In the North Island, they are most common north of a line from New Plymouth to Hastings, and in coastal Whanganui and Manawatu; scattered elsewhere. In the South Island, they are sparse with small numbers in Nelson and along rivers of the central and southern Canterbury Plains.
Population: *c.* 250,000. Up to 50,000 cocks are shot each year and numbers are reinforced in many districts by captive-reared birds. Hen pheasants are strictly protected.
Breeding: The New Zealand season is extended, and nests with eggs have been found from late July to late March; most eggs, however, are laid in October–December. The nest is a hollow scantily lined with vegetation and usually in thick cover such as hayfields, under blackberry or bracken, roadside verges, rough pasture, and crops. The female lays 7–**9**–15 olive-brown eggs (46 x 36mm) and incubates for 23–28 days. Chicks leave the nest within hours and can fly weakly at *c.* 14 days though far from fully grown. The oldest wild Pheasant recorded in New Zealand lived over 15 years.
Feeding: In their first weeks, chicks eat mainly small insects but gradually adopt the adult diet of green-leaf material, seeds, grain, berries and larger insects.
Reading: Barker, R. J. 1991. *Notornis* 38: 125–130.

15. PEAFOWL *Pavo cristatus* PLATE 2

Other name: Indian Peafowl
Size: 90cm plus male's 1m tail; male 4.5kg, female 3.5kg
Distribution: Natural range is India and Sri Lanka. They are now distributed worldwide as ornamental species in parks and private gardens. They were brought to New Zealand in the 1840s and have become truly feral in rough, mainly hill-country farmland in many warmer and drier North Island localities, especially in central Northland, North Auckland, South Kaipara Heads, northern Waikato, inland Whanganui and in Gisborne and northern Hawke's Bay. In the South Island, they are sparsely distributed in Nelson and

coastal Canterbury, including Banks Peninsula.
Breeding: Peahens lay 4–6 pale cream to warm buff eggs (69 x 51mm) between August and January, and incubate them for 28–30 days. The precocial chicks quickly leave the nest but can remain with their mother for over a year.
Behaviour: When feral, they become shy and wary. They usually form small flocks of 5–15 birds, but in autumn and winter, flocks of up to 100 birds have been reported.
Feeding: Omnivorous, eating a range of seeds, fruits and invertebrates, especially black field crickets and cicadas.
Reading: Beauchamp, A. J. 2013. *Notornis* 60: 224–232.

16. WILD TURKEY *Meleagris gallopavo* — PLATE 2

Size: Male 120cm, 8kg, but up to 10.6kg; female 90cm, 4kg
Distribution: Natural range is North America, from northeastern and central USA to Mexico. They were first introduced to New Zealand about 1890 and have become common on farms as domestic birds. Some have become truly feral on rough hilly farmland in many North Island areas, especially in Northland, South Auckland, Waikato, Taupo, coastal Bay of Plenty, Rangitikei, and the east coast from East Cape to Cape Palliser. Scarce, but widely scattered, in lowland hill country of the South Island; mainly in Marlborough, Banks Peninsula, South Canterbury and North Otago. Established on Waiheke, Great Barrier, Rakitu (Arid) islands and on Moturoa in the Bay of Islands.
Breeding: Little is known from New Zealand. Clutch size is 8–15 creamy brown eggs with darker speckles which are incubated by the female for about 28 days. The precocial chicks soon leave the nest and stay with the female, and eventually join flocks of 10–20 birds through the autumn and winter.
Behaviour: Usually quite tame and bold, but after being hunted they quickly become shy and wary. They fly strongly if flushed, or when roosting in tall trees, such as macrocarpas.
Feeding: Diet is mainly leaves of clover, grasses and weeds, supplemented with a few large insects.
Reading: Schemnitz, S. D. 1992. *Notornis* 39: 126–129.

WATERFOWL *Anatidae*

Swans, geese, ducks and mergansers are found worldwide in freshwater and coastal habitats. There are about 160 species, of which 16 (6 endemic, 4 native and 6 introduced) breed or have bred in the New Zealand region since 1920. A further endemic species, New Zealand Merganser *Mergus australis*, became extinct in the early years of the 1900s, and another 7 species are vagrants to the region.

All species have webbed feet for swimming in rivers, lakes, estuaries or coastal waters. Their bill is modified for filter-feeding – water and food are sucked in at the tip of the bill and expelled through fine comb-like lamellae at the sides, which catch minute seeds and invertebrates. Although most feed in this way, some species mainly graze on aquatic or terrestrial vegetation and pick seeds (e.g. peas or wheat) off the ground, and the mergansers have serrated bills for catching and holding fish.

In New Zealand, most introduced and some native species of waterfowl are legally harvested during a strictly controlled shooting season. Each year, Fish and Game councils determine the length and timing of the season, traditionally starting on the first Saturday in May. They also set the allowable bag limit for each species, and monitor the licensing of hunters and annual hunting statistics. They, and the voluntary organisation, Ducks Unlimited, work to create and protect wetland habitats suitable for waterfowl, and Ducks Unlimited members assist with captive breeding programmes for some threatened species.
Reading: Burns, H. 1988. *Wildfowl: An Identification Guide to the Ducks, Geese and Swans of the World.* London: Christopher Helm. Frith, H. J. 1982. *Waterfowl in Australia.* Sydney, Angus & Robertson. Madge, S. & Johnsgard, P. A. 1978. *Ducks, Geese and Swans of the World.* Lincoln: Uni Nebraska Press. Williams, M. 1981. *The Duckshooter's Bag.* Wellington: Wetland Press.

17. PLUMED WHISTLING DUCK *Dendrocygna eytoni* PLATE 5

Other name: Grass Whistling Duck
Size: 50cm, 800g
Distribution: Breeds in northeastern and tropical Australia, and the Murray–Darling Basin. Partly nomadic, following rains and floods in wet years to colonise temporary wetlands and then returning to permanent water, mainly along the eastern seaboard. Vagrant to other parts of Australia including Tasmania, and to New Guinea and New Zealand. About 15 records from New Zealand: Thames (1871), up to 14 (three shot) near Balclutha (1871), three at Ashburton (1894–96), 12 near Karamea (1975), 9–11 in the lower Waikato River area (1982), 1 at Te Aroha (1984), 6 at Haast (1990), 7 at Hokitika (1992), 5 at Woodville (2007), 1 at Tiritiri Matangi Island and Tawharanui (2007), 5 at Lake Horowhenua (2010), 7 at Fox Glacier (2011), 3 in Taradale (2011–13), and 3 at Te Whanga Lagoon, Chatham Island (2011), 9 at Whataroa (2011–13), and 3 at Barrytown (2012). Despite flocks sometimes persisting at the same site for several years, they are not known to have bred.
Feeding: In Australia, they feed mainly on land near lagoon edges, in paddocks and on open plains. Their diet is almost entirely vegetation, especially grasses, grass seedheads, legumes, herbs and sedges.
Reading: Ellis, B. A. 1975. *Notornis* 22: 244.

18. MUTE SWAN *Cygnus olor* PLATE 4

Other name: White Swan
Size: 150cm; male 12kg, female 9kg
Distribution: Natural range is northern Eurasia from Great Britain to eastern Russia. They were introduced to New Zealand from Great Britain from 1866 onwards as ornamental birds, and maintain a tenuous hold in the wild on wetlands in Hawke's Bay, North Canterbury and Lake Ellesmere. Some live in semi-feral state in many town parks, such as Virginia Lake, Whanganui, and stragglers or escapees from private collections occasionally turn up in other wetlands.
Population: *c.* 150 in the wild; *c.* 80 at Lake Ellesmere, *c.* 20 in North Canterbury, *c.* 20 in Hawke's Bay, and the rest scattered widely through the country.
Conservation: Partially protected introduced species. Mute Swans once numbered several hundred birds in the wild, but the April 1968 *Wahine* storm destroyed much feeding habitat at their stronghold, Lake Ellesmere, and the population crashed. Ducks Unlimited has a captive breeding programme aimed at eventually releasing birds into the wild.
Breeding: Birds establish their territories in August and start building their nest in September. They usually nest solitarily, but at Harts Creek, Lake Ellesmere, they formerly nested in a colony, although each nest was screened by raupo from neighbouring nests. The nest is usually floating in shallow water or beside a slow-flowing stream or lake. It is a huge mound of grass and leaves of raupo, flax and rushes, topped with a shallow bowl lined with a little down.

Laying is from late September to December. They lay 4–7–11 white eggs (120 x 70mm, 350g) at 2-day intervals. The female alone incubates for *c.* 35 days. The eggs hatch within a day of one another, and both parents lead the cygnets to water within a further day and maintain guard through their development. The cygnets are initially covered in light grey down but slowly develop brownish-white juvenile plumage and fledge at 120–150 days old. In Britain, most females start breeding at 3 years old and most males begin at 4 years old. Once paired, they remain together for life. The oldest banded bird in Britain lived over 24 years.
Behaviour: Non-breeding and moulting Mute Swans form small flocks, but breeding adults usually remain as pairs and become very territorial when breeding; the cob (male) aggressively defends his pen (female) and nest from intruding birds and people by hissing at them and striking out with his wings, and they have been known to fight other cobs to the death. Despite their name, Mute Swans are quite vocal, with a variety of quiet honks, snorts and hisses.
Feeding: Diet is mainly leaves of submerged aquatic plants which they reach by upending willow leaves plucked from overhanging trees, or grass and clover grazed near the edge of the water. These are supplemented by some aquatic invertebrates and even the odd fish, tadpole or frog.
Reading: Birkhead, M. & Perrins, C. 1986. *The Mute Swan*. London: Croom Helm.

19. BLACK SWAN *Cygnus atratus* PLATE 4

Size: 120cm; male 6kg, female 5kg
Distribution: Native to southwestern and eastern Australia and to Tasmania. Although about 100 birds were introduced to New Zealand between 1864 and 1868, it is likely that some also arrived naturally in 1867, because the Black Swan population grew and spread very rapidly. By 1880, they were well established in the wild, and are now widespread and abundant throughout the main islands and on Chatham Island. Greatest numbers are on large lowland or coastal lakes and lagoons and on some estuaries, especially Kaipara Harbour, the lower Waikato Valley, Hawke's Bay, Lake Wairarapa, Farewell Spit, Lake Ellesmere, coastal Otago and Southland, and Te Whanga Lagoon (Chatham Island). Good numbers are also found on some inland lakes such as those in the Rotorua district, Lake Taupo and Ashburton Lakes. Banding and neck-collar studies in the 1980s showed that Black Swans in New Zealand were moderately sedentary and largely divided into 10 regional populations, each with a major nesting area and one or more coastal feeding and moulting areas. At Farewell Spit, the major moulting site in the country, about 10,000 birds from all around the mainland intermingle, although most come from the Wairarapa and Marlborough.
Population: In the early 1960s, well over 100,000 Black Swans were in New Zealand, with 70,000 on Lake Ellesmere alone, however, the April 1968 *Wahine* storm destroyed much feeding habitat at Lake Ellesmere and the population there crashed to fewer than 10,000 birds by 1978. In 1981, the national population was estimated to be 63,000 birds: 60,000 on the mainland and 3000 on Chatham Island, but by 2011 the national figure had dropped to about 50,000 birds.
Conservation: Partially protected introduced species. About 7000 birds are legally shot each year during the duck-shooting season; the number taken is strictly controlled with daily bag limits and seasons set independently for each region, depending on the population trends. Before numbers fell at Lake Ellesmere in the late 1960s, special culls of birds, commercial egg-collecting, or egg-pricking were sometimes necessary to keep their numbers in check because they create a nuisance grazing on and fouling pastures adjacent to some lakes.
Breeding: Black Swans have a long breeding season, which varies according to local conditions and whether the pairs are solitary or in colonies. Solitary pairs breeding in small wetlands and large deep lakes usually nest in July–October, whereas colonial birds breeding near large shallow wetlands breed only when the lake level starts to drop, at any time from September to January. The nest is usually on land within 100m of a lake. It is a huge mound of grasses and leaves of raupo, flax and rushes, topped with a shallow bowl lined with a little down.

The clutch is of 3–**6**–14 pale green eggs (104 x 67mm, 250g), but clutches of over 10 eggs are probably laid by more than one female. The first three eggs are laid *c.* 30 hours apart, thereafter daily. Both birds share incubation in spells of 3–4 hours through the day, but the female generally incubates at night. The incubation period is 32–**36**–43 days. The eggs hatch during less than 48 hours, and both parents lead the cygnets to water within a further day.

Solitary pairs usually guard their brood on territory throughout their development, but sometimes shift to a large body of open water for safety; however, cygnets from colonies form large crèches of up to 40 birds, guarded by some of the adults. The cygnets are initially covered in light grey down, but they slowly develop the grey-brown juvenile plumage and fledge at 95–140 days old. Young birds start breeding when 2–4 years old. The oldest banded bird in New Zealand lived at least 29 years.
Behaviour: Non-breeding and moulting Black Swans form loose flocks of up to several thousand birds. In solitary pairs, the male aggressively defends a large feeding territory around the nest. Colonies of up to 5000 nests have been recorded, and only the nest site is defended. The Black Swan is quite vocal, with a musical and far-reaching bugle call given both in flight and on the water, especially at night.
Feeding: Diet is mainly leaves of submerged aquatic plants such as *Ruppia*, *Egeria*, *Elodia*, *Potamogeton*, *Myriophyllum* and *Zostera*, which they reach by upending, but they also graze on lake-side pasture grasses and clover.
Reading: Miers, K. H. & Williams, M. 1969. *Wildfowl* 20: 23–32. Williams, M. 1977. *Aust Wildl Res* 4: 289–299. Williams, M. 1979. *NZ J Ecol* 2: 34–41.

20. CAPE BARREN GOOSE *Cereopsis novaehollandiae* PLATE 4

Size: 87cm, 5kg
Distribution: Natural range is southern Australia, where they are rare but increasing with improvement of habitat on their main breeding islands. They breed mainly in grassland or wetlands on islands in Bass Strait, in the Spencer Gulf of South Australia and in the Recherche Archipelago off Western Australia, and many birds migrate to the mainland of Australia after their winter breeding season. They were first liberated at Lake Hawea in 1914, and a few persisted in open grassland and tussockland in the district until about 1946. Birds recorded from Fiordland in 1934, 1947, 1967 and 1990, Mackenzie Basin (1966), South Auckland (1986) and Takaka (1998) are considered vagrants from Australia, but most sightings are probably of birds released or escaped from private collections. A few have become established in the wild around the Kaipara Harbour, near Waikanae, at St Annes Lagoon (North Canterbury) and in lowland Canterbury.
Breeding: Not studied in New Zealand, except that goslings have been seen in spring. In Australia, they lay 3–**4**–6 creamy-white eggs (83 x 55mm) in July–August. Incubation by the female takes *c.* 35 days. Goslings leave the nest soon after hatching and can fly at *c.* 75 days old.
Behaviour: Generally feed on land, and only rarely swim. They are usually silent on the ground, but both sexes give a low-pitched grunt in flight, and the male also gives a high-pitched trumpet call.
Feeding: Mainly graze grasses, legumes, weeds and herbs in the open, often well away from standing water.
Reading: Williams, G. R. 1968. *Notornis* 15: 66–69.

21. FERAL GOOSE *Anser anser* PLATE 4

Other names: Greylag Goose, Domestic Goose
Size: 80cm, 3kg
Distribution: Natural range of the wild ancestor of this bird is the wetlands and farmland of Eurasia, from Iceland to China. Greylag Geese have been domesticated for centuries and were brought to New Zealand with the early European settlers. In many parts of the country, they have become truly feral, and numerous others live in a semi-feral state at city parks and on farms.
Population: No information available. Flocks of 100+ birds have been recorded at Lake Wairarapa, and 50+ at many other large lakes and in pastoral farmland.
Breeding: Not studied in New Zealand. In Europe, their usual clutch is of 4–**6** creamy-white eggs (85 x 58mm), incubated by the female for *c.* 30 days. Goslings leave the nest soon after hatching and can fly by *c.* 55 days old. They sometimes nest in dense colonies, with nests a few metres apart in reed beds or in thick grass under willows.
Behaviour: In New Zealand, Feral Geese are usually seen in flocks at lakes, at estuaries or on pastoral farmland. They make loud honks both on the ground and in flight.
Feeding: Graze on grass, clover and weeds, usually away from water.

22. CANADA GOOSE *Branta canadensis* PLATE 4

Size: 83cm; male 5.4kg, female 4.5kg
Geographical variation: 12 subspecies; the form in New Zealand is the Giant Canada Goose *maxima* from northern and central states of the USA (North Dakota to Arkansas), although other subspecies (*tavernii* and *canadensis*) from other parts of North America may have mixed with it.
Distribution: Natural range is North America and northeastern Asia (Kamchatka Peninsula and Japan). They were first introduced to New Zealand from North America in 1876, but only with 50 birds introduced in 1905 and other liberations up to 1920 did the present population become established. They are abundant in the wild in the eastern South Island from Marlborough to North Otago (especially at Lake Ellesmere) and common in drier tussock country of eastern Fiordland. Early attempts to introduce Canada Geese to the North Island failed, but they have become well established in the wild since the 1970s in the Waikato, Taupo–Ohakune area, northern Hawke's Bay, coastal Manawatu, and especially near Lake Wairarapa.

In the South Island, most birds breed near high-country lakes and rivers, but many adults and juveniles from inland Marlborough to the Mackenzie Basin migrate to Lake Ellesmere and other coastal lakes and estuaries in November–February for the autumn moult, and then stay through the winter to early September. Recently, more birds have remained on high-country lakes all year, moulting on inland lakes and feeding on pastures nearby, and some breed on coastal lakes such as Ellesmere and nearby Forsyth. In the North Island, most birds are resident on coastal lakes such as Whakaki Lagoon (near Wairoa) and Lake Wairarapa. Vagrants have been recorded from the Kermadec, Chatham and Auckland islands, and also Lord Howe Island, New Caledonia and mainland Australia.

Population: The post-shooting season population is *c.* 60,000 birds: 20,000 in the North Island and 40,000 in the South Island, including 10,000–15,000 overwintering on Lake Ellesmere.

Conservation: Unprotected introduced species. Up to 30,000 birds are shot each year, mainly during the normal May–July shooting season, but also when they damage arable crops such as peas and grain or eat grass and foul lake-side pastures. Sometimes special culls of moulting birds or egg-pricking have been necessary to keep numbers under control in some districts.

Breeding: Birds return to their breeding sites in early September, and the gander aggressively defends a territory of about a hectare while the female builds the nest in a site with good visibility. Laying is mainly from mid-September to late October, but replacement clutches are laid into January. They lay 2–**4–5**–10 white eggs (88 x 58mm, 200g), daily in a shallow bowl in a pile of grass and rushes gathered from within reach of the nest. The bowl is lined with feathers. Incubation, by the female only, takes 24–**26**–30 days and the eggs hatch synchronously. The goslings, which are initially covered in yellow and brown down, are led from the nest within a day of hatching and are guarded by both parents or join crèches of up to 50 goslings during the *c.* 70 days to fledging. Family groups remain together until the next breeding season, when the young are driven away. They usually start breeding at 3 years old. Most pairs remain together from year to year and return to the same nesting area each year unless nesting is disrupted. About 30% of adult Canada Geese die each year (20% shot and 10% of natural causes), giving a life expectancy of 2.8 years, but the oldest banded bird lived over 30 years.

Behaviour: When not breeding, they form flocks of up to 2000 birds and are usually very wary. Flocks are often noisy, with a constant chorus of honking as birds maintain contact, especially when they are flying. The main flight call is a musical double honk 'ah-honk'.

Feeding: Mainly graze on land and plants such as grass, clover, lucerne and brassicas. They also eat wetland and aquatic plants, especially rushes and *Egeria*, *Elodia*, and *Potamogeton*. Sometimes feed on stubble or standing crops of peas or grain, and flocks can cause considerable damage.

Reading: Imber, M. J. 1971. *Notornis* 18: 253–261.

23. PINK-EARED DUCK *Malacorhynchus membranaceus* PLATE 7

Size: 40cm, 400g

Distribution: Breeds only in Australia, mainly in the south and especially in the Murray–Darling Basin of inland New South Wales and Victoria. They disperse widely within Australia in response to inland rains and droughts, but are not common on the eastern seaboard and are only a rare visitor to Tasmania. One New Zealand record – an immature bird at Mangere Sewage Ponds, Auckland (June–July 1990).

Feeding: In Australia, Pink-eared Ducks are mainly on shallow stagnant lakes and on sewage ponds. They feed on invertebrates (especially chironomid larvae) and seeds obtained by sieving food onto comb-like lamellae inside the bill. The distinctive bill flaps are apparently used to feel invertebrates touching the bill.

Reading: Eller, G. J. 1991. *Notornis* 38: 109–110.

24. PARADISE SHELDUCK *Tadorna variegata* PLATE 5

Other names: Putangitangi, Pari

Size: 63cm; male 1700g, female 1400g

Distribution: Breeds only in New Zealand. Widely distributed in hill-country pasture, arable land, tussockland and wetlands throughout the mainland and on offshore islands with lakes or farmland such as Great Barrier, Kapiti and Stewart islands. Although they appear in subfossil and midden deposits in the Chathams, the only recent record is of one bird in January 1984. A male visited Raoul Island in October 1995, and five visited Lord Howe Island for several months from March 1950. In the North Island, the main concentrations are in Northland, in hill country of Gisborne–Hawke's Bay and Whanganui–Rangitikei, on the Manawatu dune lakes and in the Wairarapa. In the South Island, most are in coastal Marlborough, along the eastern foothills of the Southern Alps, and on the Southland plains.

Adult Paradise Shelduck are generally sedentary, but movements are complex and depend in part on the habitats being used; those breeding in tussocklands tend to be more mobile than those breeding in hill-country farmland. All birds vacate their territories and flock sites for the annual moult. Large flocks of 1000+ birds gather in December–February at traditional moulting sites on farm ponds, lakes, tarns and riverbeds. Individuals stay for 6–8 weeks and the big flocks break up in March–April. Juvenile females tend to return to breed in their natal area, but juvenile males disperse widely and often settle over 100km away from their natal area.

Population: In 2011, the population was *c.* 620,000 birds, of which *c.* 200,000 are shot annually.

Conservation: Partially protected endemic. During the summer moult, they were important food for Maori and many were killed at traditional moulting sites. Paradise Shelducks were uncommon in the 1800s and largely restricted to the eastern and southern South Island. The conversion of native forest to exotic pasture, the construction of farm ponds, the introduction of strict controls on their harvest in 1868 and liberations of Southland birds into the central North Island between 1916 and 1921 more than outweighed the effects of introduced predators and drainage of natural wetlands. They have increased greatly through the 1900s, and especially since 1990. Regional bag limits and seasons are now closely linked to productivity and movements of birds in each part of the country.

Breeding: Paradise Shelducks are found as territorial pairs except during the communal moult in summer. Birds re-establish their territory in March–April; it is often centred on a rush-covered soak, small farm pond or part of a larger lake or riverbed with an open view. The male aggressively defends the territory and maintains a lookout for predators while the female incubates. The nest is in a hollow log, under fallen logs, in a hayshed, or in a hole in the ground, but in forest patches some birds nest up to 25m above the ground in a tree hole. Laying is mostly in August–September, but a few clutches are laid into November. The clutch is of 5–**9**–15 white eggs (67 x 49mm, 85g), laid daily, but clutches of 12+ eggs are probably laid by more than one female. Clutches are only rarely replaced, but two pairs can use the same area of water, giving the false impression that Paradise Shelducks are double-brooded. The female incubates for 30–35 days, during which she leaves the nest 2–3 times a day for about an hour at a time. The eggs hatch about the same time, but late-hatching eggs are often abandoned when the female leads the brood of ducklings to open water, which can be over a kilometre away.

The ducklings have a striking pattern of brown and white down, but when they fledge at 55–65 days old they resemble adult males, except females have white patches around the eyes and base of the bill. These patches expand to the whole head after another couple of months and the body colour gradually lightens.

Most Paradise Shelducks start breeding when 2 years old, but females often delay until they are 3 years old. Pairs remain together from year to year and return to the same nesting area each year. If one bird dies, the mate occupies the same territory and re-mates. About 35% of breeding adults die each year, giving a life expectancy of 2.3 years, however, some birds live much longer, with the oldest banded bird living at least 23 years.

Behaviour: Paradise Shelducks are usually in pairs, but non-breeders flock during the breeding season, when they start their moult, and large flocks of 1000+ breeders and fledglings form for a couple of months during the summer moult. Pairs are alert, and from a high point on the ground or while circling overhead they duet their loud alarm calls: the male's deep 'zonk-zonk . . .' and the female's shrill, penetrating 'zeek, zeek . . .' Both sexes give a piercing flock call when flying to join a flock or when flying birds are approaching.

Feeding: Graze on grass and clover, and also feed on grass and weed seeds and stubble or standing crops of peas or grain. Aquatic vegetation is obtained from the surface or by upending. Flocks can sometimes cause considerable damage to young pasture and hay and grain crops, especially near major moulting sites.

Reading: Barker, R. J. 1990. *Notornis* 37: 173–181. Williams, M. J. 1972. *Wildfowl* 23: 94–102. Williams, M. J. 1979. *Notornis* 26: 213–272. Williams, M. J. 1979. *Notornis* 26: 369–390.

25. CHESTNUT-BREASTED SHELDUCK *Tadorna tadornoides* PLATE 5

Other names: Australian Shelduck, Mountain Duck

Size: 65cm; male 1600g, female 1300g

Distribution: Breeds in southwestern and southeastern Australia and in Tasmania. They are mainly sedentary, although birds move several hundred kilometres between breeding territories and traditional moulting sites, including crossing Bass Strait. In drought years, some are forced to seek more distant moulting sites; vagrants reach northern states and Norfolk Island.

First recorded in New Zealand at Hokitika in January 1973, but small invasions occurred in 1982–83 and 1984–85, with many records of singles and some flocks of up to 22 birds throughout the North and South islands, on The Snares and on Auckland and Campbell islands in 1982–86. During this period, a pair with half-grown young near Lake Tekapo in January 1985 is the only confirmed breeding record. The number seen gradually declined, except around Lakes Elterwater and Grassmere in coastal Marlborough, where a few, including immature birds, were seen regularly in late summer and autumn during the 1990s. Further individuals or small flocks have appeared from time to time, e.g. a pair at Raoul Island (March 1994), a pair at Coopers Lagoon, Canterbury (June 1995), three on Pitt Island (December 1997), three in the coastal Manawatu (March–April 1998), two at Normanby Lake, South Canterbury (March–April 2003), and two at The Neck, Stewart Island (December 2013).

Population: In 1983, at least 56 birds were in New Zealand, but 10 years later there were probably fewer than 20 birds, mostly in Marlborough, and despite having bred at least once, it is now considered a vagrant.

Breeding: Not studied in New Zealand, except that half-grown young in January point to laying in October–November. In Australia, laying is mostly in July–October, extending later in wet seasons. The nest is usually in a hole in a living or dead tree, in a hole in the ground, or under dense bushes. The clutch is 4–**9**–19 white eggs (69 x 49mm, 88g), laid daily, but those of 10+ eggs are probably laid by more than one female. The female incubates for 30–33 days and the ducklings are led from the nest to open water, which can be over a kilometre away. The ducklings have a striking pattern of brown and white down, but when the chicks fledge at *c.* 70 days old, they look like the adult but are smaller, duller and have white flecking on the face, lack the white collar and have a light brown chest and upper back.

Behaviour: In New Zealand, Chestnut-breasted Shelducks have been seen mainly in small flocks at lakes likely to be used as moulting sites, seldom at places where they are likely to breed. The male's alarm call, a loud, deep honk, is answered by the female's higher-pitched call.

Feeding: Graze on grass, clover and weeds, and also feed on grass and weed seeds, and on aquatic vegetation, which they obtain from on the surface or by upending.

Reading: Heather, B. D. 1987. *Notornis* 34: 71–77.

26. NEW ZEALAND MERGANSER *Mergus australis* PLATE 84

Other names: Auckland Island Merganser, Southern Merganser

Size: 58cm; male 650g, female 550g

Distribution: Extinct. Subfossil bones have been found in natural sites and Maori middens widely on the North, South, Stewart and Chatham islands, showing that Maori hunters and their accompanying dogs probably brought about their extinction on the mainland and at the Chathams. The only historical records are from Auckland and Adams islands of the Auckland Islands group. European attempts at settlement, together with introduced mammals, led to their decline on the Auckland Islands, but the final cause of their extinction was the shooting of about 30 birds for museum and private collections. The last pair was shot in January 1902. Extensive searches since 1907 failed to find any birds.

Breeding: The nest, eggs and clutch size of New Zealand Mergansers were not described. Two broods of four newly hatched and nearly fledged ducklings (which lacked the patterned down of northern mergansers) were recorded in January, implying egg-laying in late October–November.

Behaviour: Although their wings were reduced, they could fly. They lived on the fiord-like inlets of the eastern and southern coasts of Carnley Harbour, and also at the head of small estuaries and pools of streams.

Feeding: Little is known. They apparently fed in both freshwater and marine environments on fish, crustaceans, shellfish and marine worms. As with all mergansers, they used the backward-facing serrations on both mandibles to seize and hold their prey.

Reading: Kear, J. & Scarlett, R. J. 1970. *Wildfowl* 21: 78–86. Livesey, B. C. 1989. *Wilson Bull.* 101: 410–435. Williams, M. 2012. *Wildfowl* 62: 3–36. Williams, G. R. & Weller, M. W. 1974. *Notornis* 21: 247–249. Williams, M. et al. 2012. *Wildfowl* 62: 190–203.

27. AUSTRALIAN WOOD DUCK *Chenonetta jubata* PLATE 5

Other names: Maned Duck, Maned Goose
Size: 48cm, 800g
Distribution: Breeds widely in Australia and Tasmania. They are highly nomadic, following rains and floods in wet years to colonise temporary wetlands, and then returning to permanent water in southwestern Australia and along the eastern seaboard. Vagrant to New Zealand, with eight accepted records of lone birds: Glendhu, Wanaka (1910); Orawia, Southland (1944); Wairau River, Marlborough (1980); The Snares (1982–86); Otapiri, Southland (2002); Nelson Sewage Ponds (2010); Bromley Sewage Ponds, Christchurch (2011); and Horseshoe Lake, Christchurch (2011).
Feeding: In Australia, they prefer grassland with scattered trees near water, where they graze on grass, clover and other green foliage. They sometimes graze in shallow water on lagoon fringes, on grain stubble and in city parks.

28. BLUE DUCK *Hymenolaimus malacorhynchos* PLATE 5

Other name: Whio
Size: 53cm; male 900g, female 750g
Distribution: New Zealand only. They are mainly restricted to fast-flowing and turbulent rivers and streams in forested hill country or mountains, but are occasionally seen on mountain tarns or on sheltered harbours of Fiordland. In the North Island, they are found on rivers of the Volcanic Plateau and from the Raukumara Range to the northern Ruahine Range. They have been recently reintroduced to Egmont National Park. In the South Island, they are widespread on rivers of northwestern Nelson, the Paparoa Range and Fiordland, and in the headwaters of rivers in the Southern Alps, particularly on the western side.

Colour-banding studies have shown that breeding birds remain on their territories for life, whereas juveniles disperse up or down their natal river and attempt to settle and establish territories close to their natal territory, but will occasionally shift between catchments, even including 1000m ascents to cross mountain passes. The ability of Blue Ducks to home over long distances was shown by a pair that flew over 100km from Mt Taranaki back to their territory near Ohakune within a few days.
Population: *c.* 2000–4000 birds: up to 1500 in the North Island, mainly in and around Tongariro National Park, and up to 2500 in the South Island, widely scattered.
Conservation: Protected vulnerable endemic. The range and numbers of Blue Ducks have declined since European settlement, especially in the North Island. Clearance of lowland forest and some upland forest, grazing of riverside vegetation, and introduced predators have contributed to the decline. Introduced trout may compete for aquatic invertebrates, and the water flow of some rivers has been altered by hydroelectric dams. Aerial 1080 operations and stoat trapping along key rivers have led to improved productivity, especially in the central North Island and in the Clinton Valley on the Milford Track. Blue Ducks are being bred in captivity for release into suitable habitats such as Egmont National Park.
Breeding: Breeding adults remain on their territory all year. The nest is a simple bowl of twigs, grass and down in a hollow log, small cavity or under dense vegetation near a steep stream bank. Laying is in July–December, mostly late August–November. Many late nests are replacement clutches. They lay 3–**6**–9 creamy white eggs (65 x 45mm, 72g) at 48-hour intervals. The female incubates for 33–**34**–35 days while the male stands guard nearby.

The young are initially covered in pale creamy-white and olive-grey down. They are quickly led to the stream by the female, and can swim and dive well in fast-flowing water. They are guarded by both parents during their 10–12 week fledging period. Chicks disperse from the territory soon after fledging. Breeding in their first year of life has been recorded, but most do not manage to establish a territory and obtain a partner until their second year. The oldest Blue Duck recorded in the wild lived over 13 years.
Behaviour: Usually seen in pairs, occupying the same short stretch of river year after year. Records from the 1880s suggested that non-territorial birds sometimes flocked, but with declining numbers this is now not seen. They are usually seen in the early morning and late afternoon fossicking among rapids and small ponds in the lee of large boulders, and are rarely observed in flight. When they do fly, they fly low and direct by day, but at night they can sometimes be heard flying 50+m above the ground. Their flight call, and the male territorial call, is a shrill, somewhat hoarse whistle: 'whio' or 'whio-whio'; the female has a rattling growl: 'cr-ack'.

Feeding: Blue Ducks dabble, dive and upend in the rapidly flowing white water of mountain streams and rivers. Diet is almost entirely aquatic invertebrates; mostly chironomid larvae and cased caddisfly larvae obtained from the downstream side of stones and boulders. They occasionally catch emerging adult insects on the surface and also take some algae and fruit.

Reading: Harding, M. A. 1994. *Notornis* 41: 293–295. Kear, J. & Steel, T. H. 1971. *Notornis* 18: 187–198. Whitehead, A. L. et al. 2008. *Biol. Cons.* 141: 2784–2794. Williams, M. J. 1980. *Notornis* 26: 306–307. Williams, M. 1991. *Wildfowl* 42: 63–86. Young, D. 2006. *Whio: Saving New Zealand's Blue Duck*. Nelson: Craig Potton Publishing.

29. GREY TEAL *Anas gracilis* PLATE 6

Other name: Tete
Size: 43cm; male 505g, female 470g
Distribution: Breed only in Australia and New Zealand, and are vagrants to Indonesia, New Guinea, the Solomons and New Caledonia. In New Zealand, they were rare and local until about the 1950s, but several natural irruptions from Australia (notably in 1957 when a drought followed a year with excellent inland breeding) and the provision of nest boxes has led to a dramatic increase in numbers and range of the species. They are now common in shallow coastal lakes and lagoons with good margins of swamp and willows, in South Auckland and northern Waikato, Hawke's Bay, Manawatu, Wairarapa and the eastern South Island from Marlborough to Southland. They are also in moderate numbers on the Rotorua lakes and along the eastern foothills of the Southern Alps. After breeding, they often gather at estuaries to feed on exposed mudflats. They have been recorded on some offshore islands and most outlying islands: Chatham Island (1951, 1988), The Snares (2 in 1987), Enderby Island, Auckland Islands (2012), and Campbell Island (2012). Banding studies show that although some Grey Teal are sedentary, many are highly mobile and disperse widely in New Zealand. A bird banded in southern Australia was shot in the Waikato in 1957, and a bird banded at Mangere Sewage Ponds was shot 125km away the following day.
Population: In 1976, there were estimated to be 20,000 birds in New Zealand, but by 2005 the population had risen to well over 50,000, and has probably continued to increase.
Conservation: Protected native. Each year, even though about 6% of the population is shot accidentally in the duck-shooting season, the population has grown strongly.
Breeding: Pairs remain together all year, but most join large flocks for the late summer moult and then remain in flocks until July. In Australia, breeding is closely linked to rainfall, but in New Zealand it is more seasonal although still related to water levels. Laying is mostly in June–September, but replacement clutches can be laid through to January. The nest is a bowl of grass with a lining of down added as incubation proceeds. It is generally close to water and usually in a tree hole, nest box or among dense vegetation, e.g. *Carex secta.* They lay 5–7–9 creamy eggs (50 x 36mm), laid about dawn each day. The male guards the female during laying and incubation. The female incubates for 25–31 days. The pair leads the ducklings to water soon after they hatch. They are initially covered in dark grey-brown down with off-white facial markings and underparts, but quickly develop feathers and fledge at 35–40 days old and then disperse widely. About 68% die before they start breeding at 1 year old. Adults live on average about 3 years, but some birds live much longer; the oldest recorded in the wild in New Zealand being over 9 years old, but a bird in Australia lived at least 21 years.
Behaviour: Normally seen in small flocks of 10–50 birds, but flocks of 1000+ are recorded in autumn at Lake Wairarapa, Lake Ellesmere and at the Bromley Sewage Ponds, Christchurch. Birds in flocks chatter almost constantly. Males give a loud, short whistle and females a rapid 'cuck-cuck-cuck' call.
Feeding: Diet is mainly seeds of aquatic plants and invertebrates such as water beetles and larvae of midges, caddisflies and mosquitoes, obtained by dabbling in shallow water or by dredging exposed lake-side or estuarine mudflats and filtering out the food.
Reading: Mills, J. A. 1976. *NZ J Zool* 3: 261–267.

30. CHESTNUT TEAL *Anas castanea* PLATE 6

Size: Male 45cm, 680g; female 40cm, 590g
Distribution: Breeds only in Australia; mainly in the southwest and southeast, and particularly in coastal wetlands of Victoria and Tasmania. Most breed on small freshwater lakes but move to large lakes and estuaries after breeding. They are among the few ducks that regularly use very saline habitats. Vagrant to northern Australia, New Guinea, Lord Howe Island and New Zealand. One probable Chestnut Teal was seen at the Waikanae Estuary on 31 January 1991, and an immature bird subsequently wintered at the Manawatu Estuary from June 1991; in winter 1992, up to three birds (two immature males and an immature female) were seen at the Manawatu Estuary. Because a few adults or immatures appeared there in most subsequent years to 2003 during the annual influx of Grey Teal during the duck-shooting season, it is likely that they bred somewhere in the Manawatu wetlands. Singles at Karitane, Otago (January 1993); Kowai River, Canterbury (August 1993); Balclutha (February 2003); Coatesville, Auckland (October 2003); Bromley Sewage Ponds, Christchurch (March 2010); and Mangere Sewage Ponds, Auckland (May 2010).
Feeding: In Australia, their preferred habitats are coastal wetlands, including estuaries and brackish lagoons. They eat seeds and invertebrates by dabbling in shallow water or by dredging in mud on exposed mudflats or at the front edge of the rising tide.
Reading: Moore, J. & Moore, M. 1992. *Notornis* 39: 289–292.

31. BROWN TEAL *Anas chlorotis* PLATE 6

Other name: Pateke
Size: 48cm; male 650g, female 580g
Distribution: Breeds only in New Zealand; one bird was seen in New Caledonia three years in a row. The distribution of subfossil remains shows that Brown Teal were once very widely distributed throughout New Zealand, including in forested sites well away from permanent water. By the time of European settlement, they were still widely distributed, but largely confined to lowland swamps and swamp forest, from Northland to Stewart Island, and on the Chatham Islands, but scarce in the eastern South Island. Their numbers and range have declined dramatically as a result of drainage of wetlands, clearance of lowland forests, hunting and introduced predators. However, successful conservation management has led to a recent but sustained recovery. Their natural stronghold is Great Barrier Island and on the east coast of Northland, from the Bay of Islands to Tutukaka. Small natural populations persist on Little Barrier and Great Mercury islands and on the Coromandel Peninsula. In the South Island, a few may survive in Fiordland, but they have not been seen since 1999. Not seen on the Chatham Islands since 1925, nor on Stewart Island since 1980.

Successfully introduced to Kapiti Island (1968, 2000–01); Tiritiri Matangi Island (1987–2002); Russell (1990s); Mana Island (2000–01); Zealandia, Wellington (2000–01); Port Charles, Coromandel (2003–07); Mayor Island (2006–08); Tawharanui, North Auckland (2008–10); and Cape Kidnappers (2008–10). Many other introductions to mainland sites have failed due to predation by mustelids, cats and dogs.
Population: 2000–2500 birds in 2013; 600+ on Great Barrier Island, 500+ in eastern Northland, 700+ on the Coromandel Peninsula, 200+ in captivity and 200+ scattered widely through the rest of the country.
Conservation: Protected endemic. The decline of Brown Teal was probably caused by predation by introduced cats, dogs and mustelids, the drainage of prime lowland swamp habitats and the harvest of birds until they were protected in 1921. Conservation efforts for Brown Teal are aimed at controlling mammalian predators in suitable coastal habitat in Northland, Great Barrier Island, and at Moehau, Coromandel Peninsula, and by translocations to sites free of mammalian predators, or where predator control is done regularly. Ducks Unlimited has had great success in breeding Brown Teal in captivity, but many releases of captive-bred birds on the mainland have failed because of predation.
Breeding: Most Brown Teal lay in July–September, but clutches can be laid at almost any time of year. They lay 3–**5–6**–9 cream eggs (60 x 43mm, 61g) at about 1.5-day intervals. The nest is a down-lined bowl of grass under dense vegetation such as *Carex*, rush, fern or kikuyu grass. The male guards the territory while the female incubates for 27–**28**–30 days. The precocial ducklings leave the nest within 24 hours of hatching, and are mainly tended by the female, however the male often accompanies the female and the brood. The fledging

period is 50–55 days. The oldest Brown Teal in captivity lived 21 years.

Behaviour: Brown Teal are strongly territorial during the breeding season but some pairs, unpaired adults and juveniles form flocks at traditional sites in summer. These flocks break up in winter, but juvenile and unpaired birds continue to use the roosting sites during the breeding season. The males give soft, high-pitched wheezy whistles and popping calls; females give low quacks and growls.

Feeding: Diverse diet of terrestrial, freshwater and marine invertebrates and vegetation. Main invertebrate foods are gastropods, insects, earthworms, polychaete worms, crustaceans and molluscs taken by dabbling from just below the water surface or in mud in shallow water of estuaries, freshwater wetlands, and peaty or muddy pools or trickles on land. They also eat substantial amounts of terrestrial and aquatic vegetation, especially seeds of sedge and leaves of white clover while foraging on land, reaching up to overhanging vegetation.

Reading: Barker, D. & Williams, M. 2002. *Notornis* 49: 199–208. Hayes, F. N. & Williams, M. J. 1982. *Wildfowl* 33: 73–80. Kennedy, M. & Spencer, H. G. 2000. *Auk* 117: 154–163. Moore, S. J. et al. 2006. *NZ J Ecol* 30: 397–403. Weller, M. J. 1974. *Notornis* 21: 25–35. Weller, M. J. 1975. *Auk* 92: 280–297. Williams, M. 1995. *Notornis* 42: 219–262. Williams, M. 2002. *Notornis* 49: 199–208. Williams, M. et al. 1991. *Acta XX Cong Int Orn*: 876–884.

32. AUCKLAND ISLANDS TEAL *Anas aucklandica* PLATE 6

Size: 45cm; male 550g, female 420g

Distribution: New Zealand only. The Auckland Islands Teal has gone from the main Auckland Island, but remains on Enderby, Rose, Ewing, Dundas, Adams and Disappointment islands. The 12 birds transferred to Kapiti Island in 1907 failed to survive there.

Population: 1000+ birds.

Conservation: Protected vulnerable endemic. Auckland Islands Teal quickly declined on Auckland Island after cats and pigs arrived in the early 1800s, but a few persisted or recolonised until the last sighting in 1942. They survived in good numbers on many offshore islands in the group. The populations have increased on Rose and Enderby islands following the eradication of rabbits in 1993, due to an increase in grasses and rushes, which provide more food and better cover from predatory Southern Skuas. Auckland Islands Teal have been bred successfully in captivity.

Breeding: In December to February, Auckland Islands Teal lay 3–**4**–5 cream eggs (64 x 45mm, 75g) at intervals of 2–3 days. The nest is a down-lined bowl of sedge or grass under dense vegetation such as *Carex*, fern or tussock. The male guards the territory while the female incubates for 30–**33**–35 days. The precocial ducklings leave the nest within 24 hours, and fledge after 55–70 days. The oldest Auckland Islands Teal in captivity lived 12 years.

Behaviour: Mainly crepuscular; some are active in daylight under forest cover, but most activity is at dawn and dusk and into the night. They are strongly territorial during the breeding season and pairs remain on territory all year, but juveniles and unpaired adults form small flocks in protected bays. The males give soft, high-pitched wheezy whistles and popping calls; females give low quacks and growls.

Feeding: Diet has not been studied, but is mainly aquatic or marine invertebrates taken by dabbling in mud in shallow water of peaty pools and elephant seal wallows, trickles or water courses on land, or fossicking in rock pools on wave platforms or amongst rotting seaweed along the shoreline of sheltered bays.

Reading: Scott, D. 1971. *Wildfowl* 22: 44–45. Williams, M. 1986. *Wildfowl* 37: 63–70. Williams, M. 1995. *Notornis* 42: 219–262.

33. CAMPBELL ISLANDS TEAL *Anas nesiotis* PLATE 6

Size: 43cm; male 450g, female 350g

Distribution: New Zealand only. The Campbell Islands Teal was discovered in 1855, but rarely seen until a small population was found on Dent Island in 1975. Following a successful captive-breeding programme at Pukaha Mount Bruce and Peacock Springs, they were first introduced to Codfish Island, and then 150 captive-bred and Codfish Island-bred birds were reintroduced to Campbell Island in 2004–06, following the eradication of Norway rats there in 2001. They are now distributed widely around the coast of Campbell Island, especially in the sheltered harbours,

but also inland along creeks and around Six Foot Lake.
Population: *c.* 150 birds in 2009: Campbell Island *c.* 100 birds; Dent Island < 30 birds; Codfish Island < 30 birds.
Conservation: Protected critically endangered endemic. The species would have been extinct except that a small population persisted for over 100 years on 23ha Dent Island off the west coast of Campbell Island. Eleven birds, eight males and three females, were transferred to captivity in 1984 and 1990. Initially breeding was poor, but one female bred and she founded the entire captive stock. In 1999–2000, 24 captive birds were released on Codfish Island, as a temporary holding site pending successful eradication of Norway rats from 11,268ha Campbell Island, which was duly accomplished in 2001. A total of 150 Campbell Islands Teal were returned to Campbell Island in 2004–06, and they have bred and become established. A few birds from Dent Island have swum the 3km to join them on main Campbell Island.
Breeding: Campbell Islands Teal lay 1–**3**–**4**–6 cream eggs (63 x 43mm; 65g) in October–February. In captivity, eggs are laid at 2–2.5-day intervals. The nest is a down-lined bowl of sedge and grass hidden under dense vegetation at the base of a sedge or fern. The male guards the territory while the female incubates. In captivity, the incubation period is 30–**32**–34 days, the precocial ducklings leave the nest within a day of hatching, and fledging period is 55–70 days.
Behaviour: Mainly crepuscular; some are active in daylight, but most activity is at dawn and dusk and into the night. They are strongly territorial during the breeding season and pairs remain on territory all year, but juveniles and unpaired adults form small flocks. The males give soft, high-pitched wheezy whistles and popping calls; females give low quacks and growls.
Feeding: Diet has not been studied, but is mainly aquatic or marine invertebrates taken by dabbling in mud in shallow water of peaty pools and elephant seal wallows, trickles on land, or fossicking amongst rotting seaweed along the shoreline.
Reading: Gummer, H. & Williams, M. 1999. *Wildfowl* 50: 133–138. McLellan, P. & Gummer, H. 2006. *Cons Evidence* 3: 61–63. Williams, M. J. & Robertson, C. J. R. 1996. *Wildfowl* 47: 134–165.

34. NORTHERN PINTAIL *Anas acuta* — PLATE 7

Size: 55cm, excluding 10cm tail streamers in adult male; 800g
Distribution: Breeds in the Arctic from northern Scandinavia to Siberia, and in Alaska and northern Canada. Migrates south to winter mainly between 40° N and the equator, but some overshoot to reach Australia, New Guinea, Micronesia and Polynesia. One New Zealand record – a male in breeding plumage at Farewell Spit (October 1997).
Behaviour: Often gregarious – the bird seen on Farewell Spit was with Mallards. Holds neck very high when alert. Feeds on aquatic plants by upending. Usually silent.
Reading: Petyt, C. 1999. *Notornis* 46: 298–299.

35. MALLARD *Anas platyrhynchos* — PLATE 8

Size: 58cm; male 1300g, female 1100g
Geographical variation: Mallards in New Zealand were derived from both European and North American stock (*platyrhynchos*). In New Zealand they interbreed with Grey Ducks (*A. superciliosa*), and hybrids are common.
Distribution: Natural range is across the temperate Northern Hemisphere in Europe, Asia and North America. Birds of British game-farm stock were first introduced to New Zealand from Australia in 1867. Acclimatisation societies made many liberations up to about 1918, particularly in the southern South Island, but Mallards were not particularly successful until they were intensively bred and liberated in the 1930s and 1940s, and North American birds were introduced. Liberations continued up to 1974, by which time Mallards had become the most numerous and widespread waterfowl species on the New Zealand mainland, using a wide variety of wetlands from town parks and small farm ponds to rivers and estuaries. They have colonised many offshore islands and the Chatham, Antipodes, Snares, Auckland and Campbell island groups. Banding studies show that Mallards disperse widely throughout New Zealand, and one bird banded in Otago was shot in South Australia 16 months later.
Population: Very common. About 500,000 are legally shot each year. The Mallard population grew until about 1985, but has declined since.
Conservation: Partially protected introduced game

bird. Legally harvested in the duck shooting season, with the take controlled by daily bag limits for licensed hunters, and legally shot under permit when they damage farm crops.

Breeding: Pair formation begins in the autumn flocks, and by July pairs have formed and feeding territories are established. The nest is a bowl of grass with down added as incubation proceeds, usually under dense vegetation or sometimes simply in tall grass or in a hollow tree or fork, not far from water. First clutches are laid between late July and October, with re-nesting up to the end of December. They lay 10–**13**–16 pale greenish or creamy eggs (58 x 43mm, 60g). Eggs are laid daily, usually about dawn. The male guards the female during laying but then leaves her to incubate alone for 26–28 days. The female leads the ducklings to water soon after they hatch. Broods of up to 35 ducklings following a single female have been reported, but these may have been from a nest in which more than one female laid or when two or more broods had coalesced.

The young are initially covered in dark brown down with yellow facial markings and underparts, but they quickly develop feathers and fledge at 50–65 days old. The young disperse widely. About half die before they start breeding at 1 year old. Adults live on average 2.5 years, but the oldest bird recorded in the wild in New Zealand lived 26+ years.

Behaviour: Males commence moult in November, females start about a month later, and in December–January large flocks of moulting birds congregate on freshwater lakes. They stay well away from the shore during the day but feed on the adjacent shore at night during the 3 weeks they are flightless. At this time, flocks of 1000+ birds have been seen at Lakes Wairarapa, Ellesmere and Tuakitoto. The flocks break up in late summer, but during the duck-shooting season Mallards re-group on protected wetlands such as town lakes and reserves. In autumn and winter, Mallards have an elaborate set of courtship displays and males often gather around and harass lone females. Males have a soft, high-pitched 'quek'; females are more vocal with their characteristic loud, repeated 'quack quack quack'.

Feeding: Diet is mainly aquatic vegetation, which they get by upending or dabbling in shallow water, taking seeds from the water surface or growing plants. They often graze grass and clover. Ducklings and females forming eggs take many aquatic invertebrates such as small snails, insect larvae and water beetles. Mallards also feed on grain, peas and beans in stubble after crops have been harvested, and flocks sometimes feed in standing crops, causing considerable damage by knocking down and trampling plants.

Reading: Balham, R. W. 1952. *Emu* 52: 163–191.
Dyer, J. & Williams, M. 2010. *Notornis* 57: 178–195.
Gillespie, G. D. 1985. *J Appl Ecol* 22: 347–356.
Gillespie, G. D. 1985. *Auk* 102: 459–469.

36. GREY DUCK *Anas superciliosa* PLATE 8

Other names: Parera, Pacific Black Duck
Size: 55cm; male 1100g, female 1000g
Geographical variation: Three subspecies are recognised, but banding studies show that there is some exchange between populations, especially between Australia and New Zealand: *rogersi* breeds in Indonesia, New Guinea and Australia; *pelewensis* on islands of the southwest Pacific; and *superciliosa* in New Zealand. Grey Ducks interbreed extensively with Mallards in New Zealand, and most, if not all, remaining birds in New Zealand have a hybrid origin.
Distribution: Breeds in Australasia from Sumatra through Indonesia to New Guinea and Australia, on many islands in the southwestern Pacific, east to French Polynesia and north to the Caroline Islands, and in the New Zealand region. They were formerly in wetlands throughout New Zealand, including many offshore and outlying islands such as the Kermadec, Chatham, Antipodes, The Snares, Auckland and Campbell islands. They have largely gone from outlying islands, and pure birds are very rare on the mainland; they are generally reported in Northland, the eastern Bay of Plenty–Gisborne area, and the West Coast.

Grey Ducks prefer small lakes, slow-flowing rivers and tidal water surrounded by forest rather than farmland. They have not adapted to the agricultural landscape and are rare on town lakes. Banding studies show that they disperse widely throughout New Zealand – a bird banded in Marlborough was shot in Australia, and a New South Wales bird was shot in Otago. In recent decades, with a marked decline in numbers, they may have become more sedentary.
Population: In 1970, there were *c.* 1.5 million Grey Ducks, but now pure Grey Ducks are considered very rare, if not extinct, and are easily confused with a continuum of Grey–Mallard hybrids.
Conservation: Partially protected critically endangered native. Legally harvested in the duck-shooting season because not easily recognised on the wing from the much more common Mallard and hybrids. Decline in this species is attributed to a loss of wild habitats, and competition and widespread hybridisation with the Mallard.
Breeding: Pair formation starts in autumn flocks. By late July, most birds are paired and the males start to defend territories. The nest is a bowl of grass with a lining of down added as incubation proceeds. It is generally away from water (cf. Mallard) and usually under dense vegetation or quite often in a tree hole, fork or clump of *Astelia*, up to 10m above the ground. The first clutch is usually laid between late August and November, but pairs continue to re-nest to the end of December. They lay 5–**10**–13 pale greenish or creamy eggs (58 x 41mm, 60g) about dawn each day. The male guards the female during laying and for about the first week of incubation, but then leaves her to incubate alone for 26–28 days. The female leads the ducklings to water soon after they hatch. Broods of up to 17 ducklings have been reported, but these were probably from a nest in which more than one female laid.

The young are initially covered in dark brown down with yellow facial markings and underparts, but they quickly develop feathers and fledge at *c.* 60 days old and disperse widely. About 65% die before they start breeding at 1 year old. Adults live on average just 21 months, but some birds live much longer than this, with the oldest recorded in the wild in New Zealand being at least 20 years old.
Behaviour: Grey Ducks are sometimes seen in small flocks outside of the breeding season, but do not remain in family groups once the young have fledged. Males have a soft, high-pitched 'quek', and females the more characteristic loud 'quack quack quack', as in Mallards.
Feeding: Diet is mainly seeds sieved from the water through comb-like lamellae at the sides of the bill, and aquatic vegetation which they get by upending or dabbling in shallow water. They sometimes graze grasses along wetland margins. Ducklings and females forming eggs especially take many aquatic or marine invertebrates such as small snails, insect larvae, water beetles and crustaceans.
Reading: Balham, R. W. 1952. *Emu* 52: 163–191. Gillespie, G. D. 1985. *Auk* 102: 459–469. Muller, W. 2008. PhD thesis, Uni Canterbury. Williams, M. J. 1969. *Notornis* 16: 23–32.

37. AUSTRALASIAN SHOVELER *Anas rhynchotis* PLATE 8

Other names: Kuruwhengi, Shoveler, Spoonbill, Spoonie
Size: 49cm; male 650g, female 600g
Distribution: Breeds in southern Australia, especially in the Murray–Darling Basin, but disperses northwards in wet years. They are in wetlands throughout both main islands of New Zealand, and straggle to Stewart Island,

The Snares and the Auckland Islands. They became extinct on the Chatham Islands in 1925. Shovelers prefer fertile shallow wetlands and some sewage ponds of the lower Waikato, Hawke's Bay, Manawatu, Wairarapa, Canterbury and Otago, especially those lakes fringed with raupo. Moderate numbers are found on the Rotorua lakes and Lake Taupo. They are uncommon on flowing rivers and high-country lakes of the South Island.

They moult communally at a few remote undisturbed sites. Banding studies have shown that Shovelers are highly mobile within New Zealand, and movements between Southland and the Waikato are not uncommon. A bird banded at Waituna Lagoon was recovered 1350km away near Kaitaia just 3 months later, and a juvenile banded in coastal Manawatu was caught 800km away in Otago the following May, but by August it had returned to its natal lake to breed.

Population: *c.* 150,000 birds in the 1980s, but reduced to 15,000–30,000 birds by 2010.

Conservation: Partially protected native gamebird. About 6500 are legally harvested each year in the duck-shooting season, with the take controlled by daily bag limits for licensed hunters. Numbers of Shovelers in New Zealand are declining steadily.

Breeding: In July and August, Shovelers are in courtship flocks, but by September, pairs disperse to establish a territory. The nest is a bowl of grass, lined with down. It is usually in thick rank pasture, tussock or *Carex* away from water. Laying is mainly in October–November, but a few late or replacement clutches are laid until January. They lay 5–**11**–14 pale bluish-white eggs (52 x 38mm) about dawn each day. The male guards the female during laying and for about the first fortnight of incubation, but then leaves her to complete the incubation of *c.* 25 days. The female leads the ducklings from the nest soon after they hatch. Normally the brood is kept in dense vegetation by day but feeds in open water at night.

The young are initially covered in dark brown down with yellow facial markings and underparts, and the bill quickly develops its distinctive spoon shape. Sometimes crèches of up to 100 well-grown ducklings have been recorded. Chicks fledge at 55–60 days old and disperse widely. Males survive better than females, and adults survive better than juveniles. About 65% of Shovelers die before they start breeding at 1 year old. Adults survive on average *c.* 21 months, but some birds live much longer, with the oldest recorded in the wild in New Zealand being over 11 years old.

Behaviour: Usually seen in flocks, sometimes of 1000+ birds on large fertile lakes. They tend to shy away from city ponds. Shovelers are often silent by day, but at night they make a soft but far-carrying 'cuck-cuck-cuck . . .' call.

Feeding: Diet is mainly minute aquatic plants such as *Lemna*, seeds, and zooplankton sieved from the water by dabbling in shallow water or in mud. The food is filtered out on very fine comb-like lamellae at the sides of the bill. Large invertebrates such as water beetles and freshwater snails are also eaten.

Reading: Barker, R. et al. 2006. *J Wildl Mgmt* 69: 1508–1515. Caithness, T. et al. 2002. *Notornis* 49: 219–232. Sibson, R. B. 1967. *Notornis* 14: 22–26.

38. NORTHERN SHOVELER *Anas clypeata* PLATE 8

Size: 50cm, 650g

Distribution: Breeds in cool-temperate Northern Hemisphere from Iceland and England across northern Europe and Asia, and into western North America. They migrate to southern Europe, the Rift Valley of Africa, southern Asia and central America, and are vagrants to Micronesia and occasionally to Australasia. About eight accepted records in New Zealand, all of males in breeding plumages (when most easily distinguished from Australasian Shovelers): Waikato (May 1968), Horowhenua (May 1969, August 1971), Whanganui (August 1989), Otago (May 1990), Southland (May 1991), Bay of Plenty (May 1993) and Gisborne (June–July 1995)

Feeding: In their natural range, Northern Shovelers prefer shallow, reed-fringed, high-fertility freshwater or brackish lakes, sewage ponds and flooded paddocks. They feed on minute invertebrates, seeds and plant material obtained by dabbling in shallow water or mud.

Reading: Kinsky, F. C. & Jones, E. B. 1972. *Notornis* 19: 105–110.

39. AUSTRALIAN WHITE-EYED DUCK *Aythya australis* PLATE 7

Other names: White-eyed Duck, Hardhead, Karakahia
Size: 48cm, 900g
Distribution: Breeds only in Australia, mainly in the south and especially in the deeper swamps of the Murray–Darling catchments, along the Great Dividing Range and in coastal Victoria. Disperses widely within Australia in response to inland rains and droughts, and vagrants reach Indonesia, New Guinea, Vanuatu, New Caledonia, Norfolk Island and New Zealand. Maori had a name for the White-eyed Duck, and the many records in New Zealand in the late 1800s suggest that they may have bred here between 1865 and 1895. Since then, there have been only a few records: Rotorua (1934), Hawke's Bay (one bird shot out of a flock of eight in 1973), Auckland (1980), The Snares (1981), Otago (1990), Greymouth (2 in 1994), New Plymouth (2001), Christchurch (2005), Kaiapoi (2012–13) and Foxton Beach (2013).
Feeding: In Australia, White-eyed Ducks prefer large deep lakes with abundant aquatic vegetation, similar to those lakes used by Scaup in New Zealand. They dive to feed on aquatic plants and invertebrates, especially freshwater mussels and snails, although they occasionally upend or dabble in shallow water or mud.

40. NEW ZEALAND SCAUP *Aythya novaeseelandiae* PLATE 7

Other names: Papango, Black Teal
Size: 40cm; male 700g, female 600g
Distribution: New Zealand only. They are widespread but have a patchy distribution. Most are on dune lakes of Northland, hydroelectric lakes in the upper Waikato, and on lakes in the Rotorua district, Taupo, Hawke's Bay, West Coast, North Canterbury, and on the high-country lakes and tarns of the Southern Alps. Elsewhere they are rare, and are not recorded from offshore or outlying islands. Scaup prefer large deep lakes and are rarely found on shallow coastal lakes, lagoons, estuaries or rivers. Little information is available about movements of Scaup within New Zealand, but they are presumed to be mainly sedentary with localised rather than migratory movements.
Population: *c.* 20,000 birds in the 1990s; increasing.
Conservation: Protected endemic. Midden and subfossil evidence suggests that Scaup were formerly more widespread, including being on the Chathams. Both numbers and range have declined since European settlement through modification of habitat, shooting and the introduction of predators; however, they have recovered some ground since they were partially protected in 1921 and fully protected in 1934. Hydroelectric dams, irrigation dams and oxidation ponds have provided valuable new habitat. Ducks Unlimited has carried out a captive breeding programme and established new populations (e.g. in dune lakes from southern Taranaki to Waikanae).
Breeding: By September, most paired birds have left the winter flocks and the males have become territorial. The nest is a bowl of grass and rushes, lined with down, in dense cover close to water. Sometimes Scaup form loose colonies where suitable breeding habitat is scarce. Laying is mostly from late October to December, but a few late or replacement clutches are laid until February. The clutch is of 2–**6**–**8**–15 creamy-white eggs (64 x 45mm, 71g), but clutches of 12+ eggs are probably laid by more than one female. Only the female incubates, for *c.* 30 days. The female broods the ducklings on the nest for up to 24 hours before leading them to water; they are immediately capable of diving to feed. They are initially covered in pale brown down but with white underparts, and the bill is reddish brown. The

female guards the brood during their *c.* 75-day fledging period. Occasionally, rafts of up to 50 birds are formed by several females and their similarly aged broods. Age at first breeding and survivorship is not known, because few New Zealand Scaup have been banded.
Behaviour: Usually seen in flocks in autumn and winter, sometimes 200+ birds at traditional moulting and wintering sites such as Lakes Rotorua, Taupo and Tutira, Bromley Sewage Ponds (Christchurch), and the Ashburton Lakes. They are often silent, but males have a 3–4 note high-pitched whistle, and females 'quack'.
Feeding: They dive to at least 3m, probably much deeper, to feed on aquatic plants and invertebrates such as freshwater snails, chironomid, stonefly and beetle larvae, *Daphnia*, water boatmen, backswimmers and bivalves. They occasionally upend or dabble in shallow water or mud. Most dives last 15–20 seconds, but some last over a minute.
Reading: Soper, M. E. 1976. *New Zealand Birds.* Christchurch: Whitcoulls. Stokes, S. J. 1991. MSc thesis, Uni Canterbury. Wakelin, M. 2004. *Notornis* 51: 242–245.

GREBES *Podicipedidae*

20 species: 4 in New Zealand region, including 1 endemic.

An ancient group of diving birds, related to the family Anatidae (swans, geese, ducks). Grebes diverged very early from this lineage.

Grebes are aquatic specialists, usually living on clear, shallow freshwater lakes and ponds, particularly those with mud, clay or sand on the bottom, and emergent or floating vegetation. Their lobed, not webbed, toes propel and steer them underwater. Their tails are a vestigial tuft only, not a rudder. Their large feet are set well back, making them efficient swimmers but clumsy on land, which they avoid. Their small narrow wings are not used in swimming, but are used for flight, mainly at night. In winter, many gather on large lakes, sewage ponds or (seldom in New Zealand) in estuaries and harbours.

Sexes are alike, but males are larger than females on average and have longer bills. Fish-eating grebes have long pointed bills, whereas invertebrate-eaters have short stubby bills. Most, especially fish-eaters, swallow their own feathers, especially breast and flank feathers, which may help in the forming of pellets.

The nest is a mass of sodden waterweed and sticks, attached to submerged or emergent vegetation. The eggs, laid at intervals of about two days, are white but soon become stained brown. They are covered with vegetation when the incubating bird leaves the nest. Young chicks often ride on their parents' backs. The chicks of almost all grebes have stripes on the head and neck, remnants of which remain for several months after they have become independent juveniles. After breeding, most grebes moult all their flight feathers at once and so are flightless for several weeks; presumably true of New Zealand grebes also.

Reading: Fjeldsa, J. 2004. *The Grebes: Podicipedidae.* Oxford: OUP. Ogilvie, M. A. & Rose, C. 2002. *Grebes of the World.* Uxbridge: Malcolm Coleman Books.

41. AUSTRALASIAN CRESTED GREBE *Podiceps cristatus* PLATE 9

Other names: Puteketeke, Kamana, Southern Crested Grebe, Great Crested Grebe
Size: 50cm; 1100g
Geographical variation: Three subspecies: *cristatus* breeds in the Palaearctic, *infuscatus* in Africa, and *australis* in Australasia.
Distribution: Breeds throughout Europe, Africa and parts of Asia to Australia and New Zealand. In New Zealand, they breed in the South Island only, on lowland lakes west of the Southern Alps and on subalpine and alpine lakes within and east of the main ranges, with the greatest density in inland Canterbury and Otago.

Many move to traditional wintering sites on coastal lakes and estuaries, most notably at Lake Forsyth, near Lake Ellesmere, where up to 269 were seen in June 2012. A few, perhaps vagrants from Australia, have been seen in the North Island at Lake Rotorua (1975–76, and two in 1979). Subfossil and midden records in the North Island suggest that they formerly had a wider distribution.
Population: *c.* 600 birds in 2012, a healthy increase from the low of *c.* 250 birds in 1980 and *c.* 350 in 2004. Most of the birds are in the Canterbury and Otago high country.
Conservation: Protected vulnerable native. Since 1900, Crested Grebes have disappeared from Lakes Rotoiti

and Rotoroa in Nelson, except as occasional visitors. Declining numbers on traditional inland lakes of Marlborough, such as McRae and Guyon, and also on the West Coast, in Fiordland and western Southland. They are now absent from traditional strongholds such as Lakes Gunn and Fergus and have become very rare on Paringa, Brunner, Ianthe, Te Anau, Manapouri and Monowai; however, they have increased greatly in inland Canterbury and inland Otago at sites like the Ashburton Lakes and the man-made Lake Dunstan, mainly thanks to predator control efforts and the creation of suitable habitats by retiring lake margins.

Breeding: Prefer large clear lakes of glacial origin, provided there is some aquatic vegetation for building and anchoring the nest. Both sexes build the nest, which is attached to submerged branches, often under willows in water over a metre deep. They lay 1–**3**–7 eggs (57 x 36mm) in September–March, mostly December–January. Both sexes incubate for 23–**26**–31 days, starting when the first egg is laid. The chicks stay near the nest until all have hatched. Both adults feed the chicks and often carry them on their backs.

Behaviour: Usually breed as territorial pairs but come together in loose flocks in winter. They are silent except when breeding.

Feeding: Diet is mainly fish and aquatic invertebrates. They feed underwater and can tolerate rough water and poor underwater visibility. Larger fish are brought to the surface for swallowing. They also swallow feathers, removed mostly from their breast and flanks while preening, and feed their chicks small fish mixed with these wetted and pulverised feathers.

Reading: Jensen, L. A. & Snoyink, R. J. 2005. *Notornis* 52: 34–42. O'Donnell, C. F. J. 1981. *Notornis* 28: 212–13. O'Donnell, C. F. J. 1982. *Notornis* 29: 151–156. Sagar, P. M. 1981. *Notornis* 28: 301–10. Sagar, P. M. & O'Donnell, C. F. J. 1982. *Notornis* 29: 143–49.

42. NEW ZEALAND DABCHICK *Poliocephalus rufopectus* PLATE 9

Other names: Weweia, New Zealand Grebe

Size: 29cm, 250g

Distribution: New Zealand only. Well distributed in the North Island, on coastal lakes from North Cape to Pukekohe and from southern Taranaki to Paraparaumu; on the lakes and dams of the Volcanic Plateau, especially Rotoiti and southern Taupo; and in the east, on the lakes and dams of Gisborne, Hawke's Bay and the Wairarapa. In autumn, many birds gather on favoured lakes, especially the southern end of Taupo, on Rotoiti, Okareka (Rotorua district), Hatuma (Waipukurau), Horowhenua (Levin), Oporua Cut (Lake Wairarapa) and sewage oxidation ponds, especially those of Masterton, Waikanae and Marton. They do not flock on estuaries or coastal bays, as small grebes do elsewhere. Wintering birds appear in some localities where few breed, e.g. Lakes

Hatuma and Horowhenua. Disappeared from the South Island for many decades from 1941, but a few vagrants were seen in Marlborough and Nelson after 1987, and they have bred near Takaka since 2012.
Population: *c.* 2000 (*c.* 200 Northland, *c.* 700 Volcanic Plateau, *c.* 400 Hawke's Bay, *c.* 150 Wairarapa, *c.* 400 Manawatu). A few birds have recolonised the South Island since 2012.
Conservation: Protected vulnerable endemic. Formerly sparingly distributed on lowland lakes of the South Island but declined rapidly in the nineteenth century, of unknown causes, with the last certain breeding record on Lake Fergus, upper Eglinton Valley (1941). Vagrants appeared in Marlborough in 1987 and 2001; Puramahoi, Golden Bay 2006; and near Nelson 2010–13. Breeding recorded near Takaka since early 2012. The widespread construction of farm dams and ponds, which Dabchicks may use for breeding, and sewage oxidation ponds, which they often spend the winter on, has been to their advantage recently.
Breeding: In pairs in the breeding season, with laying in June–March, mostly September–December. They lay 2–3 eggs (43 x 29mm, 18g) in a depression in a pile of decomposing plant material, which is usually floating and anchored to a willow branch or emergent vegetation, or in shallow water resting on the bottom. The eggs are white but soon become stained brown. Both sexes incubate for 22–23 days, starting when the first egg is laid. Whenever an adult leaves the nest without being flushed, it covers the eggs. Newly hatched chicks swim and dive freely, and travel on an adult's back, where they are fed. They can fly at 5 weeks old, but may need 10 weeks to become fully independent.
Behaviour: In pairs in the breeding season but congregate to form large loose flocks in autumn and winter. They seem unaffected by duck shooting, being small and not rising from the water when disturbed. They fly from one water body to another only at night; by day they dive, swim or skitter across the surface if disturbed. In mild alarm, a Dabchick floats stern-on with the rear-end fluffed out, presenting a white eye-like pattern to the human intruder or another Dabchick approaching its territory. Dabchicks are silent.
Feeding: Diet is mainly aquatic insects (especially water boatmen) and their larvae, and small molluscs taken underwater. Larger food, such as fish and freshwater crayfish are sometimes taken. Unlike many grebes, the Dabchick does not eat feathers, presumably because of its invertebrate diet.
Reading: Buddle, G. A. 1939. *Emu* 39: 77–84. Heather, B. D. 1988. *Notornis* 35: 185–191. Lusk, C. H. & Lusk, J. R. 1981. *Notornis* 28: 203–208.

43. HOARY-HEADED GREBE *Poliocephalus poliocephalus* PLATE 9

Size: 28cm, 250g
Distribution: Breeds in Australia, mostly south of 20° S, including Tasmania. First New Zealand records were in 1975, on The Snares, Lake Horowhenua, and near Te Anau. A pair bred near Te Anau in 1975–76, and later two pairs bred until 1978. In the late 1970s, there were many widely scattered sightings, mostly of single birds that did not stay long, from Northland to Southland. Records after 1980 are few and mainly in the South Island. Now again considered a vagrant, with only three records since 1995: Gisborne (1998), Taramoa, Southland (2012), and three at Lake Elterwater, Marlborough (2014).
Breeding: Similar to New Zealand Dabchick. In Australia, they lay 4–5 eggs (40 x 28mm, 16g), mostly in October–January, and chicks are recorded November–February.
Feeding: Their diet of aquatic invertebrates taken underwater is similar to that of the Dabchick.
Reading: Barlow, M. L. 1976. *Notornis* 23: 183–187. Best, H. A. 1976. *Notornis* 23: 182–183. Storer, R. W. 1987. *Emu* 87: 150–157.

44. AUSTRALASIAN LITTLE GREBE *Tachybaptus novaehollandiae* PLATE 9

Other name: Australasian Grebe
Size: 25cm, 220g
Geographical variation: Six subspecies confined to Indonesia and Australasia; the nominate subspecies *novaehollandiae* is in Australia, southern New Guinea and New Zealand.
Distribution: Widely distributed through Australasia from Java to New Caledonia and New Zealand. They are found mainly in southern Australia, including Tasmania. The first New Zealand records were near Arrowtown (1968–69) and Dargaville (1972). In the North Island, Little Grebes have become well

established on sheltered, reed-fringed small lakes, dune lakes and farm ponds in Northland, South Kaipara Head, and since 2002 they have bred on lakes in the Rotorua area. They form small flocks of up to 20 birds in autumn, especially on the Aupouri Peninsula. In the South Island, a pair bred near Wanaka in 1977, and pairs or family parties were seen until the mid-1980s on widely scattered lakes from Marlborough to Southland. But despite a promising start, breeding pairs persisted only in coastal South Canterbury and near Farewell Spit until about 2000.

Population: Over 100 birds in 2005, mainly in Northland, North Auckland and near Rotorua.

Conservation: Protected self-introduced native, establishing a firm hold in northern New Zealand. Sometimes seen on the same lakes as Dabchicks, but it is not known if they compete.

Breeding: In New Zealand, young have been recorded in January–April. The nest is a floating pile of decomposing plant material, anchored to reeds, waterlilies or willows. In Australia, they lay 2–4–5 eggs (36 x 25mm), which both sexes incubate for *c.* 23 days. Newly hatched chicks swim and dive freely, and travel on an adult's back, during the 8 weeks to independence.

Behaviour: Very wary and secretive when nesting. At the first hint of danger, they sink silently beneath the surface, leaving only the periscope of the head above the water. Usually silent but utter loud trills when courting.

Feeding: Diet in Australia is mostly small fish, snails and aquatic insects, which they catch mainly by diving, but they also swim on the surface with head and neck immersed and turned from side to side, or snatch from the surface or from plants. They swallow feathers deliberately.

Reading: Chance, G. R. 1969. *Notornis* 16: 3–4. Marchant, S. et al. 1989. *Aust Birds* 23: 2–6. Miller, P. 1973. *Notornis* 20: 272–75.

PENGUINS *Spheniscidae*

19 species confined to the Southern Hemisphere: 16 in the New Zealand region, including 4 endemic and 5 other breeding species.

Penguins are a clearly defined group of medium- to large-sized flightless stocky seabirds standing up to 1m tall. They are a primitive group dating back to the late Eocene, about 45 million years ago; fossils of 16 named species and subfossils of one other species have been found in New Zealand, mainly in the South Island, and indicate a formerly very rich radiation of penguins in the New Zealand region.

Penguins are covered with a waterproof coat of dense, short and flattened feathers; the wings are modified into flippers, and the tail is short and stiff. They have a large head and a powerful, short, stout bill. Their legs are short and stout, with webs linking the three forward-pointing fleshy toes. On land, they walk with an ungainly waddling gait, and hop over obstacles, using their flippers to maintain balance. On ice, they sometimes toboggan. In water, they can swim rapidly, being propelled by their flippers only. Some species porpoise when travelling fast.

Penguins dive to catch fish, crustaceans (especially krill), squid and a wide range of other marine invertebrates. They can dive to extraordinary depths, with the record being an Emperor Penguin that dived to 450m, and others can stay submerged for 11 minutes.

Penguins visit land to moult and breed, and some inshore species return to land most nights to roost. During the moult of 2–5 weeks in summer or autumn, birds look ragged and 'sick' because almost all their feathers are replaced simultaneously, with the old feathers pushed out by new growing feathers. During this time, the bird fasts, and is unable to swim without getting waterlogged. If you find penguins moulting, leave them alone, and do not return them to sea; contact the Department of Conservation if a moulting penguin is in danger from humans, dogs or other predators. Many records of unusual species visiting the New Zealand region are of wandering birds forced to come ashore in autumn to moult.

They have ritualised displays, and most give a variety of loud brays, trumpets and growls. Colonial breeders often engage in fights with neighbouring birds. They usually lay a clutch of 1–2 whitish eggs each year; a few failed pairs attempt to re-lay. Nests vary from burrows in Little Blue Penguins and some Fiordland Crested Penguins to simple scrapes for most species. King and Emperor penguins build no nest and incubate the egg between the top of their feet and their body.

Penguins vary from solitary to colonial, some colonies being of millions of pairs. Eggs are small in relation to their body size, and have a long incubation period of 33–65 days depending on the species. Usually both sexes incubate, except that in the Emperor Penguin only the male incubates. Chicks hatch covered in thick down and are fed irregularly by both parents. In colonial species, chicks group together in crèches from about three weeks old until they have their natal moult into full feathers and leave the colony at 2–6 months old.

Reading: Davis, L. S & Darby, J. T. (eds). 1990. *Penguin Biology*. San Diego: Academic Press. Harrison, P. 1988. *Seabirds: An Identification Guide*. London: Christopher Helm. Serventy, D. L. et al. 1971. *The Handbook of Australian Sea-birds*. Sydney: Reed. Stonehouse, B. (ed.) 1975. *The Biology of Penguins*. London: Macmillan.

45. EMPEROR PENGUIN *Aptenodytes forsteri* **PLATE 10**

Size: 115cm, 30kg

Distribution: Circumpolar, breeding on the coast, islands and sea ice of the Antarctic continent. In the Ross Sea sector of Antarctica, there are at least six colonies: Cape Roget, Coulman Island, Cape Washington, Franklin Island, Beaufort Island and Cape Crozier. They seldom venture north of the Antarctic Circle, but a single bird came ashore at Oreti Beach, Southland (April 1967), and a juvenile (known as 'Happy Feet') came ashore at Pekapeka Beach, Wellington (June 2011) and was released northeast of Campbell Island (September 2011).

Population: 56,000 pairs in the Ross Sea sector in 2009, which is *c.* 25% of the estimated total breeding population of 238,000 pairs in Antarctica in 2009. Main Ross Sea colonies were at Coulman Island (25,000 pairs), Cape Washington (12,000 pairs) and Cape Roget (9500 pairs).

Conservation: Vagrant to mainland New Zealand. Significant declines have been noted at several colonies in the Ross Sea sector, perhaps as a result of human disturbance or changing food supplies, but a more recent increase. Cape Roget dropped from 17,000 pairs in the 1950s to 3777 pairs in 1983 but rose to 9500 pairs in 2009.

Breeding: Laying is from late April to June – the mean laying date is about a month later at southern colonies. They lay **1** white egg (123 x 82mm, 442g), which the male then incubates on the top of his feet for 62–**64**–67 days. The male also broods the chick for *c.* 10 days and feeds it an oesophageal secretion before the female returns to brood and feed the chick on demand for the next 3–4 weeks. Meanwhile, the male goes to sea to recover from his three-month fast, during which he has lost about 40% of his body weight. The male and female then alternate their attendance of the chick until it joins a crèche at *c.* 8 weeks old, and then both parents depart for sea and return about every 10 days. In December–January, the chicks depart independently of their parents at *c.* 150 days old, when they average < 50% of the normal adult weight. At some colonies, the chicks have to travel over 50km to reach the sea, and mortality on this journey is high. First breeding is at 3–5–9 years old. Birds are monogamous, but most change partners each year. At Point Geologie, to the west of Ross Sea, annual adult survivorship was 95.1%, with life expectancy 19.9 years.

Behaviour: Breeds in colonies and feeds in groups outside the breeding season. When preparing to breed, the pair vigorously defends the space around them, but once incubating, the males often huddle together to keep warm.

Feeding: Diet is mainly fish (60–250mm long) and squid (up to 280mm long), but krill and a wide range of other marine invertebrates are taken. They feed by diving to great depths (up to 450m below the surface) to capture large fish (and possibly large squid) living on or near the ocean floor, or feed on immature squid, fish and krill in shallow water near icebergs and floes. About 30% of dives are beyond 100m deep. Most dives last 2–8 minutes and are at speeds of 10–15km/hr.

Reading: Barber-Meyer, S. M. et al. 2008 *Ant Sci* 20: 3–11. Budd, G. M. 1962. *Proc Zool Soc (Lond)* 139: 365–88. Fretwell, P. T. et al. 2012. *PLOS ONE* 7(4). Henderson, L. E. 1968. *Notornis* 15: 34–35. Kooyman, G. L. et al. 1990. *Polar Rec* 26: 103–08. Kooyman, G. L. & Ponganis, P. J. 1990. In *Penguin Biology*. San Diego: Academic Press. Mougin, J-L. 1966. *L'Oiseau* 36: 167–226. Robertson, G. et al. 1994. *Ibis* 136: 19–31. Stirling, I. & Greenwood, D. J. 1970. *Notornis* 17: 277–279. Stonehouse, B. 1953. *Sci Rep Falkland Is Dep Surv* 6: 1–33. Wilson, G. J. & Taylor, R. H. 1984. *NZ Ant Rec* 6: 1–7.

46. KING PENGUIN *Aptenodytes patagonicus* PLATE 10

Size: 90cm, 13kg
Distribution: Circumpolar, breeding on many islands in the subantarctic zone, including 70,000 pairs nesting on Macquarie Island, but none breeds in the New Zealand region. A few midden remains from the Chatham Islands indicate that King Penguins may have visited or bred there in the past. Vagrants are seen regularly at Campbell Island, and birds occasionally turn up in summer and autumn to moult at the Chatham, Antipodes, The Snares and Auckland islands. Occasionally reaches the mainland: at Stewart Island and Moeraki (both before 1930), Kaikoura (1989), Timaru (1989), Punakaiki (2005) and the Catlins (2012). It is likely that a bird in Auckland Harbour in 1924 was released from a ship.
Feeding: Diet is mainly fish and squid, with some krill and other marine invertebrates. They can dive up to 240m, and stay underwater for over 9 minutes, in pursuit of prey living on or near the ocean floor.
Reading: Scarlett, R. J. 1976. *Notornis* 23: 355. Stonehouse, B. 1960. *Sci Rep Falkland Is Dep Surv* 23: 1–81. Warham, J. & Bell, B. D. 1979. *Notornis* 26: 121–69.

47. ADÉLIE PENGUIN *Pygoscelis adeliae* PLATE 11

Size: 70cm, 5kg
Distribution: Circumpolar, breeding in large colonies on ice-free coasts and islands of Antarctica and on South Shetland, South Orkney, South Sandwich and Bouvet islands. In the Ross Sea sector of Antarctica there are 34 colonies, with the largest (>50,000 pairs) being at Cape Adare, Possession Island, Cape Hallett, Cape Cotter, Franklin Island, Cape Bird and Cape Crozier. Movements are poorly known, but few are recorded north of 60° S. Two have been recorded from the New Zealand mainland: one dead on the Marlborough coast (December 1962) and one alive at Kaikoura (December 1992).
Population: 1.3 million pairs in the Ross Sea sector, which is about 30% of the total world breeding population of 4 million pairs. The largest colony in the world is at Cape Adare, with 430,000 pairs.
Conservation: Vagrant to the mainland of New Zealand. The number of birds seems to be increasing in the Ross Sea sector, but declining around the Antarctic Peninsula. Modelling suggests that the species will soon start to decline as climate change will adversely affect colonies north of about 70° S. Individual colonies seem to decline after human disturbance.
Breeding: Laying is during November and early December, mostly about the middle of November, *c.* 1–2 weeks after the birds return to the colony. They lay 1–**2**–3 pale green eggs (69 x 55mm, 120g) 2–**3**–4 days apart. If the first egg is lost shortly after laying, a third egg is often laid, bringing the clutch back to two, but this egg is much smaller than usual (66 x 51mm, 101g). The nest is a scrape surrounded by rounded stones. Colonies are on flat or gently sloping surfaces free of snow, up to 100km from open water when birds first arrive, but the sea ice quickly breaks up, letting birds reach open water easily. Incubation starts with the first egg but may be only partial until the second egg is laid. The female usually returns to sea while the male takes the first spell of about a fortnight, thereafter, incubation is roughly shared, with the length of incubation spells positively related to the distance to open water. The eggs hatch 1–2 days apart, after 30–**33**–38 days.

Chicks are guarded by their parents for the first 17–**22**–32 days, during which time they develop a thick layer of secondary down, and then start to shed this as feathers appear. The parents swap duties every couple of days and feed their chicks soon after they arrive back. The chicks join crèches, but their parents are still able to pick them out in the crowd of chicks. Chicks fledge after 41–**51**–56 days in late January and February, at *c.* 56% of adult weight. They are independent of their parents after they leave the colony. First breeding is at 3–**4**–6+ years in females, 4–**7**–8+ years in males. Birds are monogamous and usually retain their partners from year to year; most divorces are in pairs that were poorly synchronised arriving back at the colony. The oldest Adélie Penguin recorded lived at least 16 years.
Behaviour: Gregarious, with some colonies of 250,000+ pairs. At sea, they are often seen in small groups roosting on ice floes or feeding in open water.
Feeding: During the breeding season, they eat mainly krill, especially *Euphausia superba* and *E. crystallorophias*, but they also take a few fish, squid and a variety of marine invertebrates. They feed close to the surface or at moderate depths (10–100m) but are capable of diving to 175m.
Reading: Ainley, D. G. & de Master, D. P. 1980. *Ecology* 61: 522–530. Ainley, D. G. et al. 2010. *Ecol*

Monographs 80: 49–66. Cossee, R. O. & Mills, J. A. 1993. *Notornis* 40: 308–09. Davis, L. S. et al. 1988. *Notornis* 35: 15–23. Lishman, G. S. 1985. *Ibis* 127: 84–99. Reid, B. E. 1965. *NZ J Sci* 8: 503–14. Spurr, E. B. 1975. *Ibis* 117: 324–38. Taylor, R. H. 1962. *Ibis* 104: 176–204. Taylor, R. H. & Wilson, P. R. 1990. *NZ J Ecol* 14: 25–29. Van Heezik, Y. 1988. *Notornis* 35: 23–26.

48. GENTOO PENGUIN *Pygoscelis papua* PLATE 10

Size: 80cm, 5.5kg
Geographical variation: Two subspecies: the larger *papua* breeds mainly on the subantarctic islands of the Atlantic and Indian oceans, and at Macquarie Island, while the smaller *ellsworthi* breeds further south in the South Atlantic Ocean and on the Antarctic Peninsula. All that have reached New Zealand shores are presumed to have been *papua*, probably from Macquarie Island.
Distribution: Circumpolar, breeding on the Antarctic Peninsula and many islands in the subantarctic zone, including 4700 breeding pairs on Macquarie Island. They feed inshore, and so remain close to their breeding ground. A few vagrants, usually immatures, have been recorded ashore on beaches in the New Zealand region, mainly in November and December: Campbell Island (1964–65, 1985); Dunedin (1970), Bluff (1970), Catlins (1974), Banks Peninsula (1976, 1993), Antipodes Island (1978, 1995, 2002) and The Snares (1985, 2002), Shag Point, North Otago (2011).
Feeding: Diet at Macquarie Island in June–November is mainly oceanic fish (up to 18cm long) and squid. Elsewhere, Gentoo Penguins have been recorded eating mostly krill. They usually feed close to the surface but have been recorded diving to over 160m.
Reading: Croxall, J. P. & Prince, P. A. 1980. *Ibis* 122: 245–53. Darby, J. T. & Wright, A. W. 1973. *Notornis* 20: 28–30. Hindell, M. A. 1989. *Emu* 89: 71–78. Reilly, P. N. & Kerle, J. A. 1981. *Notornis* 28: 189–201. Robertson, G. 1986. *Aust Wild. Res* 13: 583–87.

49. CHINSTRAP PENGUIN *Pygoscelis antarctica* PLATE 11

Size: 75cm, 5.5kg
Distribution: Circumpolar, breeding mainly on the Antarctic Peninsula and islands in the subantarctic zone of the Atlantic Ocean, especially at the South Sandwich Islands (*c.* 5 million pairs). A very small breeding colony has been found on an islet off Sabrina Island, Balleny Islands, in the Ross Sea sector of Antarctica. Chinstrap Penguins feed inshore during the breeding season and near the northern limit of pack ice during winter, and so are rarely recorded north of 60° S. Vagrants have been recorded at Antipodes Island (November 1978), Invercargill (December 1980), Campbell Island (March 1984), Warrington, Otago (November 1992) and Kaikoura (November 2002).
Population: 13+ pairs breed at the Balleny Islands; this is a minute fraction of the total world breeding population of *c.* 6.5 million pairs.
Conservation: Vagrant to the mainland of New Zealand. Formerly they were almost entirely confined to the South American quadrant of Antarctica, but they have increased and spread eastward into the Ross Sea sector of Antarctica.
Breeding: No studies in the New Zealand region, but elsewhere laying is in late November and December, about a fortnight after birds return to their colony. They lay 1–**2**–3 creamy white eggs (67 x 52mm, 113g) 3–4 days apart. The nest is a shallow cup on a slightly raised platform of small stones on an ice-free slope, often in mixed colonies with Adélie and/or Gentoo penguins. Incubation starts after the first egg is laid, but may be only partial incubation until the second egg is laid. The male departs to sea once the second egg is laid, and the female takes the first incubation spell of *c.* 6 days. The male then incubates for 10 days. Shifts then alternate and shorten as incubation proceeds. The incubation period is 31–**35**–39 days; first eggs hatch about a day before the second egg.

Chicks are guarded for the first 3–**4**–5 weeks, during which time they are fed regularly. They then join small crèches until they fledge in late February to early March at 48–**53**–59 days old and at about 67% of adult weight. They are independent once they have left the colony. First breeding is at 3 years in both sexes.
Behaviour: Gregarious, breeding in large colonies and feeding in loose groups out of the breeding season. Compared with other penguins, they are bold and aggressive towards humans and other animals at their colony.

Feeding: Diet at Signy Island in the breeding season is mostly krill, especially *Euphausia superba*, with just a few fish and amphipods. They feed close to the surface but have been recorded diving to depths of 70m.

Reading: Conroy, J. W. H. et al. 1975. In *The Biology of Penguins*. London: Macmillan. Lishman, G. S. 1985. *Ibis* 127: 84–99. Spurr, E. B. 1985. *Notornis* 32: 1–4.

50. WESTERN ROCKHOPPER PENGUIN *Eudyptes chrysocome* PLATE 13

Size: 61cm, 2.7kg

Distribution: Breeds in reduced numbers on the Falkland Islands and islands off Cape Horn, Chile. After breeding, disperses mainly northwards to the east and west coasts of South America, but vagrants have reached Australia and New Zealand. Up to two birds visited, or were resident at, The Snares between 1985 and 2000.

Behaviour: Gregarious, breeding in huge colonies. At sea, they use both coastal and pelagic waters, and feed mainly on krill, with some fish and squid.

Reading: Banks, J. C. et al. 2006. *Polar Biol* 30: 61–67. Tennyson, A. J. D. & Miskelly C. M. 1989. *Notornis* 36: 183–189. Miskelly, C. M. et al. 2001. *Notornis* 48: 1–40.

51. EASTERN ROCKHOPPER PENGUIN *Eudyptes filholi* PLATE 13

Size: 55cm, 2.8kg

Distribution: Breeds on Marion, Prince Edward, Crozet, Kerguelen and Heard islands in the Indian Ocean; on Macquarie Island; and on Antipodes, Auckland and Campbell islands in the New Zealand region. After breeding, disperses mainly northward, and some birds reach the mainland coasts of Australia and New Zealand. In late summer, up to 20 moult at The Snares, and some reach the Otago and Canterbury coasts and the Chathams.

Population: *c.* 1.5 million pairs, of which *c.* 50,000 pairs in the New Zealand region: *c.* 2500 pairs on the Antipodes, 45,000 pairs on Campbell Island and 2500 pairs on the Auckland Islands.

Conservation: Protected critically endangered native. Although they appear to be locally common on the three subantarctic islands, they declined 94% at Campbell Island from *c.* 800,000 pairs in 1942 to 51,500 pairs in 1985, and they have continued to decline, probably because of rising sea temperatures affecting their food supply. A similar decline has been noted at Marion Island where the population declined from 137,000 pairs in 1994 to 67,000 pairs in 2001. Lesser declines have been noted at the Antipodes and Auckland islands.

Breeding: Laying is in October–November; slightly earlier at the Antipodes than at Campbell Island or the Auckland Islands. They lay 2 white eggs, the first (64 x 48mm, 80g) being much smaller than the second (71 x 54mm, 112g), which is laid 4–5 days later. The nest is a lined scrape in a large colony on terraces, scree slopes and sometimes among tussock or in caves from near the coast to several hundred metres inland. Incubation starts before the second egg is laid, but the second egg usually hatches first. The first egg is often lost from the nest during squabbles or taken by Southern Skuas, and only rarely are two chicks reared. Both sexes incubate: the female takes the first long shift of 10–19 days, followed by the male for 7–13 days. The incubation shifts shorten until the eggs hatch after 33–34 days.

Chicks are brooded initially and guarded almost continuously by the male (who fasts for 5 weeks), and occasionally by the female during daily feeding visits, until they are about 3 weeks old. Thereafter, they form small crèches and are fed only by their own parents. Chicks depart in February and early March at about 9–10 weeks old, and they are independent once they have left the colony.

Behaviour: Gregarious, breeding in colonies of over 10,000 pairs on Campbell Island, and they are seen in groups at sea. Moult usually takes place at the breeding grounds over 3–4 weeks during April, about a month after their chicks have fledged.

Feeding: At the Antipodes, satellite tracking showed that females made approximately daily trips of about 80km to feed during the guard stage, and trips of *c.* 300km in 6 days in the post-guard stage. At Campbell Island, the diet in the breeding season is mainly fish, especially dwarf cod, southern blue whiting and hake; with some small crustaceans, squid, octopus and other marine invertebrates. Overseas, krill forms most of the diet. Eastern Rockhopper Penguins feed by pursuit-diving to depths of up to 100m, but usually feed at less than 60m in dives of shorter than 2 minutes.

In the hand: Adult males have longer, deeper and wider bills than females, with little overlap at any single breeding site. At Campbell Island, males had a product (in mm) of these three bill measurements of over 8700, whereas females were under 7800; on the Antipodes the corresponding figures were 10,200 and 9400.

Reading: Cooper, W. 1992. *Notornis* 39: 66–67. Crawford, R. J. M. et al. 2003. *African J Marine Sci* 25: 487–98. Cunningham, D. M. & Moors, P. J. 1994. *Emu* 94: 27–36. Hull, C. L. 1999. *J Zool (Lond)* 247: 507–29. Hull, C. L. 2000. *Canadian J Zool* 78: 333–45. Sagar, P. M. et al. 2005. *Notornis* 52: 75–80. Warham, J. 1963. *Auk* 80: 229–256. Warham, J. 1972. *Auk* 89: 86–105.

52. MOSELEY'S ROCKHOPPER PENGUIN *Eudyptes moseleyi* PLATE 13

Other name: Northern Rockhopper Penguin
Size: 58cm, 2.8kg
Distribution: Breeds in greatly reduced numbers on Gough Island and on islands in the Tristan da Cunha group in the South Atlantic Ocean, and also on St Paul and Amsterdam islands in the Indian Ocean. After breeding, disperses mainly northwards towards the coast of South Africa, but vagrants have reached South America, Australia and New Zealand. Moseley's Rockhopper Penguins have been seen at South East Island, Chathams (August 1968 to November 1970); Moa Point, Wellington (January 1984); possibly at Gisborne (December 1976); Pitt Island and Star Keys, Chathams (several times between November 1998 and January 2004).
Behaviour: Gregarious, breeding in huge colonies and they are seen in groups at sea. They can dive to 100m and stay down for over 2 minutes. They feed mainly on krill, with some fish and squid.
In the hand: Adult males have longer, deeper and wider bills than females, with little overlap at any single breeding site. Moseley's Rockhopper Penguins have much longer flippers (175–190mm) than the other two Rockhopper penguins, *E. chrysocome* and *E. filholi* (160–175mm).
Reading: Banks, J. C. et al. 2006. *Polar Biol* 30: 61–67. Miskelly, C. & Bell, M. 2004. *Notornis* 51: 235–37. Moors, P. & Merton, D. 1984. *Notornis* 31: 262–65.

53. FIORDLAND CRESTED PENGUIN *Eudyptes pachyrhynchus* PLATE 12

Other name: Tawaki, Pokotiwha
Size: 60cm, 4kg
Distribution: Breeds only in New Zealand, in small colonies on headlands, on islets, around entrances to fiords and sometimes in sandy bays, southwards from near Bruce Bay in Westland and the Open Bay Islands, to Fiordland, Solander Island, Green Islets (Foveaux Strait), Codfish Island and on and around western and southern Stewart Island. During breeding, adults stay in continental shelf waters close to their nesting colonies. They return to their colonies to moult before dispersing in autumn. Immatures often moult away from the breeding grounds and are occasionally recorded beach-wrecked or moulting around the coast of the North and South islands in summer and early autumn, as far north as Northland. A pair attempted to breed on Banks Peninsula in 1945, and a pair bred in Palliser Bay in 1953. Yearlings and occasional older birds are common on The Snares in summer but do not breed there. Vagrants reach Auckland, Campbell and Macquarie islands and southern Australia from New South Wales to Western Australia. Subfossil and midden remains from North and South islands indicate a wider distribution in the past.
Population: *c.* 2500–3000 pairs in the 1990s; main populations are on Taumaka Island (Open Bay Islands) 150 pairs, between Paringa River and Murphy Beach 180 pairs, Breaksea Island and adjacent islets 215 pairs, Solander Islands 115 pairs, Codfish Island 140 pairs.
Conservation: Protected endangered endemic. Until recently the numbers of birds have not been assessed because most breed on the remote coastline of South Westland and on islands in Fiordland. An estimate of 5000–10,000 pairs in 1984 seems to have been optimistic. There is evidence that the breeding population on Solander Island has declined markedly since the 1950s, as have the Dusky Sound birds since Richard Henry noted 'thousands' at the beginning of the 1900s. At mainland colonies, breeding and moulting birds are threatened by dogs, mustelids and human disturbance. Weka take many eggs and chicks at some island and mainland colonies, even after the chicks are old enough to join crèches. Some are caught accidentally in fishing nets.

Breeding: Laying is in July–August. They lay 2 white eggs, the first (67 x 51mm, 99g) is smaller than the second (71 x 54mm, 117g), which is laid 3–**4**–6 days later. The nest is a shallow lined scrape in a deep cavity under tree roots, among rock falls, in crevices or caves, or under dense coastal bush or scrub; usually in a small colony of 10 or fewer pairs. Incubation starts when the second egg is laid, and it usually hatches first, after 30–**32**–35 days. Both sexes incubate; for the first week each takes short incubation spells, but then do long spells of 10–14 days. The first egg is sometimes displaced from the nest, but many pairs hatch both eggs. The chick from the smaller egg usually starves, and it is very rare that both chicks are reared successfully.

Chicks are brooded initially and guarded almost continuously by the male (who fasts), and occasionally by the female during feeding visits, until they are *c.* 3 weeks old. Thereafter, chicks form small crèches and are fed by both parents. Chicks depart in November and early December at *c.* 10–11 weeks old, and are independent once they have left the colony. First breeding is probably at 5–6 years old.

Behaviour: Moderately gregarious, breeding in small loose colonies of 10 or fewer pairs, and they are sometimes seen in small groups at sea. Adults moult at their breeding site over 20–30 days in January–March, about three months after their chicks have fledged.

Feeding: During the crèching phase in South Westland and Fiordland, adults eat mainly juvenile squid, octopus, krill and a wide variety of small fish; whereas birds feeding chicks on Codfish Island in October eat mainly small (25–35mm) fish, with a few squid and octopuses.

In the hand: Adult males have longer, deeper (generally >24mm) and wider bills than females, with little overlap in bill depth or in the product of length, width and depth within particular populations.

Reading: McLean, I. G. et al. 1993. *Notornis* 39: 60–63. McLean, I. G. et al. 1997. *Notornis* 40: 85–94. Murie, J. O. et al. 1991. *Notornis* 38: 233–38. St. Clair, C. C. 1992. *Behav Ecol Sociobiol* 31: 409–416. St. Clair, C. C. & St. Clair, R. 1992. *Notornis* 44: 37–47. Van Heezik, Y. M. 1989. *Notornis* 36: 151–56. Van Heezik, Y. M. 1990. *NZ J Zool* 17: 543–48. Warham, J. 1972. *Auk* 89: 86–105. Warham, J. 1974. *Ibis* 116: 1–27. Warham, J. 1975. In Stonehouse, B. *The Biology of Penguins*. London: Macmillan.

54. SNARES CRESTED PENGUIN *Eudyptes robustus* PLATE 12

Size: 60cm, 3kg

Distribution: Breeds only on The Snares. Most are on Main and Broughton islands, but a few nest on Toru and Rima islets of the Western Chain. While breeding, adults stay in continental shelf waters close to their nesting colonies, and they return to their colonies to moult before dispersing in winter. Some immatures moult away from the breeding grounds and are occasionally recorded beach-wrecked or moulting around the coast of Stewart Island and the South Island in summer and early autumn. Vagrants have been recorded in Hawke's Bay, on the Wellington coast, at the Chatham, Antipodes, Campbell, Auckland, and Macquarie islands, southern Australia and Tasmania, and as far afield as the Falkland Islands.

Population: Stable or slightly increasing. *c.* 28,800 pairs in 2001: Main Island 23,700 pairs, Broughton Island 4500 pairs, Toru 300 pairs, Rima 300 pairs.

Conservation: Protected endemic; little influenced by humans or introduced predators.

Breeding: Laying is from mid-September to mid-October on Main and Broughton islands, but *c.* 3–6 weeks later, in mid-November, on the Western Chain. They lay 2 white eggs, the first (68 x 52mm, 100g) smaller than the second (73 x 56mm, 130g), which is laid **4**–5 days later. The nest is a shallow lined cup often raised slightly. They breed in small dense colonies of 50–200 pairs, mostly in clearings under *Olearia* or *Brachyglottis* forest, but sometimes among boulders or in the open. Incubation starts when the second egg is laid, and it usually hatches first, after 31–**33**–37 days. Both sexes incubate. For the first few days, the pair takes short incubation spells, but then the male leaves the female to incubate for a fortnight and then returns to incubate until the chicks hatch. The first egg is sometimes displaced from the nest and is often more accessible to Southern Skuas while being incubated. Many pairs hatch both eggs, but the chick from the smaller egg often starves and it is extremely rare that both chicks are reared successfully. Chicks are guarded at the nest for the first 3 weeks; thereafter they join crèches before fledging at about 11 weeks old. First breeding is at 6 years old. The oldest banded bird lived at least 22 years.

Behaviour: Gregarious, breeding in very small to large, dense colonies of 3–**200**–1300 pairs, and they are sometimes seen in small groups at sea. Adults moult at their breeding site for 24–30 days in March–May, *c.* 3 months after their chicks have fledged.

Feeding: While breeding, they eat mainly a krill *Nyctiphanes australis*, with some small fish (especially pipefish and redbait) and squid (especially arrow squid), obtained at depths of 20–80m.
In the hand: Adult males have longer, deeper and wider bills than females, with a product (in mm) of over 17,800 being a male, and under 13,320 being a female.
Reading: Amey, J. M. et al. 2001. *NZ J Zool* 28: 432–33. Mattern, T. et al. 2009. *Emu* 109: 204–213. Miskelly, C. M. 1984. *Notornis* 31: 209–23. Miskelly, C. M. et al. 2001. *Notornis* 48: 1–40. Warham, J. 1972. *Auk* 89: 86–105. Warham, J. 1974. *J Roy Soc NZ* 4: 63–108. Warham, J. 1975. In Stonehouse, B. *The Biology of Penguins*. London: Macmillan.

55. ERECT-CRESTED PENGUIN *Eudyptes sclateri* PLATE 12

Size: 60cm, 4.5kg
Distribution: Breeds only on the Antipodes and Bounty islands. While breeding, adults stay in continental shelf waters close to their nesting colonies, and they return to their colonies to moult before dispersing in winter. Some immatures moult away from the breeding grounds and are occasionally recorded beach-wrecked or moulting on the east coast of the North and South islands and at Stewart Island and The Snares. Vagrants have been recorded on the coast of the North Island, at the Chathams, Macquarie Island, on the coast of southern Australia between Victoria and Western Australia, and two records from the Falkland Islands. A few birds bred on Otago Peninsula (late 1930s), Campbell Island (1940s), and Disappointment Island, Auckland Islands (1976).
Population: *c.* 68,500 pairs in 2011: Bounty Islands 26,000 pairs, Antipodes 42,500 pairs.
Conservation: Protected endemic; perhaps affected by changing sea temperatures and currents altering their food supply.
Breeding: Little information is available. Laying is in October–November, 2–3 weeks later on Bounty Island than on the Antipodes. They lay **2** white eggs, the first (77 x 48mm, 98g) very much smaller than the second (89 x 57mm, 149g). When the second egg is laid, the first egg is usually evicted. The nest is a shallow lined cup, often raised slightly. They nest in huge dense colonies of thousands of pairs among Shy Mollymawks or near Rockhopper Penguins, mostly among boulder-strewn slopes and terraces. Both sexes incubate. The incubation period is *c.* 36 days. About 10–11 weeks after hatching, the chicks depart in late January to February.
Behaviour: Gregarious, not only breeding in dense colonies of several thousand pairs but also forming small groups at sea. Adults moult at their breeding site for 26–30 days in March–April, *c.* 6 weeks after their chicks have fledged.
Feeding: While breeding, they eat krill and squid, and may also take small fish.
In the hand: Adult males have longer, deeper and wider bills than females, with a product (in mm) of over 16,000 being a male, and under 14,000 being a female.
Reading: Richdale, L. E. 1941. *Emu* 41: 25–53. Richdale, L. E. 1949. *Emu* 49: 153–166. Robertson, C. J. R. & van Tets, G. F. 1982. *Notornis* 29: 311–36. Warham, J. 1972. *Ardea* 60: 145–184. Warham, J. 1975. In Stonehouse, B. *The Biology of Penguins*. London: Macmillan. Warham, J. & Bell, B. D. 1979. *Notornis* 26: 121–69.

56. MACARONI PENGUIN *Eudyptes chrysolophus* PLATE 13

Size: 70cm, 4.5kg
Distribution: Breeds on many subantarctic islands in the South Atlantic Ocean and Indian Oceans, with largest numbers (1 million+ pairs) on South Georgia, Kerguelen, Crozet, Heard and McDonald islands. Disperses in the Southern Ocean, and straggles to the Ross Sea sector of Antarctica, including Cape Hallett and the Balleny Islands, and three records from New Zealand subantarctic islands, all in November–January: Campbell Island (1967–68; 1993), The Snares (1969–74).
Feeding: During breeding they make foraging trips within a 300km radius of the breeding colony to catch krill and small (6–7.5cm) lanternfish – the proportion of the latter increasing as the season progresses. They can dive to over 100m, but most dives are to 10–60m and last less than 2 minutes.
Reading: Green, K. et al. 1998. *Marine Ornith* 26: 27–34. Kinsky, F. C. 1969. *Notornis* 16: 225–36. Miskelly, C. M. et al. 2001. *Notornis* 48: 1–40.

57. ROYAL PENGUIN *Eudyptes schlegeli* PLATE 13

Size: 70cm, 5kg

Distribution: Breeds only at Macquarie Island, Australia, but feeds mainly to the south around the polar front. Vagrants reach Antarctica, islands in the southern Indian Ocean, the coasts of Tasmania and Australia, and New Zealand. About 20 records: mainly from Campbell Island, The Snares, the Chathams and on the Southland/Otago coast, but four birds in the North Island as far north as Napier. Usually seen as singletons ashore to moult for four weeks in February–March, but four seen at Campbell Island in January 1968.

Feeding: During breeding and before the post-breeding moult, they make foraging trips of around 500km to catch krill, small lanternfish and squid by diving. They can dive to over 100m, but most dives are to less than 60m and under 2 minutes' duration.

Reading: Hindell, M. A. 1988. *Emu* 88: 219–26. Hull, C. L. 1999. *J Zool (Lond)* 247: 507–529. Hull, C. L. 2000. *Canadian J Zool.* 78: 333–345. Warham, J. 1971. *Notornis* 18: 91–115.

58. YELLOW-EYED PENGUIN *Megadyptes antipodes* PLATE 11

Other name: Hoiho

Size: 65cm; male 5.5kg, female 5.25kg

Distribution: New Zealand only; breeding on the coast and some offshore islands of the southeastern South Island from Banks Peninsula to Bluff, Foveaux Strait islands, Stewart Island and its outliers (particularly Codfish), Auckland Islands and Campbell Island. Most birds are sedentary and feed within 25km of their colony while breeding, and return regularly throughout the non-breeding season to the vicinity of their breeding site. Stragglers (mainly juveniles) reach The Snares, Fiordland, the Chathams, the northern Canterbury and the Marlborough coasts, the southern North Island, and even as far north as the Bay of Plenty (1980). In some years (e.g. 1972 and 1977) moderate numbers are beach-wrecked in the southern North Island. Subfossil and midden remains only from the subantarctic islands suggest a recent colonisation of the mainland following the demise of the larger Waitaha Penguin (*M. waitaha*) before European contact.

Population: *c.* 5000 birds: *c.* 1700 breeding pairs and a similar number of non-breeders. Estimated numbers of breeding pairs: South Island 400–500, Stewart Island/Foveaux Strait 180, Auckland Islands 520–570, and Campbell Island 490–600 pairs.

Conservation: Protected vulnerable endemic. On the mainland, the breeding success fluctuates widely from year to year, but since 1980 numbers have been moderately stable at 430–530 breeding pairs, apart from a major crash in the late 1980s and early 1990s when the population declined to as few as *c.* 140 breeding pairs. A shortage of food in two successive breeding seasons (1985 and 1986) led to many adults not even attempting to breed and also saw adults starving during the annual moult. Then, on the Otago Peninsula, 30–40% of breeding adults and most chicks died during the 1989–90 breeding season, possibly as a result of an unidentified biotoxin. At the same time, Yellow-eyed Penguins on Campbell Island declined, in part due to an increase in disturbance from sea lions. They are sometimes caught accidentally in fishing nets.

Because mammalian predators (especially ferrets, stoats, cats and dogs) cause serious losses in some years, the Department of Conservation and the Yellow-eyed Penguin Trust, with support from Mainland Cheese, do intensive predator control on parts of the Otago coast, and exclude dogs from key sites. Habitat management around breeding sites aims to exclude stock (which trample or disturb nests) and restore coastal scrub and forest cover. Ecotourism, based on seeing Yellow-eyed Penguins, is an economically and culturally important activity, and is closely regulated to minimise disturbance.

Breeding: Most birds return to the same area each year, but fewer than 30% of birds use the same nest site in successive years. Laying in Otago is in September–October, mostly the second half of September; the season is about a fortnight later on Campbell Island. They lay 1–**2** pale bluish-green eggs (77 x 57mm, 138g) in a substantial open bowl, generally hard against a bank, flax bush or tussock, which provides shelter from direct sunlight and privacy from other breeding pairs. Incubation starts after the second egg is laid 3–5 days after the first. Both sexes incubate in spells of *c.* 2 days. Most eggs hatch within a day of each other, after 39–**43**–51 days.

Chicks are brooded for the first 25 days, by which time they have developed a thick layer of secondary down. They start making short forays away from the nest site, and after 40–50 days they are attended only at night. Chicks sometimes form small crèches at sites where numbers are high. They fledge after 97–**106**–118 days in February–March and are immediately able to swim and be independent of their parents. First breeding is at 2–3 years in females, 3–4 years in males. Birds are monogamous and retain their partners from year to year. The oldest tagged Yellow-eyed Penguin lived over 20 years.

Behaviour: Breeding distribution is clumped because of a shortage of suitable nesting sites rather than a need to form colonies. Small groups form outside the breeding season, or to avoid sea lions, but apparently birds feed alone.

Feeding: Yellow-eyed Penguins eat mainly small- to medium-sized fish (up to 32cm long), but squid, octopus and some krill are also taken. One-year-old birds eat more squid and less fish than adults. They dive to 160m below the surface to capture fish (and possibly squid) living on or near the ocean floor.

In the hand: Males are larger than females, but measurements overlap: over 85% of birds can be sexed correctly from a combination of skull length (from the back of the skull to bill tip) 135–**143**–150mm cf. 130–**137**–149mm, and foot length (from the back of the heel to the tip of the pad of the middle toe) 126–**131**–136mm cf. 121–**125**–131mm.

Reading: Darby, J. T. & Seddon, P. J. 1990. In *Penguin Biology*. San Diego: Academic Press. Moore, P. J. 1992. *Notornis* 39: 1–15. Moore, P. J. et al. 1995. *DOC Sci & Res Ser* 83. Wellington: DOC. Ratz, H. & Murphy, B. 1999. *Pacific Cons. Biol.* 5: 16–27. Richdale, L. E. 1951. *Sexual Behaviour in Penguins*. Lawrence: Uni Kansas Press. Richdale, L. E. 1957. *A Population Study of Penguins*. Oxford: OUP. Van Heezik, Y. 1990. *NZ J Zool* 17: 201–12. Van Heezik, Y. M. & Davis, L. 1990. *Ibis* 132: 354–65.

59. BLUE PENGUIN *Eudyptula minor* — PLATE 11

Other names: Korora, Little Blue Penguin, Little Penguin, White-flippered Penguin (Canterbury), Fairy Penguin (Australia)

Size: 40cm, 1100g

Geographical variation: Up to six subspecies have been recognised on the basis of back colour, flipper pattern and measurements, but recent genetic analysis showed only two clear, but undescribed, forms; the Otago and Southland birds being closer to Australian birds than all the others combined. The superficially distinct White-flippered Penguin of Banks Peninsula and Motunau Island is not genetically distinct.

Distribution: Breeds on the coasts of southern Australia, Tasmania and New Zealand. In the New Zealand region, Blue Penguins breed on the coasts and offshore islands of North, South, Stewart and the Chatham islands. They are generally sedentary and are often seen in shallow inshore waters and harbours within 20km of their breeding site. Some birds, especially juveniles, wander several hundred kilometres from their breeding or natal site, e.g. birds from Motunau Island have been recovered in Otago and Hawke's Bay, and vagrants occasionally reach the Three Kings and The Snares. Subfossil and midden remains indicate that Blue Penguins were widespread and common on the coasts of New Zealand in pre-European times.

Population: Widespread and locally common; the main breeding is on islands off eastern Northland, in the Hauraki Gulf, Great Barrier Island, around Cook Strait, Motunau Island, near Oamaru, around southern Otago and Foveaux Strait, and on the Chatham Islands.

Conservation: Protected native. Mainly on uninhabited islands and on remote parts of the mainland coast away from disturbance by humans, dogs, cats and mustelids, but a few persist in coastal urban areas such as around Wellington Harbour and Oamaru. Populations undergo severe crashes, and many dead birds are washed ashore in some years (e.g. eastern Northland in autumn 1974), probably as a result of food shortage or biotoxins. Occasionally caught in set nets.

Breeding: Laying is in July–December, with peaks in August and November. They lay 1–**2** white eggs (56 x 43mm, 54g), 2–5 days apart. The nest is in a burrow, natural cavity or rock pile, or sometimes under driftwood. Some Blue Penguins nest in loose colonies near the shore, but others nest hundreds of metres from any other pair and can be over 500m inland and above 200m asl on some islands; some birds are even seen occasionally at 500m near the summit of Kapiti Island. Incubation starts after the first egg is laid but may be only partial until the second is laid. Both sexes incubate with short shifts of 1–2 days, until the eggs hatch after 30–**35**–43 days.

Chicks are brooded for the first 10 days, guarded continuously for a further 1–3 weeks, guarded only at night for a further 3–4 weeks, and then in the final stages they are visited only briefly at night. Chicks fledge at 48–**56**–64 days old and at about 90% of adult weight.

They are independent once they have left the nest. First breeding is at 2–3 years in both sexes. The oldest bird recorded lived over 25 years.
Behaviour: Blue Penguins are very vocal when they come ashore at night. They have a wide range of calls, from mewing notes, not unlike those of a cat, to loud screams, trumpeting and deep-toned growls – sounds not appreciated when coming from under the floor of a crib or a bach. A complete body moult usually takes place at the breeding site for 10–18 days in December–March.
Feeding: Birds breeding on Codfish Island in October take mainly arrow squid and small (10–35mm) shoaling fish, and a few octopuses. They generally feed alone or in small groups, taking most prey within 5m of the surface, but they have been recorded diving to depths of 69m.
In the hand: Males have longer and deeper bills than females, but because of the wide geographical variation in the size of Blue Penguins, sexing of birds from bill measurements is reliable only at particular breeding sites.
Reading: Banks, J. C. et al. 2002. *Notornis* 49: 29–38. Crockett, D. E. & Kearns, M. P. 1975. *Notornis* 22: 69–72. Dann, P. 1994. *Notornis* 41: 157–66. Gales, R. 1988. *Notornis* 35: 71–75. Heber, S. 2008. *NZ J Zool* 35: 63–71. Kinsky, F. C. 1960. *Rec Dom Mus* 3: 145–218. Kinsky, F. C. & Falla, R. A. 1976. *Rec Nat Mus* 1: 105–26. Montague, T. 1985. *Emu* 85: 264–67. Van Heezik, Y. 1990. *NZ J Zool* 17: 543–48.

60. MAGELLANIC PENGUIN *Spheniscus magellanicus* PLATE 10

Size: 70cm, 3.5kg
Distribution: Breeds on the Juan Fernández Islands in the Pacific, along the coast of southern Chile to the islands near Cape Horn, along the Patagonian coast of Argentina, and in the Falkland Islands. There have been two records of Magellanic Penguins on the New Zealand mainland: Waimarama, Hawke's Bay (March 1972), and in Otago Harbour (March 1990). Both birds were moulting, but as they readily took fish from the hand they may have had an assisted passage by ship.
Reading: Boswall, J. & MacIver, D. 1975. In Stonehouse, B. *The Biology of Penguins*. London: Macmillan. Darby, J. T. 1991. *Notornis* 38: 36. Robertson, C. J. R. et al. 1972. *Notornis* 19: 111–13.

ALBATROSSES and MOLLYMAWKS *Diomedeidae*

21 species, 17 with breeding restricted to the Southern Hemisphere, 1 at the Galapagos Islands, and 3 in the North Pacific. In the New Zealand region, 17 species have been recorded,* including 7 endemic species and 4 other breeding species.

Albatrosses and mollymawks (the common name in New Zealand for the smaller *Thalassarche* albatrosses) are a clearly defined group of very large seabirds belonging to the tube-nose petrel order (Procellariiformes). Although they are among the largest of all flying birds, albatrosses are noted for their perfection of dynamic soaring flight behind boats and among the most tempestuous seas of the southern oceans. In strong winds, they wheel effortlessly on very long, narrow and stiffly held wings for hours, but in rare almost calm conditions they have a flapping flight and more usually rest on the surface until the wind picks up. Their webbed feet are used for swimming and as rudders and brakes in flight, especially when coming in to land.

Albatrosses have long bills with a strongly hooked tip and small, raised, tubular nostrils on either side at the base. The shape and colour of the bill plates can be useful in identifying beach-wrecked specimens, but at sea the head colour and pattern of black on the underwings is also important to note.

They nest in loose colonies, mainly on uninhabited and often inaccessible islands. At their breeding grounds they have an elaborate series of displays accompanied by neighs, groans, baas, wails, croaks, cackles and bill-snapping and clappering. All species lay 1 white egg, usually in a shallow depression on top of a pedestal ('chimney pot') made of vegetation and mud. Incubation takes 66–83 days. Nestlings are downy and take many months to reach flying age. With this long breeding

*The Black-footed Albatross *Phoebastria nigripes* of the North Pacific has been recorded once in the Southern Hemisphere, at Dusky Sound, Fiordland, in 1884.

cycle, some species can nest only every second year if they have bred successfully.

Albatrosses feed mainly on various squid, fish and offal, on or close to the surface. Some species are readily attracted to boats and follow them for hours, occasionally alighting to pick up scraps cast overboard or food disturbed in the wake. Some are especially attracted to fishing boats, and several species have suffered high mortality from being drowned in trawl nets, hitting trawl cables, or taking baited hooks on tuna or swordfish long lines. Various methods have been introduced to greatly reduce the accidental by-catch problems.

Reading: Harrison, P. 1987. *Seabirds of the World: A Photographic Guide*. London: Croom Helm. Onley, D. & Scofield, P. 2007. *Field Guide to the Albatrosses, Petrels and Shearwaters of the World*. London: Christopher Helm. Serventy, D. L. et al. 1971. *The Handbook of Australian Sea-birds*. Sydney: Reed. Warham, J. 1990. *The Petrels: Their Ecology and Breeding Systems*. London: Academic Press.

61. WANDERING ALBATROSS *Diomedea exulans* PLATE 14

Other name: Snowy Albatross
Size: 115cm; 6.5kg
Geographical variation: Recent taxonomic authorities have separated the Antipodean Albatross (*D. antipodensis*), which breeds in New Zealand, from the Wandering Albatross (*D. exulans*), which does not.
Distribution: Circumpolar, breeding on islands between 46° S and 55° S in the South Atlantic and South Indian oceans and at Macquarie Island. They wander widely in southern oceans between the pack ice off Antarctica and the subtropics, and banded birds from South Georgia, Crozet, Kerguelen and Macquarie islands have been found dead on the New Zealand coast or as fisheries by-catch, and larger paler albatrosses, formerly known as Snowy Albatrosses, have been seen at sea or found beach-wrecked.
Behaviour: Gregarious at breeding colonies and form flocks around fishing boats, but usually wander the oceans alone or in small groups. At sea, they are generally silent except for a hoarse croak, made when they are fighting for scraps.
Feeding: Diet is mainly squid, with occasional fish, octopuses and crustaceans, mostly caught at night on the surface or by plunging down a metre or two. During the day, food is scavenged from around whales and dolphins, and more recently from behind boats, which has made them vulnerable to accidental capture on baited fish-hooks and in trawl nets and gear.
In the hand: Wandering Albatrosses have longer bills than Antipodean Albatrosses: males 160–180mm cf. 145–160mm; females 155–170mm cf. 135–150mm.
Reading: Croxall, J. P. et al. 1990. *J Anim Ecol* 59: 775–96. Murray, T. E. et al. 1993. *Bird Cons Int* 3: 181–210. Robertson, C. J. R. & Warham, J. 1992. *Bull BOC*. 112: 74–81. Robertson, C. J. R. & Warham, J. 1994. *Bull BOC*. 114: 132–34. Weimerskirch, H. et al. 1987. *Oikos* 49: 315–22.

62. ANTIPODEAN ALBATROSS *Diomedea antipodensis* PLATE 14

Other names: Toroa, Wanderer, Gibson's Albatross (Auckland Islands)
Size: 115cm; 6.5kg
Geographical variation: Recent taxonomic authorities have separated the Antipodean Albatross (*D. antipodensis*), which breeds in New Zealand, from the Wandering Albatross (*D. exulans*), which does not. Within the Antipodean Albatross, two subspecies are recognised, *antipodensis* on the Antipodes and Campbell islands, and *gibsoni* on the Auckland Islands.
Distribution: Breeds only in New Zealand: at the Antipodes, Auckland and Campbell islands and, since 2003, at the Chatham Islands. They wander widely in southern oceans between the pack ice off Antarctica and the subtropics, from southwestern Australia in the west to South America in the east. Birds breeding on the Auckland Islands tend to feed in subantarctic and temperate waters of the Tasman Sea, west to southwestern Australia and in the southwestern Pacific, but Antipodes Island birds tend to range much further east to South American waters and over a wider latitudinal range into both Antarctic and tropical waters. Antipodean Albatrosses are seen off the New Zealand mainland in all months, but mainly in winter, especially around Stewart Island, Kaikoura and in Cook Strait.
Population: *c.* 7000 pairs breed each year, but with

mainly biennial breeding, only *c.* 60% of the breeding birds are at their colony each year, which means the breeding population is *c.* 11,500 pairs. *antipodensis*: the Antipodes *c.* 3700 pairs per year or 6200 total breeding pairs; Campbell Island <10 pairs; Chathams <5 pairs; *gibsoni*: Auckland Islands *c.* 3200 pairs per year or 5300 total breeding pairs, mostly on Adams Island, but 200–300 pairs nest on Disappointment Island each year and a few are still on the main Auckland Island.

Conservation: Protected critically endangered endemic. Antipodean Albatrosses are attracted to feed on offal behind fishing boats and are often accidentally hooked on tuna and swordfish long lines (over 300 deaths of 'wandering albatrosses' estimated in 2003–12) mainly off the eastern North Island and the Kermadecs. Females are apparently more susceptible than males. Deaths of breeding adults are particularly worrying in such a long-lived species.

Breeding: At the Auckland Islands, most eggs are laid from December to early February, but on the Antipodes and at Campbell Island they are laid about 3 weeks later, from early January to mid-February. They lay **1** white egg (126 x 78mm, 425g) in a shallow depression on top of a 20–50cm tall mound of grass and soil. The mound is built on flat ground close to a ridge, where adults can easily catch enough wind for take-off. Incubation is by both sexes in alternating shifts of 6–10 days during the incubation period of *c.* 80 days. During their breaks from the nest, satellite-tagged birds from Adams Island flew a round trip distance of up to 5000km and up to 1500km linear distance away into the Tasman Sea to feed. Chicks are initially covered in very pale grey down and are brooded by both adults for the first month, but are then left unguarded except during feeding visits and occasional longer visits until the chick fledges at 9–10 months old in late December–March and is immediately independent of its parents.

If breeding is successful, adults miss a year before breeding again, but if they fail early in the breeding cycle, most pairs breed in successive years. Pair bonds are life long, but if a bird loses its mate it can re-pair with another bird. Pairs return to the same nest location year after year, and young return to their natal colony at 3–14 years old, but usually do not start breeding until 7–16 years old. Annual adult survival on the Antipodes and Auckland islands is about 95.7%, which gives a life expectancy of about 23 years. The oldest New Zealand bird recorded was over 24 years old, but some probably live to over 40 years.

Behaviour: Gregarious at breeding colonies and forms flocks around fishing boats, but they usually wander the oceans alone or in small groups. At sea, they are generally silent except for a hoarse croak, made when they are fighting for scraps.

Feeding: Diet is mainly squid, with occasional fish, octopuses and crustaceans, mostly caught at night on the surface or by plunging down a metre or two. During the day, food is scavenged from around whales and dolphins, and recently from behind boats, which makes them vulnerable to accidental capture on baited fish-hooks.

In the hand: The subspecies are difficult to identify because of the wide variety of immature plumages and the incomplete knowledge of the rate of acquisition of a mature adult plumage. Adult females of *antipodensis* retain dark brown plumage similar to the immature plumage of other subspecies, males often have a prominent dark patch on their crown and an oily smudge across the breast, and both male and female have very little white on their upperwings. Overall, *gibsoni* is paler than *antipodensis* at all ages, and usually shows prominent white patches on the inner upperwing.

Reading: Bailey, A. M. & Sorensen, J. H. 1950. *Subantarctic Campbell Island*. Denver: Denver Mus Nat Hist. Croxall, J. P. et al. 1990. *J Anim Ecol* 59: 775–96. Murray, T. E. et al. 1993. *Bird Cons Int* 3: 181–210. Robertson, C. J. R. & Warham, J. 1992. *Bull BOC* 112: 74–81. Robertson, C. J. R. & Warham, J. 1994. *Bull BOC* 114: 132–34. Walker, K. et al. 1995. *Notornis* 42: 127–37. Walker, K. & Elliott, G. 2005. *Notornis* 52: 206–14. Walker, K. & Elliott, G. 2005. *Notornis* 52: 215–22. Walker, K. & Elliott, G. 2006. *Notornis* 53: 265–90. Weimerskirch, H. et al. 1987. *Oikos* 49: 315–22.

63. SOUTHERN ROYAL ALBATROSS *Diomedea epomophora* PLATE 14

Other name: Toroa

Size: 115cm; 9kg

Geographical variation: Recent taxonomic authorities have split the Royal Albatross into two separate species, the larger Southern Royal Albatross *D. epomophora* breeding at the Auckland and Campbell island groups, and the smaller Northern Royal Albatross *D. sanfordi* breeding at the Chathams and at Taiaroa Head, Otago. A few birds of the two species have interbred at Taiaroa Head.

Distribution: Breeds only in New Zealand; mainly on Campbell Island, a few pairs on Enderby, Adams and Auckland islands. Ranges through New Zealand coastal waters and the Tasman Sea to about 36° S all year, but mostly seen in winter, especially in Cook Strait, off East Cape and in Foveaux Strait. Most juveniles (<20 months old) move to seas off the west coast of South America, but immature birds are often found off the east coast of South America. Non-breeding adults migrate eastwards to seas off South America, returning by the South Atlantic and South Indian oceans and below Australia. Occasional stragglers have been recorded in the subtropical Pacific, e.g. in the Tuamotu Archipelago of French Polynesia.

Population: Each year *c.* 8500 pairs breed on Campbell Island and <100 pairs breed on Enderby, Adams and Auckland islands. If about 60% of pairs attempt to breed each year, this equates to a total breeding population of about 14,000 pairs.

Conservation: Protected endemic. Numbers on the subantarctic islands were much reduced by sealers, whalers, farmers and introduced animals, but since the islands have been protected, and sheep, pigs and cattle have been removed from Campbell Island and from Enderby in the Auckland Islands, numbers have increased. Royal Albatrosses are occasionally killed accidentally on fishing gear in New Zealand waters, off South America and in transit but, overall, populations seem to be moderately stable.

Breeding: About a month after returning to their colony, Southern Royal Albatrosses lay between 24 November and 25 December. They lay 1 white egg (127 x 79mm, 430g) in a shallow depression on top of a 10–30cm tall mound of tussock, thin woody branches, fern and moss. The nest is built on sheltered flat ground, often a long way from a ridge or cliff where adults can catch strong winds or an updraught for take-off. Incubation is by both sexes in alternating shifts of 2–12 days during the incubation period of 77–81 days.

Chicks hatch in February–March and are initially covered in white down. They are brooded by both parents for the first 5–6 weeks, but are then left unguarded except during feeding visits and occasional longer visits until the chick fledges at *c.* 8 months old from October to December. It is immediately independent of its parents. If breeding is successful, the adults miss a year before breeding again, but if they fail early in the breeding cycle, most pairs breed in successive years. Pair bonds are life long, but if a bird loses its mate it can re-pair with another bird. Pairs return to the same nest site year after year, and young return to their natal colony at 3–8 years old, but usually do not start breeding until 6–12 years old. The oldest banded bird lived to over 43 years old.

Behaviour: Gregarious at breeding colonies, and small flocks form around fishing boats, but at sea they are usually solitary. Generally silent at sea, but noisy when displaying at their nest.

Feeding: Diet of adults is mainly squid, especially *Histioteuthis* and post-spawning *Moroteuthopsis*, with some octopuses, fish, crustaceans and salps. Food is caught on the surface, and only rarely do birds plunge down a metre or two. Their feeding areas over continental shelf breaks and inner slopes closer to land are not used much for tuna long-line fishing, and this helps to reduce their fisheries-related mortality.

In the hand: Males are larger than females, with only a slight overlap: wing 680–705mm cf. 650–680mm; bill 180–190mm cf. 165–180mm.

Reading: Bailey, A. M. & Sorenson, J. H. 1950. *Subantarctic Campbell Island*. Denver: Denver Mus Nat Hist. Imber, M. J. 1999. *Emu* 99: 200–11. Moore, P. M. & Bettany, S. M. 2005. *Notornis* 52: 195–205. Robertson, C. J. R. & Kinsky, F. C. 1972. *Notornis*: 19: 289–301.

64. NORTHERN ROYAL ALBATROSS *Diomedea sanfordi* PLATE 14

Other name: Toroa

Size: 115cm, 9kg

Geographical variation: Recent taxonomic authorities have split the Royal Albatross into two separate species, the larger Southern Royal Albatross *D. epomophora* breeding on the Auckland and Campbell island groups, and the smaller Northern Royal Albatross *D. sanfordi* breeding at the Chathams and at Taiaroa Head, Otago. A few birds of the two species have interbred at Taiaroa Head.

Distribution: Breeds only in New Zealand – mainly at the Chatham Islands on The Forty-fours (Motuhara) and The Sisters, but a few breed at Taiaroa Head, at the southern entrance to Otago Harbour, near Dunedin. Breeding birds range through New Zealand coastal waters, mainly to the east of the main islands, but some head into the Tasman Sea as far as the southeast coast of Australia. Seen locally all year, but mostly in winter, and especially in Cook Strait, off East Cape and in Foveaux Strait. Most non-breeders, juveniles and young birds migrate eastwards to seas off South America and the Falkland Islands, returning by the South Indian Ocean and below Australia.

Population: *c.* 6500 pairs; *c.* 4000 on The Forty-fours, *c.* 2500 on The Sisters, and 30–35 pairs at Taiaroa Head, Dunedin.

Conservation: Protected endemic. On the Chathams, they were traditionally harvested by Moriori and then Maori until they were legally protected in 1921. Although some illegal harvest continued, the numbers in the Chathams have apparently remained moderately stable since the first detailed counts were made in 1972–75. However, a deterioration of nesting habitat related to soil loss in severe storms and a drier climate has led to a decline in breeding success because many eggs break in the rudimentary nests built in poor rocky habitats. The small colony at Taiaroa Head has grown steadily, mainly from returning chicks but also with continued immigration from the Chathams. Birds prospected the colony as early as the 1890s, but it was not until 1938 that they bred successfully there. Royal Albatross populations seem moderately stable despite some fisheries-related deaths in New Zealand waters, off South America and in transit through the southern oceans.

Breeding: About a month after returning to the colony, Northern Royal Albatrosses lay between 27 October and 6 December. They lay **1** white egg (124 x 78mm, 410g) in a shallow depression on top of a 10–30cm tall mound of tussock, thin woody branches, fern and moss. The nest is built on sheltered flat ground, often close to a ridge or cliff where adults can catch strong winds or an updraught for take-off. Incubation is by both sexes in alternating shifts of 2–12 days during the incubation period of 77–81 days.

Chicks hatch in January–February. They are initially covered in white down and are brooded by both parents for the first 5–6 weeks, but are then left unguarded except during feeding visits and occasional longer visits until the chick fledges at *c.* 8 months old from mid-August to November. It is immediately independent of its parents. If breeding is successful, the adults miss a year before breeding again, but if they fail early in the breeding cycle, most pairs breed in successive years. Pair bonds are life long, but if a bird loses its mate it can re-pair with another bird. Pairs return to the same nest site year after year, and young return to their natal colony at 3–8 years old, but usually do not start breeding until 6–10 years old. The oldest bird at Taiaroa Head was named 'Grandma', and she was believed to have reached a banded age of 51.5 years and a probable age of over 61 years.

Behaviour: Gregarious at breeding colonies, and small flocks form around fishing boats, but at sea they are usually solitary. Generally silent at sea, but noisy when displaying at their nest.

Feeding: Diet of adults is mainly squid, especially *Histioteuthis* and post-spawning *Moroteuthopsis*, with some octopuses, fish, crustaceans and salps. Food is caught on the surface, and only rarely do birds plunge down a metre or two. Their feeding areas over continental shelf breaks and inner slopes closer to land are not used much for tuna long-line fishing, and this helps to reduce their fisheries-related mortality.

In the hand: Males are larger than females, with only a slight overlap: wing 635–670mm cf. 615–635mm; bill 165–175mm cf. 155–165mm.

Reading: Imber, M. J. 1999. *Emu* 99: 200–211. Richdale, L. E. 1950. *Biol Monographs* 3. Dunedin: Published privately. Richdale, L. E. 1952. *Biol Monographs* 4. Dunedin: Published privately. Robertson, C. J. R. 1991. *DOC Sci & Res Ser* 35. Wellington: DOC. Robertson, C. J. R. 1993. *Emu* 93: 269–276. Robertson, C. J. R. & Kinsky, F. C. 1972. *Notornis*: 19: 289–301.

65. LAYSAN ALBATROSS *Phoebastria immutabilis* PLATE 15

Size: 80cm, 2.4kg

Distribution: Breeds mainly on islands in the north-western part of the Hawaiian Chain in the North Pacific Ocean. Some nest on a few outlying islands of Japan and on some islands in Baja California. Scatters widely across temperate and tropical waters of the North Pacific, but a few stray to the Southern Hemisphere. Recorded from Australia, Norfolk Island and once in New Zealand waters: a bird seen on the Lachlan Banks about 30km off Cape Kidnappers, Hawke's Bay (December 1995).

Feeding: Diet has not been studied in New Zealand, but elsewhere it is mainly squid, fish, offal and crustaceans, with some food scavenged from fishing boats. Prey is mainly seized on the surface, but birds occasionally surface-dive for food.

66. ATLANTIC YELLOW-NOSED MOLLYMAWK *Thalassarche chlororhynchos*

PLATE 15

Other name: Atlantic Yellow-nosed Albatross
Size: 75cm; 2.4kg
Distribution: Breeds on the Tristan da Cunha archipelago and Gough Island in the South Atlantic Ocean, and ranges through the South Atlantic between 15° S and 50° S. After breeding, some disperse to the South Indian Ocean and east to southern Australia and occasionally to New Zealand. One bird prospected on Middle Sister Island, Chathams, in January 1975. Presumably the same bird laid an egg in September 1976. A different bird was seen there in January 1996.
Feeding: Diet has not been studied in New Zealand, but elsewhere it is mainly fish, squid and crustaceans, with some fish scavenged from fishing boats. Prey is mainly seized on the surface, but birds occasionally surface-dive for food.
In the hand: Adults separable from the Indian Ocean species by having a greyer head, a prominent black triangle in front of the eye, and usually the yellow stripe on top of the bill broadens behind the nostrils and is rounded at the base.
Reading: Cuthbert, R. et al. 2003. *Condor* 105: 439–452. Latham, P. C. 1980. *Notornis* 27: 393–394. Robertson, C. J. R. 1975. *Notornis* 22: 342–344. Robertson, C. J. R. 2002. *Marine Ornith* 30: 48–49.

67. INDIAN OCEAN YELLOW-NOSED MOLLYMAWK *Thalassarche carteri*

PLATE 15

Other names: Indian Ocean Yellow-nosed Albatross, Indian Yellow-nosed Albatross
Size: 75cm; 2.2kg
Distribution: Breeds on Prince Edward, Crozet, Kerguelen, St Paul and Amsterdam islands in the Indian Ocean between 37° S and 49° S, and ranges through the South Indian Ocean and east to southern Australia and New Zealand. Both adults and juveniles have become regular autumn and winter visitors to warm coastal waters off northern and eastern Northland, the Hauraki Gulf and the Bay of Plenty, where they often loosely associate with Australasian Gannets. Numbers built up rapidly and peaked in the 1980s, when they were the most numerous mollymawk in the area, but numbers have since waned as the overall population has been hit by fisheries by-catch problems overseas. They are occasionally reported off the South Island, especially in Tasman Bay and off Kaikoura. One or two pairs have bred on The Pyramid, Chathams, since 1998.
Breeding: Not studied in New Zealand, except that nesting has been noted in summer months. Elsewhere they lay **1** white egg in September–October, which is incubated by both parents for *c.* 75 days. Fledging period is *c.* 130 days.
Feeding: Diet has not been studied in New Zealand, but elsewhere it is mainly fish, squid and shrimps, with some fish scavenged from fishing boats. Prey is mainly seized on the surface, but birds occasionally surface-dive for food.
In the hand: Adults separable from the Atlantic species by paler head, lack of a prominent black triangle in front of the eye, and usually the yellow stripe on top of the bill tapers behind the nostrils and is pointed at the base.
Reading: Latham, P. C. 1980. *Notornis* 27: 393–394. Robertson, C. J. R. 1975. *Notornis* 22: 342–344. Robertson, C. J. R. 2002. *Marine Ornith* 30: 48–49.

68. GREY-HEADED MOLLYMAWK *Thalassarche chrysostoma* **PLATE 16**

Other name: Grey-headed Albatross
Size: 80cm, 3.25kg
Distribution: Circumpolar, breeding on subantarctic islands between 46° S and 56° S, with the largest colonies being on Diego Ramirez Islands near Cape Horn, and on South Georgia. In New Zealand, Grey-headed Mollymawks breed only at Campbell Island, although about 50 pairs nest nearby on Macquarie Island. At sea, they range widely in the southern oceans, generally over deep oceanic waters between 40° S and the Antarctic coast, but especially along the Polar Front, 1000–1500km south of Campbell Island. They are occasionally seen in New Zealand coastal waters and are one of the most frequent mollymawk species to be beach-wrecked, especially in July–October when juveniles are moving north into the Tasman Sea.

Population: The annual number of breeding pairs in the world is estimated at *c.* 70,000 pairs of which *c.* 6500 pairs nest on Campbell Island. The population has declined over 80% since the 1940s.
Conservation: Protected vulnerable native. Numbers on Campbell Island are declining by about 3% per annum due to low recruitment and poor breeding success. The decline could be associated with changes in food supplies as a result of oceanic warming, and a southward shift in the Polar Front which lengthens foraging trips during breeding. Although few Grey-headed Mollymawks are accidentally caught in fishing operations in New Zealand waters because the species feeds primarily in deep water away from major fisheries, some are killed on tuna long lines in Australian waters and elsewhere in the Southern Ocean.
Breeding: Grey-headed Mollymawks, like the large albatrosses, are biennial breeders – if they raise a chick successfully, they will not attempt to breed the following year, but if they fail (especially in the early part of the nesting cycle), they will breed the following year. On Campbell Island, birds return in late August and most eggs are laid over a short period between 26 September and 9 October. They lay **1** white egg (107 x 67mm), with brownish-red speckling at the broader end, in a shallow cup on top of a small pedestal of soil and vegetation. The adults share incubation for *c.* 72 days and then share duties guarding the downy chick until it is 15–**27**–39 days old. The chick fledges at 143–**152**–157 days old in early to mid-May. Chicks are independent once they fledge. Young return to land at 5 years old, but do not start breeding until 10–**13**–17 years old. Adult survival is about 95.3%, with the oldest banded bird being over 30 years old.
Behaviour: Nests in large colonies, intermingling with New Zealand Black-browed Mollymawks on Campbell Island. At sea, Grey-headed Mollymawks usually feed alone but may form flocks with other seabirds. They seldom follow ships and, except near the Falkland Islands, tend not to congregate around fishing boats as most other mollymawks do. Generally much quieter and more docile than other albatrosses.
Feeding: Diet on Campbell Island is mainly squid, with some fish (rarely scavenged from fishing boats). Elsewhere krill and carrion, such as small seabirds, are taken. Prey is mainly seized on the surface, but occasionally birds do shallow plunges or dive for food.
Reading: Bailey, A. M. & Sorensen, J. H. 1950. *Subantarctic Campbell Island.* Denver: Denver Mus Nat Hist. Moore, P. J. & Moffat, R. D. 1990. *DOC Sci & Res Int Rep* 59. Wellington: DOC. Waugh, S. et al. 1999. *Ibis* 141: 216–225. Waugh, S. et al. 2000. *Condor* 102: 804–813. Weimerskirch, H. et al. 1986. *Ibis* 128: 195–213.

69. BLACK-BROWED MOLLYMAWK *Thalassarche melanophris* PLATE 16

Other name: Black-browed Albatross
Size: 88cm, 3.5kg
Distribution: Circumpolar, breeding on subantarctic islands between 46° S and 56° S in the South Atlantic and South Indian oceans, on Macquarie Island and, in the New Zealand region, at Bollons Island (Antipodes), the Western Chain (The Snares) and at Campbell Island. Non-breeders, juveniles and young birds of this subspecies wander extensively through the southern oceans between about 30° S and the Antarctic coast, and further north off the western coasts of South America and Africa; a few stragglers even cross the equator.
Population: The most plentiful of all albatrosses, with a world population of *c.* 3 million birds, mainly breeding on islands off southern Chile and at the Falkland Islands. Fewer than 150 pairs breed in the New Zealand region: Bollons Island (Antipodes) 120 pairs, Western Chain (The Snares) a few pairs, Campbell Island *c.* 20 pairs.
Conservation: Protected native coloniser. Internationally, this species is often caught accidentally in fishing operations when attracted to feed on offal and discards behind fishing boats, and they may be caught up on trawl wires or in nets, or on long-line hooks; however, few have been reported killed in New Zealand waters.
Breeding: On Bollons Island they nest with White-capped Mollymawks, and on Campbell Island with Grey-headed and Campbell Islands mollymawks, and rarely hybridise there with the latter species. Most eggs are laid over a short period between mid-September and early October. Pairs are stable from year to year and return to the same nest site each year. They lay **1** white egg (102 x 66mm, 230g), with pinkish speckling at the broader end, in a shallow cup on top of a small pedestal of soil and vegetation. The adults share incubation for *c.* 70 days, and then share duties guarding the downy chick until it is 15–**23**–34 days old. The chick fledges at 122–**130**–141 days old in mid-April and is independent once it leaves the nest. Young return to land from 5 years old, but do not start breeding until 6–**10**–13 years old.
Behaviour: At sea, they form large flocks to feed on

offal from fishing boats and elsewhere are found in large mixed flocks of seabirds. At their breeding ground, they have an elaborate series of displays accompanied by baas, wails, croaks, cackles, groans and bill-snapping.
Feeding: Diet has not been studied in New Zealand, but elsewhere in the southern oceans it is mainly fish (often scavenged from fishing boats), squid, krill and carrion. Prey is mainly seized on the surface, and only rarely do birds plunge or dive for food. Their affinity for feeding on scraps from fishing boats has made Black-browed Mollymawks very vulnerable to accidental capture.
In the hand: The dark-coloured eye distinguishes them from adult Campbell Islands Mollymawks, but immatures of the two species are hard to separate. They have a smaller black eyebrow and are on average larger than the Campbell Islands Mollymawk: bill 114–**117**–122mm cf. 106–**112**–118mm; wing 510–**535**–560mm cf. 490–**520**–540mm. Males are slightly larger than females in all measurements.
Reading: Moore, P. J. & Moffat, R. D. 1990 *DOC Sci & Res Int Rep* 59. Wellington: DOC. Moore, P. et al. 2001. *Emu* 101: 329–334. Waugh, S. et al. 1999. *Ibis* 141: 216–225. Weimerskirch, H. et al. 1986. *Ibis* 128: 195–213.

70. CAMPBELL ISLANDS MOLLYMAWK *Thalassarche impavida* PLATE 16

Other name: Campbell Islands Albatross
Size: 85cm, 3kg
Distribution: New Zealand only. Breeds on the northern coast of Campbell Island and nearby Isle de Jeanette-Marie, and ranges widely in New Zealand waters and through the Tasman Sea to eastern and southern Australia, reaching as far south as the Ross Sea. Most are found south of Cook Strait in the summer and East Cape in the winter. Some, especially immatures, move further northwards to the Coral Sea and to South Pacific Ocean waters around New Caledonia and Fiji, and vagrants have been recorded further east in the subtropical Pacific near Tonga, Samoa, Cook Islands, French Polynesia and even Chile, and one recorded from Kerguelen Islands in the Indian Ocean.
Population: *c.* 21,000 pairs. The population may have increased up until about 1970, but then numbers fell rapidly in the 1970s and 1980s, and have fallen slowly since then.
Conservation: Protected endemic. Most of the decline since the 1970s has been attributed to changes in food supplies as sea temperatures changed because relatively few are killed accidentally in fishing operations. Some birds are attracted to feed on offal and discards behind fishing boats and may be caught up on trawl wires or in nets.
Breeding: On Campbell Island, birds return in August and most eggs are laid over a short period between mid-September and early October. Pairs are stable from year to year and return to the same nest site each year. They lay **1** white egg (102 x 66mm, 230g), with pinkish speckling at the broader end, in a shallow cup on top of a small pedestal of soil and vegetation. The adults share incubation for 65–72 days, and then share duties guarding the downy chick until it is 15–**23**–34 days old. The chick fledges at 122–**130**–141 days old in mid-April. Chicks are independent once they fledge and apparently disperse quickly from the colony – one was found dead on Foxton Beach 7 days after it had been banded on Campbell Island. Young return to land from 5 years old, but do not start breeding until 6–**10**–13 years old. Adult survival is about 94.5%, with the oldest banded bird being over 26 years old.
Behaviour: Some hybridise with the few Black-browed Mollymawks on Campbell Island, where both species nest in large close-knit colonies, sometimes intermingling with Grey-headed Mollymawks. At sea, they form large flocks to feed on offal from fishing boats and elsewhere are found in large mixed flocks of seabirds. At their breeding ground, they have an elaborate series of displays accompanied by baas, wails, croaks, cackles, groans and bill-snapping.
Feeding: Diet is mainly fish, especially southern blue whiting, squid and krill. Prey is mainly seized on the surface, and only rarely do birds plunge or dive for food.
In the hand: The pale honey-coloured eye of adult birds is distinctive in live or freshly dead birds, but they also have a more extensive black eyebrow and are on average smaller than the closely-related Black-browed Mollymawk: bill 106–**112**–118mm cf. 114–**117**–122mm; wing 490–**520**–540mm cf. 510–**535**–560mm. Males are slightly larger than females in all measurements.
Reading: Bailey A. M. & Sorensen, J. H. 1950. *Subantarctic Campbell Island.* Denver: Denver Mus Nat Hist. Moore, P. J. & Moffat, R. D. 1990 *DOC Sci & Res Int Rep* 59. Wellington: DOC. Moore, P. et al. 2001. *Emu* 101: 329–334. Waugh, S. et al. 1999a. *Emu* 99: 29–35. Waugh, S. et al. 1999b. *Ibis* 141: 216–225.

71. BULLER'S MOLLYMAWK *Thalassarche bulleri* PLATE 16

Other names: Buller's Albatross, Pacific Mollymawk/Albatross
Size: 80cm; 3kg
Geographical variation: Two subspecies, which may eventually be reclassified as full species: the Southern Buller's Mollymawk *bulleri* breeding on The Snares and on the Solander Islands, and the Northern Buller's Mollymawk breeding at the Chatham Islands and on Rosemary Rocks, Three Kings Islands.
Distribution: Breeds only in New Zealand; near or north of the Subtropical Convergence in the Three Kings Islands, Chathams, Solander Island and at The Snares. The largest colony is on The Forty-fours (Motuhara), to the east of the Chathams. They are regularly seen in coastal waters and over the continental shelf around southern New Zealand and the Tasman Sea, and they are quite often beach-wrecked in winter, especially on the Southland, Otago and Wellington coasts. Buller's Mollymawks are uncommon in northern New Zealand waters. After breeding they disperse across the South Pacific Ocean, north of the Antarctic Convergence, to the west coast of South America; a few stray into the South Atlantic and South Indian oceans.
Population: Total population is *c*. 32,000 breeding pairs: Rosemary Rock, Three Kings Islands <20 pairs; Sisters Islands, Chathams 2150 pairs; Forty-fours, Chathams 16,000 pairs; Solander Islands 4900 pairs; The Snares 8700 pairs.
Conservation: Protected endemic. Numbers of Buller's Mollymawks breeding on The Snares increased 78% between 1969 and 1992, but declined on the Solanders between 1985 and 1996, and the nesting density has apparently declined on the Forty-fours since the 1970s. Many Southern Buller's Mollymawks (*c*. 300 a year) are caught equally on tuna long lines and in nets or cables of squid, hoki and wharehou trawling. On balance, they may have derived some benefit from the increased fishery in southern New Zealand waters, however, further close monitoring of all breeding populations is needed.
Breeding: Northern Buller's Mollymawks return to the Chathams in late September and eggs are laid between 26 October and 23 November, whereas Southern Buller's Mollymawks return to The Snares in mid-December and eggs are laid over a long season, from late December to late February. They lay **1** white egg (104 x 65mm, 246g), with brownish-red speckling at the broader end, in a shallow cup on top of a small pedestal of soil, rock chips and vegetation. The adults share incubation in stints of 2–4 days in the northern subspecies, but of 10–14 days in the southern form. Incubation lasts 68–72 days and the parents share duties guarding the downy chick until it is *c*. 21 days old. The chicks fledge at *c*. 5–6 months, in June at the Chathams but late August–early October at The Snares. Young first return to the colony from 5 years old, but probably don't start breeding until *c*. 12 years old. Most return to within 100m of where they hatched. Birds apparently mate for life and retain the same nest site from year to year – one pair banded in January/February 1948 was still using the same nest 23 years later, and the female was last seen there 45 years later in March 1993, aged at least 50, and more likely over 55 years old.
Behaviour: Nests in large colonies, generally keeping apart from other species. At sea, they are usually solitary but are sometimes seen in small groups and occasionally in large mixed flocks around fishing boats.
Feeding: Diet during the breeding season is mostly fisheries discards, salps, squid, small fish, krill, octopus and carrion such as small seabirds. Prey is mainly seized on the surface, and only rarely do birds plunge or dive for food.
In the hand: Males are slightly larger than females. Although there is much overlap, most can be sexed from a combination of tarsus width and minimum bill depth. The southern subspecies, *bulleri*, has a narrower bill (male 26.3–30.2mm, female 25.5–28.1mm) than the northern subspecies (male 30.7–34.5mm, female 28.7–32.4mm).
Reading: Francis, R. I. C. & Sagar, P. M. 2012. *NZ J Zool* 39: 3–17. Richdale, L. E. & Warham, J. 1973. *Ibis* 115: 257–263. Robertson, C. J. R. 1991. *DOC Sci & Res Ser* 35. Wellington: DOC. Robertson, C. J. R. 1994. *DOC CAS Notes* 70. Wellington: DOC. Sagar, P. M. & Warham, J. 1993. *Notornis* 40: 303–304. Sagar, P. M. et al. 1994. *Notornis* 41: 85–92. Sagar, P. M. et al. 1998. *Notornis* 45: 271–278. Sagar, P. M. & Stahl, J. C. 2005. *Emu* 105: 49–55. Spear, I. B. et al. 2003. *Ibis* 145: 253–269. Stahl, J. C. et al. 1998. *NZ J. Zool* 24: 109–137. Stahl, J. C. & Sagar, P. M. 2000. *J Roy Soc NZ* 30: 299–318. Warham, J. & Fitzsimons, C. H. 1987. *NZ J Zool* 14: 65–79. West, J. A. & Imber, M. J. 1986. *NZ J Zool* 13: 169–174.

72. WHITE-CAPPED MOLLYMAWK *Thalassarche cauta* PLATE 17

Other names: Shy Albatross/Mollymawk, White-capped Albatross
Size: 95cm, 4kg
Geographical variation: Two subspecies: Tasmanian Mollymawk *cauta* breeds around Tasmania and occasionally visits New Zealand waters, and the New Zealand White-capped Mollymawk *steadi* breeds on the Auckland Islands, with small numbers at the Antipodes and Chathams.
Distribution: Breeds on islands off southwestern Tasmania and in Bass Strait, and in the New Zealand subantarctic, especially at Disappointment Island in the Auckland Islands group. Also breeds in moderate numbers on Auckland and Adams islands; a few breed on Bollons Island, Antipodes; and one pair has nested on The Forty-fours (Motuhara), Chathams. At sea, they range widely in the southern oceans, with most records from subantarctic and subtropical waters of the South Pacific north to about 20° S, especially common off Chile, and off South Africa and Namibia. Abundant over continental shelf waters around southern and central New Zealand during most of the year, and the species of mollymawk most often beach-wrecked, mainly from early winter to late spring. One New Zealand record of the *cauta* subspecies, a banded 2-year-old bird from Mewstone, Tasmania, at the Waikato Rivermouth, but others are likely to be overlooked in New Zealand waters.
Population: *c.* 95,000 pairs in 2011–13: Disappointment Island *c.* 90,000 pairs, 5000 pairs on Auckland Island, 100 pairs on Adams Island, 20 pairs on Bollons Island and up to 3 pairs at The Forty-fours.
Conservation: Protected native. Feral pigs have almost wiped out all accessible breeding colonies on main Auckland Island. Each year, about 700 White-capped Mollymawks are killed accidentally by fishing operations in New Zealand waters, mostly drowned after having collided with and become entangled in squid trawling gear, or hooked on tuna long lines. In addition, many are killed accidentally in southern African fisheries.
Breeding: On the Auckland Islands, eggs are laid from early November to late December. They lay **1** white egg (106 x 71mm, 275g), with reddish-brown flecking at the broader end, in a shallow cup on top of a pedestal of dried mud, feathers, guano and vegetation. The adults share incubation for *c.* 70 days and then share duties guarding the downy chick for *c.* 3 weeks. Chicks fledge in June–August when *c.* 4.5 months old. The oldest bird recorded is an Australian bird aged over 16 years, but some probably live to 40+ years.
Behaviour: Gregarious; breeds in large densely packed colonies, and at sea they sometimes form huge flocks of 2000–3000 birds around fishing boats and are often in large mixed flocks of seabirds.
Feeding: Diet is mainly squid, fish, krill, salps, and offal from fishing boats, mostly seized on the surface. Their affinity for feeding on scraps near fishing boats makes them vulnerable to accidental capture or entanglement.
In the hand: Males are larger than females for all measurements, but the ranges overlap extensively. The bill and wing of *cauta* (130mm, 560mm) is shorter than *steadi* (135mm, 595mm).
Reading: Bartle, J. A. 1991. *Bird Cons Intl* 1: 351–359. Robertson, C. J. R. & van Tets, G. F. 1982. *Notornis* 29: 311–336.

73. CHATHAM ISLANDS MOLLYMAWK *Thalassarche eremita* PLATE 17

Other names: Chatham Island Albatross, Chatham Albatross
Size: 90cm, 4kg
Distribution: Breeds only at Pyramid Rock, Chatham Islands, although a few may have bred on The Snares in the 1980s and 1990s. During breeding, most forage between 38° S and 48° S to the south and east of the Chathams, but a few are seen off mainland New Zealand, especially at Banks Peninsula, Kaikoura and in Cook Strait, and 10–20 are beach-wrecked in most years. Recorded as far west as southeastern Australian waters, especially off southern Tasmania and at Albatross Island, Bass Strait, where a bird was seen ashore in 1983. After breeding, almost all winter in the seas off Chile and Peru. Two recent records from South Africa.
Population: *c.* 5300 nest sites and 4600 breeding pairs in 2001.
Conservation: Protected endemic. The Chatham Islands Mollymawk has been caught on long lines set for tuna, ling and swordfish, and in trawl nets.
Breeding: On Pyramid Rock, eggs are laid from mid-August to late September. They lay **1** white egg (102 x 66mm, 230g), with reddish-brown flecking at the broader end, in a shallow cup on top of a pedestal of dried mud, feathers, guano and vegetation. The adults share incubation in stints of 2–3 days for *c.* 70 days and

hatching is from late October to early December. Parents share duties guarding and feeding the downy chick for *c.* 3 weeks, and then feeding it at 2–3 day intervals until it fledges in late March at *c.* 4.5 months old. The youngest bird recorded back at the colony was 4 years old, but first breeding is at 7 years old. The oldest bird recorded lived over 34 years.

Behaviour: Breeds in large densely packed colonies, but less gregarious at sea and rarely follows fishing boats where it is perhaps outcompeted by larger and more aggressive White-capped Mollymawks.

Feeding: Diet is mainly squid, fish, krill, salps, and sometimes offal from fishing boats, mostly seized on the surface.

In the hand: Males are larger than females for all measurements, but the ranges overlap extensively. The bill (120mm) is much shorter than that of Salvin's Mollymawk (128mm) or the White-capped Mollymawk (135mm).

Reading: Latham, P. C. L. et al. 2004. *Notornis* 51: 47–49. Robertson, C. J. R. et al. 2000. *Notornis* 47: 174. Robertson, C. J. R. et al. 2003. *DOC Sci Internal Report Ser* 91. Wellington: DOC. Spear, I. B. et al. 2003. *Ibis* 145: 253–269.

74. SALVIN'S MOLLYMAWK *Thalassarche salvini* PLATE 17

Other name: Salvin's Albatross

Size: 95cm, 4kg

Distribution: Almost all breed on the Bounty Islands, with small numbers on Western Chain, The Snares, and just a few pairs breed at the Crozet Islands in the South Indian Ocean. Isolated pairs have attempted to breed on Pyramid Rock and The Forty-fours (Motuhara), Chathams, and at Kerguelen Island in the South Indian Ocean. During breeding, most New Zealand birds forage in coastal waters off the east coast of both the North and South islands, south of East Cape, but many also use the Tasman Sea, as far west as southeastern Australia. After breeding, most migrate to the seas off Chile and Peru between 15° S and 50° S. Occasionally seen in the South Atlantic and Indian oceans.

Population: Bounty Islands *c.* 41,000 pairs in 2010, Western Chain of The Snares 1200 pairs in 2008–10.

Conservation: Protected critically endangered native. The Bounty Island population has declined substantially from the 76,000 pairs estimated in 1978, but recent counts appear to have stabilised. Salvin's Mollymawks are the second most numerous species, after White-capped Mollymawk, to be killed accidentally by fishing operations in New Zealand waters. Each year, about 500 birds die from entanglement in nets and trawl wires, or are hooked on long lines set for ling and tuna.

Breeding: Eggs are laid in August–September. They lay **1** white egg (104 x 67mm, 240g) in a shallow cup on top of a pedestal of dried mud, feathers, guano and vegetation. The adults share incubation for 68–75 days and then share duties guarding the downy chick for *c.* 3 weeks. Chicks fledge in February–April, at *c.* 4 months old.

Behaviour: Gregarious; breeds in large densely packed colonies with nests averaging 1.2m apart on the Bounty Islands, where they intermingle with Erect-crested Penguins. At sea, they sometimes form huge flocks of 2000–3000 birds around fishing boats and are often in large mixed flocks of seabirds.

Feeding: Diet is mainly squid, fish, krill, salps, and offal from fishing boats, mostly seized on the surface. Their affinity for feeding on scraps near fishing boats makes Salvin's Mollymawks especially vulnerable to accidental capture or entanglement.

Reading: Sagar, P. M. et al. 2011. *Notornis* 58: 57–63. Spear, I. B. et al. 2003. *Ibis* 145: 253–269.

75. SOOTY ALBATROSS *Phoebetria fusca* PLATE 18

Size: 80cm, 2.5kg

Distribution: Circumpolar, breeding on subantarctic islands between 36° S and 49° S in the South Atlantic and South Indian oceans. The biggest colonies are on Gough Island and Tristan da Cunha. They disperse eastwards along the Subtropical Convergence to deep waters south of Australia and up the eastern seaboard towards the Great Barrier Reef. Four records in New Zealand: north of the Auckland Islands (February 1991), Pukaki Rise, southeast of Otago (November 1993), ashore on Antipodes Island (November 1995), and off Little Mangere Island, Chathams (December 2006).

Feeding: Diet is mainly squid, but fish, krill and carrion such as small seabirds are also taken. Most prey is seized while swimming, but birds occasionally plunge from just above the surface. Sooty Albatrosses often follow

boats and feed on scraps cast overboard, and so are often caught accidentally on long-line hooks.
Reading: Weimerskirch, H. et al. 1986. *Ibis* 128: 195–213. Weimerskirch, H. et al. 1987. *J Anim Ecol* 56: 1043–1056.

76. LIGHT-MANTLED SOOTY ALBATROSS *Phoebetria palpebrata* PLATE 18

Size: 80cm, 3kg
Distribution: Circumpolar, breeding on subantarctic islands between 46° S and 56° S, including the Antipodes, Auckland and Campbell islands. The largest colonies are on South Georgia, Kerguelen and Auckland islands. At sea, they range widely in the southern oceans, generally over deep oceanic waters between 40° S and the Antarctic coast, but are occasionally seen in New Zealand coastal waters and are most frequently beach-wrecked in July–October, especially on the Auckland west coast.
Population: World population is estimated at 20,000 breeding pairs, of which *c.* 250 are on the Antipodes, *c.* 5000 on the Auckland Islands and 1600 pairs on Campbell Island.
Conservation: Protected native. The size and trends of breeding populations in the New Zealand subantarctic are poorly known. Moderate numbers of birds (6% of seabirds identified) were caught accidentally on tuna long lines in New Zealand waters in the 1980s and 1990s, but with the introduction of by-catch mitigation devices, this mortality has dropped to almost nil.
Breeding: Biennial breeders; if they raise a chick successfully, they will not attempt to breed the following year; but if they fail (especially in the early part of the nesting cycle), they will breed the following year. On Campbell Island, birds return in early October to the same nesting site on a coastal cliff ledge or a small terrace on a steep slope of an inland peak, but they build a new nest each time. Most eggs are laid over a short period between 24 October and 7 November. They lay 1 white egg (102 x 65mm, 233g), with brownish-red speckling at the broader end, in a shallow cup on top of a small pedestal of soil and vegetation. The adults share incubation for *c.* 67 days in shifts of 12–17 days initially and then shorter shifts as hatching approaches. The parents take 2–4-day shifts brooding the downy chick until it is *c.* 19 days old. The chick fledges at *c.* 141 days old in late May to early June. Chicks are independent once they fledge. Young return to their natal colony for several years before starting to breed at an average of 12 years old. Annual survivorship is high and life expectancy is over 30 years.
Behaviour: Nest solitarily or rarely in groups of three or four pairs. At sea, they feed alone or sometimes in small flocks and sometimes gather to feed on scraps tossed from fishing boats. At their breeding ground they have an elaborate series of courtship displays accompanied by a distinctive clear two-syllable 'pee-oo', baas, and bill-snapping.
Feeding: Diet has not been studied in New Zealand, but elsewhere in the southern oceans it is mainly squid, followed by fish and krill, also some carrion such as small seabirds. Prey is mainly seized on the surface, but birds occasionally plunge for food from just above the surface.
Reading: Bailey, A. M. & Sorensen, J. H. 1950. *Subantarctic Campbell Island.* Denver: Denver Mus Nat Hist. Jouventin, P. & Weimerskirch, H. 1990. *Proc 19th Int Orn Congr.* Sorensen, J. H. 1950. *DSIR Cape Exped Series Bull* 8. Weimerskirch, H. et al. 1986. *Ibis* 128: 195–213. Weimerskirch, H. et al. 1987. *J Anim Ecol* 56: 1043–1056.

FULMARS, PRIONS, PETRELS and SHEARWATERS *Procellariidae*

The Procellariidae is the largest and most diverse family of seabirds, with about 93 species. In the New Zealand region, including the Ross Sea, 52 species have been recorded, including 10 endemic species and 22 other breeding species.

The Procellariidae includes a wide variety of seabirds from the giant petrels to the prions. All have distinctive external nostrils encased in a tube on the top or sides of the bill. They have 11 primaries; the 11th is minute but the 10th is at least as long as the 9th, giving the wing a pointed tip. All seabirds have webbed feet with three forward-pointing toes of about the same length.

Most species nest in burrows or crevices, normally clumped into colonies. Birds return to their colony months before egg-laying to claim their nest sites (usually the same site is used year after year) and to court. After copulation, females leave the colony for one to six weeks on a 'pre-laying' exodus to form the egg. Males also leave but often make occasional visits to the nest site.

All species lay one white egg, which is large relative to the size of the female. The few instances of two eggs in a nest are from two females using the same site. A long incubation period is typically split up into several incubation shifts lasting several days to several weeks between changeovers. Occasionally the changeovers do not coincide and the egg is left unattended for several days, however, eggs have hatched successfully after being chilled for six days. Incubation stints shorten as incubation proceeds, and when the egg hatches the downy chick is brooded and guarded for only a few days in hole-nesting species, but for several weeks in surface-nesting species, until it is able to maintain body temperature.

Throughout its development, the chick is fed large meals at irregular intervals. It gains weight rapidly, becoming much heavier than its parents, but this declines towards adult weight before it fledges. Chicks normally spend some time on the surface exercising their wings before they eventually leave the colony. Once they have flown, they are completely independent of their parents. Young birds usually return to their natal colony at 2–7 years old, and spend several years visiting the colony, especially when breeders are incubating or feeding chicks, before attempting to breed. The Procellariidae are typically long-lived, with several species known to live over 25 years.

Most species now breed only on predator-free offshore or outlying islands because mainland colonies have been ravaged by introduced mammalian predators. They generally return to their colonies at night, and once on land they are clumsy and unable to take flight rapidly – their only defence is by biting or by spitting stomach oil. The nestling is particularly vulnerable to predators because it is often left unattended for long periods while the parents feed at sea, and it emerges from the nest at night to exercise its wings in the week or two before it can fly.

The Procellariidae feed on a wide variety of sea life, ranging from some prions which sieve zooplankton onto comb-like lamellae along the edge of their bills, to giant petrels which scavenge dead marine mammals and occasionally kill small seabirds. Most species feed within a few metres of the sea surface, but some shearwaters dive to over 90m. The seabirds have well-developed nasal glands for extracting salt from their blood and exuding it out of their prominent nostrils.

The fulmarine petrels (*Macronectes*, *Fulmarus*, *Thalassoica*, *Daption*, *Pagodroma and Lugensa*) are a diverse group of 8 species, all of which have a robust bill with prominent joined nasal tubes, rising from the base.

The gadfly petrels (*Pterodroma*) consist of 34 species of agile seabirds with long wings and short, laterally compressed black bills with a strongly hooked nail (tip). They feed mainly on squid and small fish.

The single *Halobaena* species is sometimes placed with the fulmarine petrels. It looks like the prions but has a white-tipped tail and the upper bill has small tooth-like serrations at the base.

The six species of prion (*Pachyptila*) are small seabirds pale blue above and white below with a prominent dark M-shaped mark across the upperwings, and a dark-tipped tail. Comb-like lamellae on the inside of the bill are used to filter zooplankton.

The single *Bulweria* and *Pseudobulweria* species to occur in New Zealand have distinctly long wings and long tapering tails, and a notch on the cutting edge of the upper mandible.

The *Procellaria* are heavy, stocky seabirds with large, heavily hooked, pale bills with dark markings and prominent nostrils. They feed mainly at night on bioluminescent squid but also take offal from fishing boats.

The shearwaters (*Calonectris*, *Puffinus*) include about 29 medium to large species with long slender bills and flat nasal tubes. They are usually brown to black above and white or brown below. Some have a large sternum and dive well for fish and squid, using their wings for propulsion, while others have a small sternum and feed on, or close to, the surface.

Reading: Harrison, P. 1987. *Seabirds of the World: A Photographic Guide*. London: Christopher Helm. Harrison, P. 1988. *Seabirds: An Identification Guide*. London: Christopher Helm. Imber, M. J. 1985. *Ibis* 127: 197–229. Onley, D. & Scofield, P. 2007. *Field Guide to the Albatrosses, Petrels and Shearwaters of the World*. London: Christopher Helm. Serventy, D. L. et al. 1971. *The Handbook of Australian Sea-birds*. Sydney: Reed. Warham, J. 1990. *The Petrels: Their Ecology and Breeding Systems*. London: Academic Press.

77. SOUTHERN GIANT PETREL *Macronectes giganteus* PLATE 18

Other names: Nelly, Stinker, Pangurunguru
Size: 90cm, 4.5kg
Distribution: Circumpolar, breeding on ice-free areas of Antarctica, on small islands around the coast, on many subantarctic islands and on islands off the Chilean coast. In the New Zealand region, one pair has nested at Cape Crozier, Ross Dependency. The nearest stronghold is Macquarie Island, where *c.* 2150 pairs breed. Most remain near Antarctica and in the subantarctic zone during the summer and autumn. Some adults and many subadults disperse eastwards and northwards to about 30° S in winter and spring, and some follow the Humboldt Current to 10° S off South America.

Although the two species of giant petrels are difficult to distinguish at sea, Southern Giant Petrels are probably more common than Northern Giant Petrels in New Zealand waters in winter and spring. Of 77 banded Southern Giant Petrels recovered in New Zealand, most were first-year birds that left South Atlantic colonies in April–May and were recovered June–September.
Population: Moderately common but declining. About 30,500 pairs in 1999–2000, including large colonies (4000+ pairs) on South Shetland, South Georgia and Heard islands. Despite their close association with fishing boats, only a few are now killed accidentally in New Zealand waters since the introduction of by-catch mitigation devices.
Behaviour: At sea, they are often seen alone, but they join large mixed flocks when feeding around fishing boats, and formerly they used to gather around whaling ships, and sewer and abattoir outfalls. When feeding in flocks they are often noisy and aggressive, but otherwise they are usually silent at sea.
Feeding: Voracious scavengers and predators, feeding on dead penguins and marine mammals, and offal. Giant petrels often kill penguins and other small seabirds, and are even known to have drowned and eaten mollymawks. The diet also includes crustaceans, squid and fish taken from the sea surface.
In the hand: Separated from Northern Giant Petrel *M. halli* by having a green, not brownish, tip to the bill. Males are larger than females, and most adults can be sexed on bill length: males >97mm, females <95mm.
Reading: Hunter, S. 1984. *J Zool (Lond)* 203: 441–460. Johnstone, G. W. 1974. *Emu* 74: 209–218. Patterson, D. L. & Hunter, S. 2000. *Marine Ornith* 28: 69–74. Patterson, D. L. et al. 2008. *Marine Ornith* 36: 115–124. Powlesland, R. G. 1986. *Notornis* 33: 171–184. Warham, J. 1962. *Auk* 79: 139–160.

78. NORTHERN GIANT PETREL *Macronectes halli* PLATE 18

Other names: Nelly, Stinker, Pangurunguru
Size: 90cm, 4.5kg
Distribution: Circumpolar, breeding on many subantarctic islands, including The Sisters and The Forty-fours (Motuhara) of the Chathams, on an island in Port Pegasus in southern Stewart Island, and on the Antipodes, Auckland and Campbell islands. They range widely in the subantarctic zone during the summer and autumn. Some adults and many subadults disperse eastwards and northwards to about 35° S in winter and spring, and some follow the Humboldt Current to about 20° S off South America.

Although the two species of giant petrel are difficult to distinguish at sea, Northern Giant Petrels are probably more commonly beach-wrecked than Southern Giant Petrels in New Zealand waters in summer and autumn, but they are outnumbered by the southern species in winter and spring. Birds banded on Campbell Island have been recovered mainly around New Zealand and in the Tasman Sea, but also on the coast of Argentina. Up to the 1970s, when sewage and abattoir waste were dumped into Wellington Harbour and a whaling station operated just inside the entrance to Tory Channel in the Marlborough Sounds, hundreds of giant petrels (probably mainly of this species) were seen in the Cook Strait area, especially in October–March. Now that these sources of offal have gone, only the odd bird is now seen following fishing boats and the Cook Strait ferries.
Population: About 11,200 pairs in 1999/2000, of which New Zealand colonies total *c.* 2500 pairs; *c.* 2000 pairs in the Chathams (mainly on The Forty-fours), 230 pairs on the Antipodes, 230 pairs on Campbell Island and 50+ pairs in the Auckland Islands.
Conservation: Protected native. The size and trends of New Zealand populations are not well known, but appear to be moderately stable even though inshore offal sources have decreased. Fishing boats and increasing seal populations provide better sources of food in some places. Despite their close association with fishing boats, only a few are now killed accidentally in New Zealand

waters since the introduction of by-catch mitigation devices.

Breeding: In the New Zealand region, they lay from mid-August to early September. They lay **1** white egg (102 x 66mm) in a cup-shaped nest built of tussock and other vegetation. Eggs hatch in October–November after *c.* 60 days. Chicks are brooded for the first 2–3 weeks and then guarded for another fortnight. They fledge in February at *c.* 112 days old. Age at first breeding is as little as 4 years old, but normally at *c.* 10 years old.

Behaviour: Nest in colonies. At sea, they are often seen alone, but they join large mixed flocks when feeding around fishing boats, and they used to gather around whaling ships, sewer outfalls and abattoir outfalls. When feeding in flocks they are often noisy and aggressive, but otherwise they are usually silent at sea.

Feeding: Males tend to be voracious predators and scavengers, killing penguins and feeding on dead birds and marine mammals, whereas females tend to feed more on crustaceans, squid and fish taken from the sea surface.

In the hand: Separated from the dark phase of the Southern Giant Petrel *M. giganteus* by having a brownish, not green, tip to the bill. Males are larger than females, and most adults can be sexed on bill length: males >97mm, females <95mm.

Reading: Bailey, A. M. & Sorensen, J. H. 1950. *Subantarctic Campbell Island.* Denver: Denver Mus Nat Hist. Hunter, S. 1984. *J Zool (Lond)* 203: 441–460. McIlwaine, C. P. 1964. *Emu* 64: 33–38. Powlesland, R. G. 1986. *Notornis* 33: 171–184. Robertson, H. A. 1992. *Notornis* 39: 263–289. Wiltshire, A. & Hamilton, S. 2003. *Notornis* 50: 128–132.

79. ANTARCTIC FULMAR *Fulmarus glacialoides* PLATE 19

Other names: Southern Fulmar, Silver-grey Fulmar

Size: 50cm, 800g

Distribution: Circumpolar, breeding on ice-free areas of Antarctica and on small islands around the coast, including Sturge and Row islands in the Balleny Islands of the Ross Dependency. They also breed on southern subantarctic islands of the South Atlantic Ocean. Most remain close to the edge of the pack ice in summer, but they disperse through the southern oceans to about 35° S and further north in the Humboldt Current off South America.

Fewer than 10 Antarctic Fulmars were recorded from New Zealand beaches before 1970, but they have since become much more regular winter–spring visitors to New Zealand waters. Over 2000 birds were beach-wrecked in the 25 years following 1970, including major wrecks in 1975 (642), 1978 (471), 1985 (366) and 1999 (424). Most are beach-wrecked in September–November on the west coast of the North Island and in Southland. Because adults are starting to return to their Antarctic colonies in early October, most birds wrecked are presumably subadults.

Population: Common; colonies are scattered widely around the coast of Antarctica and southern islands. The global breeding population is estimated to be 1 million+ pairs, of which 15,000–26,000 pairs nest on the Balleny Islands.

Conservation: Protected native. The greater frequency in New Zealand waters since the mid-1970s may indicate population growth or a change in feeding patterns related to the decline in whaling, which used to provide good feeding opportunities.

Breeding: Antarctic Fulmars arrive at their ice-free colonies in early October. Laying is highly synchronous, around the second week of December. In years with warm sea temperatures, breeding can be skipped, presumably because of reduced food availability. They lay **1** white egg (76 x 51mm, 103g) in a shallow scrape on steep shingle scree, on a cliff ledge, or in a crevice. Eggs hatch in late January after *c.* 46 days, chicks are guarded for the first 2–3 weeks, and fledge in mid-March at *c.* 50 days old. Age at first breeding is *c.* 6 years old. Annual adult survival in a small colony was measured at 92.3%, giving a mean life expectancy of 13 years.

Behaviour: Breed in colonies. At sea, they are often seen alone, but when feeding they often join large mixed flocks at concentrations of krill or around fishing boats. When feeding in flocks, they are often noisy and aggressive, but otherwise they are usually silent at sea. At their colony, they give loud cackling calls, sometimes as a duet.

Feeding: Diet is mainly krill (especially *Euphausia superba*), small fish (especially *Pleuragramma antarcticum*) and offal, picked from the sea surface.

Reading: Ainley, D. G. et al. 1984. *AOU Orn Monogr* 32: 1–97. Creuwels, J. C. S. et al. 2007. *Polar Biol.* 30: 1083–1097. Creuwels, J. C. S. et al. 2008. *Ibis* 150: 160–171. Falla, R. A. 1937. *Rep BANZARE* Ser B. Hodum, P. J. 2002. *J Zool (Lond)* 256: 139–149.

Jenouvrier, S. et al. 2003. *J Anim Ecol* 72: 576–587. Mougin, J-L. 1967. *Oiseau* 37: 57–103. Mougin, J-L. 1967. *Com Natn Fr Rech Ant* 36: 1–195. Norman, F. I. & Ward, S. J. 1992. *Emu* 92: 207–222. Robertson, C. J. et al. 1980. *Nat Mus NZ Rec* 1: 271–279. Weimerskirch, H. 1990. *J Anim Ecol* 59: 867–875.

80. ANTARCTIC PETREL *Thalassoica antarctica* PLATE 19

Size: 45cm, 650g

Distribution: Circumpolar, breeding on ice-free areas of Antarctica and on small islands around the coast; in the Ross Dependency they are mainly in the Rockefeller Mountains of King Edward VII Land, and probably at the Balleny and Scott islands. Most remain within or close to the edge of the pack ice and seldom venture north of 50° S.

No confirmed records from the New Zealand mainland until 1973. In August–September 1978, during an influx into New Zealand waters, 77 were wrecked, mainly on beaches on the west coast of the North Island and Southland, and many were seen from Fiordland to Stewart Island. Since then, a few have been found beach-wrecked in most years, with small peaks in 1991 (18) and 1999 (10), indicating a possible change in their wintering distribution.

Population: The global population is 10–20 million birds, of which *c.* 3.9 million pairs breed in eastern parts of the Ross Dependency.

Conservation: Protected native. The greater frequency in New Zealand waters since the mid-1970s may indicate population growth or a change in feeding patterns related to the decline in whaling, which used to provide good feeding opportunities further south.

Breeding: Antarctic Petrels arrive at their colonies in early October. Laying is highly synchronous, in the last third of November and the first few days of December. They lay **1** white egg (70 x 49mm, 90g) in a shallow scrape on a cliff ledge or in a crevice. Eggs hatch in mid-January after *c.* 48 days. Chicks are guarded for the first 2 weeks and fledge in late February and early March at *c.* 48 days old.

Behaviour: They breed in dense colonies, but are probably forced together into sites relatively free of snow and ice. At sea, they are usually seen in flocks, with up to 5000 birds recorded feeding around whaling ships. Usually silent at sea, but at their colony they have a variety of churring, clucking and cackling calls.

Feeding: Diet is mainly krill (especially *Euphausia superba*) and small fish (especially *Pleuragramma antarcticum*) picked from the sea surface.

Reading: Ainley, D. G. et al. 1984. *AOU Orn Monogr* 32: 1–97. Barlow, M. 1979. *Notornis* 26: 313. Creuwels, J. C. S. et al. 2008 *Ibis* 150: 160–171. Falla, R. A. 1937. *Rep BANZARE Ser B.* Hodum, P. J. 2002. *J Zool (Lond)* 256: 139–149. Norman, F. I. & Ward, S. J. 1992. *Emu* 92: 207–222.

81. CAPE PIGEON *Daption capense* PLATE 19

Other names: Cape Petrel, Pintado Petrel

Size: 40cm, 450g

Geographical variation: Two subspecies: Southern Cape Pigeon *capense* breeds around the Antarctic continent and on many subantarctic islands in the Atlantic and Indian oceans, whereas the smaller Snares Cape Pigeon *australe* breeds only on subantarctic islands of New Zealand.

Distribution: Circumpolar, breeding on ice-free areas of Antarctica and on small islands around the coast, and on many subantarctic islands. In the New Zealand region, *capense* breeds at the Balleny Islands and at Scott Island in the Antarctic, and *australe* breeds at The Snares, Bounty, Antipodes, Auckland (Beacon Rock) and Campbell islands. Since 1987, *australe* has bred in the Chathams at The Forty-fours (Motuhara), and probably at The Pyramid and The Sisters.

In winter and early spring, many *capense* move north and east and mingle with *australe* in temperate seas as far north as about 25° S in the southwestern Pacific. In winter and spring, Cape Pigeons often follow fishing boats around the mainland coast, but especially to the east of the South Island. They are beach-wrecked mainly in July–November.

Population: Abundant, with many colonies, but no data are available on the size of colonies of Southern Cape Pigeons in the Ross Dependency. There are *c.* 8000 pairs of Snares Cape Pigeons, *c.* 7500 pairs on The Snares, and <50 pairs at each of the Auckland, Campbell, Bounty and Chatham islands.

Conservation: Protected native. Cape Pigeons are opportunist feeders, deriving much food as offal from fishing boats, and so have probably benefited from fishing. In the 1960s, when whales were caught in Cook Strait, huge flocks of Cape Pigeons congregated at the entrance to Tory Channel to feed on scraps from the whaling station there. Occasionally Cape Pigeons are accidentally killed in trawl nets, and on bottom long lines being hauled in, but band recoveries show that adult mortality is low and so such deaths are probably insignificant.

Breeding: Snares Cape Pigeons breed at The Snares and Bounty Islands 2–3 weeks earlier than Southern Cape Pigeons breed on the coast of Antarctica. Some birds are present on The Snares all year, but eggs are laid from 4–**11**–20 November. They lay **1** white egg (61 x 43mm, 60g) in a slight scrape on a rocky ledge, in a crevice or cave, or under a rockfall. Eggs hatch in late December to early January after *c.* 45 days. The chick is brooded for the first 8–10 days but left unguarded from 8–15 days old. Chicks fledge in mid-February at *c.* 52 days old. Young return to their natal colony from 16 months old, but do not start breeding until 3–**6**–10+ years old. The oldest bird recorded in New Zealand lived at least 28 years.

Behaviour: Breeds in loose colonies, and forms large flocks at concentrations of krill and around fishing boats, and formerly around whaling stations and sewer outfalls. They are noisy and aggressive in feeding flocks. At their colonies, they make a range of churring calls.

Feeding: Diet is mainly krill, amphipods, squid, fish and offal, mainly taken on the surface with rapid pigeon-like pecking or by diving from just above the surface. Sometimes they catch crustaceans by filtering water through their bill or by picking them from the surface while still flying.

In the hand: The subspecies *australe* is smaller than *capense*, but measurements overlap extensively. Males are larger than females: most males of *australe* on The Snares have a head and bill of >77mm, and a mid-toe and claw of >60mm, whereas females are smaller.

Reading: Beck, J. R. 1969. *Br Ant Surv Bull* 21: 33–44. Harper, P. C. 1987. *Notornis* 34: 169–192. Hodum, P. J. 2002. *J Zool (Lond)* 256: 139–149. Pinder, R. 1966. *Br Ant Surv Bull* 8: 19–47. Sagar, P. M. 1979. *Notornis* 26: 23–36. Sagar, P. M. 1986. *Notornis* 33: 259–263.

82. SNOW PETREL *Pagodroma nivea* — PLATE 19

Size: 35cm, 325g

Geographical variation: Two subspecies: the Greater Snow Petrel *nivea* breeds on the Balleny Islands in the Ross Dependency and hybridises with the other subspecies at some other colonies, and the Lesser Snow Petrel *minor* breeds widely in Antarctica, including a few in the Ross Dependency.

Distribution: Circumpolar, breeding on ice-free areas of Antarctica and on small islands around the coast, and on southern subantarctic islands in the Atlantic Ocean. Most remain within or close to the edge of the pack ice, and they are rarely recorded north of 55° S. No confirmed records from around the New Zealand mainland.

Population: Abundant, with a total population of over 4 million birds. In the Ross Dependency, there are 5000+ pairs on Sabrina Island, Balleny Islands, and they breed on Scott Island. In Victoria Land of the western Ross Dependency, there are several colonies known between Cape Adare and Cape Washington, especially near Cape Hallett (including being 'abundant' at Felsite Island). In King Edward VII Land of the eastern Ross Dependency, they breed in large numbers at Washington Ridge of the Rockefeller Mountains and hundreds breed at Mt Paterson.

Conservation: Protected native. No existing threats are known.

Breeding: Snow Petrels arrive at their colonies in October and take a pre-laying exodus of 2–3 weeks in late November. Laying is highly synchronous, in the last few days of November and the first week of December. They lay **1** white egg (55 x 40mm) in a scrape on a ledge, in a crevice, or under a rockfall. Eggs hatch in early January after *c.* 44 days, and the chick is brooded at first but left unguarded from about the fifth day. Chicks fledge in late February and early March at *c.* 48 days old.

Behaviour: They breed in scattered colonies, but are probably forced together by limited sites that are relatively free from snow and ice. At sea, they are usually alone but form small groups at food sources. They do not normally follow ships. Usually silent at sea, but at their colony they have an aerial display accompanied by a chirring call, and they are very noisy on land with a rapid burst of guttural notes.

Feeding: Diet is mainly small fish and krill, mostly obtained from the sea surface, either from the air or while resting on the surface.

In the hand: Snow Petrels show great size variation. Wing length ranges from 240 to 320mm, with 280mm being used to separate the two subspecies. At some

colonies (e.g. Balleny Islands), all are long-winged, at some all are short-winged, whereas at other colonies (e.g. Cape Hallett) there is a mix of forms, so two races may be hybridising. Overlapping this racial variation, males are heavier and have longer bills than females.
Reading: Brown, D. A. 1966. *ANARE Sci Rep Ser B* 89: 1–63. Cowan, A. N. 1981. *Notornis* 28: 169–188. Croxall, J. P. 1982. *Notornis* 29: 171–180. Croxall, J. P. et al. 1995. *Marine Ornith* 23: 69–99. Falla, R. A. 1937. *Rep BANZARE Ser B*. Greenfield, L. G. & Smellie, J. M. 1992. *Notornis* 39: 119–124. Harper, P. C. 1987. *Notornis* 34: 169–192. Jouventin, P. & Voit, C. R. 1985. *Ibis* 127: 430–441. Maher, W. J. 1962. *Condor* 64: 488–499.

83. KERGUELEN PETREL *Lugensa brevirostris* PLATE 20

Size: 33cm, 350g
Distribution: Breeds on subantarctic islands of the Atlantic and Indian oceans, including large colonies at Marion, Crozet and Kerguelen islands. They range widely in the Southern Ocean between 33° S and the edge of the pack ice. Fewer than 40 Kerguelen Petrels were recorded in New Zealand before 1973, but they have since become much more regular winter–spring visitors, with over 2000 birds beach-wrecked in the next 40 years, including major wrecks in 1981 (284), 1984 (600), 1994 (262) and 1999 (331). Most birds are wrecked on the west coast of the North Island in July–November, at a time when adults are nesting (eggs are laid 2–**13**–25 October) 8000km away, and so must be subadults.
Reading: Imber, M. J. 1984. *Notornis* 31: 89–91. Jouventin, P. et al. 1985. *Notornis* 32: 157–220.

84. GREY-FACED PETREL *Pterodroma macroptera* PLATE 20

Other names: Oi, Titi, Kuia, Great-winged Petrel, Northern Muttonbird
Size: 41cm, 550g
Geographical variation: Two subspecies: *macroptera* breeds on temperate and subantarctic islands in the Atlantic and Indian oceans and off southwestern Australia; *gouldi* breeds around the northern North Island of New Zealand.
Distribution: Breeds on Gough and Tristan da Cunha in the South Atlantic Ocean, Prince Edward, Marion, Crozet and Kerguelen islands in the South Indian Ocean, on islands off southwestern Australia and around northern New Zealand. Colonies are scattered on mainland headlands and clifftops, and on offshore islands from near New Plymouth north to the Three Kings, and down the Northland coast, Hauraki Gulf, Coromandel, Bay of Plenty to East Island off East Cape. Small mainland colonies at Mt Maunganui, Bethells Beach, and at Rapanui near New Plymouth are well known.

Grey-faced Petrels are moderately sedentary. New Zealand birds range between 20° S and 49° S in the Tasman and Coral seas and in the South Pacific to about 130° W, feeding along the edge of the continental shelf and over water 1000+m deep. They turn up off eastern Australia in February–March after breeding, and remain common there until May. Grey-faced Petrels are often beach-wrecked on Northland and Bay of Plenty beaches, especially in January and February when young have just fledged.
Population: *c.* 250,000 breeding pairs. The largest colonies, with over 100,000 pairs between them, are on Moutohora (Whale) Island and Hongiora Island (The Aldermans) in the Bay of Plenty.
Conservation: Partially protected native. Chicks are legally harvested by Maori from colonies on privately owned islands, but this take is only a fraction of what it was in the 1950s. Many island populations have benefited from the recent eradication of rats, cats and rabbits, and are increasing. Most unprotected mainland colonies are declining due to predation by rats, cats, dogs, mustelids and humans. The species has been translocated to several predator-free sanctuaries, but the long-term success has yet to be determined.
Breeding: Winter breeders. Adults return to New Zealand colonies in March to clean out their burrows and to court. They have a long pre-laying exodus of *c.* 60 days in females and *c.* 50 days in males. Laying is from 21 June to 29 July, mostly 28 June to 9 July. Females return first from their exodus and lay **1** white egg (67 x 48mm, 86g) in a burrow 0.5–2m long. Incubation is by the female for the first 0–**4**–14 days, but then in three long shifts of 8–**16**–23 days, two by the male.

Eggs hatch from mid-August to mid-September after 51–**55**–58 days, or after **54** days of incubation excluding periods of 0–**1.4**–5 days when the egg is left unattended during changeovers. The chick is

continuously guarded for the first 1–**1.7**–3 days and then fed about every 4 nights. Chicks depart from about 7 December to late January, with a peak at the end of December at 108–**118**–128 days old. Young return to their natal colony from 3 years old, but most do not start breeding until 7–10 years old. The oldest Grey-faced Petrel recorded lived over 40 years.
Behaviour: At sea, they are usually seen alone or in small feeding or roosting flocks. They are noisy over their colonies and on the ground, the main flight call being 'o-hi', which gives rise to the usual Maori name.
Feeding: Diet is mainly squid, with some fish and crustaceans. Most prey is taken at night while sitting on the surface of the sea, or dipping from the air, but they are capable of diving to depths of 23m.
In the hand: Grey-faced Petrels are all dark apart from the face and lack the prominent white patch at the base of the primaries found on similar species (Providence Petrel, and dark-phased Kermadec and Herald petrels). Wing (295–**318**–330mm) and bill (33–**37**–40.5mm) measurements help to separate beach-wrecked specimens from similar species.
Reading: Harrison, M. 1992. *DOC Sci & Res Ser* 48. Wellington: DOC. Imber, M. J. 1973. *J Anim Ecol* 42: 645–662. Imber, M. J. 1976. *Ibis* 118: 51–64. Johnstone, R. M. & Davis, L. S. 1990. *Ibis* 132: 14–19. MacLeod, C. J. et al. 2008. *Papers & Proc Roy Soc Tasmania* 142: 73–88. Taylor, G. A. 2008. *Papers & Proc Roy Soc Tasmania* 142: 189–198.

85. WHITE-HEADED PETREL *Pterodroma lessonii* PLATE 20

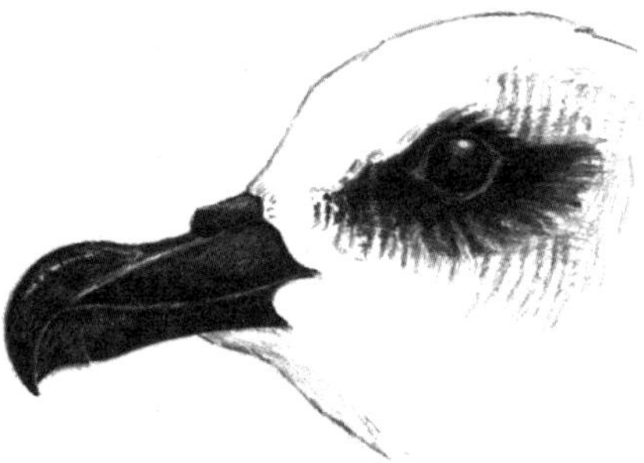

Size: 43cm, 600g
Distribution: Breeds on Crozet and Kerguelen islands in the South Indian Ocean, on Macquarie Island and in the New Zealand subantarctic on the Antipodes and Auckland islands, and possibly on Campbell Island. They range widely in the southern oceans between the pack ice and 45° S but move northwards to about 30° S in the winter. They are regularly beach-wrecked on the west coast of the North Island in winter and spring, especially around October.
Population: A common subantarctic petrel, with large colonies on Kerguelen, Macquarie, Antipodes (100,000+ pairs on the main island but few on its offshore islands) and the Auckland islands (all but the main island) including 100,000+ pairs on Disappointment Island.
Conservation: Protected native. Cats have caused massive declines of the colonies on Macquarie Island and Auckland Island. Southern Skuas kill many White-headed Petrels on the Antipodes and Auckland islands, but the populations are probably stable. The species does not seem to be adversely affected by fisheries.
Breeding: No detailed studies in New Zealand, but timing seems similar to that on Macquarie Island. Adults return to their scattered colonies in late August to clean out their burrows and to court. Laying is from mid-November to late December. They lay **1** white egg (69 x 49mm) in a burrow up to 2m long. Eggs hatch in late January and February after *c.* 60 days, and chicks depart in May at *c.* 102 days old.
Behaviour: At sea, White-headed Petrels usually feed alone or in small groups and do not follow ships. They are very vocal at their colonies from about one hour after dark, with a variety of calls, including a characteristic harsh, chattering 'ti-ti-ti' flight call.
Feeding: Feeds on squid, lanternfish, mysid crustaceans and other planktonic invertebrates.
Reading: Brothers, N. P. 1984. *Aust Wildl Res* 11: 113–131. Warham, J. 1967. *Emu* 67: 1–22. Warham, J. & Bell, B. D. 1979. *Notornis* 26: 121–169.

86. PROVIDENCE PETREL *Pterodroma solandri* PLATE 20

Other names: Bird of Providence, Solander's Petrel
Size: 40cm, 500g
Distribution: *c.* 32,000 Providence Petrels breed on Lord Howe Island and, more recently, on Philip Island (Norfolk Island) in the subtropical Tasman Sea. They were formerly abundant on both Lord Howe and Norfolk islands, but were seriously over-exploited, and died out at Norfolk Island around 1800. During the winter breeding season, they range mainly through the western Tasman Sea near the edge of the Australian continental shelf from Queensland to Tasmania. Surprisingly few have been recorded in New Zealand, with only four records: beach-wrecked birds at Muriwai (January 1921) and Dargaville (September 1984), one seen off Whangaroa Harbour (May 2004) and three off North Cape (May 2005). Most Providence Petrels migrate to the North Pacific Ocean in November–February, but some stay behind off eastern Tasmania until late December.
In the hand: Very similar to Grey-faced Petrels (*P. macroptera*), but Providence Petrels have a mottled face, a white patch on the underwing at the base of the primaries and are slightly smaller: wing 285–**304**–325mm cf. 295–**318**–330mm, and bill 32.5–**34.5**–38.5mm cf. 33–**37**–40.5mm. Dark-phased Herald Petrels (*P. heraldica*) have even shorter wings, 270–**278**–290mm, and bill, 25–**27**–29mm.
Reading: Miller, P. 1986. *Notornis* 33: 76. Priddel, D. et al. 2010. *Notornis* 57: 113–127.

87. CHATHAM ISLANDS TAIKO *Pterodroma magentae* PLATE 21

Other names: Magenta Petrel, Chatham Island Taiko
Size: 38cm, 475g
Distribution: Breeds only in dense forest near the Tuku-a-Tamatea River in the southwest of Chatham Island. Subfossil and midden evidence suggests that they formerly bred in huge numbers on Chatham Island and some on Pitt Island. During the breeding season they feed mainly in subantarctic waters to the south and east of the Chathams, but afterwards they disperse widely into the Tasman Sea and across the South Pacific to South America and north into the tropics.
Population: One of the rarest birds in the world with fewer than 200 individuals, but increasing thanks to intensive conservation efforts.
Conservation: Protected critically endangered endemic. Chicks were harvested in huge numbers by Moriori and Maori up to the start of the 1900s. Former colonies were ravaged by pigs, cats, rats and Weka, and possums compete for burrows. They were thought extinct until Ornithological Society parties led by David Crockett attracted two birds to bright lights in the Tuku Valley, Chatham Island, on 3 January 1973, and finally caught and banded two birds on 1 January 1978. Photographs and measurements confirmed that the Magenta Petrel, which had been described from a specimen collected in the central South Pacific in 1867, and the Chatham Islands Taiko were one and the same species. The known breeding sites are protected by trapping cats and poisoning rats. The Tuku Nature Reserve has been fenced to exclude cattle, sheep and pigs, and *c.* 60 chicks have been transferred to the Sweetwater Covenant, a hilltop protected by a predator-proof fence.
Breeding: Adults return in late September to clean out their burrows and to court. Females have a long pre-laying exodus of *c.* 55 days. They return to lay in late November and early December – **1** white egg (65 x 47mm) is laid in a burrow up to 3m long. There are three main incubations shifts, each lasting *c.* 15 days, and eggs hatch in mid- to late January after *c.* 55 days. Chicks are fed on average every 2–3 nights, and depart 25 April to 10 May at *c.* 105 days old. In 2014, the oldest banded bird was at least 36 years old.
Behaviour: Generally silent over their nesting area. The calls from their burrows, or rarely while being handled, are 'or-wik', 'si si si' and 'orrrr'. They sometimes emerge from their burrows in response to war-whooping.
Feeding: Apart from the regurgitated remains of squid, the diet and feeding methods are not known.
In the hand: Chatham Islands Taiko resemble Phoenix Petrels (*P. alba*), but Taiko are larger (wing 284–**302**–316mm cf. 265–**267**–290mm, and bill 30.5–**33.0**–35mm cf. 25.5–**27.9**–29.5mm). Tahiti Petrels (*Pseudobulweria rostrata)* are similar, but have a different bill structure to *Pterodroma* petrels, and their bill is larger (33–**35.7**–39mm) but wings are shorter (283–**294**–309mm).
Reading: Crockett, D. E. 1994. *Notornis* 41(S): 49–60. Imber, M. J. *et al.* 1994. *Notornis* 41(S): 61–68. Imber, M. J. *et al.* 1994. *Notornis* 41(S): 69–96. Taylor, G. A. 1991. *DOC Threatened Spec Occ Publ* 2. Wellington: DOC. Taylor, G. A. et al. 2012. *NZ J Ecol* 36: 425–432.

88. KERMADEC PETREL *Pterodroma neglecta* PLATES 20 AND 21

Size: 38cm, 500g

Geographical variation: Two subspecies: *neglecta* breeds widely across the western and central South Pacific, and *juana* breeds on islands in the eastern South Pacific.

Distribution: Breeds widely across the subtropical Pacific at Balls Pyramid (Lord Howe Island), Philip Island (Norfolk Island), Kermadec Islands, French Polynesia, Pitcairn group, Juan Fernández Islands, San Ambrosio Island and San Felix Island; in the South Atlantic at Ilha da Trinidade, Brazil; and in the Indian Ocean at Round Island, Mauritius. On the Kermadecs, they breed on Herald, Haszard, Macauley and Cheeseman islands, and they formerly bred in immense numbers on Raoul Island. They range mainly through the subtropical Pacific, but a few stragglers reach the New Zealand mainland: seven beach-wrecked on the west coast of Northland and in Hawke's Bay; singles off the Chathams (1975), at Cuvier Island (1976–81), and Kaikoura (1999). Some migrate to the tropical North Pacific between the Philippines, Japan and Mexico.

Population: Good numbers in the eastern part of the range, but only 6000–10,000 pairs on the Kermadecs, mainly on North and South Meyer islets in the Herald Islet group.

Conservation: Protected native. In 1908, *c.* 250,000 pairs of Kermadec Petrels were nesting on Raoul Island, but these were ravaged by Norway rats (eating eggs) and cats (killing adults), together with the harvesting of birds by settlers early in the 1900s. They had effectively gone from Raoul Island by 1966. Since the eradication of rats in 2002 and cats in 2004, they started to recolonise the island by 2006, when a chick was found. The eradication of Pacific rats from Macauley Island in 2006 should improve breeding conditions there.

Breeding: Kermadec Petrels can breed at any time of the year. Eggs or chicks are recorded in almost all months. Most adults return to their colonies in August, and most eggs are laid October–March, but young close to fledging have been recorded in November. Most eggs are laid on the Meyer Islets in January, a couple of months after the peak used to be on Raoul Island. They lay **1** white egg (64 x 47mm) in a shallow scrape on the surface, usually under thick vegetation. Eggs hatch after 50–52 days, and chicks depart at 110–130 days old.

Behaviour: At sea, Kermadec Petrels usually feed alone. They are noisy over their colonies and on the ground, with a distinctive loud 'yuk-ker-a-ooo-wuk' call, the explosive final note being given 0–3 times.

Feeding: Diet is squid and crustaceans, taken while sitting on the surface of the sea or dipping from the air. Unusually, they closely mimic skuas by harassing other large petrels and force them to regurgitate food.

In the hand: Kermadec Petrels have a wide range of plumages, but all have a skua-like white patch on the underwing at the base of the primaries. Equally variable Herald Petrels (*P. heraldica*), which breed in the central Pacific and have been seen in the Tasman Sea, also have white patches at the base of the primaries but lack the white shafts to the primaries on the upperwing, and have a smaller bill (25–**26.8**–28.5mm) than Kermadec Petrels (28–**30.4**–33mm).

Reading: Imber, M. J. 2005. *Notornis* 52: 168–169. Merton, D. V. 1970. *Notornis* 17: 147–199. Spear, L. & Ainley D. G. 1993. *Auk* 110: 222–233. Veitch, C. R. et al. 2004. *Notornis* 51: 61–90.

89. PHOENIX PETREL *Pterodroma alba* PLATE 21

Size: 35cm, 275g

Distribution: Breeds in the tropical and subtropical central Pacific Ocean especially on islands in the Phoenix, Line, and Marquesas groups; <20 pairs nest on Oeno Island in the Pitcairn group. Formerly bred on Henderson and Ducie in the Pitcairn group; on the Tuamotu Archipelago; possibly in Tonga; and probably on Raoul Island. Four were seen ashore there in March 1913, and one specimen was collected. They range widely in the central Pacific Ocean, but the only recent record from New Zealand was of a bird flying over Curtis Island, southern Kermadecs, in May 1982.

In the hand: Similar to Tahiti Petrels (*Pseudobulweria rostrata*), but they have a small white patch on the chin and a thin white patch along and just behind the leading edge of the base of the underwing, and Tahiti Petrels have a larger bill (33–39mm) and a different bill structure from *Pterodroma* petrels. Clearly smaller than the Chatham Islands Taiko (*P. magentae*): wing 265–**276**–290mm cf. 284–**302**–316mm, and bill 25.5–**27.9**–29.5mm cf. 30.5–**33.0**–35mm. The similar pale and intermediate phases of the Herald Petrel (*P. heraldica*), breeding in the central Pacific and seen in the Tasman Sea, have white patches at the base of the primaries (as have Kermadec Petrels *P. neglecta*), and the white patch on the inner underwing of the Herald Petrels sometimes goes right to the leading edge of the wing.

Reading: Sorensen, J. H. 1964. *Notornis* 11: 69–81. Veitch, C. R. et al. 2004. *Notornis* 51: 61–90.

90. SOFT-PLUMAGED PETREL *Pterodroma mollis* PLATE 21

Size: 34cm, 300g

Distribution: Breeds on subtropical and subantarctic islands of the South Atlantic and South Indian oceans, and recently in the New Zealand subantarctic, on Antipodes Island. They range mainly between 25° S and 60° S in the Atlantic and Indian oceans over deep water beyond the continental shelf, but are quite rare in the South Pacific Ocean, however, now regularly seen on subantarctic cruises near the Antipodes. Since 1971, an increasing number of birds have been seen at sea or beach-wrecked around the mainland of New Zealand as far north as Northland, and also at the Chathams. Most mainland records are off the east coast and around Cook Strait in May–June, when fledglings have just left their colony on the Antipodes, or in November–December.

Population: Several thousand pairs breed on Antipodes Island, where the population is growing rapidly, and very large numbers breed at Gough Island and on islands in the Indian Ocean. The total population is estimated to be over 5 million birds.

Conservation: Protected coloniser. Soft-plumaged Petrels were first discovered in the New Zealand region in February 1969, when they were seen flying over Antipodes Island. In 1978, burrows were located and the colony appeared to be expanding, and by 1994 there were several thousand pairs breeding.

Breeding: Not studied in New Zealand. Elsewhere, adults return to their colonies in August–September to clean out their burrows and to court. Laying is generally in December, and apparently some time after 5 December on the Antipodes. They lay **1** white egg (60 x 43mm, 54g) in a burrow 1–1.5m long, under dense tussock and fern. Eggs hatch in January–February after *c.* 50 days, and most chicks depart in May at *c.* 90 days old.

Behaviour: Call over their nesting area with strange, mournful, low-pitched, fluting cries like a lamb bleating; this call is sometimes uttered on the ground and in burrows, but they are generally quiet on the ground.

Feeding: Diet is mainly squid, with some small fish and crustaceans.

In the hand: Soft-plumaged Petrels have pale and dark phases, but all recorded from the New Zealand region have been of the pale phase. White-headed Petrels and Chatham Islands Taiko are the most similar species, but Soft-plumaged petrels are much smaller (wing 235–**255**–275mm, bill 25.5–**28.4**–32mm). The rare dark phase is similar to the Kerguelen Petrel but lacks the silvery outer underwing.

Reading: Harper, P. C. 1973. *Notornis* 20: 193–121. Imber, M. J. 1983. *Notornis* 30: 283–298. Jouventin, P. et al. 1985. *Notornis* 32: 157–220. Warham, J. & Bell, B. D. 1979. *Notornis* 26: 121–169.

91. MOTTLED PETREL *Pterodroma inexpectata* PLATE 22

Other name: Korure

Size: 34cm, 325g

Distribution: Breeds only on islands in southern New Zealand: in Fiordland (Shag and Front islands and an island in Lake Hauroko), Solander Islands, islands around Stewart Island including Codfish and Big South Cape, and at The Snares. Subfossil, midden and historical records indicate a former breeding distribution through the North, South and Chatham islands. During the breeding season, Mottled Petrels feed mainly in subantarctic waters to the Antarctic Polar Front and pack ice at about 65° S, but some, mainly non-breeders, are found up to about 35° S, and cross the Tasman Sea to southeastern Australia. In March–June they migrate to subarctic convergence zone of the North Pacific Ocean and into the Bering Sea, where they stay until September. They return directly to New Zealand, arriving back between mid-October and November. A few non-breeders follow the American coast south to reach cool waters of the Humboldt Current and the seas off Cape Horn. About 30 Mottled Petrels are beach-wrecked in New Zealand each summer, mostly on Southland beaches (notably Mason Bay, Stewart Island).

Population: Common. The largest colony is on Codfish Island/Whenua Hou with 300,000–400,000 pairs. Other major colonies of 10,000+ pairs are on Main Island

(The Snares) and Big South Cape Island.

Conservation: Protected endemic. Maori used to harvest chicks in the inland North Island, but colonies on the mainland have gone as a result of forest clearance, fires and predators. Weka kill many birds on islands around Stewart Island; breeding success has improved on Codfish Island since Weka were removed in 1985.

Breeding: Adults return to their colonies in late October and early November to prepare burrows and to court. Eggs are laid from early December to early January, mostly 15–23 December. They lay **1** white egg (61 x 44mm, 61g) in a burrow or crevice. Both sexes share incubation in stints of 2–**13**–22 days. Eggs hatch in early February after 48–**50**–53 days. The chick is brooded for the first couple of days and fed about every second day during the first 3 weeks of life. Chicks leave in May and early June at 90–105 days old.

Behaviour: They nest in colonies and sometimes share their cavity with Fairy Prions. At sea, they are usually alone or in small flocks. They arrive at their breeding colonies about 50 minutes after sunset, much later than Sooty Shearwaters. They are very vocal over their colonies, with rapid 'ti-ti-ti . . .' or 'kek-kek-kek . . .' calls and rarer 'oooi' and 'gorr' calls. On the ground, a wide range of calls is given, including the main flight call and the resonant 'gorr', followed by a short staccato 'wik'.

Feeding: Diet is mainly lanternfish, with some crustaceans and squid. Most prey is taken while sitting on the sea surface, or by dipping or shallow plunging from the air.

In the hand: Mottled Petrels are distinctive, with their grey belly patch and prominent black band running diagonally across the underwing from the bend in the wing towards the body. The wing length (245–275mm) is greater than that of most petrels with a similar underwing pattern. Juveniles are paler than adults and have white mottling on most tail feathers, whereas only the outer tail feathers of adults are mottled.

Reading: Harper, P. C. 1987. *Notornis* 34: 169–192. Imber, M. J. 1991. *Acta Int Orn Cong* 20: 1402–1412. Richdale, L. 1964. *Ibis* 106: 110–114. Warham, J. et al. 1977. *Auk* 94: 1–17.

92. JUAN FERNÁNDEZ PETREL *Pterodroma externa* PLATE 22

Size: 43cm, 500g

Distribution: About 1 million pairs breed only on Alejandro Selkirk Island (formerly Más Afuera) in the Juan Fernández Islands, in the eastern South Pacific Ocean. They migrate to the tropical North Pacific Ocean mainly between the equator, Hawai'i and Mexico. Vagrants reach the southwestern Pacific, including Australia and New Zealand. Five New Zealand records: one blown inland near Hamilton (October 1971); at least two birds prospected nest sites at South East Island and Mangere Island in the Chathams (1984–99); Tuku Valley, Chatham Island (October 1997); off Otago (March 2012); and off East Cape (February 2013).

In the hand: Apart from the lack of a white collar (except when in moult), they are similar to the slightly smaller White-naped Petrel. They have only flecks of grey or black on the leading edge of the outer underwing, a large white wedge on the inner shaft of the outermost primary, and a brownish-grey cap. The wing is 302–**316**–336mm cf. 299–**310**–323mm, and the bill is 34.5–**37.3**–41mm cf. 34.5–**36.3**–39mm in White-naped Petrels. The similar Barau's Petrel (*P. baraui*) of the South Indian Ocean, which has been recorded as far east as Victoria, Australia, is smaller (wing 280–300mm, bill 30–33mm).

Reading: Brooke, M. de L. 1987. *Condor* 89: 581–586. Falla, R. A. 1976. *Notornis* 23: 320–322. Imber, M. J. et al. 1991. *Notornis* 38: 60–62. Miskelly, C. M. et al. 2006. *Notornis* 53: 215–230.

93. WHITE-NAPED PETREL *Pterodroma cervicalis* PLATE 22

Other names: White-necked Petrel, Sunday Island Petrel

Size: 43cm, 450g

Distribution: Following their extirpation from Raoul Island in the northern Kermadecs in the early 1900s, the only known breeding site was on Macauley Island in the southern Kermadecs, until a few were found in 1992 on Philip Island off Norfolk Island. They may also nest on islands in Vanuatu. During the summer breeding season, they range widely within the southwestern Pacific, especially to the north and northeast of New Zealand and westwards into the northern Tasman Sea as far as eastern Australia. Regularly seen off Northland, but scarce further south: Mamaku Range (April 1968), off Muriwai Beach, (February 1972), Gisborne (1977),

1–2 in the outer Bay of Plenty (February 1991) at least two off East Cape (January–March 1997) and off eastern Stewart Island (February 2011). After breeding, they migrate in May–July to the North Pacific Ocean, mainly to the southeast of Japan. They start returning in September, but some stay until November.
Population: Macauley Island, *c.* 50,000 pairs in 1988; Philip Island (Norfolk) <100 pairs.
Conservation: Protected native. Many used to breed on Raoul (Sunday) Island, but by 1908 only about 500 pairs were breeding and were being ravaged by cats. As a result, they died out on Raoul Island before 1966. The Macauley Island population, discovered in 1966, is expanding rapidly now that the habitat has improved with removal of goats from the island in 1971. The species remains vulnerable because it is largely confined to one island.
Breeding: Little New Zealand information is available. On Raoul Island, adults returned to their colonies in late September or early October, and eggs were laid in December–January. At Philip Island, birds don't return until mid-November and eggs are laid from 8–31 January. They lay **1** white egg (66 x 47mm) in a burrow. Eggs hatch in late February and chicks depart May–June at *c.* 110 days old.
Behaviour: At sea, White-naped Petrels are usually alone or in small flocks at food. They are noisy over their colonies, with a harsh 'ka-ka-ka' call. They respond well to human war-whooping. On the ground, the main call is 'kukooowik-ka-ha', with variations on the number and pitch of the concluding notes.
Feeding: Diet is mainly squid, taken while sitting on the surface of the sea or by dipping from the air.
In the hand: The white collar is diagnostic, but this may not show up clearly in beach-wrecked specimens. White-naped Petrels can be separated from slightly larger Juan Fernández Petrels (*P. externa*) by having a brownish-black cap, the outermost primary dusky, with little or no white on the inner web (rather than having a clear white wedge on the inner web), and the underwing has a broad black leading edge beyond the bend of the wing. In *P. externa* the leading edge of the outer underwing is only flecked grey or black. The wing is 299–**310**–323mm cf. 302–**316**–336mm, and the bill is 34.5–**36.2**–39mm cf. 34.5–**37.3**–41mm in Juan Fernández Petrels.
Reading: Dowding, J. E. 1987. *Notornis* 34: 325–326. Falla, R. A. 1976. *Notornis* 23: 320–322. Veitch, C. R. et al. 2004. *Notornis* 51: 61–90.

94. BLACK-WINGED PETREL *Pterodroma nigripennis* PLATE 22

Size: 30cm, 175g
Distribution: Breeds in the southwestern Pacific, at Lord Howe Island, Philip Island off Norfolk Island, islets off New Caledonia, in the New Zealand region, Tonga, the Cook Islands, on islets off Rapa Island, and on Bass Rock in French Polynesia. In New Zealand, they breed at the Kermadecs, Three Kings Islands, Motuopao Island (off Cape Maria van Diemen), Matapia Island (off Ninety Mile Beach), Simmonds Islands (off Houhora), Piercy Island (off Cape Brett), Burgess Island (Mokohinaus), East Island, Portland Island, and in the Chathams at South East and Mangere islands. Black-winged Petrels, expanding their breeding range, have been seen prospecting for nest sites on islands off Australia and on some headlands and other islands around the northern North Island.

During the summer breeding season, they range through the subtropical southwestern Pacific and temperate waters of the Tasman Sea, as far south as Foveaux Strait. In May, they migrate to the subtropical North Pacific Ocean, mainly between the equator and 30° N, from Japan to Mexico. They return to New Zealand waters in late October. Normally <10 beach-wrecked on the New Zealand coast each year, mostly on the west coast of the North Island in December–April.
Population: Abundant. 2–3 million pairs breed on 280ha Macauley Island, making it one of the largest and densest petrel colonies in the world; the removal of goats in 1971, and Pacific rats in 1986 will have benefited the species.
Conservation: Protected native. Huge colonies on Norfolk and Raoul islands were exterminated by cats and rats, but those on predator-free islands are flourishing and Black-winged Petrels are expanding their range, including the establishment of breeding pairs on East and Portland islands off the Gisborne coast and on Mangere Island in the Chathams since 1980. This range expansion leads to prospecting birds being killed on the ground at some mainland headlands. They have quickly recolonised Raoul Island following the eradication of rats in 2002 and cats in 2004, and by 2010 at least 14 small colonies had become established.
Breeding: Adults return to their colonies in mid-October to early December to prepare burrows and to

court. Laying is from late December to mid-January in the Kermadecs and about a fortnight later on East Island and in the Chathams, where eggs are laid in mid-January. They lay **1** white egg (52 x 37mm, 37g) in a burrow 0.5–1m long. The incubation period is *c.* 45 days and the fledging period is *c.* 85 days. Chicks hatch in late February to early March at the Chathams, and fledge in April–May at the Kermadecs.

Behaviour: Very vocal over their colonies, with a low 'ahh-oo' followed by a rapid 'wi-wi-wi-wi' call. On the ground, the main calls are a rapid, hysterical 'haa-ha-haa-ha . . .', and a low 'orrrrrr . . .' lasting up to 3–4 seconds.

Feeding: Diet is squid, small fish and crustaceans caught within 2m of the surface, both by night and day.

In the hand: Black-winged Petrels have an unmistakable underwing pattern with a broad black band along the leading edge of the outer upperwing, angling diagonally across the wing towards the body from the elbow but stopping before the axillaries. The bill is more robust than in the otherwise similar Pycroft's Petrel (bill length x depth x width: 23–26 x 10.5–12 x 9–12mm cf. 22.5–26 x 9.5–10.5 x 7.5–9.5mm)

Reading: Hutton, I. & Priddel, D. 2002. *Emu* 112: 361–365. Jenkins, J. A. F. & Cheshire, N. G. 1982. *Notornis* 29: 293–310. Powlesland, R. G. 1985. *Notornis* 32: 23–41. Tanaka, Y. et al. 1985. *J Yamashina Inst Orn* 17: 23–31. Taylor, G. A. 2008. *Papers & Proc Roy Soc Tasmania* 142: 189–198. Tennyson, A. J. D. 1991. *Notornis* 38: 111–116. Veitch, C. R. et al. 2011. Pp. 372–376. In Veitch et al. 2011. *Island Invasives: Eradication and Management.* Gland: IUCN.

95. CHATHAM ISLANDS PETREL *Pterodroma axillaris* PLATE 22

Other names: Chatham Petrel, Chatham Island Petrel

Size: 30cm, 200g

Distribution: In recent times, bred only on South East Island in the Chathams, but subfossils show that they used to breed more widely in the Chatham group. Between 2002 and 2011, reintroduced to Pitt Island and southern Chatham Island, where they have started to breed. During the pre-laying exodus and incubation stage, birds forage well to the southeast of the Chathams between the Subantarctic Front and the Subtropical Convergence; however, during chick-rearing, they generally feed to the south of the Chathams and around the Bollons Seamount, 400km east of the Antipodes. After breeding, birds cross the Pacific to winter in waters about 1000km west of South America. Because movements are towards the east and south of the Chathams, they have not been beach-wrecked on the New Zealand mainland nor sighted in coastal waters.

Population: *c.* 250 pairs and a total population of *c.* 1000 birds in 2004.

Conservation: Protected vulnerable endemic. Colonies on Chatham, Pitt and Mangere island were exterminated in pre-European times, but Chatham Islands Petrels were rediscovered on South East Island in 1973 after over 30 years with no records. Because Broad-billed Prions compete for nest sites and kill chicks and even adults, they have been culled in and around known burrows, and natural burrows have been replaced with prion-proof artificial nest chambers to reduce nest competition. Breeding success has improved from 10–30% to over 70% per year. Between 2002 and 2011, 400 chicks were transferred to predator-proof enclosures on Pitt Island and southern Chatham Island, and by 2013 birds had bred successfully at both new sites.

Breeding: Adults return to South East Island in late November and early December to prepare burrows and to court. Following a pre-laying exodus of *c.* 35 days, females return to lay from 20 December to late February. They lay **1** white egg (52 x 39mm, 47g) in a deep burrow 0.5–2m long. Following an incubation period of *c.* 46 days, split into up to five shifts, eggs hatch in February to early April. Chicks fledge at 77–**87**–98 days old in May to early July. Some birds return to their natal colony at 2 years old, but generally do not breed until at least 4 years old. Mean life expectancy of adults is *c.* 20 years, and the oldest banded bird used the same burrow for 24 years and must have lived at least 28 years.

Behaviour: Nest solitarily, interspersed with nesting Broad-billed Prions, Common Diving Petrels and storm petrels. They are very vocal over their colonies, with a rapid 'chee-chee-chee . . .' call, sometimes answered by a 'coooo' or 'wikooo'. Also reported is a rapid 'wek-wek-wek . . .' and a purring ground call.

Feeding: Diet includes squid and small fish collected within 2m of the surface, mainly at night.

In the hand: Chatham Islands Petrels are similar to Black-winged Petrels, but they have black axillaries (base of the underwing), and their wings are shorter (212–228mm cf. 215–235mm).

Reading: Fleming, C. A. 1939. *Emu* 38: 380–413. Imber, M. J. 1985. *Ibis* 127: 197–229. Rayner, M. J. et al. 2012. *Emu* 112: 107–116. West, J. A. 1994. *Notornis* 41(S): 19–26.

96. COOK'S PETREL *Pterodroma cookii* PLATE 23

Other name: Titi

Size: 29cm, 190g

Distribution: Breeds only in New Zealand, on Little Barrier, Great Barrier, and Codfish islands. From 2010, chicks were transferred from Little Barrier to Cape Kidnappers to try and establish a mainland breeding site. Subfossil and midden evidence suggests that they formerly bred on the mainland of both North and South islands. During the summer breeding season, Little Barrier birds feed in the western South Pacific Ocean in two clusters, off Northland and the Coromandel Peninsula, and between East Cape and Cook Strait; and also in the Tasman Sea off Northland and in deep waters of the northern Tasman Sea. Codfish Island birds feed mainly in seas around Stewart and Solander islands and in the southern Tasman Sea, westwards from Fiordland. After breeding, Cook's Petrels migrate to the eastern Pacific Ocean, mainly between 34° S and 30° N, especially off Mexico and California, and some straggle further north into the Gulf of Alaska. Birds from Little Barrier winter mainly in the North Pacific, whereas Codfish Island birds winter mainly off Peru and Chile. They leave New Zealand waters in April and return about August, although a few remain through the winter. They are the commonest small gadfly petrel beach-wrecked on the New Zealand coast. About 25 are found each year, mainly on Auckland and Bay of Plenty beaches with peaks in December, and in March–April when chicks have just fledged.

Population: *c.* 1.3 million birds in 2008. 286,000 pairs on Little Barrier Island in 2007, <10 pairs on Great Barrier Island, and 5000 pairs on Codfish Island/Whenua Hou in 2008.

Conservation: Protected endemic. Chicks used to be collected by Maori, and adults were killed when attracted to fires lit on flight paths to colonies, but they are now fully protected. About 20,000 pairs of Cook's Petrels bred on Codfish Island in the early 1900s, but predation by Weka reduced them to <100 pairs by 1980, however, they have recovered strongly since the removal of Weka and Pacific rats in 1985 and 1998 respectively. Likewise, the numbers on Little Barrier Island have increased rapidly following the eradication of cats there in 1980, and breeding success has improved from 5% to 60% since the eradication of Pacific rats in 2004.

Breeding: Adults return to their colonies in August to prepare burrows and to court. After a pre-laying exodus of *c.* 28 days, birds lay from 23 October to 1 December on Little Barrier Island, but about a month later, from 3 to 15 December, on Codfish Island. They lay 1 white egg (53 x 39mm, 43g) in a deep burrow 1–5m long. Incubation spells are *c.* 14 days, and eggs hatch on Little Barrier from mid-December to mid-January after 46–47–50 days. Chicks are fed on average every 3 days, and reach twice the adult weight before fasting for the last 10 days before fledging, at *c.* 87 days old. Chicks fledge from mid-March to mid-April at Little Barrier, and from mid-April to early May at Codfish Island.

Behaviour: Nests in large colonies, often interspersed with Black Petrels in the north. They are very vocal over their colonies, with a rapid three-note 'kek-kek-kek' and other aerial calls, and they make high-speed dives above the colony with vibrating feathers making a whistling sound. On the ground, they give a loud purring call. Cook's Petrels often call over land as they are heading for their breeding colonies, and are heard over Northland, Auckland and Stewart Island at night.

Feeding: In the breeding season, the diet of Little Barrier birds is primarily juvenile squid and small fish, with some crustaceans and tunicates, whereas those on Codfish Island eat primarily crustaceans. Judging from the composition of the diet, and activity budgets, most prey is probably taken at night. Much is taken by surface dipping, but they also pursuit dive to a mean of 8m deep, and up to 27.5m depth.

In the hand: Cook's Petrels are similar to about 10 other small gadfly petrels, but they have a very pale underwing with only a small black line extending from the bend of the wing towards the body. Their wing (223–245mm) and bill (24.5–30mm) are longer than most similar species (Pycroft's, Stejneger's and Gould's petrels), and they have a white wedge-shaped patch covering about 60% of the inner web of the primaries, which is not as large on other species, with the exception of some Pycroft's Petrels.

Reading: Imber, M. J. 1996. *Emu* 96: 189–194. Imber, M. J. et al. 2003. *Notornis* 50: 221–230. Powlesland, R. G. 1987. *Notornis* 34: 237–252. Rayner, M. J. et al. 2007. *Biol Cons* 138: 235–247. Rayner, M. J. et al. 2007. *Emu* 107: 59–68. Rayner, M. J. et al. 2008. *Mar Ecol Prog Ser* 370: 271–284. Rayner, M. J. et al. 2008. *Bird Cons Intl* 18: 211–218. Rayner, M. J. et al. 2011. *Nat Commun* 2: 332. West, J. A. 1990. *DOC Sci & Res Int Rep* 85. Wellington: DOC.

97. STEJNEGER'S PETREL *Pterodroma longirostris* PLATE 23

Size: 28cm, 160g
Distribution: Breeds only on Alejandro Selkirk Island (formerly Más Afuera) in the Juan Fernández Islands off Chile. About 130,000 pairs breed there, but they are declining due to predation by cats. They migrate to the subtropical North Pacific between Hawai'i and Japan, where they stay from June to November. Vagrants reach temperate seas around the North and Chatham islands in November–February, with 13 recorded up to 2013.
In the hand: Stejneger's Petrels have similar plumage to Cook's and Pycroft's petrels, but they have a white forehead contrasting with the black cap, and their wing (200–220mm) is shorter than that of Cook's Petrel (220–245mm). Gould's Petrel has much more extensive black on the nape and sides to the neck.
Reading: Brooke, M. de L. 1987. *Condor* 89: 581–586. Powlesland, R. G. 1985. *Notornis* 32: 23–41.

98. PYCROFT'S PETREL *Pterodroma pycrofti* PLATE 23

Size: 28cm, 160g
Distribution: Breeds only in New Zealand, on islands off the northeastern coast of the North Island. They nest on Stephenson, Poor Knights (Aorangi), Hen and Chickens (Hen, Lady Alice, Whatupuke, Coppermine and Mauitaha) and Mercury (Red Mercury, Korapuki, Double and Stanley) islands, and successfully introduced to Cuvier Island in 2001–03. Subfossil remains from Norfolk and Lord Howe islands indicate that they formerly had a wider breeding distribution. Judging from the distribution of Pycroft's Petrels found beach-wrecked, they spend the summer in temperate or subtropical waters off the northern North Island, mainly to the east. They migrate to the central and northeastern North Pacific Ocean in the non-breeding season (May–September).
Population: *c.* 10,000 pairs, and a total population of *c.* 40,000 birds. The largest colonies are on Red Mercury Island (5000–10,000 pairs), Chickens Islands (500 pairs) and Double Island (100 pairs).
Conservation: Protected endemic. They breed only on predator-free islands or those with only the Pacific rat present. However, Pacific rats are responsible for most breeding failures, and their eradication from islands of the Mercury group (especially from Red Mercury Island in 1992) and from some of the Chickens group has led to a rapid increase in their population.
Breeding: Adults return to their colonies in October to prepare burrows and to court. Egg-laying is from *c.* 15 November to *c.* 20 December. They lay **1** white egg (49 x 35mm, 32g) in a burrow 30–130cm long. Eggs hatch in late January after *c.* 45 days. Chicks are fed on average every 2 days until the feeding frequency drops off about 3 weeks before fledging; they are rarely fed in their last week on land. Chicks reach their maximum weight of *c.* 290g (175% of adult weight) about 26 days before fledging from mid-March to mid-April at *c.* 80 days old. Birds first return to their natal island at 2–3 years old, but do not start breeding until 3–10 years old.
Behaviour: Nest in small, localised colonies, interspersed with other burrowing petrels. They are very vocal above their colonies, with a rapid, high-pitched 'kek-kek-kek...' aerial call, and a few quieter calls given on the ground.
Feeding: In the breeding season, the diet is primarily juvenile squid, crustaceans, and small fish. Most prey is taken by surface dipping, but they also make very shallow pursuit dives to 2m deep.
In the hand: Pycroft's Petrels are very similar to, though smaller than, Cook's Petrels and were not separated from them until 1933. They have shorter wings (207–229mm) than Cook's Petrels (223–245mm) and shorter bills (22.5–26mm cf. 24.5–30mm), but longer tails (88–103mm cf. 82–95mm).
Reading: Bartle, J. A. 1968. *Notornis* 15: 70–99. Dunnet, G. M. 1985. *Notornis* 32: 5–21. Gangloff, B. & Wilson, K. -J. 2004. *Notornis* 51: 26–32. Powlesland, R. G. 1987. *Notornis* 34: 237–252.

99. GOULD'S PETREL *Pterodroma leucoptera* PLATE 23

Size: 29cm, 175g
Geographical variation: Two subspecies: *leucoptera* breeds off New South Wales and has not yet been recorded in New Zealand; *caledonica* breeds on New Caledonia and straggles to New Zealand.
Distribution: Breeds only on Cabbage Tree and

Boondelbah islands, New South Wales, and along the central mountain range of New Caledonia. They migrate to the eastern tropical Pacific, especially to the southwest of the Galapagos Islands in July–October. During the breeding season, non-breeders are regularly seen in the Tasman Sea as far south as Foveaux Strait, and are occasionally beach-wrecked, mainly on the west coast of the North Island, in November–May.

In the hand: Gould's Petrels have a distinctive black cap, nape and sides to the neck and have slightly shorter wings (213–238mm) than Cook's Petrels (220–245mm) and shorter bills (23–27.5mm cf. 24.5–30mm). The most reliable feature to separate the *caledonica* subspecies from the *leucoptera* subspecies is that the inner web of the outermost tail feather of *caledonica* is white, or mainly white, with a variable amount of grey flecking near the tip, whereas in the nominate *leucoptera* the outer feather is grey to brownish grey, apart from the basal inner half being off-white. Also, *caledonica* is larger than *leucoptera*: wing 219–**229**–235mm cf. 213–**225**–238mm; bill 23.5–**25.4**–27.5mm cf. 23–**24.6**–26.5mm; and has more of a contrast in colour between the grey of its back and uppertail coverts and the dark grey of the rest of the upperparts.

Reading: Imber, M. J. & Jenkins, J. A. F. 1981. *Notornis* 28: 149–160. Powlesland, R. G. 1985. *Notornis* 32: 23–41.

100. BLUE PETREL *Halobaena caerulea* — PLATES 19 AND 24

Size: 29cm, 200g

Distribution: Circumpolar, breeding at Cape Horn and adjacent islands, and on many subantarctic islands, but not in the New Zealand region. The closest colony is of 500–600 pairs on stacks off Macquarie Island. They are sedentary during the summer breeding season, but then range widely through the southern oceans between the pack ice and about 35° S in the winter, although they have been recorded as far north as 29° S at Raoul Island and to 20° S off Peru. Blue Petrels are regular winter–spring visitors to New Zealand waters and have become more common since about 1980. Each year, 10–100 are usually beach-wrecked on North Island west coast beaches in July–November, however, subadults are occasionally wrecked in large numbers in August–October (e.g. 343 in 1981, 881 in 1984, 527 in 1985, 372 in 1991, and 438 in 1999).

Feeding: Diet is mainly crustaceans, small fish and squid, taken from the sea surface by dipping in flight or while the bird is swimming. Blue Petrels occasionally follow ships or attend feeding whales.

Reading: Jouventin, P. et al. 1985. *Notornis* 32: 157–220. Prince, P. A. 1980. *J Zool (Lond)* 190: 59–76. Reed, S. 1981. *Notornis* 28: 239–240.

101. BROAD-BILLED PRION *Pachyptila vittata* — PLATE 24

Other name: Parara, Whalebird

Size: 28cm, 200g

Distribution: Broad-billed Prions have a disjunct breeding distribution, with populations on Tristan da Cunha, Nightingale, Inaccessible and Gough islands in the South Atlantic Ocean, and on many islands about southern New Zealand: in Fiordland, Solander Islands, Foveaux Strait and on islands and stacks around Stewart Island, The Snares, and on most of the smaller islands in the Chathams group. New Zealand birds range through temperate waters close to the Subtropical Convergence between 35° S and 50° S in the Tasman Sea and Bass Strait, and in the central South Pacific. About 50–100 are wrecked on Southland and North Island west coast beaches each year in June–January, but wrecks are large in some winters (e.g. 1385 in 1961, and 1175 in 1974). A phenomenal 250,000 birds were estimated to have been killed by a severe storm in July 2011, with many beach-wrecked or blown inland mainly along the western North Island.

Population: Enormous colonies of 1 million+ pairs exist on Gough and Nightingale islands in the South Atlantic. Abundant on the Chathams (especially South East Island, *c.* 330,000 pairs) and, until the 2011 storm, they were abundant on Foveaux Strait islands.

Conservation: Protected native. Chicks used to be harvested by Maori but are now protected. Introduced predators (cats, rats and Weka) have exterminated many colonies around Stewart Island. The species was increasing, however the 2011 storm killed perhaps 80–90% of the birds breeding in southern New Zealand. The Chatham Islands population seems not to have been affected by the 2011 storm.

Breeding: Winter–spring breeder. Adults return to

their colonies from the second week of February to prepare burrows and to court. Laying is in late August to mid-September at all New Zealand colonies. They lay 1 white egg (50 x 37mm) in a burrow, rock crevice or cave. Eggs hatch in mid-October to early November after *c.* 45 days and young fledge from mid-December to late January at 55–61 days old. The oldest bird recorded on The Snares was at least 15 years old.

Behaviour: Nest in huge colonies, often interspersed with other burrowing petrels. At sea, they are often seen in flocks as they feed, roost or stream back to their colonies at dusk. They are silent at sea but very vocal at their colonies, with persistent harsh calls given both in the air and on the ground – similar to those of Fairy Prions, but louder, faster and with more notes.

Feeding: Diet is mainly copepods, other crustaceans and other planktonic invertebrates, but some small fish and squid are eaten. Most are taken from the sea surface while the bird is scurrying forwards rapidly with beak held partly open under the sea surface and moving its head from side to side, or by shallow plunging from the surface. Minute prey are sieved on to the well-developed comb-like lamellae inside the upper bill.

In the hand: Broad-billed Prions are the largest prion (wing 195–225mm) and have a large head and grotesquely wide bill (19–24mm), which does not overlap in size with that of any other prion.

Reading: Harper, P. C. 1980. *Notornis* 27: 235–286. Harper, P. C. 1987. *Notornis* 34: 169–192. Imber, M. J. 1981. In *Proc Symp Birds Sea Shore*. Cape Town: African Seabird Group. Powlesland, R. G. 1989. *Notornis* 36: 125–140. Richdale, L. E. 1944. *Emu* 43: 191–217. Richdale, L. E. 1965. *Trans Zool Soc (Lond)* 31: 87–155. West, J. A. & Nilsson, R. J. 1994. *Notornis* 41(S): 27–37.

102. SALVIN'S PRION *Pachyptila salvini* — PLATE 24

Other name: Lesser Broad-billed Prion

Size: 27cm, 170g

Geographical variation: Two subspecies: *salvini* breeds on islands in the eastern and central subantarctic South Indian Ocean and regularly reaches New Zealand waters, whereas the rare *macgillivrayi* breeds on St Paul and Amsterdam islands in the temperate South Indian Ocean and has not been recorded in New Zealand.

Distribution: Breeds only in the South Indian Ocean, on Marion, Prince Edward, Crozet, St Paul and Amsterdam islands. They remain close to their breeding colonies during summer, but in winter they disperse eastwards between 35° S and 55° S as far as New Zealand. About 50–100, mainly juveniles, are found beach-wrecked on west coast beaches each winter, but subadults are occasionally wrecked in large numbers in June–August (e.g. 1307 in 1970, and 5228 in 1974). About 10,000 birds were estimated to have been killed by a severe storm in July 2011, with many beach-wrecked or blown inland mainly along the western North Island.

Feeding: Diet is mainly crustaceans and other planktonic invertebrates, but some small fish and squid are eaten. Most are taken while the bird is swimming, by sieving minute prey onto the comb-like lamellae inside the upper bill, but sometimes while the bird is flying with beak held partly open under the sea surface.

In the hand: Salvin's Prions have a much wider bill (13.5–17.5mm) than Fairy Prions (9–12.5mm). They are similar to Antarctic Prions, except that the bill is usually wider (cf. 11–15.5mm) and more bowed, and when the closed bill is viewed from the side the lamellae are clearly visible at the base.

Reading: Harper, P. C. 1980. *Notornis* 27: 235–286. Powlesland, R. G. 1989. *Notornis* 36: 125–140.

103. ANTARCTIC PRION *Pachyptila desolata* — PLATE 24

Other name: Totorore

Size: 26cm, 150g

Distribution: Circumpolar, breeding on many subantarctic and Antarctic islands, including the Auckland Islands, Scott Island in the Ross Dependency, and possibly on islets off Campbell Island. Most remain close to their breeding colonies during summer, but they disperse widely through southern oceans to about 35° S in winter, and some straggle into subtropical waters to reach the Kermadec Islands and Vanuatu. They regularly appear in small numbers in New Zealand waters in winter. About 50 Antarctic Prions are found beach-wrecked on west coast beaches each year in May–October, but they are occasionally wrecked in large numbers in June–August (e.g. 3186 in 1974, and 1026 in 1986). About 20,000 birds were estimated to have been killed by a severe storm in July 2011, with many beach-wrecked or blown inland mainly along the western North Island.

Population: Abundant, with huge numbers breeding on South Georgia (22 million pairs) and Kerguelen Island (2–3 million pairs). In the New Zealand region, between 100,000 and 1 million pairs breed on the Auckland Islands, and fewer than 200 pairs breed on Scott Island.

Conservation: Protected native. Introduced cats and pigs have exterminated many colonies on Auckland Island, but they remain common on offshore islets. Occasional large wrecks of mainly subadults probably have little effect on the species.

Breeding: Not studied in New Zealand, but probably like other colonies, where adults return in October and lay in December. They lay 1 white egg (47 x 35mm, 33g) in a burrow or rock crevice. Eggs hatch in late January to early February after *c.* 45 days and young fledge from mid-March to early April at *c.* 50 days old.

Behaviour: At sea, they are often seen in flocks as they feed, roost or stream back to their colonies at dusk. They are silent at sea but very vocal at their colonies, both in the air and on the ground.

Feeding: Diet is mainly crustaceans and other planktonic invertebrates, but some small fish and squid are eaten. Most are taken while the bird is swimming, by sieving minute prey onto the comb-like lamellae inside the upper bill.

In the hand: Antarctic Prions have a wider bill (11–15.5mm) than Fairy Prions (9–12.5mm). They are similar to Salvin's Prions, except that the bill is usually narrower (cf. 13.5–17.5mm) and the sides are straighter, and when the closed bill is viewed from the side the lamellae are not visible at the base.

Reading: Harper, P. C. 1972. *Notornis* 19: 140–175. Harper, P. C. 1980. *Notornis* 27: 235–286. Harper, P. C. 1987. *Notornis* 34: 169–192. Powlesland, R. G. 1989. *Notornis* 36: 125–140. Tickell, W. L. N. 1962. *Falkland Is Dep Surv Sci Rep* 33: 1–55.

104. THIN-BILLED PRION *Pachyptila belcheri* PLATE 24

Other names: Narrow-billed Prion, Slender-billed Prion

Size: 26cm, 145g

Distribution: Breed on Isla Noir and Landfall Island (off the Pacific coast of Chile), Falkland Islands, East Island in the Crozet Islands and on Kerguelen Island. In autumn, birds from the Patagonian region disperse westwards into the South Pacific but are not known to reach New Zealand; however, birds from the large colonies on Kerguelen Island in the South Indian Ocean disperse eastwards through Antarctic and subantarctic seas and many, mainly young birds, reach New Zealand waters in winter. About 50 are beach-wrecked on west coast beaches of the North Island in June–August each year, but they are occasionally wrecked in large numbers (e.g. 1326 in 1974, and 1410 in 1986).

Feeding: Diet is mainly small amphipods, fish, squid and krill. Food is obtained at night by picking from the sea surface while resting on the surface, by dipping from in flight, or while pattering along the surface.

In the hand: Thin-billed Prions are one of the smallest prions: wing 165–**180**–190mm; bill 23–**25**–27mm, but with a moderately long culminicorn (8–10mm) compared with Fairy Prion (4–6mm). They have paler wingtips than other prions, and, unlike others, the undertail lacks a black terminal band.

Reading: Harper, P. C. 1972. *Notornis* 19: 140–175. Harper, P. C. 1980. *Notornis* 27: 235–286. Harper, P. C. 1987. *Notornis* 34: 169–192. Powlesland, R. G. 1989. *Notornis* 36: 125–140.

105. FAIRY PRION *Pachyptila turtur* PLATE 24

Other names: Titi Wainui, Dove Prion

Size: 25cm, 125g

Distribution: Circumpolar, breeding on many subantarctic islands, in Bass Strait and on many islands around the New Zealand mainland and at the Chathams, The Snares, Antipodes Islands and possibly on islets off Campbell Island. The main colonies around the mainland are at the Poor Knights, in Cook Strait (Stephens, Trio and Brother islands), Motunau Island, Foveaux Strait islands and the Muttonbird Islands off Stewart Island. Some small colonies exist on islands off the Otago coast and also on ledges on nearby sea cliffs on the mainland.

In summer, they range through temperate waters around the mainland coast, in the Tasman Sea and east into the South Pacific. In winter, many are in

Foveaux Strait, in the Cook Strait and Taranaki Bight area, and east of Northland, but some disperse further north into subtropical waters as far as the Coral Sea and the Kermadecs. Elsewhere, some reach waters off South America and South Africa. Birds banded on Stephens Island have been recovered mainly around New Zealand and eastern Australia. Fairy Prions are the most common bird beach-wrecked in New Zealand, with peaks of recoveries in February, when fledglings disperse to sea, and July–November, when many subadults are wrecked on west coast beaches after severe storms or persistent westerly winds.

Population: Abundant; over 2.5 million pairs in New Zealand; the largest colony is on Stephen's Island (1.83 million pairs). The Green Island (Foveaux Strait) colony which numbered 1.5 million pairs in 1941 was greatly reduced by 2012.

Conservation: Protected native. Chicks used to be harvested by Maori but are now protected. Introduced predators (cats, rats and mustelids) have exterminated most colonies on the mainland and near-shore islands, but the existing colonies seem secure as long as they remain free of predators. At Stephens Island, tuatara are responsible for the loss of over 25% of eggs and chicks, but this probably has little overall effect. Occasional large wrecks (e.g. 5118 in 1975 and 10,929 in 1985) of mainly subadults are also natural events with little long-term impact. Between 2002 and 2004, 240 chicks were transferred from Stephens Island to Mana Island, and this has resulted in a small breeding colony establishing on Mana Island, despite some returning to Stephens Island.

Breeding: Adults start returning to their breeding colonies from late March, but do not start cleaning out burrows until late July. Laying varies from mid-October at the Poor Knights, 19 October to 10 November at Stephens Island, to early November at Whero Island (Foveaux Strait) and at the Chathams. They lay **1** white egg (44 x 32mm, 23g) in a burrow 0.6–2m long, or in a shallow crevice. Incubation shifts are of 1–**2**–5 days on the Poor Knights, but the other partner often returns each night; whereas on Whero Island, incubation spells are of 6–7 days. Eggs hatch 21 November to 4 December on the Poor Knights, 3–12 December on Stephens Island, and 18 December to 19 January on Whero Island. The incubation period is 44–**47**–54 days.

Chicks are brooded continuously for the first 1–**2**–5 days and then left unguarded. Chicks fledge from the Poor Knights in January, from Stephens Island from mid-January to early February, and from Whero Island from early February to early March. The fledging period is **45** days on the Poor Knights but 43–**50**–56 days on Whero Island. Young birds return to their colonies when >2.5 years old, but usually don't breed until *c.* 4 years old. Pairs usually occupy the same nest site each year, and divorces are uncommon. Annual adult survivorship is estimated at 84%, giving a mean life expectancy of 5.9 years, but the oldest bird recorded lived over 22 years.

Behaviour: Nest in colonies. At sea, they are often seen in flocks as they feed, roost or stream back to their colonies at dusk. They are silent at sea but very vocal at their colonies, both in the air and on the ground. Males give a harsh, repeated three-note call: 'poor, pop, per', and a very rapid rattling call, whereas females give a harsh two-note call: 'errr, errr'.

Feeding: Diet is mainly krill, supplemented by other planktonic crustaceans and invertebrates, and small fish. Most prey is taken from the sea surface.

In the hand: Fairy Prions have a much wider (35–45mm) black band at the tip of the tail than other prions (except Fulmar Prions), the wing is 170–**179**–189mm, and the bill is 20–25mm long and 10–12mm wide (but note that bills of beach-wrecked birds, especially juveniles, shrink as they dry out).

Reading: Bailey, A. M. & Sorensen, J. H. 1950. *Subantarctic Campbell Island.* Denver: Denver Mus Nat Hist. Hunter, S. 1984. *J Zool (Lond)* 203: 441–460. McIlwaine, C. P. 1964. *Emu* 64: 33–38. Miskelly, C. M. & Gummer, H. 2013. *Notornis* 60: 29–40. Powlesland, R. G. 1989. *Notornis* 36: 125–140.

106. FULMAR PRION *Pachyptila crassirostris* PLATE 24

Size: 26cm, 140g

Geographical variation: Three subspecies: *crassirostris* breeds at the Bounty Islands and The Snares, *pyramidalis* breeds at the Chathams, and *flemingi* breeds at the Auckland Islands, and at Heard Island and probably McDonald Island, South Indian Ocean.

Distribution: Breeds in New Zealand and Australia. In New Zealand the main colonies are at the Chathams (The Forty-fours (Motuhara) and The Pyramid), Bounty Islands, The Snares (Western Chain), and Auckland Islands (Rose, Ewing and Ocean). They are apparently quite sedentary, but a few are storm-drifted to mainland New Zealand coasts in winter and spring, with an unusually large number in 1985 (63). An exceptionally severe storm event which killed over 300,000 prions in New Zealand in July 2011 may have killed 5000–10,000 Fulmar Prions.

Population: Uncommon; probably fewer than 50,000 pairs and 150,000 birds. Most breed in New Zealand: *c.* 30,000 nest on the Bounty Islands, 1000–5000 on the Chathams, 1000 on the Auckland Islands and 400–600 on the Western Chain of The Snares. The loss of over 5000 Fulmar Prions in July 2011 may have had a temporary severe impact on the overall population in New Zealand.

Conservation: Protected native. No information is available about historical changes in numbers or breeding distribution, but they are likely to have been on the main Auckland Island before rats and cats arrived.

Breeding: No detailed studies. As eggs hatch on The Snares in mid-December, they are probably laid in mid-late October. They lay **1** white egg (46 x 33mm) in a shallow scrape, sometimes lined with feathers, under rockfalls, in caves or in crevices. Chicks have fledged from The Snares by 11 February.

Behaviour: Nests in colonies. The birds nesting on the Bounty Islands and The Snares are unusual among prions in visiting their nests in daylight and in courting and calling by day and not at night. On the Bounty Islands, flocks of about 100 prions mob any gulls or skuas venturing over the islands in daylight. They are very vocal at their colonies, both in the air and on the ground, with males apparently giving a clear four-note call and females responding with a slurred three-note call.

Feeding: Diet is mainly small crustaceans and juvenile barnacles picked from the sea surface or by shallow dives.

In the hand: Fulmar Prions are quite similar to Fairy Prions, but Fulmar Prions have a slightly narrower tail band and generally longer wing (174–**188**–203mm, but this varies considerably with subspecies), and the bill is heavier and the hook is larger. The subspecies *pyramidalis* is the largest, with long wings (182–**193**–203mm) and wide bill (12–13mm), *crassirostris* is intermediate (175–**183**–193mm and 10–12mm respectively), and *flemingi* is the smallest (174–**179**–187mm and 9.5–11mm respectively).

Reading: Harper, P. C. 1980. *Notornis* 27: 235–286. Harper, P. C. 1987. *Notornis* 34: 169–192. Miskelly, C. M. 1984. *Notornis* 31: 209–223. Robertson, C. J. R. and van Tets, G. F. 1982. *Notornis* 29: 311–336. Sagar, P. M. 1977. *Notornis* 24: 178–183.

107. BULWER'S PETREL *Bulweria bulwerii* PLATE 30

Size: 27cm, 100g

Distribution: Breeds on islands in the tropical and warm temperate parts of the North Pacific Ocean from off China to Hawai'i, Phoenix and Marquesas islands, and in the North Atlantic Ocean. After breeding, most remain in tropical waters across the Pacific, but many Pacific birds migrate to the tropical Indian Ocean. Often recorded off northwestern Australia, and occasionally in the Tasman Sea as far south as Victoria. Two New Zealand records: Te Horo Beach, Horowhenua (January 1998); New Brighton Beach (January 2014).

108. WHITE-CHINNED PETREL *Procellaria aequinoctialis* PLATE 25

Other name: Shoemaker

Size: 55cm, 1250g

Geographical variation: Of the two subspecies, only *aequinoctialis* is known from the New Zealand region. Birds breeding at the Auckland Islands are smaller than those breeding at the Antipodes, and they may represent two different taxa.

Distribution: Circumpolar, breeding on many subantarctic islands, including Antipodes Island, the Auckland Islands (Auckland, Adams, Ewing, Disappointment) and the Campbell Islands (Dent, Jacquemart and other offshore islets). They range widely over deep water between 30° S and 65° S, but to 5° S off the western coasts of South America and Africa. Birds from the New Zealand colonies feed mainly to the south and east of New Zealand; adults feed over continental-shelf waters up to the latitude of Cook Strait during their summer breeding season and to North Cape in winter. Most Auckland Island birds apparently migrate to the west coast of South America when not breeding. Immatures are occasionally seen off the mainland coast in all seasons, and are most often beach-wrecked in November–February. Few recently fledged chicks are beach-wrecked, so they may disperse mainly to the south and east.

Population: Abundant, but declining rapidly. About

5 million birds, including *c.* 775,000 pairs on South Georgia and *c.* 235,000 pairs on the Kerguelen Islands, and large colonies at the Crozet and Prince Edward groups. In New Zealand, 100,000 pairs breed on Disappointment Island (Auckland Islands); 60,000 pairs on the Antipodes; and 10,000 pairs on Monowai Island, off Campbell Island.

Conservation: Protected native. The colony on main Campbell Island has gone because adults were killed by cats, and eggs and chicks were eaten by Norway rats. Trends in New Zealand populations are not known, but it is estimated that over 500 are killed accidentally as by-catch in New Zealand commercial fisheries each year, mainly in squid, scampi and hoki trawls, and on hooks set for ling. Elsewhere, White-chinned Petrels have the highest incidental mortality rate of any seabird in Southern Ocean long-line fisheries, primarily foul-hooked on hooks set for Patagonian toothfish, hake, tuna and sharks.

Breeding: Summer breeders – eggs are laid from late November to December. They lay **1** white egg (82 x 55mm, 135g) in a burrow 1–2 m long. The burrow is sometimes quite wet, but the nest itself remains dry because it is on a raised pedestal. Eggs hatch from late January to February after 57–**59**–62 days. Chicks are brooded initially but left unguarded from about the fifth day, and then fed at intervals of 1–6 days. Chicks fledge in April–May after 87–**97**–106 days.

Behaviour: Breeds in scattered colonies intermingled with Grey Petrels on Antipodes Island, although some colonies are dense warrens of burrows. At sea, they are usually alone but occasionally form small groups at food and sometimes follow ships. They return to their colonies in the late afternoon and circle in loose flocks. Some land in daylight, but most visits are at dusk or after dark. At the colony, they are silent in the air but very noisy on land, with two main calls given on the ground and in their burrows: a succession of clanks or rattles (apparently the origin of the sealers' name 'shoemaker') and a harsh groan or squeal.

Feeding: The diet of three birds from the Auckland and Campbell islands included squid, salps, crustaceans and fish. They readily take discards and offal from fishing boats, and this makes them especially vulnerable to fisheries by-catch. They also associate with whales and dolphins. Most prey is taken on the surface, by diving from the surface or by diving from just above the water.

Reading: Delord, K. et al. 2005. *CCAMLR Sci* 12: 53–80. Fraser, M. et al. 2005. *Notornis* 52: 175. Hall, A. J. 1987. *J Zool (Lond)* 212: 605–617. Imber, M. J. 1976. *NZ J Mar Fresh Res* 10: 119–130. Imber, M. J. 1983. *Notornis* 30: 283–298. Jouventin, P. et al 1985. *Notornis* 32: 157–220. Phillips, R. A. et al. 2006. *Biol Cons* 129: 336–347. Powlesland, R. G. 1989. *Notornis* 36: 299–310. Spear, L. B. et al. 2005. *Notornis* 52: 88–105. Warham, J. 1988. *Notornis* 35: 169–183. Warham, J. & Bell, B. D. 1979. *Notornis* 26: 121–169.

109. WESTLAND PETREL *Procellaria westlandica* PLATE 25

Other name: Westland Black Petrel

Size: 48cm, 1100g

Distribution: Breeds only in New Zealand, in the densely forested coastal foothills of the Paparoa Range, Westland. Most nest below 250m asl between the Punakaiki River and Lawson Creek. During the winter breeding season, they range mainly over continental-shelf waters between Cape Egmont and Fiordland and through Cook Strait to between East Cape and Banks Peninsula, and into pelagic waters of the Tasman Sea and Pacific about and just north of the Subtropical Convergence. A few adults and recently fledged chicks are beach-wrecked around Cook Strait in November–January. Most birds travel to the west or east coasts of South America in November, moult there, and return in March–April. This trans-Pacific migration is rapid, taking just 4–7 days on the outward journey and 8–13 days for the return journey. Over the summer, some birds remain in New Zealand waters and a few visit coastal waters of southeastern Australia.

Population: *c.* 20,000 birds, including *c.* 4000 breeding pairs.

Conservation: Protected endemic. Maori and early European settlers used to harvest chicks from colonies before they were protected. Commercial trawling for hoki within 200km of the colony since the 1960s has made much extra food (fish scraps) available, and the population more than trebled from the 3000–6000 birds in 1958; however, the population stabilised since the 1980s despite some birds, mainly adult females, being killed accidentally on tuna long lines and caught in hoki trawl nets. The sites where Westland Petrels breed are legally protected, and feral cats are trapped around the colonies.

Breeding: Westland Petrels are winter breeders. They return to their colonies on the steep sides of forested valleys from mid-February to April to court and clean out burrows. Males make frequent visits to the burrow and often stay there during the day, whereas females make only occasional visits. Although there is no clear pre-laying exodus, with females making occasional visits in the weeks before laying, one female with a forming egg was caught over 400km southwest of the colony. Eggs are laid over 3 weeks from 12 May, with a peak around 23 May. They lay 1 white egg (81 x 56mm) in a burrow 1–2m long. Eggs hatch in late July after *c.* 64 days' incubation. The chick is rarely left unattended during the first 2 weeks and is fed by each parent about every third night, but less frequently close to fledging. Chicks fledge from 5 November to 26 December at *c.* 125 days old. Young birds have been recorded back at the colonies at 5 years old, but minimum age recorded for first breeding is 10 years old. The oldest bird recorded lived at least 37 years.

Behaviour: Breed in small colonies. At sea, they are often seen alone but join large mixed flocks feeding on scraps from fishing boats. At the colony, they are normally silent in the air, apart from occasional 'quack' calls, but on the ground they are noisy and produce a wide range of sounds. The two main calls are a succession of duck-like quacks, often given in duets, and males give a barrage of pulse-like notes, reminiscent of the call of a Kookaburra.

Feeding: Nowadays, Westland Petrels take mostly fish offal during the breeding season, but their natural diet is mainly squid, fish (especially lanternfish) and planktonic crustaceans, taken on the surface or from shallow dives.

Reading: Baker, A. J. & Coleman, J. D. 1977. *Notornis* 24: 211–231. Bartle, A. J. 1990. *Notornis* 37: 146–150. Brinkley, E. S. et al. 2000. *Notornis* 47: 179–183. Freeman, A. N. D. 1998. *Emu* 98: 36–43. Freeman, A. N. D. & Wilson, K. -J. 1997. *DOC CAS Notes* 160. Wellington: DOC. Imber, M. J. 1976. *NZ J Mar Fresh Res* 10: 119–130. Landers, T. J. et al. 2011. *Condor* 113: 71–79. Murray, T. E. et al. 1993. *Bird Cons Intl* 3: 181–210. Powlesland, R. G. 1989. *Notornis* 36: 299–310. Spear, L. B. et al. 2005. *Notornis* 52: 88–105. Warham, J. 1988. *Notornis* 35: 169–183.

110. BLACK PETREL *Procellaria parkinsoni* PLATE 25

Other names: Taiko, Parkinson's Petrel

Size: 46cm, 700g

Distribution: Breeds only in New Zealand, on Little Barrier and Great Barrier islands. They formerly bred widely on mountain ranges in the North Island and the northwestern South Island. During the summer breeding season, they range mainly through subtropical waters between 30° S and 42° S, especially close to the continental shelf break or over seamounts around northeastern New Zealand. Some cross the Tasman Sea to the southeastern coast of Australia. A few birds are wrecked on North Island beaches in November–April. Recently fledged chicks are sometimes found beach-wrecked on the east coast of the North Island in May.

Black Petrels migrate in March–July to the eastern tropical Pacific Ocean from west of the Galapagos Islands to southern Mexico (15° N) and northern Peru (5° S). Adults return in October–December, but some younger birds may stay there all year.

Population: *c.* 8000 birds, including non-breeders. Little Barrier *c.* 100 pairs, Great Barrier *c.* 1650 breeding pairs, mainly at Mt Hobson.

Conservation: Protected vulnerable endemic. Although Maori and early Europeans harvested chicks from mainland colonies, introduced predators probably caused their demise. The colony on Little Barrier Island was severely reduced until cats were eradicated in 1980. Since then the number of chicks raised has improved and the colony is increasing. On Great Barrier Island, where breeding was not discovered until 1964, cat predation at the colony is slight and productivity is high, probably because, unlike the former situation on Little Barrier, there are few nesting Cook's Petrels to sustain high numbers of cats near the colony.

The overall population is declining; the most likely cause is that Black Petrels associate with fishing boats and they are one of the species most at risk from by-catch in fisheries operations. They are sometimes accidentally caught on long-line hooks set for snapper, bluenose and tuna, or in fishing nets, especially in the Hauraki Gulf, but probably also off South America. Mortality of juveniles appears high, with only about 50% surviving their first three years at sea, and annual adult survival of 90.3% is unusually low for a large seabird. Between 1986 and 1990, 249 fledglings were transferred from Great Barrier to Little Barrier Island in the hope of boosting the small Little Barrier colony, however, it was only partially successful because most returned as adults to Great Barrier.

Breeding: Black Petrels are summer breeders. They

return to their mainly high, ridge-top colonies between mid-October and December to court and clean out burrows. Males make frequent visits to the burrow and often stay there during the day, whereas females make only occasional visits. The pre-laying exodus of each pair lasts *c.* 23–24 days. Eggs are laid in November–January, mostly between 20 November and 25 December. They lay **1** white egg (69 x 51mm, 99g) in a burrow 0.5–2m long. The female incubates for the first 0–4 days, then the male takes a long shift of 4–17 days, and then alternating shifts get shorter towards hatching. Eggs hatch in January–February after *c.* 57 days. The chick is rarely left unattended during the first 2–3 days but is then fed every 2–3 nights until close to fledging, when feeding becomes infrequent. Chicks emerge from their burrows about 10 nights before they finally fledge from mid-April to early July at 96–**107**–122 days old. Young birds can first return to their colony at 3 years old, but they first breed at 5–7–10 years old. Annual survival of 90.3% equates to a life expectancy of adults of 10.3 years, but the oldest banded bird lived at least 29 years.
Behaviour: Breeds in loose colonies intermingled with Cook's Petrels. At sea, they are often seen alone but sometimes form flocks of up to 300 birds around feeding cetaceans, or fishing boats. At the colony, they are usually silent in the air but sometimes give a low moan followed by a series of clacks. On the ground they have loud, far-carrying calls, the main one being a rapid series of staccato clacks. Quieter clacks and moans are given from the burrow.
Feeding: While breeding, Black Petrels feed mainly on squid, supplemented by fish, crustaceans and other marine invertebrates. Judging from the diet composition and the importance of bioluminescent forms, much food is probably taken at night; however, observations in the eastern tropical Pacific show that much squid is scavenged from around feeding melon-headed whales and false killer whales by day. Some prey is taken by sitting on the surface with head immersed and then taking a shallow dive, but they are capable of diving down at least 10m.
Reading: Freeman, R. et al. 2010. *PLOS ONE* 5(2). Imber, M. J. 1976. *NZ J Mar Fresh Res* 10: 119–130. Imber, M. J. 1987. *Notornis* 34: 19–39. Imber, M. J. et al. 2003. *Notornis* 50: 183–190. Pitman, R. L. & Balance, L. T. 1992. *Condor* 94: 825–835. Powlesland, R. G. 1989. *Notornis* 36: 299–310. Warham, J. 1988. *Notornis* 35: 169–183.

111. GREY PETREL *Procellaria cinerea* PLATES 25 AND 26

Other name: Pediunker
Size: 48cm, 1000g
Distribution: Circumpolar, breeding on many sub-antarctic islands, including the Antipodes (Antipodes and Bollons) and Campbell islands. They range widely over deep water between 25° S and 60° S and follow the Humboldt Current to the seas off Peru. During the winter breeding season, adult females move further north than adult males, with a concentration of adult females in nutrient-rich waters north of East Cape and off the coast of Gisborne. After breeding, most cross the Pacific to the Humboldt Current off Chile and Peru from November to March, but at this time some immature Grey Petrels use the seas off the east coast of the North Island, where they are sometimes found beach-wrecked.
Population: Uncommon; only *c.* 400,000 birds and *c.* 80,000 breeding pairs. Many overseas colonies have declined rapidly, making the colony of *c.* 53,000 pairs on the Antipodes by far the largest. The colonies on islands off Campbell Island are small, and fewer than 100 pairs remain in the remnant colonies on main Campbell Island.
Conservation: Protected native. The eradication of rats and cats from Campbell Island will improve breeding opportunities and success there. Of greatest concern is that Grey Petrels are attracted to feed on offal discarded from fishing boats, and because breeding females feed in important fishery areas, they are especially susceptible to being drowned after being accidentally hooked on long lines in ling and tuna fisheries, and in blue whiting trawl nets. Grey Petrels made up 27% of seabirds reported killed in New Zealand waters in 1988–97, and despite the introduction of improved by-catch mitigation measures, an average of over 100 were estimated to have been killed in New Zealand fisheries each year between 2003 and 2011.
Breeding: No detailed study has been made in New Zealand. The timing of breeding seems similar to that on Tristan da Cunha and at Kerguelen, with laying in April–May. They lay **1** white egg (81 x 56mm) in a burrow 1–3m long. Eggs hatch in May–June after 52–65 days, and chicks fledge October–December after 110–160 days.
Behaviour: Breed in loose colonies intermingled with White-headed Petrels on Antipodes Island. At sea, they are often seen alone, but occasionally they form large

mixed flocks around fishing boats or feeding whales. They are silent while flying but noisy on land, with two main calls given on the ground and in their burrows: a drawn-out moan and, more commonly, a few wheezy moans followed by loud, far-carrying, staccato bleats.
Feeding: Diet is mostly squid, fish and offal, mainly taken on the surface or by diving from about 3m.

Reading: Bartle, J. A. 1990. *Notornis* 37: 146–150. Imber, M. J. 1983. *Notornis* 30: 283–298. Jouventin, P. et al. 1985. *Notornis* 32: 157–220. Murray, T. E. et al. 1993. *Bird Cons Int* 3: 181–210. Warham, J. 1988. *Notornis* 35: 169–183. Warham, J. & Bell, B. D. 1979. *Notornis* 26: 121–169. Zotier, R. 1990. *Emu* 90: 180–184.

112. TAHITI PETREL *Pseudobulweria rostrata* PLATE 21

Size: 38cm, 400g
Geographical variation: Two subspecies: *trouessarti* of New Caledonia, Fiji and American Samoa, and *rostrata* of French Polynesia. The subspecies may not be valid and those recorded in New Zealand have not been identified to subspecies level.
Distribution: Breeds mainly on mountainous tropical and subtropical islands of the South Pacific Ocean, but occasionally on atolls. Breeds in the central mountains of New Caledonia and on at least 12 small islets in the southern lagoon; on Taveuni and Gau islands of Fiji; on Ta'u, Tutuila and possibly Olosega in American Samoa; and on Tahiti, Moorea, Raiatea, Marquesas and Gambier islands of French Polynesia. They range over deep water of the tropical Pacific and into the Coral and northern Tasman seas, and a few reach the Indian Ocean, off northwestern Australia. One New Zealand specimen from Dargaville Beach (June 1988), but four others were seen east of Northland and in the Bay of Plenty in the winter of 1988.
In the hand: Tahiti Petrels (and other *Pseudobulweria*) have disproportionately large feet, and a notch in the cutting edge of the upper mandible like that found in *Procellaria*. The notch is formed by the latericorn having a blunt end, rather than a pointed end as in *Pterodroma*. The Tahiti Petrel is larger than the other three *Pseudobulweria* species.
Reading: Gangloff, B. et al. 2012. *Conserv Genet* 13: 39–52. Imber, M. J. 1985. *Ibis* 127: 197–229. Plant, A. R. et al. 1989. *Notornis* 36: 149–150. Powlesland, R. G. & Pickard, C. R. 1992. *Notornis* 39: 27–46. Villard, P. et al. 2006. *Ibis* 148: 285–291.

113. CORY'S SHEARWATER *Calonectris borealis* PLATE 27

Size: 46cm, 900g
Distribution: Breeds on islands in the eastern North Atlantic Ocean, including Berlengas, Azores, Porto Santo, Madeira, Desertas, Salvages and Canary islands. They range extensively in the North Atlantic Ocean and migrate to spend November–May in temperate and tropical waters of the western South Atlantic and in temperate and cooler waters of the southwestern Indian Ocean. One New Zealand record: Foxton Beach (January 1934).
Feeding: Diet is mainly fish and squid, mostly seized on the surface or during shallow plunges. Cory's Shearwaters often associate with cetaceans and follow fishing boats to feed on scraps tossed overboard.
In the hand: Males are larger than females: bill depth 21.0–**22.6**–24.1mm cf. 19.3–**20.4**–21.6mm, and bill length 54.4–**58.8**–61.7mm cf. 52.0–**55.7**–59.9mm.
Reading: Oliver, W. R. B. 1934. *Emu* 34: 23–24. Robertson, H. A. & James, P. C. 1988. *Bull BOC* 108: 79–87. Zino, P. A. 1971. *Ibis* 113: 212–217.

114. STREAKED SHEARWATER *Calonectris leucomelas* PLATE 27

Size: 48cm, 500g
Distribution: Breeds on islands in the northwest Pacific Ocean, especially around Japan, but also off Russia, Korea and China. They migrate south to spend October–April in the western Pacific off the Philippines, Palau and especially off northern New Guinea; in the South China Sea; in waters around Indonesia; in the Arafura Sea between Indonesia and Australia; and in the Coral Sea. Some birds straggle east through the Indian Ocean as far as the Red Sea, west to Hawai'i and California, and south into the Tasman Sea. One New Zealand record: Kawhia Beach, Waikato (February 2006).

Feeding: Diet is mainly fish and squid, mostly seized on the surface or during shallow plunges when shoals of fish are forced to the surface by marine predators such as skipjack tuna. Streaked Shearwaters are generally gregarious and they often follow ships and fishing boats to feed on scraps tossed overboard.

Reading: Scofield, R. P. et al. 2010. *Notornis* 57: 212–215. Yamamoto, T. et al. 2010. *Auk* 127: 871–881.

115. WEDGE-TAILED SHEARWATER *Puffinus pacificus* PLATES 26 AND 28

Size: 46cm, 450g

Geographical variation: Two subspecies: *pacificus* breeds only in the southwestern Pacific, at the Kermadecs, Norfolk Island, Fiji and Tonga; *chlororhynchus* breeds widely in the South Indian Ocean, around Australia and across the subtropical and tropical Pacific, including Lord Howe Island and New Caledonia. Most specimens and sightings off mainland New Zealand have not been identified to subspecific level.

Distribution: Breeds on islands of the tropical and subtropical Indian and Pacific oceans and ranges widely in adjacent seas. Some populations are migratory; band returns show that birds from southeastern Australia migrate to the western North Pacific. In the New Zealand region, Wedge-tailed Shearwaters breed only at the Kermadec Islands and apparently migrate to the southeastern part of the North Pacific. They are recorded at sea to the northeast of New Zealand in autumn, and a few stragglers of both subspecies have been recorded beach-wrecked on the North Island coast, mainly November–April.

Population: A very common and widely distributed shearwater with a total population of over 5 million birds. In New Zealand, they breed only at the Kermadec Islands, where *c.* 40,000 pairs nest on Macauley Island, *c.* 10,000 pairs nest on the Meyer Islets and Dayrell Island off Raoul Island, and 2500 pairs nest on Curtis Island.

Conservation: Protected native. On Raoul Island, 'immense numbers' were recorded in 1908, but its status was only 'abundant' by 1944, and by 1966 they were virtually extinct because of predation by feral cats and Norway rats. Since the eradication of rats in 2002 and cats in 2004 on Raoul Island, and the eradication of Pacific rats on Macauley Island in 2006, the populations of Wedge-tailed Shearwaters are expected to return to their former abundance. By 2008, at least 13 active burrows were found in two clusters on Raoul Island, indicating a rapid recolonisation.

Breeding: No detailed studies in New Zealand through the whole season. In the Kermadecs, timing of breeding varies a week or two from year to year. Birds return to their colonies in October and clean out their burrows in November. The colony is virtually abandoned during the first half of December while birds are on their pre-laying exodus, but they return and lay in mid- to late December, mostly around 18 December. They lay 1 white egg (67 x 43mm) in a burrow up to 2.5m long, but sometimes they lay on the surface under an overhanging rock, in a small cave or under vegetation. Both sexes incubate for 50–54 days.

Chicks hatch in early February and are initially covered in pale grey down. They are left unattended within days after hatching and fledge from late May to early June, at *c.* 90 days old, at which time they are immediately independent of their parents. Some yearlings attend colonies, but they do not start breeding until at least 4 years old. The oldest bird recorded was an Australian one aged over 19 years.

Behaviour: Breeds in large dense colonies on some islands, sometimes interspersed with other petrels and shearwaters, especially Black-winged Petrels at the Kermadecs. At sea, Wedge-tailed Shearwaters are usually solitary but sometimes form small feeding flocks or large rafts off colonies. They are generally silent at sea and over their colonies, but occasional wails are given by circling birds. Wedge-tailed Shearwaters are very noisy on land at the colony. They often come ashore in the late afternoon, with numbers increasing towards dusk, and the noise builds to a peak in the first couple of hours of darkness. The main call given on the ground is a soft wailing moan: 'ka-whoooo-ahh'.

Feeding: Diet is mainly fish, but squid, krill and jellyfish are also taken. Feeding birds sometimes look for prey by gliding along with head and neck just under the water. Prey is seized near the surface or sometimes by pursuit-plunging. They scavenge around whales and dolphins, and from behind boats.

Reading: Crockett, D. E. 1975. *Notornis* 22: 1–9. Jenkins, J. A. F. 1979. *Notornis* 26: 331–348. Merton, D. V. 1970. *Notornis* 17: 147–199. Veitch, C. R. et al. 2011. Pp. 372–376 in Veitch et al. 2011. *Island Invasives: Eradication and Management*. Gland: IUCN.

116. BULLER'S SHEARWATER *Puffinus bulleri* PLATE 26

Other name: New Zealand Shearwater (North America)
Size: 46cm, 425g
Distribution: Breeds only on the Poor Knights Islands off the eastern coast of Northland. Between early September and mid-May, birds disperse widely throughout New Zealand seas, mainly over North Island continental-shelf waters, particularly off Northland, in the Hauraki Gulf and the Bay of Plenty, and off East Cape; but they reach Foveaux Strait, seas off Fiordland and the Chatham Islands. From December, some birds move across the Tasman Sea to coastal waters off eastern Australia.

During April to late May, Buller's Shearwaters depart on migration to the central South Pacific and then on to the northern and eastern North Pacific, from Japan across to the western coast of North America. Most reach the subarctic waters off Japan in June, then many drift northwards to the Gulf of Alaska and eastwards to be off the North American coast by August, and then they head directly back in early September. Some non-breeders remain all year in the North Pacific, with many seen off the west coast of North America in September–October, and some even move south to spend the summer in the Humboldt Current, off Peru and Chile.
Population: *c.* 2.5 million birds estimated in the 1980s, but no recent data.
Conservation: Protected endemic. Numbers breeding on the Poor Knights Islands increased greatly since the removal of feral pigs from Aorangi Island in 1936. On Aorangi Island, the population was estimated at 100 pairs in 1938, but *c.* 200,000 pairs were breeding by 1981, the increase probably coming from a mix of recruitment and immigration from nearby Tawhiti Rahi Island. The Poor Knights Islands are protected as a nature reserve and are predator free.
Breeding: Birds return to their colonies in mid-September, and court and clean out their burrows during October. They are then virtually absent from the colony for *c.* 30 days from late October on their pre-laying exodus. Most eggs are laid during just a few days from 26 to 30 November, with a few laid through to mid-December. They lay **1** white egg (65 x 43mm, 67g) in a burrow 0.5–**1**–3m long, but occasionally in caves, cavities and old stone walls. Both sexes incubate in stints of 4–7 days for *c.* 51 days. The chick is initially covered in smoky blue-grey down and is left unattended within days after hatching between 17 and 26 January. Most chicks fledge in the second half of May, at 90–100 days old.
Behaviour: Breed in large dense colonies, interspersed with Fairy Prions. They have apparently ousted Fluttering Shearwaters and Grey-faced Petrels from Aorangi Island since the 1930s while their numbers increased. At sea, Buller's Shearwaters are usually found alone or in small flocks, but they migrate across a broad front in ones and twos and in groups of up to 12 birds. Feeding aggregations or resting rafts of 50–600 birds are often seen off the east coast of New Zealand in summer, and occasionally flocks of 5000–10,000 birds are seen off the eastern coast of Northland and off North America. They are generally silent at sea but noisy in the air and on the ground at their colonies, especially when they return in the first couple of hours of darkness.
Feeding: Diet is small (9–17mm) krill, small fish, salps and jellyfish, taken while sitting on the surface. Birds searching for food glide along with head and neck just under the water. Buller's Shearwaters rarely plunge into the sea or dive underwater. Since the 1990s, they have started to scavenge scraps from around fishing boats.
Reading: Harper, P. C. 1983. *Notornis* 30: 299–318. Jenkins, J. A. F. 1974. *Notornis* 21: 109–120. Jenkins, J. A. F. 1988. *Notornis* 35: 203–215. Wahl, T. R. 1985. *Notornis* 32: 109–117.

117. FLESH-FOOTED SHEARWATER *Puffinus carneipes* PLATES 25 AND 28

Other name: Toanui
Size: 44cm, 600g
Distribution: Breeds on temperate islands at St Paul Island (Indian Ocean), around the southern coast of Western Australia, off Eyre Peninsula (South Australia), at Lord Howe Island and in northern New Zealand. The main colonies in the New Zealand region are off the eastern coast of the North Island from Northland to East Cape, especially at Coppermine, Whatupuke and Lady Alice islands in the Hen and Chickens group, Green and Middle islands of the Mercury group, and Karewa Island in the western Bay of Plenty. Smaller colonies are at Kauwahaia Island (Bethells Beach), Ohinau Island, East Island, Saddleback Island (off New Plymouth) and the Titi Islands in Cook Strait.

During the breeding season, they range over

continental-shelf waters off the eastern North Island and in Cook Strait, and some move into the Tasman towards Lord Howe and Norfolk islands. Non-breeders also move south to the eastern Cook Strait and to the Subtropical Convergence from Foveaux Strait east to the Chathams. In March to late May, New Zealand birds migrate north past Fiji and Tonga to winter in the North Pacific Ocean, mainly off the eastern coast of Korea and off Japan, but some winter off the western coast of North America. They return to New Zealand waters in late September.

Population: In 2004, the global population was estimated to be 650,000+ birds, but recent data, including from New Zealand, suggests that this is too high because of high fisheries-related mortality. The New Zealand estimate of 25–50,000 pairs has been revised downwards to *c.* 12,000 pairs. The largest New Zealand colony is on Coppermine Island (Hen and Chickens).

Conservation: Protected vulnerable native. Subfossil and midden records from the North Island and Chatham Island indicate a wider breeding distribution in the past, and this has probably been reduced by predators and 'muttonbirding'. Current breeding colonies are largely protected, and only a few chicks are illegally harvested. Flesh-footed Shearwaters are attracted to feed on discards and offal behind fishing boats and their populations are at very high risk from fisheries by-catch. The main threats are from being hooked on baited snapper long lines in the Hauraki Gulf, and on tuna long lines off Gisborne, or becoming entangled in trawl nets catching scampi in the Bay of Plenty.

Breeding: No detailed studies in New Zealand. Birds return to their colonies in late September to early October, and eggs are laid over about three weeks from 21 November to 12 December. They lay **1** white egg (69 x 46mm, 75g) in a burrow 1–4m long. Both sexes incubate for *c.* 53 days. The chick is initially covered in pale grey down and is guarded by either parent for 2–3 days and fed about every second night for 12 days, then increasingly infrequently until the chick fledges in late April or early May, at *c.* 92 days old. Young first return to their natal colonies at 4 years old, and start breeding at 5–6 years old. The oldest bird recorded was an Australian one over 30 years old.

Behaviour: Breed on some islands in large dense colonies, on others interspersed with Grey-faced Petrels, Sooty Shearwaters and Little Shearwaters. Early in the season, they sometimes take over a burrow occupied by a Grey-faced Petrel chick (winter bred) that is about to leave, and at some northern colonies they share burrows with tuatara. Grey-faced Petrels in turn oust Flesh-footed Shearwater chicks when they return to their colonies in April.

At sea, Flesh-footed Shearwaters are usually solitary, but they form feeding flocks and rafts off their colonies. They are generally silent at sea except when they are fighting for scraps. At their colonies, they are noisy on moonless nights, especially just after dusk and before dawn. The main call, given on the ground and sometimes in the air, is a series of high-pitched moans somewhat resembling the sound of cats fighting.

Feeding: Diet is mainly squid and fish. Much food is probably caught at night on the surface or by pursuit-plunging. Dive depths are to a mean of 13m and a maximum of 28m. During the day food is scavenged from around whales and dolphins, and more recently from behind boats, which makes them especially vulnerable to accidental capture on baited fish-hooks and in trawl nets.

Reading: Brown, R. G. B. et al. 1978. *Condor* 80: 123–125. Falla, R. A. 1934. *Rec Auck Inst Mus* 1: 245–260. Taylor, G. A. 2008. *Papers & Proc Roy Soc Tasmania* 142: 189–198. Warham, J. 1958. *Auk* 75: 1–14.

118. PINK-FOOTED SHEARWATER *Puffinus creatopus* PLATE 27

Size: 48cm, 900g

Distribution: Breeds on the Juan Fernández Islands of Robinson Crusoe (Más a Tierra) and Santa Clara, and on Mocha Island off central Chile. They migrate north to the eastern North Pacific, usually in continental-shelf waters from Mexico to British Columbia, but as far north as Alaska. Stragglers reach Hawai'i, and vagrants reach the Line Islands, eastern Australia and New Zealand. Six accepted New Zealand records: 2–4 in the outer Canterbury Bight (June 1979), and singles off Kaikoura (January 1994, December 1998, February 1999, December 2001 and January 2003).

Feeding: Diet is mainly fish and squid seized on the surface or during shallow plunge-dives. Pink-footed Shearwaters follow boats and feed on scraps tossed overboard.

Reading: Tunnicliffe, G. A. 1982. *Notornis* 29: 85–91. Tunnicliffe, G. A. 1984. *Notornis* 31: 130.

119. GREAT SHEARWATER *Puffinus gravis* PLATE 27

Size: 48cm, 800g

Distribution: Breeds on Inaccessible and Nightingale islands in the Tristan da Cunha group, Gough Island, and Kidney Island in the Falklands. During breeding, forages in the South Atlantic Ocean and into the south-western Indian Ocean. They migrate north to spend April–October in the North Atlantic Ocean, mainly along the Gulf Stream, but a few venture into the South Pacific Ocean near the Straits of Magellan. They straggle along the Pacific coast north to Alaska, and also to Australia and New Zealand. The first accepted record was in December 2006, east of Pitt Island, Chathams, following several earlier unconfirmed sightings near the Kermadecs and in Cook Strait. Six subsequent sightings: Kaikoura (February 2010), Foveaux Strait (April 2011), Puysegur Point (April 2011), off South Otago (April 2011), Canterbury Bight (November 2011) and Mayor Island (November 2013).

Feeding: Diet is mainly fish, squid, euphausiids and octopus, mostly seized on the surface or during shallow plunges, but they commonly dive deeply. Great Shearwaters are generally gregarious and they regularly follow ships and fishing boats to feed on scraps tossed overboard.

Reading: Gaskin, C. P. et al. 2008. *Notornis* 55: 222–223.

120. SOOTY SHEARWATER *Puffinus griseus* PLATE 28

Other names: Titi, Muttonbird

Size: 44cm, 800g

Distribution: Circumpolar, breeding in the subantarctic and temperate zones on islands off the coast of Chile and around Cape Horn; on Kidney Island, Falklands; on Tristan da Cunha; on islands off Tasmania and New South Wales; Macquarie Island; and in New Zealand on many islands and some headlands on the mainland, from the Three Kings Islands to Campbell Island and Chatham Islands. The main colonies in the New Zealand region are on islands off Stewart Island (especially Codfish and Big South Cape), The Snares, Auckland, Campbell and Chatham islands. Subfossil and midden evidence and historical records suggest that Sooty Shearwaters formerly bred in large colonies on the mainland, but only small colonies persist on Banks Peninsula; at Cape Wanbrow, Oamaru; at eight or more sites on the Otago coast; and on isolated headlands along the west coast of the South Island.

Between September and mid-May, breeding and pre-breeding birds disperse widely throughout New Zealand seas, mainly over continental-shelf and deeper waters off southern New Zealand, but some disperse south to the pack ice. Most adults depart on migration to the North Pacific between late March and early May, moving along the east coast of the South and North islands. Fledglings leave their colonies from mid-April to late May and follow a similar route.

The migration path is directly north over a broad front to subarctic waters between Japan and the west coast of North America, which they reach in April–May. Some then drift northwards to reach the Gulf of Alaska in June. Breeding birds return directly south in August and arrive back in New Zealand waters in September, but non-breeders return a month or two later. Sooty Shearwaters are often found dead on the New Zealand coast during the northward migration of fledglings in May, and again in November–December when pre-breeders return to New Zealand waters.

Population: Abundant, but declining. The global population is estimated at over 20 million birds, of which about half breed in New Zealand; the largest colony is at The Snares, where *c.* 2.75 million pairs breed.

Conservation: Partially protected native. A large traditional annual take of *c.* 250,000 of the fattest chicks (muttonbirds) takes place on 36 islands in Foveaux Strait and around Stewart Island. Sooty Shearwaters have undoubtedly declined since 1840, with the demise of many mainland and some island colonies being due to the spread of introduced predators and the conversion of forest for farming. The more recent widespread decline observed since 1960 may be due to increased harvesting of muttonbirds following the introduction of new technologies such as helicopter and small boat access to islands; increased mortality from fisheries by-catch, especially drift-netting in the North Pacific; and the effects of climate change. Because the huge colonies on The Snares, Auckland Island and the Chathams are protected and free of mammalian predators and yet some are showing declines, the most likely factor is the change in abundance or distribution of food at sea brought about by a shift in the Subantarctic Convergence, which is a consequence of global climate change.

Breeding: Adults return to their colonies in September,

and court and clean out their burrows through October. After a pre-laying exodus of *c.* 3 weeks in early November, most eggs are laid in late November and early December. They lay **1** white egg (77 x 48mm, 93g) in a burrow 0.3–4m long, or occasionally in a crevice, under bushes or huts. Both sexes incubate. Eggs hatch from mid-January after *c.* 53 days. Chicks are initially covered in smoky blue-grey down and are left unattended within days of hatching. Chicks reach their maximum weight of 1000–1800g at *c.* 7 weeks old, but then lose weight to fledge at *c.* 750g at 86–**97**–106 days old in late April to mid-May. Young return to their natal colony at 3–4 years old but do not start breeding for several years. The oldest bird recorded in New Zealand lived over 34 years.
Behaviour: Breeds in large dense colonies, interspersed with other seabirds. At sea, Sooty Shearwaters are gregarious, with huge flocks of up to 500,000 birds recorded feeding, on migration or in the seas near breeding colonies. They are generally silent at sea but noisy in the air and on the ground at their colonies when they return in the two hours after dusk, and are even noisier as they depart just before dawn. The main call is a series of hoarse moans: 'oo-oo-ah', getting louder and faster each time.
Feeding: Diet is small fish, squid, krill and other small crustaceans, taken mainly by plunging and then swimming with half-opened wings and feet. Usual dive depth is 10–70m under the surface, exceptionally up to 93m. Males dive deeper than females during the incubation period.
Reading: Ainley, D. G. & Boekelheide, R. J. 1983. *Studies in Avian Biol* 8: 2–23. Lyver, P. O'B. 2000. *NZ J Ecol* 24: 169–180. Moller, H. et al. 2009. *NZ J Zool* 36: 325–341. Richdale, L. E. 1963. *Proc Zool Soc (Lond)* 141: 1–117. Scofield, R. P. & Christie, D. 2002. *Notornis* 49: 158–165. Spear, L. B. & Ainley, D. G. 1999. *Condor* 101: 205–218. Taylor, G. A. 2008. *Papers & Proc Roy Soc Tasmania* 142: 189–198. Warham, J. & Wilson, G. J. 1982. *Notornis* 29: 23–30. Warham, J. et al. 1982. *Notornis* 29: 269–292.

121. SHORT-TAILED SHEARWATER *Puffinus tenuirostris* PLATE 28

Other name: Tasmanian Muttonbird
Size: 42cm, 550g
Distribution: Breeds only on islands off southern Australia from Western Australia to northern New South Wales, especially in Bass Strait and around Tasmania. Subfossil and midden records from the North, South and Chatham islands suggest they may once have bred in the New Zealand region. From September to April, adults range through waters south of Australia to the edge of the pack ice and across the Tasman Sea to continental-shelf waters of the Hauraki Gulf and Bay of Plenty.

After breeding, adults go directly to the northern North Pacific and the Bering Sea in March–April, but fledglings leave between late April and mid-May, and some drift across the Tasman and are beach-wrecked on the west coast of New Zealand in May–June (e.g. 587 birds in May 1986). Adults return past Fiji and Samoa to their colonies in Australia in late September, but subadults return a month or two later. Many returning birds pass through New Zealand waters as far south as Foveaux Strait, and 100–300 are beach-wrecked in most years, however, unusually large wrecks occur in October–December in some years (e.g. 1968, 2000 and 2013). The 2000 wreck coincided with unusually warm waters in the Tasman Sea, and so their usual food species may have been adversely affected.
Population: *c.* 23 million birds. The main colonies are on islands in Bass Strait and around Tasmania, with vast colonies (1 million+ pairs) on Babel Island and Trefoil Island. Each year an estimated 200,000 chicks are harvested, and up to 50,000 birds, mainly subadult, are accidentally caught in fishing nets in the North Pacific, however, the population is apparently close to being stable.
Behaviour: At sea, they are seen in large flocks of up to 500,000 birds while on migration, but in smaller flocks most of the time.
Feeding: Diet is mainly krill, amphipods, and small fish and squid. Although similar to that of the Sooty Shearwater, this diet probably has more plankton. They catch most food beneath the surface after plunging in or diving from the surface.
Reading: Bradley, J. S. et al. 1991. *Ibis* 133 Suppl 1: 55–61. Holmes, G. 1977. *Notornis* 24: 286–287. Serventy, D. L. 1967. *Proc 14th Int Orn Congr* 165–190. Skira, I. J. 1986. *Aust Wildl Res* 13: 481–488. Skira, I. J. 2003. *Corella* 27: 81–84. Wooller, R. D. et al. 1990. *J Anim Ecol* 59: 161–170.

122. CHRISTMAS ISLAND SHEARWATER *Puffinus nativitatis* PLATE 28

Size: 37cm, 350g

Distribution: Breeds on tropical and subtropical islands throughout the central Pacific Ocean from Kure Atoll in the northwest Pacific and the Leeward Islands of Hawai'i to the Austral group of French Polynesia and Easter Island, including Christmas Island (Kiribati). Their distribution at sea is not well known, but most are seen in tropical waters of the central and eastern Pacific. Two New Zealand records: a bird wrecked at Dargaville Beach (February 1976) after a tropical cyclone, and a bird found alive on Curtis Island in the southern Kermadecs (November 1989).

Reading: Crockett, D. E. 1977. *Notornis* 24: 285–286. Taylor, G. A. & Tennyson, A. J. D. 1994. *Notornis* 41: 287–291.

123. NEWELL'S SHEARWATER *Puffinus newelli* PLATE 29

Size: 33cm, 390g

Geographical variation: Two subspecies: the numerous *newelli* in Hawai'i, and the very rare *myrtae* in French Polynesia could appear here.

Distribution: Breeds in Hawai'i, especially on Kauai, and a tiny population on four islands off Rapa Island in French Polynesia. Breeding in Hawai'i is from June to November. Winters in the eastern tropical Pacific, but some also wander westwards to the Mariana Islands and south to tropical or temperate waters of the Southern Hemisphere. One bird caught in American Samoa (January 1993), one ashore on Philip Island, Norfolk Island group (December 1997), and a single New Zealand record: a dead female found on Dargaville Beach (November 1994).

Reading: Taylor, G. A. 1996. *Notornis* 43: 187–196.

124. MANX SHEARWATER *Puffinus puffinus* PLATE 29

Size: 36cm, 450g

Distribution: Breeds on islands in the temperate and subarctic North Atlantic. They migrate to the South Atlantic, mainly to seas off Brazil and Argentina, but sometimes to waters of southern Africa. A few wander to Australasia; a British-banded yearling was found dead in South Australia in November 1961, and three immature birds have since been beach-wrecked in New Zealand: Pukerua Bay (June 1972), Waikanae (January 1985) and Otaki (July 2002).

In the hand: As the Manx Shearwater is very difficult to distinguish at sea from the Fluttering Shearwater, most acceptable records are likely to be from beach-wrecked specimens. It can be separated from Fluttering and Hutton's Shearwaters on measurements and undertail and underwing colours. Bill length is 31–**34.5**–38mm and wing length is 225–**237**–245mm, the side feathers of the undertail coverts have black outer vanes (as in Hutton's Shearwater), the longest axillaries reach near the trailing edge of the wing and are white with a broad black subterminal band (immatures) or a moderate black band (adults) and white tip, and apart from the dark leading edge (especially at the elbow) the underwing is mainly white.

Reading: Brooke, M. de L. 1990. *The Manx Shearwater*. London: T. & A. D. Poyser. Kinsky, F. C. & Fowler, J. A. 1973. *Notornis* 20: 14–20. Tennyson, A. J. D. 1986. *Notornis* 33: 59–61.

125. FLUTTERING SHEARWATER *Puffinus gavia* PLATE 29

Other name: Pakaha

Size: 33cm, 300g

Distribution: Breeds only in New Zealand, on many islands and islets along the northeastern coast of the North Island from the Three Kings Islands to islands near Gisborne, and on islands in the Marlborough Sounds. In spring and summer, they are seen in inshore waters close to their breeding colonies, but in autumn, many fledglings migrate to the southeastern seaboard of Australia, from South Australia to Queensland, and stragglers have been recorded from New Caledonia and Vanuatu. Most return in July–August, when they are often found beach-wrecked. Subfossil and midden remains from North, South and Chatham islands suggest a wider breeding distribution in the past.

Population: A very common shearwater in the Hauraki Gulf, in the Bay of Plenty and in Cook Strait. The total is 100,000+ breeding pairs, with the largest colonies being on the Three Kings Islands, Channel Island, the Aldermens, and the Trio Islands in Cook Strait.

Conservation: Protected endemic. Chicks were harvested by Maori until legal protection in 1953. Numbers of Fluttering Shearwaters have declined with the spread of predators such as cats and rats to headlands on the mainland, and to offshore islands. Colonies on Little Barrier, Cuvier, and Moutohora (Whale) islands were destroyed by cats and rats, but are now recovering following eradication of these predators. Within the Mercury Islands, Fluttering Shearwaters are common only on islands free of Pacific rats. Efforts to eradicate mammalian predators from offshore islands have undoubtedly helped small seabirds such as the Fluttering Shearwater. Chicks have been successfully transferred to establish new breeding populations on Maud and Mana islands, and playback of calls has attracted birds to new sites at Tawharanui Peninsula, Young Nick's Head and to Matiu/Somes Island in Wellington Harbour. Fluttering Shearwaters are vulnerable to accidental capture by inshore fisheries, especially in set nets.

Breeding: Poorly known. Some birds visit their colonies throughout the year. Most return to their colonies on forest- or scrub-covered islands in August to court and clean out their burrows. Eggs are laid from early September to mid-October. They lay **1** white egg (57 x 40mm) in a burrow 0.5–1m long, or occasionally in a crevice or among rockfalls. Eggs hatch in November and chicks fledge in late January and early February. First breeding is at 5–7–10 years old.

Behaviour: Breeds in dense or scattered colonies, often interspersed with other seabirds, especially Common Diving Petrels, Little Shearwaters and Grey-faced Petrels in northern colonies, and with Fairy Prions around Cook Strait. At sea, Fluttering Shearwaters are sometimes found in flocks of up to 20,000 birds while feeding, roosting or on passage. When feeding they occasionally give a soft chattering cackle, but when they are circling their breeding colonies they are very noisy with rapid, staccato two-syllable calls, with much variation on the main call: 'ka-how ka-how ka-how ka-how, kehek kehek kehek kehek – errr'.

Feeding: Diet is mostly small fish (especially pilchards and sprats) and krill, taken mainly by plunging from a few metres above the surface or paddling slowly forwards searching with their head submerged, then diving with their partly opened wings used for propulsion. Maximum dive depth for one individual was 29m.

In the hand: Fluttering Shearwaters can be separated from Hutton's and Manx shearwaters on measurements and on undertail and underwing colours. Bill length is 28–**33.5**–37mm and wing length is 190–**210**–225mm, the side feathers of the undertail coverts are normally white, the longest axillaries do not reach the trailing edge of the wing and are light buff-grey, squarish-ended and white-tipped, and apart from the dark leading edge the underwing is mainly white.

Reading: Bell, M. et al. 2005. *Notornis* 52: 11–15. Edgar, A. E. 1962. *Notornis* 10: 1–15. Powlesland, R. G. & Pickard, C. R. 1992. *Notornis* 39: 27–46.

126. HUTTON'S SHEARWATER *Puffinus huttoni* PLATE 29

Size: 36cm, 350g

Distribution: Breeds only in New Zealand, 1200–1800m asl in the Seaward Kaikoura Range of the northeastern South Island, and at a new colony on the Kaikoura Peninsula established through translocations of chicks. Formerly bred in the Inland Kaikoura Range. Because subfossil and midden material is not readily distinguishable from that of Fluttering Shearwaters, it is not possible to tell if they used to have an even wider breeding distribution. During spring and summer, they range over continental-shelf and deeper waters mainly east of the South Island from Cook Strait to Otago, especially north of Banks Peninsula.

In autumn, Hutton's Shearwaters migrate to coastal and continental-shelf waters of Australia as far north as Torres Strait and around the southern and western coasts to northwestern Western Australia. It is not yet clear whether they circumnavigate the continent or follow the same route outwards and back. Adults return to New Zealand in August, followed by subadults in October–November, but younger pre-breeders apparently remain in Australian waters all year. The pattern of recovery of beach-wrecked birds reflects this migration pattern: very few specimens are found between April and August, but numbers increase to peak in October–November, when the subadults return.

Population: *c.* 114,000 breeding pairs, nesting in one large colony in a nature reserve at the head of Kowhai Stream, and one small colony (8000 pairs) on private land in Shearwater Stream, both in the Seaward Kaikoura Range.

Conservation: Protected endemic. Although the species was first described in 1912, its breeding grounds were not found until 1965. Reports from high-country runholders indicated that Hutton's Shearwaters used to breed in the Inland Kaikoura Range, where Maori formerly collected the young as muttonbirds. Pigs destroyed lower altitude colonies and are the main threat. Some parts of the colonies are in steep, unstable sites, and erosion (perhaps induced by browsing by deer, chamois, goats, pigs, hares and possums) has obliterated some. Control of pigs and browsing mammals has led to better vegetation cover at the colonies and less destruction of burrows. Stoats are trapped at the accessible main subcolonies, but many nesting sites are too remote to be protected. Between 2005 and 2013, 496 chicks were transferred to establish a new small colony at a predator-free site, Te Rae o Atiu, on the Kaikoura Peninsula, where breeding commenced in 2010.

Breeding: Birds return to their colonies on soil-covered slopes high in the mountains from late August to mid-September. In some years the colonies are still snow-covered and birds wait up to a month before they can clean out their burrow. Eggs are usually laid between 25 October and 18 November, but later in years when snow persists long into the spring. They lay **1** white egg (60 x 41mm) in a burrow 0.6–**1.2**–2.5m long, but usually running parallel with and just below the surface. Eggs hatch in late December–January after *c.* 50 days' incubation, and most chicks fledge during March–early April at 75–94 days old. Young return to the colony from 3 years old, but do not start breeding until 4–6 years old. Annual adult survival is 93.1%, giving a mean life expectancy of adults of *c.* 19 years.

Behaviour: Breeds in large, patchily dense colonies. At sea, Hutton's Shearwaters are difficult to distinguish from Fluttering Shearwaters, with which they may mix. Large flocks of 20,000 birds, presumed to be primarily of this species, have been seen feeding and roosting off the Marlborough coast. Off Australia, they have been seen in small flocks, sometimes intermingling with other shearwaters. When circling above their breeding colonies they are noisy, uttering a rapid staccato cackle, more wheezy than that of the Fluttering Shearwater. There is much variation on the main call: 'ko-uw ko-uw ko-uw ko-uw, kee kee kee kee – aaah'.

Feeding: Diet is mostly small fish and krill, taken mainly by plunging from a few metres above the surface or by paddling slowly forwards searching with their head submerged, then diving with their partly opened wings used for propulsion. They can dive to *c.* 20m.

In the hand: Hutton's Shearwaters can be separated from Fluttering and Manx shearwaters on measurements and on undertail and underwing colours. Bill length is 32–**36**–39mm and wing length is 210–**225**–235mm, the side feathers of the undertail coverts have dark brown edges in most birds, the longest axillaries reach near the trailing edge of the wing and are dark brown, rounded at the tip, and only rarely or slightly tipped with buff or white, and the underwing is smudged with brown, especially near the base of the wing.

Reading: Cuthbert, R. 2002. *Biol Cons* 108: 69–78. Cuthbert, R. & Davis, L. S. 2002. *Emu* 102: 323–329. Cuthbert, R. & Davis, L. S. 2002. *Ibis* 144: 423–432. Halse, S. A. 1981. *Emu* 81: 42–44. Halse, S. A. & Halse, N. J. 1988. *West Aust Nat* 17: 97–106. Harrow, G. 1965. *Notornis* 12: 59–65. Harrow, G. 1976. *Notornis* 23: 269–288. Powlesland, R. G. & Pickard, C. R. 1992. *Notornis* 39: 27–46. Sommer, E. et al. 2009. *Notornis* 56: 144–153. Tarburton, M. K. 1981. *Notornis* 28: 9–10.

127. LITTLE SHEARWATER *Puffinus assimilis* PLATE 29

Other name: Allied Shearwater

Size: 28cm, 240g

Geographical variation: Four subspecies, two of which breed in the New Zealand region: the Kermadec Little Shearwater *kermadecensis* and the North Island Little Shearwater *haurakiensis.* The Norfolk Island Little Shearwater *assimilis* occasionally visits New Zealand waters.

Distribution: Little Shearwaters breed on islands in the Indian Ocean at St Paul Island and on islands off the coast of Western Australia, on Lord Howe, Norfolk and the Kermadec islands, and around northern New Zealand. All subspecies are moderately sedentary. Kermadec Little Shearwaters breed on the Herald Group, on Macauley Island, and have an especially large colony on Curtis Island; young birds are sometimes beach-wrecked on western and northern North Island beaches in November–December.

North Island Little Shearwaters breed on islands around the northern North Island, with main colonies on the Poor Knights, Chickens, Mokohinau, Mercury and Aldermen islands, and smaller colonies on the

Cavalli Islands and Ohena Island; they are commonly seen in the outer Hauraki Gulf and the Bay of Plenty.

Norfolk Island Little Shearwaters breed at Lord Howe and Norfolk Islands and stray to the west coast of the North Island.

Population: The Kermadec race has 100,000+ breeding pairs, with most on Curtis Island, and several hundred on Macauley and the Meyer islands. The North Island race has *c.* 10,000 pairs, with moderate numbers on the Poor Knights, Hen and Chickens (especially Lady Alice Island), Mokohinau group (especially Lizard Island), Mercury group (e.g. *c.* 1000 pairs on Red Mercury Island) and the Aldermens (4000+ pairs).

Conservation: Protected native. Being a very small shearwater, Little Shearwaters are easily preyed on by introduced mammals and do well only on islands without mammalian predators, although they survive in reduced numbers in the presence of Pacific rats. The recent eradication of rats and other predators from many northern offshore islands and from Raoul Island should result in an increase in both native subspecies.

Breeding: Mostly winter or spring breeders, but birds return to their colonies irregularly all year. Laying is from mid-June to late July in the Kermadecs, and from early July to mid-August around the northern North Island. They lay **1** white egg (54 x 37mm) in a burrow 0.3–2m long. Eggs hatch after 52–58 days. Chicks fledge at 70–75 days old, in mid-October to late November at the Kermadecs, and November–December around the northern North Island.

Behaviour: Breeds in colonies ranging from small, loose aggregations mingling with Grey-faced Petrels and Pycroft's Petrels on such islands as Red Mercury, to large, dense colonies on Curtis Island (Kermadecs). At sea, Little Shearwaters are usually solitary or in small flocks, and seldom associate with other seabirds. They are noisy over and at their breeding colonies, particularly just after dusk and before dawn, with their main call being a rapidly repeated 'kakakakakakak-urrr'.

Feeding: Diet is mostly small fish, krill, squid and octopus, taken mainly by diving from the surface or by plunging from a few metres above the surface.

In the hand: This and the Subantarctic Little Shearwater are the only shearwaters with bright blue feet. The subspecies are impossible to determine at sea, and even in the hand, plumage differences are slight and measurements overlap extensively: *kermadecensis*: bill 24–**25.3**–27mm, wing 180–**189**–195mm; *haurakiensis*: bill 23–**26.1**–29mm, wing 181–**192**–201mm and greater upperwing coverts have white tips; *assimilis*: bill 22–**23.3**–24.3mm, wing 173–**182**–189mm.

Reading: Fleming, C. A. & Serventy, D. L. 1943. *Emu* 43: 113–125. Powlesland, R. G. & Pickard, C. R. 1992. *Notornis* 39: 27–46.

128. SUBANTARCTIC LITTLE SHEARWATER *Puffinus elegans* PLATE 29

Size: 28cm, 250g

Distribution: Subantarctic Little Shearwaters have disjoint breeding distribution; in the South Atlantic Ocean on Gough Island and islands in the Tristan da Cunha group, and in New Zealand on the Star Keys in the Chathams, and on the Antipodes Islands, especially Bollons Island. This species has been recorded in skua middens at Mangere and Little Mangere Island (Chathams), and seen at the Solander, Bounty and Auckland islands, and on The Snares, and it is occasionally wrecked on South Island and southern North Island beaches.

Population: *c.* 150 pairs on the Star Keys in the Chathams, but 100,000+ pairs on Bollons, Archway and Inner Windward islands of the Antipodes Islands.

Conservation: Protected native. Being a very small shearwater, Subantarctic Little Shearwaters are easily preyed on by introduced mammals, and their absence from Antipodes Island suggests that even the presence of mice will eliminate them.

Breeding: Spring breeder, with eggs laid in August to October. They lay **1** white egg (56 x 37mm) in a burrow 0.3–1m long. Eggs of closely related Little Shearwaters hatch after 52–58 days and chicks fledge at 70–75 days old, which fits observed fledging in January–February.

Behaviour: Breeds in colonies ranging from small, loose aggregations mingling with other species on the Star Keys, to large dense colonies on Bollons Island. At sea, Subantarctic Little Shearwaters are usually solitary or in small flocks, and seldom associate with other seabirds. They are noisy over and at their breeding colonies, particularly just after dusk and before dawn, with their main call being a rapidly repeated 'kakakakakakak-urrr'.

Feeding: Diet is mostly small fish, krill, squid and octopus, taken mainly by diving from the surface or by plunging from a few metres above the surface.

In the hand: This and the Little Shearwater are the only shearwaters with bright blue feet. These species are difficult to separate at sea, but in the hand Subantarctic Little Shearwaters have many lower back feathers and upperwing coverts with distinctive narrow white tips. Measurements, e.g. bill 23–**24.5**–26mm, wing 170–**187**–197mm, overlap those of all three Little Shearwater subspecies that occur in New Zealand.

Reading: Fleming, C. A. & Serventy, D. L. 1943. *Emu* 43: 113–125. Imber, M. J. 1983. *Notornis* 30: 283–298. Powlesland, R. G. & Pickard, C. R. 1992. *Notornis* 39: 27–46. Warham, J. & Bell, B. D. 1979. *Notornis* 26: 121–169.

STORM PETRELS *Hydrobatidae*

The storm petrels are very small seabirds, ranging from Antarctic waters to the tropics. There are 22 species, of which 6 breed in the New Zealand region, and 1 is a vagrant.

The storm petrels are small delicate birds with weak black bills. They have very prominent nostrils encased in a single, often upturned tube at the base of the bill. They have 11 primaries, but the 11th (outermost) is minute. The 10th primary is shorter than the 9th, giving the wings a rounded tip. The legs and webbed toes are long and are used to skip or patter across the sea surface as birds look for zooplankton.

The biology of the storm petrels and threats to them are like those of the Procellariidae. The main differences are that females are larger than males, they lay the heaviest egg relative to female weight of any bird (typically in the range of 25–29% of female weight for the smaller species), and the egg is regularly left unattended for one or more days at a time during incubation, which makes the incubation period highly variable.

Reading: Harrison, P. 1988. *Seabirds: An Identification Guide*. London: Christopher Helm. Lockley, R. M. 1983. *Flight of the Storm Petrel*. Newton Abbot: David & Charles. Onley, D. & Scofield, P. 2007. *Field Guide to the Albatrosses, Petrels and Shearwaters of the World*. London: Christopher Helm. Serventy, D. L. et al. 1971. *The Handbook of Australian Sea-birds*. Sydney: Reed. Warham, J. 1990. *The Petrels: Their Ecology and Breeding Systems*. London: Academic Press.

129. WILSON'S STORM PETREL *Oceanites oceanicus* PLATE 31

Size: 18cm, 35g

Geographical variation: Two subspecies: *oceanicus* breeds on subantarctic islands in the South Atlantic and South Indian Ocean; *exasperatus* breeds on coasts and islands off Antarctica and is an uncommon passage migrant through New Zealand waters.

Distribution: Circumpolar, breeding at many sites on the coast of Antarctica and on many islands in Antarctic and southern subantarctic waters north to 46° S. In the Ross Dependency, they breed at many sites along the coast of the Ross Sea and on Balleny and Scott islands. After breeding, they migrate to the Northern Hemisphere and are occasionally beach-wrecked or seen passing through New Zealand waters in March–May. The main northward migration route appears be to the east of New Zealand, judging by many records at sea off the East Coast, near the Chathams, and on the Chatham Rise, but also recorded off North Cape. There are fewer records from the southward migration in November–December but they are often seen at Campbell Island, especially in Perseverance Harbour.

Population: The global population is 4–10 million pairs; *c.* 128,000 pairs breed in the Ross Dependency.

Conservation: Migrant to the mainland of New Zealand. Numbers are huge despite skua predation and reductions in some subantarctic colonies after the introduction of cats and rats.

Breeding: Not studied in Ross Dependency, but elsewhere in Antarctica, adults return to their colonies in November to early December to claim nest sites and to court. Laying is in December–January. They lay 1 white egg (33 x 24mm, 10g) in a crevice in a cliff or scree slope. Eggs hatch in January–February after *c.* 45 days, and chicks depart March–April at *c.* 60 days old. Young breed at 3 years old, and average life expectancy of adults is at least 13 years.

Behaviour: Breeds in large dense colonies and often feeds and migrates in flocks, often following well back in the wake of fishing boats.

In the hand: Wilson's Storm Petrels are like Leach's Storm Petrels, the only other black storm petrel with a white rump known from the region, but Wilson's

Storm Petrels have a smaller bill: 11–**12.5**–13.5mm cf. 13.5–**16.0**–17.5mm. The white rump patch of Wilson's Storm Petrel is not divided or partially divided by a dark central line of feathers as in Leach's Storm Petrel.

Reading: Falla, R. A. 1933. *Rep BANZARE B* 2: 1–288. Lacan, F. 1971. *Oiseau* 41: 65–89. Petyt, C. 2001. *Notornis* 48: 54–55. Pryor, M. E. 1968. *Ant Res Ser (Wash)* 12: 57–82.

130. GREY-BACKED STORM PETREL *Garrodia nereis* PLATE 31

Size: 18cm, 35g

Distribution: Circumpolar, breeding on many subantarctic islands in the Atlantic and Indian oceans, and in the New Zealand region. They breed at the Chathams on many small islands and stacks, with main colonies on South East and Mangere islands; also on the Antipodes and Auckland islands, and on islets off Campbell Island. Breeding birds return to their colonies almost all year round, but some New Zealand birds move north to about 30° S and westwards into the southern Tasman Sea, and they are regular visitors to coastal waters off southeastern Australia. Grey-backed Storm Petrels are occasionally beach-wrecked in June–December, especially around Cook Strait. Several times they have been recorded well inland in the southern South Island, and so may also breed somewhere in Fiordland.

Population: Moderate numbers, with a global population of *c.* 200,000 birds. Possibly 10,000–12,000 pairs breed in the Chathams, 10,000+ pairs on the Antipodes, and smaller colonies at the Auckland Islands and on islands off Campbell Island.

Conservation: Protected native. Little is known of the numbers of this species, but because they nest above ground they are especially vulnerable to mammalian predators, and so most are now on islands free of ground predators and grazing mammals, except that some fall prey to Antipodes Islands Parakeets. The eradication of rats from Campbell Island in 2001 will have improved breeding opportunities there.

Breeding: Adults return to their colonies at almost any time of year. Numbers build up in August and eggs are laid from mid-September to December. They lay 1 white egg (31 x 23mm, 8.5g) in a shallow cup of leaf fibres above ground in a 'rat hole' at the base of flax, ferns, herbs or tussock clumps, or under iceplants. The incubation period is 39–45 days; because the egg is often left unattended for a day or more, the period is quite variable. The chick is brooded for only a few hours and then guarded for up to 4 days. It is fed every 1–**1.6**–3 days and reaches adult weight by 17 days old, but it does not fledge until *c.* 50 days old.

Behaviour: Breeds in loose colonies and feeds alone or in small flocks. Silent in the air. A monotonous cricket-like chirping is given on the ground.

Feeding: Studies at the Chathams have found that Grey-backed Storm Petrels specialise in feeding on the free-swimming stage of immature barnacles, supplemented with other zooplankton.

In the hand: Grey-backed Storm Petrels are the smallest storm petrel in the New Zealand region (wing 117–**131**–139mm). Females average longer in the wing and tail than males, but measurements overlap. The outermost primary is rounded in adults but pointed in juveniles.

Reading: Greene, T. C. 1999. *Notornis* 46: 301–310. Imber, M. J. 1981. In *Proc Symp Birds Sea Shore*. Cape Town: African Seabird Group. Imber, M. J. 1983. *Notornis* 30: 283–298. Plant, A. R. 1989. *Notornis* 36: 141–147. Tennyson, A. et al. 2002. *Notornis* 49: 241–245. Warham, J. & Bell, B. D. 1979. *Notornis* 26: 121–169.

131. WHITE-FACED STORM PETREL *Pelagodroma marina* PLATE 30

Other names: Takahikare-moana, Frigate Petrel, Jesus Christ Bird

Size: 20cm, 45g

Geographical variation: Five subspecies, of which two have been recorded in New Zealand: *dulciae*, breeding around southern Australia, and *maoriana*, breeding around the mainland of New Zealand and at the Chatham and Auckland islands.

Distribution: There are widespread colonies of White-faced Storm Petrels in subantarctic to subtropical parts of the Atlantic, Indian and southwestern Pacific oceans. In New Zealand, *maoriana* breed on many islands of northern New Zealand from Motumahanga (off New Plymouth) in the west to Motunau (Bay of Plenty) in the east. They also breed on Sentinel Rock (Cook Strait), Motunau Island (North Canterbury), several islands around Stewart Island, and at the Chatham Islands (especially South East Island) and Ewing Island in the Auckland Islands group. After breeding, most New Zealand birds migrate to warmer tropical waters of the eastern Pacific in May–August; a bird banded on South East Island in February was recovered 1000km west of Peru three months later. About 30 White-faced Storm Petrels are beach-wrecked each year, mostly on Northland and Bay of Plenty beaches in spring and summer.

One of the few White-faced Storm Petrels beach-wrecked in winter, at Muriwai Beach (May 1983), was a bird of the Australian subspecies, *dulciae*. Unconfirmed sightings suggest that part of the population of this subspecies may migrate to the seas north of New Zealand in winter.

Population: The New Zealand subspecies *maoriana* is common and breeding on many islands. The total population is probably over 1 million breeding pairs. The largest colony is on South East Island, Chatham Islands, with *c.* 850,000 breeding pairs.

Conservation: Protected native. Despite declines caused by the introduction of cats, rats and Weka to many islands, the populations are secure on many islands without mammalian predators.

Breeding: Adults return to their colonies in September to early October, and eggs are laid from late October to mid-December. They lay **1** white egg with pink spots at the larger end (36 x 26mm, 12g). Burrows are usually 0.5–1m long. Incubation spells are of 1–**4**–9 days, but the egg is often left unattended between shifts and can hatch even after being left for 92 hours. The incubation period is 50–55 days, but the period depends on the nest attentiveness of the adults. The chick is continuously guarded for 2–3 days and fed nightly during the 52–**57**–67-day fledging period. Chicks fledge from mid-February to mid-March. A few remain to mid-April.

Behaviour: Breeds in dense colonies. At sea, they feed alone or in large flocks. They are silent in the air but give a mournful twitter and a cackling call from burrows and on the surface.

Feeding: Studies at the Chathams have found that White-faced Storm Petrels feed on a wide variety of krill, amphipods and other planktonic crustaceans, and small fish. They take most prey from the surface while flying or pattering along, occasionally while resting on the surface.

In the hand: Females are slightly larger than males, but measurements overlap greatly. The outermost primary is rounded in adults but pointed in juveniles. Subspecies *maoriana* has a deeply forked tail (5–**10.5**–15mm), whereas *dulciae* has only a shallow fork (2–**5.0**–8.5mm).

Reading: Imber, M. J. 1981. In *Proc Symp Birds Sea Shore*. Cape Town: African Seabird Group. Imber, M. J. 1984. *Emu* 84: 32–35. Richdale, L. E. 1943. *Trans Proc Roy Soc NZ* 73: 97–115, 217–232, 335–350. Underwood, M. & Bunce, A. 2004. *Emu* 104: 213–220. West, J. A. & Nilsson, R. J. 1994. *Notornis* 41(S): 27–37.

132. KERMADEC STORM PETREL *Pelagodroma albiclunis* PLATE 30

Size: 20cm, 50g

Distribution: New Zealand only. Breeding in the southern Kermadec Islands; confirmed on Haszard Island, and possibly also on cliffs of Macauley Island. Possibly also nesting on South Meyer Island off Raoul Island. Many records at sea in the Kermadec group and to the southwest towards New Zealand; a group of four seen in the Tasman Sea in October 1981 may have been of this species, and one seen off Lord Howe Island suggests some dispersal to the east in May to November.

Population: The Kermadec Storm Petrel *albiclunis* is very rare, with perhaps 100–300 pairs.

Conservation: Protected critically endangered endemic. The eradication of goats (1970) and recent (2006) eradication of Pacific rats from Macauley Island, only 220m from Haszard Island, should allow the species to increase its breeding range and numbers, and the eradication of cats and rats from Raoul Island will provide further opportunities for expansion.

Breeding: Little known. In August, they lay **1** white egg (36 x 26mm) with red spots at the larger end, in a burrow. Incubation period is likely to be 50–55 days, and fledging period about 50–70 days, and so chicks would fledge from mid-November to January.

Behaviour: At sea, they feed alone or in small flocks, sometimes associated with dolphins and tuna.

Feeding: Likely to be similar to that of the White-faced Storm Petrel: krill, amphipods and other planktonic crustaceans, and small fish. They take most prey from the surface while flying or pattering along, occasionally while resting on the surface.

In the hand: Kermadec Storm Petrels have a distinctive white rump and only a slightly forked tail (1.5–**3.6**–6mm).

Reading: Imber, M. J. & Stephenson, B. M. 2008. *Notornis* 55: 166–170.

133. NEW ZEALAND STORM PETREL *Pealeornis maoriana* PLATE 31

Size: 18cm, 33g
Distribution: Breeding known only on Little Barrier Island. In the breeding season, it ranges through waters off the northeastern North Island, from the Mercury Islands group to North Cape and the Three Kings Islands, but especially in the outer Hauraki Gulf around Little Barrier Island and the Mokohinau Islands. Records in the nineteenth century, from off East Cape (two in 1827) and Banks Peninsula (before 1895) suggest a broader historical distribution. A few sightings off the eastern seaboard of Australia from Victoria to Queensland, and possibly off New Caledonia, in the non-breeding season indicate a post-breeding movement to the western Tasman and Coral seas.
Population: For over 100 years, the New Zealand Storm Petrel was thought to be extinct, until it was rediscovered on 25 January 2003 when a bird was seen at sea off Whitianga, Coromandel Peninsula. There have been many subsequent sightings and searches for its breeding grounds on islands in the Hauraki Gulf. Radio-tagged birds were eventually traced to land at Little Barrier Island, and breeding was confirmed in February 2013. From the number of sightings, and from low recapture rate of birds banded at sea, it is estimated that there are hundreds, if not low thousands, of birds and the population is growing.
Conservation: Protected endangered endemic. The eradication of cats from Little Barrier Island in 1980, and eradication of Pacific rats in 2004, will have undoubtedly helped the species.
Breeding: Little known. From the timing of the presence of brood patches on birds caught at sea, it seems that eggs are laid in February–March. They lay **1** white egg in crevices in rocky banks and cliffs under forest cover. Chicks fledge in May–June.
Behaviour: Breeds in loose colonies. At sea, they usually feed alone, but small flocks of 10–20 birds have been recorded where 'chum' has been fed out.
Feeding: Little known. Some birds handled at sea have regurgitated remains of small crustaceans. They take most prey from the surface while flying or pattering along, occasionally while resting on the surface.
Reading: Gaskin, C. P. & Baird, K. A. 2005. *Notornis* 52: 181–194. Gaskin, C. P. et al. 2011. *Notornis* 58: 104–112. Gaskin, C. 2013. *NZ Geographic* 121: 36–57. Stephenson, B. M. et al. 2008. *Notornis* 55: 77–83. Stephenson, B. M. et al. 2008. *Notornis* 55: 191–206.

134. BLACK-BELLIED STORM PETREL *Fregetta tropica* PLATE 31

Size: 20cm, 55g
Distribution: Breeds widely on subantarctic islands in the Atlantic (South Shetland, South Orkney and South Georgia islands) and Indian oceans (Prince Edward, Crozet and Kerguelen islands), and in New Zealand at the Antipodes and Auckland islands. Recorded from the Chathams in subfossil deposits and seen there in January 1979, and on Campbell Island in 1963. During summer, they feed in the subantarctic and around the Bounty Platform and Pukaki Rise. After late summer breeding, New Zealand birds migrate to warmer subtropical waters of the Coral Sea and the southwestern Pacific Ocean. They are occasionally seen east of New Zealand and around the Chathams on passage during May–June as they head north, and in October–November as they return south. Only seven birds have been beach-wrecked up to 2012, mainly in Southland or on beaches near Cook Strait.
Population: The global population is estimated to be *c.* 500,000 birds. About 50,000–100,000 pairs breed in New Zealand, mainly in the Auckland Islands. At the Antipodes there are 10,000+ pairs.
Conservation: Protected native. Little is known of the trends of New Zealand populations.
Breeding: Little is known in New Zealand. At Signy Island (South Orkney), adults return to their colonies in November and lay in late December and January, which is consistent with the discovery of two freshly laid eggs on the Auckland Islands on 1 February. They lay **1** white egg (37 x 27mm, 15g) in a burrow up to 0.5m long in stream banks and peat hummocks. The incubation period is 35–45 days, and chicks fledge at 65–70 days old from mid-April to late May.
Behaviour: Breeds in small scattered colonies. At sea, they feed alone or in small flocks. Silent in the air, but on the ground they give a piercingly shrill whistle, which is often hard to pinpoint.
Feeding: Little known, but probably feed on krill, amphipods and other planktonic crustaceans, and small fish and squid. They take most prey from the surface while flying or pattering along. Sometimes feed around whales and trawlers.

In the hand: The few Black-bellied Storm Petrels lacking a central black stripe down the belly are almost identical to some White-bellied Storm Petrels, however, the feet of the former extend well beyond the tail (*c*. 10mm), and they have white (not black) bases to their throat feathers.
Reading: Beck, J. R. & Brown, D. W. 1971. *Ibis* 113: 73–90. Imber, M. J. 1973. *Notornis* 30: 283–298. Imber, M. J. et al. 2005. *Notornis* 52: 125–132. Petyt, C. 2001. *Notornis* 48: 54–55. Tennyson, A. et al. 2002. *Notornis* 49: 241–245. Turner, D. 1980. *Notornis* 27: 94–95. Warham, J. & Bell, B. D. 1979. *Notornis* 26: 121–169.

135. WHITE-BELLIED STORM PETREL *Fregetta grallaria* PLATE 31

Size: 20cm, 50g
Geographical variation: Four subspecies: the nominate *grallaria*, which breeds in the Kermadecs and at Roach Island, Lord Howe group, is the only form known from New Zealand.
Distribution: Breeds widely on subtropical or temperate islands in the South Atlantic (Tristan da Cunha group), South Indian (Roche Quille off St Paul Island) and South Pacific oceans (Lord Howe, Kermadec, Rapa and Juan Fernández islands). In the Kermadecs, they breed in the southern group on Macauley and Curtis islands, and possibly also on Haszard and Cheeseman islands. Throughout their range, White-bellied Storm Petrels migrate northwards into the tropics after the summer–autumn breeding season; however, birds have been caught on Macauley Island in September and on Curtis Island in October–November, and so some birds remain close to their breeding colonies. They are rare vagrants to waters off the New Zealand mainland at any time of year, with only seven records (three beach-wrecked) as far south as Farewell Spit, however, some of these may have been New Zealand Storm Petrels *Pealeornis maoriana*, which were not considered because they were believed to be extinct.
Population: Macauley and Curtis islands have up to 700 birds, with most on Curtis. The Roach Island colony at Lord Howe has 1000+ pairs.
Conservation: Protected endangered native. Little is known of the status and trends of New Zealand populations, but the eradication of rats from Macauley Island in 2006 should allow improved breeding success.
Breeding: Apparently breed in late summer and autumn as on Lord Howe Island; a downy chick seen on Curtis Island on 21 May 1982 and dead chick close to fledging on Macauley Island on 3 August 1966 suggests that eggs are laid in March–May. They lay 1 white egg (36 x 26mm) in a crevice, short burrow or small caves. No information on incubation or fledging periods.
Behaviour: Silent in the air, but on the ground they give a soft twittering call and a high-pitched whistle – 'pee-pee-pee . . .' – repeated 20 or more times.
Feeding: Diet is planktonic crustaceans and small squid, taken from the surface while flying or pattering on the water.
In the hand: White-bellied Storm Petrels can be distinguished from the few Black-bellied Storm Petrels that lack a central black stripe down the belly, and from the New Zealand Storm Petrel, by having the feet extending to about the tip of the tail, not *c*. 10mm beyond.
Reading: Lovegrove, T. G. 1978. *Notornis* 25: 291–298.

136. LEACH'S STORM PETREL *Oceanodroma leucorhoa* PLATE 31

Size: 20cm, 45g
Geographical variation: Four subspecies: *leucorhoa* breeds widely in the North Atlantic and North Pacific, and straggles to New Zealand; three others (*chapmani*, *cheimomnestes* and *socorroensis*) breed on the Pacific coast of North America.
Distribution: Breeds mainly on small islands in the North Atlantic and North Pacific between 42° N and 68° N, except down the Pacific coast of North America to northern Mexico (30° N), and a small recent colony found off South Africa. They migrate to tropical and subtropical waters after breeding, and stay there from September to March, with some non-breeders remaining all year. A few have straggled to New Zealand: Muriwai Beach (August 1922); Matamata (April 1978); Dargaville Beach (August 1978); Rabbit Island, Chathams (two prospecting in November 1980) and Ninety Mile Beach (October 1998).
Behaviour: At Rabbit Island, two birds gave soft chuckles – 'kuk-ku-huk' – in flight and on the ground; and a prolonged loud churring with a rising pitch, interspersed with 'ik' notes, was given by a bird in a burrow.

Feeding: Diet is planktonic crustaceans, small fish, juvenile squid and offal, taken from the surface while flying or pattering on the water.
In the hand: Leach's Storm Petrels are similar to Wilson's Storm Petrel, the only other black storm petrel with a white rump known from the region, but have a much larger bill: 13.5–**16.0**–17.5mm cf. 11–**12.5**–13.5mm. The white rump patch of Leach's Storm Petrel is divided or partially divided by a dark central line of feathers, whereas Wilson's Storm Petrel has a pure white rump.
Reading: Imber, M. J. & Lovegrove, T. G. 1982. *Notornis* 29: 101–108.

137. COMMON DIVING PETREL *Pelecanoides urinatrix* PLATE 30

Other name: Kuaka
Size: 20cm, 130g
Geographical variation: Six subspecies, three of which breed in the New Zealand region: Northern Diving Petrel *urinatrix* breeds from the Three Kings Islands to the Marlborough Sounds; Southern Diving Petrel *chathamensis* breeds off Stewart Island, Solanders, The Snares and the Chathams; and the Subantarctic Diving Petrel *exsul* breeds on the Antipodes, Auckland and Campbell islands.
Distribution: Circumpolar, breeding on islands between 34° S and 55° S and staying mainly in adjacent seas. Northern Diving Petrels breed on islands off Tasmania and in Bass Strait, and on many islands from the Three Kings to the Bay of Plenty, Sugarloaf Island near New Plymouth, and on islands in Cook Strait and the Marlborough Sounds. Southern Diving Petrels breed on many islands in Foveaux Strait and around Stewart Island, and on the Solander Islands, The Snares, and small islands in the Chathams. Subantarctic Diving Petrels are circumpolar, breeding mainly in the subantarctic zone of the South Atlantic and Indian oceans, Macquarie Island, and at the Antipodes and Auckland islands and on islets off Campbell Island.

All subspecies are quite sedentary, remaining mainly near the breeding colonies, which they visit occasionally during the non-breeding season. Common Diving Petrels are quite often wrecked on beaches close to breeding colonies with peaks of recoveries in winter and again in early summer, when young have just left the nest. Normally a few hundred birds are found each year, but an exceptional wreck of 3155 birds occurred in July 1975.
Population: Global population 16 million+ birds, of which 1 million+ pairs nest in New Zealand. Large colonies are on scattered islands off Northland and in the Bay of Plenty, on Sugarloaf Island, on the Brothers and Trio islands in Cook Strait, on South East Island in the Chathams, on Little Solander Island, at The Snares, and on the Antipodes.
Conservation: Protected native. Common Diving Petrels are vulnerable to predation by introduced mammals and survive best on islands without mammalian predators. They have become extinct or rare on islands with rats or cats, or where grazing mammals accidentally destroy burrows. The eradication of rats from many offshore islands will benefit Common Diving Petrels. Chicks have been transferred to Mana and Motuora islands and to Cape Kidnappers to establish new colonies at predator-free sites.
Breeding: The breeding season is a couple of months earlier in northern New Zealand than in Foveaux Strait. On Green Island in the Mercury Group, Common Diving Petrels return to their colony from March onwards, with a peak of activity around the end of May to prepare burrows. Eggs are laid in August in northern New Zealand, but from late September to early October in Foveaux Strait. They lay **1** white egg (38 x 30mm, 16g) in a burrow 0.25–1.5m long. Unusually for petrels, they can lay a replacement egg if the first fails early in incubation. Eggs hatch after *c.* 53 days. Chicks are brooded for 10–15 days and fledge at 45–**52**–59 days old in late November–December in northern New Zealand, and in January–February in Foveaux Strait. Some young birds return to their natal colony to breed as yearlings, but most start breeding at 2–3 years old. The oldest bird lived over 18 years.
Behaviour: Breeds in colonies, and at sea they are seen in small groups. They are noisy at their breeding colonies with a variety of calls given in the air, on the ground and from their burrows. The main calls are a harsh 'kuaka-did-a-did' and 'kuaka' given by females only; 'kooo-ah', given by males only.
Feeding: Diet is mostly small krill and copepods, taken mainly by diving into the sea from a metre or two above surface, then swimming underwater using their short, flipper-like wings for propulsion to depths of up to 64m.
In the hand: The two species of diving petrel can be reliably separated only in the hand. The Common Diving Petrel has dusky-brown inner webs on its three outer primaries, not white or very pale grey as in the South Georgian; the septal process is near the base of

the nostril rather than near the centre; and the underwing coverts vary from heavily smudged brown-grey to pale-grey, but never white as in the South Georgian, which usually also has a black line on the rear of the tarsus. The wing length declines with increasing latitude, but measurements overlap between subspecies: *urinatrix* 117–**131**–137mm; *chathamensis* 115–**123**–130mm; and *exsul* **119**mm.

Reading: Miskelly, C. M. & Taylor, G. A. 2004. *Emu* 104: 205–211. Payne, M. R. & Prince, P. A. 1979. *NZ J Zool* 6: 299–318. Powlesland, R. G. et al. 1992. *Notornis* 39: 101–111. Richdale, L. E. 1943. *Emu* 43: 24–48, 97–107. Richdale, L. E. 1965. *Trans Zool Soc (Lond)* 31: 1–86. Thoresen, A. C. 1969. *Notornis* 16: 241–260.

138. SOUTH GEORGIAN DIVING PETREL *Pelecanoides georgicus* PLATE 30

Size: 18cm, 120g

Distribution: Circumpolar, breeding in the subantarctic zone. The only colony in New Zealand is at Sealer's Bay on Codfish Island/Whenua Hou, although 3–4 pairs nest on the nearby Bishop and Clerk Islets. As recently as 1943 they bred on Dundas and Enderby in the Auckland Islands, and subfossil remains indicate huge colonies used to be in dunes at Mason Bay, Stewart Island, and probably on Chatham Island. They are thought to be sedentary, but judging by stomach contents of Codfish Island birds, they apparently feed well offshore near the edge of the continental shelf.

Population: A common species, with a global population of *c.* 15 million birds, including millions of pairs nesting on South Georgia, the Kerguelen, Prince Edward, Crozet and Heard islands. Codfish Island has fewer than 100 pairs, and the Bishop and Clerk Islets have 3–4 pairs.

Conservation: Protected critically endangered native. The colony on Codfish Island, identified in 1978, was previously assumed to be of Common Diving Petrels. The former colonies in sand dunes on Dundas and Enderby islands were probably destroyed by trampling of cattle and activity of Hooker's sea lions, and by the interference of rabbits. The eradication of Weka (1986) and Pacific rats (1998) from Codfish Island has reduced predation pressure. The breeding habitat on Codfish Island is limited to a small area of sand dunes. People are prevented from walking over these dunes, but weed encroachment and storm erosion still pose threats.

Breeding: On Codfish Island, birds spend September–October cleaning out their deep burrows in unstable and sparsely vegetated sand dunes, 1–5m above the high-tide line. Eggs are laid in early November, a month earlier than at other, more southern breeding colonies. No other New Zealand information on breeding due to the fragile nature of the only breeding grounds. Elsewhere, they lay **1** white egg (39 x 32mm), incubation is for 44–**47**–52 days, and chicks fledge at 43–**50**–60 days old.

Behaviour: On Codfish Island, they breed in a loose colony scattered along about 1km of sand dunes, separate from other seabirds. Adults call in the air over the colony but return directly to their burrows, spending little time on the surface.

Feeding: Diet of the Codfish Island birds is small krill, fish and squid, taken mainly by diving into the sea from a metre or two above the surface, then swimming underwater using their short, flipper-like wings for propulsion to depths of up to 50m.

In the hand: The two species of diving petrel can be reliably separated only in the hand – see Common Diving Petrel.

Reading: Imber, M. J. & Nilsson, R. J. 1980. *Notornis* 27: 325–330. Jouventin, P. et al. 1985. *Notornis* 32: 157–220. Payne, M. R. & Prince, P. A. 1979. *NZ J Zool* 6: 299–318. Weimerskirch, H. et al. 1989. *Emu* 89: 15–29. West, J. & Imber, M. J. 1989. *Notornis* 36: 157–158. Worthy, T. H. 1998. *Notornis* 45: 229–246.

TROPICBIRDS *Phaethontidae*

3 species: 2 in the New Zealand region, including 1 species breeding at the Kermadec Islands.

Sailors called tropicbirds 'bos'n birds' because the projecting middle tail feathers resembled the marlin spike of the boatswain, and their call is like his whistle. These white seabirds are confined to tropical and subtropical seas, often far from land. They are usually solitary or in pairs, flying strongly well above the sea surface, approaching ships with a steady flight and briefly escorting them. Tropicbirds feed on fish and squid, taken mostly by plunge-diving. They breed on the ground, solitary or in loose colonies, the density depending on available nest sites rather than social need.

139. RED-TAILED TROPICBIRD *Phaethon rubricauda* PLATE 32

Other names: Amokura, Bosun Bird
Size: 46cm, plus up to 40cm for tail streamers; 800g
Geographical variation: A single species but with a gradual increase in size and of the pink suffusion on the white plumage from the northern Pacific to the Kermadecs.
Distribution: Breeds on many islands of the tropical Indian and Pacific oceans, including Lord Howe, Norfolk and the Kermadec islands. They remain at sea when not breeding, although a few are seen near the Kermadecs in winter. Each summer, usually associated with the passage of tropical cyclones, a few birds are seen around northern New Zealand, mainly off Northland or in the Hauraki Gulf, or beach-wrecked on the coasts of Northland and occasionally as far south as the Waikato, Taranaki and Wellington west coasts. They have been recorded inland, e.g. twice at Lake Taupo. The only South Island record is of a bird at Akaroa in the 1950s.
Population: *c.* 120 pairs breed at the Kermadec Islands, mainly on the Herald Islets off Raoul Island, and on Macauley Island.
Conservation: Protected nationally endangered native. No information is available on population trends, but the eradication of Pacific and Norway rats (in 2002) and cats (in 2004) from Raoul Island, and the eradication of Pacific rats from Macauley Island in 2006 is expected to improve their breeding prospects.
Breeding: Laying is in December–May, mostly December–January. They lay 1 fawn egg, spotted and blotched reddish brown (67 x 47mm, 80g) in a scrape on the ground, often in inaccessible positions in cavities and fissures of rugged cliffs. Both sexes incubate in shifts of 2–7 days for 40–46 days. The young stay at the nest for 65–90 days. Most leave in April–May, but there are records of large chicks at Macauley Island in August.
Behaviour: When not breeding, Red-tailed Tropicbirds are usually seen as singles, pairs at the most. They are silent at sea but noisy, especially in aerial display in pairs, at breeding islands. In display, they have a special hover that makes them seem to fly in reverse. Their short legs can barely support them, and they shuffle along, their breast touching the ground.
Feeding: Fish and squid are caught by plunge-diving from both high and low altitudes; most prey is caught in the top 5m of the ocean, but dives of up to 13m have been recorded.
In the hand: Much larger than White-tailed Tropicbird (wing 330–360mm cf. 260–280mm), and adult plumage is very different. Juvenile upperparts barring is similar, but the bill tends to be all blackish or blackish with red base, whereas the bill of juvenile White-tailed Tropicbirds tends to be yellowish with a blackish tip.
Reading: Merton, D. V. 1970. *Notornis* 17: 147–199. Powlesland, R. G. et al. 1992. *Notornis* 39: 101–111. Tarburton, M. K. 1984. *Notornis* 31: 92–94. Tarburton, M. K. 1989. *Notornis* 36: 39–49. Veitch, C. R. et al. 2004. *Notornis* 51: 61–90.

140. WHITE-TAILED TROPICBIRD *Phaethon lepturus* PLATE 32

Other name: Yellow-billed Tropicbird
Size: 38cm, plus up to 40cm for tail streamers; 300g
Distribution: Breeds on islands in the tropical Atlantic, Indian and western Pacific oceans, and remains at sea when not breeding. The nearest breeding sites to New Zealand are New Caledonia, Tonga, Niue and Rarotonga. Regularly seen in subtropical waters between New Zealand and Fiji. Rare vagrants

to waters off the New Zealand mainland are mainly birds blown south by tropical cyclones. There have been about 18 records, mainly of beach-wrecked immature birds on Northland coasts but as far south as the Whakatane and Taranaki coasts.
Behaviour: Similar to Red-tailed Tropicbirds but tend to accompany ships more often.

PELICANS *Pelecanidae*

7 species; 1 vagrant reaches New Zealand.

Pelicans are very large freshwater or marine birds with four webbed toes and a very long bill with a massive fleshy pouch for catching fish. Small flocks surround a shoal of fish and then feed synchronously by dipping their heads into the centre of the shoal. Unlike some marine pelicans, the Australian species rarely dives for food. Pelicans have a laboured take-off, but their flight is easy and graceful as they soar on thermals and glide effortlessly, reminiscent of a jumbo jet, as they come in to land. They often fly in flocks in a V-formation, roost in flocks and breed in colonies.

141. AUSTRALIAN PELICAN *Pelecanus conspicillatus* PLATE 38

Size: 170cm, 5kg
Distribution: Breeds only in Australia, mainly in the north and east. Usually found on inland and coastal lakes rather than in harbours or estuaries, and often breeds near inland lakes, although some colonies are on islands in Bass Strait. They disperse widely from their breeding colonies and are regular visitors to New Guinea, the Bismarck Archipelago and Solomon Islands. Rare vagrant to New Zealand with five records: Whanganui River (1890); Kaipara Harbour (August–September 1976); Southland (November 1977); three or four birds in South Canterbury (December 1977–June 1978); and at least 14 birds on the Wairoa River, between Dargaville and Ruawai, northern Kaipara Harbour (August 2012). This flock later split up, with individuals or small flocks presumably mainly from the original invasion, seen from Parengarenga Harbour to the Waikato River at Meremere. With no evidence of breeding in 2012–13, further vagrants arrived to boost the original influx, with a maximum of 18 birds seen at Tapora, mid-Kaipara Harbour, in April 2013, shortly after four had reportedly been shot near Dargaville.
Behaviour: Australian Pelicans are gregarious; they breed in colonies, roost in flocks on sand or mudbanks, and feed in parties to surround shoals of fish and then plunge their heads simultaneously below the water to catch their prey.
Reading: Sagar, P. M. 1978. *Notornis* 25: 353–354. Vestjens, W. J. M. 1977. *Aust Wildl Res* 4: 37–58.

GANNETS and BOOBIES *Sulidae*

9 species; 2 breed in the New Zealand region and 2 visit New Zealand waters.

Gannets and boobies are marine birds, mainly feeding close to shore rather than in open oceans. All plunge-dive – gannets for fish, boobies mainly for flying fish. Whereas gannets are typical of temperate coastal waters, boobies are typical of tropical and subtropical seas. Breeding adults tend to stay permanently around their colony and in local seas, whereas non-breeding birds and young disperse or migrate to distant waters.

Their bill is sturdy and cone-shaped, with its cutting edges serrated for seizing fish. The forehead is flattened, and much of the face is covered with bare skin. Three webbed toes, sometimes with all or some skin very brightly coloured. The sexes are alike, but juveniles take 2 to 4 years to gain full adult plumage. They breed in colonies, and gannetries are particularly dense, mostly on islands and typically on the ground.
Reading: Nelson, J. B. 1978. *The Sulidae: Gannets and Boobies*. Oxford: OUP.

142. CAPE GANNET *Morus capensis* PLATE 33

Size: 90cm, 2.6kg
Distribution: Breeds mainly on islands off South Africa and Namibia, and disperses to coastal waters of southern Africa from the Gulf of Guinea to Mozambique. A few reach islands in the Indian Ocean and off Australia, but since the early 1980s a few have nested with Australasian Gannets in Bass Strait. One New Zealand record, a male at the Australasian Gannet colony at Cape Kidnappers, Hawke's Bay, between 1997 and 2005, which bred successfully with an Australasian Gannet in 1999–2000. The male hybrid offspring bred at Cape Kidnappers in October 2005.
Behaviour: Very similar to that of the Australasian Gannet, but some breeding displays are performed markedly slower and with a deeper voice.
Reading: Robertson, C. J. R. & Stephenson, B. M. 2005. *Notornis* 52: 238–242.

143. AUSTRALASIAN GANNET *Morus serrator* PLATE 33

Other name: Takapu
Size: 89cm; 2.3kg
Distribution: Breeds in New Zealand, Philip Island (Norfolk group) and Australia. In New Zealand, they breed in 28 colonies, from the Three Kings Islands south to Little Solander Island. In 1980–81, the largest gannetries were at Gannet Island, west of Kawhia (8000 pairs), White Island (6800 pairs), Three Kings Island (5850 pairs), and at Cape Kidnappers (5200 pairs), although the latter had grown to *c.* 7300 pairs by 2008. There are three mainland colonies: the Muriwai (West Auckland) and Cape Kidnappers colonies are on plateaus on coastal headlands, whereas the recent Farewell Spit colony is on shellbanks near the tip of the spit.

Adults and a few juveniles range widely in New Zealand seas during the winter, mostly north of Cook Strait, but vagrants reach the Chatham, Snares, Auckland and Campbell islands. Almost all juveniles and some adults disperse to coastal waters off Australia, as far west as the Indian Ocean and as far north as Rockhampton, Queensland. Most young New Zealand gannets stay in Australian waters until they are 3–7 years old, but a few return at 1–2 years old. Of the 100–300 gannets beach-wrecked annually, most are found on Northland coasts in November–February, during chick-rearing and with the departure of juveniles across the Tasman.
Population: National counts were 21,100 breeding pairs in 1946–47, 37,800 pairs in 1969–70, and 46,000 pairs (of the global population of 53,000 breeding pairs) in 1980–81. The annual increase over the 34 years from 1946 to 1980 was 2.3%. The Farewell Spit colony has grown rapidly from *c.* 75 breeding pairs in 1983, to *c.* 600 pairs in 1987, and to *c.* 3900 pairs in 2011.
Conservation: Protected native. Numbers are increasing rapidly, and mainland colonies have benefited from strict control of access by sightseers because birds are easily disturbed.
Breeding: The breeding season varies from year to year and between gannetries, depending on latitude. Hauraki Gulf males return in mid-June, eggs are laid between late July and mid-October, and chicks leave the nest from late December. At Cape Kidnappers, they return in late July, eggs are laid in late September to December, and chicks leave the nest from early February.

The nest is a depression in a mound built mostly of seaweed and guano. Nests are spaced out according to the striking distance of neighbouring sitting birds. They lay **1** pale blue-green, chalky-covered egg (77 x 47mm), which both sexes incubate under the webs of their feet for 43–**45**–53 days. Some replacement eggs are laid if the first is lost early in incubation. The young leave the nest at about 42 days old, but do not fledge until 91–**102**–119 days old. Most cross the Tasman Sea soon after leaving the gannetries, arriving there from January onwards. They first breed at 3–7 years old. The oldest banded bird in New Zealand lived over 30 years.
Behaviour: Usually solitary away from the colony, but loose flocks form over shoals of fish, and sometimes the birds commute in small flocks. Except when feeding in flocks, they are usually quiet away from the gannetry.
Feeding: The diet varies from colony to colony, for example, Farewell Spit birds feed mainly on pilchards, anchovy and jack mackerel from shallow water in Golden Bay and Tasman Bay, whereas Cape Kidnappers birds feed on deep-water fish species such as saury, kahawai and cubiceps well offshore in Hawke Bay. Small squid are also taken. They are almost entirely marine, feeding primarily over continental-shelf and inshore waters, but also enter harbours and estuaries. They either dive at an angle from *c.* 5m above the surface to *c.* 3m deep, or they dive straight down from up to 30m high to *c.* 4m deep, but sometimes to depths of over 20m. Just

before hitting the water, they fully stretch their wings backwards, entering the water at tremendous speed. Inflatable air sacs beneath the skin on the lower neck and breast cushion the shock of entry. In shallow water, such as surf, they dive at a narrow angle. They can stay underwater for up to 40 seconds and catch up to five fish in a single dive. Most prey is swallowed at the surface.
Reading: Fleming, C. A. & Wodzicki, K. A. 1952. *Notornis* 5: 39–78. Hawkins, J. M. 1988. *Notornis* 35: 249–260. Ismar, S. M. H. et al. 2011. *Wilson Bull* 123: 121–125. Machovsky-Capuska, G. E. et al. 2011. *Mar Ecol Prog Ser* 422: 255–261. Machovsky-Capuska, G. E. et al. 2013. *J Ornith*: doi: 10.1007/s10336-013-1018-4. Robertson, D. A. 1992. *NZ J Ecol* 16: 77–81. Schuckard, R. et al. 2012. *Notornis* 59: 66–70. Wingham, E. J. 1984. Emu 84: 129–136, 211–224. Wingham, E. J. 1985. *Emu* 85: 231–239. Wodzicki, K. A. et al. 1984. *Notornis* 31: 232–261.

144. BROWN BOOBY *Sula leucogaster* PLATE 33

Size: 70cm, 1300g
Geographical variation: Four subspecies; the only one recorded in New Zealand is *plotus* of eastern Africa, islands of the Indian Ocean, Indonesia, Micronesia, northern Australia, New Guinea and much of the Pacific Ocean.
Distribution: Breeds in tropical seas. The nearest breeding sites to New Zealand are on many of the islands and cays off the Queensland coast. Occasionally seen off the Kermadec Islands, and a few reach the New Zealand mainland in most summers. They are seen mostly as singles in Northland and in the Bay of Plenty, but have been recorded as far south as Canterbury, and sometimes reside for several months and associate with nesting Australasian Gannets.
Feeding: They feed by vertical plunging, but from a lower height than Australasian Gannets. Flying fish are the main prey in the tropics, but they take other fish and some squid.
Reading: Miskelly, C. M. 1980. *Notornis* 27: 395.

145. MASKED BOOBY *Sula dactylatra* PLATE 33

Other names: Blue-faced Booby, Tasman Booby, Masked Gannet
Size: 80cm, 2.1kg
Geographical variation: Of the four subspecies, *tasmani* breeds at Lord Howe, Norfolk and Kermadec island groups, and is the most likely form to appear at the mainland of New Zealand.
Distribution: Breeds in tropical and subtropical seas in the Pacific, Indian and Atlantic oceans, and in the Caribbean Sea. In New Zealand, they breed on the Kermadec Islands at Meyer, Dayrell, South Chanter, Macauley, and Curtis islands. They are a rare vagrant to the New Zealand mainland; seven records: Gannet Island (1883), west of North Cape (1964), Firth of Thames (two in October 1977–March 1978), Hamilton (July 1983), Dargaville (May 1988), Paraparaumu Beach (September 1995) and Charleston (May 2007).
Population: The global population of the *tasmani* subspecies is probably fewer than 2000 birds, of which 200+ pairs breed at the Kermadec Islands, mainly on Macauley Island (100 pairs in 1988), Curtis Island (70 pairs in 1989) and the Herald Islets (50 pairs in 1966–67).
Conservation: Protected endangered native. The number of Masked Boobies breeding at the Kermadecs has increased in recent decades, partially owing to an influx of birds from colonies at Norfolk Island.
Breeding: At the Kermadecs, they breed almost all year, with the peak of laying in July to November. They lay 1–2–3 dull white eggs (66 x 46mm, 75g) on the ground, often in a site exposed to the wind. Both sexes incubate under the webs of their feet for *c.* 44 days, starting after the laying of the second egg, *c.* 5 days after the first. Hatching is not synchronous and, although both sexes brood chicks at first and feed them, usually only one is raised. Fledging period is *c.* 120 days, but the fledglings are fed for a further month or two. The young may breed as early as 2 years old. A bird banded in Australia lived over 25 years.
Behaviour: Masked Boobies fly high and fast, soaring and circling. Like Brown Boobies, they often perch on buoys and posts marking channels. They are silent at sea but noisy at breeding colonies.
Feeding: Mostly flying fish; also other fish and some squid, taken by plunging from high above, usually in deep oceanic water far from land.
Reading: Ismar, S. M. H. et al. 2010. *Marine Ornith* 38: 105–109. Priddel, D. et al. 2005. *Emu* 105: 105–113. Veitch, C. R. et al. 2004. *Notornis* 51: 61–90.

SHAGS *Phalacrocoracidae*

33 species worldwide in freshwater and marine habitats; 12 species breed in the New Zealand region, including 8 endemic species.

In New Zealand, all members of the Phalacrocoracidae are popularly called 'shags', whereas elsewhere the term 'cormorant' is used for members of the genus *Phalacrocorax*. Foot colour varies between the three genera in New Zealand: black in the mainly freshwater *Phalacrocorax*, pink in the marine *Leucocarbo*, and yellow in the marine *Stictocarbo*.

Shags are medium to large, long-necked, aquatic birds with a stiff, wedge-shaped tail, and moderately short, rounded wings, which black-footed shags hold out to dry when perched. Shags feed by diving from the water surface to catch fish and crustaceans with their long, hooked bill. They use their webbed feet to swim underwater. The outermost toe is longest, and a web connects the inner toe with the long hind toe. In the breeding season, bare skin on the face becomes brightly coloured and contrasts with the eye and bill.

Shags sometimes feed in flocks. They typically roost in flocks and breed in colonies on cliffs or rocky islets, or in trees overhanging water, sometimes together with other shags. The have an elaborate series of ritualised courtship displays at or near the nest, a bulky platform made of sticks or seaweed. Their eggs have a chalky encrustation on the surface. Both sexes share incubation. The chicks are naked at hatching but soon develop down. Both parents regurgitate food for the chicks. If a predator approaches, chicks in trees overhanging water will jump well before they can fly, but they are adept at climbing back up to the nest.

146. LITTLE SHAG *Phalacrocorax melanoleucos* PLATE 34

Other names: Kawaupaka, Little Pied Cormorant
Size: 56cm, 700g
Geographical variation: Three subspecies: *melanoleucos* breeds in Palau, Indonesia, New Guinea, Australia, New Caledonia and Solomon Islands (except Renell Island, where *brevicauda* is endemic) and was briefly established on Campbell Island in the late 1960s, and is a vagrant to The Snares; and *brevirostris* breeds in the rest of New Zealand. The New Zealand birds have a wide range of plumage forms, from pied (like those elsewhere in Australasia) to the common 'white-throated' form, smudgy adults and an almost completely black juvenile form. Paler phases are more common in the north. Pied birds make up 60% of the population in the Far North, 32% in Auckland, 15% in the rest of the North Island, but just 8% in the South Island.
Distribution: Breeds in Australasia east of Java and the Moluccas, in New Caledonia and New Zealand. Colonies are scattered throughout the North, South and Stewart islands, and nearby offshore islands. Little Shags are found in sheltered coastal waters, estuaries, harbours, rivers, dams and lakes up to the subalpine zone. There is much local movement between feeding and roosting or nesting areas. After breeding, they disperse widely from their colonies and large flocks congregate around good food sources (e.g. sewer outfalls) or good roosting sites (e.g. 300+ birds roosting at Freemans Pond at the base of Farewell Spit, and 300+ about Wellington Harbour, places where few are found in summer). Stragglers have been recorded from The Snares and Auckland Island, and a small colony of Australian origin was established on Campbell Island in 1967–69.
Population: Widespread and locally common (5000–10,000 pairs), especially in the central North Island. Colonies of 200+ pairs have been recorded at Lakes Rotomahana, Rotorua and Taupo. The number of Little Shags seems to be declining in the northern North Island, but increasing in the southern North Island and the South Island.
Conservation: Protected native. Little Shags are sometimes illegally shot by fishermen who regard them as competitors for fish, and some birds are caught accidentally in fishing nets. Shags are now known to have a minimal impact on fish stocks, and few are now shot – this may have contributed to the increase in numbers of Little Shags.
Breeding: Nests in large colonies, sometimes together with other shags, especially Pied Shags. Colonies are commonly in willows or silver poplars overhanging fresh water or estuaries, but sometimes they nest on maimai or on ledges in river gorges or on sea cliffs. The nest is usually a platform of sticks and leaves, about 30cm in diameter. The breeding season is very long: nest-building starts in late July, and laying is August–February, with a peak in September–November. They lay 1–4–5 pale blue-green eggs (48 x 31mm, 25g)

2 days apart. Incubation lasts *c.* 4 weeks, and chicks fledge 5–**6**–8 weeks later. They can start breeding at 2 years old. The oldest bird in Australia lived over 20 years.
Behaviour: Normally they feed alone or in small groups of up to 10 birds, but often they roost in flocks of up to 50 birds on logs, piers, rocks and in trees. They are silent away from their colonies and make little noise at their colonies, except while displaying, and a loud, repeated 'coo' is given when an aerial predator approaches the colony.
Feeding: Diet varies greatly with habitat, but is mainly small fish (<13cm long) and freshwater crayfish, with the occasional frog and tadpole. The main inland prey are smelt, bullies and goldfish, whereas the main marine species taken are bullies, flounder, sole and smelt. Little Shags generally feed close inshore in water less than 3m deep; their dives last *c.* 15 seconds, but up to 37 seconds in deep water. Rests between dives last *c.* 6 seconds.
Reading: Dickinson, P. 1951. *Aust J Mar Fresh Res* 2: 245–251. Dowding, J. E. & Taylor, M. J. 1987. *Notornis* 34: 51–57. Lalas, C. 1983. PhD thesis, Uni Otago. Matthews, C. W. & Fordham, R. A. 1986. *Emu* 86: 118–121. Millener, P. R. 1972. MSc thesis, Uni Auckland. Potts, K. J. 1977. *Wildlife - A Review* 8: 34–38. Powlesland, R. G. & Luke, I. J. 2000. *Notornis* 47: 1–5. Stonehouse, B. 1967. *Ibis* 109: 600–605. Taylor, M. J. 1987. *Notornis* 34: 41–50.

147. BLACK SHAG *Phalacrocorax carbo* — PLATE 34

Other names: Kawau, Black Cormorant, Great Cormorant
Size: 88cm; male 2.5kg, female 1.9kg
Geographical variation: Of the six subspecies, *novaehollandiae* breeds throughout Australia, New Guinea, Solomon Islands, New Caledonia and New Zealand.
Distribution: Breeds widely from eastern North America (Newfoundland to Maine), Greenland, Iceland, across Europe and Asia, Africa and Australasia. In New Zealand, they breed throughout the main islands and on the Chatham Islands; vagrant to the Kermadecs, The Snares and Campbell Island. They are found in sheltered coastal waters, estuaries, harbours, rivers, streams, dams and lakes up to the subalpine zone. It seems that some young disperse widely – a nestling banded at Lake Wairarapa was recovered at Lord Howe Island, and one banded in New South Wales was recovered near Westport. There is much local movement between feeding, roosting, and nesting areas, but no evidence for regular long-distance migration in New Zealand.
Population: Widespread and moderately common (5000–10,000 birds). Most nest in small colonies of 5–20 pairs, but colonies of over 50 pairs have been recorded in the Waikato, in the Lake Wairarapa wetlands, and at several sites on Chatham Island.
Conservation: Protected native. For many years, Black Shags were persecuted by fishermen who saw them as competitors for commercial fish species and for young trout. Black Shags were given partial protection in 1986 after studies had shown that they ate many young eels and so were probably of some benefit to game-fishers. They are often caught in fishing nets and occasionally on hooked lines.
Breeding: Nesting colonies are commonly in willows, pines, pohutukawa or beech trees overhanging water, or on cliff ledges in river gorges. Some are on coastal cliffs or in low scrub on offshore stacks, and occasionally they nest on old maimai, on the ground (e.g. Wairau Lagoons, Farewell Spit) or in trees well away from water (e.g. in karaka trees in Gollans Valley, near Wellington). The nest is usually a large platform of sticks, twigs, and flax, raupo and cabbage tree leaves, up to 10m above the water or ground. Nests are often reused in a season or between years.

The breeding season is variable from colony to colony, and breeding may be delayed at some sites by disturbance from duck-shooters. Most eggs are laid in June–October, but birds at Gollans Valley regularly lay in late April. They lay 2–**3**–5 bluish-green eggs (61 x 38mm) 2 days apart. Incubation lasts 27–31 days. Chicks are able to scramble from the nest at *c.* 4 weeks old, but fledge at *c.* 7 weeks old. They are fed by their parents for 7–10 weeks after fledging. Some young breed at 2 years old, but most start at 3 years old. A Black Shag banded in Europe lived nearly 20 years.
Behaviour: Generally feed alone, but sometimes they form flocks of 100+ birds where food is abundant. They often roost in small groups on logs, rocks and in trees. They are generally silent away from their colonies, but at the nest they make a variety of croaks, grunts and wheezy whistles.
Feeding: Diet is mainly small- and medium-sized fish (<35cm long), including mullet, wrasse, red cod, spotties, smelt, eels, bullies, galaxiids, trout, carp and perch; the proportion of species varies greatly according to habitat. Freshwater crayfish, large invertebrates and

molluscs are also taken. Black Shags feed in lakes, pools in rivers, estuaries and tidal inlets, and stay close inshore, mainly in water less than 3m deep, but have been caught in craypots set 12m deep. Their dives usually last *c.* 20 seconds, with *c.* 6 seconds' rest between dives, but dives of up to 58 seconds have been recorded.

Reading: Dickinson, P. 1951. *Aust J Mar Fresh Res* 2: 245–251. Falla, R. A. & Stokell, G. 1945. *Trans Roy Soc NZ* 74: 320–331. Sim, D. & Powlesland, R. G. 1995. *Notornis* 42: 23–26. Stonehouse, B. 1967. *Ibis* 109: 600–605.

148. PIED SHAG *Phalacrocorax varius* PLATE 34

Other names: Karuhiruhi, Pied Cormorant
Size: 81cm; male 2.2kg, female 1.7kg
Geographical variation: Two subspecies: *varius* breeds in New Zealand, and *hypoleucos* breeds in Australia.
Distribution: Breeds in coastal mainland Australia and in New Zealand. Pied Shags have a patchy breeding distribution within New Zealand, mainly in warmer areas on sheltered coasts, harbours and offshore islands. The main breeding areas are around the Kaipara and Hokianga harbours, on the east coast of the North Island from Doubtless Bay to Gisborne, in the South Island from Tasman Bay through the Marlborough Sounds and south to Banks Peninsula, in Fiordland, and around the east coast of Stewart Island. Colonies are on freshwater lakes at Pupuke (Auckland), Hakanoa (Huntly), Waimanu Lagoon (Waikanae), Zealandia (Wellington), Elterwater (Marlborough) and Rotorua (Kaikoura). Pied Shags are generally sedentary and, unlike their Australian counterpart, rarely venture inland. A few birds, mainly juveniles, disperse well away from breeding areas and can turn up in coastal sites almost anywhere.
Population: Widespread and moderately common (*c.* 5000 birds), especially in the Bay of Islands, inner Hauraki Gulf, Coromandel Peninsula and Marlborough. Most nest in small colonies of 5–30 pairs, but over 50 pairs have been recorded in Whangarei Harbour, in Panmure Basin (Auckland) and near Nelson.
Conservation: Protected nationally vulnerable native. Counts suggest a decline in northern and southern New Zealand, but an increase in central parts. Pied Shags are sometimes illegally persecuted by fishermen who regard them as competitors for fish, and some birds are caught accidentally in fishing nets and craypots. Shags are now known to have a minimal impact on fish stocks, and few are now shot.
Breeding: Nest in colonies, sometimes together with other shags, especially Black and Little shags. Colonies are commonly in pines, pohutukawa or rata growing on cliffs and overhanging the sea, but occasionally they nest in pohutukawa, willows or silver poplars, or on navigation lights and artificial structures over estuaries or lakes. The nest is usually a large platform 0.5m across, built of sticks and seaweed, up to 10m above the water. Nests are generally reused through the season and from year to year.

Most colonies are active all year round, but laying peaks in August–October and February–April. They lay 2–**3–4**–5 pale bluish-green eggs (59 x 38mm, 47g) 2 days apart. Incubation lasts 25–**29**–33 days, but this varies within a clutch so that first eggs take *c.* 31 days to hatch and fourth eggs take *c.* 27 days. The chicks hatch over the space of a few days. Chicks first leave the nest at *c.* 4 weeks old, but fledge at 47–**53**–60 days old. They are fed by their parents for up to 11 weeks after fledging. In Australia, a banded Pied Shag lived over 20 years.
Behaviour: They mostly feed alone but sometimes form flocks of 20+ birds where food is abundant. They often roost in small groups on logs, on rocks and in trees. Generally silent away from their colonies, but at the nest they are noisy, making a variety of harsh croaks, squeals and wheezy whistles.
Feeding: Diet is mainly fish 6–15cm long. Flounder, mullet, perch, smelt and eels are usually taken in water less than 10m deep. Dives usually last 20–30 seconds, depending on water depth. The longest dive recorded was of 225 seconds in 20m deep water. Rest time between dives is 5–10 seconds.
Reading: Lalas, C. 1979. *Notornis* 26: 94–95. Millener, P. R. 1972. MSc thesis, Uni Auckland. Powlesland, R. G. et al. 2008. *Notornis* 55: 69–76. Stonehouse, B. 1967. *Ibis* 109: 600–605. Taylor, M. J. 1987. *Notornis* 34: 41–50.

149. LITTLE BLACK SHAG *Phalacrocorax sulcirostris* PLATE 34

Other name: Little Black Cormorant
Size: 61cm, 800g
Distribution: Breeds in Australasia east of Borneo and Java, in New Caledonia and the North Island of New Zealand, with a few large colonies in the Auckland, Waikato, Rotorua Lakes, Lake Taupo, Hawke's Bay and Lake Wairarapa wetlands. They disperse widely in autumn after breeding, with an influx of birds into coastal areas around Northland and Auckland and into Wellington Harbour. An increasing number winter in the South Island, as far south as Southland, and a straggler has reached The Snares. Fledglings banded at Lake Rotorua have been recovered in the Hauraki Gulf and from Wellington.
Population: Widespread and moderately common (1000–5000 pairs), especially in the North Island. Colonies of 300+ pairs have been recorded at Lakes Whangape (Waikato), Rotorua and Taupo, but these normally last only a few years before the birds shift elsewhere. The number of Little Black Shags seems to be increasing, with a marked increase in numbers seen in winter in the southern North Island and in the South Island since about 1980.
Conservation: Protected native. Little Black Shags are sometimes illegally persecuted by fishermen who regard them as competitors for fish, and some birds are caught accidentally in fishing nets. Shags are now known to have a minimal impact on fish stocks, and few are now shot – this may have contributed to the recent increase in numbers of Little Black Shags.
Breeding: Nests in large colonies, sometimes together with other shags, especially Little Shags. Colonies are commonly in willows overhanging fresh water, but sometimes nests are constructed on the ground on small islands. The nest is usually a platform of sticks about 30cm in diameter. Laying is mostly in November–December, but some autumn nesting has been recorded. They lay 2–4–5 pale bluish-green eggs (48 x 32mm) 2 days apart. No information is available on incubation or fledging periods. In New Zealand, the oldest recorded Little Black Shag lived at least 9 years.
Behaviour: Feeds in flocks of 10–150 birds that work as a group to herd a shoal of fish. They often roost in large groups on logs, piers, rocks and in trees. They are silent away from their colonies, but at the nest they are noisy, making a variety of harsh croaks and whistles.
Feeding: Diet is mainly small fish and freshwater crayfish. The main inland prey are smelt, bullies and goldfish. Smelt and whitebait are probably the main marine species taken, judging by the flocking behaviour of birds in estuaries and sheltered harbours. Most fish are taken close to the surface, and dive times are generally 5–10 seconds. Rest times between dives last only 2–3 seconds.
Reading: Potts, K. J. 1977. *Wildlife – A Review* 8: 34–38.

150. KING SHAG *Leucocarbo carunculatus* PLATE 35

Size: 76cm, 2.5kg
Distribution: New Zealand only. Breeds on very small islands in the outer Marlborough Sounds – Duffers Reef, North Trio Islands, White Rocks, Sentinel Rock, Stewart Island (southeast of D'Urville Island) and Rahuihui Island. They are sedentary and generally remain within the Marlborough Sounds, especially favouring 20–40m deep water in the outer parts of Pelorus and Queen

Charlotte sounds. Sight records from Lake Horowhenua (1966), and Kaikoura (2011).
Population: Between 1992 and 2002, the population was estimated to be about 645 birds, with 102–126 pairs, mainly on North Trio, Duffers Reef and White Rocks.
Conservation: Protected endangered endemic. King Shags are sometimes illegally shot by fishermen, and a few birds are caught accidentally in fishing nets. Shags are now known to have a minimal impact on fish stocks, and few are now shot. King Shags are very wary, and some nests fail if boats approach colonies too closely.
Breeding: Nests in winter in colonies on small exposed islands, sometimes only a few metres above high-water mark. The nest is usually a level platform about 0.5m in diameter, made of twigs, branchlets and kelp, and cemented with guano. Nest-building activity picks up in March and reaches a peak in May. Laying is mostly in May–June. They lay 1–2–3 pale blue eggs (65 x 41mm). There is no information on incubation or fledging periods.
Behaviour: Sometimes roosts in flocks on rocks or on mussel-farm buoys, but feeds solitarily. Birds from the Duffers Reef colony fly low and directly to their feeding grounds on average 8km away. They spend much time early in the season collecting nest material or circling the colony. They are silent away from their colonies and make little noise at their colonies, except while displaying.
Feeding: Diet is mainly 10–15cm long seafloor-dwelling fish such as flatfish (especially witch), sole, opalfish, triplefins, blue cod, red cod and red scorpionfish. Crabs and crayfish are occasionally taken. Dives can be up to 90m deep, but preferred feeding sites are in 20–40m deep water with a flat bottom. Average dive times are *c.* 120 seconds, with a maximum of 190 seconds recorded. Most rests between dives last 70–140 seconds.
Reading: Bell, M. 2010. *Notornis* 57: 33–36. Brown, D. 2001. *Notornis* 48: 177–178. Lalas, C. & Brown, D. 1998. *Notornis* 45: 129–140. Nelson, A. 1971. *Notornis* 18: 30–37. Schuckard, R. 1994. *Notornis* 41: 93–108. Schuckard, R. 2006. *Notornis* 53: 297–307.

151. STEWART ISLAND SHAG *Leucocarbo chalconotus* PLATE 35

Other name: Bronze Shag (dark phase)
Size: 68cm, 2.5kg
Geographical variation: The two main colour forms, pied and bronze, interbreed freely. Birds breeding in Otago are much larger and have more developed papillae above the bill than those in Foveaux Strait. The bronze phase predominates in the north, while the pied phase predominates in the south; a few birds have intermediate plumage.
Distribution: New Zealand only. Breeds from near Moeraki (North Otago) to Foveaux Strait and around Stewart Island. About 15 colonies of 10–500 pairs are occupied each year, but numbers fluctuate widely at particular colonies, and some colonies are abandoned only to be reoccupied several years later. Colonies are on small islands and on sea cliffs on the mainland. After breeding, some birds disperse northwards to about the Waitaki River and west to Te Waewae Bay. Vagrants have reached Lake Ellesmere and The Snares.
Population: Moderately common around the south-eastern South Island and Foveaux Strait. The total population is 1600–1800 pairs.
Conservation: Protected vulnerable endemic. Stewart Island Shags are sometimes illegally shot by fishermen, and a few birds are caught accidentally in fishing nets. Colony sizes fluctuate from year to year, making long-term population trends hard to assess.
Breeding: Nests in colonies on islands and on sea cliffs, sometimes only a few metres above high-water mark. The nest is usually a level pedestal about 0.5m in diameter, made of twigs and seaweed and cemented with guano. The breeding season is long and variable, but laying is mostly in September–November. They lay 1–2–3 pale blue eggs (66 x 42mm). There is no information on incubation or fledging periods.
Behaviour: Sometimes roosts on headlands, islands and wharves in huge flocks of 1000+ birds, particularly in April–May. They are silent away from their colonies, and only the male calls at the nest.
Feeding: Diet in Otago is mainly bullies and sea-floor-dwelling fish such as flounder and sole. Marine invertebrates such as crabs, shrimps, octopus and polychaete worms are occasionally taken. Most food is taken in water less than 30m deep, but they feed up to 15km from land. Average dive times are 50–70 seconds, but the maximum recorded is 169 seconds. Most rests between dives last 20–40 seconds.
Reading: Lalas, C. 1983. PhD thesis, Uni Otago. Sansom, M. L. 1956. *Notornis* 7: 16–20. Watt, J. P. C. 1975. *Notornis* 22: 265–272.

152. CHATHAM ISLANDS SHAG *Leucocarbo onslowi* PLATE 35

Size: 63cm, 2.25kg
Distribution: Breeds only on Chatham Island (including Motuhinahina Island in Te Whanga Lagoon), Pitt Island, including nearby Rabbit Island, and the Star Keys. They feed through coastal waters of the Chatham group and occasionally in brackish water in Te Whanga Lagoon.
Population: Widespread and locally common, Breeds in small colonies of up to about 40 pairs, but formerly of up to 300 pairs. The population has declined rapidly in recent decades, going from 842 pairs at 10 colonies in 1997 to only 355 pairs in 2011.
Conservation: Protected critically endangered endemic. The widespread decline, even at remote colonies, suggests changes in food supplies at sea, but some are accidentally caught in craypots. Some are illegally shot by fishermen, and several accessible mainland colonies (e.g. Cape Fournier) have been abandoned because of disturbance by people or farm stock, and associated gull predation. Colonies are sometimes disturbed by fur seals.
Breeding: Nests in colonies on islands and exposed rocky headlands, usually well above high-water mark. The nest is a level platform about 0.5m in diameter, made of twigs, iceplant and seaweed. Laying is mostly in August–December, but there is variation both between and within colonies – the Te Whanga Lagoon colony usually starts several months before the coastal colonies. They lay 1–2–3–4 pale blue eggs (61 x 44mm). Incubation period is *c.* 30 days, and fledgling period is *c.* 30–40 days.
Behaviour: Sometimes roosts in flocks of 100+ birds, but generally feeds alone.
Feeding: Diet is mainly small (<25cm long) fish, especially flatfish, opalfish and bullies, and the occasional squid, cuttlefish and octopus. Most are taken from deep offshore waters, but birds occasionally feed close inshore or in rockpools.
Reading: Bell, D. & Bell, M. 2000 *Notornis* 47: 148–153. Bester, A. J. & Charteris, M. 2005. *Notornis* 52: 6–10. Fleming, C. A. 1939. *Emu* 38: 380–413. Imber, M. J. 1994. *Notornis* 41(S): 97–108. Lalas, C. 1983. PhD thesis, Uni Otago.

153. BOUNTY ISLANDS SHAG *Leucocarbo ranfurlyi* PLATE 35

Size: 71cm, 2.5kg
Distribution: Breeds only on the Bounty Islands; commonly feeds within the group, but some venture into the open ocean. Two birds seen at Bollons Island, Antipodes, in 1950 were probably of this species.
Population: A significant decline has occurred since November 1978, when 569 pairs were counted, including 165 pairs on Lion Island alone. In 1997, there were 120 nests counted and population was estimated to be *c.* 330 birds, but in 2005 and 2011, the population was estimated to be *c.* 300 pairs.
Conservation: Protected endangered endemic. The rapid decline in the 1980s and 1990s is likely to have been a result of changes at sea in their food supply, because there are few other possible impacts at such a remote site. The population may have now stabilised at a lower level.
Breeding: Nests mainly in colonies on narrow cliffside ledges, but a few nests are on rocky ridges. The nest is a flattened bowl 35cm in diameter, made of seaweed, feathers, stones and mud. Laying is in October–November. They lay 2–3 eggs (64 x 41mm). There is no information on incubation or fledging periods.
Behaviour: Sometimes feeds in flocks of up to 300 birds. They are generally silent, but the male only makes calls during displays.
Feeding: Diet includes small fish and squid, snails, isopods and sea urchins.
Reading: Robertson, C. J. R. & van Tets, G. F. 1982. *Notornis* 29: 311–336.

154. AUCKLAND ISLANDS SHAG *Leucocarbo colensoi* PLATE 35

Size: 63cm, 2kg
Distribution: Breeds only on the Auckland Islands. Commonly seen around the sheltered harbours and inlets of the southern and eastern side of the islands, and at Port Ross in the north; uncommon elsewhere. A vagrant was resident on The Snares from 1994 to 2001.
Population: Probably *c.* 4500 birds in 2011, with the largest breeding concentration on Enderby Island where

there were *c.* 1350 nests in 10 colonies.
Conservation: Protected vulnerable endemic. The population is limited to one island group, where nests are either on predator-free islands or on Auckland Island in sites that are largely inaccessible to pigs and cats.
Breeding: Nests in colonies on cliff-side ledges, usually under an overhang or under trees to afford protection from skuas. The nest is a flattened bowl made of twigs, tussock, seaweed, peat and guano. Laying is in November–February. They lay 3 pale blue eggs (62 x 39mm) at intervals of 2–4 days. The incubation period is about 28 days. The fledging period is not known.
Behaviour: Sometimes feeds and roosts in flocks. During courtship displays, the male utters barks and ticking sounds, and females give a soft purr.
Feeding: No detailed studies, but their diet includes small fish, squid, and marine invertebrates such as sea urchins and snails.

155. CAMPBELL ISLANDS SHAG *Leucocarbo campbelli* PLATE 35

Size: 63cm, 2kg
Distribution: Breeds only on the Campbell Islands, and has not been recorded far from the group, except that Otago Museum has a male specimen labelled from Antipodes Island that may have been collected in 1888. Commonly seen around the sheltered harbours and inlets of the eastern and southern coast of Campbell Island, especially in winter.
Population: In 1975, *c.* 2000 nests and an estimated population of 8000 birds. No recent estimates.
Conservation: Protected endemic. The population is limited to one island group, but no known threat exists.
Breeding: Nests in inaccessible colonies of up to 150 nests on cliff-side ledges, islets and in caves. The nest is a flattened bowl, made of twigs and tussock. Laying is in November–February. They lay 2 pale blue eggs (64 x 39mm). There is no information on incubation or fledging periods. A banded bird lived at least 13 years.
Behaviour: In winter 1960, a flock of 2000 birds was recorded in Perseverance Harbour, but usually they hunt in coordinated packs of 30–100 birds. These flocks spread out as they start to feed but maintain synchronous diving, so that all birds are submerged at once. During courtship, males utter barks and females apparently remain silent.
Feeding: No detailed studies, but their diet includes small shoaling fish and marine invertebrates.
Reading: Bailey, A. M. & Sorensen, J. H. 1962. *Subantarctic Campbell Island.* Denver: Denver Mus Nat Hist.

156. SPOTTED SHAG *Stictocarbo punctatus* PLATE 35

Other names: Parekareka, Kawau Tikitiki, Blue Shag (southern subspecies)
Size: 70cm, 1200g
Geographical variation: Two subspecies: the Spotted Shag *punctatus* breeds in the North Island and the northern and eastern South Island, and the Blue Shag *steadi* breeds around the southwestern South Island and Stewart Island.
Distribution: Breeds only in New Zealand. In the North Island, Spotted Shags breed in the inner Hauraki Gulf, on the west coast of Auckland and the Waikato, on Kapiti Island and in Wellington Harbour on Matiu/Somes, Mokopuna and Makaro/Ward islands. In the South Island, they nest in Tasman Bay and the Marlborough Sounds, down the Kaikoura coast to Banks Peninsula, and from North Otago to the Catlins. Blue Shags nest in a few scattered colonies in Westland (e.g. Perpendicular Point at Punakaiki, and the Open Bay Islands) and on islands in Foveaux Strait and around Stewart Island. There is much local movement between feeding and nesting areas.

Spotted Shags favour the marine environment off rocky shores and rarely venture into enclosed estuaries, freshwater habitats or sandy sea coasts. After breeding, most form large winter flocks and often fly in long lines between their feeding and roosting sites. Most birds remain within 200km of their breeding grounds, but some long-distance movement occurs, such as the annual appearance of a mixed-age flock of 20–50 birds in Hawke's Bay over 300km from the nearest known breeding site. Odd birds (especially juveniles) can appear almost anywhere, including several records from Lake Taupo; a juvenile banded on Matiu/Somes Island in July was caught five months later on the Coromandel Peninsula, 500km away.
Population: Widespread and locally common (10,000–50,000 pairs), Spotted Shags are probably increasing, with marked increases recorded on Banks Peninsula

and in Wellington Harbour in the past 40 years.
Conservation: Protected endemic. Spotted Shags are sometimes illegally shot by fishermen, and some birds are caught accidentally in fishing nets and craypots. Shags are now known to have a minimal impact on fish stocks, and few are now shot. Spotted Shags often breed at sites where nests are difficult to count and often change sites, so population trends are hard to assess.
Breeding: Nests in colonies of 10–700 pairs, normally apart from other shags. The colonies are usually on coastal cliff ledges or rocky islets. The nest is a platform about 0.6m in diameter, made of seaweed, grass and iceplant. The breeding season is variable from year to year and in different parts of the country; in the Hauraki Gulf, peaks of laying are in March, August and December; on Matiu/Somes Island, the two peaks are in June and November; but at Banks Peninsula and Otago Harbour, the only peak is in September–November. Laying of Blue Shags at Punakaiki is quite variable, March–April in some years but August in others.
They lay 1–**3**–4 pale blue eggs (58 x 36mm, 42g) at 2-day intervals. The incubation period is 28–**31**–35 days. Chicks are guarded continuously until *c.* 30 days old and are fed about four times a day by both parents. Chicks leave the nest and fledge at 57–**62**–71 days old. The oldest Spotted Shag recorded was over 10 years old.
Behaviour: Form large flocks of up to 2000 birds when feeding, or roosting on headlands, sandspits or beaches out of the breeding season. They are silent away from their colonies. Displaying males are noisy, but females remain silent.
Feeding: Diet is mainly small fish less than 15cm long and marine invertebrates. The main fish taken are ahuru, red cod, gudgeon, bullies and sprats; arrow squid are also taken frequently. Spotted Shags feed mainly in deep water up to 15km from the shore, but they sometimes feed in harbours. Their average dive time is *c.* 30 seconds, with a rest of 10–15 seconds between dives. The longest dive recorded lasted 70 seconds.
Reading: Doherty, J. L. & Brager, S. 1997. *Notornis* 44: 49–54. Fenwick, G. D. & Browne, W. M. M. 1975. *J Roy Soc NZ* 5: 31–45. Kinsky, F. C. 1970. *Notornis* 17: 102–104. Lalas, C. 1983. PhD thesis, Uni Otago. Stonehouse, B. 1967. *Ibis* 109: 600–605. Turbott, E. G. 1956. *Rec Auck Inst Mus* 4: 343–363.

157. PITT ISLAND SHAG *Stictocarbo featherstoni* PLATE 35

Size: 63cm, 1200g
Distribution: Breeds on Chatham and Pitt islands and on many of the smaller islands in the group. Not recorded elsewhere.
Population: Widespread and locally common. Breeds in small colonies of up to about 40 pairs. Numbers have declined steeply in recent decades from 729 breeding pairs in 1997, to 547 pairs in 2003, and 434 pairs in 2011.
Conservation: Protected critically endangered endemic. The causes for the recent decline are not clear, but at-sea effects are implicated because remote colonies away from human disturbance have also shown declines. Some are accidentally caught in fishing nets and craypots, and a few are illegally shot by fishermen.
Breeding: Nests in small colonies of 5–20 pairs, normally apart from Chatham Island shags. The colonies are usually on coastal cliff ledges or rocky islets. The nest is a platform *c.* 30cm in diameter, made of seaweed, grass and iceplant. The breeding season is extended. The peak of laying is in August–September, but laying continues as late as December. They lay 1–**3**–4 pale blue eggs (58 x 35mm) probably at 2-day intervals. Adults share incubation for *c.* 30 days. The parents guard their chicks for the first fortnight, but then leave them unattended for long periods during the 6–8 week fledging period.
Behaviour: Breeds in much smaller colonies than Chatham Island Shags or the closely related Spotted Shag. They usually feed alone. Silent away from their colonies; displaying males are noisy, but females remain silent.
Feeding: Diet is mainly small fish, especially bullies, and marine invertebrates such as snails and polychaete worms. They feed mostly in coastal waters up to 20m deep, but occasionally feed in the brackish water of Te Whanga Lagoon. Their average dive time is *c.* 30 seconds, with a 15-second rest between dives. The longest dive recorded lasted 68 seconds.
Reading: Bell, D. & Bell, M. 2000. *Notornis* 47: 148–153. Bester, A. J. & Charteris, M. 2005. *Notornis* 52: 6–10. Fleming, C. A. 1939. *Emu* 38: 380–413. Imber, M. J. 1994. *Notornis* 41(S): 97–108. Lalas, C. 1983. PhD thesis, Uni Otago.

DARTERS *Anhingidae*

2 species; 1 vagrant reaches New Zealand.

Between them, the two species of darter have a near worldwide distribution in freshwater habitats, except for Europe, the Pacific Islands and high latitudes. These large birds resemble shags but are slimmer and have a long, thin, unhooked bill and a very long snaky neck. They have long stiff tails and long rounded wings, which are held out to dry, shag-like, when the birds perch after swimming.

158. DARTER *Anhinga melanogaster* PLATE 34

Size: 90cm, 1750g
Geographical variation: Of the three or four subspecies, *novaehollandiae* of Australia and New Guinea is seen occasionally in New Zealand.
Distribution: Breeds widely, from Africa through Asia to Australia. In Australia, most breeding colonies are in the Murray–Darling Basin and along the eastern seaboard, but after breeding they use columns of rising hot air to soar and glide from one place to another and disperse widely. The only confirmed New Zealand records are a fresh skin of an adult female found nailed to the wall of a shed near Hokitika (January 1874), Lake Waiharahara, Kaitaia (December 1992), Lake Daniells, Lewis Pass (November 2003), and Wellington Harbour (December 2003).
Feeding: Feeds in lakes, ponds and slow-moving streams by sinking slowly underwater and then swimming with webbed feet to dart the neck out and stab fish on the needle-like bill. On surfacing, the bird tosses the fish into the air and catches it head first. Sometimes they eat insects caught above the water. Dives last *c.* 30 seconds, with only a 5-second pause between dives.
Reading: van Tets, G. F. & Scarlett, R. J. 1972. *Notornis* 19: 85–86.

FRIGATEBIRDS *Fregatidae*

5 species, of which 2 reach New Zealand.

Sailors called frigatebirds 'man-o'-war birds' because of their piratical habits. They inhabit tropical seas, often hundreds of kilometres from land, soaring high on thermals. Away from the breeding grounds, they are most often seen over land gracefully gliding on updraughts over the windward shore when a tropical storm is approaching. They feed entirely on the wing, taking flying fish and squid by surface dipping and, to a lesser extent, pursuing other seabirds, particularly boobies, and forcing them to disgorge their food. They breed on remote islands and atolls, nesting in colonies in trees or bushes, or, if necessary, on the ground. The nest is made of loosely woven sticks. They lay a single white egg.

159. GREAT FRIGATEBIRD *Fregata minor* PLATE 32

Other names: Greater Frigatebird, Man-o'-war Bird.
Size: 95cm; 1450g
Geographical variation: Of the five subspecies, *palmerstoni* of the western and central Pacific Ocean is the form recorded in New Zealand.
Distribution: Breeds on islands in the Indian and Pacific oceans, and a few nest in the southwestern Atlantic Ocean. The nearest breeding places to New Zealand are on islands off New Caledonia (Chesterfield, Surprise and Walpole), Tonga and American Samoa. Great Frigatebirds probably get swept south in summer and autumn by tropical storms. About 15 New Zealand records since 1855, between the Kermadec Islands and Westport, mostly on the east coast of the North Island or inland at lakes.
Behaviour: In New Zealand, usually seen drifting effortlessly high above the water or shore facing into the prevailing wind, or chasing terns or gannets, skua-like, and forcing them to drop or disgorge food, which is deftly caught in mid-air.

160. LESSER FRIGATEBIRD *Fregata ariel* PLATE 32

Other name: Least Frigatebird
Size: 76cm, 1000g
Geographical variation: Of three subspecies, *ariel* of the central Indian Ocean, Australia and the southwestern Pacific is the form recorded from New Zealand waters.
Distribution: Breeds on islands of the tropical Indian, Pacific and southwestern Atlantic oceans. They are more often recorded in New Zealand than Great Frigatebirds because the nearest breeding sites are on islands off Queensland, New Caledonia, Fiji, Tonga and Samoa. Lesser Frigatebirds probably get swept south in summer and autumn by tropical storms. About 40 specimens have been recovered dead in New Zealand since 1907, mostly in the north, but including Cook Strait and the Chatham Islands; also over 25 sightings, mostly at the Kermadecs and in Northland, but as far south as the Catlins.
Behaviour: In New Zealand, usually seen effortlessly drifting high above the shore facing into the prevailing wind, or chasing terns or gannets, skua-like, and forcing them to drop or disgorge food, which is deftly caught in mid-air.

HERONS, EGRETS and BITTERNS *Ardeidae*

About 65 species; 10 in New Zealand, including 5 breeding species. An endemic species, the New Zealand Little Bittern *Ixobrychus novaezelandiae,* became extinct in the late 1800s.

This family occurs worldwide, mainly in the tropics. Their broad-winged, flapping flight is ponderous but strong, though the smaller species are faster. Apart from the bitterns and night herons, they are active by day. They have a slender body and long neck and legs; night herons have a stouter body and shorter neck, giving them a hunched appearance. All have a straight, dagger-like bill and a short tail. The bill, on a long, often kinked neck, is ideal for seizing and skewering fish.

Patches of powder down are on the breast and rump of bitterns, and the thighs also in egrets. The middle of the three long, forward-pointing toes has serrations along the side like teeth of a comb and is thought to remove fish slime and mud during grooming and preening. All species give a low-pitched croak when alarmed but feed silently.

Egrets and herons are very similar; for example, all have bare facial skin, often distinctively coloured. Egrets are white; herons are usually grey – the distinction is useful but not absolute. Egrets are gregarious and breed in colonies, often mixed with other egrets and with ibises; true herons are solitary. Both typically have plumes when breeding. Their nest is an untidy platform of sticks and twigs. Incubation starts with the first or second egg, and so chicks are of different ages and sizes. Adults feed the young with regurgitated food, not offering whole food. The young start breeding at 1 or 2 years old, sometimes still in immature plumage.

Herons, egrets and bitterns feed mainly on fish, also frogs and insects. Larger species may take small mammals and birds as chance offers.

Reading: Hancock, J. & Elliot, H. 1978. *The Herons of the World*. London: London Editions. Hancock. J. & Kushlan, J. 1984. *The Herons Handbook*. London: Croom Helm.

161. PACIFIC HERON *Ardea pacifica* PLATE 39

Other names: White-necked Heron
Size: 90cm, 900g
Distribution: Despite its name, it breeds only in Australia and New Guinea. Nine records in New Zealand: Methven (April–July 1952), Matamata (July 1978), Houhora, Far North (October 1981), Waipu (January 1984), Hokitika (June–July 2002), Oamaru (January–March 2003), Toko, Taranaki (June 2003), northern Southland (May 2013–April 2014) and Wayby, Wellsford (September 2013).
Behaviour: Favours margins of freshwater swamps and dams and damp pasture inland. Similar to White-faced Herons in feeding and flight behaviour.

162. WHITE HERON *Ardea modesta* PLATE 36

Other names: Kotuku, Eastern Great Egret, Great White Heron
Size: 92cm, of which length of body is under half; 900g
Distribution: Breeds from India through Southeast Asia, China and Japan, to Australia and New Zealand. In New Zealand, they breed only at the Waitangiroto River, near Okarito, Westland. After breeding, they disperse widely, especially northwards; therefore they can appear at any shallow freshwater lake, swamp, damp pasture, estuary, or mangrove creek at some time. Some have reached the Chatham, The Snares, Auckland and Campbell islands as strays blown off course during this dispersal. From time to time, their winter number is augmented by irruptions from Australia, such as small ones in 1952 and 2013, and a large irruption in winter 1957, when *c.* 150 extra birds were recorded, mainly in Northland, Waikato, Bay of Plenty, Canterbury and Otago. These extra birds did not appear to join the existing breeding population.
Population: 150–200 birds; half are non-breeders.
Conservation: Protected, nationally critically endangered, native. The White Heron colony at Okarito is in a reserve, and public access is controlled to minimise disturbance to breeding birds but allow viewing from observation hides. As the colony has grown, the number of fledglings per nest has declined and the total population has remained reasonably stable between the periodic irruptions.
Breeding: The Okarito colony has been known since pre-European times. It is in a kahikatea swamp through which the sluggish Waitangiroto River crawls. Some of the nests are in the crowns of tree ferns; others are in kowhai or kamahi. Associated Royal Spoonbills prefer adjacent taller kahikatea. Both sexes share nest-building. Laying is in September–October. They lay 3–4–5 pale bluish-green eggs (52 x 36mm). Both sexes incubate for *c.* 25 days and care for the young. The fledging period is *c.* 42 days, and the young leave the colony at *c.* 64 days old.
Behaviour: White Herons make a harsh grating call in flight; otherwise silent, except at the breeding colony.
Feeding: Diet is mainly small fish and eels, frogs, shrimps and aquatic insects, which they swallow whole, and occasionally small mammals such as mice and small birds such as silvereyes. They feed by quietly walking or standing motionless, lunging with their dagger-like bill and a kinked neck at prey whenever it comes within range.
Reading: Andrew, I. G. 1963. *Notornis* 10: 311–315. Miller, C. 2001. *Notornis* 48: 157–163.

163. CATTLE EGRET *Ardea ibis* PLATE 36

Size: 50cm; male 390g, female 340g
Geographical variation: Two subspecies: *ibis* of Africa spread in the twentieth century to South and then North America. The larger *coromanda* of southern and eastern Asia, including Japan and southern Korea and China, spread south to Indonesia, Australia and New Zealand.
Distribution: Breeds widely in the Americas, Africa, Asia and Australasia. In Australia, they are common and widespread but breed especially in Queensland and New South Wales. First records in New Zealand were in 1963, possibly 1956, and from then they have been recorded annually as steadily increasing winter visitors until they reached a peak in 1986 of well over 3000 birds. They arrive mainly in April–May, making a landfall somewhere on western coasts, stay for a while to feed, and then move to a few favoured farms or open habitats in the North, South, Stewart and Chatham islands. Vagrants have been recorded from the Kermadecs, The Snares, Auckland and Campbell islands. Most return to Australia in October–November, but some, mostly juveniles, remain throughout the summer. They have not bred in New Zealand.

The main wintering sites in the North Island are: Awanui (Far North), Ruawai (Northland), Parakai (Auckland), Aka Aka and Piako (South Auckland), Rangiriri and Lake Ngaroto (Waikato), Awaiti (Bay of Plenty), Lake Hatuma (Hawke's Bay), Featherston (Wairarapa), Whirokino and Lake Horowhenua (Manawatu); and in the South Island: Takaka (Nelson), Grovetown (Marlborough), Karamea, Westport and Kokatahi (West Coast), Ellesmere (Canterbury), West Taieri and Inch Clutha (Otago), and Wyndham and Thornbury (Southland).
Population: National counts in late August rose from 293 in 1977 to a peak in 1986 of 3000+, fell to 2000+ in 1987, and to 1000+ in 1988. Since 2000, numbers have dropped to fewer than 500 each year.
Behaviour: Cattle Egrets are gregarious. In Australia, they nest colonially in trees or beside swamps and lakes or on islands in settled or industrial areas, often with

other egret species and with ibises. In New Zealand, they feed in small parties or in flocks of up to several hundred birds, and they roost in tall trees, mostly macrocarpas, or on or near the ground in swamp or lake-side vegetation. They are shy and wary, and seldom allow close approach.
Feeding: In New Zealand, they associate with cattle and with other domestic stock, especially sheep. They walk slowly forward, neck outstretched, peering at the ground, with backward and forward movement of the head. Mostly they search independently, but sometimes they seem coordinated: those at the back of the flock fly to the front and the flock rolls forward along a drain or across a paddock. Their diet is mainly earthworms, grass grubs, larvae of moths and flies, and in the north, crickets. Young birds that oversummer also feed on flies, grasshoppers and a few mice. They may sway their necks from side to side before lunging at flies on grass. Occasionally they perch on resting cattle or sheep, but do not seem to use them as vantage points to scan for prey or to feed on ticks and other parasites of large animals, as they do in tropical countries.
Reading: Bridgman, H. A. & Maddock, M. 1994. *Notornis* 41: 189–204. Heather, B. D. 1991. *Notornis* 38: 165–169. Jackson, W. R. & Olsen, M. 1988. *Notornis* 35: 83–85. Maddock, M. 1993. *Corella* 17: 93–99. McKilligan, N. G. 1985. *Ibis* 127: 530–536.

164. PLUMED EGRET *Ardea intermedia* PLATE 36

Other name: Intermediate Egret
Size: 64cm, 450g
Geographical variation: Three subspecies: *brachyrhyncha* of Africa, *intermedia* of southern Asia, Japan and the Philippines, and *plumifera* of eastern Indonesia, Australia and New Guinea.
Distribution: Breeds in Africa, south of the Sahara; southern and eastern Asia and Australasia. In Australia they breed only on the mainland, in the north and east from Broome to Victoria, and mostly in the Murray–Darling Basin. About 15 New Zealand records: Manawatu Estuary (early 1970s); lower Waikato, near Lakes Whangape and Ohinewai (1979, 1981, 1985, 1993); Kaikohe (1986); Avon–Heathcote Estuary (1986); Cobden, Greymouth (1990); Lake Ellesmere (three in 1998, four in 2011); Whangapoua Estuary, Coromandel (2001); Motueka (2004); Lawrence (2004); Auckland (2006–07).
Behaviour: Similar to White Herons in their feeding methods, but they prefer freshwater habitats and seldom visit estuaries or other saline coastal places. They sometimes feed in pasture, often in the presence of Cattle Egrets.

165. WHITE-FACED HERON *Egretta novaehollandiae* PLATE 37

Other names: Blue Heron, Blue Crane
Size: 67cm, 550g
Geographical variation: Two subspecies: *nana* in New Caledonia and the Loyalty Islands, and *novaehollandiae* throughout the rest of Australasia.
Distribution: Breeds in southern Indonesia, New Guinea, Australia, Lord Howe and Norfolk islands and New Zealand. Occasionally reported in New Zealand from 1865 to the 1930s, they became established and are now the most common heron, having benefited from the widespread conversion of forest to farmland. They are open-country generalists and are found in swamp margins, lake shores, farm dams and creeks, riverbeds, town parks; also mudflats, estuaries, rocky shores, and sandy beaches inside harbours and estuaries.

Breeding was initially confirmed in 1941 at Shag River, Otago, but they became widespread on the New Zealand mainland in the 1940s and increased explosively in the late 1950s and early 1960s. They colonised the Chatham Islands by the early 1970s, and vagrants have been recorded from the Kermadecs, Antipodes, The Snares, Auckland and Campbell islands.
Population: Widespread and common, especially in lowland districts with rough pasture and nearby lakes and estuaries.
Conservation: Protected self-introduced native. White-faced Herons spread and increased rapidly between the 1940s and 1970s, but numbers have stabilised or declined slightly.
Breeding: Breeds solitarily or in loose groups, usually high up in belts of macrocarpas, pines or eucalypts, not necessarily near water. The nest is an untidy bundle of sticks and twigs, not easy to see, in a fork or well out on a branch. At the Chathams especially, they nest on cliff ledges and under rocks just above high-water mark, in sites usually used by Reef Herons. Very long breeding season: laying starts in June in the north, later further south, with the peak about October. They lay 3–4–5 pale blue-green eggs (45 x 33mm), which both sexes incubate for *c.* 26 days. Usually only two young are raised, fed by both adults. Unlike other herons, the young stay at or near the nest until they are able to fly, at about 6 weeks old.
Behaviour: Mainly solitary, but they form loose flocks in winter on damp and flooded pasture, often with Cattle Egrets and Black-backed Gulls. When not breeding, they may roost together. They are often seen perched on a fencepost or the lip of a stock water-trough. In flight, a harsh 'graaw' is quite common.
Feeding: Diet is mainly fish, frogs and tadpoles, aquatic and pasture insects, spiders, earthworms and mice. They stalk through the shallows of wetlands, darting a dagger-like bill forwards by straightening out their long neck, or pausing to rake one foot rapidly back and forth.
Reading: Hemmings, A. D. & Chappell, R. G. 1988. *Notornis* 35: 245–247. Lo, P. L. 1984. *Notornis* 31: 95. Lo, P. L. 1991. *Notornis* 38: 63–71. Lo, P. L. & Fordham, R. A. 1986. *Notornis* 33: 233–245. Lowe, K. W. 1983. *Corella* 7: 101–108. Moore, P. J. 1984. *Notornis* 31: 285–299.

166. LITTLE EGRET *Egretta garzetta* PLATE 36

Size: 60cm, 400g
Geographical variation: Three subspecies, of which *immaculata* of Australasia is the form seen in New Zealand.
Distribution: Breeds from Africa and southern Europe, east to India, Southeast Asia, China, Japan, Indonesia and Australia, including Tasmania. Since the first records in 1944 and 1951, they have become scarce annual migrants or stragglers to New Zealand from Australia, usually arriving in autumn and departing in early spring. They sometimes oversummer. Little Egrets have been recorded at many localities, mainly coastal, throughout the North and South islands. Most are in singles, but occasionally groups of up to five are recorded. Two vagrants reached Raoul Island, Kermadecs (1974).
Behaviour: Little Egrets are quite unlike White Herons or Intermediate Egrets in their feeding methods – they are very active, chasing after fish and other animal food with a high-stepping gait, wings upraised. They prefer estuaries and other tidal wetlands to freshwater habitats.

167. REEF HERON *Egretta sacra* PLATES 36 AND 37

Other names: Matuku moana, Eastern Reef Egret
Size: 66cm, 400g
Geographical variation: Two subspecies, *albolineata* of New Caledonia and the Loyalty Islands, and *sacra* elsewhere. Reef Herons are usually dimorphic, with a dark phase (the only one seen breeding in New Zealand) and a white phase (common in the Pacific Islands but recorded only once in New Zealand). Occasionally there is also a third, mottled phase, which is intermediate.
Distribution: Eastern Asia from Bangladesh to southern Korea and Japan, Australia and New Zealand, and eastward through the tropical Pacific to the Marquesas, Tuamotu and Austral islands. Reef Herons are widespread in the North, South and Stewart islands and adjacent islands, mainly along rocky shores or in mangrove-filled estuaries and tidal streams, not on long, sandy beaches. They are seldom inland, although occasionally seen at Lake Taupo. Scarce on Stewart Island and a rare vagrant to the Kermadec, Chatham and Auckland islands. The white phase has been seen in New Zealand once: Avon–Heathcote Estuary (June 1987).
Population: *c.* 500 birds. Moderate numbers on the coasts of Northland, Coromandel Peninsula and in the Marlborough Sounds.
Conservation: Protected nationally endangered native. In New Zealand, Reef Herons are less widespread than they used to be, probably not because of competition with White-faced Herons but largely owing to increased human disturbance on the coast and mammalian predation.
Breeding: Solitary nesters in caves, in crevices between or behind rocks, on rock shelves under an overhang, in cliff-side vegetation under clumps of flax or *Astelia*, or among the roots of pohutukawa. Nests are a platform of sticks or twigs, made up of seaweed or such trees and shrubs as are washed up by the tide. Laying is mainly in September–December, with a peak in October. They lay 2–3–5 pale blue-green eggs (46 x 35mm), and both sexes incubate for 25–28 days. The young fledge at 5–6 weeks old. The oldest recorded Reef Heron in Australia lived at least 14 years.
Behaviour: Usually solitary but roost in small flocks, especially in Northland mangroves at high tide. Their daily movements are influenced by the tides – they feed mainly on falling and low tides.
Feeding: Diet is mainly small fish, including eels and flounder, also crabs and molluscs. They feed largely by crouching, body and head horizontal, neck retracted, jabbing at prey, sometimes flicking their wings. Sometimes they stalk with the body above the horizontal, the neck curved but not retracted, and the head above the level of the body.
Reading: Bell, M. 2010. *Notornis* 57: 152–155. Edgar, A. T. 1978. *Notornis* 25: 25–58.

168. NANKEEN NIGHT HERON *Nycticorax caledonicus* PLATE 37

Other name: Rufous Night Heron
Size: 60cm, 800g
Geographical variation: Of the five subspecies, *australasiae* of eastern Indonesia, New Guinea and Australia has colonised New Zealand.
Distribution: Breeds in the Philippines, Micronesia, Indonesia, New Guinea, Bismarck Archipelago, Solomon Islands, New Caledonia, Australia, and recently in New Zealand. In Australia, they are a vagrant to Tasmania but common in the north, east and southwest, and are especially common along the coastal rivers of southeastern Australia and the inland rivers of the Murray–Darling Basin.

First recorded in 1842, and unsuccessfully liberated in Wellington in 1852. About 25 records of vagrants since then, including a sighting of an adult and two immatures near Blenheim in 1958, which suggested possible breeding. Banded birds released from Wellington Zoo in 1982 were later reported as far away as Pakawau, Golden Bay (1983) and Warkworth, North Auckland (1984), as well as at Lower Hutt (1984).

In 1994, nine birds (six immatures and three adults) were seen in willows along the Whanganui River between Pipiriki and Jerusalem, and breeding was proven on this stretch of river in 1995. Roosts have become established at Jerusalem and three sites downriver as far as Upokongaro. An immature bird seen near Blenheim in March 2012 may have come from this population.
Population: *c.* 50 birds, but difficult to count except at known roosts.
Conservation: Protected coloniser. This apparently natural colonisation is unlikely to have any adverse effects on existing native species.
Breeding: In Australia, Nankeen Night Herons breed in the dense cover of trees, e.g. mangroves and eucalypts, often high above water level in saline or fresh wetlands,

both adults building the usual platform of sticks. They lay 2–**3**–5 pale green to blue eggs (52 x 37mm), which both sexes incubate for 21–22 days. Hatching is not synchronous. The young leave the nest 6–7 weeks after hatching. In New Zealand, the only nest discovered was in a tree fern, high above a side-stream of the Whanganui River. The presence of nestlings in November, and sightings of recently fledged juveniles in February–March, suggests that eggs are laid in October–January.
Behaviour: Gregarious all year but feeds solitarily. They roost by day in groups in leafy trees, e.g. willow, often low to the ground and within convenient flying distance of water.
Feeding: In Australia, diet is mostly fish, also frogs, freshwater crayfish and insects, taken as opportunities arise. They usually stand and wait, upright or crouched, or walk slowly, in the manner of most herons. They feed mainly at night or in the evening but may feed by day, especially when breeding. They fly out from their roost at dusk with slow, heavy wingbeats to their feeding sites.
Reading: Marsh, N. 1995. *Notornis* 42: 282–283. Marsh, N. & Lovei, G. L. 1997. *Notornis* 44: 152–155.

169. AUSTRALASIAN BITTERN *Botaurus poiciloptilus* PLATE 37

Other name: Matuku
Size: 71cm; male 1400g, female 1000g
Distribution: Breeds in southern Australia (including Tasmania), New Zealand, New Caledonia and the Loyalty Islands. In New Zealand, they are widely distributed in the North, South and Stewart islands, and formerly on the Chatham Islands. Most are found in Northland, lower Waikato wetlands, Bay of Plenty, southern Lake Taupo, coastal Whanganui and Manawatu, inland Hawke's Bay, Lake Wairarapa wetlands, Golden Bay, Lake Ellesmere, inland Canterbury lakes, the West Coast, and coastal Southland. Resident on Great Barrier and Mayor islands. They are found in tall, dense beds of raupo and reeds in freshwater wetlands, wet habitats with a mixture of water purslane and willow weed, and damp pasture infested with large clumps of rush or introduced tall fescue.
Population: *c.* 1000 birds in New Zealand, though easily overlooked.
Conservation: Protected nationally endangered native. Bitterns have declined through drainage and 'reclamation' of wetlands, and cattle grazing in swamps which damages breeding cover. They are possibly more common than estimated because they are cryptic and can live in small swamps not included in national estimates.
Breeding: They nest in dense stands of raupo and reeds surrounding lakes and in swamps. Nests are built by the female, who breaks down all reeds within reach until a platform is made 250–300mm above water level. Laying is in August–December, with a peak in November. The female alone incubates the clutch of 3–**4**–6 olive-brown eggs (51 x 37mm) for *c.* 25 days, and then feeds the young. The chicks fledge at *c.* 7 weeks old.
Behaviour: Usually solitary and stealthy. If disturbed, they may stand tall, neck fully stretched up, head and bill pointing skywards, or drop slowly down into the vegetation by retracting their head and crouching down, their plumage looking very reed-like. This cryptic 'freeze' posture is a surveillance posture; their eyes can look all around from this pose. On windy days they may also sway to match the movement of the vegetation. When startled and put to flight, Australasian Bitterns may make their version of the usual heron croak. Calling from within the reedbeds, males advertise their territories by booming – making sounds rather like a muffled foghorn, or the sound produced by blowing across an open bottle.
Feeding: Diet is fish (especially eels), frogs, freshwater crayfish and aquatic insects, caught mostly on or near edges of ponds or waterways. They feed alone, sometimes from traditional feeding platforms made by flattening clumps of reeds. Holding their head and neck parallel to the surface, they sway the head from side to side or keep still for up to 10 minutes; they then lunge and swallow the prey whole or, if too big, by shaking and battering it first. They feed mostly at night, and so are seen mainly at dawn and dusk.
Reading: O'Donnell, C. F. J. 2011. *Emu* 111: 197–201. Teal, P. J. 1989. MSc thesis, Waikato Uni. Whiteside, A. J. 1989. *Notornis* 36: 89–95.

170. LITTLE BITTERN *Ixobrychus minutus* PLATE 37

Size: 30cm, 150g
Geographical variation: Of the four subspecies, *dubius* of Australia and southern New Guinea is the form recorded from New Zealand. The little-known New

Zealand Little Bittern *Ixobrychus novaezelandiae*, which has been extinct since the late nineteenth century, was much larger (53cm).
Distribution: Breeds widely in Europe, Africa, Asia, southern New Guinea and Australia. One New Zealand record: a juvenile that walked past a Westport supermarket in February 1987 and was caught, held in captivity for three weeks, and released.
Behaviour: Usually more secretive than the much larger Australasian Bittern, and males do not boom, advertising instead with a hoarse, monotonous croaking. In Australia, they skulk in thick reedbeds, flooded shrubland and other dense vegetation in swamps, marshes, the edges of freshwater wetlands.
Reading: O'Donnell, C. F. J. & Dilks, P. 1988. *Notornis* 35: 153–157.

IBISES and SPOONBILLS *Threskiornithidae*

30 species; 1 breeds in New Zealand and 4 are vagrants from Australia.

The bills of this group are highly distinctive: long and down-curved in the ibises, long and spatulate in spoonbills. All are gregarious, breeding, roosting and feeding in flocks. They feed mainly in shallow freshwater lakes, brackish coastal lagoons and estuaries, but the ibises that visit New Zealand feed also in dry habitats in Australia, e.g. pasture and public parks. The mid-toe is specialised as a comb-claw in ibises, but not in spoonbills. Most develop ornamental plumes when breeding. They disperse widely after breeding and are silent away from the breeding colonies.

171. GLOSSY IBIS *Plegadis falcinellus* PLATE 39

Size: 60cm, 500g
Distribution: Breeds widely in eastern North America, Europe, parts of Africa, central Asia, India, Malaysia, Indonesia, New Guinea and Australia. They are frequent vagrants to New Zealand, sometimes irrupting in small flocks (of up to 24 birds), as in 1953, 1968, 1975 and 1988, but there is no sign that they have bred here. One record from Chatham Island (December 1984). In New Zealand, they frequent damp pasture and rough pasture and rushes on the muddy margins of freshwater lakes.
Behaviour: Gregarious all year. They are easily overlooked, resembling the hunched posture of a feeding Pukeko, and in flight they have head and bill extended and can be mistaken for a shag. They are usually extremely wary.
Feeding: Peck and probe rapidly for food in soft ground, taking food in the tip of the curved bill. In Australia, they take all sorts of aquatic invertebrates and pasture insects. In New Zealand, they have been known to take fish, small eels, frogs and tadpoles from swamps and insects and earthworms from pasture.
Reading: Lowe, K. W. 1983. *Emu* 83: 31–34. Sansom, O. et al. 1954. *Notornis* 6: 18–19.

172. AUSTRALIAN WHITE IBIS *Threskiornis molucca* PLATE 39

Size: 70cm, 2kg
Geographical variation: Of the three subspecies, *strictipennis* of Australia and southern New Guinea reaches New Zealand.
Distribution: Breeds in Australasia from the Moluccas to New Guinea, Solomon Islands and Australia. Adults are sedentary, but immatures move widely. First recorded in New Zealand at Appleby, Nelson, in March 1925. There have been minor irruptions in 1925, 1957 and 1975, but no sign that they have bred here. These irruptions occurred when a dry spell followed widespread flooding in inland New South Wales. Birds were recorded at four localities in 1925: Appleby, Riwaka, Rotomanu (Westland) and South Taranaki. Ten or more immature birds arrived in 1957 at scattered localities from Northland to Southland, including up to four seen at the mouth of the Rangitikei River. They were seen at various places during the following five years but died out. A similar influx in 1975 was at first in Northland and the Bay of Plenty, but later elsewhere in the North Island. Most remained through 1976, but had gone by 1980. The only subsequent records have

been of single birds near Oamaru (1984), Westport (1986) and Helensville (1989). In New Zealand, they frequent damp pasture and rough pasture and rushes on the muddy margins of freshwater lakes.
Behaviour: Usually gregarious; feeds with herons and often roosts with herons or shags. Usually silent.

173. STRAW-NECKED IBIS *Threskiornis spinicollis* PLATE 39

Size: 65cm, 1400g
Distribution: Breeds in Australia and New Guinea. Some adults are sedentary, but some adults and immatures travel long distances seasonally from inland breeding sites to coastal wetlands, or are nomadic and exploit temporary wetlands created by heavy rains. One New Zealand record: Tarras, Central Otago (January–February 2009).
Behaviour: Usually gregarious, breeding in colonies with other waterbirds, and feeding in flocks at concentrated food sources such as outbreaks of grasshoppers and locusts.

174. ROYAL SPOONBILL *Platalea regia* PLATE 38

Other name: Kotuku-ngutupapa
Size: 77cm, 1700g
Distribution: Breeds in northern, eastern and south-eastern Australia and New Zealand. A vagrant to Indonesia, New Guinea and some Pacific islands.

After a century of vagrant records, Royal Spoonbills have successfully colonised New Zealand. They were first reported at Castlepoint in 1861 but did not start breeding until 1949, next to the White Heron colony near Okarito. This colony slowly built up, with most birds wintering at the Manawatu Estuary, but then breeding tapered off and the population declined from its peak in the early 1960s. Perhaps with fresh immigrants from Australia, a new colony was formed at the Vernon Lagoons, Marlborough, in 1978. They nested among Black-backed Gulls and Pied Shags on or near the ground. This was soon followed by the establishment of about a dozen colonies, mainly among nesting shags, on the Otago and Southland coast, starting with Maukiekie Island (1984), Green Island (1988) and Omaui Island (1992). Colonies also formed about this time at Parengarenga Harbour (1993) and among Black-backed Gulls on Kapiti Island (1994). Now also breeding at Lake Ellesmere and Lake Wairarapa.

They disperse in autumn, mainly to traditional wintering sites at Parengarenga, Rangaunu and Whangarei harbours (Northland), Mangere oxidation ponds (Auckland), Kaituna Cut/Maketu (Bay of Plenty), Ahuriri Estuary (Hawke's Bay), Foxton Estuary (Manawatu), Farewell Spit, Motueka and Waimea estuaries (Nelson), Avon–Heathcote Estuary and Lake Ellesmere (Canterbury). Individually colour-banded birds move widely; juveniles from the Vernon Lagoon colony have been reported from Parengarenga Harbour to Invercargill Estuary.
Population: From a total of 52 birds in August 1977, Royal Spoonbills have increased rapidly, perhaps at first supplemented by Australian birds but mainly through successful breeding at several new colonies. Winter censuses gave national totals of 242 birds in 1991, 377 in 1992, 502 in 1993, 560 in 1994, 610 in 1995, 659 in 1996, 956 in 2000, and 2361 in 2012.
Breeding: At Okarito, they nest in tall kahikatea, whereas the more recently established colonies are on the ground near Black-backed Gull colonies or on top of low-growing taupata and boxthorn scrub near shag colonies. Laying is in September–December. They lay 2–3–4 dull white eggs with brown blotches (66 x 43mm). Both sexes incubate for 20–25 days. The fledging period is about 7 weeks. Birds can breed at 3 years old.
Feeding: Diet is mainly small invertebrates, fish and frogs, taken at night as much as by day because they rely on touch rather than sight to detect food. They feed mostly in tidal mudflats or around the margins of shallow lakes, by walking along and sweeping their bill, slightly open, in smooth, sideways arcs, by which the water movement pulls small prey from the bottom or from the water column.
Reading: Holdaway, R. N. 1980. *Notornis* 27: 168–169. Lowe, K. W. 1982. *Emu* 82: 163–168. Robertson, H. A. & Preece, B. E. 1980. *Notornis* 27: 170–171.

175. YELLOW-BILLED SPOONBILL *Platalea flavipes* PLATE 38

Size: 88cm, 1900g
Distribution: Breeds only in Australia. Two New Zealand records: Rangaunu Harbour and Kaitaia area (1976–81) and Te Whiti, Wairarapa (December 1981).
Behaviour: In Australia, they prefer feeding in shallow dams and pools of fresh or brackish waters rather than tidal mudflats. They feed with typical spoonbill action of sweeping the bill from side to side. They also feed on damp or flooded pasture.
Reading: Billing, A. E. 1977. *Notornis* 24: 192.

RAPTORS *Accipitridae and Falconidae*

The raptors, or diurnal birds of prey, are found worldwide from inshore marine habitats to the mountain tops. There are about 220 species of eagle, kite, hawk and harrier (Accipitridae), of which 1 breeds in New Zealand and 1 is a vagrant, although there is an old Te Papa specimen of a White-bellied Sea Eagle *Haliaeetus leucogaster* with no date or locality data. There are 61 species of falcon and kestrel (Falconidae) – again only 1 species breeds in New Zealand, but 2 are vagrants. Subfossil bones of the very large, long-legged, moa-killing Haast's Eagle *Aquila moorei* and the large endemic Eyles' Harrier *Circus teauteensis* show that New Zealand once had a greater variety of large raptors.

Current New Zealand raptors are medium to large, mainly brown birds. Raptors have long wings and tail; long, unfeathered, powerful feet with very sharp talons on the three forward-pointing toes and on the hallux, the backward-pointing toe; a small, broad hook-shaped bill with a waxy cere at the base of the upper bill; and large eyes.
Reading: Cade, T. J. 1982. *The Falcons of the World.* London: Collins. Ferguson-Lees, J. & Christie, D. A. 2001. *Raptors of the World.* London: Christopher Helm. Newton, I. 1976. *Population Ecology of Raptors.* Berkhamsted: Poyser.

176. BLACK KITE *Milvus migrans* PLATE 40

Other name: Fork-tailed Kite
Size: Male 50cm, 550g; female 55cm, 600g
Distribution: Breeds widely in Africa and from southern Europe across Asia and Australasia to the eastern states of Australia. In Australia, most breed in inland parts of South Australia, New South Wales and Queensland, but they have frequent but irregular irruptions to other states and to coastal areas in response to droughts and local abundance of food. Vagrant to New Zealand, with seven records: Waihopai Valley, Marlborough (1992–94; 2000–14), Mackenzie Basin (1994), Wanaka (1996), South Auckland (2001–02), Pirinoa, South Wairarapa (2002) and Inglewood (2009). Probably overlooked, because most Swamp Harriers are not examined critically.
Feeding: In Australia, Black Kites scavenge road-killed animals, other dead animals, offal and garbage, but also catch live prey such as young rabbits, birds, reptiles, frogs and large insects. They hunt by soaring, high quartering and low, hedge-top quartering.

177. SWAMP HARRIER *Circus approximans* PLATE 40

Other names: Kahu, Harrier Hawk, Australasian Harrier
Size: male 55cm, 650g; female 60cm, 850g
Distribution: Breeds widely in southeastern New Guinea, Australia and the southern Pacific, including Vanuatu, New Caledonia, Fiji, Tonga, Wallis Island, French Polynesia (introduced), and in New Zealand. Vagrants have been recorded from Samoa and the Cook Islands. Swamp Harriers are widespread and common throughout open country on the New Zealand mainland, offshore islands and the Chathams. They visit the Kermadec Islands each winter and wander to The Snares, Auckland and Campbell islands.

In New Zealand, Swamp Harriers are common in wetlands, farmland, high-country tussockland, scrubland, along forest margins and riverbeds and around the coast. The only habitats they rarely use are large stands of dense native or exotic forest, and urban areas. Banding studies show much movement both north and south across Cook Strait, especially of young birds wandering in autumn and early winter. Adults also disperse from their breeding home range in February–March and sometimes use a regular wintering area up to 100km away each year.

Population: Widespread and very common, especially compared with the number of other raptor species seen in other parts of the world.

Conservation: Partially protected native. Swamp Harriers undoubtedly benefited from the conversion of forest to farmland since European settlement and the introduction of small mammals (especially rabbits) and birds, which form the main part of their diet. For many years they were persecuted by some farmers for attacking young lambs and cast sheep, and sportsmen shot many because Swamp Harriers sometimes attack young gamebirds. During the 1930s and 1940s, bounties were paid by Acclimatisation societies for hundreds of thousands of birds, but Swamp Harriers remained abundant. Since the 1950s, numbers have declined as rabbit control removed a key part of their diet, but they remain common. They were partially protected in 1985.

Breeding: Males establish their territories in May–June, but females do not return until June–August. In June, some pairs start courtship soaring, and on warm calm days from late July to October pairs are often seen doing their spectacular 'sky dance' or courtship diving, a series of U-shaped dives accompanied by loud calls. In September–October, females start building the nest. It is a low platform of bracken, manuka, raupo and flax stalks, topped with rushes, cabbage tree leaves and grass. It is sited on the ground in swamps, in wet patches covered in rushes, in bracken fern or rank grass in young pine plantations or on road verges, or in grain crops. Rarely, nests are built on a platform in a tree.

In September–December, they lay 2–3–5–7 off-white eggs (52 x 39mm) at 48–72-hour intervals. Only the female incubates for 31–34 days, but the male feeds the female throughout. The eggs hatch over several days and some eggs are abandoned once a few chicks have hatched. Only the female feeds the chicks, but the male gathers food for the female and the chicks, and passes it to the female by dropping it as both birds fly close to the nest. When the chicks are older, both adults hunt,

and when the female is away the male occasionally drops food at the nest but does not stay to feed the nestlings.

The chicks fledge at 43–46 days old, in December–February. They remain with their parents for a week after leaving the nest, but gradually venture further and finally disperse about 7 weeks after fledging. Yearling females have been recorded breeding, but males probably do not start breeding until 2–3 years old. Pairs return to the same territory year after year, but occasionally a male will mate with two females. The oldest Swamp Harrier recorded in New Zealand lived over 18 years.

Behaviour: Strongly territorial in the breeding season but otherwise usually solitary. In winter, they often have large (100+ birds) communal roosts in a secluded swamp, and they sometimes form loose flocks when dispersing long distances or when feeding at abundant sources. Swamp Harriers are silent outside the breeding season, except for an occasional whistle. During display flights, especially dives, they are very vocal, the male giving a repeated high-pitched 'kee-a', and the female a 'kee-o' response.

Feeding: Diet is varied, with both carrion and live prey eaten. The main carrion are sheep (especially in winter and spring), possums and hedgehogs (from roads), and waterfowl and other gamebirds (during the shooting season). Live prey is mainly small mammals (especially rabbits, hares, hedgehogs, rats and mice), small birds (introduced species, ducks and eggs), frogs, fish, lizards and large invertebrates such as grasshoppers and crickets (in summer and autumn). They are sometimes controlled when they create a nuisance at free-range poultry farms or at sites where endangered species are being protected.

Swamp Harriers hunt by day and usually search for prey by low, slow quartering followed by a dive attack or by briefly hovering and then dropping vertically.

Swamp Harriers sometimes soar high, especially when searching for carrion, and they sometimes stoop like a falcon to flush small birds from a crop. Young birds often hunt insects on the ground with a series of pounces and snatches with the feet. Prey is caught by the sharp talons, not with the bill, which has a very weak bite, but the hooked tip is used to lever skin and flesh from the carcass.

In the hand: First-winter Swamp Harriers have brown eyes, dark brown plumage with an obvious white nape patch, and do not moult their flight feathers. In females, the eye colour changes to mid-brown in the second winter and yellow in later years; whereas in males yellow specks have appeared at 9 months of age and by the second year they have golden yellow eyes, which in later years turn sulphur-yellow. As birds get older, their plumage gets paler, and so very old birds can appear almost grey. Females are larger than males, with little overlap in leg and bill measurements: the hind-claw length of females is 21.5–**24.5**–31mm cf. 18–**21**–26.5mm in males, and bill length (including cere) is 33–**36.5**–40.5mm in females and 30–**33**–37mm in males. Females are also heavier in all seasons, usually weighing over 800g, whereas males rarely exceed 750g, even with a full crop.

Reading: Baker-Gabb, D. J. 1979. *Notornis* 26: 325–329. Baker-Gabb, D. J. 1981. *Notornis* 28: 103–119. Baker-Gabb, D. J. 1981. *Notornis* 28: 241–254. Pierce, R. J. & Maloney, R. F. 1989. *Notornis* 36: 1–12. Robertson, H. A. 1980. *NZ J Zool* 7: 579–583.

178. NANKEEN KESTREL *Falco cenchroides* PLATE 40

Other name: Australian Kestrel

Size: Male 32cm, 160g; female 34cm, 180g

Geographical variation: Two subspecies: *cenchroides* in Australia and on Lord Howe and Norfolk islands and a vagrant to New Zealand; *baru* in New Guinea.

Distribution: Widespread and common on mainland Australia but scarce in Tasmania. They are mainly sedentary, but occasionally inland droughts force them to move northwards or towards the coast. They colonised Lord Howe Island in the 1940s and bred on Norfolk Island in the 1970s. Frequent vagrants appear anywhere in New Zealand, especially in the autumn and early winter. The numerous records since 1889 include small irruptions in 1969 and 1990 when birds were seen widely in both North and South islands. There is no firm evidence that they have bred in New Zealand, despite conditions being suitable for them, judging from repeated sightings of two birds near Te Mata Peak, Hawke's Bay, for over five years from the late 1980s.

Feeding: Kestrels have an unmistakable hunting method of hovering, poised in mid-air with head facing into the wind and tail depressed according to the strength of the wind. They drop by stages before plunging to the ground to seize prey in their talons. Small birds are sometimes taken on the wing. Kestrels are typically seen in open country, sometimes riding updraughts around hilltops or sand dunes as they search short grass for mice, small birds, lizards and large insects.

Reading: Edgar, A. T. & Grant, P. 1969. *Notornis* 16: 288–298. Powell, W. J. 1978. *Notornis* 25: 94–95.

179. BLACK FALCON *Falco subniger* PLATE 40

Size: Male 50cm, 600g; female 54cm, 800g

Distribution: A rare species endemic to Australia. They breed inland and occasionally near the coast of southern Australia, but droughts occasionally force birds into coastal areas and cause small irruptions east of the Great Dividing Range. Following an irruption in 1982–83, a probable juvenile male reached Gisborne (November 1983).

Feeding: Black Falcons often glide on slightly drooped wings but can accelerate to very swift flight when chasing small birds, their main prey. Small food items are eaten on the wing or at a perch, rarely on the ground.

Reading: Blackburn, A. 1984. *Notornis* 31: 6.

180. NEW ZEALAND FALCON *Falco novaeseelandiae* PLATE 40

Other names: Karearea, Bush Hawk, Sparrow Hawk

Size: Male 43cm, 300g; female 47cm, 500g

Geographical variation: Treated as one highly variable species, with three forms that differ in size, colour and habitat: the 'Bush Falcon' of forests of the North Island and the northwestern South Island; the 'Eastern Falcon' of the open country of the eastern South Island; and the 'Southern Falcon' of coastal Fiordland, Stewart Island and the Auckland Islands. The forms intergrade and show clinal variation with habitat rather than latitude.

Distribution: New Zealand only. They breed in native and exotic forest in the North Island, mainly south of a line from northern Taranaki to Whakatane (Bay of Plenty), although a few pairs breed in the Coromandel Range. In the South Island, they breed in dry tussockland and rough farmland in hills along the eastern side of the Southern Alps from Marlborough to Southland, and in forests of northwestern Nelson, the Southern Alps, West Coast and Fiordland. Rare on Stewart Island and its outliers. Well established on the Auckland Islands. Known from the Chathams from an egg collected before 1888 and from subfossil bones. Adults are quite sedentary, but juveniles wander widely in autumn and winter and account for most sighting of falcons on offshore islands, in farmland and orchards, and in towns and cities.

Population: Widespread but uncommon; in the 1970s there were *c.* 4000 pairs: 3150 pairs of Eastern Falcons, 650 pairs of Bush Falcons and 200 pairs of Southern Falcons.

Conservation: Protected endemic. Falcons may never have been common in New Zealand, but the clearance of much lowland native forest has reduced their range; selective logging of large podocarps up to the 1980s removed some of their preferred nesting sites; and introduced stoats, cats, possums and pigs are known nest predators. These changes were offset by the good hunting opportunities along forest edges created by roading or partial forest clearance and by the introduction of mammals (especially rabbits and hares) and of small birds (especially finches and Skylarks). Although Falcons have been protected since 1970, they are sometimes shot by pigeon fanciers and poultry farmers when a young bird discovers an easy source of food. Trained Falcons bred in captivity under permit have been used in experiments to scare birds from airfields and vineyards.

Breeding: Most established pairs remain on territory all year. Territory size in central North Island pine forests is about 9km^2, but in open country of the eastern South Island it is about 15km^2, and even larger in native forest. In late winter and early spring, pairs are often seen together doing aerial displays, including food passes and aerobatics. The nest is a simple scrape on a sheltered cliff ledge, on a slip face, under a rock overhang or a fallen log, or up to 40m high in a tree in a clump of *Astelia*. Laying is in August–January. They lay 1–3–4 eggs (49 x 37mm, 45g), which are buff to rich reddish brown with rusty brown speckles. Incubation is shared in shifts of 1–4 hours and takes 25–35 days.

The chicks are brooded by mainly the female for the first 10–14 days and are fed by the female only. However, the male gathers most of the food for the female and the chicks, and passes the food to the female by dropping it as both birds fly close to the nest. When the chicks are *c.* 2 weeks old, the female starts hunting too. Male chicks fledge at *c.* 32 days, but females stay until *c.* 35 days old. They retain some natal down until about 6 weeks old. Their parents continue to feed them with aerial food passes (drops or talon-to-talon transfers) and at perches for over a month, but chicks start hunting when about 7 weeks old and most are independent 2 months after fledging. They soon disperse widely. Although a few breed at 1 year old, most do not start until they are 2 years old.

Behaviour: Falcons are fiercely territorial in the breeding season and make repeated dive attacks on people near the nest; this is often the first sign that a pair has established a territory in an area. This attack is accompanied by a characteristic 'kek-kek-kek' call, which is also the main call heard from both sexes outside the breeding season.

Feeding: Falcons are fierce and fearless predators of live prey, especially small birds (especially finches, Bellbirds, Silvereyes, Skylarks, Blackbirds and Song Thrushes), small mammals (young rabbits and hares) and large insects (huhu beetles, grasshoppers, cicadas, manuka beetles and cockchafer beetles). They take some large birds, including New Zealand Pigeons and Rock Pigeons, Magpies, and even White-faced Herons, Black-backed Gulls and Pheasants. On the Auckland Islands and on Codfish Island, petrels and prions are often taken.

Falcons usually wait on a perch until they see the quarry and then directly attack, or sometimes head off in another direction to gain height before turning to dive from behind. Some attacks are mounted by the Falcon flying swiftly over the brow of a hill, or around a corner of forest or a building to startle a feeding flock, and then it selects and attacks one bird. They catch prey by the sharp talons, not the bill, but kill large prey by biting the back of the neck. They rarely feed on carrion.

In the hand: Juveniles are like adults, except the upperparts of juveniles are uniformly coloured rather than having pale feather-tips, and they lack barring on the flanks. Females are much larger than males, and wing measurements of adults do not overlap, despite marked differences in size between the various forms: females 268–308mm cf. males 226–267mm. Bush Falcons are smallest, e.g. wing averages 273mm in females and 236mm in males cf. 281mm and 248mm respectively for Southern Falcons and 297mm and 255mm in Eastern Falcons.

Reading: Barea, L. P. et al. 1999. *Notornis* 46: 257–267. Fox, N. C. 1978. *Notornis* 25: 203–212. Fox, N. C. 1978. *Notornis* 25: 317–331. Fox, N. C. 1988. *Notornis* 35: 270–272. Lawrence, S. B. & Gay, C. G. 1991. *Notornis* 38: 173–182. Seaton, R. 2007. PhD thesis, Massey University. Stewart, D. & Hyde, N. 2004. *Notornis* 51: 119–121.

RAILS, GALLINULES and COOTS *Rallidae*

About 140 species, of which 8 breed in New Zealand.

Midden remains show that 5 other endemic species became extinct between the arrival of Maori and 1840, and the Chatham Island Rail *Cabalus modestus* became extinct in 1893 and the North Island Takahe *Porphyrio mantelli* was last reported in 1894. Two other species are vagrants to New Zealand, and a Corncrake *Crex crex* was reputedly killed near Nelson in 1865.

The rails are mainly aquatic birds, all capable of swimming well. In New Zealand, they range in size from the small Marsh Crake to the large, flightless Takahe. Apart from the Pukeko and Weka, rails and crakes are secretive birds, usually skulking in freshwater swamps, and estuarine mangroves and rushes. On some mammal-free islands, however, they live on the forest floor.

Rails have slim bodies that help them move through dense vegetation, moderately long, powerful legs with long or very long, unwebbed toes that help them walk in wetlands, a short tail, which is flicked up and down as they walk or swim, and short, broad wings. Apart from the flightless Weka and Takahe, rails have low, laboured flight by day, but at night they fly higher and show good ability to colonise isolated islands. Island forms tend to become flightless.

The two species of gallinule currently breeding in New Zealand, the Takahe and the Pukeko, are believed to represent multiple invasions from Australia of the Southwest Pacific Swamphen (*Porphyrio melanotus*) or its ancestor. The founders of the Takahe arrived millions of years ago, and North and South island species (*P. mantelli* and *P. hochstetteri*) may have even been from separate invasions. The Pukeko arrived much more recently and is only subspecifically distinct from its Australian cousins. Typical of ancient New Zealand birds, the Takahe became larger and flightless.

The gallinules and coots have a bony frontal shield extending from the bill to cover the forehead. The legs of coots are quite short, and the toes have lobes of skin that help them swim and dive.

Most species nest solitarily, but Pukeko form groups and several females can lay in the same nest. The cup-shaped nest is generally well concealed in dense swamp vegetation or among *Carex* clumps; however, coots construct an exposed floating platform attached to raupo or rushes. The downy young are capable of walking, running and swimming within days of hatching.

Reading: Ripley, S. D. 1977. *Rails of the World*. Toronto: M. F. Feheley.

181. AUCKLAND ISLANDS RAIL *Lewinia muelleri* PLATE 41

Size: 21cm, 90g

Distribution: New Zealand only. Known only on Adams and Disappointment islands in the Auckland Islands. On Adams Island, they are widespread in habitats with a dense canopy about a metre above ground but with open runways beneath. They are found throughout the tussock and herb fields on Disappointment Island.

Population: Locally common on Adams Island, with an estimated population of *c.* 1500 birds. Common on Disappointment Island, with *c.* 100 birds.

Conservation: Protected endemic. Auckland Islands Rails were first collected in the late 1800s but were not seen again until one was caught on Adams Island in 1966 and taken to Mount Bruce Wildlife Reserve (now Pukaha Mount Bruce). In 1989, they were found to be moderately common on Adams Island, once their habitat preferences were known. Another healthy population was discovered on Disappointment Island in 1993. With

two populations, the subspecies is probably safe as long as rats are not accidentally introduced to these islands.
Breeding: Little is known. Two nests were found in November 1989, and at the same time young chicks were heard squeaking. Eggs are therefore laid in October–November. The only clutch recorded was of **2** cream eggs (35.1 x 26.5mm, 12g; 32.8 x 24.2mm, 8.5g), marked with brown, red-brown and pale grey spots and blotches concentrated at the blunt end. The cup-shaped nests are well hidden among tussock and sedge. Incubation and fledging periods are unknown. An immature bird caught in the wild lived 9 years in captivity at Mount Bruce.
Behaviour: Little known, because birds are shy and cryptic; they live under dense vegetation and rarely fly. In summer, they are active from just before sunrise to just after sunset, and although they do not call at night, they may remain active. The usual distinctive call is a loud, descending 'crek', repeated about 10 times at 1-second intervals. The second call is a loud, sharp, whistle-like note, repeated about 50 times in about 12 seconds. They also make a variety of grunts and clicks, and chicks squeak. They respond to their taped calls.
Feeding: Unknown, but presumably the diet is invertebrates such as snails, worms and insects.
Reading: Elliott, G. P. et al. 1991. *Notornis* 38: 199–209. Falla, R. A. 1967. *Notornis* 14: 107–113.

182. BANDED RAIL *Gallirallus philippensis* PLATE 41

Other names: Moho pereru, Mioweka (Stewart Island)
Size: 30cm, 170g
Geographical variation: Up to 15 subspecies are recognised, of which the subspecies *assimilis* breeds in New Zealand.
Distribution: Breeds in the South Pacific from Indonesia and the Philippines through Melanesia, Australia, New Zealand, and western Polynesia as far east as Niue. In New Zealand, Banded Rails were formerly common throughout the three main islands and their outliers, but had declined by the 1930s owing to habitat loss and the introduction of mammalian predators.

Found mainly in mangrove forests, salt marshes and rush-covered (not raupo-covered) freshwater wetlands in Northland (including the Three Kings and Poor Knights islands), around Auckland, Great Barrier Island, Coromandel Peninsula and Bay of Plenty. They are rarely recorded inland or south of a line from northern Taranaki to Opotiki, except for breeding reported at Mahia. Probably overlooked in inland swamps; after 60 years without sightings, one was killed by a cat at Lake Wairarapa in 1992. In the South Island, they are now largely confined to unmodified salt marshes of the northern coast in Whanganui Inlet, Golden Bay, Tasman Bay and at the head of the Pelorus and Queen Charlotte sounds in the Marlborough Sounds. Banded Rails are occasionally recorded from Stewart Island and are still in moderate numbers on some of its offshore islands without Weka, and on Little Solander Island.
Population: Locally common near the coast of the northern North Island and on mustelid- and/or rat-free offshore islands. The northern South Island population was *c.* 100 breeding pairs in the early 1980s.
Conservation: Protected native. Populations appear to be declining through habitat modification with reclamation of estuaries and mangrove swamps, clearance of mangroves, and predation by introduced mammals, especially ferrets and stoats. Successful translocations to Moturoa Island, Bay of Islands (1996), and Kundy Island, off Stewart Island (1999).
Breeding: Pairs remain on their territories all year. Territory size varies from *c.* 1.5ha in suitable habitat in the northern South Island to about 4ha in northern New Zealand. Most eggs are laid in September–December, but clutches have been recorded as late as March, and dependent chicks have been seen in April. They probably lay several clutches each season, comprising 3–**5**–6 buff or pale pinkish eggs (40 x 29mm, 16g), marked with dark reddish-brown and purplish-grey spots and blotches. The cup-shaped nest is well hidden in thick grasses or rushes. The pair incubates for 19–25 days. The chicks, which are initially covered in black down but change to dark brown by a week old, are led from the nest within 24 hours and are accompanied by both parents throughout the *c.* 60 days to fledging.
Behaviour: Pairs remain together on territory year after year but often only emerge from dense cover at dawn and dusk or in heavy rain, or feed under mangrove cover. Sometimes a family party emerges to forage in a secluded creek or ditch, especially on a falling tide, when there are young chicks to be fed. The best way to see Banded Rails is to play tapes of their calls, especially their high-pitched 'quee-quee-' or creaky 'swit-swit-' calls often heard at dusk.
Feeding: Diet is mainly snails (*Potamopyrgus estuarinus*, *Ophicardelus costellaris* and *Amphibola crenata*), crabs (especially *Helice crassa*), spiders, beetles and worms. They also take seeds, fruits and succulent leaves. Most

feeding is in the morning and evening and straight after high tide when crabs are most active and the tide has dislodged snails.

Reading: Elliott, G. P. 1987. *NZ J Ecol* 10: 109–115. Elliott, G. P. 1989. *Notornis* 36: 117–123. Schodde, R. & de Naurois, R. 1982. *Notornis* 29: 131–141.

183. WEKA *Gallirallus australis* PLATE 41

Other name: Woodhen
Size: 53cm; male 1000g, female 700g
Geographical variation: Four subspecies: the North Island Weka *greyi* breeds in the North Island, the Western Weka *australis* breeds in the northern and western South Island, the Buff Weka *hectori* was introduced to the Chatham Islands before it died out from the eastern South Island, and the Stewart Island Weka *scotti* is largely confined to the islands around Stewart Island.
Distribution: New Zealand only. Formerly bred throughout the mainland of New Zealand, but in the 1920s and 1930s they disappeared from most of the North Island, where they are naturally confined mainly to the Opotiki–Motu district, although they have been successfully introduced to the Russell Peninsula (Bay of Islands) and Kawakawa Bay (South Auckland), and to a number of islands: Kawau, Pakatoa, Rotoroa, Whanganui (off Coromandel), Rakitu (Arid) and Mokoia. Numerous reintroduction attempts have failed, and they have hybridised with Western and possibly Stewart Island subspecies on Kapiti Island.

In the South Island, Western Weka are locally common in the Marlborough Sounds, Golden Bay and northwestern Nelson, northern Westland south to about Hokitika, and on some Fiordland islands; uncommon in Tasman Bay, from Hokitika to Fiordland and inland Southland. They have been introduced to Totaranui (Abel Tasman National Park), D'Urville Island and smaller islands in the Marlborough Sounds, and to Kapiti Island.

Buff Weka became extinct in the eastern South Island by the late 1920s, but luckily they had been introduced to the Chathams, where they thrived. They are now abundant throughout Chatham and Pitt islands. They have been reintroduced to Banks Peninsula, Harwich and Stevensons islands in Lake Wanaka, and Pigeon and Pig islands in Lake Wakatipu.

Stewart Island Weka are scarce on Stewart Island but have been introduced to many of the nearby islands and to Macquarie Island, where they have since been eradicated. The origin of Weka introduced to several islands (e.g. Solander and Open Bay) has not been established.
Conservation: Protected endemic, except on the Chatham Islands, where a legal harvest is permitted. Maori and early European settlers used Weka for food, oil and feathers, and carried them to many offshore islands. Weka declined dramatically between 1900 and 1940, and became extinct in most of the North Island and disappeared from the eastern South Island. The causes of the rapid decline are not clear, but habitat changes during the conversion of forest and scrubland to farmland, disease, the use of poison baits and predation by mustelids, cats, and dogs may have contributed.

With a few exceptions, the many attempts to reintroduce Weka back into their former range on the mainland have been unsuccessful, despite some birds persisting and even breeding for a few years. Mainland populations undergo major fluctuations and some become locally extinct for several years before reinvasion and rapid breeding and they become common again. These declines are often attributed to disease, but there is no supporting evidence and it seems more likely that they are due to widespread breeding failure and adult mortality during periods when food is scarce.
Breeding: Pairs remain on territory or in fixed home ranges all year. The breeding season is highly variable and depends on local weather patterns, food availability and population size. Weka can breed all year if conditions are suitable, but the majority of clutches are laid in August–January. Up to four broods can be raised in a year. The nest is a bowl of grasses, sedges, rushes and cabbage tree leaves, lined with finer grasses, feathers, moss and wool; it is on the ground at the hollow base of a tree, in a short burrow, under or inside fallen logs, or in a dry site under tussock, sedges or fern. Weka lay 1–2–3–6 creamy white or pinkish eggs (59 x 41mm) about 2–3 days apart.

Both sexes incubate, the female for most of the day, the male from late afternoon to early morning. They incubate for 25–26 days from after the last egg is laid; the chicks hatch over several days and leave the nest at 2–3 days old when still covered in dark brown down. Both adults brood the chicks during cold weather in the first week and feed the chicks until they are nearly fully grown at 6–10 weeks old. The young disperse at 3–4 months old and can breed at 5 months old. The oldest Weka recorded in the wild lived over 19 years.
Behaviour: Adult Weka stay on their territory or home

range all year, but juveniles disperse from their natal area. Although Weka are flightless, they can swim across a kilometre or more of river, lake or sea. Weka are usually shy and retiring, and are seen only fleetingly as they run from one patch of cover to another, but some birds, especially those on islands or living around tramping huts, become very bold and readily take food from the hand.

Weka are more often heard than seen. Their main call is a shrill, far-carrying, double-note 'coo-eet', normally heard at dusk and in the early evening. Often when one Weka starts calling, others respond and the hills come alive with calls. Other calls include soft, deep, resonant booming and high-pitched peeping from young begging for food.

Feeding: Diet is mainly invertebrates and fruit, but they take seeds, small vertebrates and carrion. The main invertebrates are worms, beetles, orthopteran larvae, snails, amphipods and isopods found in leaf litter, in long grass or along the tideline. They feed by flicking the litter aside with their bill (surprisingly, not with their feet). They can sometimes become serious pests by feeding on newly sown crops, and come into conflict with conservation programmes by killing invertebrates, reptiles and seabirds, and eating eggs of seabirds and other ground-nesting birds.

Reading: Beauchamp, A. J. 1987. PhD thesis, Victoria University. Beauchamp, A. J. 1987. *Notornis* 34: 317–325. Beauchamp, A. J. 1988. *Notornis* 35: 282–284. Beauchamp, A. J. et al. 1993. *Notornis* 40: 309–312. Beauchamp, A. J. & Chambers, R. 2000. *Notornis* 47: 82–89. Carroll, A. L. K. 1963. *Notornis* 10: 281–300. Coleman, J. D. et al. 1983. *Notornis* 30: 93–107.

184. SPOTLESS CRAKE *Porzana tabuensis* PLATE 41

Other names: Puweto, Putoto, Sooty Rail

Size: 20cm, 45g

Distribution: Widely distributed in Australasia and the South Pacific from the Philippines and Micronesia east to the Marquesas Islands of French Polynesia. Within New Zealand, they are in raupo- and sedge-dominated swamps throughout the North Island, but are sparsely yet very widely distributed in raupo swamps and reed beds in the South Island and on Stewart Island. Flax-dominated wetlands are usually crakeless spots. They are common on some offshore islands such as the Three Kings, Motukawanui, Poor Knights, Tiritiri Matangi and Great Barrier islands. They are also on small islands in the Kermadecs, and on Chatham Island.

Spotless Crakes are secretive and rarely seen; many records are of cat-killed birds being brought to houses, or from duck-shooters who have seen crakes lurking near their maimai. They are apparently quite mobile, probably flying at night, judging by occasional records of birds found in towns, far from their usual habitats; and by their widespread distribution around New Zealand and in the Pacific. In the Waikato, a bird released 25km from its banding site had returned there within 6 weeks.

Population: Locally common on mammal-free offshore islands such as the Meyer Islets in the Kermadecs, the Poor Knights Islands, and in many raupo and sedge swamps in the northern North Island and in the Manawatu/Horowhenua dune lakes.

Conservation: Protected native. The drainage of many lowland wetlands and introduced mammalian predators have undoubtedly had a major impact on Spotless Crakes, but because of their very secretive nature, they are probably more common than the number of records suggest.

Breeding: Pairs remain on territory all year. They lay from late August to January, mostly September–October, 2–3–4–5 pinkish cream eggs (30 x 22mm, 9g) in a bulky, cup-shaped nest loosely woven out of grass and sedge. In swamps, the nest site is usually raised 30–50cm above the water level beside the pedestal of a *Carex*, and often under a canopy of dead *Carex* tillers and an overstorey of tall raupo, willow, manuka or cabbage trees to protect the nest from the elements. On islands, they nest on the ground, under dense cover. Clutch size and egg size increases through the season. Both sexes incubate for 20–22 days. The chicks, which are initially covered with black down, leave the nest within 4 days and are looked after by both parents during the 4–5 months until they reach adult size.

Behaviour: Little is known, as the birds are shy and cryptic, and live in dense vegetation. Spotless Crakes are more often heard than seen, and usually they are found by playing their taped calls in suitable habitat. They have a wide variety of calls; those usually heard from swamps are sharp 'pit-pit' calls, a single or repeated 'book' and a distinctive rolling 'purrrrrrr' call like an alarm clock going off and gradually running down. Most unsolicited calls are heard at dawn and dusk, when the birds are probably most active.

Feeding: Diet is a mixture of invertebrates such as worms, spiders, beetles, snails and insect larvae, and seeds of aquatic plants or fallen fruits. In swamps, they rarely come into the open but sometimes feed on muddy margins or in channels through raupo; however, on predator-free islands they readily feed in leaf litter on the forest floor by day.
In the hand: From a small sample (n=12), it appears that male Spotless Crakes have longer bills than females (18–21mm [8] cf. 16–17.5mm [4]).
Reading: Hadden, D. 1970. *Notornis* 17: 200–213. Kaufmann, G. 1987. *Notornis* 34: 207–216. Kaufmann, G. & Lavers, R. 1987. *Notornis* 34: 193–205. O'Donnell, C. F. J. 1994. *Notornis* 41: 211–213. Onley, D. 1982. *Notornis* 29: 9–21.

185. MARSH CRAKE *Porzana pusilla* PLATE 41

Other names: Koitareke, Baillon's Rail
Size: 17cm, 35g
Geographical variation: Five subspecies; three in Africa, Europe and Asia to Irian Jaya, *palustris* in Papua New Guinea, Australia and Tasmania, and *affinis* in New Zealand.
Distribution: Breeds throughout the Old World from Africa and Europe across Asia to Australasia. In New Zealand, they are scattered sparsely in raupo swamps of the North, South and Stewart islands, but are also in salt-marsh habitats and high-altitude wetlands of the South Island. They were last seen in the Chatham Islands in the early 1900s.

Marsh Crakes are secretive and rarely seen; many records are of cat-killed birds being brought to houses, or from duck-shooters who have seen crakes lurking near their maimai. They are apparently quite mobile, probably flying at night, judging from occasional records of birds found at lighthouses or in towns, far from their usual habitats.
Population: Locally common in some salt-marsh habitats, such as on the southern side of Farewell Spit, and generally more numerous than Spotless Crakes in the South Island.
Conservation: Protected native. The drainage of many lowland wetlands and introduced mammalian predators have undoubtedly had a major impact on Marsh Crakes, but because of their very secretive nature, they are probably more common than the number of records suggest.
Breeding: Little information is available from New Zealand, because very few nests have been found. Pairs apparently remain on territory all year. They lay in September–December, 4–**6**–7 olive-brown eggs (28 x 20mm) in a shallow dished platform made of short lengths of rushes or sedge. The nest is usually 30–40cm above the water beside the pedestal of a *Carex* and with a hood of dead *Carex* tillers to protect the nest from the elements. Unlike the Spotless Crake, nests are generally not in dense raupo stands. Both sexes incubate for 16–20 days. The chicks are initially covered with black down and have yellow bills.
Behaviour: Little is known because Marsh Crakes are extremely shy and cryptic, and live in dense vegetation. By day, they are less vocal than Spotless Crakes and seldom respond to taped calls, however, they occasionally respond aggressively to taped calls of Spotless Crakes. At dusk and at night, especially in spring and early summer, they give a variety of calls – that most often heard being a harsh trill 'krek', like the sound of a fingernail being drawn along a comb.
Feeding: Diet is a mixture of invertebrates and seeds of aquatic plants. In swamps, they rarely come into the open, but sometimes feed on muddy margins of swamps or in tidal runnels in salt marshes.
Reading: Barlow, M. & Sutton, R. R. 1975. *Notornis* 22: 178–180. Elliott, G. 1989. *Notornis* 36: 117–123. Kaufmann, G. 1987. *Notornis* 34: 207–216. Kaufmann, G. & Lavers, R. 1987. *Notornis* 34: 193–205.

186. BLACK-TAILED NATIVE-HEN *Gallinula ventralis* PLATE 42

Size: 35cm, 400g
Distribution: Breeds only in mainland Australia. They are widespread and highly nomadic, moving inland to breed following heavy rain and dispersing back towards the coast in drier spells. They are vagrants to Tasmania and New Zealand, with at least six New Zealand records: Colac Bay, Southland (June 1923); Tukituki River, Hawke's Bay (May 1957 to mid-1958); Karamea (August–November 1984); lower Waikato (May 1986); Lake Hood, Ashburton (August 2002); and

Greenstreet, Ashburton (December 2011).
Behaviour: They feed on open ground in irrigated pasture or at the margins of wetlands on plants and seeds. They also run swiftly to disturb and then catch large insects.
Reading: Braithwaite, D. H. 1963. *Notornis* 10: 228–233.

187. DUSKY MOORHEN *Gallinula tenebrosa* PLATE 42

Size: 37cm, 500g
Distribution: Breeds in eastern Indonesia, Timor, New Guinea, and in southern parts of Western Australia, and the eastern states of Australia, including Tasmania. Some are nomadic, heading inland to breed following heavy rains, and back to coastal areas when temporary wetlands dry out. Two New Zealand records: Lake Hayes, near Arrowtown (August–October 1968), and near Lake Ellesmere (February 2005).
Behaviour: Prefers densely vegetated freshwater wetlands, in reed beds, rushes and willows, though ventures out onto nearby pasture.
Reading: Barlow, M. L. 1969. *Notornis* 16: 81–84.

188. PUKEKO *Porphyrio melanotus* PLATE 42

Other names: Purple Swamphen, Southwest Pacific Swamphen
Size: 51cm; male 1050g, female 850g
Geographical variation: Five subspecies, of which *melanotus* breeds in Australia and New Zealand.
Distribution: Breeds in northern and eastern Australia, Tasmania, Norfolk Island and New Zealand. It is found throughout the North, South and Stewart islands and many of their offshore islands, including Great Barrier, Great Mercury, Waiheke and Kapiti islands, and on the Chatham Islands. A few are resident in the Denham Bay swamp and the Blue Lake on Raoul Island, Kermadecs. A vagrant to L'Esperance Rock, the Kermadecs, the Three Kings Islands and Campbell Island. Because few are known from subfossil material or middens on the New Zealand mainland, it seems likely that the Pukeko became established within the past 500 years and became abundant only several hundred years ago as forest was cleared.
Population: Abundant in most districts throughout their range, especially favouring rough damp pasture near wetlands.
Conservation: Partially protected native. Legally harvested during the duck-shooting season in most parts of New Zealand, but not a highly prized gamebird. In some areas, Pukeko are sometimes regarded as a pest for grazing pasture and damaging grain and vegetable crops. They have adapted well to the changes humans have made to swamps and forests, and so have prospered, particularly on irrigated or damp pastures.
Breeding: Eggs are usually laid in August–February, with a peak in October–November, but a few may breed in any month. Pukeko build their nests on a clump of rushes, tussock or raupo, usually standing in or near water, the vegetation being beaten down into a platform. Usually several nests are made at once. Territories are often occupied by groups rather than pairs and they have highly variable mating systems. Groups will often consist of two laying females and at least two males, and all share the incubation. Groups can contain non-breeding 'helpers', offspring from previous broods that help in feeding and caring for the chicks. Each adult female lays 2–5–7 buff eggs (51 x 35mm) with blotches of brown distributed evenly or in a ring at the larger end, but because several females can lay in the same nest, clutches of 10–15 eggs are not uncommon. The incubation period is 23–25–29 days. Chicks are capable of leaving the nest within hours of hatching, but often remain for 4–5 days. They are fed for about 2 months after hatching. Young Pukeko can breed at the end of their first year but usually do not breed until their second year. Life expectancy depends on the harshness of the climate; it averages 3–4 years in Otago, but 5–6 years near Auckland. The oldest Pukeko recorded in New Zealand lived over 9 years.
Behaviour: In places with plenty of cover, Pukeko prefer to run or swim to safety, but in more open places they readily take flight for short distances. When they do fly, their take-off is laboured: running across the surface with rapid wingbeats, taking to the air with feet dangling and head and neck stretched out. Sometimes they land in the top of raupo, scrub or willows, and clumsily perch and clamber about there. They often call loudly, with a harsh screech.
Feeding: Diet is a wide variety of swamp and pasture

vegetation; also animals, mainly insects and spiders, but also frogs, small birds and eggs. From late summer to mid-winter, they form flocks to graze on pasture, especially clovers, usually near a swamp, pond, ditch or clump of rushes, to which they return if disturbed. Larger food, e.g. raupo (*Typha*) or other seed-head stem, may be held by one foot, parrot-like, and stripped or macerated by the powerful bill.

Reading: Carroll, A. L. K. 1966. *Notornis* 13: 133–141. Carroll, A. L. K. 1969. *Notornis* 16: 101–120. Craig, J. L. 1980. *Anim Behav.* 28: 593–603. Craig, J. L. et al. 1980. *Notornis* 27: 287–291. Fordham, R. A. 1983. *NZ J Ecol* 6: 133–142. Jamieson, I. G. 1994. *NZ Geographic* 21: 54–70. Jamieson, I. G. & Craig, J. L. 1993. *Natural History* 102: 50–57.

189. TAKAHE *Porphyrio hochstetteri* PLATE 42

Other names: Notornis, South Island Takahe
Size: 63cm; 3kg
Distribution: New Zealand only. Takahe are widespread as subfossils and in middens, in lowland and upland areas of both North and South islands, but they are now considered to be of two separate species: *P. mantelli* in the North Island and *P. hochstetteri* in the South Island. There were only four confirmed sightings of Takahe in the South Island during the nineteenth century, all in or near Fiordland. They were thought extinct until November 1948, when G. B. Orbell rediscovered them in Takahe Valley in the Murchison Mountains, and later in the Kepler and Stuart mountains, west of Lake Te Anau, Fiordland. Their natural range is now confined to the Murchison Mountains. Successful small groups are established on five islands: Tiritiri Matangi (Hauraki Gulf), Kapiti and Mana (western Wellington), Maud (Marlborough Sounds) and Rarotoka (Centre Island) (Foveaux Strait), and recently introduced to Secretary and Motutapu islands. A few birds are in Maungatautari, Cape and Zealandia sanctuaries; and captive birds are held at the Te Anau Wildlife Centre and Burwood Bush.
Population: At their rediscovery in 1948, the total was *c.* 250, at most 300, birds. They declined steadily through the 1960s and 1970s, and reached a minimum of 110 birds, but they have since recovered. In 2012, there were *c.* 275 birds: *c.* 110 in the Murchison Mountains, *c.* 105 on offshore islands or mainland sanctuaries, and *c.* 60 in captivity.
Conservation: Protected critically endangered flightless endemic. The aims of current management efforts are to try to protect the natural population in the Murchison Mountains with an extensive stoat trapping network and deer control programme covering the entire 50,000ha peninsula; and by transferring birds between the existing and new island, sanctuary and captive populations to increase productivity and reduce the risks of genetic problems such as inbreeding.
Breeding: Laying is in October–January. They lay 1–**2**–3 pale buff eggs (74 x 49mm, 97g) with irregular, widely spaced reddish purple blotches. Both sexes incubate for 29–**30**–31 days. Eggs hatch *c.* 48 hours apart, and the chicks soon leave the nest and are attended by both adults. Young are capable of breeding at the end of their first year but usually do not begin until their second year. They may stay with their parents for 1–2 years and share the chick-rearing role. They are potentially very long-lived, up to 20 years.
Behaviour: Takahe are fiercely territorial in the breeding season, and some males will attack human intruders. Following breeding, the family party usually stays together close to the nesting territory, and sometimes yearlings will help their parents with incubation and care of young. The main contact call by day or night is a loud, Weka-like 'coo-eet', and the alarm note is a very deep, resonant 'oomf'. Pairs often duet.
Feeding: The main foods of the naturally distributed high-altitude birds are snow tussocks (*Chionochloa* spp.) and, in winter in the beech-forested valleys, the rhizomes of the fern *Hypolepis millefolium*. On islands, they take mainly introduced grasses. They dig up fern rhizomes and pull out snow-tussock leaf bases with their bill. Holding them in one foot, they macerate the bases, digesting only the plant juices, not the fibres, which remain as typical green, sausage-shaped droppings of largely unaltered fibres.

Reading: Hegg, D. et al. 2012 *NZ J Ecol* 36: 75–89. Lee, W. G. & Jamieson, I. G. (eds) 2001. *The Takahe: Fifty Years of Conservation Management and Research.* Dunedin: Uni Otago Press. Mills, J. A. & Mark, A. F. 1977. *J Anim Ecol* 46: 939–958. Mills, J. A. et al. 1984. *NZ J Ecol* 7: 57–70.

190. AUSTRALIAN COOT *Fulica atra* PLATE 42

Other name: Eurasian Coot
Size: 38cm; male 570g, female 520g
Geographical variation: Of four subspecies, *australis* breeds throughout Australasia, including New Zealand.
Distribution: Ranges from Europe and parts of northern Africa across Asia to Japan, south to New Guinea, Australia and New Zealand. Coots were recorded in New Zealand as vagrants on eight occasions between 1875 and 1953, all in the South Island. One was recorded at Lake Tutira, Hawke's Bay, in 1954. Then Coots invaded from Australia in 1957, when nine were shot in Southland, one was shot on Lake Wairarapa and another was seen on Lake Pupuke, Auckland. The first breeding record in the South Island was at Lake Hayes, near Arrowtown, in 1958, and in the North Island at Lake Okareka, near Rotorua, in 1962. Coots spread to all districts in the 1960s and 1970s and are now widespread and common on certain lakes. Vagrants have reached Stewart Island and The Snares.

Coots favour shallow, sheltered bays fringed with extensive raupo beds and willows, especially in Auckland, Hamilton Lake, on the Volcanic Plateau lakes, Lake Tutira, Virginia Lake (Whanganui), Centennial Lagoon (Palmerston North), Queen Elizabeth Park and Henley Lake (Masterton), Lake Elterwater (Marlborough), St Annes Lagoon (near Cheviot), Lake Heron and the Ashburton Lakes (inland Canterbury). They are still largely absent from Wellington, Nelson, the West Coast and Southland.

Population: *c.* 2000 birds in 1995, but still increasing.
Conservation: Protected self-introduced native. Coots are now widespread and firmly established in New Zealand, and slowly increasing as they colonise new lakes.
Breeding: Eggs are laid in August–February, and often two broods are raised. The nest is an untidy, floating platform of twigs, rushes and waterweed anchored in emergent vegetation on the margins of inland waters. Rushes are often bent over to form the nest itself or a cover above it. Both sexes collect nest material. They lay 3–8 creamy white eggs (50 x 34mm), uniformly marked with dark spots. Both sexes incubate for 22–26 days and care for the young. The chicks are precocial and quickly leave the nest. They are fed by their parents for the first 5 weeks, and fledge at 55–60 days old. The age of first breeding of the smaller Eurasian Coot is at 1–2 years old, and the oldest known banded bird in Europe lived over 18 years.
Behaviour: Coots form large flocks in the non-breeding season, but in spring and summer, while territorial breeding birds are occupied in or near reed beds, non-breeders form small flocks in more open water. Although highly mobile, they are presumed to move at night, because they are rarely seen to fly by day; rather, they skitter across the surface, rather like Dabchicks, feet trailing and with rapid, shallow wingbeats, to splash down breast first. Their usual call is a series of loud, harsh notes uttered singly, sometimes rendered 'krark'.
Feeding: Diet is mainly vegetarian but includes some aquatic invertebrates. They reach most of the plants in submerged weed beds by diving; they jump upwards and forwards, disappearing bill first. Their lobed feet alone propel them underwater. They bring plants to the surface, jerkily swallowing what is in the bill. Dives last 2–15 seconds, depending on the water depth. They sometimes graze mown lawns at some city lakes.
Reading: Bakker, B. J. & Fordham, R. A. 1993. *Notornis* 40: 131–136. Granville, I. 1973. BSc (Hons) thesis, Uni Canterbury. Macdonald, R. 1968. *Notornis* 15: 234–237.

SNIPES, SANDPIPERS, GODWITS and ALLIES *Scolopacidae*

About 80 species, of which 3 endemic non-migratory snipes breed in New Zealand, 3 endemic snipes, *Coenocorypha barrierensis*, *C. iredalei* and *C. chathamica* have become extinct since European settlement, and 39 transequatorial species reach New Zealand in spring–summer as migrants, vagrants or stragglers.

Apart from the stints (known as peeps in North America), these waders have a slender bill that is as long as or longer than the head. In curlews and godwits, the bill is sensitive and flexible at the tip, and the mandibles open during probing in soft mud or shallow water. All have long, pointed wings, rapid flight, and, for birds, a short tail; most have long legs. Their eyes are smaller than those of plovers and dotterels, as suits their more tactile, less visual feeding. Gregarious when not breeding.

Their food has not been studied in detail in New Zealand; however, they are known to take a variety of mudflat burrowing crabs, small amphipod and ostracod crustaceans, polychaete worms and small gastropod and bivalve molluscs. Their diet also includes larvae and pupae of craneflies (Tipulidae), midges (Chironomidae), beetles and other flies; they may also take spiders, crickets and earthworms. They swallow grass, sedge and rush seeds, but whether by accident or design is not known. The various species probe to different depths according to their bill length. Most of the rapid, vigorous, sewing-machine probing of smaller waders is exploratory, as often is the slower, more careful probing of the godwits, curlews or whimbrels.

Most of the waders that migrate to New Zealand breed in the Arctic or subarctic tundra of the Northern Hemisphere, from the largest curlews to the smallest stints. The routes taken by the various species of wader are being determined by an extensive cooperative research programme throughout the East Asian–Australasian Flyway. Waders are captured in mist-nets or cannon-nets, then banded and marked with a white leg-flag to denote capture in New Zealand. In addition, geolocators and satellite transmitters have been attached to birds to determine the routes, stopover sites, times of movements, and breeding grounds for Bar-tailed Godwits and Red Knots. These studies have shown that waders undertake astonishing flights, including Bar-tailed Godwits flying non-stop for 8–9 days from Alaska to New Zealand. The coast of the Yellow Sea has been proven to be a critical pressure spot on the northward migration because it is used by most of our migrant waders as a stopover site to refuel before the final migration leg to the breeding grounds, and is also used by many as a stopover on the southward migration, but huge areas of the intertidal habitat are being claimed for massive industrial and port developments.

The first Arctic migrants arrive in September–October, but others trickle into the country through November and December. Most leave in March–April, but a variable proportion of the summer population stays behind to overwinter in New Zealand; although a few are adults that adopt breeding plumage, most are yearlings or two-year olds, and so the number left behind provides an indication of the success of the previous northern breeding season.

New Zealand is at the southern limit of many species; and some of the distances travelled, by birds as light as House Sparrows, are huge. In order to undertake such long journeys, waders feed voraciously in the weeks before departure and often arrive late to their high-tide roosts. They lay down extensive fat deposits: their weight can increase to 75% above their normal non-breeding level. On arrival, they are often emaciated and exhausted, and quite approachable, but they quickly regain their condition. The adult Arctic migrants moult all of their flight feathers during the southern summer, and so can be distinguished from juveniles, which do not moult, or lose only a few feathers, until the next southern autumn.

The sexes are alike, but females are often noticeably larger than males. The non-breeding plumage, as is mostly seen in New Zealand, is dull, the upperparts mottled or a uniform brown and/or grey, the underparts paler, sometimes with streaks and spots. Before leaving and while breeding, they are brighter and more boldly marked, many species becoming much more rufous above and rufous or black below. The age at first breeding is 1–2–3 years old, and many birds live at least 15 years.

Reading: Chandler, R. 2009. *Shorebirds of the Northern Hemisphere*. London: Christopher Helm. Hayman, P. et al. 1986. *Shorebirds: An Identification Guide to the Waders of the World*. Beckenham: Croom Helm. Pringle, J. D. 1986. *The Shorebirds of Australia*. Sydney: Angus & Robertson. Woodley, K. 2012. *Shorebirds of New Zealand: Sharing the Margins*. Auckland: Penguin.

191. SOUTH ISLAND SNIPE *Coenocorypha iredalei* PLATE 85

Other names: Stewart Island Snipe, Tutukiwi
Size: 22cm, 95g
Distribution: Extinct; formerly New Zealand only. Subfossil bones of this species were found throughout the South Island, but they had gone before European settlement. They survived on Stewart Island and outlying islands into the 1900s, but dwindled and were last recorded on Big South Cape Island in August 1964 shortly after the arrival of ship rats.
Conservation: Extinct endemic. Snipe were widespread on the South Island mainland before human settlement, but probably died out following the arrival of Pacific rats and dogs when Maori colonised about 1000 years ago. An attempt to save the Stewart Island Snipe by

transferring them to a predator-free island in August 1964 failed when the two birds caught died before release.
Breeding: Laying was in September–December. The nest was a simple depression in leaf litter, or a bowl of grass, sedge, or *Dracophyllum* leaves and bark, twigs, lichen and moss. It was on or near the ground, under dense vegetation such as manuka and *Dracophyllum*. They laid 2 pale brown eggs (40 x 30mm, 19g) with dark spots and blotches. Incubation was shared. Chicks left the nest on the day of hatching.
Behaviour: On islands off Stewart Island, South Island Snipe lived mainly in thick vegetation under dense *Olearia* forest cover, or in low heathland scrub of stunted manuka and *Dracophyllum*, with *Cladia* lichen. Although cryptically patterned and shunning open areas, South Island Snipe were confiding and allowed close approach. They were the source of the Maori legend of the hakawai, a frightening creature that called only at night. This nocturnal aerial display, two syllable calls followed by the roaring sound of vibrating tail feathers during the birds' rapid descent, was mainly performed on moonlit nights.
Feeding: Diet comprised a wide variety of invertebrates, including earthworms, amphipods, insects and their larvae. They probed in the peaty soil and around the bases of plants.
Reading: Guthrie-Smith, H. 1925 *Sorrows and Joys of a New Zealand Naturalist*. Reed: Dunedin. Miskelly, C. M. 1987. *Notornis* 34: 95–116. Miskelly, C. M. 2012. *Notornis* 59: 15–31. Miskelly, C. M. & de Lange, P. 2006. *Notornis* 53: 339–352. Wilson, R. A. 1959. *Bird Islands of New Zealand*. Whitcombe & Tombs: Christchurch.

192. CHATHAM ISLANDS SNIPE *Coenocorypha pusilla* PLATE 43

Size: 20cm, 80g
Distribution: Chatham Islands only. Formerly on Chatham, Pitt and Mangere islands, but after cats eradicated them from Mangere Island in the 1890s they were confined to South East Island. Reintroduced to Mangere Island in 1970, from which they have colonised Little Mangere Island and Rabbit Island. More recently found on the Star Keys (1974), and now a vagrant to Pitt Island.
Population: *c.* 2000 birds. Common on South East Island, increasing elsewhere.
Conservation: Protected vulnerable endemic. Although capable of strong flight, Chatham Islands Snipe rarely fly during the day, and their confiding nature makes them easy prey to ground-hunting predators. Successfully reintroduced to Mangere Island from South East Island in 1970 and 1972 after cats had died out. Attempts to rear young in captivity have had little success.
Breeding: Eggs are laid from late July to early April, but mostly September–January. The nest is on or near the ground, among dense vegetation such as tussock, sedge or fern. It is a simple depression in leaf litter, or a bowl of grass or sedge leaves. They lay 2–4 pale pinkish-brown eggs (39 x 28mm, 16g) with spots and blotches of dark brown and grey around the widest part. Incubation is shared, and lasts 18–20 days. Chicks leave the nest on the day of hatching and the brood is split between the adults. The chicks are fed entirely by their parents initially, but become independent at about 6 weeks old.
Behaviour: Chatham Islands Snipe remain under forest or among dense cover during the day but will feed in open areas at night. They fly during the day only if disturbed at close range, but do so readily at night when they display aerially.
Feeding: Diet includes earthworms, amphipods, insects and their larvae. They obtain all their food by probing in soil and at the base of plants.
Reading: Miskelly, C. M. 1990. *Ibis* 132: 366–379. Miskelly, C. M. 1990. *Emu* 90: 28–32. Miskelly, C. M. 1999. *Notornis* 46: 207–221. Miskelly, C. M. & Munn, A. 2011. *Notornis* 58: 93–94.

193. SNARES SNIPE *Coenocorypha huegeli* PLATE 43

Other name: Tutukiwi
Size: 22cm, 110g
Distribution: New Zealand only. Until recently, confined to The Snares, where it is common on North East and Broughton islands, and recorded from Alert Stack. In 2005, successfully introduced to Putauhina Island off southwestern Stewart Island, and in 2012, introduced to Codfish Island.
Population: *c.* 400 pairs on The Snares, 320 birds on Putauhina Island in 2011, and 30 introduced to Codfish Island in 2012.
Conservation: Protected endemic. This species has been

introduced to a couple of islands off Stewart Island, where it is being used as an ecological substitute for the extinct South Island Snipe (*C. iredalei*), and these populations are also an insurance measure should rats ever get to The Snares.

Breeding: Laying is in November–April, with a peak in early December. The nest is on or near the ground, among dense vegetation such as tussock, sedge or fern. It is a simple depression in leaf litter, or a bowl of grass or sedge leaves. They lay 2 pale brown eggs (44 x 33mm, 25g) with dark spots and blotches. Incubation is shared equally by the sexes and lasts *c.* 22 days. The chicks leave the nest on the day of hatching, and each is cared for independently by one of the adults. The chicks are fed entirely by their parents for the first 2 weeks and remain with them for 9–11 weeks. Snipe can breed at 1 year old, but most cannot obtain a territory until 2–3 years old. The oldest known banded bird lived to at least 16 years and 10 months.

Behaviour: Snares Snipe prefer areas of dense ground cover, where they can reach densities of 10 birds per hectare. They are capable of flight but rarely do so unless disturbed at close range. Although they have not been recorded doing aerial displays, tail feather wear suggests that some birds do the diving display when their vibrating tail feathers make a roaring sound. Although cryptically patterned and shunning open areas, snipe are confiding and allow close approach. Their presence is often revealed by the male territorial calls: 'chuup-chuup-chuup' and 'queeyoo queeyoo queeyoo'.

Feeding: Diet comprises a wide variety of invertebrates, including earthworms, amphipods, insects and their larvae. They favour damper areas of tussock, scrub or forest, where they get all their food by probing in the peaty soil and around the base of plants.

Reading: Miskelly, C. M. 1987. *Notornis* 34: 95–116. Miskelly, C. M. 1990. *Ibis* 132: 366–379. Miskelly, C. M. 1999. *Notornis* 46: 207–221. Miskelly, C. M. & Sagar, P. M. 2005. *Notornis* 52: 120–121. Miskelly, C. M. et al. 2012. *Notornis* 59: 32–38.

194. SUBANTARCTIC SNIPE *Coenocorypha aucklandica* PLATE 43

Other names: Hakawai, New Zealand Snipe

Size: 23cm, 110g

Geographical variation: Three subspecies described: *meinertzhagenae* on the Antipodes Islands, *aucklandica* on the Auckland Islands, and *perseverance* on the Campbell Islands.

Distribution: New Zealand only. Subantarctic Snipe are now confined to subantarctic islands which large mammalian predators have not reached. Antipodes Island Snipe are on all islands in the Antipodes group, Auckland Islands Snipe are on all islands in the group except the main island, where there are cats and pigs. In November 1997, a small population of snipe was rediscovered in the Campbell Islands, living on Jacquemart Island, and they have since recolonised the main island following the eradication of rats in 2001.

Population: Common on predator-free islands in the subantarctic, but no estimate of numbers is available.

Conservation: Protected endemic. Snipe nest on the ground, are confiding and rarely fly, and so are extremely vulnerable to ground-hunting predators such as cats and rats. The only introduced mammal that snipe have survived alongside is the house mouse on Antipodes Island.

Breeding: Laying is in September–January on Auckland and Campbell islands, but the season is extended from August–March, and apparently bimodal with laying in August–early November and again in late January–March on the Antipodes. The nest is on or near the ground, among dense vegetation such as tussock, sedge or fern. It is a simple depression in leaf litter, or a bowl of grass or sedge leaves. They lay 2 pale brown eggs (42.8 x 31.4mm, 23g) with dark spots and blotches especially around the broadest part of the egg. Incubation is shared by the sexes. The chicks leave the nest on the day of hatching, and each is cared for independently by one of the adults. The chicks are fed entirely by their parents initially and remain with them for at least 9 weeks.

Behaviour: Subantarctic Snipe prefer areas of dense ground cover, only venturing into more open areas at night. They are capable of flight but rarely do so unless disturbed at close range or when displaying. Although cryptically patterned and shunning open areas, snipe are confiding and allow close approach. Their presence is often revealed by the male territorial calls: 'trerk trerk trerk' and 'queeyoo queeyoo', particularly at dawn or dusk. They have a nocturnal aerial display, a call followed by the roaring sound of vibrating tail feathers as the bird plunges towards the ground.

Feeding: Diet comprises a wide variety of invertebrates, including earthworms, amphipods, insects and their larvae. They favour damper areas of tussock, scrub or forest, where they get all their food by probing in the peaty soil and around the base of plants.

Reading: Miskelly, C. M. & Baker, A. J. 2010. *Notornis* 56: 113–123. Miskelly, C. M. et al. 2006. *Notornis* 53: 375–381. Miskelly, C. M. & Fraser, J. R. 2006. *Notornis* 53: 353–359. Miskelly, C. M. 1987. *Notornis* 34: 95–116. Miskelly, C. M. 1990. *Ibis* 132: 366–379. Miskelly, C. M. 1990. *Emu* 90: 28–32. Miskelly, C. M. et al. 2006. *Notornis* 53: 361–374.

195. JAPANESE SNIPE *Gallinago hardwickii* PLATE 43

Other name: Latham's Snipe
Size: 24cm, 160g
Distribution: Breeds in Japan, especially in the north, on the southern Sakhalin Peninsula and the southern Kurile Islands, and on the mainland coast of eastern Siberia. They migrate to winter in New Guinea and Australia, mainly in the eastern and southeastern states. They have been recorded in New Zealand about 15 times, from Auckland to The Snares, usually at freshwater wetlands surrounded with rank rushes, sedges and reeds. Apart from two early specimens (Auckland 1898 and Whanganui 1914) and recent records from Manawatu Estuary (1999–2000) and Lake Ellesmere (2002), the rest are sight records where the identity of Japanese Snipe is assumed in preference to the other similar, but less likely, snipes. Seen as singles, except for two at Cooper's Lagoon (1973), two at Lake George, Colac Bay (1984–86) and three at Lake Wairarapa (1993).
Behaviour: Solitary or in small groups. When approached, they generally crouch in thick vegetation, blending with their surroundings, but if disturbed they rise suddenly, zigzag up steeply and pitch suddenly, or circle fairly high calling a harsh 'krek' repeatedly, before landing.

196. RED KNOT *Calidris canutus* PLATE 44

Other names: Huahou, Lesser Knot
Size: 24cm, 120g
Geographical variation: Five or 6 subspecies of Red Knot: the Lesser Knot, *rogersi*, which breeds on the Chukotka Peninsula and eastern Siberia, and *piersmai* from the New Siberian Islands, are the forms that migrate to Australasia, including New Zealand. These subspecies are inseparable in non-breeding plumage, but most Red Knots that visit New Zealand are believed to be Lesser Knots, *rogersi*.
Distribution: Breeds in widely separated parts of the high Arctic and winters in temperate and tropical estuaries of both hemispheres. In New Zealand, they are unevenly distributed around the coast, with large concentrations (5000+ birds) regularly at the Kaipara and Manukau harbours and at Farewell Spit. Flocks of 1000–5000 birds are often recorded from Parengarenga, Houhora, Rangaunu, Whangarei and Waitemata harbours, and the Firth of Thames. Smaller flocks of 200–1000 birds regularly spend the summer at Mangawhai Estuary, Golden and Tasman bays, in Southland coastal lagoons and estuaries, at Paterson Inlet (Stewart Island), and Te Whanga Lagoon (Chatham Island). Smaller groups are at many other estuaries and coastal lagoons. A surprisingly rare bird on the Aotea, Kawhia and Ohiwa harbours, Ahuriri Estuary, Avon–Heathcote Estuary and the Otago coast. A straggler to the Kermadec, Auckland and Campbell islands. Usually 4–10% of summer visitors remain to overwinter, mainly in the Manukau Harbour.

The New Zealand Wader Study Group has shown from banding recoveries and leg-flag sightings that adult Red Knots reach New Zealand in September–October from their breeding grounds in far-eastern Siberia after 4 to 5 flights down through eastern Asia and Australia or Irian Jaya. Many juveniles stop in Australia before moving on to New Zealand in their second year. The return from New Zealand to eastern Siberia, starting in March–April, is apparently mainly through staging areas in the Gulf of Carpentaria and New Guinea, and then on the Yellow Sea coast of China and Korea, especially in Bohai Bay.
Population: Red Knots are the second most numerous Arctic wader to reach New Zealand. Between 1983 and 1993, 33,000–**51,000**–67,000 were counted by Ornithological Society members each summer, but numbers dropped to 27,000–**42,000**–67,000 between 1994 and 2003, and further to 27,000–**31,000**–40,000 between 2008 and 2012. This equates to decline of 2.4% per annum over the 30-year period since 1983. About 2000–4000 birds overwinter.

Behaviour: Gregarious; flying, roosting and feeding in packed masses. In flight, a flock will twist and turn like swirling smoke clouds. In New Zealand, Red Knots are usually silent, but feeding flocks and roosting flocks disturbed by the rising tide may keep up a subdued, not unmusical chatter. Birds in flight may utter a throaty 'knut, knut', and before migration they give a clear 'weet, weet' call.
Feeding: Diet is mainly small (5–15mm) thin-shelled bivalves *Myodora*, *Tellina* and *Nucula*, with other thicker-shelled molluscs (e.g. the cockle *Chione*) and gastropods, which are swallowed whole. They feed close to the tideline on intertidal mudflats and sandflats, often with Bar-tailed Godwits. A tactile rather than visual feeder, feeding as a flock with remarkable coordination, they rapidly drill soft mud or wet sand with a sewing-machine action, head held low and bill nearly vertical.
Reading: Barter, M. et al. 1988. *Stilt* 12: 29–32. Piersma, T. 1991. *Stilt* 19: 30–36. Riegen, A. C. 1999. *Notornis* 46: 123–142. Sagar, P. M. et al. 1999. *Notornis* 46: 1–43. Southey, I. 2009. *DOC Res Dev Ser* 308. Wellington: DOC.

197. GREAT KNOT *Calidris tenuirostris* PLATE 44

Size: 27cm, 160g
Distribution: Breeds in northeastern Siberia and migrates to southern Asia, the Philippines and Australasia, especially to the northern and northwestern coasts of Australia, where over 150,000 spend the southern summer. A rare migrant to New Zealand, with about 30 records up to 2012, from Northland to Mason Bay, Stewart Island. Mostly singletons, except at Firth of Thames (two in 1970), Manukau Harbour (three in 2004), Wanganui Estuary (three in 1992) and Manawatu Estuary (three in 1967, four in 2003).
Behaviour: Gregarious. In New Zealand, they are usually found roosting or feeding with Red Knots, and may be overlooked amongst huge flocks of these at some sites.
Reading: Andrew, I. G. 1968. *Notornis* 15: 207–210.

198. SANDERLING *Calidris alba* PLATE 52

Size: 20cm, 50g
Distribution: Breeds in the high Arctic in Greenland, Spitzbergen and parts of Siberia, including the Taimyr Peninsula and the delta of the Lena River, and on northern islands of Canada. They winter widely on coasts in tropical and temperate regions of both hemispheres. A rare but probably annual visitor to New Zealand. They have been recorded from Northland to Southland, and from Chatham Island. Usually singles, but sometimes in small flocks, e.g. five at Parengarenga Harbour (1950); four at Tapora, Kaipara Harbour (1999); five (1967) and four (1988) at Kaituna Cut/Maketu; six at Farewell Spit (1983); five (1966) and four (1971) at Waituna Lagoon, Southland.
Behaviour: Sanderlings always seem in a hurry as they feed busily close to the tideline; on the sandy ocean beaches that they prefer, they rush in and out of the wave line, following each backwash and jabbing and probing rapidly. They also peck and probe on estuarine and mudflat pools, but prefer the sandier parts. They hold their body horizontal and move their legs so fast that they have been likened to clockwork toys.

199. DUNLIN *Calidris alpina* PLATE 44

Size: 18cm, 50g
Distribution: Breeds from eastern Greenland, across northern Europe and Siberia to Alaska and northern Canada. Dunlins winter mainly north of the tropics, in the southern United States and Caribbean, and from Europe east to southern China, Korea and Japan. The few records in Australia and New Zealand are of rare vagrants, including four accepted records of single birds seen at Kaipara Harbour (1974), the Firth of Thames (1977) and Manukau Harbour (1979, 1986).
Behaviour: In general behaviour, including feeding, very much like the Curlew Sandpiper. In flight, they give a high, flat 'trreee'.
Reading: Brown, B. 1975. *Notornis* 22: 241–243. Brown, B. 1979. *Notornis* 26: 202–203.

200. CURLEW SANDPIPER *Calidris ferruginea* PLATE 46

Size: 19cm, 60g

Distribution: Breeds in high arctic central Siberia between the Yenesei and Kolyma rivers. A few have bred in Alaska, well to the east of their normal range. They winter in Africa, southern Asia and Australasia, and are a regular migrant to New Zealand estuaries and coastal lagoons from Northland to Southland. Recorded from the Kermadec, Chatham and Auckland islands.

Population: Flocks of 10–50 (exceptionally 100+) Curlew Sandpipers were recorded at Parengarenga and Manukau harbours, the Firth of Thames, Lake Ellesmere and Awarua Bay in the 1980s and early 1990s. Between 1983 and 1993, a total of 29–75–136 birds were recorded each summer in Ornithological Society counts, making them the seventh most numerous Arctic wader in New Zealand; but numbers have since plummeted, and perhaps only 10–20 visit New Zealand each year. A few overwinter.

Behaviour: They roost and feed mainly with Wrybills, when they are present, or with Banded Dotterels or Red Knots. Their call is a clear, soft, liquid 'chirrup'.

Feeding: Curlew Sandpipers feed in wet mud or in shallow water, often belly-deep, probing deeply and often submerging their head to do so.

Reading: Sagar, P. M. et al. 1999. *Notornis* 46: 1–43. Southey, I. 2009. *DOC Res Dev Ser* 308. Wellington: DOC.

201. STILT SANDPIPER *Calidris himantopus* PLATE 44

Size: 21cm, 50g

Distribution: Breeds in Arctic regions of Alaska and Canada, and migrates to southern South America. A few vagrants have reached Australia, and two New Zealand records, both at Lake Ellesmere – in September to November 1998, and in December 2000.

202. SHARP-TAILED SANDPIPER *Calidris acuminata* PLATE 45

Size: 21cm; male 75g, female 60g

Distribution: Breeds in northeastern Siberia, in a limited range from the Lena River to the Kolyma River. Most birds migrate to New Guinea and Australia, particularly in eastern South Australia, Victoria and southern New South Wales, but some reach New Zealand, Vanuatu, New Caledonia and Fiji. In New Zealand, they are a regular migrant in small numbers. Small flocks of 5–10 birds are often recorded on Parengarenga and Manukau harbours, the Firth of Thames, Lakes Wairarapa and Ellesmere, and at the Southland coastal lagoons and estuaries. Smaller numbers are found at other estuaries or coastal lagoons from Northland to Southland in October–March. A transient at the Kermadec Islands, and a straggler to the Chathams and The Snares.

Population: Sharp-tailed Sandpipers are the eighth most numerous Arctic wader to reach New Zealand. Between 1983 and 1993, 14–68–173 were counted each summer, but their numbers have since progressively declined to only 15–30 each summer, perhaps as a result of reclamation of important staging habitats around the Yellow Sea. A few overwinter.

Behaviour: Gregarious, often feeding and roosting quietly in small flocks at pools in beds of *Sarcocornia*, roosting on shellbanks or sandbanks with Wrybills, Red Knots, Curlew Sandpipers and Red-necked Stints, or sharing marsh-turf of coastal lagoons with Banded Dotterels and Pectoral Sandpipers. They are usually silent in New Zealand, but birds, when flushed, may utter soft, metallic 'pleeps'.

Feeding: Sharp-tailed Sandpipers forage on the shallow edges of lagoons, both fresh and brackish, preferring low-growing salt-marsh vegetation to open mudflats, although in New Zealand they may also visit higher parts of the shore away from the tideline.

Reading: Sagar, P. M. et al. 1999. *Notornis* 46: 1–43. Southey, I. 2009. *DOC Res Dev Ser* 308. Wellington: DOC.

203. PECTORAL SANDPIPER *Calidris melanotos* PLATE 45

Size: 22cm; male 80g, female 70g
Distribution: Breeds across northern Siberia from the Taimyr Peninsula to the Bering Sea, enclosing the known breeding range of the Sharp-tailed Sandpiper, and in northern Alaska and Canada. Most migrate through the United States and Mexico to winter in southern South America, but a few apparently migrate due south to Australia and New Zealand, with occasional records in southeastern Asia, Micronesia, New Guinea, Kiribati and Vanuatu. In New Zealand, they favour eastern estuaries and coastal lagoons, especially Lakes Wairarapa, Ellesmere and Wainono, and at Te Whanga Lagoon, Chatham Island, but they have been recorded at many sites from Northland to Southland.
Population: Usually fewer than 10 Pectoral Sandpipers visit New Zealand each year, mainly in November–April. The largest flock recorded was 11 at Lake Ellesmere in February 1993.
Behaviour: Gregarious, usually in small flocks or with, but feeding apart from, Sharp-tailed Sandpipers and Banded Dotterels. They are usually silent in New Zealand but, when disturbed into flight, they call a clear, husky 'prrrt, prrrt'.
Feeding: Like Sharp-tailed Sandpipers, they prefer the edges of wet grassy areas and shallow pools with scattered low vegetation, but are even more likely to avoid the open tideline.

204. BAIRD'S SANDPIPER *Calidris bairdii* PLATE 46

Size: 16cm, 40g
Distribution: Breeds from the Chukotski Peninsula and Wrangel Island of far-eastern Siberia, across arctic Alaska and Canada to northwestern Greenland, and winters in western and southern South America. Rare vagrants to Australia and New Zealand, including seven records of single birds, perhaps sometimes of the same individual, all in the North Island: Manukau Harbour (1970, 1976), Firth of Thames (1970, 1971, 1972) Portland Island (2002), and Manawatu Estuary (1976).
Reading: McKenzie, H. R. et al. 1971. *Notornis* 18: 58–60.

205. WHITE-RUMPED SANDPIPER *Calidris fuscicollis* PLATE 46

Size: 17cm, 35g
Distribution: Breeds in far-northern Alaska and Canada, and winters in southern South America. Rare vagrants to eastern and southeastern Australia and New Zealand, including two at Manukau Harbour (December 1969) and one at Parengarenga Harbour (March 1971).
Behaviour: If flushed, they often utter a distinctive, high-pitched 'jeet', like a mouse's squeak.
Reading: Edgar, A. T. 1971. *Notornis* 18: 116–117. McKenzie, H. R. 1970. *Notornis* 17: 236–237.

206. LITTLE STINT *Calidris minuta* PLATE 47

Size: 14cm, 25g
Distribution: Breeds in the Arctic from Scandinavia east to Siberia, and migrates mainly to southern Europe, Africa and southern Asia. They are rare vagrants to Australasia, including three accepted records at Lake Ellesmere (1992–93, 1995, 2010) and several other possible sightings at Kaipara Harbour, the Firth of Thames and Lake Ellesmere. Probably often overlooked and mistaken for Red-necked Stints.
Behaviour: Like Red-necked Stints in habits and habitat; the acceptable records were each of birds in mixed flocks that allowed direct comparisons of plumage and morphology to be made.
Reading: Crocker, T. C. et al. 2002. *Notornis* 49: 182–184.

207. RED-NECKED STINT *Calidris ruficollis* PLATE 47

Size: 15cm, 30g
Distribution: Breeds in northern Siberia from the Taimyr Peninsula to the Bering Sea, and in northwestern Alaska. They migrate to the coasts of the Bay of Bengal, Malaysia, the Philippines, Indonesia and Australasia, especially to southeastern Australia. In New Zealand, they are widespread in small flocks that seldom exceed 25 birds. Favoured sites are Parengarenga and Manukau harbours, the Firth of Thames, Porangahau Estuary, Farewell Spit, Lakes Grassmere, Ellesmere and Wainono, and Awarua Bay, but they use many coastal lagoons and estuaries from Northland to Southland. Stragglers have been recorded at Chatham Island and the Auckland Islands.
Population: The fifth most numerous Arctic wader to reach New Zealand. Between 1983 and 1993, 65–**158**–231 were counted each summer; however, numbers have subsequently declined to about 60–150 birds, possibly due to major reclamation of migration stopover sites in the Yellow Sea. In winter, fewer than 25 remain, mainly at Lake Ellesmere.
Behaviour: Gregarious; feeding in small single-species flocks, or with Banded Dotterels and Wrybills, and usually roosting with Wrybills, if present. Quiet in New Zealand; in flight, they sometimes utter a thin, high-pitched call.
Feeding: Red-necked Stints feed mainly on tidal mudflats, sandflats and coastal lagoons with a thin film of moisture. They feed eagerly, with legs flexed and bodies low to the mud, running about with mouse-like rushes, their bills busily probing up and down like sewing machines. They also snatch and jab at the surface.
Reading: Sagar, P. M. et al. 1999. *Notornis* 46: 1–43. Southey, I. 2009. *DOC Res Dev Ser* 308. Wellington: DOC. Thomas, D. G. and Dartnall, A. J. 1971. *Emu* 71: 20–26.

208. LONG-TOED STINT *Calidris subminuta* PLATE 47

Size: 14cm, 25g
Distribution: Breeds near the treeline in the subarctic of Asia from Kazakhstan to Siberia, and most winter in Southeast Asia and the Philippines, but about 200 regularly reach Australia, especially in the west and north. Two accepted New Zealand records, at Lake Ellesmere in August–September 1997 and December 2000.
Reading: Petch, S. et al. 2002. *Notornis* 49: 185–186.

209. LEAST SANDPIPER *Calidris minutilla* PLATE 47

Size: 14cm, 25g
Distribution: Breeds in subarctic North America from Alaska through northern Canada to Labrador, Nova Scotia and Maine. They migrate to southern United States, the Caribbean, Central America and northern South America. A rare vagrant to Australasia, including a sight record of a yellow-legged stint at Wairoa Estuary (1952) that fits this species, and two other probable sight records (certainly of yellow-legged stints) at Ahuriri Estuary (1953) and the Firth of Thames (1972).
Reading: Stidolph, R. H. D. 1953. *Notornis* 5: 115.

210. SEMIPALMATED SANDPIPER *Calidris pusilla* PLATE 46

Size: 14cm, 25g
Distribution: Breeds in far-eastern Siberia and in subarctic North America, from Alaska through northern Canada and Baffin Island to Labrador. This is the most common wader of North America, and they migrate to winter in estuaries of Central America, the Caribbean, and northern and central South America. One New Zealand record: Westshore Lagoon, Ahuriri Estuary, Hawke's Bay (January 1966).
Reading: Sibson, R. B. & Mackenzie, N. B. 1967. *Notornis* 14: 84.

211. WESTERN SANDPIPER *Calidris mauri* PLATE 47

Size: 16cm, 30g
Distribution: Breeds on Chukotka Peninsula of far-eastern Siberia, and in western and northern Alaska. Winters in coastal California, Mexico, Central America and northern South America. Rare vagrants to Australasia, including six New Zealand records: Farewell Spit (October 1964), Rangaputa Bank, Rangaunu Harbour (November 1970), Firth of Thames (February 1971, November 1984) and Parengarenga Harbour (April 1976, January 1979).
Reading: Blackburn, A. & Bell, B. D. 1965. *Notornis* 12: 109–110.

212. BROAD-BILLED SANDPIPER *Limicola falcinellus* PLATE 44

Size: 17cm, 35g
Geographical variation: Two subspecies: *falcinellus* breeds in Scandinavia and northwestern Russia and migrates to East Africa and southern Asia; *sibirica* breeds in northern Siberia and migrates mainly to southeastern Asia and northwestern Australia.
Distribution: Breeds in widely scattered parts of the Arctic from Scandinavia to eastern Siberia, and winters in Africa, southern Asia and in Australasia. In most years, a few reach New Zealand. They were first recorded at the Firth of Thames, January–March 1960, and since then singles, or at most two birds, have been recorded occasionally between Northland and Lake Ellesmere. Most sightings have been at the Manukau Harbour and on the Firth of Thames.
Behaviour: Often solitary, but also with Wrybills or Red-necked Stints at high-tide roosts.
Feeding: In New Zealand, they feed on soft intertidal mudflats with the bill held vertically, probing vigorously up and down, sometimes inserting the full length of the bill and submerging the head; occasionally they peck at the surface.
Reading: Sibson, R. B. & McKenzie, H. R. 1960. *Notornis* 8: 233–235.

213. BUFF-BREASTED SANDPIPER *Tryngites subruficollis* PLATE 45

Size: 20cm, 60g
Distribution: Breeds mainly in in the high Arctic tundra of northern Alaska and northern Canada; a few in northeastern Siberia. Winters mostly inland in Argentina, Paraguay and Uruguay. A scarce vagrant to Australasia, including about 10 confirmed records from Australia, and one confirmed record from New Zealand: South Kaipara Harbour, March 2014.
Behaviour: Usually silent when not breeding, and often solitary. They favour short damp grassland rather than estuaries. Known for their lek breeding, in which males congregate to display, raising their stiffly-held wings.

214. RUFF *Philomachus pugnax* PLATE 45

Other name: Reeve (female)
Size: male 29cm, 170g; female 22cm, 110g
Distribution: Breeds from northern Europe east to eastern Siberia, and winters mostly in southern Europe, Africa and India. A scarce vagrant to Australasia, including about 18 sight records in New Zealand: Manukau Harbour, (possible in 1964, 2001, 2006–07), Lake Ellesmere (two in 1984–85, 1991–92, 1999–2000), Colac Bay, Southland (1984–85), Lake Poukawa (1985), Lake Wainono (1987, 2002), Miranda (2001, 2005), Ahuriri Estuary (2001), Taranaki (2002), Rakaia River mouth (2003), Kaiapoi (2004), Maketu (2005) and Nelson (2007).
Behaviour: Gregarious and usually silent when not breeding. They favour muddy edges of shallow fresh-water lagoons, probing and pecking to feed. Well known for their lek breeding, in which males congregate to display their spectacularly variable ruffs and ear tufts of breeding plumage. Females visit the lek solely to copulate.

215. ASIATIC DOWITCHER *Limnodromus semipalmatus* PLATE 49

Size: 35cm, 180g
Distribution: Asiatic Dowitchers are uncommon. Breeds patchily in lower Siberia, Mongolia and Manchuria. In winter they are thinly distributed on the coast of the Bay of Bengal, Thailand, Sumatra, Java and northwestern Australia, where several hundred may spend the southern summer. Five records in New Zealand: Avon–Heathcote Estuary (August–September 1985), Firth of Thames (February–May 1987), Farewell Spit (January 1988), Maketu (November 1998) and Ohiwa Harbour (December 2002).
Reading: Fennell, J. et al. 1985. *Notornis* 32: 322–323. Paige, J. P. 1965. *Ibis* 107: 95–97.

216. FAR-EASTERN CURLEW *Numenius madagascariensis* PLATE 48

Other name: Eastern Curlew
Size: 63cm, 900g
Distribution: Far-eastern Curlews are uncommon, with an estimated population of *c.* 38,000 birds in 2006, but they are declining rapidly. Breeds in north-eastern Asia, including lower Siberia, eastern Mongolia and Manchuria, and migrates to coasts of Asia and Australasia, especially northern and eastern Australia. In New Zealand, Eastern Curlews are an annual migrant in ever-decreasing numbers. Favoured places for small flocks of 3–10 birds are Manukau Harbour, the Firth of Thames, Farewell Spit and the Southland coast. Birds are often recorded at Parengarenga, Kaipara and Kawhia harbours, Kaituna/Maketu in the Bay of Plenty, and the Manawatu, Ashley and Avon–Heathcote estuaries. Recorded at the Kermadec, Chatham, Stewart and Campbell islands.
Population: Far-eastern Curlews are the ninth most common Arctic wader in New Zealand. Numbers have declined dramatically in southeastern Australia and New Zealand since the 1960s, when probably *c.* 100 birds visited New Zealand each summer. By the 1980s and early 1990s, only 20–50 birds visited New Zealand each year, and numbers have declined even further, perhaps as a result of ongoing loss of intertidal habitats at stopover sites in the Yellow Sea. Since 2008, fewer than 10 have visited New Zealand each summer. A few non-breeders stay in New Zealand over the southern winter.
Behaviour: Gregarious and wary when roosting on sand dunes and shellbanks and among mangroves. Their call, given mostly in flight, is a loud, haunting 'croo-lee, croo-lee'.
Feeding: Diet is mainly crustaceans, especially ghost shrimps and crabs, and marine polychaete worms, caught by probing down their burrows deep into the mud, by probing sideways into shallow burrows or by picking at the surface. They feed mainly in muddy, tidal estuaries and harbours.
Reading: Close, D. & Newman, O. M. G. 1984. *Emu* 84: 38–40. Robertson, H. A. & Dennison, M. D. 1979. *Notornis* 26: 73–88.

217. WHIMBREL *Numenius phaeopus* PLATE 48

Size: 43cm, 450g
Geographical variation: Four to six subspecies are recognised, of which two reach New Zealand. The Asiatic Whimbrel *variegatus* breeds in eastern Siberia and is the common form in Australasia, and the American Whimbrel *hudsonicus* breeds in northern North America and regularly reaches New Zealand in small numbers.
Distribution: Breeds widely around the globe in the lower Arctic and northern temperate regions, and migrates to many estuaries and coasts in tropical regions and in the temperate Southern Hemisphere. Asiatic Whimbrels are a regular summer visitor to New Zealand, while American Whimbrels are also regular visitors, but make up only 5–10% of the Whimbrels seen here. The most favoured places for small flocks of 5–20 Whimbrels are Parengarenga, Rangaunu, Whangarei, Kaipara and Manukau harbours, the Firth of Thames, and Farewell Spit. Smaller groups, usually ones and twos, may appear at any estuary or coastal lagoon in New Zealand. Recorded at the Kermadec and Chatham islands.
Population: Whimbrels are the sixth most common Arctic wader to visit New Zealand, but numbers are declining. Between 1983 and 1994, 33–**89**–178 Whimbrels were counted in New Zealand each summer, but since 2008 fewer than 50 have visited each year. A few birds

of both subspecies overwinter.
Behaviour: Gregarious, usually seen feeding in small groups of up to five birds, but they form small flocks at roost. Often they stay warily in water at the edge of a flock of Bar-tailed Godwit roosting on the tideline. They take off before the godwits take any notice of a distant intruder. Their tittering call – 'ti-ti-ti-ti-ti-ti-ti' – is sometimes readily heard from within a passing flock of godwits.
Feeding: Diet is mainly crabs and marine worms, picked from the surface or taken by shallow probing.

218. LITTLE WHIMBREL *Numenius minutus* PLATE 48

Other name: Little Curlew
Size: 30cm, 160g
Distribution: Breeds on the dry, open steppes of central and northeastern Siberia, and mainly winters in New Guinea and Australia, especially inland in the north and northwest. In New Zealand, they are a rare annual migrant, but many probably go undetected because they frequent habitats away from usual wader haunts. Usually singles, occasionally twos and threes, feed in short grassland or ploughed paddocks near estuaries and coastal lakes from Parengarenga to Wainono Lagoon, but especially at Lake Ellesmere, Manukau Harbour and the Firth of Thames.
Behaviour: In New Zealand, they are usually alone or roost with Pacific Golden Plovers, New Zealand Dotterels or Pied Stilts. The usual flight call is a soft chattering 'te-te-te', changed to a harsh 'tchoo-tchoo-tchoo' when flushed or alarmed.
Feeding: Diet is mainly large insects, picked from the surface in grassland or on the drier parts of mudflats.
Reading: Heather, B. D. & Mackenzie, N. B. 1973. *Notornis* 20: 167. McGill, A. R. 1960. *Emu* 60: 89–94.

219. BRISTLE-THIGHED CURLEW *Numenius tahitiensis* PLATE 48

Size: 42cm, 400g
Distribution: A rare species numbering *c.* 10,000 birds. Breeds in tundra of western Alaska on Seward Peninsula and Yukon Delta, and winters on oceanic islands and atolls of the Pacific Ocean from Guam to Hawai'i in the north, and from Fiji to Pitcairn Islands in the south. Records from Papua New Guinea, Solomons, New Caledonia and the Kermadec Islands (Macauley Island 1966, North Meyer Island 1972, and Raoul Island 1972) are at the southwestern limit of their range.
Feeding: Diet includes invertebrates, molluscs and hermit crabs. In French Polynesia and in Rarotonga, they feed in open grassland, in marsh turf, in channels and pools of the outer coral reef, and on sandy beaches along the water's edge or along the line of beach wrack. Unusually for curlews, they are known for stealing the eggs of seabirds.
Reading: Gill, R. E. & Redmond, R. L. 1992. *Notornis* 39: 17–26.

220. BAR-TAILED GODWIT *Limosa lapponica* PLATE 49

Other name: Kuaka
Size: male 39cm, bill 8.5cm, 300g; female 41cm, bill 10.5cm, 350g
Geographical variation: Three subspecies are currently recognised, but this is under review: *lapponica* breeds from Scandinavia east to central Siberia, and migrates to Europe, Africa and southern Asia; *menzbieri* breeds in northern Siberia and migrates to southeastern Asia and northwestern Australia; *baueri* breeds in Alaska and migrates to Australasia, especially New Zealand.
Distribution: Breeds from northern Scandinavia across northern Siberia to Alaska. They migrate mainly to estuaries and coasts of tropical and temperate regions from Europe and Africa to Australasia and southwestern Pacific islands, such as Vanuatu, New Caledonia and particularly Fiji. In New Zealand, they are found on estuaries and sandy coasts throughout, but especially on inlets and estuaries with broad intertidal mudflats; south to Stewart Island and east to Chatham Island. Over 10,000 birds visit the Kaipara and Manukau harbours and Farewell Spit each southern summer, and flocks of over 3000 birds visit Parengarenga, Houhora, Rangaunu, and Whangarei harbours in Northland; and the Firth of Thames, Kawhia Harbour, Tauranga

Harbour, Ohope–Ohiwa, and Tasman Bay. They are a regular visitor to the Kermadecs, and a few straggle to subantarctic islands.

Data from banding, leg-flagging, geolocators, and satellite transmitters show that adult Bar-tailed Godwits reach New Zealand in late September or early October after flying 8–9 days non-stop the 11,700km across the Pacific, from staging sites around the Kuskokwim Shoals of the Yukon Delta in southwestern Alaska. Some birds, especially juveniles, may travel a longer route through eastern Asia and Australia, arriving here in October–December; at least some of the juveniles stay in Australia until moving here in their second year. Bar-tailed Godwits leave New Zealand from the second week of March to the first week of April; individual godwits have very consistent departure dates within that four-week departure window. They usually fly non-stop for *c.* 7 days to cover the 10,000km to the Yellow Sea and Japan, where most congregate near Yalu Jiang on the China–North Korea border. They stopover for *c.* 40 days to refuel, before going on the last 7000km to reach their breeding grounds in Alaska, in May and early June.

Population: Bar-tailed Godwits are the most common Arctic wader to visit New Zealand. Ornithological Society counts at most major estuaries throughout New Zealand revealed 67,000–**83,000**–102,000 birds between 1983 and 1993, 60,000–**77,000**–101,000 between 1994 and 2003, and 77,000–**87,000**–101,000 between 2008 and 2012. Despite the apparent recent increase, over the 30 years after 1983 there was an overall downward trend of 0.4% per annum. About 75% are found in the North Island and 25% in the South Island. Each year, 8000–15,000 birds remain for the southern winter; presumably mainly youngsters, because few are in breeding plumage in winter.

Conservation: Protected declining migrant. The main factor causing their decline seems to be loss of huge areas of intertidal habitat at their main stopover sites on the shores of the Yellow Sea, but perhaps climate change is also affecting feeding and breeding conditions in the Arctic.

Behaviour: Gregarious; they feed in loose flocks on mudflats and fly and roost in large tight flocks, often in company with Lesser Knots. Just before landing, a flock may split apart, its members side-slipping erratically; on landing they run together with an excited chattering. Their call in a flying flock is a clear, excited 'kew-kew'; and a soft 'kit-kit-kit-kit' is heard from passing flocks. Roosting flocks, if uneasy, may keep up a steady conversational chatter.

Feeding: Diet is mainly polychaete worms and molluscs. They feed on tidal flats, most moving with the tideline, but birds slowly scatter as the tide falls. They make trial probes at intervals as they walk across mud or wet sand and probe, for the full length of the bill if necessary and sometimes with head underwater, often walking round the bill to reach down better to where their prey is hiding. They also dig out crabs with their bill from sandy burrows or in beds of eelgrass.

Reading: Barter, M. 1989. *Stilt* 14: 43–48. Battley, P. F. et al. 2012. *J Avian Biol* 43: 1–12. Conklin, J. R. & Battley, P. F. 2011. *Behav Ecol* 22: 854–861. Riegen, A. C. 1999. *Notornis* 46: 123–142. Sagar, P. M. et al. 1999. *Notornis* 46: 1–43. Southey, I. 2009. *DOC Res Dev Ser* 308. Wellington: DOC. Woodley, K. 2009. *Godwits: Long-haul Champions*. Auckland: Raupo/ Penguin.

221. BLACK-TAILED GODWIT *Limosa limosa* PLATE 49

Size: 39cm, 350g

Geographical variation: Three subspecies: *islandica* breeds in Iceland; *limosa* breeds in northern Europe and western Asia; and *melanuroides* breeds in eastern Asia.

Distribution: Breeds in the subarctic from Iceland across Asia to the Bering Sea. The Asiatic Black-tailed Godwit *melanuroides* breeds in northern Asia from Mongolia and the upper Yenesei River eastwards to the Bering Sea. They winter in a wide arc from eastern India to Australasia, especially in Arnhem Land and the Gulf of Carpentaria in northern Australia. Since they were first recognised in New Zealand in 1952, they have been seen annually in many estuaries between Parengarenga and the Southland coast, and have strayed to the Chatham Islands (2000) and the Auckland Islands (1963 and 1976). Occasionally they are in small flocks, with a maximum group of 11, at Lake Ellesmere in 1985. A few sometimes overwinter.

Behaviour: Very like that of Bar-tailed Godwits, which the usual singles or small groups normally associate with in New Zealand.

222. HUDSONIAN GODWIT *Limosa haemastica* PLATE 49

Size: 39cm, 300g

Distribution: Breeds in two disjunct regions of northern North America: one in northwestern Canada and Alaska, the other along the southern side of Hudson Bay. Most migrate to South America, but some reach the southwestern Pacific, including New Zealand. A few are recorded on estuaries and coastal lagoons every year from Parengarenga to the Southland coast, and once from Te Whanga Lagoon, Chatham Island (2004). A few sometimes overwinter.

Behaviour: Very like that of Bar-tailed Godwits, which the usual singles or twos normally associate with in New Zealand.

Reading: Sibson, R. B. 1950. *Notornis* 3: 199.

223. UPLAND SANDPIPER *Bartramia longicauda* PLATE 55

Other name: Bartram's Sandpiper

Size: 28cm, 140g

Distribution: Breeds in North America, mainly on grasslands east of the Rockies. They migrate to South America, from southern Brazil to southern Argentina and Chile. A rare vagrant to Australasia, including a sight record of a single bird at Karaka, Manukau Harbour (February 1967).

Behaviour: They feed mainly inland in grassland, away from water. They readily perch on fenceposts, being in the habit of holding their wings upward briefly when landing, revealing the black barring on the underwing and flanks. Their rolling trill is rather like that of curlews.

Reading: McKenzie, H. R. 1968. *Notornis* 15: 216–218.

224. WANDERING TATTLER *Tringa incana* PLATE 50

Size: 27cm, 120g

Distribution: Breeds in far-eastern Siberia, coastal Alaska, the Yukon and northwestern British Columbia. Most winter on the coast of America from California to Peru and on islands of the central and eastern Pacific Ocean as far south as French Polynesia, Cook Islands, Tonga and Fiji. A few wander to the coasts of New Zealand and eastern Australia. In New Zealand, they are rare but probably annual visitors to mainly rocky shorelines. Recorded from the Kermadecs; on the mainland from Northland to Canterbury, mainly in the east, except for Farewell Spit; and from the Chatham and Auckland islands.

Behaviour: Usually wary and solitary. They bob their head and teeter up and down with their tail. Wandering Tattlers prefer rocky shores to tidal mudflats and beaches. Their usual flight call is a clear, sweet whistle or rippling trill of 6–10 notes, with the accent on the second note, the following notes diminishing a little in volume and given more rapidly than the first two or three.

225. GREY-TAILED TATTLER *Tringa brevipes* PLATE 50

Other name: Siberian Tattler

Size: 25cm, 100g

Distribution: Breeds patchily across northern Asia from the upper Yenesei River and Lake Baikal to the mountains of eastern and far-eastern Siberia and the Kamchatka Peninsula. They migrate to spend winter in southeastern Asia, the Philippines, Australasia and islands in the southwestern Pacific as far east as Fiji.

They are regular at the Kermadecs and a scarce annual visitor to the New Zealand mainland. There have been numerous sight records of ones and twos, especially from the northern North Island and at Farewell Spit, but recorded as far south as Southland and Stewart Island. Stragglers have reached the Chatham, Snares and Auckland islands. A few birds may overwinter.
Behaviour: Usually wary and solitary. They bob their head and teeter up and down with their tail. Siberian Tattlers prefer tidal mudflats but also frequent rocky coasts. Their usual flight call is a sharp, high-pitched two syllable: 'tloo-weet'.

226. COMMON SANDPIPER *Tringa hypoleucos* PLATE 52

Size: 20cm, 50g
Distribution: Breeds across Europe and Asia from Spain and Britain to the Kamchatka Peninsula and Japan. They winter on the coasts of Africa, Madagascar, southern and southeastern Asia, the Philippines, and Australasia, especially in New Guinea. They are an uncommon visitor to tidal rivers, estuaries, coastal lagoons and sewage ponds in New Zealand, often in habitats not usually checked by ornithologists. Of the *c.* 35 accepted sight records, only seven sightings have been in the South Island, and one on Stewart Island.
Behaviour: Usually solitary and often in places not frequented by other waders; a bird in Whanganui Inlet, northwest Nelson, was by itself for three years, feeding on the same stretch of muddy tidal creek apart from other species.
Reading: Crossland, A. C. 2012. *Stilt* 62: 31–32.

227. GREENSHANK *Tringa nebularia* PLATE 50

Other name: Common Greenshank
Size: 32cm, 170g
Distribution: Breeds from Scotland and Scandinavia, across the taiga and tundra of Asia to the Kamchatka Peninsula. They winter widely in Africa, Arabian Peninsula, India, Myanmar, Thailand, China, Malaysia, the Philippines and Australasia. A few reached New Zealand annually in the 1980s and 1990s, mostly seen as singles or in small parties of up to four birds, but they have since become scarce visitors. Recorded from Parengarenga Harbour to the coastal lagoons and estuaries of Southland, and stragglers have reached the Chatham, Snares and Campbell islands.
Behaviour: Gregarious; in New Zealand they are usually seen in the company of Pied Stilts on shallow brackish or freshwater lagoons and muddy tidal creeks rather than on tidal mudflats – which, however, they occasionally use. One bird remained in the Bay of Plenty for nine years and assumed breeding plumage in the New Zealand summer.

Their flight call is a loud, ringing 'tchew-tchew-tchew', and they sometimes utter a quiet 'tchew' during feeding.
Feeding: Greenshanks prod and probe at the margins of pools and lagoons, walking briskly, sometimes up to their belly in water, and often running after small fish.

228. MARSH SANDPIPER *Tringa stagnatilis* PLATE 50

Size: 22cm, 70g
Distribution: Breeds across central Asia to Mongolia, and formerly in eastern Europe. They winter in Africa, southern Asia and Australasia. In New Zealand, they were first recognised in 1959. Since about 1980, they have been recorded in most years at coastal lagoons, lakes and estuaries from Parengarenga to Southland. Usually seen alone, but up to four seen together at Kaituna, Bay of Plenty (1969–70), Lake Ellesmere (1981–82), Kaipara Harbour (1989, 1994) and Mangere Ponds (1993), and six at Miranda (1998). A few overwinter.
Behaviour: Very like that of Greenshanks but more graceful in all their activities. They, too, prefer the company of Pied Stilts, and also prefer freshwater lakes and pools, both inland and coastal, to tidal mudflats or even the upper reaches of estuaries.
Reading: Battley, P. 1991. *Stilt* 19: 28–29.

229. LESSER YELLOWLEGS *Tringa flavipes* PLATE 50

Size: 24cm, 75g

Distribution: Breeds in Alaska and Canada east to Hudson Bay, migrating to Central and South America. A rare vagrant to Australasia, including 18 records of single birds in New Zealand from Auckland to South Canterbury, and at the Chathams; all in the period 1962 to 2004, but not subsequently. Most sightings have been in coastal marshes and pools, including four widely spaced records from Ahuriri Estuary, and two records each from Manukau Harbour, Farewell Spit and Lake Wainono. Three sightings have been inland on the muddy edges of freshwater lakes (Lake Wanstead, Pukepuke Lagoon and Lake Wairarapa).

Behaviour: In New Zealand, very like that of Greenshanks and Marsh Sandpipers, and often in the company of Pied Stilts. Their flight call is a double 'wheep-wheep'. Lesser Yellowlegs walk gracefully and snatch invertebrates from the surface. Often wading up to their bellies and holding the bill and neck stretched forward, they jab at the water surface.

230. TEREK SANDPIPER *Tringa cinerea* PLATE 52

Size: 23cm, 70g

Distribution: Breeds from the Baltic coast of Finland, across Siberia to the Kolyma River. They migrate to the coasts of Africa, Madagascar, Arabian Peninsula, southern and southeastern Asia, the Philippines and Australasia; especially common in many parts of northern and eastern Australia. Terek Sandpipers are a scarce but probably annual visitor to New Zealand; their numbers have declined since the 1980s and 1990s when 5–10 were present most summers. Seen especially at estuaries of Northland and Auckland, Manawatu Estuary, Farewell Spit, and the Southland lagoons. The largest flock recorded was eight at Kaipara Harbour in 1986. Sometimes overwinters.

Behaviour: Terek Sandpipers often remain alert and active at high-tide roosts, which they usually share with Wrybills. They bob their heads and teeter up and down with their tail. Their call is a musical trill: 'weeta-weeta-weet'.

Feeding: The restlessly active feeding of these birds draws attention as they abruptly change direction to dash after animals they have seen, which they get by pecking eagerly at the surface. They also probe deeply into soft mud. They favour places where shallow water covers mud such as tidal creeks, both within and apart from mangroves, coastal lagoons and estuarine mudflats.

231. TURNSTONE *Arenaria interpres* PLATE 52

Other name: Ruddy Turnstone

Size: 23cm, 120g

Geographical variation: Two subspecies: the nominate *interpres*, which breeds in the Arctic from northeastern Canada through Scandinavia and northern Asia to Alaska, and migrates to tropical and temperate coasts of both hemispheres; and *morinella*, which breeds in central subarctic North America and migrates to South America and the Pacific Islands. Both are likely to visit New Zealand.

Distribution: Breeds along the northern coasts and islands of Greenland, Scandinavia, Siberia, Alaska and the islands of northern Canada. Almost worldwide in autumn and winter on the coasts of the Americas, Africa, Madagascar, southern and southeastern Asia, the islands of the Pacific, and Australasia. In New Zealand, they concentrate in certain favoured localities: Parengarenga, Rangaunu, Kaipara, Manukau and Tauranga harbours and the Firth of Thames in the North Island; Farewell Spit, Motueka Estuary, Lake Grassmere, Kaikoura Peninsula and the coastal lagoons and estuaries of Southland in the South Island; Chatham Island and the Auckland Islands. Small numbers are likely to turn up at any coastal lagoon or estuary, especially when they are migrating southwards in late September to October, or northwards in March–April. A straggler to The Snares, Kermadec, Antipodes and Campbell islands. The migration route taken by New Zealand birds is not known; some may come through the Pacific, as a geolocator-bearing Australian bird did, while others may follow the East Asian–Australasian Flyway. A bird banded near Auckland by the New Zealand Wader Study Group was recaptured in Queensland on its southward migration and then recaptured a month later

back at its original capture site. It seems likely that New Zealand birds follow the same northward migration route through East Asia as Australian birds, using the Taiwan province of China and the Yellow Sea as stopover sites.
Population: Turnstones are the third most numerous of the arctic waders to visit New Zealand. Numbers have declined 5.5% per annum from the 2394–**4227**–5915 birds counted each summer by the Ornithological Society between 1983 and 1994, to fewer than 2000 seen each year since 1997. Turnstones are evenly divided between the North and South islands, but substantial numbers visit the Chatham Islands (*c.* 500) and Auckland Islands (*c.* 100). Between 100 and 1500 (3–45% of the previous summer's visitors) overwinter, perhaps mainly yearlings, and so reflecting the highly variable breeding success in the previous northern summer.
Behaviour: Gregarious, in small flocks of the same species or with Banded Dotterels, sometimes visiting rough farmland near the sea. Flocks in flight or when disturbed utter a twittering 'kititit'.
Feeding: Feed actively by deftly flicking over shells, seaweed and pieces of wood with their longish, wedge-shaped bills in search of food items such as sandhoppers. They tend to avoid smooth, sandy beaches and open mudflats, preferring to feed on shelly or stony foreshores, among rockpools or on exposed rocky reefs. Their actions depend on what is available; at Farewell Spit, some feed on the Ocean Beach, bustling between waves to dab at wet sand and fossick through stranded debris. Most feed on the Bay Flats; on the falling tide flicking aside or pushing into eelgrass strands, looking for animals hidden underneath; on the rising tide probing for crabs in their burrows in the small runnels among the plants. On rocky coasts, they feed differently; in Victoria, Australia, they take mostly small gastropod molluscs and some barnacles.
Reading: Houston, P. & Barter, M. 1990. *Stilt* 17: 17–23. Minton, C. et al. 2010. *Wader Study Group Bull* 117: 9–14. Minton, C. et al. 2011. *Wader Study Group Bull* 118: 87–96. Robertson, H. A. & Dennison, M. D. 1979. *Notornis* 26: 73–88. Sagar, P. M. et al. 1999. *Notornis* 46: 1–43. Southey, I. 2009. *DOC Res Dev Ser* 308. Wellington: DOC.

232. GREY PHALAROPE *Phalaropus fulicaria* PLATE 51

Other name: Red Phalarope
Size: 20cm; male 50g, female 60g
Distribution: Breeds through the high Arctic in Greenland, Iceland, Spitzbergen and extreme northern parts of Asia, Alaska and Canada. They migrate to three zones of plankton-rich oceanic upwelling: off Senegal and Sierra Leone, off Namibia and western South Africa, and off the western coast of South America. Vagrants, presumably from the group that winters off South America, have been recorded 10 times in New Zealand, mainly in the east and all but one in June or July, when they should have been breeding: Lake Wainono (1883, 1987); Lake Ellesmere (1925); Hastings (1934); Kaituna Cut, Bay of Plenty (1977); Manukau Harbour (1992); Inch Clutha, South Otago (1993); Ninety Mile Beach (2003), Farewell Spit (March 2005) and Napier (2012). Except for the 1987 Lake Wainono record, all birds seen in June or July were in full or partial breeding plumage, with a bicoloured bill.
Reading: Brown, B. & Latham, P. C. M. 1978. *Notornis* 25: 198–202.

233. RED-NECKED PHALAROPE *Phalaropus lobatus* PLATE 51

Other name: Northern Phalarope
Size: 19cm; male 35g, female 40g
Distribution: Breeds on arctic tundra in Greenland, Iceland, Scandinavia and the northern parts of Asia, Alaska and Canada. They migrate to three main zones of oceanic upwelling: off western North America, off Arabia, and between the Philippines and New Guinea, although some also winter off Namibia. They are an annual migrant in small numbers to most Australian states, particularly in the northwest and southeast. Twelve New Zealand records scattered throughout the year: Lake Ellesmere (1929, December 2000, January 2002), Whanganui Estuary (April 1935), Washdyke Lagoon (March 1961), Manukau Harbour (June 1985), Miranda (December 1996), Farewell Spit (November 2000, October 2002), Lake Grassmere (November 2002, up to two between May 2005 and January 2007), and Ahuriri Estuary (June 2010).
Reading: Crockett, D. E. 1961. *Notornis* 9: 266. Jenkins, J. A. F. et al. 1986. *Notornis* 33: 191–192.

234. WILSON'S PHALAROPE *Phalaropus tricolor* PLATE 51

Size: 22cm; male 50g, female 65g
Distribution: Breeds on the prairie marshes of central North America and migrates to wetlands in southern South America, particularly Argentina. Unlike the other two phalaropes, they do not go to sea but prefer wetlands of the interior. They are a rare vagrant to Australasia, including a single bird at the Manawatu Estuary (September 1983), up to two birds at Lake Ellesmere (November 1983–April 1984), and one at Taharoa, Waikato (October 2004).
Reading: Moore, J. L. & Moore, M. 1984. *Notornis* 31: 330–333. Sagar, P. M. & Harrison, K. C. 1984. *Notornis* 31: 333–334.

PAINTED SNIPE *Rostratulidae*

2 species; 1 is a rare vagrant to New Zealand.

Superficially like the true snipes of the Scolopacidae, but they are closer to the rails (Rallidae) and jacanas (Jacanidae). Sex roles are reversed, females being brighter coloured and bigger, and they visit males purely for courtship and mating. The rest of nesting duties are the responsibility of the male. They are polyandrous, i.e. a female mates with more than one male.

235. PAINTED SNIPE *Rostratula benghalensis* PLATE 43

Size: 25cm, 120g
Geographical variation: Two subspecies: *benghalensis* breeds in Africa and Asia, and *australis* breeds in Australia; the latter is most likely to reach New Zealand.
Distribution: Breeds in central and southern Africa, southern Asia, southern Japan, China, the Philippines, western Indonesia and Australia. Mainly following heavy rains, they breed at inland swamps and lakes of the eastern states of Australia from Queensland to Victoria along the Murray–Darling rivers, but also in southern parts of Western Australia and the Northern Territory. When the interior dries out, they return to coastal lakes and swamps along the northern and eastern seaboard, vagrants have reached Tasmania and Lord Howe Island. A single vagrant has reached New Zealand: a male at Lake Ellesmere (August 1986).
Behaviour: Little is known about Painted Snipe because they feed mainly in thick vegetation at dusk and at night, and they freeze rather than fly when disturbed. When they do fly, they fly low, directly and only briefly, unlike the steep, towering flight of true snipe. Like rails, they jerk the rear of their body up and down.
Reading: Harrison, K. C. & Mulligan, S. 1987. *Notornis* 34: 87–88.

OYSTERCATCHERS *Haematopodidae*

8 species worldwide; 3 endemic to New Zealand.

Oystercatchers are all black, or black and white, shorebirds with a very long, straight, reddish-orange bill, a squat body and short, thick, pinkish-red legs. They have loud shrill calls and elaborate 'piping' displays, in which several birds gather and move around with neck stretched, bill pointed downwards and body hunched with wings touching the ground, accompanied by loud, insistent calling.

Oystercatchers are gregarious, feeding in loose flocks but generally roosting and flying in tight flocks. They are mainly coastal, although South Island Pied Oystercatchers are unusual in that they breed well inland on gravel riverbeds and on farmland. Their nest is a simple scrape, partially lined with small twigs. Both sexes share incubation and feed the precocial young.
Reading: Baker, A. J. 1973. *Notornis* 20: 128–144. Hayman, P. et al. 1986. *Shorebirds: An Identification Guide to the Waders of the World*. Beckenham: Croom Helm. Woodley, K. 2012. *Shorebirds of New Zealand: Sharing the Margins*. Auckland: Penguin.

236. VARIABLE OYSTERCATCHER *Haematopus unicolor* PLATE 53

Other names: Torea, Torea Pango (black phase), Black Oystercatcher
Size: 48cm; 725g
Geographical variation: The distribution of the three colour phases (black, pied and intermediate) varies with latitude: in the northern North Island, 43% are black, 22% are pied and 35% are intermediates; in central New Zealand (39–44° S), 85% are black and 7% pied; and in the southern South Island and Stewart Island, 94% are black and 5% pied.
Distribution: New Zealand only. They are on coasts of the main islands and offshore islands but not the outlying islands. Breeding and wintering distributions are similar, but there is some local movement to estuaries outside the breeding season. In the North Island, they are most abundant along the northeastern coast from North Cape to Mahia Peninsula, and near Wellington, but scattered along the west coast between Manawatu and Auckland. In the South Island, they are common around Tasman and Golden bays, Marlborough Sounds, and in Fiordland, but less numerous on the east coast between Cloudy Bay and Dunedin, and on the West Coast. Common on the beaches of Stewart Island and its offshore islands.
Population: *c.* 6000 birds: North Island 3000 (Northland 1100, Coromandel–Bay of Plenty 800, Gisborne 250, Wellington 200); South Island 3000 (Nelson 750, Marlborough Sounds 730, Fiordland 450); Stewart Island 150.
Conservation: Protected endemic. In the early 1900s, they were in serious decline from hunting; however, since they were protected in 1940 they have increased dramatically. This is especially so in the northern North Island, where many nests on sandspits are now also protected from predators and human disturbance. Growth has been seen in areas without nest protection, but this may be due to immigration from nearby predator-free islands or from protected sites further afield. The total population has trebled from *c.* 2000 birds in the early 1970s.
Breeding: Pairs remain stable from year to year; some occupy their territory all year, but others join small winter flocks or join flocks of Pied Oystercatchers. The nest is a shallow scrape, usually on a sandy beach just above spring-tide level, but also on shingle beaches, rock platforms and rarely on lake shores up to 30km inland (e.g. Lake Wairarapa). Eggs are laid in September–February, mostly November–December; earlier in southern New Zealand. They lay 1–**2**–**3**–5 stone to pale olive eggs (59 x 41mm; 49g), spotted dark brown. They are laid 2 days apart, mainly in the afternoon. Both sexes incubate, but the female does most during daylight, for 25–**28**–33 days, starting when the last egg is laid. The downy chicks remain in the nest 1–2 days and then stay in their parents' territory and are fed solely by them for the first 3 weeks. They first fly at 39–50 days old, but stay close to their natal territory for at least 2–3 months before dispersing to join winter flocks. They can start breeding at 2 years old, but most do not begin until 4–6 years old. The oldest bird recorded lived over 30 years.
Behaviour: Much behaviour is highly ritualised, and many displays are common to other oystercatchers. The most conspicuous breeding display is 'social piping'. Birds mob aerial predators and lead ground predators away from the nest or chicks with conspicuous walking, false brooding and feigning wing injury.
Feeding: Diet is mainly molluscs (especially bivalves), worms and crabs, also other small invertebrates and occasionally small fish. They take these mainly from rocky or sandy shores and estuaries, occasionally lake shores and grassland, by surface picking and deep probing. They open bivalves by stabbing between the shells and twisting the bill to part the shells; some birds hammer through the shell.
In the hand: Females are larger than males, especially for bill length, but measurements overlap: males **82**mm, females **91**mm. First-year birds are distinguished by their dull brown-black upperparts, brownish bill, grey legs and brown eyes, and they retain juvenile primaries through their first year. Second- and third-year birds still have a brownish tinge to their backs but develop the pink legs and orange-red eyes of adults.
Reading: Baker, A. J. 1973. *Notornis* 20: 128–144, 330–345. Baker, A. J. 1974. *Notornis* 21: 219–233. Baker, A. J. 1974. *NZ J Mar Fresh Res* 8: 211–219. Baker, A. J. 1975. *J Zool (Lond)* 175: 357–390. Bell, M. 2010. *Notornis* 57: 169–172. Rowe, L. 2008. *Notornis* 55: 146–154.

237. SOUTH ISLAND PIED OYSTERCATCHER *Haematopus finschi* PLATE 53

Other names: Torea, SIPO ('sigh-po')
Size: 46cm; 550g
Distribution: Breeds only in New Zealand, mainly on braided riverbeds, farmland, fringes of lakes and in subalpine bogs east of the Southern Alps in the South Island. Some breed on rivers west of the Alps and on Southland rivers and, since 1980, a few pairs have bred on the Ngaruroro River, Hawke's Bay and around 1990 a few pairs bred in South Wairarapa. After breeding, some shift to estuaries of the South Island, but in late December to early March most of the population migrates directly to estuaries and sandy beaches of the North Island and the northern South Island, although many also remain through the winter at estuaries of the South and Stewart islands. Stragglers have reached Australia, Vanuatu and the Kermadec, Chatham, Snares and Campbell islands.

The largest wintering populations (10,000+ birds) are at Kaipara and Manukau harbours, the Firth of Thames, and the coast between Nelson and Farewell Spit. 1000+ birds are regularly at Whangarei and Kawhia harbours, the Avon–Heathcote Estuary, near Dunedin and at Southland harbours. Birds start returning to their South Island breeding grounds from early June, but most breeding birds return in late July to early August. In spring and summer, about 18,000 (20% of the total population), mainly subadult birds, stay at the main wintering sites, especially in the Manukau–Firth of Thames area (8000) and the Nelson region (3000).
Population: South Island Pied Oystercatchers are the most common native wader in New Zealand. Ornithological Society counts at most major estuaries throughout New Zealand revealed 69,000–**81,000**–88,000 birds between 1984 and 1994, 62,000–**83,000**–102,000 between 1995 and 2003, and 73,000–**79,000**–83,000 between 2008 and 2012. Allowing for birds at sites not surveyed, the total population was *c.* 90,000 birds in 2010. Almost all breed in the South Island and *c.* 70,000 winter in the North Island, especially at Kaipara Harbour (18,000), Manukau Harbour (29,000) and Firth of Thames (18,000). The main wintering site in the South Island is between Nelson and Farewell Spit (10,000 birds).
Conservation: Protected endemic. From the mid-1800s, the population was in serious decline from hunting; however, with conversion of tussockland to pasture, and their protection in 1940, they have increased rapidly. This is especially obvious at the northern North Island wintering sites of Manukau Harbour and the Firth of Thames, where their combined numbers increased from fewer than 1000 in the 1940s to 17,000 in 1972 and to 38,000 in the 1990s. At southern wintering sites, they have also increased, but not to the same extent. The total population more than doubled from the 49,000 birds estimated in 1970–71 to reach a peak of *c.* 112,000 birds in 1993, but the population, especially at South Island wintering sites, has since fallen, and the overall population has stabilised at about 90,000 birds.
Breeding: Pairs usually reclaim the same territory year after year, even though the birds generally spend winter at different sites. The nest is a shallow scrape; on riverbeds it is usually on a slightly raised area of

sand, often near a piece of driftwood or a prominent stone, but on farmland it is often placed randomly, although away from fences or trees. Eggs are laid in August–December, mostly September–November; earlier in lowlands. They lay 1–**2**–3 brownish-stone eggs (56 x 39mm; 44g), blotched dark brown. Eggs are laid 2 days apart, mainly in the afternoon. Both sexes incubate for 25–**28**–30 days, starting when the penultimate egg is laid. The downy chicks remain in the nest 1–2 days and then stay in the parents' territory until they first fly at *c.* 5 weeks old. Young return to their natal area at 3–4 years old but generally do not start breeding until 4–5 years old. Annual survival of breeding adults has been measured to be about 90%. The oldest bird recorded in New Zealand lived over 27 years.

Behaviour: Much behaviour is highly ritualised, and many displays are common to other oystercatchers. The most conspicuous breeding display is 'social piping'. Birds mob aerial predators and lead ground predators away from nest or chicks with conspicuous walking, false brooding and feigning wing injury.

Feeding: Diet is mainly molluscs (especially bivalves), estuarine worms, earthworms and insect larvae (especially grassgrub), but other small invertebrates and small fish are taken. They feed in estuaries, on sandy shores, in pasture, on ploughed paddocks and riverbeds by surface picking and deep probing. They open bivalves by stabbing between the shells and twisting the bill to part the shells; some birds hammer through the shell.

In the hand: Females are larger than males, especially for bill length, but measurements overlap slightly: males **81**mm, females **91**mm. First-year birds are distinguished by their dull brown-black upperparts, brownish-orange bill, grey legs and brown eyes, and they retain juvenile primaries through their first year. Second- and third-year birds still have a brownish tinge to their back but develop the pink legs and orange-red eyes of adults.

Reading: Baker, A. J. 1973. *Notornis* 20: 128–144. Baker, A. J. 1974. *Notornis* 21: 219–233. Baker, A. J. 1974. *NZ J Mar Fresh Res* 8: 211–219. Baker, A. J. 1975. *J Zool (Lond)* 175: 357–390. Baker, A. J. 1975. *Notornis* 22: 189–194. Sagar, P. M. & Geddes, D. 1999. *Notornis* 46: 89–100. Sagar, P. M. et al. 1999. *Notornis* 46: 1–43. Sagar, P. M. et al. 2000. *Notornis* 47: 71–81. Sagar, P. M. et al. 2002. *Notornis* 49: 233–240. Sibson, R. B. 1966. *Notornis* 13: 94–97. Southey, I. 2009. *DOC Res Dev Ser* 308. Wellington: DOC. Twydle, M. & Twydle, W. 1983. *Notornis* 30: 197–198. Veitch, C. R. 1978. *Notornis* 25: 1–24.

238. CHATHAM ISLANDS OYSTERCATCHER *Haematopus chathamensis* PLATE 53

Size: 48cm; 600g

Distribution: Confined to the Chatham Islands. Most are on the northern coast of Chatham Island where conservation management has been most active. Others are widely scattered on the coast of southern Chatham Island, Pitt Island, and on wave platforms of South East and Mangere islands and the Star Keys. Breeding and wintering distributions are similar, but some local movement of juveniles between islands has been noted, and some pairs breeding on South East Island regularly feed 2km away on Pitt Island.

Population: *c.* 309 birds in 2010. Of 109 known or likely breeding pairs in 2006, 74 were in northern Chatham Island, 14 in southern Chatham Island, 14 on Pitt Island, four on South East Island and three on Mangere Island.

Conservation: Protected critically endangered endemic. In the 1930s, the Chatham Islands Oystercatcher was widely distributed but scarce. Numbers have increased spectacularly since 1970, when the population was estimated at 52 birds. By 1987 there were 112 birds, and by 1998, 144 birds. Following a period of intensive conservation effort in 1998–2004, the population peaked at 313–351 birds in 2006. Recruitment has declined since conservation efforts were reduced and the population has fallen back a little. The main increase in the population has been in the northern part of Chatham Island, where nests have been protected from feral cats and Weka, from trampling or disturbance by farm stock, and from storm surges since the early 1990s. Marram, an introduced dune plant, causes the shape of the beach–dune profile to change and make oystercatcher nests more vulnerable to storm surges. Trials in which marram was replaced with native dune vegetation resulted in a more gradual slope to the beach profile and hence more room for oystercatchers to nest successfully above the high-tide line. The population on South East Island has, however, declined from 13 pairs in 1978 to eight pairs in 1989 and to just four pairs since 2004.

Breeding: Most pairs occupy their territory all year, but juveniles and subadults form small flocks or settle alone on a vacant section of coast. The nest is a shallow scrape, usually on a sandy beach just above spring-tide level, or among rocks above the shoreline. On offshore islands, nests are usually well away from centres of Southern Skua territories and are often under the cover of small bushes or rock overhangs. Eggs are laid in October–February, mostly November–December. They lay 1–2–3 olive-grey eggs (57 x 40mm; 46g), spotted dark brown. They are laid 2 days apart. Both sexes incubate, but the female does most during daylight, for about 25 days. The downy chicks remain in the nest 1–2 days and are then led away by their parents; they continue to be brooded at least during the first week. They first fly at *c*. 7 weeks old but stay close to their natal territory for several months before dispersing. They start breeding from 3 years old, but most start at 5–6. Mean adult life expectancy is 12.7 years; the oldest known bird lived over 19 years.

Behaviour: Much behaviour is highly ritualised, and many displays are common to other oystercatchers. The most conspicuous breeding display is 'social piping'. Birds mob aerial predators, including Southern Skuas, and lead ground predators away from nests or chicks with conspicuous walking, false brooding and feigning wing injury.

Feeding: Diet is mainly molluscs and marine worms, supplemented with other small invertebrates. They take these mainly from rocky shores (especially from small pools on wave platforms and from algal mats) or sandy shores by surface picking and deep probing. They open bivalves by stabbing between the shells and twisting the bill to part the shells; some birds hammer through the shell. Limpets and chitons are struck vertical blows, prised off rocks and eaten whole.

In the hand: Females are larger than males, especially for bill length, but measurements overlap slightly: males **68**mm, females 77mm. First-year birds are distinguished by their dull brown-black upperparts, pinkish-brown bill, grey legs and brown eyes, and they retain juvenile primaries through their first year. Second- and third-year birds still have a brownish tinge to their back but develop the pink legs and orange-red eyes of adults.

Reading: Baker, A. J. 1973. *Notornis* 20: 128–144. Baker, A. J. 1974. *Notornis* 21: 219–233. Baker, A. J. 1974. *NZ J Mar Fresh Res* 8: 211–219. Baker, A. J. 1975. *J Zool (Lond)* 175: 357–390. Moore, P. J. 2008. *Notornis* 55: 20–31. Schmechel, F. & O'Connor, S. 1999. *Notornis* 46: 155–165.

STILTS and AVOCETS *Recurvirostridae*

Of 7 species worldwide; 2 breed in New Zealand and 1 is a vagrant that may have bred here in the 19th century.

These are medium-sized elegant waders with long, slender bills, necks and especially legs, which allow them to wade belly-deep when feeding in shallow fresh, salt or brackish water. Stilts have a fine, almost straight bill. Avocets have a fine, upturned bill, more sharply turned in females, with complex lamellae which they use to sift out tiny food particles. Sexes are alike, but males have longer legs. Most species have a pattern of black above and white below. Webbing between the front three toes is much reduced in stilts. Although they have long legs, which trail behind the short, square tail in flight, they are slim and graceful. Adult plumage is gained in their first or second year; they first breed at 2–3 years old.

Reading: Hayman, P. et al. 1986. *Shorebirds: An Identification Guide to the Waders of the World.* Beckenham: Croom Helm. Pringle, J. D. 1986. *The Shorebirds of Australia.* Sydney: Angus & Robertson. Woodley, K. 2012. *Shorebirds of New Zealand: Sharing the Margins.* Auckland: Penguin.

239. PIED STILT *Himantopus himantopus* PLATE 54

Other names: Poaka, Black-winged Stilt, White-headed Stilt

Size: 35cm, 190g

Geographical variation: Of the five subspecies, *leucocephalus* extends from the Philippines, Indonesia and the Bismarck Archipelago to Australia and New Zealand.

Distribution: Pied Stilts, more generally known as Black-winged Stilts overseas, breed right around the world in tropical and warm temperate regions. They breed throughout New Zealand but are rare on Stewart and Chatham islands and absent from Fiordland and the subantarctic islands. They may have colonised New Zealand as recently as the early 1800s. They expanded rapidly from about the 1870s to the early 1900s, and continued to increase at least until the 1940s.

The migration routes taken by the various regional populations of Pied Stilts have been studied by the Ornithological Society by a national programme of colour-banding adults and juveniles. Many birds on riverbeds in the southern North Island and the South Island move in December–February to coastal sites and some, especially those from inland Southland, Central Otago, Mackenzie Basin and mid-Canterbury, move to northern North Island harbours. Coastal breeders in both main islands and birds breeding in the north are usually sedentary. Pied Stilts can be heard calling as they fly high overhead on migration.

Population: In June 1984–94, Ornithological Society counts at most major estuaries throughout New Zealand in June revealed 15,000–**18,000**–21,000 birds; however, the overall population at the time was estimated to be about 30,000 birds because many winter on rivers, wet paddocks and at lake margins. About 85% of the population wintered in the North Island. Mean winter counts at favoured sites were: Parengarenga (700), Kaipara Harbour (2650), Manukau Harbour (3350), Firth of Thames (3450), Ahuriri/Westshore (600), Lake Wairarapa (1000) and Lake Ellesmere (550). Favoured also, but accommodating hundreds of birds, are Houhora, Rangaunu, Whangarei, Kawhia/Aotea, Tauranga, Maketu, Whakaki Lagoon, Lake Poukawa, Lake Hatuma and Manawatu Estuary in the North Island, and Nelson Haven, Lake Grassmere, Avon–Heathcote Estuary, Green Island Lagoon and Southland lagoons and estuaries in the South Island. Smaller flocks are at many places around the New Zealand coast and inland lakes. They are least common where the coastal habitat is largely unsuitable, e.g. in Taranaki and on the West Coast. Since the early 1990s, their numbers have remained reasonably stable, with means of 16,000 counted in the winters of 1995–2003, and 18,000 in the winters of 2008–12, and so the national population estimate remains at about 30,000 birds.

Conservation: Protected native. Pied Stilts are probably a relatively recent colonist of New Zealand and have thrived with the conversion of lowland swamp forest into seasonally wet farmland. In South Canterbury, some Pied Stilts have hybridised with the endemic Black Stilt when its numbers dwindled to such a level that Black Stilt had difficulty finding a mate of their own species.

Breeding: Pied Stilts return to their breeding grounds in June–July in lowland places and August–October in inland places. They breed in loose colonies of up to 100 pairs, but typically 3–20 pairs, on mounds surrounded by or near water in wetlands in open country, both coastal and inland. Mainly in flooded pasture, muddy pasture resulting from chewed-down, trampled turnips and choumoellier, margins of swamps, edges of ponds and estuaries and other permanent wetlands, and gravel riverbeds. Both sexes build the nest. In lowland places, the peak of laying is in August–October; October–November inland. They lay 2–**4**–6 greenish eggs (44 x 32mm) with blackish-brown blotches and streaks. Starting with the last egg, both sexes incubate for about 25 days. The fledging period is 28–37 days. Pied Stilts usually start breeding at 2 years old, occasionally at 1 year old. The oldest banded bird of the European subspecies lived over 12 years.

Behaviour: Gregarious at all seasons; adults breed together in loose colonies, feed together and, in autumn and winter, roost together in often large, compact flocks. Their yapping is persistent and noisy when feeding and flying, including at night; juveniles utter a higher-pitched chipping, sometimes hoarse, until their first winter.

Feeding: Diet is mainly aquatic and terrestrial invertebrates. If the habitat is tidal, they feed at low tide, day or night. At inland ponds and swamps, they take mainly insects; on inland riverbeds mainly larvae of mayflies, caddisflies, stoneflies and midges, plus adult water boatmen and molluscs. Common methods of feeding are: plunging, in which birds peck underwater; snatching, in which birds capture flying insects; probing, in which birds insert their bill into mud or wet soil; and scything, in which birds sweep the bill from side to side in soft mud, like avocets, particularly when wind or darkness makes prey less visible.

Reading: Pierce, R. J. 1984. *Notornis* 31: 7–18. Pierce, R. J. 1984. *Notornis* 31: 106–130. Pierce, R. J. 1985. *NZ J Zool* 12: 467–472. Pierce, R. J. 1986. *Auk* 103: 273–280. Sagar, P. M. et al. 1999. *Notornis* 46: 1–43. Southey, I. 2009. *DOC Res Dev Ser* 308. Wellington: DOC.

240. BLACK STILT *Himantopus novaezelandiae* PLATE 54

Other name: Kaki
Size: 40cm, 220g

Distribution: New Zealand only. In the nineteenth century, Black Stilts bred on the braided shingle riverbeds and associated wetlands of the lower North Island and the whole South Island (except Fiordland) on both sides of the Southern Alps. In the 1930s and 1940s, 500–1000 birds were scattered through lowland South Canterbury, Central Otago and the Mackenzie Basin. They declined steeply in the 1950s, and by 1960 most of the remaining 50–100 birds bred in the Mackenzie Basin. They now breed only in the Mackenzie Basin of the upper Waitaki River system, from the Godley and Macaulay rivers in the north to the Cass, Tasman, Tekapo, Ohau, Hopkins, Dobson and Ahuriri rivers in the centre and south. After nesting, most move to ponds or lakes before wintering on the nearby river deltas around major lakes in the Mackenzie Basin, but a few Black Stilts and hybrids move to coastal Canterbury or migrate to the North Island, mainly to Kawhia and Kaipara harbours, leaving in January and returning in July–August.

Population: *c.* 70 adult birds in 2013: 61 adults in the wild and 5 breeding pairs in captivity at Twizel and Peacock Springs, Christchurch.

Conservation: Protected critically endangered endemic. The decline of Black Stilts has been from predation by introduced mammals, loss of habitat, and hybridisation with Pied Stilts. The main predators are feral cats and ferrets. They breed alone on the banks of small streams and sidebraids of major rivers, but also on islands or swamps. Unlike Pied Stilts, they do not have the mutual protection of nesting in colonies; they have lost some of their distraction displays; and their fledging period is a long *c.* 40 days, cf. the Pied Stilt's 30–37 days. Habitat was lost to hydroelectric development, to drainage of swamps, and to the spread on riverbeds of introduced plants such as willows and lupins.

As Black Stilts declined, they became so widely separated that often not enough Black Stilts were on a river, and as Pied Stilts became abundant they interbred, resulting in hybrids. Management now focuses on controlling predators and weeds in breeding areas, and collecting eggs from the wild, artificially incubating them, and captive-rearing up to 90 chicks each year. They are released in late winter and given supplementary food for several months as they acclimatise to life in the wild.

Breeding: Nests as solitary pairs in braided shingle rivers and nearby wetlands such as sidestreams, swamps, tarns and ponds. They arrive on territory in July or August and select a nest site on stable shingle, usually on islands or the banks of a river. Both sexes build the nest. Eggs are laid in September–December. They lay 3–**4**–5 eggs (45 x 32mm), greenish with dark brown or black blotches and streaks. Incubation starts after the third or fourth egg is laid. Both sexes incubate for 24–**25**–27 days. The chicks leave the nest at 2–3 days old, and fledge at 30–**40**–55 days. They can breed at 2 years old, but most start breeding at 3 years old. The oldest bird known in the wild lived over 19 years.

Behaviour: Less gregarious than Pied Stilts. They make a loud, monotonous yapping, like that of Pied Stilts but higher-pitched.

Feeding: Largely insectivorous, taking mostly larval aquatic invertebrates, especially mayflies, caddisflies and stoneflies in rivers, and larval midges and damselflies, worms and molluscs in tarns and swamps. Other foods of some importance are several kinds of small fish, and water boatmen. They catch their prey by pecking at them in the water column, probing beneath shingle or rocks or, in mud, scything sideways by feel only, in the manner of avocets. Favourite feeding places are the riffles of braided rivers.

Reading: Pierce, R. J. 1986. *Black Stilt.* Wellington: John McIndoe & NZ Wildlife Service. Pierce, R. J. 1996. *Bird Cons Intl* 6: 81–88. Reed, C. E .M. 1986. MSc thesis, Massey Uni. Reed, C. E. M. et al. 1993. *Black Stilt Recovery Plan.* Wellington: DOC. Van Heezik, Y. et al. 2005. *Zoo Biol* 24: 459–474.

241. RED-NECKED AVOCET *Recurvirostra novaehollandiae* PLATE 54

Size: 44cm, 300g

Distribution: Breeds only in Australia, mainly in southern parts. Between 1859 and 1892, avocets were reported widely from Whangarei to Invercargill, and they attempted breeding at several estuarine localities in Canterbury. Since then, there have been only two accepted records, both of single birds: Lake Ellesmere (1912), and Westport (1968–70).

Behaviour: Gregarious. They feed in flocks at shallow wetlands of fresh, brackish or preferably saline water. In Australia, they are often inland at salt lakes, especially when evaporation has raised the salinity, but they move to coastal wetlands in summer–autumn. They utter loud barking and wheezing whistles.

Reading: Kaigler, C. G. 1968. *Notornis* 15: 123.

PLOVERS, DOTTERELS and LAPWINGS

Charadriidae

About 66 species, most of which are migratory. There are about 42 plovers and dotterels, of which 5 (formerly 6) breed in New Zealand, 7 are transequatorial migrants and 1 is a vagrant from Australia; 24 lapwings, 1 of which breeds in New Zealand.

In New Zealand, the terms plover and dotterel mean the same thing; there is no clear distinction in the way they are used. All are plumpish with a thick short neck, short tail, and small rounded head with a high forehead; bill shorter than the head, pointed and slightly swollen towards the tip. The plumage is a blend of black, white, brown and grey, sometimes with rufous added in breeding plumage. They often have bold patterning in flight. They have a characteristic 'walk or run-stop-look-step-peck' way of feeding.

Lapwings tend to be inland on pasture and around coastal wetlands. They have wattles on the face and spurs on the bends of the wing, and are noisy on the ground and in flight, by night as well as by day.

Reading: Chandler, R. 2009. *Shorebirds of the Northern Hemisphere*. London: Christopher Helm. Hayman, P. et al. 1986. *Shorebirds: An Identification Guide to the Waders of the World*. Beckenham: Croom Helm. Pringle, J. D. 1986. *The Shorebirds of Australia*. Sydney: Angus & Robertson. Woodley, K. 2012. *Shorebirds of New Zealand: Sharing the Margins*. Auckland: Penguin.

242. PACIFIC GOLDEN PLOVER *Pluvialis fulva* PLATE 55

Other names: Eastern/Least/Asiatic Golden Plover
Size: 25cm, 130g
Distribution: Breeds on the Arctic and subarctic tundra of Siberia and western Alaska. They migrate south on a broad front, mainly to the coasts of India, Pakistan, Sri Lanka, Southeast Asia, southern China, Japan, Malaysia, the Philippines, Australasia and most Pacific Islands. In New Zealand, they are the fourth most common Arctic migrant wader. They are seldom seen far from the coast. Favoured places are Parengarenga and Rangaunu harbours, Lake Ohia (Far North), Whangarei, Kaipara and Manukau harbours, the Firth of Thames, Bay of Plenty estuaries, Muriwai Lagoon (Gisborne), Wairoa and Ahuriri estuaries, Manawatu Estuary, Lake Wairarapa, Farewell Spit, Lake Ellesmere, the Southland coastal lagoons and estuaries, and Te Whanga Lagoon, Chatham Island. They are recorded regularly at the Kermadecs, and stragglers have reached the Auckland Islands.

The earliest birds arrive in September, but most arrive from October to early November. Almost all depart New Zealand in late March to early April.

Population: Between 1983 and 1993, 151–**466**–1120 birds were counted in New Zealand, and allowing for sites not counted the estimated average population was *c.* 650 birds each summer, but only 0–**2**–7 overwintered. Since 1983, the population has declined by 4.7% per annum, and only 63–**166**–265 were counted each summer from 2008–12.

Behaviour: Pacific Golden Plovers usually stay separate from other waders at high-tide roosts and sometimes roost away from the water's edge, often in a ploughed paddock or on short pasture. Flocks are usually small, 10–50. In New Zealand, unlike in the Pacific Islands, they are notably alert and wary. They are usually silent on the ground. In flight, which is fast, they give a clear, melodious, two-syllable 'tlu-ee'.

Feeding: They feed on grassland, salt marsh and the upper levels of tidal flats on a wide range of animal food. On grassland, they eat insects and their larvae, including beetles, crickets, grasshoppers, caterpillars, flies, ants and earwigs; also spiders, earthworms and plant seeds. On tidal flats, they take mainly molluscs, marine worms, and small crustaceans such as crabs.

Reading: Robertson, H. A. & Dennison, M. D. 1979. *Notornis* 26: 73–88. Sagar, P. M. et al. 1999. *Notornis* 46: 1–43.

243. AMERICAN GOLDEN PLOVER *Pluvialis dominicus* PLATE 55

Size: 26cm, 165g
Distribution: Breeds on the Arctic and subarctic tundra from northern and central Alaska east to Baffin Island (Canada). They migrate to winter in the interior of South America from Bolivia and southern Brazil to central Argentina. Two New Zealand records accepted: Karikari Peninsula (January 1991) and Little Waihi Estuary, Bay of Plenty (January 2011); but three other possible records: two birds on Farewell Spit (November 1981); one at Pollen Island, Auckland (January 1989); and one at Ahuriri Estuary (March 2011). Birds have been in non-breeding plumage but with Pacific Golden Plovers.

244. GREY PLOVER *Pluvialis squatarola* PLATE 55

Other name: Black-bellied Plover
Size: 29cm, 250g
Distribution: Breed throughout the Arctic tundra and are almost circumpolar, except for Greenland, Iceland and Scandinavia. They migrate to the coasts of North and South America, Africa, southern Asia and Australasia. In New Zealand, they are a rare but generally annual visitor between mid-August and mid-April; a few birds have overwintered. Since they were first recorded in the 1940s, there have been sightings from Parengarenga Harbour to the Southland coast, and in the Kermadec and Chatham islands. Most records are from Northland, the Firth of Thames and Farewell Spit. The largest group seen together was 12 at Farewell Spit in 1994.
Population: Usually fewer than 5 visit New Zealand each summer, the maximum was *c.* 15 in 1994; whereas *c.* 12,000 visit Australia. Numbers visiting Australasia have declined since the mid-1990s.
Behaviour: In New Zealand, they usually roost on the coast on sandbanks or shellbanks rather than in ploughed fields or on short pasture, as Pacific Golden Plover do. Their call in flight is a loud, far-carrying, three-syllable, slurred whistle: 'tlee-oo-ee', the second syllable lower in pitch.
Feeding: Grey Plovers are birds of tidal estuaries, feeding in wet, muddy conditions, close to and often wading in the tideline.

245. NEW ZEALAND DOTTEREL *Charadrius obscurus* PLATE 56

Other names: Tuturiwhatu, Rako, Red-breasted Dotterel
Size: 25cm; 160g (*obscurus*), 145g (*aquilonius*)
Geographical variation: Two subspecies: the larger and more boldly coloured Southern New Zealand Dotterel *obscurus* breeds on Stewart Island, and the smaller Northern New Zealand Dotterel *aquilonius* breeds on the coast of the North Island.
Distribution: New Zealand only. Two discrete populations: North and Stewart islands. In the North Island, New Zealand Dotterels breed on beaches, especially near stream mouths, of Northland, Auckland, South Auckland, the Waikato and the Bay of Plenty, and since 1990 they have colonised the Gisborne, Hawke's Bay and Wairarapa coast. They breed from North Cape to Taranaki in the west, and to Riversdale (Southland) in the east. They also breed on some offshore islands, including the Cavalli, Hauraki Gulf (Great Barrier, Motuora, Waiheke, Motuihe, Browns, Ponui, and Beehive), Great Mercury and Moutohora (Whale) islands, Rurima Rocks and Portland Island. A scarce visitor to the coasts of Taranaki and Manawatu. Some northern birds are sedentary and stay in their breeding places; others move a short distance to a flocking site at an estuary. The first arrivals are in mid-January; most arrive by late February. Most leave the flock site and return to their breeding places by the end of April.

New Zealand Dotterels were apparently breeding till the mid-1800s throughout the South Island, particularly in the Southern Alps and their foothills and on the braided riverbeds of Canterbury, moving to the coast in winter. They were probably exterminated by introduced predators and by being shot for food. The remaining population breeds only on Stewart Island, above the bushline. Some descend to tidal estuaries, mudflats and beaches to feed. In January–March, most move down to overwinter at estuaries in Paterson Inlet (Stewart Island) or on the Southland coast, especially near Cow Island in Awarua Bay. The Paterson Inlet birds roost at high tide on sandflats behind the dunes near Duck Creek, Mason Bay. A few birds disperse much further and have been recorded in winter at Farewell Spit and Motueka Sandspit, on the West Coast, in Marlborough and in Canterbury. Southern birds usually arrive back at their breeding grounds in September.

Population: *c.* 2400 birds. A total of 2175 birds of the northern subspecies *aquilonius* was counted in the 2011 breeding season; this increase from *c.* 1350 birds in the mid-1990s is thanks to ongoing predator control and protection of nests from human disturbance at many nesting sites. The southern subspecies has increased from *c.* 60 birds in 1992 to *c.* 250 in 2012 following cat and rat control at their main breeding sites.

Conservation: Protected vulnerable endemic. The dune areas and beaches preferred by northern birds are often affected by housing, pine plantations and plantings of marram grass to stabilise foredunes and sandspits. Disturbance by people, their vehicles, dogs and stock may crush eggs and chicks, or leave eggs, chicks and adults vulnerable to predation by Black-backed Gulls. Efforts to protect northern birds at many breeding sites have generally improved breeding success and may have led to their recent expansion of range. With the southern birds, the control of feral cats and rats in the main breeding areas is carried out each summer. The encouraging gains by both subspecies since the mid-1990s are entirely dependent on ongoing conservation management.

Breeding: Northern New Zealand Dotterels breed on sandspits, at stream mouths, on beaches, shellbanks, sandbanks and among low dunes from August to February. The nest is a scrape in the sand with little or no lining, often near an obvious marker such as a piece of driftwood, seaweed or a clump of vegetation. Southern New Zealand Dotterels breed inland on open subalpine mountain tops, usually where vegetation is sparse or very low and often in rocky places. The nest is a depression among cushion plants lined with dried vegetation.

From August to January, but mainly September to December, Northern New Zealand Dotterels lay 2–**3** pale olive to buff-brown eggs (44 x 31mm), heavily marked with dark brown or black blotches. Up to three replacement clutches can be laid in a season. Southern New Zealand Dotterels lay 2–**3** eggs (46 x 33mm) in October to January. Both sexes incubate for 27–**29**–33 days, females mostly by day, and males mostly by night. Chicks leave the nest within 24 hours of hatching and fledge at 36–46 days old. Juveniles of both subspecies are likely to wander, usually until *c.* 18 months old. Most young first breed in their second year, occasionally in their third year. The oldest known bird lived over 32 years, but one individual, 'Wimble', may have lived at least 42 years (if worn band numbers were read correctly).

Behaviour: Tame and approachable; often heard before being seen. The common call, often accompanied by head-bobbing, is a penetrating 'chrp', 'trrt' or 'prrp'. It is associated with alertness and mild alarm in the presence of a human or other intruder.

Feeding: Commonest habitats are tidal estuaries, stream mouths and sandy beaches. They use a version of the 'walk or run-stop-look-step-peck' method typical of plovers. Diet is mainly aquatic and terrestrial invertebrates but includes some small fish. Crabs are commonly taken, the larger ones bashed and eaten in pieces. Foot-paddling is recorded, as is sand-scratching, which is a means of flushing sandhoppers.

On the subalpine breeding grounds of Stewart Island, some birds fly down to tidal flats in Paterson Inlet to feed, but they also feed on wet herb fields and in seepages, eating a variety of invertebrates, including insects, spiders and earthworms.

Reading: Barlow, M. 1993. *Notornis* 40: 15–25. Dowding, J. E. 1994. *Notornis* 41: 221–233. Dowding, J. E. & Chamberlin, S. P. 1991. *Notornis* 38: 89–102. Dowding, J. E. & Murphy, E. C. 1993. *Notornis* 40: 1–13. Dowding, J. & Davis, A. 2007. *New Zealand Dotterel (*Charadrius obscurus*) Recovery Plan, 2004–2014*. Wellington: DOC. Edgar, A. T. 1969. *Notornis* 16: 85–100.

246. SEMIPALMATED PLOVER *Charadrius semipalmatus* PLATE 57

Size: 18cm, 55g

Distribution: Breeds in northern Canada and Alaska. Most migrate to winter in South America, but some remain in Central America and on the coast of California and southern states of the USA; vagrants have been reported from Europe, Australia and New Zealand. The first accepted New Zealand record was of a bird photographed at the Firth of Thames from November 1983 to October 1985 that was originally misidentified as a Ringed Plover (*Charadrius hiaticula*). Another bird identified as a Ringed Plover was at the Firth of Thames from December 1970 to May 1971, and may well have been this species too. Further records were at Manukau Harbour (December 2009–March 2010) and

Miranda (October–December 2010).
Behaviour: Gregarious and often joins flocks of Wrybills in New Zealand. General behaviour and feeding methods are similar to those of the Banded Dotterel.

247. RED-CAPPED PLOVER *Charadrius ruficapillus* PLATE 57

Other name: Red-capped Dotterel
Size: 15cm, 38g
Distribution: Breeds only in Australia, mainly on coasts in the southeast and in Tasmania, or at ephemeral inland lakes after rains. For a short period they bred in New Zealand. The first record was an adult male collected near Waikanae in 1878; the next was a female mated to a Banded Dotterel in 1947–50 on the Ashley River, Canterbury, raising hybrid young. In the 1960s and 1970s, several pairs of Red-capped Plovers bred on the Ashley, Leader and Waipara rivers of northern Canterbury, and raised chicks. Between 1955 and 1981, there were several records of birds at the Ashley and Waipara river mouths, and further afield at Manukau Harbour, Firth of Thames, Lake Ellesmere and Lake Tuakitoto, presumably all associated with this failed colonisation attempt. Birds were not found in an intensive search of former breeding grounds in 1986–87.
Behaviour: Gregarious and often join flocks of Banded Dotterels in New Zealand. General behaviour and feeding methods are similar to those of the Banded Dotterel.
Reading: Hughey, K. F. D. 1989. *Notornis* 36: 24–26.

248. BANDED DOTTEREL *Charadrius bicinctus* PLATE 56

Other names: Pohowera, Tuturiwhatu, Double-banded Plover (Australia)
Size: 20cm, 60g; Auckland Islands birds larger
Geographical variation: Two subspecies: *bicinctus*, the common breeding bird of the North, South and Chatham islands and partial migrant to Australia; and *exilis*, confined to the Auckland Islands.
Distribution: Breeds only in New Zealand. They are found throughout the North and South islands, and on several offshore islands (including Great Mercury and Ruapuke), Stewart Island, the Chatham and Auckland islands. A high proportion of the population migrates to southeastern Australia in winter, a few regularly visit Lord Howe and Norfolk islands, and some straggle to Vanuatu, New Caledonia and the Kermadecs.

Some Banded Dotterels breed around the sandy coasts, especially near stream or river mouths of both main islands, but their breeding concentrations are on the shingle riverbeds of Hawke's Bay, Manawatu and the Wairarapa in the southern North Island, and especially on the braided riverbeds of Marlborough, Canterbury, Otago and Southland in the South Island. The main stronghold is Canterbury, where 5000 pairs breed on riverbeds and river terraces, and at coastal lakes, lagoons and beaches; another 5000 pairs breed on rivers in the Mackenzie Basin.

The migration routes taken by the various regional populations of Banded Dotterel have been studied in a cooperative programme of colour-banding in New Zealand and Australia. Birds breeding at coastal sites, from Northland beaches to the Stewart Island coast, are generally sedentary. Birds breeding inland in the North Island generally winter on nearby coasts or coastal lakes, or move to Auckland or the Bay of Plenty in January–February. Westland birds move mainly to Farewell Spit. After breeding, most birds from the Mackenzie Basin and the high-altitude southern South Island migrate to Australia in March, whereas those breeding in the Canterbury lowlands and in Marlborough mostly migrate to northern New Zealand in February. The percentage of winter band recoveries in Australia are: Southland 74%, Central Otago 95%, Mackenzie Basin 65%, Canterbury 27%, Westland 15%, Marlborough–Nelson 3%, North Island 1%. Movements of birds breeding in the Chatham and Auckland islands are not known.
Population: In June of 1984 to 1994, 5250–**7400**–9250 Banded Dotterels were counted at New Zealand estuaries, split evenly between North and South islands. Because some birds had already started returning to their breeding grounds in June, and because many inland sites, rivers, small estuaries and beaches were not surveyed, these totals were underestimates. At the time, based on banding studies, the population was estimated to be *c.* 50,000 birds, of which *c.* 30,000 wintered in Australia. Numbers wintering in New Zealand appear to have declined about 15%, because winter counts from 2008 to 2012 revealed only 5200–**6350**–7350 birds. Banded Dotterels are common on the Chatham Islands, especially around Te Whanga Lagoon and the northern

coast of Chatham Island. On the Auckland Islands, there were at least 730 *exilis* in November 1989.

Conservation: Protected vulnerable endemic. Widespread and moderately common. They suffer considerable nest predation by introduced mammals, especially cats, ferrets, stoats and hedgehogs, loss of riverbed habitats to hydroelectric development and irrigation schemes, and consequent weed encroachment onto riverbeds downstream. Human disturbance, especially from off-road vehicles, affects both riverbed and coastal breeding populations.

Breeding: Banded Dotterels start returning to their North Island breeding sites in June or July, and to inland Canterbury sites in August–September. Nests are in consolidated sand, shingle, shell and dirt, with or without prostrate vegetation. Males prepare a series of scrapes, one of which is chosen as the nest. Eggs are laid in July–November in lowland areas, September–December in the Rangipo Desert of the central North Island and in the Mackenzie Basin; but starting as late as November on the mountain ranges of Central Otago. They lay 2–**3**–**4** eggs (34 x 25mm, 12g), pale grey through blue-green to olive and brown, with black spots, streaks and blotches. Both sexes incubate for 25–27 days, starting usually after the second or third egg; the female incubates for most daylight hours; the male incubates mainly at night. Hatching is synchronised. The chicks soon leave the nest and feed independently. The fledging period is 5–6 weeks. Most birds breed in their first year. The oldest banded bird lived over 12 years.

Behaviour: Gregarious at winter roosts, but they often form loose flocks and are even territorial while feeding. They often return to the same feeding territory year after year. They breed solitarily with well-defended territories. Their usual calls are a fast, rolling 'che-ree-a-ree', accented on the second syllable, in defence of the breeding or winter feeding territory; and a loud, high-pitched, far-carrying 'pit' or 'chip', given in flight or on the ground.

Feeding: Diet includes a variety of terrestrial and aquatic invertebrates, supplemented by occasional berries of prostrate plants. On pasture and tilled ground, they mostly take earthworms and beetles. On riverbeds, marsh turf habitats of lakeshores and estuarine mudflats, they take worms, the larvae of midges, mayflies and caddisflies, and emerging adult insects. Like all plovers, they feed visually by using 'run-stop-look-step-peck' on dry sand and 'run-stop-peck' on wet sand and salt marsh; they also foot-tremble in damp habitats.

Reading: Bomford, M. 1988. *Notornis* 35: 9–14. Falla, R. A. 1978. *Notornis* 25: 101–108. Pierce, R. J. 1980. *Notornis* 27: 309–324. Pierce, R. J. 1989. *Notornis* 36: 13–23. Pierce, R. J. 1999. *Notornis* 46: 101–122. Robertson, H. A. & Dennison, M. D. 1979. *Notornis* 26: 73–88. Sagar, P. M. et al. 1999. *Notornis* 46: 1–43. Walker, K. et al. 1991. *Notornis* 38: 257–265.

249. LESSER SAND PLOVER *Charadrius mongolus* PLATE 56

Other names: Mongolian Dotterel, Mongolian Plover

Size: 20cm, 60g

Geographical variation: Five subspecies, split into two geographically distinct subgroups, *mongolus* and *atrifrons*. Those seen in New Zealand in breeding plumage are mostly from the two easternmost subspecies *mongolus* and *stegmanni*, but at least one individual from the *atrifrons* group of central Asia has been seen.

Distribution: Breeds in two widely separated groups: one in central Russia, the Tibet region of China and the Himalayas of central Asia; and the other in eastern and northeastern Siberia. The species winters on coasts of eastern and southern Africa, southern Asia and in Australasia, east to Fiji. In Australia, they are common on northern coasts and down the eastern seaboard to Victoria, Tasmania and South Australia. In New Zealand, Lesser Sand Plovers are a scarce but regular visitor, mostly in late September to mid-April or even early May. Most records are in the Manukau Harbour, the Firth of Thames and Farewell Spit, but they have been recorded at estuaries from Parengarenga Harbour to the Oreti Estuary, Invercargill. The most seen together is 4 at Karaka, Manukau Harbour, in 1981. Several birds have overwintered, and an individual stayed at Porangahau Estuary from March 1986 to January 1988 without going into breeding plumage.

Population: Normally, fewer than 5 visit New Zealand each summer, whereas *c.* 20,000 visit Australia.

Behaviour: Gregarious; in New Zealand they feed and roost with Banded Dotterels on mudflats and estuaries. They feed in the 'run-and-stop' manner typical of plovers, pausing often to crouch and lunge at prey seen moving. Their voice is similar to that of the Banded Dotterel but distinctive to the experienced observer, with a rolled 'r' component not present in a Banded Dotterel's voice.

Reading: Heather, B. D. & Robertson, H. A. 1981. *Notornis* 28: 82–83. Hirschfeld E. et al. 2000. *British Birds* 93: 162–189. Parrish, G .R. 2000. *Notornis* 47: 125–126. Sibson, R. B. 1975. *Notornis* 22: 347–349.

250. GREATER SAND PLOVER *Charadrius leschenaultii* PLATE 56

Other names: Large Sand Dotterel
Size: 24cm, 90g
Geographical variation: Of the three subspecies, *leschenaultii* breeds in eastern central Asia and migrates to Australasia.
Distribution: Breeds across central Asia from Turkey to northwestern China, and winters in Africa, southern Asia and Australasia. The subspecies *leschenaultii* breeds in southern Siberia, Mongolia and northwestern China, and migrates to Australasia, especially to the coasts of northern Australia and down the eastern seaboard to Victoria and Tasmania. In New Zealand, they are recorded almost annually as a rare visitor, mostly in September–April. Favoured sites are the Kaipara and Manukau harbours, the Firth of Thames and Farewell Spit, but they have been recorded on estuaries from Parengarenga Harbour to coastal Southland. The most seen together is 9 at the Firth of Thames in 1983.
Population: Normally, fewer than 5 visit New Zealand each summer, whereas about 75,000 visit Australia.
Behaviour: Gregarious, feeding and roosting with other species, especially with Banded Dotterels on mudflats and estuaries. They feed in the 'run-and-stop' manner typical of plovers. The call is a soft trill similar to that of the Lesser Sand Plover.
Reading: Hirschfeld E. et al. 2000. *British Birds* 93: 162–189. Sibson, R. B. 1953. *Notornis* 5: 179–181.

251. ORIENTAL DOTTEREL *Charadrius veredus* PLATE 55

Other name: Oriental Plover
Size: 24cm, 95g
Distribution: Breeds in Mongolia and Manchuria, and migrates to winter mostly in Indonesia and Australia. Up to 150,000 birds visit the coasts and open grassy plains, airfields and sports fields of northern Australia, but they are stragglers to southern states, and a rare straggler to Lord Howe Island and New Zealand. Eighteen New Zealand records, mainly of single birds: Raoul Island, Kermadecs (1908, 1982); Parengarenga Harbour (1955, 1968, 1969), Manukau Harbour (1975, three in 1994), Firth of Thames (1953, 10 in 1954–55), Greymouth (1982, 1987), Lake Wainono (1977), Greymouth airfield (1982), Lake Ellesmere (1989), Invercargill Estuary (1988), Waituna Lagoon (1988), Te Whanga Lagoon, Chathams (2000), and Port Waikato (2013).
Behaviour: Gregarious, feeding in loose flocks. They take mainly insects, such as grasshoppers and crickets, by the usual plover 'run-and-stop' method. Their call is a whistled 'chip' in flight, but a sharp, rippling trill when chasing one another on the ground.

252. WRYBILL *Anarhynchus frontalis* PLATE 52

Other names: Ngutuparore, Wrybill Plover
Size: 20cm, 55g
Distribution: New Zealand only. Wrybills breed in Canterbury and parts of inland Otago on the braided rivers that flow east from the Southern Alps or their foothills, from the Waiau and Hurunui rivers in the north to the Matukituki and Dart rivers in the south. The main breeding rivers are the Waimakariri, Rakaia, Rangitata, and the upper Waitaki and its tributaries in the Mackenzie Basin.

After breeding, most birds fly north to the large tidal harbours of Northland, Auckland and South Auckland – Kaipara, Manukau and, above all, the Firth of Thames. Flocks of 100+ birds reach Parengarenga, Houhora, Whangarei and Waitemata harbours. Smaller flocks regularly winter at other Northland estuaries, Tauranga Harbour, Muriwai Lagoon (Gisborne), Porangahau Estuary and Manawatu Estuary. A few Wrybills remain in the South Island in winter, mainly on the Waimea Estuary and at Farewell Spit. A vagrant has reached the Chathams.

Fledglings and failed breeders start leaving in late November, often staging at Lake Ellesmere. The main northward movement of birds is in the last couple of weeks of December and early January. The last adults and late fledglings leave in early February. Their return from northern mudflats starts in early August, the peak being in mid-August, often staging in flocks at Lakes Ellesmere and Wainono. Some 2–10 % of winter visitors, presumably mainly yearlings, stay in the north through the summer.

Population: *c.* 5300 in 2010. Ornithological Society counts since 1983 have shown that about 90% of Wrybills overwinter at the Firth of Thames and Manukau Harbour, and that less than 1% remain in the South Island through the winter.

Conservation: Protected vulnerable endemic. The breeding of Wrybills has apparently been confined to eastern South Island rivers in historical times. In the late 1800s and early 1900s, many were collected for museum specimens, especially because of their unique sideways-bent bill. They were legally protected in 1940 and the population gradually increased from about 1500–2000 birds to just over 5000 now. Numbers have fluctuated over recent decades, with major threats being predation by mustelids and cats, floods, water extraction for irrigation, and invasion of shingle riverbeds by exotic weeds such as willows, gorse and lupins; however, control of predators has led to recent population increases.

Breeding: Eggs are laid from late August to January; many adults lay two clutches. The usual nesting sites are on islands of bare shingle, with the stones slightly larger than the eggs, or on a shingle bank near water at a high point without vegetation. The blue-grey adults, eggs and chicks blend well with the blue-grey of the greywacke shingle. A few nest on the shores of adjacent lakes, e.g. Lake Tekapo. Males scrape a hollow in the shingle by bulldozing with their breast.

They lay **2** pale grey eggs (35 x 26mm, 11g), tinged blue or green, and covered with minute dark-brown spots and lines. Both sexes incubate for *c.* 30 days. Hatching is synchronous, and the chicks are led away to a riffle, backwater or other suitable feeding place. The fledging period is 36–37 days. About 50% of first-year birds return to the breeding grounds, but few breed until they are 2 years old. The oldest bird recorded lived over 22 years.

Behaviour: Gregarious when not breeding; they roost quietly together, almost all on one leg, which they keep to, preferring to hop rather than lower the second leg when disturbed. They swirl as one in the air, especially before southward migration, when a flock has been likened to smoke or to a flung scarf. Their usual call is not prominent, on the ground or in flight.

Feeding: The last third of the long bill turns to the bird's right at an angle of 15–22°, and the upper mandible is slightly broader than the lower and overlaps it on the outside of the curve; inside the curve the two halves do not meet, and so the lower mandible collects invertebrates from under stones. Feeding is by pecking directly or by tilting the head to the left followed by clockwise movements of the bill under stones in shallow riffles. Diet is mainly aquatic or near-aquatic mayflies, caddisflies, bugs, beetles, flies and stoneflies. When rivers are in flood, they are forced onto stream banks and the water's edge, where their diet is more general – beetles, flies, mayflies and spiders.

On tidal mudflats in the north, they prefer silty mud with a surface film of water. They catch small crustaceans by scything the wet mud, the bill dabbing slightly from left to right.

In the hand: Young birds arrive on wintering grounds in fresh plumage and do not moult until the following year. Adults moult their primaries between January and April, and so have fresh plumage throughout the winter. No reliable sexing method is available for non-breeding birds.

Reading: Davies, S. 1997. *Notornis* 44: 1–14. Hughey, K. E. D. 1985. *Notornis* 32: 42–50. Hughey, K. E. D. 1997. *Notornis* 44: 185–193. Pierce, R. J. 1979. *Notornis* 26: 1–21. Rawlings, M. 1993. *Forest & Bird* 24: 10–15. Sagar, P. M. et al. 1999. *Notornis* 46: 1–43. Stead, E. F. 1932. *The Life Histories of New Zealand Birds*. London: Search. Veitch, C. R. & Habraken, A. M. 1999. *Notornis* 46: 45–70.

253. BLACK-FRONTED DOTTEREL *Elseyornis melanops* PLATE 57

Other name: Black-fronted Plover

Size: 17cm, 33g

Distribution: Breeds throughout Australia and, since the late 1950s, in New Zealand.

They first colonised Hawke's Bay, then spread to Manawatu, Wairarapa and across Cook Strait to Marlborough and South Canterbury in the late 1960s. Now they breed on the shingle riverbeds of the eastern and southern North Island, south of Wairoa and Whanganui, and are found sparsely in the northeastern South Island and in increasing numbers on the shingle beds of smaller rivers in Canterbury,

Otago and Southland. Elsewhere they are seen only as rare non-breeding vagrants, except that a small number regularly visit estuaries in the eastern Bay of Plenty, and a few have bred near Auckland since 2002.

When not breeding, most birds stay on the rivers, but in autumn some move to dried lake beds (e.g. Pukepuke and Omanuka lagoons), and when river levels rise in winter they gather on nearby muddy places and wetlands such as Whakaki Lagoon, Ahuriri Estuary, Lakes Poukawa, Hatuma and Wairarapa, and sewage ponds near Feilding, Otaki and Masterton. A regular few are in winter on the Bay of Plenty coast, their origin unknown. Some non-breeding flocking in the South Island has begun at Lakes Elterwater and Ellesmere, and at Spider, Wainono and Washdyke lagoons.

Population: *c.* 2000 in New Zealand. North Island *c.* 1700 (Hawke's Bay 800, Wairarapa 400, Manawatu 400); South Island *c.* 300 (Marlborough 100, Canterbury 100, Otago 50, Southland 50).

Conservation: Protected coloniser. Black-fronted Dotterels have recently established as a breeding species in New Zealand, and do not seem to compete significantly with any native species.

Breeding: Eggs are laid *c.* 2–3 days apart in August–February, early in Hawke's Bay, where riverbeds are wider, and late in Wairarapa, where floods are common in early summer. The nest is a shallow depression on the ground, usually lined with fine pebbles or wood chips, dry grass and leaves, often on the shingle ridge nearest to the feeding area. They lay 2–**3** khaki eggs (29 x 21mm), with the grey or cream background obscured by a mass of brown spots, flecks and fine wavy lines. Both sexes incubate for 22–**25**–26 days. Chicks leave the nest within days of hatching and fledge at 23–30 days old.

Behaviour: Some birds remain on territory all year in solitary pairs, but in winter others form loose groups of up to 100 birds. The contact call is a sharp 'pit', more high-pitched and metallic than that of Banded Dotterels and given more often in flight. The threat call is a vigorous rippling 'ree-ree-ree-ree-ree'. The main territorial call is a languid churring 'rrrr-reep' given by the male while circling above its territory in butterfly flight. In the presence of a human intruder, they crouch back-on in the shingle, becoming almost invisible. When more alarmed, they spread and depress their tail, rocking from side to side. They run among stones rather than over them, as other riverbed waders do.

Feeding: Diet is mainly molluscs, crustaceans, insects and earthworms, taken by the 'walk or run-stop-peck' typical of plovers. They also foot-tremble, followed by pecking to take prey disturbed by tapping (on hard surfaces) or leg-shaking (over soft soil or mud).

Reading: Child, P. & Child, M. 1984. *Notornis* 31: 31–39. Dennison, T. C. & Robertson, H. A. 1999. *Notornis* 46: 187–193. Heather, B. D. 1977. *Notornis* 24: 1–8. Robertson, H. A. & Heather, B. D. 1999. *Notornis* 46: 79–88. Tarburton, M. K. 1989. *Notornis* 36: 249–259.

254. SHORE PLOVER *Thinornis novaeseelandiae* PLATE 57

Other name: Tuturuatu

Size: 20cm, 60g

Distribution: Found naturally only on South East Island, and until recently on Western Reef in the Chathams; rarely wandering to other islands of the group. They live on the coastal rocky wave platforms and on the 'Clears', an open, exposed area of salt meadow at the southern end of the island.

Shore Plovers were recorded in the South Island at Queen Charlotte Sound (Marlborough Sounds) and Dusky Sound (Fiordland) in 1773, and were probably distributed widely round the South Island coast until exterminated soon after the arrival of Norway rats and feral cats. The last reliable mainland record was at Waikawa River, Otago, about 1871. At the time they were still on Mangere and Pitt islands in the Chathams, but they disappeared soon after the introduction of cats to those islands.

Between February 2001 and January 2003, 40 juvenile Shore Plovers were transferred from South East Island to Mangere Island and have established a small but apparently self-sustaining population. Between 1994 and 2012, a total of 364 juvenile and 28 adult birds reared in captivity were released at five islands around the New Zealand mainland, including Motuora, Motutapu, Waikawa (Portland), and Mana islands. These transfers were only partially successful or too recent to judge success, with major problems caused by avian predators and incursions from mammalian predators. The largest population, of up to 37 pairs in 2011, established on Waikawa Island after releases in 1998–2006, but a predator incursion in 2012 eliminated most birds. The Mana Island population was removed after a setback in 2011 when a single Norway rat killed many breeding adults. Some Shore Plovers have wandered to the mainland from these release sites, generally to nearby coasts and estuaries, but some birds have returned over 250km to captive institutions where they were hatched, and an adult female from Mana was seen in order at Plimmerton (adjacent to Mana), Lake Ellesmere, Manawatu Estuary, and back at Plimmerton between November 2012 and January 2013, a round trip of 850km.

Population: *c.* 200 birds in 2012, including 60–65 pairs in the wild (43–45 pairs on South East Island) and 6–10 pairs in captivity.

Conservation: Protected critically endangered endemic. Very vulnerable to predators such as cats, stoats and rats; they survived naturally on two small predator-free islands, despite hundreds being collected for museum specimens between 1890 and 1910. For unknown reasons, they disappeared from Western Reef within a few years of being discovered there in 1999. Faced with the constant risk of introduced predators reaching South East Island, the loss of marsh-turf habitat since the removal of sheep in 1961, and the risk of fire, disease or the encroachment of breeding fur seals onto key feeding and breeding areas. The aim is to establish several self-sustaining populations on islands and in captivity, but to date, these transfers have been only partially successful.

Breeding: Eggs are laid from mid-October to January. One brood per year on South East Island, but double-brooding has been recorded at some new release sites. Nests are hidden under thick vegetation, occasionally under boulders near the shore or under large rocks inland. They lay 2–3 pale buff eggs (37 x 26mm, 13g), blotched or spotted darker brown, at 3–5 day intervals. Both sexes, but mostly females, incubate for about 28 days, usually starting when the last egg is laid. The fledging period is normally 35–45 days. Some young breed at 2 years, but most start when 3 years old. A bird banded as an adult lived to over 20 years old.

Behaviour: Strongly territorial in the breeding season, but in winter they may roost and feed in flocks of up to 35 birds. They are noisy, making loud, ringing calls, especially in aggression with neighbours. The normal call of both sexes is a quiet 'kleet' or 'pip', higher-pitched in females.

Feeding: Diet includes crustaceans (copepods, ostracods, amphipods, and isopods), spiders, molluscs (gastropods, bivalves), and insects and their larvae. They glean and peck among the tide-wrack and on wet rock platforms covered in algae and barnacles. Birds at release islands and at mainland sites often feed on sandy or gravel beaches and are not confined to wave platforms. They may take rapid, short steps – 'step-peck-peck-peck-step' – or foot-tremble on algae-covered rock platforms.

Reading: Aikman, H. 1999. *Notornis* 46: 195–205. Davis, A. 1994. *Notornis* 41 (S): 171–194. Davis, A. 1994. *Notornis* 41 (S): 195–208. Dowding, J. E. & Kennedy, E. S. 1993. *Notornis* 40: 213–222. Dowding, J. E. & O'Connor, S. M. 2013. *Notornis* 60: 70–84. Fleming, C. A. 1939. *Emu* 39: 1–15.

255. RED-KNEED DOTTEREL *Erythrogonys cinctus* PLATE 57

Size: 18cm, 50g

Distribution: Breeds only in Australia, mainly on inland freshwater lakes and swamps. They head inland to breed following heavy rains, but when the interior dries out they move towards estuaries and brackish coastal lagoons. A vagrant to southern New Guinea and Tasmania. One seen in New Zealand: Manawatu River Estuary (March 1976).

Behaviour: Usually solitary and seen gleaning and probing for invertebrates on the edge of freshwater wetland margins or brackish coastal ponds. They swim readily.

Reading: Robertson, H. A. & Dennison, M. D. 1977. *Notornis* 24: 193–194.

256. SPUR-WINGED PLOVER *Vanellus miles* PLATE 53

Other names: Masked Lapwing, Masked Plover

Size: 38cm; male 370g, female 350g

Geographical variation: Two subspecies: *miles* in northern Australia and New Guinea and *novaehollandiae* from mid-Queensland to southeastern Australia, Tasmania and New Zealand. The subspecies overlap extensively and hybridise in Queensland and in the interior of the continent.

Distribution: New Guinea, Australia, Lord Howe Island and New Zealand. A vagrant to the Moluccas, Christmas Island (Indian Ocean), Norfolk Island and the Cook Islands. Vagrants were recorded at Kai Iwi (1886) and at Hokitika (1892). A pair bred for the first time in New Zealand near Invercargill Airport about 1932. By

1951, there were *c.* 100, and by 1971 *c.* 1250 breeding birds within a 16km radius of the original breeding site. During the 1950s, they expanded to inland Southland and appeared near Lake Wanaka, Central Otago, but remained rare outside Southland until the mid-1960s. From the late 1960s to the 1980s, they spread to Stewart Island and to the rest of the South Island, where they are very common in open country throughout. The first breeding records in the North Island were in the early 1970s near Gisborne, Dannevirke and Paraparaumu, but they are now abundant in coastal Manawatu and southern Wairarapa, and common throughout the North Island. They have become well established on the Chatham Islands since breeding was first recorded there in 1981, and have apparently established at Raoul Island, Kermadecs, since 1993. Vagrants recorded from Bounty, Snares, Antipodes, Auckland and Campbell islands.

Population: Abundant in Southland, coastal Otago and Canterbury, Manawatu and southern Wairarapa; common or becoming so elsewhere. Numbers in some districts appear to have peaked and then stabilised at a lower level.

Conservation: Unprotected self-introduced native. Spur-winged Plovers are a recent arrival in New Zealand and are clearly suited to the arable and pasture habitats. They are probably beneficial to farmers because they eat a wide range of invertebrates, including pests such as grass grubs and porina larvae; however, they are much maligned because they are noisy and aggressive in defence of their nests or chicks. They are a common cause of bird-strike incidents at airports due to their slow flight and use of grassland habitats.

Breeding: Laying is from June to late November, with the peak in August. Several clutches are laid each year. The preferred site is rough, open pasture without farm animals, or a flat, wet area with some surface irregularity and a wide outlook. They also breed on bare ground (e.g. chewed-down turnips or choumoellier, or consolidated riverbed shingle). The nest is a scrape in the ground, unlined or scantily lined with whatever material is nearby.

They lay 1–4 khaki eggs (49 x 35mm, 31g) with brownish-black spots and blotches. Both sexes incubate for 30–31 days after the last egg is laid. The chicks soon leave the nest and follow the adults, but find their own food. The fledgling period is 7–8 weeks. Young are capable of breeding at the end of their first year, but most pair for life in their first year and breed in their second year. The oldest bird recorded in New Zealand lived over 16 years.

Behaviour: Often gregarious when not breeding; flocks of up to 600, presumably juveniles and non-breeders, have been recorded at Lake Wairarapa in October–December. Spur-winged Plovers are extremely noisy; their main call is a loud, penetrating and staccato 'rattle', often at night, on the ground and in the air. Among their various displays is the conspicuous piping party; in a loose circle on raised ground, six or seven birds face one another in an upright stance with legs straight, breast pushed out and wings held slightly open, exposing the spurs; they call harshly at one another, alternating with silence; some birds stiffly advance and retreat.

When alarmed, they are wary and alert with an upright stance, although an incubating bird usually creeps unobtrusively away from the intruder. They are aggressive in defence of their nest and chicks, screaming and dive-bombing to divert intruders, and attacking Harriers and Australian Magpies as they fly over.

Feeding: Diet on short-grassed pasture and ploughed paddocks is mainly earthworms, insects and their larvae, and also seeds and leaves; in tidal and other coastal habitats, crustaceans and molluscs are taken. They feed

with a slow, stalking walk; shoulders hunched and head forward, with a sudden dip to catch prey.
Reading: Barlow, M. 1972. *Notornis* 19: 201–211. Barlow, M. 1983. *The Year of the Spur-winged Plover*. Invercargill: Craig Printing. Barlow, M. L. et al. 1972. *Notornis* 19: 212–249.

PRATINCOLES and COURSERS *Glareolidae*

Of the 15 species, 1 reaches New Zealand as a vagrant.

Pratincoles are graceful and highly aerial birds, similar to terns. They have very long, narrow wings, a forked tail and a wide gape with which they seize flying insects on the wing. They also feed on the ground like other waders; in spite of their short legs, they can run fast. Their bill is short and strongly arched. The sexes are alike.

257. ORIENTAL PRATINCOLE *Glareola maldivarum* PLATE 51

Size: 23cm, 75g
Distribution: Breeds in southern Asia from Pakistan and India to Mongolia, China, the Taiwan province of China and the northern Philippines. They are partially sedentary in winter, but many migrate to winter in northern Australia, often in thousands, and in February 2004 almost 3 million congregated at Eighty Mile Beach (Western Australia) to feed on yellow-winged locusts. Small numbers reach southern and eastern Australia, and a few occasionally wander to New Zealand. Thirteen records: Westport (1898), a flock of at least five at Appleby, Nelson (1959); Port Adventure, Stewart Island (1963); Raoul Island, Kermadecs (1976); Wainono Lagoon (1977); South Turnbull (1977); Kaipara Harbour (1985, 1986); Ruapuke Island, Foveaux Strait (1988, 1989); Farewell Spit (1994); New Plymouth (1999); Lake Ellesmere (2002).
Behaviour: Oriental Pratincoles fly like over-large swallows, usually near water. Normally they are found in small flocks, but all New Zealand sightings have been of single birds apart from the small flock at Appleby in 1959.
Reading: Falla, R. A. 1959. *Notornis* 8: 126–127. Pierce, R. J. 1978. *Notornis* 25: 290.

SKUAS *Stercorariidae*

8 species: 2 breed in the New Zealand region, 2 are regular transients especially in spring and autumn as they pass between their Arctic breeding grounds and Southern Ocean seas, and 1 is a straggler from its non-breeding range in the central Pacific.

Skuas are strong-flying pelagic birds allied to the gulls. They have hooked beaks with a distinctive sheath covering the base of the upper bill. Most species have light- and dark-plumage phases, with some intermediate forms; all have conspicuous white flashes in the outer wing. The three small species have highly developed central tail feathers that extend well beyond the remainder of the tail, but these are rarely seen on birds in New Zealand waters.

Skuas are piratical, pursuing terns, gulls, shags and shearwaters, and forcing them to drop or disgorge their food. These spectacular aerobatic chases are most often seen in autumn when large flocks of White-fronted Terns usually have Arctic and/or Pomarine Skuas in attendance.

During breeding, the large native skuas feed mainly on shoaling fish, petrels and their eggs and chicks, or penguin eggs and chicks. They also eat carrion on beaches or coastal farmland. They are renowned for their fierce territorial defence, diving noisily at people and other large intruders venturing into their breeding area. They strike at people with their feet as they pass close overhead.

Reading: Furness, R. W. 1987. *The Skuas*. Calton: Poyser. Harrison, P. 1983. *Seabirds: An Identification Guide*. Beckenham: Croom Helm. Serventy, D. L. et al. 1971. *The Handbook of Australian Sea-birds*. Sydney: A. H. & A. W. Reed. Young, E. C. 1994. *Skua and Penguin: Predator and Prey*. Cambridge: CUP.

258. SOUTHERN SKUA *Catharacta antarctica* PLATE 59

Other names: Hakoakoa, Brown Skua, Subantarctic Skua

Size: 63cm; male 1675g, female 1950g

Geographical variation: Three subspecies: *antarctica* breeds in the Falklands and Patagonia, *hamiltoni* breeds on Tristan da Cunha and Gough islands in the South Atlantic Ocean, and *lonnbergi* breeds on the Antarctic Peninsula and circumpolar on many subantarctic islands, including in New Zealand.

Distribution: Breeds on many subantarctic islands around the globe. In New Zealand, they breed on the Chathams, Solander, Stewart and outliers, Snares, Antipodes, Auckland and Campbell islands, and also on the Balleny Islands of the Ross Dependency. A few pairs have nested in southern Fiordland. In the summer, they remain close to their breeding grounds, but transients appear at the Bounty Islands and vagrants reach the Ross Sea. Although most northern breeding birds remain on their territory all year, most birds leave southern colonies and disperse northward in autumn, especially to southern Australia and the western Tasman Sea. In winter, they are occasionally seen along the coast of the North and South islands; and seldom inland, usually feeding on dead sheep and lambs.

Population: Widespread in the subantarctic, with many small populations. New Zealand probably has fewer than 2000 birds; the main populations are on the Chathams (*c.* 200 birds), Snares (*c.* 170 birds), Antipodes, Auckland (especially Enderby) and Campbell islands.

Conservation: Protected native. In the Chathams, some Southern Skuas are illegally shot by fishermen and farmers, but elsewhere few are harmed.

Breeding: Most breeding birds at the Chathams and Snares defend their territory all year, although the winter defence is less aggressive. In these colonies, about 30% of territories are defended by trios (two unrelated males and a female), but groups of up to 7 birds have been recorded At more southerly colonies, birds rarely overwinter and almost all breed in simple pairs. Numbers at the colonies build up from September with members of each territorial group arriving back independently.

Laying is from mid-September to December, with a clear latitudinal gradient from the Chathams, where birds start laying in mid-September, to Campbell Island, where laying starts in early November. The nest is usually a bowl of dry grass, moss and lichen. They lay 1–**2**–3 brown eggs (74 x 52mm) with dark brown blotches. Eggs are laid about 2 days apart. The adults share incubation for 28–**29**–32 days and feed the chicks during the 55–60 day fledging period. They continue to feed the young for at least 70 days after fledging. On the Chathams, young birds return to the natal colony at 4–5 years old, but do not start breeding until 5–**8**–14 years old. Many birds live to 20–30 years old.

Behaviour: Non-breeding birds normally form 'clubs' near the colony before and during the breeding season. They fill gaps as territorial members disappear. Southern Skuas normally maintain the same breeding territory and partner(s) year after year. Territorial displays include a conspicuous 'heraldic' display, in which a bird holds its wings stiffly upwards to show off the white wing patches, and extends its neck and head and utters a descending long call 'charr-charr-charr. . .' They defend their territory very aggressively against other skuas and, with a screeching call, repeatedly and fearlessly dive at people or other intruders, striking out with their feet as they pass close overhead. Usually solitary at sea away from the breeding grounds.

Feeding: While breeding, the diet is mainly penguin eggs and chicks, or petrels. The latter are caught at night on the ground, or are sometimes forced to the ground and then killed. Southern Skuas carry seabirds to a 'midden' where they leave the wings, head and legs in a pile, or they regurgitate pellets containing the remains of small seabirds, especially storm petrels. They also feed on fish, eggs of other birds, dead marine mammals and seal placenta, and scavenge dead sheep and cattle in the Chathams. Goose barnacles and Broad-billed Prions form the main part of their winter diet in the Chathams. Away from their colonies, their winter diet is presumed to be mainly pelagic fish, although the few seen on the New Zealand mainland coast are often feeding on carrion such as fish remains or beach-washed sheep. They occasionally harass other birds such as albatrosses, petrels, gulls and shags and force them to regurgitate or drop their prey.

Reading: Hemmings, A. D. 1989. *J Zool (Lond)* 218: 393–405. Hemmings, A. D. 1990. *Emu* 90: 108–113. Hemmings, A. D. 1994. *J Roy Soc NZ* 24: 245–260. Moors, P. J. 1980. *Notornis* 27: 133–146. Young, E. C. 1978. *NZ J Zool* 5: 401–416. Young, E. C. 1994. *Notornis* 41(S): 143–163. Young, E. C. 1994. *Condor* 100: 335–342. Young, E. C. et al. 1988. *NZ J Ecol* 11: 113–117.

259. SOUTH POLAR SKUA *Catharacta maccormicki* PLATE 59

Other name: Antarctic Skua
Size: 59cm; male 1275g, female 1425g
Distribution: Breeds on the coast and offshore islands of Antarctica, mainly near penguin and petrel colonies. They winter at sea, some ranging into the North Pacific, northern Indian and North Atlantic oceans. In New Zealand territory, they breed at over 50 sites around the Ross Dependency; the main colonies (>300 pairs) are at Cape Crozier, Possession Island, Cape Bird, Sven Foyn Island and Cape Adare. They presumably migrate well offshore, because there are only about 20 records from New Zealand waters between the Kermadecs and Campbell Island, and only a few have been beach-wrecked, mainly along the west coast of the North Island. A bird banded at Cape Hallett in 1964 was recovered in Japan in 1966.
Population: Moderately common around Antarctica; in 1981–83 *c.* 15,000 birds were at 55+ sites in the Ross Dependency, with Cape Crozier (*c.* 1000 pairs) having the largest population.
Conservation: Protected native. About 80% of breeding South Polar Skuas are associated with penguin colonies, and in the long term, numbers may change in line with penguin populations as they are affected by climate change.
Breeding: Birds arrive at their Ross Sea colonies in mid- to late October, slightly earlier at more northern colonies. Usually a pair occupies the same territory year after year; however, a pair will occasionally shift their territory several kilometres between years. They rarely change mates, except when one bird dies. A single communally breeding trio has been reported from Ross Island. Laying is from mid-November to late December, but the season varies slightly from colony to colony and year to year, depending on weather and food availability. They lay **2** tan eggs (71 x 50mm) speckled brown, 1–4 days apart, in a simple scrape in gravel or sand, with no nest lining. Both birds incubate evenly in spells of 90–180 minutes, and the female is regularly fed by the male during this time, however, where pairs have access to penguin eggs or chicks, both sexes forage. Incubation starts when the first egg is laid, and the eggs hatch 1–**2**–5 days apart, after 24–**29**–35 days. Chicks are brooded in the nest for the first 1–2 days, but spend increasing time away from the nest. At Cape Crozier in 1993–94, two chicks were raised in about one-third of nests, but in almost all other nests with two chicks, the youngest chick was evicted from the nest by the older one when about 3 days old and subsequently died or was adopted by a neighbouring pair. The fledging period is 49–59 days. The fledglings continue to be fed by their parents for several weeks. Young normally return to their natal colony at 1–**3**–5 years old. A few females breed at 4 years old, and males at 5, but most females start breeding at 6–7 years old, and most males start at 8–9. South Polar Skuas are very long-lived; the annual survivorship of birds aged over 10 years at Cape Crozier is 96%, giving a mean life expectancy of over 35 years. As a further indication of the good survival at Cape Crozier, 42 of 224 chicks banded in 1961 were still alive 22 years later.
Behaviour: Non-breeding birds normally form 'clubs' near the colony before and during the breeding season, and they start courting and forming pairs. Territorial displays are similar to those of the Southern Skua, with a conspicuous 'heraldic' display, in which a bird holds its wings stiffly upwards to show off the white wing patches, and calls 'charr-charr-charr'. They defend their territory very aggressively against other skuas and, with a screeching call, repeatedly dive at people or other intruders. Little is known of the social behaviour of South Polar Skuas away from the breeding grounds, but they appear to be solitary at sea.
Feeding: While breeding, the incubating or brooding female is mainly fed by the male, who disgorges food a short distance from the nest. Diet is mainly a shoaling fish, the Antarctic silverfish *Pleuragramma antarcticum*, but if a territory includes a penguin rookery or petrel colony, a major part of the owners' diet during part of the season will be eggs and chicks and spilt krill. Some skuas specialise in attacking breeding penguins to gain eggs and chicks, and a pair sometimes works as a team to displace an incubating or brooding penguin from its nest. They also feed on dead birds and seals. In the non-breeding season, they feed on shoaling fish, and in the seas off Japan, they constantly harass feeding shearwaters and get much food by piracy.
In the hand: Females are 10–15% heavier than males and are generally larger, but measurements overlap: bill 47–**51**–53.5 cf. 48–**49.5**–51.5mm and wing 400–**415**–430 cf. 390–**410**–420mm.
Reading: Ainley, D. G. et al. 1985. *Condor* 87: 427–428. Ainley, D. G. et al. 1986. *Notornis* 33: 155–163. Ainley, D. G. et al. 1990. *J Anim Ecol* 59: 1–20. Hemmings, A. D. 1994. *J Roy Soc NZ* 24: 245–260. Pietz, P. 1987. *Auk* 104: 617–627. Reid, B. E. 1966. *Notornis* 13: 71–89. Spellerberg, I. F. 1970. *Notornis* 17: 280–285. Spellerberg, I. F. 1971. *Ardea* 59: 189–229. Wang, Z. & Norman, F. I. 1993. *Notornis*

40: 189–203. Young, E. C. 1963. *Ibis* 105: 203–233, 301–318. Young, E. C. 1994. *Skua and Penguin: Predator and Prey*. Cambridge, CUP. Young, E. C. & Millar, C. D. 1999. *Notornis* 46: 287–197. Young, E. C. & Millar, C. D. 2003. *NZ J Zool* 30: 79–93.

260. POMARINE SKUA *Coprotheres pomarinus* PLATE 58

Size: 48cm, excluding central tail feathers; 600g
Distribution: Circumpolar breeder on dry tundra and mountains in the Arctic and subarctic of North America, Greenland, Iceland, Scandinavia and Russia. They migrate south in September and pass through the tropics to winter at sea in the Southern Hemisphere. A common visitor to eastern and southeastern coasts of Australia, but an uncommon though regular visitor to New Zealand waters from Northland to Foveaux Strait and east to the Chathams in December–April. They are mainly pelagic but occasionally join Arctic Skuas inshore to harass White-fronted Terns, and sometimes chase Red-billed, Black-billed and even Black-backed gulls. On the New Zealand coast, they tend to be seen off sandy ocean beaches such as Farewell Spit and the Manawatu coast, rather than in sheltered waters, and they quite often fly over land near the sea.
Behaviour: Pomarine Skuas are conspicuous as they rather clumsily chase White-fronted Terns or small gulls and harry them until they are forced to drop their fish or to regurgitate. This food is caught and eaten in mid-air. Between chases, they usually fly low and purposefully between feeding flocks of terns or gulls, or settle on the water with a characteristic posture of high head and high tail. They usually feed solitarily, but sometimes join small flocks of Arctic Skuas working a flock of terns and gulls. An exceptional gathering of 38 birds was reported in the Tasman Sea, 100km off the Waikato coast, in February 1984.

261. ARCTIC SKUA *Stercorarius parasiticus* PLATE 58

Size: 43cm, excluding central tail feathers; 400g
Distribution: Circumpolar breeder on lowland tundra in the Arctic and subarctic of North America, Greenland, Iceland, Scandinavia and Russia. They migrate south in September and pass through the tropics to winter at sea in temperate parts of the Southern Hemisphere. A common visitor to New Zealand waters from October to May, and they are easily the most numerous skua seen off the coasts of the mainland and the Chatham Islands. Also recorded from the Kermadecs and the Antipodes.

A few immatures remain over the winter. They are often seen in coastal waters and in large sheltered harbours and sounds, but are seldom seen over land, except when they join roosting flocks of terns or gulls.
Behaviour: Arctic Skuas are conspicuous as they twist and turn in aerobatic chases of White-fronted Terns, Black-fronted Terns or small gulls, continually harrying them until they are forced to drop their fish or to regurgitate. This food is caught and eaten in mid-air. Sometimes they feed on scraps discarded from fishing boats. Between chases, they usually fly low and purposefully between feeding flocks of terns, or settle on the water with a characteristic posture of high head and high tail. They usually feed solitarily, but sometimes small flocks of four or five birds work a flock of terns. Gatherings of over 60 birds have been reported off the northern North Island.
In the hand: Non-breeding Arctic Skuas and Long-tailed Skuas are hard to separate, even in the hand; Arctic Skuas recorded in Australasia generally have longer wings (298–**315**–325mm cf. 272–**295**–315mm), bill (29–**31**–33mm cf. 26.5–**28**–31mm), and mid-toe and claw (41–**43.5**–45mm cf. 34.5–**38**–41.5mm) than Long-tailed Skuas. A combination of these measures should reliably separate most birds.
Reading: Melville, D. S. 1985. *Notornis* 32: 51–73.

262. LONG-TAILED SKUA *Stercorarius longicaudus* PLATE 58

Size: 36cm, excluding central tail feathers; 300g
Geographical variation: Two subspecies: *longicaudus* breeds in Scandinavia and western Russia, and *pallescens* breeds in eastern Russia, Siberia, North America and Greenland, and is assumed to be the form that migrates to New Zealand through the Pacific.
Distribution: Circumpolar breeder on dry tundra and mountains in the Arctic and subarctic. They migrate south in September and pass through the tropics to winter at sea in the Southern Hemisphere. In the South Pacific, most winter in central and eastern waters, but a few visit the southwestern Pacific. The first accepted record in New Zealand was a beach-wrecked bird at Muriwai (January 1964). Since then there have been occasional records in New Zealand between September and April, especially when El Niño weather patterns force birds west from their usual wintering range to New Zealand. Recorded mainly off the North Island from Northland to Wellington, but occasionally as far south as Foveaux Strait, and also seen off the Chatham Islands. More frequently recorded since the early 1980s, with a large influx in January–February 1983, when 50+ birds were seen or found beach-wrecked, and 20+ seen off northern Northland in March 2011. An extraordinary insight into the movement of the species was a record of a bird hit by an aircraft at 4000m, about 3000m above the Coromandel Peninsula in November 2010 – what it was doing there is a mystery.
Behaviour: Little is known of the wintering behaviour of Long-tailed Skuas, but generally they are more pelagic than Arctic Skuas and are usually solitary. They feed on small fish at the sea surface by dipping and hovering tern-like, rather than through piracy more typical of other skuas. None of the birds seen in New Zealand have been noted harrying terns, as is the usual behaviour of Arctic Skuas.
In the hand: Non-breeding Long-tailed Skuas and Arctic Skuas are hard to separate; however, about 50% of Long-tailed Skuas have diagnostic blue tarsi, the rest have grey tarsi like Arctic Skuas. Long-tailed Skuas recorded in New Zealand generally have shorter wings (272–**295**–315mm cf. 298–**315**–325mm), bill (26.5–**28**–31mm cf. 29–**31**–33mm, and mid-toe and claw (34.5–**38**–41.5mm cf. 41–**43.5**–45mm) than Arctic Skuas in Australasia. A combination of these measures should reliably separate most birds.
Reading: Melville, D. S. 1985. *Notornis* 32: 51–73.

GULLS *Laridae*

47 species: 3 breed in the New Zealand region and 2 are vagrants.

Gulls are coastal or inland birds in New Zealand. Adults have white bodies and grey or black backs, and broad wings with black and white patterning at the tips. Juvenile plumage has a distinctive buff barring on the backs and wings. Gulls have a strong bill with a distinctive shape, deepest about a third of the way back from the tip. They walk well on quite long legs. Gregarious;

breeding in colonies, and feeding and roosting in large flocks. The nest is a shallow cup in a low, well-formed mound of vegetation on the ground. Chicks are fed by regurgitation. Gulls feed on a wide variety of foods, including human refuse, fish, shellfish, crustaceans and other invertebrates (including earthworms and grubs exposed by ploughing) and eggs of other birds.

Reading: Grant, P. J. 1987. *Gulls: An Identification Guide*. Calton: Poyser. Harrison, P. 1983. *Seabirds: An Identification Guide*. Beckenham: Croom Helm. Serventy, D. L. et al. 1971. *The Handbook of Australian Sea-birds*. Sydney: A. H. & A. W. Reed.

263. PACIFIC GULL *Larus pacificus* PLATE 59

Size: 63cm, 1300g

Distribution: Breeds in southern Australia only. Pacific Gulls are found along the coast and offshore islands from Shark Bay, Western Australia, through the Great Australian Bight to Bass Strait and Tasmania, and north to about Sydney, New South Wales. Rare inland or far offshore, and rare in northern Australia. Outcompeted by Black-backed Gulls in southeastern Australia since their arrival in the 1940s, and numbers are declining. One New Zealand record: an immature bird at Dargaville Beach (January 2010).

Behaviour: Pacific Gulls are usually gregarious, breeding in small loose colonies, and found in small flocks in the non-breeding season. Adults are sedentary, but immature birds disperse.

Feeding: At sea and in estuaries they take crabs, fish, chitons and other molluscs, and eat carrion from near the tideline. They eat discarded fish scraps, visit refuse tips and abattoirs in coastal towns, steal fish from Australasian Gannets, and are known to eat eggs and kill birds up to the size of Short-tailed Shearwaters.

Reading: Coulson, R. & Coulson, G. 1993. *Emu* 93: 50–53.

264. BLACK-BACKED GULL *Larus dominicanus* PLATE 59

Other names: Karoro, Kelp Gull, Southern Black-backed Gull

Size: 60cm; male 1050g, female 850g

Geographical variation: Five subspecies: *vetula* in southern Africa, *judithae* in the South Indian Ocean, *melisandae* in Madagascar, *austrinus* in Antarctica, and *dominicanus* in South America, Australia and New Zealand.

Distribution: Breeds on the coast of Antarctica, in the subantarctic, and through the temperate Southern Hemisphere, including Australia and New Zealand. In New Zealand, they breed in colonies or in scattered pairs along mainland coast, on most offshore islands, and on the Chathams, Bounty, Snares, Antipodes, Auckland and Campbell islands, but strangely absent from the Three Kings. Vagrants reach the Ross Dependency and the Kermadec Islands, and as far afield as Norfolk and Lord Howe islands, Niue and the Cook Islands. They also breed on riverbeds and lake shores, and a few nest at subalpine tarns high in the mountains of the North and South islands.

Black-backed Gulls use estuaries, harbours and open coastlines, rivers, lakes, wet pasture, lambing paddocks, freshly ploughed farmland, rubbish tips, and city parks. They are mainly sedentary, but flocks will commute 30km or more each day between roosting sites near the coast and inland feeding sites. At sea, they are mainly restricted to coastal waters; however, they readily follow ships out into pelagic waters.

Population: Widespread and locally abundant.

Conservation: Unprotected native. Black-backed Gulls have benefited from human settlement in New Zealand, especially with the creation of readily available food supplies from rubbish tips, fish processors and fishing boats, meatworks and sewer outfalls. With offal and sewage discharges into the sea now greatly reduced, and with improved waste management limiting refuse available, numbers are declining in many areas. Numbers are often controlled near airports, by shooting or egg-pricking, to reduce the risk of birdstrike on aircraft.

Breeding: Most Black-backed Gulls nest in large colonies of up to 2000 pairs on coastal dunes, sandspits, boulderbanks, gravel beaches, rocky islets and riverbeds, but some nest solitarily on coastal rock stacks and headlands, near mountain tarns up to 1500m asl, and they sometimes nest on roofs of city buildings. Numbers of birds at colonies start to build up in late July, and nest-building commences almost immediately. The nest is built mainly by the male. It is a substantial mound of dry grass, seaweed, twigs, feathers and tidal flotsam, measuring about 20cm in diameter, with a small but deep depression in the centre.

Most eggs are laid between mid-October and late November, with a peak in early November, but some repeat clutches are laid through to late January. The clutch is of 1–**2**–**3**–5 eggs, but rare clutches of more than 3 eggs may be laid by two females. The eggs (69 x 47mm, 80g) are greyish-green in ground colour with brown spots and blotches, but there is usually considerable variation in the ground colour within a clutch. Eggs are laid 2–3 days apart, at any time of day, and egg size declines through a clutch. Both sexes incubate for 23–**27**–30 days and brood the nestlings for 2–3 days. The chicks then leave the nest for increasingly long periods. Until chicks fledge at *c.* 50 days old, they are usually guarded by one of the parents. They remain with their parents for a couple of months after fledging, and juveniles up to 6 months old are seen begging for food. Some 2-year old birds display at colonies, but most probably do not start breeding until at least 4 years old. Annual survival of adults is about 93%, giving a mean life expectancy of about 14 years; the oldest Black-backed Gull recorded in New Zealand lived 31.5 years.

Behaviour: Generally gregarious; nesting in large colonies, roosting in large flocks and often feeding in loose flocks of hundreds of birds at locally abundant food. When breeding, they vigorously defend a small area around their nest site and attack other birds or people entering the area. Young non-breeding birds normally form 'clubs' near the colony during the breeding season. Black-backed Gulls have a large variety of breeding calls, but the most characteristic calls are a contagious 'long call' heard especially in breeding colonies or in feeding flocks, described as 'uh uh eeah-ha-ha-ha-ha-ha' or 'kaloo-kaloo-kloo-kloo-kloo-kloo-kloo', and a non-contagious 'gorah gorah' call mainly from breeding adults.

Feeding: Black-backed Gulls are opportunists, taking a wide variety of food, including offal, refuse, carrion, marine invertebrates and shellfish, fish, frogs, lizards, birds, eggs, mammals and even small fruit and other plant material. They are often seen feeding on offal and food scraps at rubbish tips, sewer outfalls, along the shoreline, behind boats or behind tractors ploughing. At sea, they feed on algae and plunge-dive for small fish and marine invertebrates. Along the coast, they can be seen carrying shellfish aloft and dropping them to break open the shells. During bad weather, Black-backed Gulls often head inland to feed on worms and insects forced to the surface of wet pasture or sports fields. They also congregate in lambing paddocks to feed on placentas and dead lambs, and will occasionally attack weak lambs and sick or cast sheep. Undigested food items are regurgitated as pellets at roosts and breeding colonies.

In the hand: Males are larger than females, but measurements overlap, e.g. wing 400–**427**–440mm cf. 373–**404**–428mm; and bill 49–**54**–59mm cf. 44.5–**49**–53mm. Males have a positive score from the equation 0.126 x head length + 0.289 x bill depth – 19.707, and females have a negative score.

Reading: Fordham, R. A. 1964. *Notornis* 11: 3–34, 110–126. Fordham, R. A. 1968. *Proc NZ Ecol Soc* 15: 40–50. Fordham, R. A. 1970. *J Anim Ecol* 39: 13–27. Kinsky, F. C. 1963. *Rec Dom Mus* 4: 149–219. Nugent, G. 1982. *Notornis* 29: 37–40. Powlesland, R. G. & Robertson, H. A. 1987. *Notornis* 34: 327–338. Powlesland, R. G. & Powlesland, M. H. 1994. *Notornis* 41: 117–132.

265. FRANKLIN'S GULL *Larus pipixcan* PLATE 60

Size: 35cm, 280g

Distribution: Breeds in marshes among the prairies of Canada (Alberta, Saskatchewan and Manitoba) and the northern United States (Montana, North and South Dakota and Minnesota), and feeds over adjacent pasture and cropland. Migrates south to the Pacific coast of South America where it feeds along the coast and offshore in the Humboldt Current. Vagrants have been reported from Europe and South Africa, but more often through the Pacific and as far as Australia, where it has even made its way to Western Australia. Four New Zealand records: Raoul Island, Kermadecs (July 1988), Tomahawk Lagoon, Dunedin (June–July 2002), Manukau Harbour (September–October 2009) and Marlborough (July 2013).

Behaviour: Franklin's Gulls are usually gregarious and occur in huge flocks in their wintering grounds. They often associate with other small gulls and waders. Silent away from their breeding colonies.

Feeding: At sea and in estuaries they take small invertebrates from near the surface by dipping and shallow dives, or when swimming. On land, they hawk insects and feed on earthworms and other invertebrates, and will take discarded scraps.

Reading: Onley, D. J. & Schweigman, P. 2004. *Notornis* 51: 49–50. Veitch, C. R. et al. 2004. *Notornis* 51: 61–90.

266. RED-BILLED GULL *Larus novaehollandiae* PLATE 60

Other names: Tarapunga, Silver Gull
Size: 37cm; male 300g, female 260g
Geographical variation: Four subspecies: *hartlaubii* breeds in South Africa, *novaehollandiae* in Australia, *forsteri* in the southwestern Pacific from Torres Strait to New Caledonia, and *scopulinus* in New Zealand.
Distribution: Breeds on coasts and offshore islands of South Africa, Australia and New Zealand, and on islands in Melanesia. In New Zealand, they breed in about 80 colonies on the mainland coasts and offshore islands, and on the Three Kings, Chatham, Snares, Auckland and Campbell islands. They are stragglers to the Kermadecs and are strangely absent from the Bounty Islands and the Antipodes. There is an inland colony in the North Island at Lake Rotorua, where they nest with – and, rarely, hybridise with – Black-billed Gulls. Red-billed Gulls frequent estuaries, harbours and open coastlines, and parks of coastal cities. They sometimes venture inland onto wet paddocks, sportsfields and freshly ploughed farmland, and a few use lakes in the central North Island.

They are moderately mobile – most birds abandon the breeding colony in autumn, and many individuals undertake regular seasonal movements of several hundred kilometres between breeding sites and their traditional wintering sites, e.g. between Kaikoura and Wellington Harbour. Most birds remain within 400km of their breeding colony, but birds banded at Kaikoura have been seen in Auckland and in Invercargill. Individuals commute 20km or more each day between roosting or breeding sites and offshore feeding sites. At sea, they are mainly in coastal waters, however, they occasionally follow ships out into pelagic waters.
Population: Widespread and locally common. The two largest colonies, each with 5000+ breeding pairs, are at the Three Kings Islands and at Kaikoura. The New Zealand population has increased substantially since European settlement but is now declining, perhaps because the important winter food supplies of offal and sewage discharged into the sea have been greatly reduced since 1970 as environmental standards have improved.
Conservation: Protected vulnerable native. Red-billed Gulls initially benefited from human settlement in New Zealand, especially with the creation of readily available winter food supplies from meatworks, whaling stations, fish processors, fishing boats, sewer outfalls and scraps discarded in city parks. The recent decline may be due to a reduction in important winter food supplies, or perhaps due to other changes in natural food supplies at sea, caused by climate change or fisheries.
Breeding: Red-billed Gulls nest in large, densely packed colonies of up to 6000 pairs on sandspits, boulderbanks, shellbanks, gravel beaches, rocky headlands and rocky islets, usually near marine upwellings. Numbers of birds at colonies start building up in mid-July, but nesting sites are not occupied until early August. Pairs usually remain together year after year, but their nesting site changes within the colony. Both birds help to build the nest, but the male does most of the work. The nest is a small mound of dry grass, seaweed, twigs, feathers and tidal flotsam, measuring about 15cm in diameter, with a shallow depression in the centre.

On the mainland, most eggs are laid from early October to late December, but on the subantarctic islands the season is about a month later. Older birds lay earlier in the season than younger ones. The clutch is of 1–**2**–5 brownish-ochre eggs (52.5 x 37.5mm) with purple or brown spots and blotches. Clutches of 4 or 5 are laid by two females. Egg size declines through a clutch and through the season. Both sexes incubate for 24–**25**–27 days and then brood and feed the nestlings. The chicks remain close to the nest and are usually guarded by one of the parents. The fledging period is *c.* 37 days and then the fledglings remain dependent on their parents for a further 3 weeks. A few males start breeding at 1 year old, but most do not start nesting until 3–**4**, about a year younger than females. Females have a higher annual survival rate (89%) than males (84%), with corresponding life expectancies of 9 and 6 years respectively. The oldest bird recorded lived at least 28 years.
Behaviour: Highly gregarious; nesting in large colonies, roosting in large flocks and often feeding in flocks of thousands of birds at locally abundant food. When breeding, they vigorously defend a small area around their nest and attack other birds or people entering the area. Young non-breeding birds normally form 'clubs' near the colony during the breeding season. Red-billed Gulls have a variety of breeding calls, but the most characteristic call heard through the year is a strident and discordant scream.
Feeding: During the breeding season, Red-billed Gulls feed mainly in inshore waters on the planktonic euphausiid *Nyctiphanes australis*, although some other marine invertebrates, small fish, terrestrial insects and earthworms are also taken. A few birds specialise in stealing eggs from other Red-billed Gulls or White-fronted Terns. In autumn and winter, the diet is much more varied and they feed on offal, refuse,

carrion, marine invertebrates, shellfish and fish. They are usually seen feeding on offal from fishing boats, fish-processing plants or meatworks, at sewer outfalls, along the shoreline, at rubbish tips or on scraps in city parks. During bad weather, they often head inland to feed on worms and insects forced to the surface in wet pastures or sportsfields.

In the hand: Males are larger than females, but measurements overlap. Bill measurements provide a good discrimination between the sexes; males have a positive score from the equation: 0.26 x bill length + bill depth at gonys (deepest part) -22.875, and females have a negative score.

Reading: Gurr, L. 1967. *Ibis* 109: 552–555. Gurr, L. & Kinsky, F. C. 1965. *Notornis* 12: 223–240. Mills, J. A. 1969. *Notornis* 16: 180–186. Mills, J. A. 1971. *NZ J Mar Fresh Res* 5: 326–328. Mills, J. A. 1973. *J Anim Ecol* 42: 147–162. Mills, J. A. 1979. *Ibis* 121: 53–67. Mills, J. A. 1989. In Newton, I. (ed.) *Lifetime Reproduction in Birds*. London: Academic Press. Powlesland, R. G. & Powlesland, M. H. 1994. *Notornis* 41: 117–132.

267. BLACK-BILLED GULL *Larus bulleri* PLATE 60

Size: 37cm; male 300g, female 250g

Distribution: New Zealand only. Breeds mainly on braided riverbeds of the South Island from Marlborough to Southland, with about 70% of the population in the mid-1990s in Southland. Some nest on Hawke's Bay and Wairarapa riverbeds, and they also nest inland at lakes in the central North Island, especially at Lake Rotorua where they nest with and, rarely, hybridise with Red-billed Gulls. There are also a few colonies on the North Island coast (Kaipara Harbour, Manukau Harbour, near Clevedon, Firth of Thames, Coromandel Harbour, Bay of Plenty, Gisborne, Portland Island, Wairoa, Black Reef and Porangahau). In spring and summer, Black-billed Gulls are mainly inland on the larger rivers and lakes of the South Island and on nearby arable farmland and rivers where they are often seen following the plough. In winter, they are mainly coastal, frequenting estuaries, harbours, open coastlines, and parks of coastal towns, often in association with Red-billed Gulls. In bad weather, they head inland to feed on flooded pasture and wet sportsfields. A few are permanent residents of the lakes in the central North Island, and Lake Wairarapa. They are moderately mobile, with many South Island birds moving to the southern North Island in winter; some birds reach Stewart Island and vagrants appear at The Snares.

Population: *c.* 30,000 pairs in 2012. For some unknown reason, numbers of Black-billed Gulls have crashed in the South Island since the 1970s. For instance, the number nesting on the four main rivers in Southland (Waiau, Aparima, Oreti and Mataura) declined from 137,000 birds in 1977 to *c.* 30,000 birds in 2006, a decline of over 5% per annum. However, they are slowly increasing in numbers and range in the North Island; before 1970, the only known regular breeding colony was at Lake Rotorua, but several inland and coastal colonies have established recently.

Conservation: Protected critically endangered endemic. Although Black-billed Gulls are less reliant on man than the other gulls, they have probably benefited from human settlement in New Zealand, especially with the creation of arable farmland near their South Island riverbed breeding sites. The causes of the recent declines in the South Island are not clear, but are probably mainly due to predation by introduced mammals at breeding colonies. Water extraction from rivers and dam construction leads to lower flows and hence a loss of safer islands within rivers. It also leads to an encroachment of weeds, which provides cover for predators and forces colonies into sites more vulnerable to flooding. Illegal shooting of adults and disturbance of colonies take a further toll. Changes in the coastal environment may have affected overwintering survival.

Breeding: Black-billed Gulls nest in large, densely packed colonies of up to 3000 pairs on open shingle islands or margins in braided riverbeds, or on the coast on sandspits, boulderbanks or shellbanks. Most birds form pairs in their winter flocks. On South Island rivers, birds return in September to the region of their previous colony, but with changes in riverbed patterns and in vegetation growth, they rarely use the same site for more than a few years, and many colonies shift to another catchment. Once a site has been chosen, they quickly build their nests and start laying, and further nest material is added as incubation proceeds. Both birds help to build the nest, but the male does most of the work. The nest is a small mound of dry grass and twigs, measuring about 15cm in diameter, with a shallow depression in the centre. Nests are 45–60cm apart in the centre of colonies, further apart towards the edge.

Laying is from late September to December; later clutches are generally replacements after a colony has been destroyed by floods or predators, deserted following human disturbance, or if food supplies dwindle in the early stages of the nesting cycle. Within each colony, most birds start laying within a few days, and usually within a fortnight of occupying the site, although some late arrivals lay near the edge of the colony well after the majority are incubating.

They lay 1–**2**–4 pale olive-green to pale grey eggs (55 x 37mm) with sparse light and dark brown blotches. Both sexes incubate for 20–**24**–27 days. The chicks are capable of walking within 24 hours of hatching. The family abandons its nest site 1–2 days after the final chick hatches and becomes nomadic within the vicinity of the colony, though the parents continue to brood, feed and guard the young. They are fed by regurgitating onto the ground, but older chicks feed from their parents' bills. From about 2 weeks old the chicks are capable of swimming, and at about this age the chicks tend to congregate in loose crèches guarded by a few adults. These are usually near the water's edge, and if a ground predator approaches, the chicks swim out in a tightly packed raft, with the adults mobbing the predator by swooping and calling noisily. The chicks fledge at *c.* 26 days old. They first breed at 2 years old and can live for over 23 years.

Behaviour: Highly gregarious; nesting in large colonies, roosting in large flocks and often feeding in flocks of hundreds of birds at locally abundant food. When breeding, they defend a small area around their nest site; they will attack other birds entering the area, and mob predators and people approaching the colony. Black-billed Gulls have a large variety of breeding calls, but the most characteristic call heard through the year is a loud and discordant screech.

Feeding: Inland-breeding Black-billed Gulls usually feed in flocks on unpredictable but temporarily rich food supplies such as invertebrates (especially earthworms and grass-grub adults and larvae) exposed by ploughing or brought to the surface by irrigation or rains, and shoals of small fish such as whitebait and young flatfish. They are also adept at hawking above flowing water for aquatic invertebrates. In the winter, their diet is more varied and includes marine and freshwater invertebrates and shellfish, small fish, scraps in city parks, and worms and insects forced to the surface in wet pastures or sportsfields.

Reading: Beer, C. G. 1965. *Auk* 82: 1–18. Beer, C. G. 1966. *Ibis* 108: 394–410. Black, M. J. S. 1955. *Notornis* 6: 167–170. Burger, J. & Gochfeld, M. 1996. *Emu* 96: 73–80. Dawson, E. W. 1958. *Notornis* 8: 32–38. Evans, R. M. 1982. *Ibis* 124: 491–501. Gurr, L. 1967. *Ibis* 109: 552–555. McClellan, R. K. 2009. PhD thesis, Uni Otago. Powlesland, R. G. & Powlesland, M. H. 1994. *Notornis* 41: 117–132.

NODDIES and TERNS *Sternidae*

About 41 species worldwide (4 noddies and 37 terns): all 4 noddies and 6 of the terns breed in the New Zealand region, and 9 terns visit regularly or as rare vagrants.

Noddies and terns are mostly pelagic or coastal, except some terns are inland on rivers and lakes. Noddies breed only in the tropics or subtropics, and sailors may have named them for their absurd-seeming nodding courtship displays. Noddies are quite uniformly white, pale grey or brown, whereas terns are usually white below and shades of black or grey above. Juvenile plumage has buff barring, especially on the back and wings.

Noddies and terns are more aerial than gulls and are more delicate; their wings are narrower and more pointed and their tail is often forked, sometimes deeply. They have straight, slender, tapering bills. They shuffle or waddle along on short legs. Gregarious; breeding in colonies, and feeding and roosting in tight flocks. The nest is a simple scrape or depression in sand, shingle, shell or stones, but some noddies build a small platform nest in a tree or shrub, and the White Tern, actually a noddy, simply lays its egg in a depression on a tree branch.

Whole fish, caught mainly by plunge-diving or by picking from the surface of the water and held crosswise in the bill, are usually brought in courtship display and to the chicks, but some tropical terns and noddies feed their chicks by regurgitation. Chicks go on begging for months after they can fly.

Reading: Harrison, P. 1983. *Seabirds: An Identification Guide*. Beckenham: Croom Helm. Serventy, D. L. et al. 1971. *The Handbook of Australian Sea-birds*. Sydney: A. H. & A. W. Reed.

268. BROWN NODDY *Anous stolidus* PLATE 61

Other name: Common Noddy
Size: 39cm; 200g
Geographical variation: Of the four subspecies, *pileatus* breeds on islands in the Indian Ocean and the tropical South Pacific Ocean, including the Kermadecs.
Distribution: Tropical and subtropical islands of the Atlantic, Indian and Pacific oceans. In the South Pacific, they breed on many tropical islands from the northern Great Barrier Reef east to French Polynesia, but also in the subtropics at Norfolk and Lord Howe islands, and at Curtis Island in the southern Kermadecs. There were two unverified New Zealand records in the 1800s, and then in 1989 they were discovered breeding on cliff ledges of Curtis Island. Subsequently, beach-wrecked birds have been found at Muriwai (June 1992) and at Waitara (June 2002).
Population: *c.* 25 pairs nesting on Curtis Island in 1989.
Conservation: Protected coloniser. This common species has recently established as a breeding species in the New Zealand region.
Breeding: In some tropical places they breed year-round, but in the South Pacific they breed in spring and early summer. Eggs are laid on Curtis Island in September–November. The nest is usually an untidy heap of sticks, leaves and seaweed, cemented by guano, in trees, scrub and sometimes on the ground; at the Kermadecs, all nests are on cliff ledges and steep slopes. They lay **1** creamy-white egg (53 x 36mm, 36g), blotched reddish brown. Both adults incubate for 30–35 days and brood the white downy chick for a couple of weeks, and then care for the chick during and after the 42–56 day fledging period.
Behaviour: Gregarious; in New Guinea and Australia, they breed in large colonies, often with Sooty Terns, but at Curtis Island they nest alone. After breeding, Brown Noddies disperse and may be seen hundreds of kilometres from land.
Feeding: At sea, they often feed in mixed-species flocks where small fish have been driven to the surface by predatory fish; huge feeding flocks have been likened to smoke on the horizon. When feeding, they hover and dip at the surface mainly taking small fish, squid, pelagic molluscs and medusae. Sometimes they feed on offal discarded by fishing boats.
Reading: Veitch, C. R. et al. 2004. *Notornis* 51: 61–90.

269. BLACK NODDY *Anous minutus* PLATE 61

Other names: White-capped Noddy, Lesser Noddy
Size: 37cm; 120g
Geographical variation: Of the seven subspecies, the nominate *minutus* breeds on islands in the southwestern Pacific Ocean, including the Kermadecs.
Distribution: Breeds on tropical and subtropical islands of the Atlantic, Indian and Pacific oceans. The Black Noddy breeds widely in the tropical Pacific from New Guinea and the Great Barrier Reef east to French Polynesia, but also in the subtropics at Norfolk Island and the Kermadecs. In New Zealand, they breed on North and South Meyer islets in the Herald Group off Raoul Island, and at Macauley, Curtis and Cheeseman islands and L'Esperance Rock in the southern Kermadecs. Rarely strays far outside subtropical waters. About 20 records from near the New Zealand mainland, from the Three Kings Islands to the Taieri Estuary, Otago. Most appear after northerly gales between September and May.
Population: *c.* 1100 pairs: Meyer Islets 1000 pairs, Macauley Island 50 pairs, Curtis Island 40 pairs, Cheeseman Island 20 pairs, and a few pairs on L'Esperance Rock.
Conservation: Protected native. This common species formerly bred on Raoul Island, but rats and cats eliminated them. Rats were eradicated in 2002 and cats in 2004, and so it is hoped that Black Noddies will soon re-establish there.
Breeding: In some tropical places they breed year-round, but at the Kermadecs, they have a defined breeding season. The timing varies from year to year; eggs are usually laid in August–January, mostly in October–November. The nest is usually an untidy heap of sticks, leaves, *Cyperus* sedge and seaweed, cemented by guano, in trees and scrub. Sometimes, such as on Macauley Island when there were no trees or scrub, the nest is on a rock ledge or in a cave. They lay **1** creamy-white egg (44 x 31mm, 23g), blotched reddish brown. Both adults incubate for 30–37 days and brood the black downy chick for a couple of weeks, and then care for it during and after the 40–55 day fledging period.
Behaviour: Gregarious; they breed in large colonies. After breeding, Black Noddies stay near the breeding islands, feeding at sea during the day and roosting at the colonies at night.

Feeding: At sea, they often feed in mixed-species flocks where small fish have been driven to the surface by predatory fish. They hover and dip at the surface, mainly taking small fish, squid and plankton. Chicks are fed by regurgitation, not whole small fish like most terns.
Reading: Soper, M. F. 1969. *Notornis* 16: 71–75. Veitch, C. R. et al. 2004. *Notornis* 51: 61–90.

270. GREY TERNLET *Procelsterna cerulea* PLATE 62

Other names: Blue-grey Noddy, Grey Noddy
Size: 28cm; 70g
Geographical variation: Of the four subspecies, *albivitta* breeds on islands in the subtropical South Pacific Ocean from Lord Howe Island to Chile, including the Kermadecs and islands off the northern North Island.
Distribution: Breeds on many tropical and subtropical islands of the Pacific Ocean. In New Zealand, most breed on islands of the Kermadecs, especially on Macauley and Curtis. Known only as an occasional vagrant to the New Zealand mainland before the summer of 1969–70, mostly single birds off the coast of Northland from Cape Maria van Diemen to Waipu. That summer, many frequented the waters off eastern Northland and the Bay of Plenty, and *c.* 1000 apparently bred at the Volkner Rocks off White Island; they were also seen at Sugarloaf Rock in the Aldermen Islands. Small groups have since bred irregularly at West Island, Three Kings Islands; Sugarloaf Rock, Poor Knights Islands; Cathedral Rocks, Mokohinau Islands; Sugarloaf Rock, The Aldermen Islands; and at Volkner Rocks. One inland at Lake Taupo in 1994. One South Island record, at Banks Peninsula, following the *Wahine* storm of April 1968.
Population: *c.* 21,000 pairs: Macauley 10,000 pairs, Curtis 5000 pairs, Meyer and Napier islets of the Herald Group 3000 pairs, L'Esperance Rock 1500–2000 pairs; Cheeseman Island *c.* 1000 pairs; northern North Island 50+ pairs.
Conservation: Protected native. This common species formerly bred on Raoul Island, but rats and cats eliminated them. Rats were eradicated in 2002 and cats in 2004, and so it is hoped that they will soon re-establish there.
Breeding: In the Kermadecs, eggs are laid in August–October. They are laid on a bare rocky surface sheltered from the sun, in cavities and crevices, on cliff ledges, under clumps of vegetation along clifftops, and in the shade of boulders on beaches. They lay **1** creamy-white egg (42 x 28mm) with small dark and light brown blotches. Both adults incubate for *c.* 32 days. The fledging period is *c.* 35 days. Maximum lifespan recorded overseas was 15 years.
Behaviour: Gregarious; breeding in loose colonies and feeding in sometimes immense flocks of 5000+ birds at concentrations of plankton or where small fish have been driven to the surface by predatory fish. Some disperse after breeding, but most stay within 20km of their breeding site, and a few come ashore during the non-breeding period. Their flight is graceful, floating, and unhurried.
Feeding: Flocks work into the wind, hovering and fluttering over the water, repeatedly dipping down to pick up plankton from the surface, sometimes skipping on the surface like a storm petrel, getting only bill and feet wet. As they run out of the feeding area, they veer away to the side, circle around to rejoin the rear of the flock and start working their way forward again. Their main food is tiny fish, marine insects, plankton and tiny squid. Chicks are fed by regurgitation, not whole small fish like most terns. They peck at first at the webs of the adult's feet to induce regurgitation, not at the bill as is usual.
Reading: Falla, R. A. 1970. *Notornis* 17: 83–86. Latham, P. C. M. 2003. *Notornis* 50: 118–121. Soper, M. F. 1969. *Notornis* 16: 75–80. Veitch, C. R. et al. 2004. *Notornis* 51: 61–90.

271. WHITE TERN *Gygis alba* PLATE 62

Size: 31cm; 110g
Geographical variation: Many subspecies of doubtful validity, of which *candida* breeds on many islands in the tropical Indian and Pacific oceans, including Lord Howe Island, Norfolk Island and the Kermadecs.
Distribution: Breeds on many tropical and some subtropical islands of the Atlantic, Indian and Pacific oceans. In New Zealand, a few breed on Raoul Island in the Kermadecs. During breeding, they are usually seen at sea within 100km of their main breeding islands. For several months after fledging, young birds feed with their parents during the day and return to their

breeding trees to roost at night. In autumn and winter, they become more pelagic and are absent from Raoul Island in April–August. Vagrants occasionally reach the North Island of New Zealand in autumn and early winter: Waipu (two in March 1883), Bethells Beach (May 1960), Pakotai, inland Northland (May 1964), Palmerston North (June 1972), Otaki Beach (May 1986), Te Horo Beach (April 1988), Dargaville Beach (July 1990, July 1998), Muriwai Beach (May 1990), Taupiri, inland Waikato (May 1998), a loose flock of six and perhaps up to 13 seen between North Cape and the Three Kings Islands (March 2011). Three South Island records: Ettrick, Otago (March 1945), Greymouth (January 2002) and Hokitika.

Population: Probably fewer than 10 pairs breed annually on Raoul Island.

Conservation: Protected native. This internationally common species was in a very precarious state on Raoul Island before rats were eradicated in 2002 and cats in 2004, and so it is hoped that they will soon recover.

Breeding: At Raoul Island, White Terns return to their breeding sites in September, and are often seen over land as pairs. Eggs are laid in October–December. They particularly favour pohutukawa as breeding trees on Raoul Island, laying their single egg in a depression or slight irregularity on a bare, horizontal branch, often many metres above the ground. They lay **1** white egg (44 x 33mm), heavily marked with brown and grey blotches. Both adults incubate for 27–35 days and, unlike other noddies, feed their chicks on whole fish. The chick, which takes 45–60 days to fledge, clings to the bark tenaciously with its long, sharp claws.

Behaviour: White Terns seldom associate with other noddies and terns. Their flight is fluttering and ethereal. Inquisitive and tame, they hover in front of a human intruder's face, uttering strange wheezing and twanging sounds.

Feeding: They flutter over the water surface and repeatedly dip down to catch tiny fish from near the surface without submerging themselves.

Reading: Tarburton, M. K. 1984. *Notornis* 31: 86–89. Vanderwerf, E. A. 2003. *Wilson Bull* 115: 258–262. Veitch, C. R. et al. 2004. *Notornis* 51: 61–90.

272. SOOTY TERN *Onychoprion fuscatus* PLATE 63

Other name: Wideawake Tern

Size: 43cm; 210g

Geographical variation: Of the several subspecies, some of which are of doubtful validity, *serratus* of the southwestern Pacific from the Great Barrier Reef and Norfolk Island east to French Polynesia is the one that breeds at the Kermadecs.

Distribution: Widespread in tropical and subtropical parts of the Atlantic, Indian and Pacific oceans. In New Zealand, they breed throughout the Kermadecs, but now mainly at Macauley and Curtis islands and in the Herald Group (North and South Meyer and Dayrell islets). After breeding they become much more pelagic and are rarely seen at the Kermadecs between April and August. Vagrants reach the North Island in most years, and a few reach the South Island as far south as Foveaux Strait. The sighting of 13 on Pakiri Beach in July 1986 was exceptional.

Population: *c.* 24,000 pairs: Macauley 10,000 pairs, Curtis 5500 pairs, Herald Group 4000 pairs, Raoul 4000 pairs.

Conservation: Protected native. This globally abundant species formerly bred in huge numbers on Raoul Island, especially at Denham Bay and the Hutchinson Bluffs areas (e.g. 40,000 pairs each in 1966). By 1997, these colonies had been wiped out by Norway rats (taking eggs and chicks) and cats (taking chicks and adults). Following rat eradication in 2002 and cat eradication in 2004, Sooty Terns re-established breeding colonies near the Hutchinson Bluffs by 2006, and about 4000 pairs were counted there in 2008; Denham Bay, however, remained unoccupied in 2010.

Breeding: Much more seasonal in the Kermadecs than in the tropics, where breeding can be continuous on a 9-month cycle. Laying at the Kermadecs is in October–December and is remarkably synchronised within large colonies; most eggs are laid over a few days. The nest is an unlined scrape in sand and low vegetation at the top of the beach. They lay **1** cream egg (53 x 36mm) spotted and blotched dark brown and black. Both adults incubate for *c.* 28 days. The fledging period is *c.* 30 days, but the young stay at the colony for several months, sometimes forming a crèche. A chick banded at the Kermadecs was found breeding in the Indian Ocean on Aride Island, Seychelles, aged 33.5 years.

Behaviour: Gregarious during breeding; their colonies are noisy, day and night, both from their harsh 'wideawake' calls and from the incessant nocturnal activity. The 'wideawake' calls are also heard among feeding flocks.

Feeding: Diet is mainly squid, small fish and crustaceans, caught mostly at night by surface dipping. Sooty Terns feed far out to sea, and so regurgitate to feed their young, whereas other terns that feed close to shore give whole undigested fish to their young.

Reading: Cossee, R. O. 1995. *Notornis* 42: 280. Veitch, C. R. et al. 2004. *Notornis* 51: 61–90.

273. GREY-BACKED TERN *Onychoprion lunatus* PLATE 63

Other name: Spectacled Tern

Size: 38cm; 150g

Distribution: Breeds widely in the central tropical Pacific Ocean between Tonga, the Northern Mariana Islands, Hawai'i and French Polynesia. Becomes pelagic after the breeding season, and so is rarely seen. Vagrants recorded west to the Philippines, New Guinea and the Solomons, east to Easter Island and south to New Zealand. Two records: Papakanui Spit, Kaipara Harbour (February 1999) and Pungaereere Stream mouth, Taranaki (January 2002).

Behaviour: At sea, they often feed in mixed-species flocks where small fish have been driven to the surface by predatory fish. They hover and dip at the surface, but sometimes plunge-dive, to take small fish and squid.

274. BRIDLED TERN *Onychoprion anaethetus* PLATE 63

Other name: Brown-winged Tern

Size: 38cm; 120g

Geographical variation: Of the four subspecies, the nominate *anaethetus* of the Indian Ocean, Southeast Asia, Australia and the western Pacific east to Samoa and Tonga is by far the most likely form to be found in New Zealand.

Distribution: Breeds widely in the tropics of the Atlantic, Indian and Pacific oceans, and usually remains in tropical or subtropical waters in the non-breeding season. One record in New Zealand, a beach-wrecked bird at New Brighton, Canterbury (November 1987).

Behaviour: At sea, they often feed in mixed-species flocks where small fish have been driven to the surface by predatory fish. They shallow plunge-dive or dip to the surface to take small fish, squid and crustaceans. Sometimes they rest on the water or roost on flotsam and jetsam.

Reading: Hulsman, K. & Langham, N. P. E. 1985. *Emu* 85: 240–249. Tunnicliffe, G. A. & Langlands, P. A. 1990. *Notornis* 37: 131–139.

275. LITTLE TERN *Sternula albifrons* PLATE 62

Size: 25cm; 50g

Geographical variation: Three subspecies, of which the Eastern Little Tern *sinensis* breeds from southeastern Asia to Australia, and reaches New Zealand.

Distribution: Breeds widely from Europe and Africa east to Asia and Australasia. Eastern Little Terns breed east from Sri Lanka to the Solomon Islands, north to Japan and Korea and south to Australia, including Tasmania. The arrival in September of Little Terns in Australasia, including three birds banded as nestlings in Japan and re-sighted at Miranda, shows that many eastern Asian birds head south to New Zealand in the northern winter. Some of these Asian birds reach New Zealand as annual migrants, arriving in October–November and gaining breeding plumage in February–April as they are about to leave. They favour the large harbours of Northland and South Auckland, especially Rangaunu and Kaipara harbours, and some visit estuaries and coastal lagoons south to Stewart Island, and at the Chathams. A few overwinter.

Population: Not recognised in New Zealand until January 1949. The summer total in New Zealand is probably 10–50 birds.

Behaviour: Gregarious; at high tide, Little Terns may roost loosely together near flocks of White-fronted Terns, Wrybills, Bar-tailed Godwits or Red Knots, but they may also continue to feed over high tide, appearing only when the tide is falling, so are easily missed.

Feeding: Diet is mainly small fish, caught by fluttering, hovering and then plunge-diving, usually in shallow water over mudflats or in brackish ponds.

Reading: Habraken, A. 2002. *Miranda News* 47: 16.

276. FAIRY TERN *Sternula nereis* PLATE 62

Other name: Tara-iti
Size: 25cm; 70g
Geographical variation: Three subspecies: the nominate *nereis* breeds in southern and western Australia, *exsul* breeds in New Caledonia, and the New Zealand Fairy Tern *davisae* breeds in northern New Zealand.
Distribution: Fairy Terns are the smallest and rarest of the terns that breed in New Zealand. Up to the early 1900s, they were apparently widespread and bred on the coasts of the North Island and inland on the braided riverbeds of the eastern South Island. By the 1950s, only about 18 pairs remained, all confined to the east coast of Northland from Skull Creek (Whangarei Harbour) in the north to Pakiri in the south, including Ruakaka, Waipu, Mangawhai and Te Arai. Some were discovered breeding on the west coast at Papakanui Spit (South Kaipara Head) in 1969. Their breeding range further contracted to only three sites by 1985: Waipu Estuary, Mangawhai Estuary and Papakanui Spit, but birds have since attempted to breed at Pakiri (from 2003) and Te Arai (from 2012). The east coast birds form post-breeding flocks at or near the breeding sites from late December to the end of March, and then most move to the Kaipara Harbour for the winter, although a few singletons have been seen as far afield as the Firth of Thames, Bay of Plenty and Manawatu Estuary. Flocks of 8–18 birds are regularly seen from late February to July on the Kaipara Harbour, mostly at Tapora, or at Papakanui Spit, where breeding birds probably stay all year. In July, flocks disband and birds return to their east coast breeding places.
Population: In 2012, the New Zealand total was *c.* 35 birds, including 8 breeding pairs.
Conservation: Protected critically endangered native subspecies. The decline of the New Zealand Fairy Terns was largely a result of degradation of breeding habitat, disturbance by people during the breeding season and predation by gulls and introduced mammals. Fairy Terns nest in exposed areas of mobile sand, and so their habitat is degraded when sand is stabilised by plantings of marram, lupin and pines, or levelled for housing development. Fairy Terns nest on beaches used by people and frequented by gulls, cats, mustelids, hedgehogs and dogs. Protection by trapping mammals, erecting temporary fences and signs to exclude people and vehicles, and regular patrols by wardens resulted in the population increasing slowly. Attempts to release captive-reared chicks failed because they were not adept at foraging after release.
Breeding: Fairy Terns nest solitarily. Nests are on low-lying sand and shell, mostly above the reach of spring tides, but exposed to storm surges. First clutches are laid from mid-November to early December, but they may re-lay through to mid-January if earlier clutches are lost. They lay 1–2 buff eggs (35 x 25mm, 13g), spotted and blotched dark brown. Both adults incubate for 23–25 days. Young first fly at 22–23 days old. The oldest recorded Fairy Tern in New Zealand lived at least 18 years.
Behaviour: Solitary when breeding, but several pairs may inhabit the same sandspit. They form flocks shortly after breeding and stay in small feeding and roosting flocks through the winter. Fairy Terns are generally silent in flight.
Feeding: Diet is mainly small fish, caught inside estuaries and at sea just beyond the breaking waves. When feeding, they flutter, hover, and then plunge-dive to catch their prey.
Reading: Hansen, K. 2006. *New Zealand Fairy Tern Recovery Plan, 2005–15.* Wellington: DOC. Parrish, G. R. & Pulham, G. A. 1995. *Tane* 35: 161–173, 175–181. Preddy, J. M. 2008. *Notornis* 55: 159–161.

277. GULL-BILLED TERN *Gelochelidon nilotica* PLATE 60

Size: 43cm; 230g
Geographical variation: Of the six or seven subspecies, *macrotarsa* of Australia and New Guinea reaches New Zealand, but some birds could be the Asian migrant *affinis*.
Distribution: Almost cosmopolitan, breeding in the Americas, Africa, across temperate Europe and Asia to China, Indonesia, New Guinea and inland Australia, mainly in the southeast. They are common on most Australian coasts but rare in Tasmania. In New Zealand, a few vagrants were seen in most years since they were first recorded near Invercargill in 1955, usually as singles or in small flocks of up to eight birds. However, there was major influx from June 2011, with numerous sightings of individuals or small flocks from Northland to Southland through to at least 2013. The largest flocks seen during this invasion were of 16 birds at Manukau Harbour, and 15 at Lake Forsyth and Lake Ellesmere,

but there was no sign of breeding.

Behaviour: Most New Zealand records have been at estuaries or coastal lagoons and marshes, but they are as likely to feed over grassland and ploughed fields. They fly low and swoop from time to time to snatch invertebrates or small fish from the surface.

Reading: McKenzie, H. R. 1955. *Notornis* 6: 163–164. Rogers, D. I. et al. 2005. *Emu* 105: 145–158.

278. CASPIAN TERN *Hydroprogne caspia* PLATE 61

Other name: Tara nui

Size: 51cm; 700g

Distribution: Almost cosmopolitan, breeding locally in temperate or subtropical parts of Central and North America north to the Great Lakes, in Africa, from Europe across central Asia to China, and in Australasia. In New Zealand, they breed on both main islands, usually coastal but small numbers sometimes breed inland, especially near Rotorua and on Canterbury rivers. A rare vagrant to the Kermadec and Chatham islands. The main colonies are on estuarine shellbanks and sandspits: Rangaunu, Whangarei, Kaipara, Whangapoua and Kawhia harbours; Mangawhai Estuary; Bowentown, Tauranga Harbour; Matakana Island; Ohope Spit; Lake Onoke Spit, Palliser Bay; Farewell Spit; Waimea Estuary; Vernon Lagoon; Lake Ellesmere; and Invercargill Estuary. Single pairs or small colonies breed on sandy beaches and at many harbours and estuaries, sometimes in association with colonies of Black-backed Gulls, less often with Red-billed Gulls or Black-billed Gulls.

After breeding, North Island birds tend to stay within 100km of their breeding places; birds banded in Northland feed and roost on such harbours as the Kaipara, Manukau and the Firth of Thames, but some birds move much further south. South Island birds tend to move north in autumn, and adults return to breed again in spring. Birds banded near Invercargill travel in stages to main wintering places at the Avon–Heathcote Estuary and Lake Ellesmere, but some reach southern North Island estuaries and coastal lagoons, and one even regularly used the Manukau Harbour, 1170km away. Most Caspian Terns stay on or near the coast, or at lowland lakes such as Lake Wairarapa, but single birds may be seen working rivers well inland, e.g. to Palmerston North, Masterton and Upper Hutt, and a few visit inland lakes such as Rotorua and Taupo.

Population: The New Zealand total is *c.* 4000 birds including 1300–1400 breeding pairs. Colony sizes and some colony locations are quite variable from year to year, but they rarely exceed 100 pairs.

Conservation: Protected vulnerable native. Caspian Terns may be a quite recent colonist of New Zealand because they were rare in fossil deposits and middens, and were not recorded by early naturalists until about 1860. They remained scarce until about the 1930s, but became increasingly common up to the 1970s. The population was reasonably stable through to the 1990s despite several major colonies being disturbed by increased human activity and planting pine trees and marram on favoured bare sandspits, but numbers appear to have declined since the 1990s. Some colonies are now fenced off to prevent damage from off-road vehicles and from people and dogs.

Breeding: Most Caspian Terns nest in large loose colonies. The nest is a shallow, unlined scrape in sand or shingle. Laying is from late September to early December. They lay 1–**2**–3 light stone-coloured eggs (64 x 45mm, 75g), evenly sprinkled with dark brown spots and blotches. Eggs are laid 1–**2**–4 days apart. Both adults incubate for 26–**27**–29 days and brood the chicks for 5–10 days. The chicks hatch over several days, and, when food is in short supply, the youngest starve. The chicks fledge at 33–**35**–39 days old and continue to beg and be fed for up to 8 months. The fledglings accompany their parents to their sometimes separate wintering sites, leaving when 7–9 weeks old. The juveniles usually stay at the wintering site, or wander locally, but some become nomadic and wander widely. Most return to their natal colony to breed at 3–5 years old, but some juveniles return to the colony with a parent at 8–9 months old and have been seen still begging for food at 18 months old. The oldest banded Caspian Tern in New Zealand lived at least 24 years.

Behaviour: Gregarious; many breed in loose colonies of up to 100 pairs, though up to 350 pairs nested at South Kaipara Heads in the 1970s. They roost in small flocks between feeding bouts at estuaries and on sandy beaches, but they usually feed alone.

Caspian Terns are often heard first, the usual call in flight being a loud, harsh 'kaaa', or a repetitive variant of it; there are other less frequent calls. Juveniles are often very audible, uttering a persistent high-pitched mewing call as they beg to be fed.

Feeding: Diet is mainly small surface-swimming fish such as juvenile yellow-eyed mullet, smelt and piper; also stargazers and small flounders, which are caught by plunging into the water at a steep angle, often fully submerging. Inland they catch smelt, whitebait, bullies, trout and small eels. Juveniles sometimes dip-feed while standing in shallow water at the tide's edge, taking worms and small flounders.

Reading: Barlow, M. L. 1998. *Notornis* 45: 193–220. Barlow, M. L. & Dowding, J. E. 2002. *Notornis* 49: 76–90. Bell, M. & Bell, B. D. 2008. *Notornis* 55: 84–88. Pierce, R. J. 1984. *Notornis* 31: 185–190. Sibson, R. B. 1992. *Notornis* 39: 87–93.

279. WHITE-WINGED BLACK TERN *Chlidonias leucopterus* PLATE 64

Size: 23cm; 65g

Distribution: Breeds in marshes from eastern Europe to Siberia, in eastern China, Mongolia and Manchuria. They migrate south to winter in Africa, southern and southeastern Asia, and in Australasia. They are a regular migrant to New Zealand, from the harbours of Northland to the lagoons and estuaries of Southland, but especially around the Auckland isthmus and in coastal Canterbury from Banks Peninsula to the Waitaki River. The earliest record in New Zealand was a pair in breeding plumage on the Waihopai River, Marlborough, in 1868, they bred in Canterbury in the early 1900s and a pair bred among Black-fronted Terns at a lagoon at the mouth of the Opihi River, South Canterbury, in 1973–74.

Population: Usually fewer than 10 reach New Zealand each year, except for occasional small influxes, e.g. 12 at Ahuriri Estuary (1972), 5 at Opihi River mouth (1973), and 14 at Cooper's Lagoon, Canterbury (1995). A few overwinter in some years.

Behaviour: In New Zealand, some birds have reversed plumage sequence, and stay as though to breed. In the South Island, single birds often associate with colonies of Black-fronted Terns, and a pair attempted to breed twice in 1973–74. Normally the nest is a rough mass of vegetation, floating or moored in fresh water, but those in New Zealand were on shingle close to a coastal lagoon.

Feeding: Gregarious; overseas they forage in noisy flocks, but in New Zealand they are usually in singles, beating into the wind and contact-dipping (i.e. submerging the bill only) to pick invertebrates from the water surface.

Reading: Pierce, R. J. 1974. *Notornis* 21: 129–134.

280. WHISKERED TERN *Chlidonias hybridus* PLATE 64

Size: 26cm; 90g

Geographical variation: Three subspecies: *hybridus* breeds in Europe, Asia and North Africa, *delalandii* in southern and eastern Africa and Madagascar, and *javanicus* in Australia, and a vagrant to New Zealand.

Distribution: Breeds in marshes in several widely separated populations. In Australia, they are nomadic and follow the rains. Most breed inland on rivers, and on temporary freshwater or brackish wetlands and flooded claypans, especially in the Murray–Darling River system in the southeast. Australian birds generally migrate north after breeding into northern Australia, eastern Indonesia and New Guinea in April–December, with some reaching New Caledonia. The few vagrants seen in New Zealand are assumed to come from Australia, judging by the timing of plumage changes: Lake Horowhenua (two in August–October 1977, and May–September 1978), lower Waikato River (August–September 1978), Pukekohe (March 1980), Lake Rotorua (May 1987), Bromley Sewage Ponds, Christchurch (December 2005), coastal Marlborough (January–February 2006), Travis Wetlands, Christchurch (May 2007), and North Kaipara Head (October 2009).

Behaviour: Breeding and feeding habits are very like those of the White-winged Black Tern. Their flight is buoyant, typical of marsh terns, flying upwind over fresh or brackish water and contact-dipping to seize invertebrates, small fish and tadpoles at the surface, then dropping downwind to start again. In New Zealand, they sometimes patrol and feed over the same stretch of still inland water and use the same roosting places for months.

Reading: Heather, B. D. & Jones, E. B. 1979. *Notornis* 26: 185–195.

281. BLACK-FRONTED TERN *Chlidonias albostriatus* PLATE 64

Other name: Tara piroe
Size: 29cm; 90g
Distribution: New Zealand only. Black-fronted Terns breed on the shingle riverbeds of the eastern South Island from Marlborough to Southland, and on the upper Motueka and Buller rivers in southern Nelson. They feed over the rivers and nearby fields. In late summer and autumn, they disperse north, occasionally reaching Northland, and south to the waters off Stewart Island, and once to The Snares; however, most feed at sea within 10km of the eastern South Island and in Cook Strait north to Waikanae Estuary and west to Farewell Spit. Autumn and winter flocks of 100–300 birds are regularly seen at Farewell Spit, Lake Grassmere, Kaikoura Peninsula, Hurunui, Ashley, Ashburton and Opihi river mouths, and at Aramoana. Smaller wintering flocks of 20–50 birds regularly appear in the North Island at the Bay of Plenty, in Hawke's Bay and at Lake Onoke, Palliser Bay. In the non-breeding season, they sometimes feed over coastal fields or lagoons, and come ashore to roost in the middle of the day, often roosting near flocks of White-fronted Terns.
Population: *c.* 8000 birds in 2008, based on sums of breeding season counts from a large number of rivers. Repeated counts showed significant declines on 8 of 29 rivers, and a significant increase at only one river, where there was a history of predator control.
Conservation: Protected endangered endemic. Black-fronted Terns are declining in number throughout their breeding range. Their colonies are easily disturbed by predators and people, and many of their riverbed nesting sites have been invaded by exotic plants such as willows and lupins, especially where rivers are dammed or where water is taken for irrigation. The development of farmland beside their nesting sites may have created feeding opportunities, because they often follow the plough to catch exposed insects and worms.
Breeding: They nest in small loose colonies of up to 50 pairs, some on riverbeds near the coast or beside coastal lagoons, but most are well inland, often near colonies of Black-billed Gulls. The nests, scrapes in the shingle, are spaced well apart. First clutches are laid from early October to late November, but replacement clutches are laid through to January. They lay 1–**2**–4 dark stone-coloured eggs (40 x 29mm, 18g) with brown blotches. Both adults incubate for 22–**23**–26 days. The eggs may hatch a day or two apart. The young fledge at *c.* 30 days old.
Behaviour: Black-fronted Terns attack intruders at their colonies by diving, calling harshly, and often striking the intruder's head with their feet. The usual call is a repetitive 'kit'; they usually feed silently.
Feeding: While breeding, they feed in flocks over rivers and nearby riverflats and fields. They work their way up rapidly flowing rivers and return repeatedly to their starting point. They contact-dip from about 2m above the water (i.e. dipping to touch the surface with the bill only) to take mainly emergent nymph and subimago mayflies and stoneflies. They sometimes plunge-dive to take small fish, such as upland bullies. On riverflats and farmland, their main food is earthworms and grass-grub larvae exposed by ploughing and cultivation, but they also feed on large insects such as grasshoppers, and on lizards. After breeding, most move to the coast for the autumn and winter, taking mostly planktonic crustaceans from the sea, as well as earthworms from wet coastal pasture.
Reading: Keadwell, R. 2005. *Emu* 105: 39–47. Lalas, C. 1977. MSc thesis, Uni Otago. Lalas, C. & Heather, B. D. 1980. *Notornis* 27: 45–68. Latham, P. C. M. 1981. *Notornis* 28: 221–239. O'Donnell, C. F. J. & Hoare, J. M. 2009. *Notornis* 56: 167–168. O'Donnell, C. F. J. & Hoare, J. M. 2010. *NZ J Ecol* 35: 30–43.

282. WHITE-FRONTED TERN *Sterna striata* PLATE 65

Other names: Tara, Kahawai Bird, Sea Swallow
Size: 42cm; 160g
Distribution: New Zealand only, apart from a few that have bred on Flinders and Cape Barren islands in Bass Strait, Australia, since 1979. White-fronted Terns breed commonly from Northland to Southland, especially on the eastern coast and offshore islands. They are abundant at the Chatham and Auckland islands, and breed around the coast of Stewart Island. An occasional visitor to The Snares and Campbell Island. Colonies are often ephemeral; a site used successfully one year may be abandoned and a new site used, but some sites are in regular use. In autumn, large numbers of young birds and some adults migrate to the southeastern coast of Australia, where they are widespread in May–November in New South

Wales, Victoria and Tasmania, and a few range west to Western Australia or north to Queensland. Most adults stay on New Zealand coasts throughout the winter. They are rarely recorded inland, usually on rivers in Canterbury, but some have visited Lakes Taupo and Rotorua.

Population: 15,000–20,000 pairs in 1997. They are by far the commonest tern on the New Zealand shore and coastal waters. Some colonies contain thousands of pairs, but usually 50–200 pairs. Some birds nest alone or in small groups of only a few pairs.

Conservation: Protected native. For unknown reasons, the number of birds seems to be declining, but the capriciousness of colonies makes them difficult to monitor. Large numbers persist despite severe predation of breeding adults by cats and mustelids, and of eggs and chicks by mustelids, rats, cats, hedgehogs, Red-billed Gulls and Black-backed Gulls.

Breeding: Large colonies are generally on sandy beaches, low-lying sandspits, shingle- or shellbanks and rocky islets, and smaller colonies are usually on rock stacks, steep cliffs and offshore islands. White-fronted Terns often nest close to colonies of Red-billed Gulls. Laying is from mid-October to January, during which several replacement clutches are laid if eggs or chicks are lost to predators or storm surges. Colonies form rapidly and laying is highly synchronised. They lay 1–2 eggs (46 x 33mm) on the mainland of New Zealand, but 1–2–3 eggs (46 x 32mm) on the Chathams. Eggs vary from pale green-blue to light brown with an array of spots. The first egg is larger than the second, and birds over 6 years old lay on average larger eggs than younger birds. Both adults incubate for *c.* 24 days and then brood the chicks for several days; the chicks then join others in a crèche. On the New Zealand mainland, each pair usually rears only one chick to fledging at 29–35 days old. The adults continue to feed their young for up to 3 months after leaving the colony. They usually retain pair-bonds from year to year, even when the colony shifts. Young birds can start breeding at 2 years old, but most start when at least 7 years old. The oldest banded bird lived over 26 years.

Behaviour: Gregarious. Most breed in large, tightly-packed colonies with less than a metre between nests. White-fronted Terns attack intruders at their colonies, by swooping and calling 'keark' repeatedly. They feed in coastal waters in large flocks of hundreds or thousands of birds, often forming great 'swirls' over shoaling fish, in company with shearwaters, gannets and gulls. They roost in tight flocks of up to 2000 birds on beaches, shellbanks, piers and at the mouth of estuaries. The usual call is a single high-pitched note 'siet', repeated at intervals and given particularly in flight by day or night.

Feeding: Diet is mainly small surface-shoaling fish such as smelt and pilchards, caught by shallow plunge-diving from 3–10m. They often work a shoal that kahawai and kingfish have driven to the surface, and sometimes accompany feeding dolphins. They are often pursued by skuas, which harass them and force them to disgorge and drop the fish they have caught.

Reading: Mills, J. A. & Shaw, P. W. 1980. *NZ J Zool* 7: 147–153.

283. ANTARCTIC TERN *Sterna vittata* PLATE 65

Size: 36cm; 140g
Geographical variation: Of the five subspecies, *bethunei* breeds in the New Zealand region.
Distribution: Circumpolar in the Southern Hemisphere, breeding on the Antarctic Peninsula, on islands of the South Atlantic and South Indian oceans, and on subantarctic islands of Australia and New Zealand. In the New Zealand region, they breed on islands off Stewart Island (in Port Pegasus, and at Stage, Solomon and Moggy islands), Antipodes, Bounty, The Snares, Auckland and Campbell islands. At the northern breeding sites, adults and young stay in nearby coastal waters all year, but further south they are absent in April–October, apparently in the southern oceans, because the only Antarctic Tern recorded north of Foveaux Strait was seen at the Chathams in 1997.
Population: *c.* 1000 breeding pairs in New Zealand, fairly evenly spread through the subantarctic.
Conservation: Protected native. Populations in the subantarctic appear to be secure as long as rats and cats do not reach their breeding grounds. The eradication of rats and disappearance of cats from Campbell Island is expected to allow some recovery there.
Breeding: Colonial whenever possible but usually in small groups. On The Snares, they are mostly solitary on cliff ledges overlooking the sea; on Auckland and Campbell islands they nest on rocks close to the sea and on rock outcrops in areas of scrub well inland. Laying is prolonged and varies from island to island with no clear latitudinal pattern: mid-September to late March on The Snares, October–February on Campbell Island, November–February on the Auckland Islands, and December–March on Antipodes Island. The nest is a scrape or a depression on the ground or on a ledge. They lay 1–2 buff-olive eggs (46 x 32mm, 25g) with brown and black blotches. Both adults incubate for 24–25 days. In two-egg clutches, the eggs hatch 2–3 days apart, or the second egg does not hatch. The fledging period is 27–32 days. Young can start breeding at 3 years old. Annual survival estimates are 91–94%, giving mean lifespans of 13–17 years. The oldest banded bird in New Zealand lived at least 14 years.
Behaviour: Gregarious; feeding and roosting in small flocks of up to 100 birds.
Feeding: Antarctic Terns feed close inshore, taking fish and crustaceans. Their feeding methods vary depending on the prey type and sea conditions. In calm seas, they feed on crustaceans by contact-dipping (i.e. submerging the bill only) or take fish by plunge-diving to become completely or partially submerged. As seas become rough, they mainly contact-dip to take crustaceans and small fish, but may also partially plunge for crustaceans and plunge for fish.
Reading: Sadleir, R. M. F. S. et al. 1986. *Notornis* 33: 264–265. Sagar, P. M. 1978. *Notornis* 25: 59–70. Sagar, P. M. & Sagar, J. L. 1989. *Notornis* 36: 171–182. Sagar, P. M. et al. 2003. *Notornis* 50: 36–42. Sagar, P. M. et al. 2007. *Notornis* 54: 214–219.

284. ARCTIC TERN *Sterna paradisaea* PLATE 65

Size: 34cm; 110g
Distribution: Circumpolar, breeding in the Arctic and subarctic regions of the Northern Hemisphere in Greenland, Iceland, northern Europe, Siberia and North America. Arctic Terns have the longest annual migration of any bird studied at about 50,000km, not including an extra 40,000km travelled when at staging sites and at their wintering areas. After breeding, they travel south to the edge of the Antarctic pack ice in the Southern Ocean, taking three routes, down the western or eastern sides of the Pacific Ocean, or down the eastern side of the Atlantic Ocean. They have regular staging sites en route, including the Peru and Benguela currents and in the South Indian Ocean near Amsterdam Island; return routes are less clearly defined.

They are a rare but annual visitor to New Zealand as they pass by on their way to and from Antarctic waters. Most records are of single birds on beaches and at river mouths from October to June, but mainly in November, and so a flock of four birds at Manawatu Estuary in September 2010 was unusual. Recorded from Northland to Stewart Island; also at the Chathams, Antipodes and The Snares. They are regular visitors to the Auckland and Campbell islands during the summer. A few subadults may overwinter in New Zealand waters. A juvenile banded in Sweden on 27 June 2003 was recovered freshly dead at Mason Bay, Stewart Island, on 1 December 2003, after a likely journey of 25,000km. An adult from the Netherlands carrying a geolocator was recorded in New Zealand waters on its way to Antarctica.
Behaviour: Gregarious; often joining roosting flocks of White-fronted Terns, in which they are easily

overlooked. Feed mainly on small fish near the surface by shallow plunge-diving.

Reading: Fijn, R. C. et al. 2013. *Ardea* 101: 3–12. Latham, P. C. M. 1986. *Notornis* 33: 69–76.

285. COMMON TERN *Sterna hirundo* PLATE 65

Size: 36cm; 120g
Geographical variation: Three subspecies are recognised: *hirundo* breeds in North and Central America, Canaries, Azores, North Africa, and Eurasia; *tibetana* in western China; and *longipennis* in Siberia east of Lake Baikal, northeast China, and North Korea. Birds of the *longipennis* subspecies have been recorded in New Zealand and Australia, but *hirundo* has also been recorded in Australia and could occur here.
Distribution: Breeds in eastern North America, Central America, temperate North Atlantic, North Africa, and across temperate Europe and Asia. They migrate to tropical and subtropical waters of Atlantic, Indian and Pacific oceans. Since the 1960s, they have become commonplace each summer in New Guinea, the Solomons, and in northern and eastern Australia. In New Zealand, one was recorded at Lake Horowhenua in 1977, but the first confirmed record was at Pukerua Bay in 1984. Since then, singles have been seen almost annually between November and April in the North Island, mainly in the Bay of Plenty and on the Kapiti–Manawatu coast, but three records in the South Island, as far south as the mouth of the Ashburton River.
Behaviour: Gregarious; often joining roosting flocks of White-fronted Terns, in which they are easily overlooked, but they are usually found on the edge of the flock. Feeds mainly on small fish near the surface by shallow plunge-diving.
Reading: Latham, P. C. M. 1986. *Notornis* 33: 69–76.

286. CRESTED TERN *Sterna bergii* PLATE 61

Other name: Swift Tern
Size: 47cm, 350g
Geographical variation: Of four subspecies, probably *cristata* of New Guinea, Australia and the tropical South Pacific east to French Polynesia reaches New Zealand.
Distribution: Breeds in South Africa, islands and coasts of the Indian Ocean, Australia and islands of the tropical South Pacific. Rare vagrants have been seen in New Zealand 14 times: Raoul Island, Kermadecs (1910), Spirits Bay (1951), Farewell Spit (1960), Firth of Thames (1974), Napier (1981), Wellington Harbour and the Kapiti Coast (1981–95), Kaikoura (1985), Manawatu Estuary (1995), Washdyke Lagoon (1995), New Plymouth (1995–97), Kaipara Harbour (1996), Wellington Harbour (2002), Whatipu (2011), and Christchurch (2012).
Behaviour: Adults in breeding and non-breeding plumage, and immatures have all been seen, often roosting with White-fronted Terns. One bird apparently remained on, or regularly visited, the Wellington coast for 15 years.

PIGEONS and DOVES *Columbidae*

About 320 species worldwide; 2 are endemic to New Zealand and 3 have been introduced.

Usually the larger members of the family are called pigeons, and the smaller ones, doves. Pigeons and doves have plump bodies with short necks and legs, small heads, and short, straight bills. The plumage is soft, dense and loose, and some species have brilliant or iridescent colouring. They feed mainly on vegetable matter and can be split into two groups: grain-eaters and fruit-eaters. Both groups supplement their diet with foliage, buds and flowers. Pigeons and doves have a large crop for storing grain or fruit. The fruit-eating pigeons play an important ecological role in forest regeneration, transporting intact seeds of trees and shrubs to new sites in exchange for a nutritious reward from the digested flesh.

Unlike most birds, pigeons and doves can drink without raising their heads to swallow. They are strong fliers and have aerial displays in which the bird rises, stalls and then dives with wings and tail held stiffly, and they also clap their wings together above their backs during display flight.

The nest is rudimentary, usually a flat tray of interwoven twigs in a tree, or on the ledge of a cliff or building. All species lay only one or two small eggs; most granivorous species lay two eggs, and most fruit pigeons lay only one. The total clutch weight, at on average 9% of the female body weight, is the lightest of all bird groups. The breeding season is usually determined by suitable food being available, and normally several broods are reared each year. This is helped by having very short incubation and fledging periods, and young usually fledge well below adult weight. Clutches are sometimes overlapped, eggs being incubated in one nest while chicks are being fed in another.

Apart from Emperor Penguins and flamingos, pigeons and doves are the only birds to produce food for their chicks. They feed their chicks (sometimes called squabs) crop-milk, a protein-rich, cottage cheese-like secretion from the crop wall. At first, crop-milk is the only food, but as the chicks grow, regurgitated foods form an increasingly large part of the diet.

Reading: Gibbs, D. et al. 2001. *Pigeons and Doves: A Guide to the Pigeons and Doves of the World*. London: Christopher Helm. Goodwin, D. 1970. *Pigeons and Doves of the World*. London: British Museum. Robertson, H. A. 1988. *J Zool (Lond)* 215: 217–229.

287. ROCK PIGEON *Columba livia* **PLATE 66**

Other names: Feral Pigeon, Rock Dove

Size: 33cm, 400g

Geographical variation: Over 200 varieties of dovecote or racing pigeons have been selected through thousands of years of domestication. Rock Pigeons in towns are continuously supplemented by lost dovecote or racing pigeons, and so have more variable plumages than rural birds, which are mainly like the original Rock Pigeon plumage type.

Distribution: Natural range is Europe, North Africa, western Asia and India. Domesticated birds were taken from Europe to most parts of the world. Early European settlers brought birds to New Zealand, and they quickly reverted to the wild and established feral populations in the North and South islands, but mainly in the cropping districts of the North Island and the northern and eastern South Island, and in cities and large towns. Vagrants have been recorded from the Chathams and Antipodes islands and The Snares. In cities, Rock Pigeons are sedentary, frequenting city parks and grain-handling and storage facilities, but rural birds often commute over 20km between their roosting and breeding sites and their feeding grounds on newly sown crops or stubble.

Population: Widespread and locally common.

Breeding: Breeds solitarily on buildings or under bridges, and the nest site is defended all year, but they also nest in small colonies on cliffs high above a river or the sea, on offshore rock stacks or in sea caves, and rarely in a tall tree where a broken branch or old nest provides a flat platform. The nest is a simple platform of straw and twigs on a ledge. They can breed at any time of year, depending on food being available, but the peak is in spring and summer, and the low is late autumn. Rock Pigeons re-nest up to five times each season, sometimes while they are still feeding young in another nest. In a normal season, they probably raise 2–3 broods each year.

The clutch is 1–2–4 white eggs (39 x 29mm; 19g), but those of over three eggs are probably laid by more than one female. Both adults incubate for *c.* 17 days and brood the chicks for the first week. Chicks are at first fed just crop-milk, a protein-rich secretion from the crop wall of both adults, but as they grow, regurgitated food forms an increasingly large part of the diet. The chicks fledge at *c.* 30 days old at about 84% of adult weight and quickly become independent. The young are capable of breeding at 6 months old.

Behaviour: Rock Pigeons are usually seen feeding or roosting in loose flocks, and they commute in tight, fast-flying flocks between roosts and feeding places. In parks, birds can be seen displaying at any time of year, the male bowing and strutting around the female with his neck arched and chest puffed out. They also perform aerial displays where the male flies with slow, deliberate wingbeats interspersed with gliding with wings held stiffly upwards. Calls are variations on a rippling coo of three notes: 'oor-roo-cooo'.

Feeding: In cities, Rock Pigeons readily take scraps of food from people, and spilt grain. In rural areas, they feed on newly sown or stubble grain, stored grain, peas, maize, beans, clover and weed seeds, supplemented with occasional invertebrates such as snails, worms and slugs. Rock Pigeons can cause serious damage to newly sown pea and bean crops, as a flock can work systematically through a crop day after day.

Roosting or nesting Rock Pigeons can foul buildings and footpaths in cities.

Reading: Dilks, P. J. 1975. *NZ J Ag Res* 18: 87–90. Dilks, P. J. 1975. *Notornis* 22: 295–301. Murton, R. K. et al. 1972. *J Appl Ecol* 9: 835–874. Robertson, H. A. 1988. *Ibis* 130: 261–267.

288. BARBARY DOVE *Streptopelia risoria* PLATE 66

Size: 28cm, 140g

Distribution: Natural range is across the Sahel zone of northern Africa from Senegal to Ethiopia, and into Arabia. Domesticated birds were taken to Europe and many other parts of the world. They were brought to New Zealand as cage birds but have become feral. A few established in Masterton in the 1970s, but this population did not expand. Small feral populations are now established in the Bay of Islands, near Whangarei, in Auckland, Waikato, Hawke's Bay, and on the Horowhenua coast near Waikawa. Barbary Doves are occasionally reported in Taranaki, Whanganui, Levin, Masterton, Blenheim, Christchurch and Dunedin.

Population: The population of Barbary Doves in New Zealand is increasing, but with probably fewer than 2000 birds, mostly near Whangarei, Auckland, and around Havelock North and Hastings.

Breeding: Breeds solitarily in shrubs, hedges or trees. They can breed at any time of year if food is available, but the peak is in spring and summer, and the low is in late autumn. Barbary Doves re-nest several times each season. They lay **2** white eggs (29 x 23mm, 8g) on a simple platform of twigs. Both adults incubate for *c.* 15 days and brood the chicks for the first week. Chicks are at first fed just crop-milk, a protein-rich secretion from the crop wall of both adults, but as the chicks grow, regurgitated seeds form an increasingly large part of the diet. They fledge at *c.* 15 days old and quickly become independent.

Behaviour: Barbary Doves are usually seen alone or in pairs, occasionally in small flocks at good food sources. Calls are a mellow 'coo-crroo', the second note being lower and longer; also a high-pitched excitement cry: 'heh-heh-heh', sounding like a jeering laugh.

Feeding: In towns, they readily take scraps of food from people, and spilt grain. In rural areas, they feed on newly sown or stubble grain, and clover and weed seeds, supplemented with occasional invertebrates such as snails.

Reading: Stidolph, R. H. D. 1974. *Notornis* 21: 383–384.

289. SPOTTED DOVE *Streptopelia chinensis* PLATE 66

Other names: Spotted Turtle-Dove, Malay Spotted Dove

Size: 30cm, 130g

Geographical variation: Five subspecies, of which *tigrina*, from Bangladesh and Myanmar through south-eastern Asia to the Philippines and Indonesia, has been introduced to New Zealand.

Distribution: Natural range is Asia, from India and Sri Lanka to southern China, Philippines and Timor. Introduced to Hawai'i, Fiji, New Caledonia, Australia, California, Mauritius and New Zealand as a cage bird. The main population of Spotted Doves in New Zealand is in the Auckland area, from Warkworth to Pukekohe and west to Waitakere. They probably originated from escaped cage birds and especially from a substantial liberation at Mt Eden in the 1920s. They are mainly found in well-treed suburbs and city parks, and in rural areas around Howick, Whitford, Clevedon and Karaka; a few birds have been recorded as far south as Miranda on the Firth of Thames. Small populations have established recently around Whangarei, and in coastal Bay of Plenty from Katikati to Opotiki. Birds have been reported from Hamilton, Te Kuiti, Taupo, Murupara and Wairoa.

Population: Locally common and steadily increasing its range around Auckland; increasing rapidly around Whangarei and in the Bay of Plenty.

Breeding: Spotted Doves breed solitarily. The nest is a flimsy platform of twigs, well concealed in a large shrub, hedge or tree, up to 12m above the ground. They can breed at any time of year if food is available, but the peak is in spring and summer, and the low is in late autumn. Spotted doves re-nest several times each season. They lay **2** white eggs (27 x 21mm, 7g). Both sexes incubate for *c.* 16 days and brood the chicks for the first week. Chicks are at first fed just crop-milk, a protein-rich secretion from the crop wall of both adults, but as the chicks grow, regurgitated seeds form an increasingly large part of the diet. They fledge at *c.* 15 days old and

quickly become independent.
Behaviour: Spotted Doves are more often heard than seen. When seen, they are normally alone or in pairs as they search for food on the ground; however, they sometimes form flocks where grain has been spilt or where weeds are seeding prolifically. A spectacular display is a steep upward flight and downward glide with wings and tail stiffly spread. Their calling reaches peaks in autumn and spring, 2–4 coo notes varying in rhythm and emphasis, e.g. 'croo-croo' or 'cu-cu-croo-crook'.
Feeding: In towns, they feed on grass and weed seeds in lawns and along paths, but in rural areas they feed on spilt grain, especially where horses and other livestock have been fed, around poultry yards and on grass, clover and weed seeds in short cover. Their diet is supplemented with occasional invertebrates such as snails.

290. NEW ZEALAND PIGEON *Hemiphaga novaeseelandiae* PLATE 66

Other names: Kereru, Kukupa (northern North Island), Wood Pigeon
Size: 51cm, 650g
Distribution: New Zealand only. New Zealand Pigeons are found throughout the North, South and Stewart islands, and until the mid-1800s, on Raoul Island, Kermadecs. They are also on many forested offshore islands. On the mainland, they are most common in Northland, the King Country, Taranaki–Whanganui, Wellington, Nelson district, the West Coast, Dunedin, and Stewart Island. They favour native lowland forests dominated by podocarps, tawa, taraire and puriri, bush patches on farmland, gardens, and parks and botanical gardens of cities. Their breeding and wintering distributions are similar, but birds can move long distances (100+km) to good sources of fruit or foliage outside the breeding season. A satellite-tagged bird in Southland crossed Foveaux Strait four times and travelled over 480km in just over 3 months.
Population: New Zealand Pigeons are widespread and locally common, and generally increasing in numbers.
Conservation: Protected endemic. In the early 1900s, the New Zealand Pigeon was in serious decline from overhunting and clearance of lowland forest, but with protection since 1921, and perhaps the planting of food plants such as tree lucerne and willows, it increased. Landscape-scale and intensive control of predators, especially possums and rats, has improved breeding at many sites on the mainland, and the overall population has grown rapidly. Illegal hunting, predation by rats, cats, stoats and possums, and competition for food from possums still affect many populations. New Zealand Pigeons increased greatly on Kapiti Island in the decades since possums were eradicated. The conservation of New Zealand Pigeons is particularly important because they play a key ecological role in the regeneration of native forests by dispersing the seeds of large fruited trees and shrubs, some of which (e.g. miro, tawa, taraire, puriri and karaka) are too large to be dispersed by other birds.
Breeding: The timing of breeding is closely linked to the availability of certain fruits; they can lay at any time of the year, but also some or all pairs fail to breed in years when fruit is in poor supply. New Zealand Pigeons lay mainly in September–March. During the season, each pair can lay 2–3 clutches, which can be overlapping, i.e. birds incubating while still feeding a chick in another nest. Pairs usually occupy the same area each breeding season. The nest is a platform of sticks on a horizontal fork or in a tangle of vines 2–15m above the ground, and the egg or chick can often be seen through the nest.

They lay **1** white egg (48 x 33mm, 30g). Both adults incubate for 27–30 days; females incubate from late afternoon to mid-morning, males through the middle of the day. Both adults brood the chick. It is at first fed just crop-milk, a protein-rich secretion from the crop wall of the adults, but as it grows, regurgitated fruits form an increasingly large part of the diet. The chick fledges at 35–45 days, well below adult weight and with a conspicuously short tail. The chick is fed by regurgitation for several weeks after fledging. The first chicks raised in a season are evicted when their parents re-nest, but the last chick raised stays close to its natal territory for at least 2–3 months. First breeding can be at less than 12 months old, but is usually at 1–2 years old. The oldest banded bird in the wild lived at least 23 years.
Behaviour: The most conspicuous breeding display is the display dive: a bird flaps upward from a perch, stalls, then dives on stiffly held wings. This display is done by both sexes, but particularly by males close to the time of egg-laying, often, but not always, close to the nesting area. Other breeding displays include close chases, head and neck-bobbing, and a display where the male bounces up and down on a branch while posturing and calling. Incubating or brooding birds defend their nest with grunts and wing-flicking, and birds defend their favoured fruiting tree from competitors.

Feeding: Herbivorous; fruits are preferred and in some parts of the country are the sole diet. The preferred fruits eaten by New Zealand Pigeons are of miro, tawa, taraire, puriri and pigeonwood; other main fruits are of kahikatea, coprosma, titoki, nikau, karaka, privet, elder and plums. Supplejack and cabbage-tree fruits are also eaten but are much less preferred. When fruit is in short supply, New Zealand Pigeons feed on foliage, especially old leaves of kowhai, tree lucerne, broom and clover, leaves of coprosma, hoheria and *Parsonsia*, and young leaves or buds of willow, elm and poplar. Flowers of kowhai, tree lucerne, broom and laburnum also form an important seasonal part of their diet.

Reading: Clout, M. N. et al. 1986. *Notornis* 33: 37–44. Clout, M. N. et al. 1988. *Notornis* 35: 59–62. Clout, M. N. et al. 1995. *Ibis* 137: 264–271. Emeny, M. T. et al. 2009. *NZ J Ecol* 33: 114–124. McEwen, W. M. 1978. *NZ J Ecol* 1: 99–108. Pierce, R. J. & Graham, P. J. 1995. *S & R Series* 91. Wellington: DOC. Powlesland, R. G. et al. 1994. *S & R Series* 66. Wellington: DOC. Powlesland, R. G. et al. 2011. *NZ J Ecol* 35: 229–235.

291. CHATHAM ISLANDS PIGEON *Hemiphaga chathamensis* PLATE 66

Other name: Parea

Size: 55cm, 800g

Distribution: Chatham Islands only. They are mainly in the forests of southern Chatham Island, especially around the Tuku River, but a few are seen elsewhere on the island, and on Pitt and South East islands.

Population: *c.* 600 in 2009. Chatham Islands Pigeons are locally common around the Tuku River, but scarce elsewhere in the Chathams.

Conservation: Protected vulnerable endemic. The Chatham Islands Pigeon was critically endangered but is now increasing. They were common in the 1870s, but by 1989 the population had declined to as few as 45 birds. Predator control and fencing in and around the Tuku Valley have led to improved breeding and rapid population growth. Birds are now venturing into parts of Chatham Island where they have not been seen for many years. The conservation of Chatham Islands Pigeons is important because they play a key ecological role in the regeneration of native forests by dispersing the seeds of large-fruited trees and shrubs.

Breeding: The timing of breeding is closely linked to certain fruits, especially hoho (*Pseudopanax chathamicus*), being available. They lay mainly in June–November, but can lay as early as May and as late as February. During the season, each pair can lay 2–3 clutches, which can be overlapped, i.e. an egg in one nest while a chick is being fed in another nest. Pairs usually occupy the same area each breeding season. The nest is a platform of sticks on a horizontal fork or in a tangle of vines 1–10m above the ground, and the egg or chick can often be seen through the nest. They lay **1** white egg (51 x 34mm, 33g). Both adults incubate for 27–**28**–29 days; females incubate from late afternoon to mid-morning, males through the middle of the day. Both adults brood the chick. It is at first fed just crop-milk, a protein-rich secretion from the crop wall of the adults, but as it grows, regurgitated fruits form an increasingly large part of the diet. The chick fledges at 36–**46**–53 days old, well below adult weight and with a conspicuously short tail. The chick is fed by regurgitation for several weeks after fledging. First breeding can be at less than 12 months old, but is usually at 1–2 years old.

Behaviour: The most conspicuous breeding display is the display dive: a bird flaps upward from a perch, stalls, and then dives on stiffly held wings. This display is done by both sexes, but particularly by males, close to the time of egg-laying, often, but not always, close to the nesting area. Other breeding displays include close chases, head and neck-bobbing, and a display where the male bounces up and down on a branch while posturing and calling. Incubating or brooding birds defend their nest with grunts and wing-flicking.

Feeding: Herbivorous; fruits are preferred, but leaf buds, leaves, flower buds and flowers form an important seasonal part of their diet. The main fruits eaten are hoho, matipo, mahoe and karamu. When fruit is in short supply, Chatham Islands Pigeons feed on foliage, especially clover and hoho.

Reading: Dilks, P. J. et al. 2010. *Notornis* 57: 156–161. Flux, I. A. et al. 2001. *Notornis* 48: 197–206. Millener, P. R. & Powlesland, R. G. 2001. *J Roy Soc NZ* 31: 365–381. Powlesland, R. G. et al. 1994. *S & R Series* 66. Wellington: DOC. Powlesland, R. G. et al. 1997. *Ibis* 139: 353–365.

COCKATOOS, PARROTS and PARAKEETS

Strigopidae, Cacatuidae and Psittacidae

About 330 species worldwide; 3 endemic members of the Strigopidae, 2 introduced Cacatuidae, and 6 endemic and 3 introduced Psittacidae.

These three families of parrots are all part of the Psittaciformes. This order is well known for its colourful, sometimes gaudy plumage and high intelligence, making them attractive subjects to be held in captivity.

All have large heads and eyes, a short neck, and a short, deep bill. The upper mandible is strongly curved, sharply pointed, and hinged at the base so the parrot can crack nuts or other unyielding food. Parrots can use the bill as an extra limb, showing great agility at climbing. They have a large fleshy cere surrounding the nostrils. Two toes are pointed forwards and two back (zygodactyl), giving a strong grip. Parrots can hold food with a foot while shredding it and passing it to their mouth. Mainly herbivorous, although some also eat invertebrates.

Most parrots are gregarious, and many have loud harsh or chattering voices, though some also give beautiful liquid notes. They mostly lay their clutch of white eggs in tree holes or in rock crevices.

Reading: Forshaw, J. M. & Cooper, W. T. 1978. *Parrots of the World*. Melbourne: Lansdowne. Juniper, T. & Parr, M. 1998. *Parrots: A Guide to Parrots of the World*. Sussex: Pica Press.

292. KAKAPO *Strigops habroptilus* **PLATE 67**

Other names: Owl-parrot, Night Parrot

Size: 63cm; male 2.1kg, female 1.5kg

Distribution: New Zealand only. Subfossil and midden records show that Kakapo were throughout the North, South and Stewart islands before and during early Maori times. By the early 1800s, they were still in the central North Island and the forested parts of the South Island. Their range contracted rapidly after stoats and ship rats were introduced in the 1880s, and by 1900 they were common only in parts of the southern and western South Island. By the mid-1970s, only 18 males were known from remote parts of Fiordland, and they probably died out there in the early 1990s.

In 1977, however, a population of about 100 birds was found living south and east of the Tin Range in southern Stewart Island. This population was also in serious decline because of predation by feral cats. The remaining 61 Kakapo were moved to several cat-free and mustelid-free islands, but by 2005 they, and a few transferred Fiordland birds, were mostly on Codfish Island/Whenua Hou. Some birds have been translocated to Little Barrier, Anchor and Chalky islands.

Population: In 2013, the total was 125 birds, a substantial increase from the minimum of 51 birds known to be alive in 1995–96.

Conservation: Protected critically endangered endemic. Kakapo evolved without mammalian predators, and although their nocturnal habits and camouflaged plumage were presumably effective against the avian predators of ancient New Zealand, they are particularly susceptible to mammalian predators, being large, flightless, relatively slow-moving, placid, and strongly scented. To make matters worse, they often roost and nest on the ground, and in a breeding year males congregate on traditional display grounds and boom loudly for 6–8 hours every night for 3–5 months. They also have a long breeding period (100+ days), during which the female leaves the eggs and chicks unattended for long periods on most nights while she forages. Their productivity is naturally low and is dependent on an abundant supply of fruits being available, and much of this is removed by competing introduced herbivores such as possums, deer, goats and chamois, and introduced omnivores such as rats, pigs and introduced birds.

Recent conservation attempts have concentrated on clearing predators from suitable islands, and shifting Kakapo to these islands once predators have been eradicated. The fate of individual birds and all breeding attempts are closely monitored, and if chicks are doing poorly, they are removed and hand-raised in captivity. Supplementary food (mainly fruit, nuts and formulated artificial pellets) has been supplied in some years to try to stimulate breeding more frequently than the once every 3–5 years in nature. Unlike some parrots, wild-raised adults have not been kept successfully in captivity.

Breeding: Successful breeding requires an abundant supply of high-quality food throughout the 8-month breeding cycle. This 'masting' seems to happen every

3–5 years, e.g. in Fiordland the seeds that have high protein value are of tussock grasses and beech trees, and on Stewart and Codfish islands the key fruits are rimu and pink pine. With supplementary food, however, Kakapo may breed more often than every 3–5 years, e.g. two supplementary-fed females on Little Barrier laid eggs in consecutive years.

Kakapo are unique among New Zealand birds, parrots, and flightless birds in having a lek, or arena mating system. In good fruiting years, males establish a miniature display territory that has no connection with feeding or nesting sites. The display area is a 'track and bowl' system consisting of a series of bowls, each a shallow depression about 50cm across, connected by tracks 30–60cm wide, mostly clustered within an 'arena' on a prominent vantage point, a ridge or hilltop with low-growing and sparse vegetation, where calls can be projected a long distance. Males remove encroaching vegetation from their track and bowl system. They give three major types of call during the booming season (December–March): non-directional, low-pitched 'booming', which is highly resonant and can carry several kilometres on a suitable night; highly directional, high-pitched 'chinging', which may reveal to an approaching female the exact position of the male; and harsh 'skrarking', which is apparently related to territorial defence and aggression between neighbouring males. When booming, males inflate their thoracic air sacs hugely, and by holding their head low, the sacs act as a resonating chamber. They utter 20–50 booms at about 2-second intervals, and then pause for 30–120 seconds between sequences. Booming continues throughout the night for 6–8 hours each night for 3–5 months. Females travel several kilometres to briefly visit the displaying males to mate. The dominant males mate with several females, and males take no part in tending or defending the nest.

Nests on Stewart and Codfish islands are in the decayed centre of fallen tree trunks, in the hollow centre of a standing stump, and under tussock clumps. Between January and March, they lay 1–3–4 white eggs (51 x 38mm, 41g) at intervals of 3–5 days. The female alone incubates for 27–**30**–31 days, starting when the first egg is laid, so hatching may be staggered over many days. During the first 2 weeks of incubation, the female rarely leaves the nest, but later she leaves to feed for several hours. The chicks are usually brooded for the first 3–4 weeks all day, but for only part of the night, then she broods for less of the night, and finally, when the chicks are about 8 weeks old, she visits only once or twice a night and roosts elsewhere by day. The fledging period is *c.* 72 days, and the chicks associate with their mother until about 6 months. The young may first breed when 6–8 years old. Kakapo are long-lived; the oldest known bird in the wild lived at least 40 years, but some probably live to 100 years old.

Behaviour: Solitary, unlike other parrots. Kakapo are the heaviest parrot and are flightless. The keel on the sternum is rudimentary, but the broad wings are used to maintain balance when climbing and running, and they slow the bird's steep fall from low trees.

Feeding: Herbivorous. Kakapo eat a wide variety of fruits, seeds, leaves, stems and roots. The stout bill is used for grubbing and grinding; the inside of the upper mandible has a series of ridges that work with the tongue and the lower mandible to grind fibrous foods, acting as a kind of juice extractor. Tussock and other grass seeds are removed by using the foot to pass stems through the bill from the base to the end. Foliage is browsed while attached to the plant; the fibrous material is ejected as tightly compressed, kidney-shaped 'chews', often still attached to the plant.

Reading: Ballance, A. 2010. *Kakapo: Rescued from the Brink of Extinction*. Nelson: Craig Potton Publishing. Butler, D. 1989. *Quest for the Kakapo*. Auckland: Heinemann Reed. Cemmick, D. & Veitch, D. 1987. *Kakapo Country*. Auckland: Hodder & Stoughton. Lloyd, B. D. & Powlesland, R. G. 1994. *Biol Cons* 69: 75–85. Merton, D. et al. 1984. *Ibis* 126: 277–283. Powlesland, R. G. et al. 1992. *Ibis* 134: 361–373. Powlesland, R. G. et al. 1995. *NZ J Zool* 22: 239–248. Williams, G. R. 1956. *Notornis* 7: 29–56. Various authors. 2006. *Notornis* 53: 1–197.

293. KAKA *Nestor meridionalis* — PLATE 67

Size: 45cm; male 475g, female 425g (North Island); male 575g, female 500g (South Island)

Geographical variation: Two subspecies: the North Island Kaka *septentrionalis*, and the South Island Kaka *meridionalis*, but recent genetic research suggests that there is a latitudinal cline rather than any clear split between the two islands.

Distribution: New Zealand only. Kaka were common as subfossils throughout the three main islands and in middens in the North Island. They were abundant when Europeans arrived, but by the early 1900s they had declined to localised flocks. North Island Kaka are still in the large forest tracts from Coromandel Peninsula to the Aorangi Range in southern Wairarapa. They are moderately common in the central North Island, especially Pureora and Whirinaki forests. They are most numerous on the larger offshore islands: Hen and Chickens, Great Barrier, Little Barrier, Mayor and Kapiti. Kaka commute freely between the northern islands and wander to mainland forests and towns, e.g. Northland, Auckland, Hamilton and Greytown, and to other offshore islands where they are not normally resident. Recent translocations to Zealandia and Pukaha Mount Bruce have been successful, and they are now commonly seen in Wellington.

South Island Kaka are in the forested parts of the South and Stewart islands and on some offshore islands, e.g. the Chetwodes, Codfish and Big South Cape, but are nowhere common. They are chiefly west of the Southern Alps and in Fiordland and western Southland. They extend east of the Alps into Canterbury at lower mountain passes. Some birds wander occasionally to coastal Canterbury and Otago.

Population: Probably fewer than 10,000 birds, mostly on large offshore islands, especially Little Barrier, Kapiti and Codfish.

Conservation: Protected vulnerable endemic. The range and number of Kaka have been greatly reduced by clearfelling and 'sustainable logging' of beech and mixed podocarp/hardwood forests, competition with possums and rats for fruit and nectar-bearing plants such as mistletoe and rata, competition from wasps for beech honeydew in the South Island, and predation by introduced mammals, especially stoats. Nesting females are often killed by stoats and possums, and this produces a very skewed sex ratio in favour of males in many mainland populations. Numbers of Kaka increased greatly on Kapiti Island in the decades since possums were eradicated. Other island and pest-free sanctuary populations are reasonably secure; and reducing numbers of possums, rats, stoats and wasps in mainland forests may safeguard mainland birds.

Breeding: Nests are a shallow bowl of decayed wood dust in hollow branches or trunks of large canopy or emergent trees, with the entrance usually 5–20m above the ground, but on pest-free islands they often use the bases of hollow trees. On the mainland, Kaka need mature and dying trees to provide suitable nest sites; however, they readily use nest boxes when natural nest sites are scarce. The timing and extent of breeding is closely associated with mast fruiting or seeding of key tree species; in years when food is scarce, few pairs breed. In October–March, they lay 1–2 clutches of 1–**4–5**–8 white eggs (42 x 31mm, 23g). Eggs are laid 3–4 days apart. The female alone incubates for 23–25 days and broods the nestlings for the first 15–20 days. The eggs hatch about a day apart, and so the chicks vary in size and development. The male regurgitates food to the female during incubation 8–12 times a day, and shares in feeding the chicks, which take about 70 days to fledge and another 5 months to become fully independent of their parents. They first breed from 4 years old. The oldest banded Kaka in the wild lived to over 27 years old.

Behaviour: Kaka can be very conspicuous when in a flock and when flying, but cryptic when feeding alone; the sound of falling pieces of wood often betrays their presence. They delight in acrobatics and aerobatics, jumping through the trees and using their bill as an extra appendage, and tumbling through the air for enjoyment. The calls consist of a wide variety of melodious liquid whistling notes, and harsh grating calls. Kaka are active by both day and night; brooding females often come and go from their nest during the night, and leave their nestlings alone for hours at a time.

Feeding: Diet is mainly fruit, nectar and insects. They use their powerful bill to tear off loose bark and break up decaying wood to extract the grubs of wood-boring beetles such as the huhu beetle and kanuka longhorn beetle, and to tap into sap from the bark of beech, mountain totara, rimu, and especially southern rata trees. They eat many kinds of seeds and succulent fruit, such as hinau and tawa, and use their delicate brush-tipped tongue to take honeydew, and nectar from flowers of flax and trees such as rata and pohutukawa.

Reading: Beggs, J. R. & Wilson, P. R. 1987. *NZ J Ecol* 10: 143–147. Beggs, J. R. & Wilson, P. R. 1991. *Biol Cons* 56: 23–38. Greene, T. C. & Fraser, J. R. 1998. *NZ J Ecol* 22: 11–16. Moorhouse, R. 1997. *NZ J Ecol* 21: 141–152. Moorhouse, R. et al. 2003. *Biol Cons* 110: 33–44. O'Donnell, C. J. F. & Dilks, P. J. 1989. *Notornis* 36: 65–71. Powlesland, R. G. et al. 2009. *Notornis* 56: 11–33. Sainsbury, J. P. et al. 2006. *Emu* 106: 329–338.

294. KEA *Nestor notabilis* PLATE 67

Size: 46cm; male 950g, female 775g

Distribution: South Island only. Kea are in high country from northwestern Nelson and Marlborough southward to Fiordland. They are mostly in high-altitude forest, the mountains, and high alpine basins and steep valleys; but they often come down to the lowland flats, mainly on the west of the Southern Alps, and have also been recorded as far afield as Farewell Spit lighthouse. Subfossils at one North Island site indicate a previously wider range, and odd records from the Tararua Range could be of birds crossing Cook Strait or cage escapees from nearby collections.

Population: Difficult to assess given the broad but sparse distribution, and mobility of birds within regions. From breeding densities, probably *c.* 2000 pairs and 6000 individuals in 2013.

Conservation: Protected endangered endemic. They have received much publicity as sheep killers, and had the nickname of 'feathered wolf'; but while they certainly feed on dead sheep, and occasionally kill sick and injured sheep or those trapped in heavy snow, only a few birds actually attack healthy sheep. There was a government bounty paid for them, and an estimated 150,000 Kea were killed between 1880 and 1971, when they became partially protected. They were fully protected in 1986.

Kea are playful and inquisitive, but are destructive, and soon make themselves unwelcome at skifields and subalpine car parks, and on hut roofs and tents. The worst offending birds are caught and transferred to distant sites or taken into captivity.

Breeding: Males may often be polygamous, i.e. support more than one nesting female. Kea nest in holes in the ground, under logs and in cavities among the jumbled boulders of old moraines overgrown with scrub and trees, usually in the upper forest. The nest comprises twigs, grasses, moss and lichens. In July–January, they lay 1–**4**–5 white eggs (44 x 33mm). The female alone incubates for 22–26 days. The male feeds her by regurgitation while she is incubating and brooding, and she in turn feeds the nestlings by regurgitation. The fledging period is 90–100 days. Young are probably over 3 years old before they breed. The oldest Kea recorded in the wild lived over 22 years.

Behaviour: Gregarious; flocks of mainly juvenile and subadult males gather at skifield carparks and refuse dumps, and small groups of 5–15 birds are seen elsewhere. Their call is a ringing, far-carrying 'keee-aa', an evocative sound, especially when heard in the swirling mists of the alpine tops. They fly strongly and delight in tumbling in air currents.

Feeding: Mostly herbivorous, feeding on berries and shoots. Many have learnt to fossick through refuse dumps and eat carrion and food scraps. A few may specialise in using their bill to dig into the flesh of healthy sheep above the kidneys; the sheep may develop a large festering area above the kidneys, or blood poisoning.

In the hand: Males are about 5% bigger than females in most linear measurements, except that their bill is 12–14% longer, and they are 20% heavier. There is some overlap in measurements, but over 80% of wild birds are sexed correctly using a bill length of 43.9mm as the cut-off point, and weight is useful as an additional factor for separating the sexes. Fledglings have a yellow wash on their crown, bright yellow-orange eye-ring, cere and bill. Juveniles in their second year have a pale crown and pale yellow eye-ring, cere and lower bill. Subadults in their third and fourth year have an incomplete yellow eye-ring but dark cere and bill.

Reading: Bond, A. B. & Diamond, J. 1992. *Notornis* 39: 151–160. Bond, A. B. et al. 1991. *Emu* 91: 12–19. Clarke, C. M. H. 1970. *Notornis* 17: 105–114. Wilson, K. J. 1990. *Forest & Bird* 21: 20–26.

295. SULPHUR-CRESTED COCKATOO *Cacatua galerita* PLATE 68

Other name: White Cockatoo

Size: 50cm, 900g

Distribution: Natural range is northern, eastern and southeastern Australia and Tasmania, New Guinea and adjacent islands. They were introduced to New Zealand in the early 1900s and have become well established in coastal Waikato, and in the Turakina and Pohangina river catchments of the southwestern North Island. Smaller populations are found in the Waitakere Ranges, Auckland; near Wainuiomata, Wellington; and on Banks Peninsula. Other very small groups have established at scattered sites from Northland to the Catlins, and single stragglers (perhaps even from Australia) or cage escapees have been recorded widely, including on the West Coast.

Population: Probably fewer than 1000 birds; the main

sites of coastal Waikato, Turakina Valley and Pohangina Valley each have *c.* 200 birds. The population has been held in check or is declining, because chicks are taken from nests and adults are trapped to supply the cage-bird trade.
Breeding: Nests are in hollow limbs and trunks of tall trees, especially podocarps, usually above 20m. The nest is a hollowed-out funnel lined with wood chips. Eggs are laid in August–November. They lay 1–2–3 white eggs (48 x 33mm). Both sexes incubate for *c.* 30 days and brood the young, which fledge at *c.* 70 days old.
Behaviour: Gregarious when not breeding. Small, widely dispersed flocks and pairs gather into large flocks (up to 100+ birds) at winter communal roosts or on cereal stubble in the early morning or late afternoon. In the middle of the day, they travel and feed in smaller groups. In spring, the large flocks split up as pairs begin nesting and non-breeders adopt a more nomadic lifestyle. Sulphur-crested Cockatoos remain alert and are hard to approach. Birds perched high in trees while the flock feeds on the ground or in neighbouring trees scream at the approach of an intruder, and the whole flock flies up.
Feeding: In New Zealand, they feed on maize, the seeds of grasses, cereals and weeds (including thistles), fruit of podocarps, seeds of introduced conifers, walnuts, orchard fruit, and insect larvae dug out of rotting wood. Despite causing localised damage to maize crops, they do not seem to cause major damage.
Reading: Styche, A. 2000. PhD thesis. Victoria Uni.

296. GALAH *Eolophus roseicapillus* PLATE 68

Size: 36cm, 325g
Distribution: Native to Australia, where they are widespread except that they are less common along the wetter eastern seaboard and in Tasmania. Introduced to New Zealand as a cage bird. Although first recorded in the wild in 1959 at Clevedon, it was not until about 1975 that cage escapees became well established in South Auckland and the northern Waikato, with records north to Wellsford and south to Hamilton. Their stronghold is on Ponui Island, and they have been recorded from several islands in the Inner Hauraki Gulf, including Pakihi, Waiheke, Rakino and Tiritiri Matangi. Most sightings are around Ponui Island, Hunua Ranges, Mangatawhiri, Pukekohe and Port Waikato. Galahs in a consignment of smuggled birds that was released at sea off the Horowhenua coast in the 1970s were seen in the Manawatu and Horowhenua lowlands for some years, but failed to establish.
Population: Probably fewer than 150 birds; the largest flock recorded is 50 birds.
Breeding: Few details are available about breeding in the wild in New Zealand. Courtship and mating have been noted in August. In Australia, they lay 3–6 white eggs on a bed of green leaves and twigs in a tree cavity.
Behaviour: Gregarious; they are often in small flocks and pairs during the summer and early autumn, but gather into larger flocks in the winter and early spring. The flocks are highly mobile and somewhat nomadic.
Feeding: In Australia, they feed mostly on the ground on seeds of grasses, cereals and weeds; they have been recorded feeding on maize stubble in New Zealand. Because they are a major pest of grain crops in Australia, their increase and spread could also cause problems here.

297. RAINBOW LORIKEET *Trichoglossus haematodus* PLATE 68

Size: 28cm, 150g
Distribution: Native to eastern Indonesia, New Guinea, Solomons, Vanuatu, New Caledonia and the eastern and southeastern seaboard of Australia. Commonly held in captivity in New Zealand, and cage escapes are occasionally seen. The deliberate and illegal release near Lake Rotoiti, Rotorua, in the 1980s apparently failed to establish; however, the release of *c.* 120 birds in 1992, mainly on the North Shore of Auckland, led to the temporary successful establishment of the species in an area from the Whangaparaoa Peninsula in the north to Clevedon in the south. Because they have the potential to compete with native honeyeaters and parrots for food or nesting sites, and to spread diseases to wild birds, an eradication programme was begun in 1999. By 2002, the viable populations had been eliminated, however, further birds have since been released, but have been captured before becoming fully established.
Population: At its peak, 150–200 birds.
Breeding: Rainbow Lorikeets bred in the wild in New Zealand in the 1990s and early 2000s, but few details are available. In southeastern Australia, they lay multiple

clutches of 2–3 white eggs (27 x 22mm) in a hollow tree, from July to January.

Behaviour: Gregarious; they are often in small flocks and pairs during the summer and early autumn, but gather into larger mobile flocks in the winter and early spring. In Auckland, birds travelled over 30km from roosting sites to feeding sites.

Feeding: In Australia, they eat nectar, pollen, fruit, leaf buds, and occasionally seeds of grasses, cereals and weeds.

298. CRIMSON ROSELLA *Platycercus elegans* PLATE 68

Size: 35cm, 130g

Distribution: Native to eastern Australia, from northern Queensland to eastern South Australia. Introduced to Norfolk Island and New Zealand. A small number established near Dunedin about 1910 but died out by the 1950s. A few established and bred in the wooded parks and suburbs in Wellington between 1963 and about 2000; they were most often seen around Central Park, Brooklyn, and at the Botanical Gardens. A few birds, probably recent cage escapees, have been seen elsewhere in the country.

Population: Possibly extinct in the wild.

Breeding: Not studied in New Zealand, but juveniles have been seen in October–March. In Australia, the nest is a shallow bowl of decayed wood dust in a hollow limb of a tree. In August–February, they lay 3–5–8 white eggs (29 x 24mm) at 2-day intervals. The female alone incubates from about midway through the clutch for *c.* 21 days. The fledging period is *c.* 35 days. Males feed incubating and brooding females until the brood is about 5 days old, thereafter both parents feed the nestlings and recent fledglings, and the young remain with their parents for several months after fledging.

Behaviour: In New Zealand, Crimson Rosellas were usually seen as singles or in small family groups, but in Australia immatures form small flocks in autumn and winter while adults remain in pairs or small parties. Their usual call is a low-pitched 'kweek-kweek-kweek', lower in tone than the similar Eastern Rosella call.

Feeding: Diet is mainly seeds of grasses, weeds and trees, and fruit.

Reading: Hamel, J. 1970. *Notornis* 17: 126–129. Krebs, E. A. et al. 2002. *Behav Ecol Sociobiol* 51: 447–451.

299. EASTERN ROSELLA *Platycercus eximius* PLATE 68

Size: 32cm, 110g

Geographical variation: Of the three doubtfully distinct subspecies, *eximius* of southern New South Wales, Victoria and eastern South Australia was introduced to New Zealand.

Distribution: Native to southeastern Australia, from southern Queensland to eastern South Australia and Tasmania. Introduced to New Zealand as a cage bird. Birds were released or escaped in Dunedin around 1910. They became well established and spread through southeastern Otago until about the 1940s, when they declined in range back to the Dunedin area. There are isolated records from near Nelson, Kaikoura, near Christchurch, Invercargill and Stewart Island. A separate population became established in Auckland before 1920; they spread northwards to reach Wellsford and Leigh in the early 1940s, and by 1970 had spread throughout Northland and to many offshore islands in the Hauraki Gulf. They have also spread southwards into the Waikato and Taranaki in the west and to the Coromandel and Bay of Plenty in the east. Another population became established in the Wellington area in the 1960s, and they have since spread northwards along the foothills of the ranges into the Horowhenua and Manawatu in the west and to the Wairarapa and Hawke's Bay in the east. Isolated records from Gisborne. They favour open or lightly timbered country, such as farmland with scattered totara, and orchards, but may also occupy dense native forest.

Population: Common in many parts of the North Island, especially Northland, Auckland, Coromandel Peninsula, eastern Wairarapa and the Hutt Valley.

Breeding: Nests are mostly in cavities in tree trunks or branches, but where large trees are absent, they use the crowns of tree ferns. They lay 4–5–6–7 white eggs (27 x 22mm) in October–February. The female alone incubates for 18–22 days, and the fledging period is 28–36 days. The female is fed by the male during incubation and for the first few weeks of brooding, and she feeds the young chicks. Older chicks are fed by both parents, and after fledging, they remain with their parents for several months.

Behaviour: Gregarious when not breeding; often in small flocks of 5–25 birds. Their usual call, often uttered in flight, is a loud, ringing, bell-like 'kwink', sometimes a single note, but usually repeated two or three times. Other calls are a loud 'chitty-chew', and a strident screech when alarmed. Their flight is undulating, steady wingbeats alternating with long glides, often ending in an upward swoop into a tree.
Feeding: Diet includes a wide range of seeds, fruits, flowers, buds, shoots and occasional insects, especially case moths. Seeds are often taken on or near the ground, e.g. Scotch thistles in paddocks. They have been reported to cause some minor damage to citrus fruit and kiwifruit in Northland, and occasionally eat tomatoes, apples and other orchard fruit.
Reading: Fleming, C. A. 1944. *Notornis* 1: 60. Galbraith, J. A. 2010. MSc thesis, Uni Auckland. Hamel, J. 1970. *Notornis* 17: 126–129. Woon, J. A. et al. 2002. *Notornis* 49: 91–94. Wright, D. 2001. MSc thesis, Uni Auckland. Wright, D. & Clout, M. N. 2001. *DOC Sci Int Ser* 18. Wellington: DOC.

300. RED-CROWNED PARAKEET *Cyanoramphus novaezelandiae* PLATE 69

Other name: Kakariki
Size: Male 28cm, 80g; female 25cm; 70g
Geographical variation: Of five subspecies, two are extinct (*subflavescens* of Lord Howe Island and *erythrotis* of Macquarie Island), and the other three subspecies are in New Zealand: the Kermadec Parakeet *cyanurus* breeds in the Kermadec Islands; the Red-crowned Parakeet *novaezelandiae* breeds on the main islands, many offshore islands, and at the Auckland Islands; and the Chatham Island Red-crowned Parakeet *chathamensis* breeds in the Chatham Islands.
Distribution: Now New Zealand only. Kermadec Parakeets are common on the Herald Islets and have become common on Raoul Island since cats and rats were eradicated; common on Macauley Island. In the North and South islands, Red-crowned Parakeets formed mixed flocks with Yellow-crowned Parakeets, and were an occasional serious pest of crops, orchards and gardens in the 1870s and 1880s, but with the introduction of ship rats and stoats they became rare. In the North Island, a few are now found naturally in heavy forest of western Northland, the central North Island and the Ruahine Ranges, and vagrants visit bush patches along the eastern coast of Northland from nearby islands; they are common on many offshore islands from the Three Kings, through the Hauraki Gulf to the Bay of Plenty, and on Kapiti Island. Successfully introduced to Tiritiri Matangi, Motuihe, Cuvier, Moutohora (Whale) and Matiu/Somes islands, and to Zealandia in Wellington. Recently transferred to Tawharanui Sanctuary (North Auckland) and to Cape Kidnappers. Now largely gone from the South Island, although a few may persist in Nelson, the Catlins and South Westland. Widespread on Stewart Island and its outliers; vagrant to The Snares. Common at the Auckland Islands, except for Auckland Island itself. Chatham Island Red-crowned Parakeets are moderately common in the southwest of Chatham Island and on Pitt Island, scarce elsewhere on Chatham Island and on Mangere and Little Mangere islands, but abundant on South East Island.
Population: Common to abundant on many offshore islands free of predatory mammals. Very rare on the mainland apart from introduced populations in sanctuaries, and local dispersal from sanctuaries and from adjacent offshore islands.
Conservation: Protected endemic. Red-crowned Parakeets are particularly susceptible to mammalian predators (especially cats, stoats and ship rats) because they often feed on the ground and nest in holes close to the ground. They are secure and stable on many island reserves; however, the Macauley Island population of Kermadec Parakeet fell by 90–95% over two months from *c.* 20,000 in September 1988 to less than 2000 in November 1988 as a result of a drought, but they had recovered to *c.* 3500 by 2002.
Breeding: Red-crowned Parakeets favour holes in branches and trunks of trees, particularly decaying trees, but they also use crevices in cliffs or among rocks, burrows in the ground or densely matted vegetation. Most eggs are laid in October–December, but re-laying can continue through to March. They lay 4–**7**–9 white eggs (26 x 21mm, 6g) which the female incubates for 23–**24**–25 days. These are usually laid daily at the start, but the interval increases through the clutch to up to a 3–4-day interval between the final eggs. Because incubation starts after about the fourth egg is laid, hatching is highly asynchronous and there is considerable variation in the age and size of chicks within a brood. During incubation, and for the first 14 days of brooding, the male calls the female off the nest and feeds her by regurgitation. Both sexes feed the older chicks. The fledging period is 36–**41**–49 days, but sometimes the

chicks leave the nest earlier and are fed on the ground before they can fly. First breed at less than a year old.
Behaviour: Usually solitary or in pairs, and defend the area around their nest, however, in autumn and winter they form small flocks. Non-migratory, though they may fly long distances to get to good sources of food or fresh water. In flight, they make a loud, rapid chatter: 'ki-ki-ki-ki-ki'. Silent or chatter and babble when feeding.
Feeding: Mainly herbivorous. Diet varies seasonally and includes seeds of many kinds (particularly flax, beech, sedges, grasses, tussocks, *Mariscus* and *Muehlenbeckia*), fruits (particularly *Coprosma*, ngaio and *Solanum*), flower buds, flowers, nectar, leaves, shoots; also invertebrates especially during breeding. They often feed on the ground rather than in the canopy.
Reading: Bellingham, M. 1987. *Notornis* 34: 234–236. Boon, W. M. et al. 2001. *Bird Cons Intl* 10: 211–239. Dawe, M. R. 1979. MSc thesis, Uni Auckland. Greene, T. C. 1998. *NZ J Ecol* 22: 161–171. Greene, T. C. 2003. *Notornis* 50: 83–99. Nixon, A. J. 1994. *Notornis* 41(S): 5–18. Sagar, P. M. 1988. *Notornis* 35: 1–8. Taylor, R. H. 1975. *Notornis* 22: 110–121.

301. YELLOW-CROWNED PARAKEET *Cyanoramphus auriceps* PLATE 69

Other name: Kakariki
Size: Male 25cm, 50g; female 23cm; 40g
Distribution: New Zealand only, breeding widely on the main islands and many offshore islands. They favour podocarp forest and beech forest on the mainland, and forest and taller scrub on offshore islands. Mixed flocks with Red-crowned Parakeets were an occasional serious pest of crops, orchards and gardens in the 1870s and 1880s; but with the introduction of ship rats and stoats they became uncommon. In the North Island, they are now mainly in forested areas across the centre from Taranaki through the King Country and the Urewera to the Raukumara Range, and in the Tararua and Rimutaka ranges; also on some offshore islands, including the Three Kings, Hen and Chickens, Little Barrier and Great Barrier, and successfully introduced to Mana Island. In the South Island, they are widespread: western Marlborough (including Chetwode and Titi islands, and successfully transferred to Motuara and Long islands), Nelson, Westland, inland North Canterbury, western Otago, the Catlins and Fiordland. They are on Codfish Island, and Stewart Island and its outliers. In the Auckland Islands, they are common on the main Auckland Island but outnumbered by the Red-crowned Parakeet on the other islands.
Population: Yellow-crowned Parakeets are widespread but uncommon throughout, even on predator-free islands.
Conservation: Protected endemic. Yellow-crowned Parakeets are susceptible to mammalian predators (especially cats, stoats and ship rats) because they sometimes feed on the ground and nest in holes, but have probably survived better on the mainland than Red-crowned Parakeets because they generally have more arboreal feeding and nesting sites. They are probably secure on island reserves, but they are nowhere common and are well outnumbered by Red-crowned Parakeets.
Breeding: Yellow-crowned Parakeets favour holes in branches and trunks of trees, particularly holes in mature or old trees. Eggs can be laid at almost any time of year, but mostly in October–December. They lay 2–**5**–**6**–9 white eggs (23 x 19mm). The female alone incubates for 18–20 days starting part-way through the clutch. During incubation and early stages of brooding, she is called from the nest and is fed by the male. Both sexes feed the older chicks by regurgitation. The fledging period is 37–47 days.
Behaviour: Usually solitary or in pairs, but in autumn and winter they form small flocks. In flight, they make a rapid high-pitched chatter: 'ki-ki-ki-ki-ki'. Silent or chatter and babble when feeding. On Little Barrier, a frequent call of males, perhaps territorial, is a loud 'err-e-e'.
Feeding: Diet varies seasonally, but is dominated for most of the year by invertebrates (particularly scale insects, leaf miners and aphids), flower buds and flowers (especially of kanuka, rata and beech) and seeds (especially beech). Leaves, shoots and fruits are also taken as they become seasonally available. They feed in the canopy rather than on the ground, and often follow mixed feeding flocks led by Whiteheads in the North Island and Yellowheads in the South Island.
Reading: Boon, W. M. et al. 2000. *Bird Cons Intl* 10: 211–239. Kearvell, J. C. et al. 2003. *Notornis* 50: 27–35. Elliott, G. P. et al. 1996. *NZ J Zool* 23: 249–265. Elliott, G. P. et al. 1996. *NZ J Zool* 23: 267–278. Greene, T. C. 1988. MSc thesis, Uni Auckland. Kearvell, J. C. et al. 2003. *Notornis* 50: 27–35. Kearvell, J. C. et al. 2003. *Notornis* 50: 27–35. Nixon, A. J. 1994. *Notornis* 41(S): 5–18.

302. ORANGE-FRONTED PARAKEET *Cyanoramphus malherbi* PLATE 69

Other name: Kakariki
Size: Male 22cm, 45g; female 20cm; 35g
Distribution: New Zealand only. Formerly found throughout the North and South islands, but now found naturally in only three beech forest valleys in inland Canterbury: South Hurunui, Poulter and Hawdon. Captive-reared birds have been introduced to Chalky Island (2005–07), Maud Island (2007–08), Mayor Island (2009–11) and Blumine Island, Marlborough Sounds (2011–12).
Population: Probably 500–600 birds in the wild, and increasing.
Conservation: Protected endangered endemic. It has been long debated whether the Orange-fronted Parakeet was just a colour morph or subspecies of the Yellow-crowned Parakeet, however, genetic data and field observations of assortative mating where the two forms overlap has established that they are separate species. Being hole-nesters, Orange-fronted Parakeets are susceptible to mammalian predators, especially ship rats and stoats which are irruptive following periodic mast seeding of beech. They survive in the wild because of intensive predator control and nest site protection programmes. They have bred well in captivity.
Breeding: Orange-fronted Parakeets favour holes in branches and trunks of trees, particularly holes in mature or old red beech trees, and in standing dead trees. Eggs can be laid at almost any time of year, but mostly in December–April. They can have up to four clutches in a year, especially in years when beech seed is abundant. They lay 1–7–10 white eggs (24 x 19mm) at 2-day intervals. The female alone incubates for 21–26 days starting part-way through the clutch. She is called from the nest and is fed by the male during incubation and the early stages of brooding. Both sexes feed the older chicks by regurgitation. The fledging period is 35–45 days. If the pair re-nests, the male tends the chicks and also provides food for the incubating female.
Behaviour: Usually solitary or in pairs, but in autumn and winter they form small flocks. In flight, they make a rapid high-pitched chatter: 'ki-ki-ki-ki-ki'. Silent or chatter and babble when feeding.
Feeding: Diet varies seasonally, but includes seeds, fruit, flower buds and flowers, and invertebrates, especially scale insects and caterpillars. Compared with Yellow-crowned Parakeets, they feed more on invertebrates, and in lower layers of the forest and on the ground.
Reading: Boon, W. M. et al. 2000. *Bird Cons Intl* 10: 211–239. Kearvell, J. C. 2002. *Notornis* 49: 261–263. Kearvell, J. C. et al. 2002. *NZ J Ecol* 26: 139–148. Kearvell, J. C. et al. 2003. *Notornis* 50: 27–35. Nixon, A. J. 1991. *Notornis* 28: 292–300. Taylor, R. H. et al. 1986. *Notornis* 33: 17–22.

303. FORBES' PARAKEET *Cyanoramphus forbesi* PLATE 69

Other name: Chatham Islands Yellow-crowned Parakeet
Size: Male 28cm, 80g; female 26cm, 70g
Distribution: New Zealand only. Assumed to have been throughout forested parts of the Chatham Islands, but subfossil parakeets cannot be distinguished to species level. Now resident on Little Mangere and Mangere islands, and vagrants occasionally reach Pitt, South East and Chatham islands.
Population: In the 1970s, the population was only 50–60 birds, mostly on Little Mangere Island. By 2002 they had recovered to *c.* 800 birds, mainly living on Mangere Island.
Conservation: Protected endangered endemic. Forbes' Parakeet is susceptible to mammalian predators (especially cats and ship rats) which caused their demise on all but Little Mangere Island. Between the early 1900s and late 1960s, Forbes' Parakeets were virtually confined to 10ha Little Mangere Island. With the disappearance of feral cats, and subsequent removal of stock and the resultant flush of vegetation, Mangere Island was colonised by Forbes' Parakeets in the early 1970s; however, in this artificial environment they hybridised with the much more numerous Chatham Islands Red-crowned Parakeet. Since the mid-1970s, conservation effort has concentrated on removing hybrids and keeping the Red-crowned Parakeet population at less than about 10% of the total parakeet population on the island, and this will continue until the habitat improves sufficiently to allow the usual habitat segregation between these two species. A massive tree planting programme, and the provision of nest boxes, is increasing the forested area suitable for Forbes' Parakeets.
Breeding: Forbes' Parakeets favour holes in branches and trunks of trees, particularly holes in mature or old trees, but they readily use nest boxes, and will nest in rock crevices and under dense vegetation. Eggs are

laid October–March. They lay 1–**5–6**–10 white eggs (23.5 x 19mm). The female alone incubates for 20–**22**–26 days, starting after the second egg is laid, which results in varied sizes and ages of chicks in a brood. The female is called from the nest and is fed by the male during incubation and during the first couple of weeks of brooding; thereafter, both parents feed the chicks by regurgitation. The fledging period is 32–**39**–49 days.
Behaviour: Usually solitary or in pairs, but in autumn and winter they form small flocks. In flight, they make a rapid high-pitched chatter: 'ki-ki-ki-ki-ki'. Silent or chatter and babble when feeding.
Feeding: Prefer mature and dense seral (young) forest to more open habitats. Diet varies seasonally, but includes seeds, fruit, flower buds and flowers, and invertebrates. They generally feed in the canopy rather than on the ground.
Reading: Boon, W. M. et al. 2000. *Bird Cons Intl* 10: 211–239. Chan, C. -H. et al. 2006. *Cons Genetics* 7: 493–506. Greene, T. C. 1989. *Notornis* 36: 326–327. Kearvell, J. C. et al. 2003. *Notornis* 50: 27–35. Nixon, A. J. 1994. *Notornis* 41(S): 5–18.

304. ANTIPODES ISLANDS PARAKEET *Cyanoramphus unicolor* PLATE 69

Size: Male 32cm, 160g; female 29cm, 130g
Distribution: New Zealand only. Confined to Antipodes Island and its associated islets, including Bollons Island. They are most numerous in tall, dense tussocks and sedges, especially on lower parts of the islands, on steep slopes and along watercourses.
Population: 2000–3000 birds.
Conservation: Protected endemic. At present there are no threats, but, with their very restricted natural range, they would be soon threatened if rats ever got to the Antipodes. They adapt readily to captivity and some are held in collections.
Breeding: They nest in well-drained burrows in fibrous peat beneath vegetation, or in the thick, matted bases of tall tussocks. The burrow is often over a metre deep. Eggs are laid in October–January. In captivity, they lay 5–6 white eggs (27 x 23mm, 7.7g). The only clutch in the wild had five eggs, but because only 1–3 newly fledged young are usually seen, the mean clutch may be smaller. In captivity, the female alone incubates for *c.* 28 days. The male helps by feeding the female while incubating and brooding, and feeds older chicks by regurgitation. The young probably start breeding at 1 year old. They are probably quite long-lived; of 38 birds banded on Antipodes Island in 1969, 2 were recaptured 10 years later.
Behaviour: Solitary or in pairs or family groups. They are sedentary and, although they can fly well, they prefer to walk and climb through the vegetation, especially when feeding. With care, they can be approached closely. Their calls are similar to those of other parakeets, but are distinctly lower-pitched.
Feeding: They feed mainly on tussock and sedge leaves, holding them in one foot and chewing towards the tip, extracting the juices. They also eat seeds, buds, berries and flowers, and fossick round the colonies of Rockhopper and Erect-crested Penguins for scraps of fat left on skua-killed penguin and petrel carcasses, and for remains of broken eggs. Unusually, some kill and eat Grey-backed Storm Petrels.
Reading: Greene, T. C. 1999. *Notornis* 46: 301–310. Taylor, R. H. 1975. *Notornis* 22: 110–121. Warham, J. & Bell, B. D. 1979. *Notornis* 26: 121–169.

305. REISCHEK'S PARAKEET *Cyanoramphus hochstetteri* PLATE 69

Other name: Antipodes Islands Red-crowned Parakeet
Size: male 28cm, 125g; female 26cm, 95g
Distribution: New Zealand only. Confined to the Antipodes Islands; common on more open parts of the central plateau and around the coast of Antipodes Island, and on Bollons Island; fewer on Archway, Windward and Leeward islands.
Population: 4000–5000 birds.
Conservation: Protected endemic. Their population appears to be stable, but may benefit from the proposed removal of mice, which presumably compete for seeds.
Breeding: Reischek's Parakeets nest in burrows at the base of tussocks and ferns. Most eggs are laid in November–December. Breeding is poorly known, but like other parakeets, the female alone incubates. The fledging period is 32–**39**–49 days.
Behaviour: Usually solitary or in pairs, and defend the area around their nest; however, in autumn and winter they form small flocks which gather at good sources of food or fresh water. In flight, they make a loud, rapid

chatter: 'ki-ki-ki-ki-ki'. Silent or chatter and babble when feeding.
Feeding: Mainly herbivorous. Diet varies seasonally and includes seeds of sedge and tussocks; leaves of tussocks, *Anisotome* and *Colobanthus*; leaf buds and berries of *Coprosma*; occasional invertebrates and carrion from dead seabirds. They often feed on the ground.
Reading: Greene, T. C. 1999. *Notornis* 46: 301–310.

CUCKOOS *Cuculidae*

About 144 species worldwide; 2 endemic and 4 vagrants to New Zealand.

Most cuckoos are parasitic, laying their eggs in nests of other insectivorous bird species, and then letting the host pair rear their young, fledging often well after it is capable of flying well. Cuckoos lay their eggs while the host's clutch is being formed, or a day or two after completion of that clutch. The cuckoo removes one of the host's eggs with its bill and replaces it with one of its own. The cuckoo egg develops very rapidly and usually hatches first. The cuckoo chick then ejects all other eggs and chicks from the nest, or simply dominates the smaller chicks and they starve to death. Young cuckoos make persistent, high-pitched begging calls even after leaving the nest, and this stimulates its foster parents and other birds of the same or different species to feed it, thus causing confusion about the true identity of the foster parents.

Cuckoos are strong fliers, and most migrate between temperate breeding territories and tropical wintering grounds. During the breeding season, they are conspicuously vocal, but at other times they remain silent and cryptic.
Reading: Erritzøe, J. et al. 2012. *Cuckoos of the World.* London: Christopher Helm.

306. ORIENTAL CUCKOO *Cuculus optatus* PLATE 70

Size: 33cm, 100g
Distribution: Breeds in central and eastern Asia from Himalayas and western Siberia to Japan, parasitising nests of warblers and flycatchers. In September, they migrate south to winter from southern India eastwards to the Philippines, New Guinea, the Solomon Islands and northern and eastern Australia. A few birds straggle to New Zealand, with a total of about 35 records from Raoul Island to The Snares, all in October–April.
Behaviour: Oriental Cuckoos are usually seen in open areas with trees, such as willows along riverbanks, trees around farmhouses, or near a forest edge. They typically perch on a branch or post and make repeated forays to catch insects and earthworms from the ground nearby. They are generally silent in New Zealand, but a bird on Little Barrier Island uttered a quiet, regular 'tsoo-tsoo-tsoo' about a dozen times at 1-second intervals.

307. PALLID CUCKOO *Cuculus pallidus* PLATE 70

Size: 32cm, 85g
Distribution: Breeds in southwestern, southern and eastern Australia, including Tasmania, parasitising open-nesting species such as honeyeaters and flycatchers. After breeding, they move northwards to central and northern Australia, New Guinea and the western parts of Indonesia. A rare vagrant to New Zealand, with only seven records: Craig Flat, Otago (one bird seen in May–October 1939, 1940 and 1941); Okarito (December 1941); Greymouth (March 1942); Wairarapa (1977); Omarama, North Otago (January 1990); Riverton, Southland (1998); Wellington (November 2006).
Behaviour: In New Zealand, Pallid Cuckoos have usually been seen perched on power poles or fenceposts in open country, then gliding down to the ground to catch insects and earthworms. The first bird recorded in New Zealand appeared on the same farm for three years in a row during the non-breeding season. The distinctive call of the male is a monotonously repeated phrase, consisting of an ascending and accelerating series of melancholy notes: 'too too . . . too too'. The female utters a hoarse 'kheer'.
Reading: Marples, B. J. 1942. *Notornis* 2: 10–11.

308. FAN-TAILED CUCKOO *Cacomantis flabelliformis* PLATE 70

Size: 26cm, 60g

Geographical variation: Five subspecies. The Australian subspecies *flabelliformis*, which parasitises mainly dome-nesting species such as thornbills and scrub-wrens, strays to New Zealand.

Distribution: Breeds in southern and eastern Australia, including Tasmania; New Guinea, Solomons, Vanuatu, New Caledonia and Fiji, parasitising mainly dome-nesting species but also some cup-nesting ones. After breeding, some Australian birds migrate northwards, but many remain sedentary or become nomadic. Very rare vagrant to New Zealand. Six records, including a small invasion in 1991: Lyttelton Harbour (subadult female killed by a cat in June 1960); Wanaka (September 1991); Haast (October 1991); Karikari Peninsula, Northland (October 1991); Culverden, North Canterbury (December 1999); Maungatoroto, Northland (September 2010).

Behaviour: Fan-tailed Cuckoos often perch on low branches, power poles or fenceposts in open country or open forest, then glide down to the ground to hop around in search of insects and earthworms. On landing on a perch, they typically cock and fan their tail. Their call is a repeated phrase consisting of a rapid descending trill.

309. SHINING CUCKOO *Chrysococcyx lucidus* PLATE 70

Other name: Pipiwharauroa

Size: 16cm, 25g

Geographical variation: Four subspecies are currently recognised, of which the nominate *lucidus* breeds in New Zealand.

Distribution: Breeds in southwestern and eastern Australia (including Tasmania), Vanuatu, New Caledonia and New Zealand. In New Zealand, they breed throughout the mainland and offshore islands, mainly in scrub and forest habitats (to about 1200m asl) where Grey Warblers, their main host species, live, but they are also heard in suburban gardens. A few Shining Cuckoos reach the Chathams each summer, and stragglers have reached the Kermadecs, The Snares, Auckland Islands and Rarotonga. In March, they migrate north to winter in western Indonesia, New Guinea and the Bismarck Archipelago (New Britain, New Ireland and Bougainville) and the Solomons. It is believed that many New Zealand birds migrate through eastern Australia to or from their wintering grounds in the Bismarck Archipelago and the Solomons, but many are recorded on passage at Lord Howe Island, which suggests that some take a more direct route. A few birds overwinter in New Zealand, especially in the northern North Island, but they remain quiet and inconspicuous in winter. Shining Cuckoos return to New Zealand in September and early October, and adults return to the same site year after year.

Population: Widespread and locally common. Adults are especially conspicuous in late spring and early summer; fledglings are very conspicuous in late summer.

Conservation: Protected native. Numbers appear to be moderately stable, because their main host, the Grey Warbler, has adapted well to human settlement in New Zealand. Continuing clearance of large tracts of subtropical rainforest at the wintering grounds of Shining Cuckoos could, however, have a severe impact.

Breeding: Like other cuckoos, Shining Cuckoos parasitise other breeding birds by laying in nests of other species, and so take no part in the incubation of their eggs or in raising their young. Despite anecdotal reports of a wide variety of birds, the only good evidence is that Grey Warblers are the host species on the mainland, and the Chatham Islands Warbler is the host on the Chathams. Shining Cuckoos return to the same general area each year and establish a territory that encompasses several Grey Warbler territories. The male frequently feeds his partner during the spring, and the birds are often seen together. Shining Cuckoos lay their eggs in the dome-shaped nest of Grey Warblers by entering head first, taking a host egg in their bill, laying their own egg, and then backing out. This usually happens a few days either side of the host clutch being completed and incubation starting. Shining Cuckoos also pull Grey Warbler chicks from nests, perhaps to stimulate re-nesting, and so provide an opportunity to parasitise the new nest.

Eggs are laid from mid-October to mid-January, usually into the second, late or replacement clutches of Grey Warblers, whose first clutch is usually laid in September before Shining Cuckoos arrive back from their wintering grounds. The olive-green egg (18.5 x 12.5mm, 1.8g), which is slightly larger than those of the Grey Warbler and stands out clearly by its different colour, hatches after 14–**15**–17 days, *c.* 4 days faster than those of the host. When the cuckoo chick is 3–**4**–7 days old, it evicts the other Grey Warbler eggs or chicks in the nest and is then raised alone. Fledging period is **19**–21 days, and the fledgling begs incessantly – 'eee-eee-eee' – and is fed by both Grey Warblers for at least 4 weeks, before becoming independent. Juvenile Shining Cuckoos migrate to winter in the tropics, and they possibly remain there until 2 years old, when they have been recorded back in their natal area.

Behaviour: The arrival of Shining Cuckoos in spring is often heralded by clear, descending 'tsee-ew' calls heard at night as birds fly overhead. They advertise their territory in spring with a loud and far-carrying, highly distinctive song: 'coo-ee coo-ee . . . coo-ee', usually repeated 10–20 times, followed by one or two descending notes: 'tsee-ew'. They become silent after December, their continued presence known only from occasional sightings and as a relatively common casualty from flying into windows. Although usually a solitary bird, small groups sometimes gather in spring and summer to display excitedly with wing-flicking and uttering trilling notes and the descending 'tsee-ew' notes from the territorial song. Large pre-migratory flocks of several hundred birds have been reported in autumn.

Feeding: Diet is mainly invertebrates, especially the small green caterpillars that feed on kowhai leaves and the black hairy caterpillars of the Magpie Moth *Nyctemera annulata*; Shining Cuckoos are often killed by cats among the cinerarias.

Reading: Briskie, J. V. 2007. *Notornis* 54: 15–19. Gill, B. J. 1982. *Notornis* 29: 215–227. Gill, B. J. 1983. *Ibis* 125: 40–55. Gill, B. J. 1983. *NZ J Zool* 10: 371–381.

310. LONG-TAILED CUCKOO *Eudynamys taitensis* PLATE 70

Other names: Koekoea, Long-tailed Koel (Australia), Karavia (Cook Islands)

Size: 40cm, 125g

Distribution: Breeds in New Zealand only. Long-tailed Cuckoos breed throughout forests of the mainland, and on forested offshore islands such as Little Barrier, Kapiti, Codfish and Stewart. Stragglers have reached the Chathams, The Snares and Auckland Islands. In December–April, they migrate to winter in the tropical Pacific in an arc from the Bismarck Archipelago and Micronesia in the west to the Marquesas and Tuamotu islands of French Polynesia in the east, but mainly to the east of Fiji. Some migrate through the Kermadecs and Lord Howe Island, a few pass through Norfolk Island and there have been unconfirmed records on the eastern coast of Australia. Adults migrate a couple of months before the juveniles. A few adults appear in the Cook Islands in late December, but most do not arrive until March. Juveniles migrate north in April–May and apparently remain in their Pacific wintering grounds during their first summer.

In New Zealand, the breeding distribution is governed by the distribution of the host species – the Whitehead in the North Island, and the Yellowhead and Brown Creeper in the South Island – however, during migration, birds are heard well away from the range of these species (e.g. Northland and Manawatu). A few birds overwinter in New Zealand, especially in the northern North Island, but they remain quiet and inconspicuous. Adult Long-tailed Cuckoos return to New Zealand in early October, and adults return to the same site year after year.

Population: Widespread and sometimes moderately common, especially conspicuous in late spring and early summer.

Conservation: Protected endemic. The numbers of Long-Tailed Cuckoos in New Zealand are probably declining in line with the decline of the host species (especially Yellowheads) on the mainland. Clearance of subtropical rainforest in parts of their wintering range could have an impact on the numbers of Long-tailed Cuckoos visiting New Zealand.

Breeding: Like other cuckoos, Long-tailed Cuckoos lay their eggs in nests of other species, and take no part in the incubation of their eggs or in raising their young. Despite anecdotal reports of their eggs being laid in the nests of a wide variety of birds, including Robins, Fantails, Silvereyes and Tomtits, clearly the main host species are the Whitehead in the North Island, Yellowhead in the South Island, and the Brown Creeper in the South, Codfish and Stewart islands. Banding has shown that Long-tailed Cuckoos return to the same general area each year. Little is known of the social behaviour of Long-tailed Cuckoos, but they may have a lek-type breeding system, because groups of adults (possibly males) gather to call and Long-tailed Cuckoos are not encountered in simple pairs.

Laying is mainly from mid-November to mid-December. They lay a single creamy-white or very pale pink egg (23 x 17mm) covered in brownish blotches.

It is noticeably larger than those of the host but is usually accepted. The incubation period is estimated to be *c.* 16 days. The cuckoo chick evicts the host's eggs and chicks and is then raised alone. The fledging period is estimated to be *c.* 21 days, and the fledgling begs incessantly and is then fed by both foster parents and their helpers for at least 4 weeks, before the young becomes independent. Juvenile Long-tailed Cuckoos migrate to winter in the tropics and probably remain there until at least 2 years old.
Behaviour: The arrival of Long-tailed Cuckoos in late spring is often heralded by their harsh, piercing, long drawn-out shriek – 'zzwheesht' – heard at night as birds migrate southward. This is also the typical daytime call during the breeding season, but they also give a loud, rapid, ringing chatter: 'zip, zip, zip, zip' or 'rrrp pe-pe-pe-pe-pe'. When calling, they usually sit on a high perch in the canopy. When giving the shriek call in combination with the chatter call, they often display by fanning their tail, slowly flapping their wings and adopting a hunched posture. Several birds (possibly males) gather in a tight group only a few metres apart as they display, and others (possibly females) watch from 20–30m away. Long-tailed Cuckoos continue to call into January and February, well after breeding has finished, and they are also vocal during their northward migration. They are a relatively common casualty from flying into windows.
Feeding: Diet is mainly large invertebrates such as weta, stick insects, spiders, beetles and bugs. Skinks, geckos, small birds, eggs, nestlings, berries and fruit are also taken.
Reading: Gill, B. J. & Hauber, M. 2012. *Emu* 112: 326–332. Gill, B. J. & Hauber, M. E. 2013. *Notornis* 60: 158–170. McLean, I. G. 1988. *Notornis* 35: 89–98.

311. CHANNEL-BILLED CUCKOO *Scythrops novaehollandiae* PLATE 70

Size: 61cm, 700g
Distribution: Breeds in northern and eastern Australia, parasitising nests of magpies, crows and currawongs. After breeding, they migrate north to winter in eastern Indonesia, New Guinea and the Bismarck Archipelago. Rare vagrant to New Zealand, with seven records including a minor influx in 1996: Invercargill (December 1924); Aupouri Peninsula, Northland (October 1986 to January 1987); Raglan (October 1996); Te Paki, Far North (October 1996); Pukerua Bay, Wellington (November 1996); Mangawhai Heads, Northland (October 2002), Motiti Island and Tauranga (January 2007).
Behaviour: Channel-billed Cuckoos are usually found in open country with scattered trees. In Australia, they fly with slowly flapping wings in small noisy groups and are often harassed by corvids. They have a loud, melodious trumpet call.
Reading: Tennyson, A. J. D. & Brackenbury, G. 1998. *Notornis* 45: 223–226.

TYPICAL OWLS *Strigidae*

223 species worldwide; 1 extinct species that was endemic to New Zealand, 1 native and 1 introduced.

Owls are mainly nocturnal birds of prey, although overseas some species hunt by day. They have a large head and very flexible neck, so that the whole of the head can be rotated through 270° to look for prey at the side or the rear. The large eyes, directed forward as in humans, give good binocular vision in low-intensity light. The yellow eyes are set in a brown circular disc of feathers. This facial disc helps to direct sound to the large ear openings. The bill is short and hooked. Legs are well feathered, except for the bare powerful feet with needle-sharp talons. Their plumage is soft and cryptically coloured, and wing feathers have softened edges to allow silent flight. They specialise in catching rodents, small birds and large insects. Prey is usually eaten whole, and the indigestible parts are regurgitated in a sausage-shaped pellet, lined with bones and hard pieces and coated with fur and feathers. Their eggs are white and usually laid in a hollow tree or crevice.
Reading: Burton, J. A. 1973. *Owls of the World: Their Evolution, Structure and Ecology*. Netherlands: Lowe. Hollands, D. 1991. *Birds of the Night: Owls, Frogmouths and Nightjars*. Balgowah, NSW: Reed. Konig, C. et al. 2008. *Owls: A Guide to the Owls of the World*. London: Christopher Helm.

312. MOREPORK *Ninox novaeseelandiae* PLATE 71

Other names: Ruru, Boobook (Australia)
Size: 29cm, 175g
Geographical variation: Currently one species is recognised in Australasia, with multiple subspecies that are often confined to an island group; for example, the subspecies *albaria* formerly bred on Lord Howe Island, *undulata* breeds on Norfolk Island, and *novaeseelandiae* breeds in New Zealand.
Distribution: Australasia, including Timor, New Guinea, Australia and New Zealand. Moreporks are found throughout forested areas of the North, South and Stewart islands from sea level to the upper bushline, and on most larger forested offshore islands from Three Kings to islands off southern Stewart Island. Vagrants have reached The Snares. Widespread, but sparingly distributed in drier eastern areas, except moderately abundant on Banks Peninsula. They live in native and exotic forest and in open country with clumps of mature trees for shelter and nesting.
Population: Widespread and moderately common.
Conservation: Protected native. The subfossil records of Moreporks are all within the last 1000 years, perhaps indicating that they were scarce before human settlement of New Zealand. Although much forest was cleared by Maori and then by European settlers, their food supply may have been increased with the introduction of small mammals – the Pacific rat brought by Maori, and then mice, ship rats and Norway rats brought by Europeans.
Breeding: The nest site is usually in a hollow tree or branch, but sometimes in a clump of epiphytes, a cabbage tree, a pile of pine needles in a tree fork, on the ground under tree-fern fronds or a rock, in petrel burrows, or among the roots of pohutukawa. Laying is in September–February, mainly October–November. They lay 1–**2**–3 white eggs (38 x 34mm, 25g). The female alone incubates for 25–30 days but is called from the nest and fed by the male. The fledging period is 35–40 days. Both parents feed the young in the nest.
Behaviour: Moreporks roost in trees, preferably in gullies with plenty of shelter overhead for concealment, but they may still be found and mobbed by small birds. Their usual call is a clear 'more-pork'. Other calls include a monotonous, deep, repeated 'more-more-more. . .', and a repeated 'cree' when hunting. They rarely call during daylight, usually starting from dusk.
Feeding: Diet is mainly large insects such as weta and cicadas, and night-flying insects such as moths and huhu beetles, including those attracted to lights; also spiders, mice, young rats and small birds. When eating large prey, they hold it in one foot or stand on it with both feet and tear off pieces. Pellets of indigestible material are regurgitated and cast beneath their daytime perches.
Reading: Imboden, C. 1975. *Notornis* 22: 221–230. Lindsay, C. J. & Ordish, R. G. 1964. *Notornis* 11: 154–158. Stephenson, B. M. & Minot, E. O. 2006. *Notornis* 53: 308–315.

313. LAUGHING OWL *Sceloglaux albifacies* PLATE 84

Other name: Whekau
Size: 38cm, 600g
Geographical variation: Two subspecies: *rufifacies* of the North Island, and *albifacies* of the South Island and Stewart Island.
Distribution: Subfossil remains of the North Island subspecies are found at numerous sites, including swamps, caves, dunes and a few middens. There were only four records since European settlement: skins collected on Mt Taranaki (1854) and in the Wairarapa (1868), and sightings near Gisborne (1889) and near Porirua (before 1892). The southern subspecies is also widespread as subfossils, including a few midden records from the South and Stewart islands. In the mid-1800s, Laughing Owls were fairly common and reported widely from Nelson, Canterbury, Otago and Fiordland, and skins came from Stewart Island in about 1880. They seemed to prefer forest and scrub edges, and rocky places in open country such as limestone outcrops. They declined rapidly and were rare by 1880. The last known bird was found dead at Blue Cliffs, South Canterbury, in 1914.
Conservation: The rapid decline suggests predation by introduced mammals, finished off by the introduction of stoats and ferrets to control rabbits.
Breeding: A few nests, lined with dry grass, were found in deep, dry, crevices among rocks, mostly with such narrow entrances that birds had to be smoked out. The usual clutch was **2** white eggs (48 x 40mm), laid in September–October.
Behaviour: The calls of the Laughing Owl were described as 'a loud cry made up of a series of dismal shrieks frequently repeated' and 'a peculiar barking noise . . . just like the yelping of a young dog'.
Feeding: Cave deposits indicate their diet was mainly

birds, geckos, bats and rodents. Earthworms and insects such as beetles were also eaten.

Reading: Holdaway, R. N. & Worthy, T. H. 1996. *J Zool (Lond)* 239: 545–572. Tennyson, A. & Martinson, P. 2006. *Extinct Birds of New Zealand*. Wellington: Te Papa Press. Williams, G. R. & Harrison, M. 1972. *Notornis* 19: 4–19.

314. LITTLE OWL *Athene noctua* — PLATE 71

Other name: German Owl

Size: 23cm, 180g

Distribution: Natural range is continental Europe, northern Africa and western Asia. In an endeavour to control the numbers of small introduced birds, the Otago Acclimatisation Society imported 219 Little Owls from Germany between 1906 and 1910, and others were liberated in Canterbury about the same time. They are now widespread in farmland and towns in Nelson, Marlborough, Canterbury, Otago and Southland. A few are seen in Westland and Fiordland. No confirmed records from Stewart Island or the North Island since the 1950s. They live in hedgerows, haysheds, old farm buildings, clumps of trees; in daylight they often sun themselves on fenceposts, hedges, tree branches, roof ridges, and telegraph poles near old farm buildings.

Population: Widespread and moderately common in drier coastal areas of the eastern South Island.

Breeding: The usual nesting sites are holes in trees, old farm buildings, haystacks, stacks of hay bales, rabbit burrows, and banks, e.g. disused quarry walls. Most eggs are laid in October–November. They lay 2–**3–4**–5 white eggs (35 x 29mm), which the female alone incubates for *c.* 28 days. The fledging period is 30–35 days. The age of first breeding is 1 year, though not all breed then. The oldest bird banded in Britain lived to at least 10 years old.

Behaviour: Solitary. They are usually seen in the late afternoon sunning themselves rather than looking for food, or are disturbed from roosts in farm buildings or hedgerows. Their usual call, heard mostly in autumn and winter, is a clear, high-pitched 'kiew'. They bob up and down when alarmed. Their flight is undulating.

Feeding: Although introduced to control small birds that had become pests in orchards and cereal crops, their diet in New Zealand is mainly insects (caterpillars, beetles and earwigs), spiders and earthworms. They also take a few small birds, frogs, lizards, mice and rabbits. Little Owls often feed on the ground, walking and running freely, sometimes by day as well as at night.

Reading: Marples, B. J. 1942. *Trans Proc Roy Soc NZ* 72: 237–254.

BARN OWLS *Tytonidae*

27 species worldwide; 1 has colonised New Zealand recently, having previously been a vagrant.

The barn owls are mainly nocturnal birds of prey. They have a large head and very flexible neck, so that the whole of the head can be rotated to look for prey at the side or the rear. The large, dark eyes, directed forward as in humans, give good binocular vision in low-intensity light. The eyes are set in a white, heart-shaped disc of short feathers. This facial disc helps to direct sound to the large ear openings. The bill is short and hooked. Legs are well feathered, except for the bare powerful feet with needle-sharp talons. Unlike typical owls (Strigidae), the inner toe is as long as the middle toe, and the claw of the middle toe has comb-like serrations. Because their plumage is soft and wing feathers have softened edges, the flight of barn owls is silent. They specialise in catching rodents, small birds and large insects. Prey is usually eaten whole, and the indigestible parts are regurgitated in a sausage-shaped pellet, lined with bones and hard pieces and coated with fur and feathers. Their eggs are white and usually laid in a hollow tree or crevice.

Reading: Burton, J. A. 1973. *Owls of the World: Their Evolution, Structure and Ecology*. Netherlands: Lowe. Hollands, D. 1991. *Birds of the Night: Owls, Frogmouths and Nightjars*. Balgowah, NSW: Reed. Konig, C. et al. 2008. *Owls: A Guide to the Owls of the World*. London: Christopher Helm.

315. BARN OWL *Tyto alba* PLATE 71

Size: Male 30cm, 300g; female 35cm, 400g
Geographical variation: More than 30 subspecies, of which *delicatula* of Australia and the Solomon Islands is assumed to reach New Zealand.
Distribution: The landbird with the widest natural distribution, being found almost worldwide. They are widespread in mainland Australia but rare in Tasmania. Some vagrants naturally reach New Zealand: Barrytown (1947), Haast River mouth (1955), Runanga (1960), South Kaipara Head (1986), New Plymouth (1990), Waikato (2001) and Kaitaia (2008). Others are believed to have come from Australia or the South Pacific as stowaways in aircraft or ships: live birds at Papatoetoe, near Auckland Airport (1983), and at Whenuapai RNZAF Base (1992) – presumably the same bird was seen on Little Barrier Island 6 weeks later, and stayed 4 months; and at Lyttelton (2001).

In April 2008, an injured 7-month-old Barn Owl was found with its parents near Kaitaia. By the time of the discovery, this pair had already made several nesting attempts, dating back to spring 2007, and they have continued to breed twice a year through to at least 2013. Barn Owls have been seen up to 5.5km from the nest site, but no other pairs have been found.
Population: Only one pair known, but about 10 offspring from successful breeding may be alive and breeding.
Conservation: As a natural immigrant to New Zealand, the species is fully protected, and classified as a colonising native bird. Wingspan Birds of Prey Trust has provided nest boxes, and local farmers have controlled possums in the vicinity of the nest site.
Breeding: Barn Owls can breed at almost any time of the year. In New Zealand, recent fledglings have been seen in April, June, July, August, November and January, and it has been deduced that eggs have been laid twice a year, once in spring and once in late summer. They lay 2–3–4 white eggs (43 x 32mm) in a deep hole in a tree trunk. The nests in New Zealand have been about 11m up a dead puriri tree in open farmland with patches of scattered open forest. Incubation is by the female only, for 30–35 days. The fledging period is 45–55 days, but fledglings are fed for a similar length of time after first leaving the nest.
Behaviour: At night, Barn Owls are seen sitting upright on fenceposts or branches, or are caught in car headlight beams like a buoyant white ghost. Their call is a menacing, long-drawn-out, cat fight-like screech, 'skiirrr'.
Feeding: In New Zealand, their diet is typical in consisting of a mix of small rodents and birds. Numerically, mice are the main prey item, followed by introduced passerines and rats.
Reading: Gill, B. J. & Turbott, E. G. 1984. *Notornis* 31: 177–179. Hyde, N. et al. 2009. *Notornis* 56: 169–175.

SWIFTS *Apodidae*

92 species; 2 are stragglers to New Zealand.

The swifts are somewhat swallow-like in appearance and behaviour, but are not closely related at all, and are actually grouped with hummingbirds. Compared with swallows, swifts are larger and have long scythe-like wings and short tails. They are perhaps the most aerial of all birds, some landing only at their nest sites. They fly rapidly and wheel in broad arcs. In fine weather, they fly very high and so easily escape notice, but at dawn and dusk, and in poor weather, they often fly low over open water or around headlands, hilltops or stands of tall trees. They have short, broad bills that open extremely wide for catching aerial insects. Their feet are tiny and their toes all point forward, so swifts rest by clinging to the sides of trees, rocks or walls, not perched on branches, wires, or on the ground.
Reading: Chantler, P. 2000. *Swifts: A Guide to the Swifts and Treeswifts of the World.* London: Croom Helm.

316. SPINE-TAILED SWIFT *Hirundapus caudacutus* PLATE 72

Other names: White-throated Needletail, Needle-tailed Swift
Size: 20cm, 100g
Geographical variation: Two subspecies, of which *caudacutus* of northeastern Asia and Japan is a straggler to New Zealand.

Distribution: Breeds in eastern Asia from western Siberia to Korea and Japan, and south to Myanmar. The subspecies *caudacutus* migrates south through China and the Philippines to winter in New Guinea, Australia and Tasmania from October to April. In most years, a few overshoot their normal wintering grounds or are carried ahead of storm fronts to reach New Zealand. There are many records dating back to 1888, mainly from the North Island, but as far south as The Snares, and from the Chathams (2004). Most records are from mid-November to March, but a few have been seen as late as May. From time to time, invasions are considerable, the most notable being in 1942–43, when birds were reported from Northland to Stewart Island. In 1968–69, flocks appeared in Westland, and in February 1979, a flock of 60+ birds was seen in southern Otago.
Behaviour: Usually gregarious; small flocks circle hilltops, clifftops or stands of trees. Swifts fly rapidly and wheel around in sweeping glides as they catch insects in mid-air. They feed high in fine, calm weather, but in windy or stormy weather, or at dusk, they feed close to the ground and so are more easily seen.
Reading: McCaskill, L. W. 1943. *Notornis* 1: 38–40. Miller, P. 1980. *Notornis* 27: 44.

317. FORK-TAILED SWIFT *Apus pacificus* PLATE 72

Size: 18cm, 45g
Geographical variation: Four subspecies, of which *pacificus* of northeastern Asia and Japan is a straggler to New Zealand.
Distribution: Breeds in eastern Asia from Siberia to Korea and Japan, and from north India to Malaysia. The subspecies *pacificus* migrates south through China and the Philippines to winter in New Guinea, Australia and Tasmania from October to April. They occasionally reach New Zealand, probably carried along ahead of storm fronts. Since the first record of four birds in Taranaki in 1884, there have been about 20 records of Fork-tailed Swifts in New Zealand, from Northland to Campbell Island, and also at Pitt Island, Chathams (1991) and the Antipodes (2002). Mostly seen as single birds or small flocks in October–February, but others have been seen unexpectedly in May–September, when they are usually breeding in the Northern Hemisphere.
Behaviour: Usually seen alone or in small flocks circling hilltops or clifftops. Swifts fly rapidly and wheel around in sweeping glides as they catch insects in mid-air. They feed high in fine, calm weather, but in windy or stormy weather they feed close to the ground and so are more easily seen. They are usually quite vocal, with a shrill whistle or excited chattering.
Reading: Turbott, E. G. 1964. *Notornis* 11: 107–109.

KINGFISHERS *Halcyonidae*

About 86 species worldwide; 1 is native to New Zealand, and 1 is introduced but probably also a vagrant.

The kingfishers are generally brightly coloured birds with a plump body, short neck, tail and legs, a large head and a long, broad and dagger-like bill. Their flight is fast and direct. They often perch on posts, branches and powerlines and dart down to the ground, or dive into water, to catch their prey. Despite their name, kingfishers do not necessarily eat fish; some species are entirely terrestrial.

They nest in tree hollows or earth banks, which they excavate by repeatedly flying at the vertical surface and spearing it with their closed bill; the skull has special shock-absorbing structures to cushion the blows.

318. LAUGHING KOOKABURRA *Dacelo novaeguineae* PLATE 71

Other names: Kookaburra, Laughing Jackass
Size: 45cm, 350g
Geographical variation: Two subspecies: *minor* of Cape York Peninsula, and the more common *novaeguineae*, which is the subspecies in New Zealand.
Distribution: Despite the scientific name, this species

is native to Australia, not New Guinea. Laughing Kookaburras are common in eastern and southeastern Australia, and have been successfully introduced to southwestern Australia, Tasmania and New Zealand. Sir George Grey introduced them to Kawau Island in the Hauraki Gulf in the early 1860s. Introductions to Wellington, Nelson and Otago in the 1860s and 1870s did not establish. They are now found in open country and on forest margins from near Whangarei in the north to the Waitakere Ranges in the south. The main places where they are reported include: Glenbervie, Whangateau, Dome Valley, Warkworth, Kaukapakapa, Kawau Island, Puhoi, Wenderholm and Waiwera. Single birds reported elsewhere, from Waikato and Gisborne to Westland and Otago, are vagrants from Northland or, more likely, Australia.
Population: Scarce and with a limited distribution in New Zealand; probably fewer than 500 birds.
Breeding: Little New Zealand information. Pairs remain on territory all year; their young stay with them as helpers. The nest is in a tunnel bored in a rotten tree trunk, e.g. in a Phoenix palm at Wenderholm, or in a natural cavity in a pohutukawa. Eggs are laid in November–February. They lay 2–**3**–4 white eggs (44 x 33mm). The incubation period is *c.* 23 days, and the fledging period is 33–39 days. Chicks may be fed for several weeks after fledging. Laughing Kookaburras are long-lived; the oldest known in Australia lived over 13 years, but some probably live much longer.
Behaviour: Family groups roost and breed together. The common call is a loud, boisterous 'koo-hoo-hoo-hoo . . . hoo-hoo-ha-ha-ha-ha-ha', often uttered in undisciplined chorus by a family group. It is heard all year, mostly at dawn and dusk, and both advertises the territory and keeps the family together.
Feeding: Laughing Kookaburras sit rigidly on a prominent branch or post, bill pointing down, and suddenly swoop to the ground or into shallow water. They catch mainly earthworms, snails, insects, freshwater crayfish, frogs, lizards, rats, mice and small birds.
Reading: Parry, V. A. 1970. *Kookaburras*. Melbourne: Landsdowne Press. Parry, V. A. 1973. *Emu* 73: 81–100.

319. KINGFISHER *Todiramphus sanctus* — PLATE 71

Other names: Kotare, Sacred Kingfisher, New Zealand Kingfisher
Size: 24cm, 65g
Geographical variation: Of eight subspecies in Australia, New Caledonia, the Loyalty, Lord Howe, Norfolk and Kermadec islands and New Zealand, the New Zealand subspecies is *vagans*.
Distribution: Widespread on the Kermadecs, in the North, South and Stewart islands and on most offshore islands; vagrant to the Chathams (four records, 1985–2004), but not reported from any of the subantarctic islands. In the breeding season, they are common throughout the North Island and lowland South Island, except rare in Southland; scarce well inland in the eastern South Island. They occupy many habitats, especially bush patches near the coast, in tidal estuaries, and in mangrove swamps in the north. They also live in developed farmland with scattered trees, and breed inland along river and stream edges or by lake shores, along forest margins and well into forests, both native and exotic. In winter, most birds that breed at high altitude (500+m asl) or in forests move to lowland farms and the coasts of both islands, including Southland.
Population: Common and widespread, especially in coastal districts and lowlands in winter.
Conservation: Protected native. Although Kingfishers occasionally live well into forests, they have probably benefited from the clearance of forest and the creation of forest-edge habitats and riparian margins of willows and poplars along rivers and near lakes. Artificial structures such as powerlines and posts in estuaries are excellent elevated perches to hunt from.
Breeding: Kingfishers nest in rotten tree trucks, knot-holes or hollow branches, in the soil held by the roots of blown-over trees, in riverbanks, roadside cuttings, heads of slips, and coastal cliffs. The nest is in a chamber at the end of a short tunnel that slopes slightly upwards. To start a tunnel, they sit on a branch slightly above and several metres from the site and fly straight at it, neck outstretched and uttering a peculiar whirring call, and strike it forcefully with the bill tip. They continue until the hole is big enough to perch in, and the rest is pecked and scooped out. Eggs are laid in October–January. They lay 3–**5**–7 white eggs (29 x 24mm), which the female mostly incubates for 20–21 days. The chicks fledge at 26–27 days old, but are fed for another 7–10 days after leaving the nest.
Behaviour: Usually solitary or in pairs, spaced widely apart when breeding and when perching on posts or powerlines between feeding flights. Their usual call is a loud, penetrating 'kek-kek-kek-kek'.
Feeding: On tidal mudflats, diet is mainly small crabs,

especially *Helice crassa*; in fresh water, tadpoles, freshwater crayfish and small fish; in open country and forest, earthworms, large insects such as cicadas, weta, stick insects, dragonflies, chafers, wasps and beetles, spiders, lizards, mice and small birds, especially Silvereyes. They often perch for long periods on any elevated object such as a rock, post, powerline, driftwood or bare branch, especially those that overlook pasture or tidal mudflats. When a bird sees prey, it suddenly darts with a direct, descending flight, snatches its victim and immediately returns to its perch, carrying the food crosswise in its bill. Larger animals may be battered against the perch. Kingfishers regurgitate pellets of indigestible material below their perch and nest hole.

Reading: Fitzgerald, B. M. et al. 1986. *Notornis* 33: 23–32. Hayes, L. M. 1989. *Notornis* 36: 107–113.

ROLLERS *Coraciidae*

16 species worldwide; 1 reaches New Zealand as a vagrant.

Rollers are colourful birds of the tropics and subtropics, with a large head, plump body, short neck and legs, long wings and a wide, short, and slightly hooked bill. They spend a lot of time perched high on bare branches, making harsh noises. They feed mainly early morning or late afternoon, diving from their perch to take large insects on the wing, often with aerobatic twisting and turning, and then circling back to their perch with an upward swoop.

320. DOLLARBIRD *Eurystomus orientalis* PLATE 73

Other name: Eastern Broad-billed Roller
Size: 29cm, 130g
Geographical variation: Of the 10 subspecies, *pacificus* breeds in northern and eastern Australia and then migrates to winter in Indonesia and New Guinea; vagrants reach New Zealand.
Distribution: Asia and Australasia. Dollarbirds arrive in Australia from tropical Australasia from late September to November, and the adults leave in February–April, soon after their young have fledged, and the young follow about a month later. Vagrant Dollarbirds, single birds or small groups are reported two or three times each decade, anywhere from Northland to Southland. Some sightings are of adults in October–December, but most are of young birds caught up by adverse winds when on northward passage in March–May.

NEW ZEALAND WRENS *Acanthisittidae*

An ancient family of 7 species endemic to New Zealand, but only 2 are still alive. Three species were extinct by the time of first European contact; the Stephens Island Wren (*Traversia lyalli*) became extinct in 1894; and the Bush Wren (*Xenicus longipes*) died out by about 1970.

The New Zealand wrens are an ancient family of tiny passerines (Order Passeriformes, or perching birds) with no close affinity to other passerines. They have short, rounded wings and a very short tail. Females are larger than males.

321. RIFLEMAN *Acanthisitta chloris* PLATE 75

Other name: Titipounamu
Size: 8cm; male 6g, female 7g
Geographical variation: Two subspecies: the North Island Rifleman *granti* on the North Island, Great and Little Barrier islands; and the South Island Rifleman *chloris* on the South Island and its offshore islands in the Marlborough Sounds and Fiordland, Codfish Island, and formerly on Stewart Island and its outliers.

Distribution: New Zealand only. Subfossil remains are scarce, but Riflemen were apparently widespread at the time of European settlement, and then declined with the loss of lowland forest and the spread of introduced predators. In the North Island, apart from small remnant populations either side of the Hokianga Harbour (in Northland), they are now absent north of the Waikato and the Coromandel Peninsula. Elsewhere, they are patchily distributed in forests and older stands of scrub, but rare in the large forest tracts of inland Whanganui and Taranaki. They are common on Little Barrier Island, a few are on Great Barrier Island, and they have been successfully introduced to Tiritiri Matangi Island. In the South Island, they are widely distributed from Marlborough and northwestern Nelson to Fiordland. They are common on D'Urville Island and Codfish Island. They disappeared from Stewart Island by 1990, but have been successfully reintroduced to Dancing Star Preserve near Oban, and to Ulva Island. In general, best numbers are in high-altitude beech forest and in lowland podocarp forest, and they like mature tawa forest in the North Island, and manuka/kanuka scrub in the dry eastern South Island. They also use some older exotic forests, especially those with a dense understorey of native shrubs and with old native trees left in gullies; but they are uncommon in young stands of pine, kahikatea and scrub where nest-holes are rare.

Population: Widespread and locally common, especially in beech forest and older stands of tawa and podocarp forest.

Conservation: Protected endemic. Riflemen seem to have a stable distribution on the mainland, but their poor dispersal across water or open habitats has led to a fragmented distribution in some parts of the country, such as small isolated pockets on Mt Taranaki, on the Maraetotara Plateau in eastern Hawke's Bay, around Ngaumu and Aorangi forests in the Wairarapa coastal hill country, and on Banks Peninsula.

Breeding: Pairs remain on their territory all year. Some pairs have one or more helpers attending their nests. The male starts building several nests before the female finally joins in. The usual tree-hole nest is completely enclosed except for a small side entrance tunnel, and is well lined with leaf skeletons, fern roots, twigs and feathers. It is placed from near the ground to about 18m (usually 3–6m), but occasionally they use a small crevice in a bank or a disused rabbit burrow. They readily use a 15cm square nest box with a 2cm diameter entrance hole, especially where natural holes are scarce.

First clutches are laid in late September to early October, with replacement clutches and some second clutches being laid to the end of December. Courtship feeding is common early in the breeding season from about 12 days before laying to the completion of the clutch. They lay 2–**4**–5 white eggs (16 x 12.5mm, 1.3g) at 48-hour intervals. Both sexes incubate for 19–20 days; males incubate about 50% more during daylight hours than females. Chicks hatch about the same time. Both parents brood them for the first 10–12 days and feed them (mainly the male and occasionally helpers) until they fledge at 21–**24**–27 days old. After fledging, the chicks continue to be fed for 4–5 weeks, when they become fully independent. Riflemen often start building a second nest while still feeding chicks in the first nest and start incubating while still feeding fledglings. Most pairs lay replacement clutches if their first nest fails, and about 50% of pairs lay a second clutch after successfully raising a brood. Pairs remain together year after year. Young females sometimes pair up with a regular male helper on reaching independence, and young of both sexes can start breeding at *c.* 9 months old. Annual survival of adult Riflemen near Kaikoura was *c.* 73% for males and 53% for females, giving life expectancies of 3.2 and 1.6 years respectively, but two banded males are known to have lived at least 6 years.

Behaviour: Pairs remain on territory all year, but helpers assist in raising young, especially late in the breeding season. Regular helpers are mainly unpaired males, some of which subsequently pair with one of the offspring raised. Casual helpers occasionally feed chicks in one or more broods; they are sometimes unpaired adults, but most are chicks from the first brood helping with their parents' second brood. Males guard their female closely early in the season until she lays, but later in the season they allow unpaired males to assist in raising their broods. The main call of Riflemen is a very high-pitched, sharp 'zipt-zipt-zipt-zipt', often uttered by a pair as they feed a few metres apart.

Feeding: Diet is almost entirely invertebrates; beetles, spiders, small weta, flies, moths and caterpillars are the most important food, with bugs, snails and lacewings also recorded. Some ripe fruit is taken. Riflemen glean most of their food from small crevices and epiphytic mosses and lichens on the trunks and large branches of trees at almost any level of the forest, although they only rarely feed on the forest floor.

Reading: Gaze, P. D. 1978. *Notornis* 25: 244. Gray, R. S. 1969. *Notornis* 16: 5–22. Leech, T. J. et al. 2007. *Oryx* 41: 369–375. Moeed, A. & Fitzgerald, B. M. 1982. *NZ J Zool* 9: 391–403. Sherley, G. H. 1990. *Behaviour* 112: 1–22. Sherley, G. H. 1993. *NZ J Zool* 20: 211–217. Sherley, G. 1994. *Notornis* 41: 71–81.

322. BUSH WREN *Xenicus longipes* PLATE 85

Other name: Matuhi
Size: 9cm, 16g
Geographical variation: Three subspecies: the North Island Bush Wren *stokesii* of the North Island, the South Island Bush Wren *longipes* of the South Island, and Stead's Bush Wren *variabilis* of Stewart Island and its outliers.
Distribution: Extinct; formerly in New Zealand only. Subfossil remains are scarce, but Bush Wrens were apparently widely distributed before European settlement. The North Island Bush Wren was probably absent from Northland but otherwise widespread in mainland forests until the late 1800s, though not as common as the Rifleman. In the 1900s, the only authentic records are from Kapiti Island (1911), the southern Rimutaka Range (1918) and the Urewera Ranges (several records up to a sighting in the Aniwaniwa Valley in 1955).

The South Island Bush Wren was reported as common throughout forested mountain country, especially high-altitude beech forest, from northwestern Nelson and the Richmond Range south on both sides of the Southern Alps to Fiordland. By the early 1900s, they were declining rapidly, and by the 1950s they were recorded only sporadically, and mainly in Fiordland; however, the last two authentic records are from the Little Wainihinihi River, Arthur's Pass (1966), and Moss Pass, Nelson Lakes National Park (1968). Subsequently there have been a few rumours of birds in the Nelson Lakes areas and Fiordland.

Stead's Bush Wren was common in forest on Stewart Island and in coastal 'muttonbird' scrub of *Olearia* and *Hebe* on several outlying islands. They survived on Stewart Island up to 1951, on Kotiwhenua (Solomon) Island to the early 1960s and on Taukihepa/Big South Cape Island to 1965. In 1964, ship rats invaded Big South Cape, and six birds were transferred to Kaimohu Island, where they persisted until the last sighting in 1972.
Population: Extinct. Some hope of their survival stems from the rediscovery of Riflemen in dense forest in Northland where they were long thought to have been extinct. The most likely places that a few birds could persist are in the Urewera, northwestern Nelson, Nelson Lakes area, Fiordland or Stewart Island.
Conservation: Protected presumed extinct endemic. The Bush Wren declined about the time of European settlement with the loss of much lowland forest, and then disappeared from most of the country in the late 1800s with the arrival of ship rats and mustelids. The extinction of Stead's Bush Wren is directly attributable to the arrival of ship rats at Kotiwhenua and Big South Cape islands in the early 1960s. The attempt to relocate six birds to a predator-free island failed, probably because of chance events in such a small founder population.
Breeding: The nest was often built low to the ground among the roots of standing or fallen trees, in a low hole or fork of a tree, among clumps of fern or in petrel burrows. It was spherical with a small side entrance near the top; built of moss, fern rootlets and leaves, and lined with feathers. Eggs were found in November–December. They laid 2–3 white eggs (20 x 14.5mm). Incubation and fledging periods were not known, but both parents incubated and fed nestlings. Two birds transferred from Big South Cape to Kaimohu Island were at least 8 years old when last seen.
Behaviour: Pairs were territorial during the breeding season, but at other times of the year single birds, pairs or small family parties were recorded. The common call was a 'subdued trill' or a loud 'seep', sometimes rapidly repeated like the 'whirring' call of the Rock Wren.
Feeding: Diet was almost entirely invertebrates, with moths, flies and spiders recorded being fed to chicks. In the South Island, Bush Wrens fed by running along outer branches of trees, and not close to the trunk like Rifleman; however, on the 'muttonbird' islands they often fed on or close to the ground, which probably made them especially vulnerable to mammalian predators. They moved swiftly and furtively while searching for prey on branches, among plants on the forest floor or around the base of trees, with a characteristic hopping or bobbing movement.
Reading: Blackburn, A. 1965. *Notornis* 12: 191–207. Creswell, R. A. 1968. *Notornis* 15: 168. Guthrie-Smith, H. 1925. *Bird Life on Island and Shore.* Edinburgh: Blackwood. Miskelly, C. M. 2003. *Notornis* 50: 113–114. Stead, E. F. 1936. *Trans Roy Soc NZ* 66: 313–314.

323. ROCK WREN *Xenicus gilviventris* PLATE 75

Size: 10cm; male 16g, female 20g

Geographical variation: At one time a subspecies, *rineyi*, was proposed for greener birds found in Fiordland, however, they are now considered to be just a colour phase. Birds in northwestern Nelson are green, those in the central South Island are distinctly browner, whereas those in Westland and Fiordland are again much greener and the sexes are very distinct.

Distribution: South Island only, although subfossil remains have also been found in the North Island. Rock Wrens are patchily distributed in alpine and subalpine habitats of the Tasman Mountains of northwestern Nelson, especially the upper Cobb Valley and the Victoria Range of northern Westland, down both sides of the Southern Alps and on some side ranges to the east, to Fiordland. They are apparently sedentary and remain close to or above the bushline throughout the year. Successfully introduced to Secretary Island (2008–10).

Population: Widespread and locally common, especially in Mt Cook and Mt Aspiring National Parks, and in the Murchison Mountains, but declining in many places. Often seen on the nature trail near the eastern portal of the Homer Tunnel. They are commonest close to the bushline, especially where screes or rockfalls are interspersed with stable areas of low subalpine scrub, fellfield and cushion vegetation.

Conservation: Protected endangered endemic. Rock Wrens disappeared from the North Island before European settlement, but in the South Island their range has changed little since European settlement, however, the distribution has become patchy and numbers have declined steeply in many areas. Fires and introduced mammalian predators, especially stoats and mice, are major reasons for their decline. Being a high-altitude species, they are susceptible to long-term climate changes affecting their habitat, overwinter survival and timing of breeding.

Breeding: Contrary to popular speculation, pairs remain on their territory all year and do not migrate to low altitudes in winter. The female selects the nest site, but both birds work together to excavate a hollow in a bank, rocky crevice, or a soil-covered ledge for the nest. The large enclosed nest has an entrance tunnel in the side. It is made of tussocks, grasses and sedges, and is lined with feathers. During the week of nest-building and the next 5 days before eggs are laid, the female is frequently fed by the male. Most first clutches are laid from mid-October to mid-November, but replacement clutches are laid until late December. They lay 1–**3**–5 creamy eggs (20 x 15.5mm, 2.5g). Both sexes incubate equally for 18–**20**–22 days. The chicks, which hatch over 1–3 days, are brooded throughout the fledging period of 21–**24**–26 days. Towards fledging, they are brooded only about 40% of daylight hours by both parents, but all night by the female. Both parents feed the chicks until they disperse 2–4 weeks after fledging. Many juveniles form pairs in the summer they are hatched and then breed when 11 months old. The oldest bird recorded lived at least 8 years.

Behaviour: Pairs remain on territory all year and, unlike the Rifleman, there is no indication that they have helpers at their nests. They have quite weak flight and bob their body on alighting. A conspicuous display involves bobbing and wing flicking. The main calls are a high-pitched and far-carrying three-note call, with the first note being accentuated, and a 'whirring' call. Pairs sometimes duet.

Feeding: Diet is mainly invertebrates, especially beetles, spiders, centipedes, caterpillars, flies, and larvae of caddisflies, but *Coprosma* and *Gaultheria* fruit and grass seeds are also eaten.

Reading: Heath, S. 1986. Pp. 277–288 in *Flora & Fauna of Alpine Australasia: Ages and Origins.* Melbourne: CSIRO. Michelsen-Heath, S. 1989. MSc thesis, Uni Otago. Michelson-Heath, S. & Gaze, P. D. 2007. *Notornis* 54: 71–78. Riney, T. 1953. *Notornis* 5: 186–188. Soper, M.F. 1961. *Notornis* 9: 158–161.

NEW ZEALAND WATTLEBIRDS *Callaeidae*

An ancient family of 5 species, endemic to New Zealand.

The origin and affinities of the New Zealand wattlebirds are obscure and ancient. They have colourful fleshy wattles at the gape; short, rounded wings; limited flight, and they prefer to progress with leaps and bounds on strong legs. The tail is long and drooping. The bill size is highly variable within the group, but all feed on forest invertebrates and fruits. Their calls are loud and varied.

324. NORTH ISLAND KOKAKO *Callaeas wilsoni* PLATE 76

Other name: Blue-wattled Crow
Size: 38cm; male 230g, female 220g
Distribution: At the time of European settlement, North Island Kokako were widespread in the forests of the North Island and Great Barrier Island. They have gone from forests in Hawke's Bay, the Whanganui hinterland, the Ruahine, Tararua and Rimutaka ranges, and the Wairarapa. The few that survived at the north end of Great Barrier Island have been transferred to Little Barrier. They are now in low numbers in the much-reduced native forests of Northland, and southern Waikato and northern Taranaki. Their main strongholds are tall, mixed lowland forest of podocarp and hardwood in parts of the Bay of Plenty (Mamaku, Horohoro and Rotoehu forests), Pureora and Mapara forests of the King Country, and the northern Urewera Ranges of East Cape. Kokako prefer tall, mixed lowland forest of podocarp and hardwood that has a high diversity of plant species. They have been successfully transferred to Little Barrier, Tiritiri Matangi and Kapiti islands, and to mainland sites in the Waitakere and Hunua ranges (Auckland), Otanewainuku and Whirinaki (Bay of Plenty), Ngapukeriki (East Cape), Boundary Stream (Hawke's Bay) and Pukaha Mount Bruce (Wairarapa). A transfer to Secretary Island (Fiordland) in 2008–09 apparently failed.
Population: *c.* 1600 birds in 2011; mainly in the northern Urewera, Pureora, and on Little Barrier Island.
Conservation: Protected endemic. The decline of Kokako probably has many causes. In the North Island, the clearance and fragmentation of tall lowland forest has turned prime Kokako habitat into isolated pockets. Logging, including 'selective logging', removed many of their main food plants. Predation of eggs, chicks and incubating females by introduced mammals, especially ship rats and possums, and by Australasian Harriers, and the destruction of understorey food plants by the browsing of goats, deer and possums have limited their breeding success. Experimental control of introduced mammals has increased the number of Kokako at Kaharoa and especially at Mapara, and is being tried elsewhere on the mainland. Birds have been shifted from the mainland to predator-free islands and intensively managed mainland sanctuaries with the aim of improving the total to over 2500 birds.
Breeding: Kokako remain in territorial pairs all year. The female builds the nest over several days in dense foliage or beneath the cover of the canopy, 3–**16**–30m above ground. It is always well concealed from above, and the birds approach from below. Nests are a twig base on which is woven a cup of long stems of epiphytic orchid, filmy fern, rata vine and lycopod, often lined with tree-fern scales, moss, lichen or rotten wood, or they are built directly in a clump of epiphyte. Eggs are usually laid in October–December, but in years when there is a good supply of fruit they may continue laying until March and raise two, exceptionally three, broods.

They lay 2–**3** eggs (37 x 26.5mm), pinkish grey with brown and mauve spots and splotches. The female incubates for *c.* 20 days and both parents feed the chicks during the *c.* 31-day fledging period. The young stay in the adults' territory and are fed by them for up to 12 months, but they are usually independent after 4 months. Females are known to breed in their first year. The oldest Kokako recorded lived at least 11 years, but some probably live to 20+ years.
Behaviour: Pairs or solitary birds (probably mainly males) hold their territory all year and for many years. They sing loudly and for prolonged periods, mainly about dawn, rarely during the rest of the day. Pairs sing delightful organ- or flute-like duets of long, melodic syllables, short clucks and buzzes. The main call is a slow, rich 'ko-ka-ko-o-o-o', tailing off at the end. The singing bird flaps its wings as it calls. Kokako prefer to bound along branches and from branch to branch rather than fly. Flights are usually short and seldom sustained for more than 50m.
Feeding: Diet is mainly foliage and fruit, supplemented with invertebrates. All year, they feed on leaves at all levels of the forest. When available, they feed on the fruits of podocarp and hardwood trees and on berries from a variety of shrubs, epiphytes and vines. They take insects during summer and autumn, especially when feeding chicks.
Reading: Basse, B. et al. 2003. *Biol Cons* 109: 259–270. Flux, I. et al. 2006. *Notornis* 53: 199–207. Innes, J. 1999. *Recovery Plan for North Island Kokako.* Wellington: DOC. Innes, J. & Hay, R. 1995. *Notornis* 42: 79–93. Innes, J. et al. 1999. *Biol Cons* 87: 201–214. Innes, J. et al. 2013. *Notornis* 60: 107–114. Lavers, R. B. 1987. *Notornis* 25: 165–185. MacMillan, B. W. H. & McClure, B. R. 1990. *Notornis* 37: 107–119. Meenken, D. S. et al. 1994. *Notornis* 41: 109–115.

325. SOUTH ISLAND KOKAKO *Callaeas cinerea* PLATE 76

Other name: Orange-wattled Crow
Size: 38cm, 230g
Distribution: Subfossil and midden remains suggest that South Island Kokako were throughout the South Island and Stewart Island, but forest clearance and burning eliminated them from the eastern lowlands. At the time of European settlement, South Island Kokako were common throughout the western South Island from northwestern Nelson to Fiordland, in large areas of beech forest east of the Southern Alps, on Banks Peninsula and in the Catlins, They were also in mixed podocarp forest and scrub on Stewart Island. They declined rapidly and were uncommon by 1900 and had largely disappeared from both the South Island and Stewart Island by about 1960. They are now functionally extinct, with perhaps only a few individuals remaining in widely scattered locations. The most recent accepted records were of individuals seen in Mt Aspiring National Park in 1967, and near Reefton in 2007.
Population: Probably extinct, or down to just a handful of scattered birds.
Conservation: Protected critically threatened or recently extinct endemic. The decline of South Island Kokako probably had many causes, but introduced predators, especially possums, rats and stoats, are likely to have been the main factor because large areas of suitable habitat remain intact.
Breeding: Little work has been done on South Island Kokako compared with the North Island Kokako, but their breeding ecology is likely to have been similar. Nests are a bulky twig base on which is woven a cup lined with moss, lichen or tussock, or they are built directly in a clump of epiphyte. Eggs laid in November–January. They lay 2–3 eggs (40 x 27.5mm), stone-coloured, with brown and mauve spots and splotches. The female incubates for *c.* 18 days and both parents feed the chicks.
Behaviour: Pairs likely hold their territory all year and for many years, but there are records of small feeding flocks, and it seems that they spent more time on the ground compared with North Island Kokako. They sing loudly and for prolonged periods, mainly about dawn, rarely during the rest of the day. Pairs sing delightful organ- or flute-like duets of long, melodic syllables, short clucks and buzzes. The main call is a slow, rich 'ko-ka-ko-o-o-o', tailing off at the end. The singing bird flaps its wings as it calls. Kokako prefer to bound along branches and from branch to branch rather than fly. Flights are usually short and seldom sustained for more than 50m, though they reputedly fly better than the North Island species.
Feeding: Diet is mainly foliage and fruit, supplemented with buds and invertebrates. All year, they feed on leaves and fruits at all levels of the forest and on the ground, where they grub amongst moss and litter. When available, they feed on the fruits of podocarp and hardwood trees and on berries from a variety of shrubs, especially *Coprosma* species, epiphytes and vines. They take insects during summer and autumn, especially when feeding chicks.
Reading: Clout, M. N. & Hay, J. R. 1981. *Notornis* 28: 256–259. Tennyson, A. & Martinson, P. 2006. *Extinct Birds of New Zealand*. Wellington: Te Papa Press.

326. NORTH ISLAND SADDLEBACK *Philesturnus rufusater* PLATE 76

Other name: Tieke
Size: 25cm; male 80g, female 70g
Distribution: At the time of European settlement, Saddlebacks were plentiful and widely distributed in the forests of the whole of the North Island and on offshore islands such as the Hen and Chickens, Great Barrier and Little Barrier, and Cuvier Island. They declined during the 1800s after the spread of Norway rats and feral cats, and by 1870 they had largely gone from north of the Waikato. The decline accelerated late in the century as ship rats and mustelids spread, and they had virtually gone from the rest of the North Island by about 1890, and died out in the early 1900s. About 500 North Island Saddlebacks survived on Hen Island. Since 1964, they have been successfully transferred to many islands: Whatupuke (1964), Red Mercury (1966), Cuvier (1968), Lady Alice (1971), Stanley (1977), Kapiti (1981–89), Little Barrier (1984–88), Tiritiri Matangi (1984), Mokoia (1992), Motuohora (1999), Motuihe (2005) and Motutapu (2011), and to several fenced mainland sanctuaries: Zealandia (2002), Bushy Park (2006), Tawharanui (2012), Cape Kidnappers (2013) and Maungatautari (2013). Coppermine Island in the Hen and Chickens was colonised when birds flew the 150m gap from neighbouring Whatupuke Island. Transfers to Motukawanui Island in the Cavalli group

(1983, 1984) failed when a stoat invaded in 1986, and transfers to Fanal Island in the Mokohinau group (1968, 1985) failed for unknown reasons.

Population: *c.* 10,000 birds; reaching very high densities on some offshore islands.

Conservation: Protected endemic. The decline of North Island Saddlebacks seems to have been linked to the spread of rats, cats and mustelids. Although they can survive in tall forest in the presence of Pacific rats, numbers increased dramatically in young forest on Red Mercury Island after Pacific rats were eradicated. Because of island and sanctuary transfers, provision of nest boxes, and better rodent control, and plans to eradicate rodents from many island reserves, the species is now secure.

Breeding: North Island Saddlebacks usually nest within 2–3m of the ground in tree holes (especially in pohutukawa), in rock crevices, tree-fern crowns and in dense epiphytes. The female makes the nests of rootlets, leaves and twigs, lined with fine grasses, bark fibres and tree-fern scales. Eggs are usually laid in October–January, and one brood is normally raised, but at recently colonised sites where resources are unlimited they can breed from August to May and raise up to 4 broods. They lay 1–**2–3**–4 grey or white eggs (29 x 22mm) with dark blotches and streaks, mainly at the larger end. Females alone incubate for *c.* 18 days. Both adults feed the young, which fledge at *c.* 26 days old. The oldest bird lived at least 17.5 years.

Behaviour: Pairs hold their territory all year and defend it loudly. The main call is a loud, far-carrying 'cheet, te-te-te-te'; the long, steady, introductory note is followed by up to 30 short notes. Saddlebacks are active and inquisitive. They prefer to bound along branches, from branch to branch and across the forest floor rather than fly. Flights are noisy, rapid and usually short, seldom sustained for more than 50m. Saddlebacks roost in cavities that are often on or near the ground, under overhanging stream banks or several metres up in tree holes or beneath epiphytes.

Feeding: Diet is mainly invertebrates, but in season they also take a wide variety of fruits and nectar. They take invertebrates from the forest floor to the canopy. On the forest floor, they rummage in the litter and dig into rotting logs with their strong, chisel-shaped bills. On trunks and branches, they examine crevices, sometimes inserting one mandible only, or forcibly open their bills to prise off bark or to unroll dead, curled leaves. This feeding is vigorous and noisy, often attracting Fantails and Whiteheads, which feed on insects that have been disturbed. They hold large insects such as weta with one foot and pull them apart with the bill.

In the hand: Males have longer tarsi, with little overlap: 40–**41.8**–44 cf. 36.5–**38.8**–40.5mm.

Reading: Hooson, S. & Jamieson, I. G. 2002. *Bird Cons Intl* 13: 79–95. Jenkins, P. F. 1978. *Anim Behav* 26: 50–78. Jenkins, P. F. & Veitch, C. R. 1991. *NZ J Zool* 18: 445–450. Lovegrove, T. G. 1996. *Biol Cons* 77: 151–157. Lovegrove, T. G. 1996. *Notornis* 43: 91–112. Merton, D. V. 1965. *Notornis* 12: 208–212. Merton, D. V. 1965. *Notornis* 12: 213–222. Ruarus, S. P. et al. 2011. *NZ J Ecol* 35: 220–228.

327. SOUTH ISLAND SADDLEBACK *Philesturnus carunculatus* PLATE 76

Other names: Tieke, Jackbird (juvenile)

Size: 25cm; male 85g, female 75g

Distribution: At the time of European settlement, Saddlebacks were plentiful and widely distributed in the forests of the northern, western and southern South Island, and on Stewart Island and some of its outliers. They declined during the 1800s after the spread of Norway rats and feral cats, and further with the arrival of ship rats and stoats in the late 1800s. South Island Saddlebacks had virtually disappeared from the South and Stewart islands by 1905 and were gone by 1950; however, they survived on Big South Cape/Taukihepa Island (930ha) and two adjacent islets, Pukeweka (2ha) and Solomon/Kotiwhenua (25ha), off the southwest corner of Stewart Island, until the accidental arrival of ship rats in 1963. In 1964, 36 were shifted successfully to nearby Big and Kaimohu islands, thus saving them from extinction. Since 1965, they have been transferred to many islands off Stewart Island and reintroduced back to Big South Cape (2011) and Solomon (2012) islands. Further afield, there have been successful translocations to Breaksea (1992), South Passage (2001) and Chalky (2008) islands in Fiordland; to Motuara (1994), Long (2005) and Blumine (2009) islands in the Marlborough Sounds, and to Orokonui Ecosanctuary near Dunedin (2009).

Population: *c.* 2000 birds; increasing through successful translocations to many islands.

Conservation: Protected endemic. The decline of Saddlebacks seems to have been linked to the spread of rats, cats and mustelids. Because of island transfers, provision of nest boxes, and better control and eradication of rats in island reserves, the species is now secure and increasing.

Breeding: Saddlebacks nest in tree holes, especially in southern rata and kanuka; in rock crevices, in tree-fern crowns, and in flax and dense epiphytes, usually within 2m of the ground. The female builds the nest of twigs, bark, rootlets and ferns, lined with fine grasses, bark fibres and tree-fern scales. Eggs are usually laid in October–January, and one brood is raised, but at recently colonised sites where resources are unlimited they can raise 2 broods. They lay 1–**2** off-white eggs (32 x 22mm) with brown and purplish blotches and streaks, mainly at the larger end. Females alone incubate for 20–21 days, and brood the nestlings. Both adults feed the young, which fledge at *c.* 26 days old, including for some time after leaving the nest. Some males breed at 1 year old, but most birds do not breed until 2 years old. The oldest bird lived at least 17.5 years.

Behaviour: Pairs hold their territory all year and defend it loudly. The main call is a loud, far-carrying 'cheet, te-te-te-te'; the long, steady, introductory note is followed by up to 30 short notes. Saddlebacks are active and inquisitive. They prefer to bound along branches, from branch to branch and across the forest floor rather than fly. Flights are noisy, rapid and usually short, seldom sustained for more than 50m. Saddlebacks roost in cavities that are often on or near the ground, under overhanging stream banks or several metres up in tree holes or beneath epiphytes.

Feeding: Diet is mainly invertebrates, but in season they also take a wide variety of fruits and nectar. They take invertebrates from the forest floor to the canopy. On the forest floor, they rummage in the litter and dig into rotting logs with their strong, chisel-shaped bills. On trunks and branches, they examine crevices, sometimes inserting one mandible only, or forcibly open their bills to prise off bark or to unroll dead, curled leaves. This feeding is vigorous and noisy, often attracting Fantails, which feed on insects that have been disturbed. They hold large insects such as weta with one foot and pull them apart with the bill.

In the hand: Males have longer tarsi, with little overlap: 39–**42.2**–44 cf. 33.4–**39.5**–41.9mm, and this in combination with weight (75.5–**84.1**–90 cf. 64–**73.2**–83g) can distinguish over 90% of birds correctly.

Reading: Blackburn, A. 1965. *Notornis* 12: 191–207. Hooson, S. & Jamieson, I. G. 2003. *Bird Cons Intl* 13: 79–95. Hooson, S. & Jamieson, I. G. 2003. *Notornis* 50: 191–201. Hooson, S. & Jamieson, I. G. 2004. *Ibis* 146: 417–426. Lovegrove, T. G. 1996. *Biol Cons* 77: 151–157. Lovegrove, T. G. 1996. *Notornis* 43: 91–112. Michel, P. et al. 2010. *NZ J Ecol* 34: 237–246. Pierre, J. P. 1999. *Biol Cons* 89: 153–159. Pierre, J. P. 2000. *Notornis* 47: 7–12. Rasch, G. & McClelland, P. 1993. *Notornis* 40: 229–231. Roberts, A. 1994. *South Island Saddleback Recovery Plan.* Wellington: DOC. Taylor, S. S. & Jamieson, I. G. 2007. *Notornis* 54: 61–64.

328. HUIA *Heteralocha acutirostris* — PLATE 84

Size: Male 45cm (bill 60mm); female 48cm (bill 104mm), 350g

Distribution: Extinct. Formerly North Island only. Subfossil and midden remains have been found from North Cape to Wellington. Huia were recorded after European settlement only from forests from the Raukumara Range and the Turakina River south to the Wairarapa and the Rimutaka Range, near Wellington. The last accepted record was of three birds seen by W. W. Smith in 1907, but quite credible reports were made up to about 1920.

Conservation: A long period of Polynesian settlement, during which the birds' range shrank markedly, was followed by extensive destruction of prime habitat of lowland forest after European settlement, especially in the Manawatu, southern Hawke's Bay and the Wairarapa. Introduced predators, especially ship rats, cats and mustelids, probably killed many birds. The final demise of Huia may have been aided by the collection of many specimens for museum skins, e.g. 646 skins were collected from the southern Hawke's Bay in a month in 1863.

Breeding: Little is known. The nest was a large structure of sticks and twigs with finer material lining the cup. The clutch was 2–4 (45 x 30mm) eggs, greyish with brown and purplish markings.

Behaviour: Huia were almost always found in pairs, readily attracted and easily caught or shot. They travelled on the ground or in the canopy in long leaps and bounds, flying only short distances on their rounded wings. Their alarm call was a shrill whistle, which was easily imitated, bringing them to investigate.

Feeding: Huia were one of the few birds in the world whose sexes differed in bill shape. The male had a short, chiselling bill and concentrated on the outer surfaces of wood; it had a special ability to insert its bill into rotting wood and then force it open to split the wood. The female probed its long, decurved bill deeply so as to retrieve insects unobtainable to the male. They were seen to take huhu grubs and weta, and took other insects, spiders and berries.

Reading: Medway, D. G. 1968. *Notornis* 15: 177–192. Phillips, W. J. 1963. *The Book of the Huia.* Christchurch: Whitcombe & Tombs. Tennyson, A. & Martinson, P. 2006. *Extinct Birds of New Zealand.* Wellington: Te Papa Press.

STITCHBIRD *Notiomystidae*

An ancient family of just 1 species, endemic to New Zealand.

The Stitchbird was formerly placed within the honeyeater family (Meliphagidae), but genetic work has established that they are closer to the New Zealand wattlebirds, and so they must have independently evolved some morphological characters shared with the honeyeaters, such as their body shape and a brush-like tongue.

Reading: Driskell, A. C. et al. 2007. *Aust J Zool* 55: 73–78.

329. STITCHBIRD *Notiomystis cincta* PLATE 77

Other name: Hihi

Size: 18cm; male 37g, female 30g

Distribution: North Island and its offshore islands only. Subfossil and midden remains and historical records show that Stitchbirds were throughout the North Island and on offshore islands such as Great Barrier, Little Barrier and Kapiti up to the 1840s. They have never been reported from the South Island. Up to the early 1870s, they were comparatively common in southern parts of the North Island, as far north as the Waikato. They then declined rapidly, and by 1885 had vanished from the mainland, Great Barrier and Kapiti islands. They survived only on Little Barrier Island from 1885 to 1980. Transfers to Hen (1980–81), Cuvier (1982–85) and Mokoia (1994) islands and the Waitakere Ranges (2007–08) have been unsuccessful. Transfers to Kapiti (1983–2002) and Tiritiri Matangi (1995–2010) islands, Zealandia in Wellington (2005–10) and to Maungatautari, Waikato (2009–11) have been successful, but at least partially maintained through supplementary feeding. Also released at Bushy Park Sanctuary, Whanganui (2013).

Population: Several thousand are probably now on Little Barrier Island and fewer than 200 at each of the other sites.

Conservation: Protected vulnerable endemic. The cause of the rapid decline in the late 1800s is not known but may be due to avian disease (perhaps introduced with European passerines) or, more likely, the spread of tree-climbing ship rats, stoats and feral cats. The extermination of cats (by 1980) and Pacific rats (by 2004) on Little Barrier Island allowed that population to increase and be more secure. Management aims to establish self-sustaining populations of Stitchbirds on several islands, in case ship rats or stoats get to Little Barrier Island. The other islands tried to date, although lacking ship rats and stoats, may not have enough variety of nectar- and fruit-producing plants, especially since the more aggressive Tui and Bellbirds dominate the best sources. Although Kapiti Island is large (2000ha) and the habitat is improving with the eradication of possums (by 1985) and rats (by 1997), it is still short of nectar- and fruit-producing plants and, for some time yet, may not be self-sustaining without the supply of artificial nectar from feeders.

Breeding: Although Stitchbirds are apparently monogamous on Little Barrier, which is their one remaining natural habitat, on Kapiti Island, where there may be a shortage of suitable tree holes for nests and a lack of food plants, they are polygynandrous, i.e. many males and females breeding in the same nest; this is rare among passerines. Stitchbirds nest in tree holes, usually high in live, mature trees. On Little Barrier, these are mainly in pohutukawa, tawa and puriri; on Kapiti, in pukatea, rata, kamahi and hinau. Nests are usually level with or above the entrance holes, often on top of previous nests. The nest is a platform of sticks with a cup on top made of tree-fern rhizomes, lined with tree-fern scales and feathers. Uniquely among birds, some copulate face to face. Eggs are laid in September–March; up to four clutches are laid if nests fail, but a maximum of two broods are raised each year. They lay 1–**4**–6 white eggs

(19 x 15mm), which females incubate for 14–**16**–20 days. Both sexes feed the nestlings, and the young take 21–**27**–34 days to fledge. The oldest Stitchbird recorded lived over 9 years.

Behaviour: Stitchbirds are quite nomadic, travelling several kilometres in a day between good feeding sites. During their first winter, the young may form loose flocks with an adult male. The adult male has a loud, explosive whistle: 'wee-a-wee' or 'see-si-ip', a territorial call given near the nest and when feeding. Both sexes give the familiar, loud 'stitch' note – the probable origin of the name Stitchbird. It is also given as a warning call whenever birds are worried, e.g. by intruding humans. Among other calls is a penetrating alarm call: 'yeng, yeng, yeng', like a Bellbird's but higher pitched.

Feeding: Diet is a wide variety of nectar and fruits whenever available, also invertebrates gleaned from foliage and bark. Normally, whenever Tui and Bellbird are present, Stitchbirds tend to feed in lower strata of the forest, taking low-grade sources of nectar; however, when nectar is abundant they feed in the canopy with the two honeyeaters.

Reading: Anderson, S. 1993. *Notornis* 40: 14. Castro, I. et al. 2003. *Biol Cons* 114: 271–280. Driskell, A. C. et al. 2007. *Aust J Zool* 55: 73–78. Gravatt, D. J. 1970. *Notornis* 17: 96–101. Low, M. & Pärt, T. 2009. *J Anim Ecol* 78: 761–771. Low, M. et al. 2007. *J Anim Ecol* 76: 459–470. Rasch, G. 1989. *Notornis* 36: 27–36. Rasch, G. & Craig, J. L. 1988. *NZ J Zool* 15: 185–190.

PIOPIO *Turnagridae*

A primitive family of 2 extinct species, both endemic to New Zealand.

The affinities of the Piopio are not clear, but some authors have aligned them with the bowerbirds and catbirds (Ptilonorhynchidae), the whistlers (Pachycephalidae), or the birds-of-paradise (Paradisaeidae) of Australia and New Guinea. Whatever their relationships, this lineage has recently come to an abrupt end with the introduction of mammalian predators to New Zealand.

Reading: Tennyson, A. & Martinson, P. 2006. *Extinct Birds of New Zealand.* Wellington: Te Papa Press.

330. NORTH ISLAND PIOPIO *Turnagra tanagra* PLATE 85

Other name: North Island Thrush

Size: 26cm, 130g

Distribution: Extinct. Subfossil and midden records are widely distributed throughout the North Island. Piopio were widespread and locally common on mainland forests at the time of European settlement. They soon disappeared from Northland, and had all but disappeared from the central and southern North Island by the 1880s. The last confirmed specimen was shot at Ohura, southern King Country, in 1902. Reports of sightings, mainly in the Ureweras, Raukumara Range, and inland Whanganui/Taranaki up to the 1970s could not be confirmed.

Conservation: The rapid decline of the North Island Piopio suggests introduced predators or avian disease as possible causes, because much suitable forest habitat remained. The spread of introduced mammals, particularly cats and Norway rats, probably contributed significantly to their demise, which largely preceded the arrival of ship rats and mustelids.

Breeding: The nest was a cup built of twigs and moss, lined with grasses, tree-fern scales or other fine material, in a tree fork usually *c.* 2m high. The usual clutch was 2 white or pinkish-white eggs (35 x 25mm) with scattered black or brown spots.

Behaviour: Piopio lived in forest and scrub from the coast to the mountains. They were very tame and readily came around people camping, where they were easily killed. They had a variety of song and calls.

Feeding: Diet included invertebrates, often obtained by grubbing with its bill from the forest floor, plus fruits, seeds and foliage.

Reading: Johansson, U. S. et al. 2011. *PLOS ONE* 6(9): doi: 10.1371/journal.pone.0024317. Mead, W. P. 1950. *Notornis* 4: 3–6. Medway, D. G. 1968. *Notornis* 15: 177–192. Medway, D. G. 2004. *Notornis* 51: 231–232. Olson, S. L. et al. 1983. *Notornis* 30: 319–336. Tennyson, A. & Martinson, P. 2006. *Extinct Birds of New Zealand.* Wellington: Te Papa Press.

331. SOUTH ISLAND PIOPIO *Turnagra capensis* PLATE 85

Other name: South Island Thrush
Size: 26cm, 130g
Geographical variation: Two subspecies: the South Island Piopio *capensis* of the South Island and Stewart Island, and the Stephens Island Piopio *minor* of Stephens Island in the Marlborough Sounds.
Distribution: Extinct. Subfossil and midden records are widely distributed throughout the South Island, and on Stewart Island. Piopio were widespread and locally common on mainland forests and on some islands in Fiordland at the time of European settlement, but they had all but disappeared by 1900. Unconfirmed sight records were made in northwest Nelson and Fiordland up to 1963. The Stephens Island subspecies was common in 1894, but died out soon thereafter following the clearance of most of the forest cover and the introduction of cats by the lighthouse keepers.
Conservation: The rapid decline of the South Island Piopio suggests introduced predators or avian disease as possible causes, because much suitable forest habitat remained. The spread of introduced mammals, particularly cats, Norway rats, ship rats and mustelids, probably contributed significantly to their demise. Cats were probably entirely responsible for the demise of the Stephens Island Piopio.
Breeding: They were territorial and lived in pairs. The nest was a cup built of twigs and moss, lined with grasses, tree-fern scales or other fine material, in a tree fork usually *c.* 2m high. The usual clutch was **2** white or pinkish-white eggs (35 x 25mm) with scattered black or brown spots.
Behaviour: South Island Piopio lived in forest and scrub from the coast to the mountains. They were very tame and readily came around people camping, where they were easily killed by dogs; Sir James Hector on one occasion counted over 40 near his camp on the West Coast. They had a variety of song and calls.
Feeding: Diet included invertebrates, often obtained by grubbing with its bill, from the forest floor, plus fruits, seeds and foliage.
Reading: Child, P. 1965. *Notornis* 12: 53. Johansson, U. S. et al. 2011. *PLOS ONE* 6(9): doi: 10.1371/journal.pone.0024317. Medway, D. G. 2004. *Notornis* 51: 231–232. Olson, S. L. et al. 1983. *Notornis* 30: 319–336. Tennyson, A. & Martinson, P. 2006. *Extinct Birds of New Zealand*. Wellington: Te Papa Press.

AUSTRALASIAN WARBLERS and ALLIES

Acanthizidae

About 60 species in Southeast Asia, Australasia and the southwestern Pacific; 2 endemic species in New Zealand.

A diverse group of very small or small forest and scrub birds. Many, like the scrubwrens, thornbills, and warblers, have short, fine bills for gleaning insects on foliage or, more distinctively, by hovering and picking insects from leaves. Some species have distinctive, loud and beautiful song.

332. GREY WARBLER *Gerygone igata* PLATE 75

Other names: Riroriro, Grey Gerygone
Size: 10cm, 6.5g
Distribution: New Zealand only. Subfossil remains are scarce, but Grey Warblers were apparently widespread historically. They are one of the few native passerines to have benefited from human modification of the landscape. They are common through many forest, scrub, rural and city habitats from sea level to the subalpine zone on the main islands and most offshore islands, but absent from the outlying islands, except for the vagrants at The Snares. Scarce on Little Barrier and Kapiti islands, where native forest-bird communities are relatively intact.
Population: Widespread and abundant. They are especially common in manuka, kanuka and gorse scrub.
Conservation: Protected endemic. The Grey Warbler is common and widespread, and no specific conservation management is necessary.
Breeding: Grey Warblers establish their territories in late July and August. The female takes up to 27 days to build

the enclosed nest with a 3cm-diameter hole in the side. About half the nests are pensile (hanging freely from an attachment at the top), and the rest are also secured elsewhere. It is made of rootlets, moss, lichen, leaves, bark, tree-fern scales and fibres, twigs, cobwebs, spider egg-cases, wool, hair and feathers, and is lined with a thick layer of feathers, downy seeds and tree-fern scales. Nests are 1–10m above the ground, usually in the lower half of the forest. Eggs are laid in August–December; in the South Island usually two broods are raised each year with peaks of laying in September and November, but in the northern North Island usually only one brood is raised each year.

They lay 2–**4**–5 white eggs (17 x 12mm, 1.5g) with reddish-brown speckling concentrated near the larger end. Eggs are laid at 2-day intervals, and incubation starts once the final egg is laid. The female alone incubates for 17–**19.5**–21 days, and then broods the chicks for the first 10 days. The chicks are fed by both parents during the 15–**17**–19 day fledging period and for up to 35 days after leaving the nest. The male does most of the later care of the first brood as the female prepares to lay the second clutch. Once independent, the young become mobile and disperse several kilometres from their natal territory. First breeding is probably at 1 year old. Pairs are monogamous and persist all year and between years. At Kowhai Bush, adult survivorship was at least 82% and life expectancy was 5 years. The oldest recorded lived 5.8 years, but some are likely to live to 10+ years old.

The Grey Warbler is the only host to the Shining Cuckoo on the New Zealand mainland. First clutches escape parasitism because they are laid before the cuckoos arrive, but often Shining Cuckoos replace an egg in the second clutch with one of their own, and eventually the bigger and faster-growing cuckoo chick expels all other eggs or chicks.

Behaviour: Males defend their breeding territory with long chases interspersed with bouts of loud and prolonged singing; females join in the chases, especially when the intruder approaches a nest. The territories expand into overlapping home ranges between the breeding seasons, and flocks of up to 25 birds form in the winter. Grey Warblers occasionally join flocks of other insectivorous birds such as Silvereyes, Brown Creepers and Whiteheads.

Feeding: Diet is almost entirely invertebrates, especially spiders, caterpillars, flies, beetles and bugs, but also includes a few small fruits. Grey Warblers take most of their food by gleaning from leaves, but they often feed in a highly distinctive way by catching prey near the ends of branches while hovering in mid-air.

In the hand: Sexes are indistinguishable for most of the year, but only females develop a brood patch; sexes are best distinguished by the behaviour of birds during the breeding season. Juveniles have brown, not red, eyes, and their legs are dull grey, not black, and some have a pale yellow eye-ring. Juveniles moult into adult plumage in January–March, at about the same time that adults moult.

Reading: Anderson, M. G. et al. 2013. *Emu* 113: 187–191. Briskie, J. V. 2007. *Notornis* 54: 15–19. Gill, B. J. 1982. *Ibis* 124: 123–147. Gill, B. J. 1982. *Emu* 82: 177–181. Gill, B. J. 1983. *Notornis* 30: 137–165.

333. CHATHAM ISLANDS WARBLER *Gerygone albofrontata* PLATE 75

Size: 12cm; male 10g, female 8.5g

Distribution: Chatham Islands only. Subfossil remains and records in the first half of the 1900s indicate that they used to be throughout all of the Chatham Islands. They are now confined to the forested areas of the southern half of Chatham Island, Pitt, Mangere, Little Mangere and South East islands, and the Star Keys.

Population: Locally common, and abundant on South East and Mangere islands.

Conservation: Protected vulnerable endemic. Chatham Islands Warblers do not seem to have adapted to human-modified habitats as well as Grey Warblers have done on the New Zealand mainland. Those on Chatham Island have declined during this century and have disappeared from the northern half of the island, but they remain the commonest native bird in the southern forests and scrub. On predator-free offshore islands, such as South East and Mangere, they are abundant in native forest and scrub, and their future seems assured so long as these islands remain free of rats and cats. Chatham Islands Warblers are sometimes parasitised by Shining Cuckoos, and so they were used to host broods of Black Robins in the early stages of the recovery of that critically endangered species. However, although able to successfully hatch Black Robin eggs and raise Black Robin chicks through the first couple of weeks, they were unable to fledge them successfully.

Breeding: Pairs establish territories in August, and the female takes up to 13 days to build the enclosed hanging nest. It has a 3cm-diameter hole in the side and is made of rootlets, mosses, lichens, leaves, bark, twigs, grass stems, flowers, cobwebs, spider egg-cases and feathers, and is lined with a thick layer of feathers. On Chatham Island, most nests hang in the open, often on terminal branches of *Dracophyllum arboreum* about 6m above the ground. On offshore islands, however, they are only 2–3m above the ground and in dense foliage, presumably to protect them from damage from petrels landing at night. Most eggs are laid in September–December, and only one brood is raised each year, but some replacement clutches are laid late in the season.

They lay 2–**3**–4 white eggs (18 x 13mm; 1.8g) with reddish speckling concentrated near the larger end. Eggs are laid at 2-day intervals. The female alone incubates for 17–**19.5**–21 days and broods the chicks, but both parents feed the chicks. The fledging period is 19–**20**–23 days, and chicks are fed by their parents for up to 24 days after leaving the nest; normally the male and female split their brood and care for one or two chicks each. When the population density is high, small juvenile flocks form late in the breeding season. First breeding is probably at 2 years old, because 1-year-old birds are in subadult plumage and are non-territorial in the following breeding season. The oldest bird recorded in the wild lived over 7 years.

Some nests late in the season are parasitised by Shining Cuckoos.

Behaviour: Males defend their territory with long chases interspersed with bouts of loud and prolonged singing; females occasionally join in the chases but have only a weak subsong.

Feeding: Diet is entirely invertebrates, especially spiders, caterpillars, flies, beetles and bugs. They glean most of their food from leaves and from crevices in trunks and branches. Unlike the Grey Warbler, they seldom hover to catch food, but quite often feed on the ground in the leaf litter.

In the hand: Sexes are distinguished by colour and size: the adult male has white underparts and a prominent white face with contrasting dark eyestripe, and the adult female has grey-white underparts and a face with a yellow tinge, especially on the throat. Only females develop a brood patch. Males are larger in all measurements, with little overlap in wing length: 60–**64**–67mm cf. 57–**60**–62mm. Juveniles are like females, but their upperparts have an olive-grey tone rather than brownish olive, underparts are yellower, outer webs of primaries are green-yellow not buff-yellow, and their iris is brown, not red. Juveniles moult into adult plumage in November–January, while adults probably do not moult until January–March, several weeks after breeding.

Reading: Dennison, M. D. et al. 1984. *Notornis* 31: 97–105. Robertson, H. A. & Dennison, M. D. 1984. *Emu* 84: 103–107.

HONEYEATERS *Meliphagidae*

About 170 species in Australasia and the islands of the Pacific, to the Bonin Islands and Hawai'i: 3 endemic species, of which 1 is extinct. The Red Wattlebird *Anthochaera carunculata* was twice recorded in New Zealand as a vagrant in the 1800s, but is not covered here.

Honeyeaters are medium-to-large forest birds with a slightly decurved bill and a protrusile brush-tipped tongue, which is divided at the tip and has its edges frayed. It is used to reach deeply into flowers and drink nectar, or to extract sugar secretions from cracks in bark. Despite their name, all New Zealand honeyeaters feed on a mixture of nectar, fruits and insects. They follow the seasonal flowering of certain plant species and play an important ecological role in pollinating the flowers of many native trees and shrubs, and dispersing the seeds of many plants with small- to medium-sized fruits.

334. BELLBIRD *Anthornis melanura* PLATE 77

Other names: Korimako, Makomako

Size: 20cm; male 34g, female 26g

Geographical variation: Three subspecies; the Bellbird *melanura* shows clinal variation in plumage colour from Northland to Stewart and Auckland islands; the Three Kings Bellbird *obscura* is confined to the Three Kings Islands; and the Poor Knights Bellbird *oneho* breeds only on the Poor Knights but occasionally visits the nearby mainland of eastern Northland.

Distribution: New Zealand only. Present and often

common in forest and scrub areas in the North, South, Stewart and Auckland islands and on many offshore islands. Vagrant to Campbell Island (2003–04). In the South Island they have expanded into settled districts and large exotic plantations, and are common in orchards, gardens, parks and farm shelterbelts, and on river margins. On the mainland north of the Waikato, they became extinct in the 1860s, although, in winter, a few males fly to eastern Northland, e.g. to Tutukaka from the Poor Knights Islands, to Whangarei Heads from the Hen and Chicken Islands, to Leigh from Little Barrier Island, and to Whangaparaoa Peninsula from Tiritiri Matangi Island. Females seldom fly to the mainland, however, Bellbirds have recently become established at Tawharanui Peninsula and Shakespear Regional Park in North Auckland.

Population: Common in many parts of the South Island and in some forested parts and offshore islands of the North Island. Their distribution is sometimes strangely patchy, being common in one area, but absent from apparently suitable habitat 10km away, and translocations to new mainland sites have generally failed.

Conservation: Protected endemic. The cause of the rapid decline of the Bellbird from Northland and around Auckland in the 1860s may have been caused by some disease, because island populations offshore were not affected and Bellbird survive well elsewhere on the mainland in the presence of the same array of introduced mammalian predators.

Breeding: Bellbirds keep the same breeding territory year after year. Mainland Bellbirds lay in September–January, rarely to March, during which they commonly raise two broods. On the Poor Knights Islands, the laying period is from late September to late November, and usually only one brood is raised. The female makes the nest, which is loosely built of twigs and fibres with a deep cup, lined with feathers and fine grass. Most nests are in dense cover in a fork, but on islands with nesting petrels many are sheltered in a rock or trunk cavity. At daily intervals, they lay **3–4–5** pinkish-white eggs (23 x 16mm, 3.1g) with reddish-brown spots and blotches, densest at the larger end; 2–3–4 eggs on the Poor Knights and Three Kings islands. The female incubates, from laying the last egg, for *c.* 15 days. Both parents feed the chicks, which fledge at *c.* 19 days old. Mainland birds can breed at 1 year old. The oldest Bellbird recorded lived 8+ years.

Behaviour: Bellbirds are territorial in the breeding season but may leave the territory to feed at a nearby nectar source. After breeding, they become nomadic and are usually solitary; even though several may be feeding simultaneously in a tree, they defend a feeding territory within the tree. The famous bell notes are impressive only when given by many birds at once, mostly at dawn and dusk in places of high density and few other species.

Feeding: Diet is mainly nectar from many native and introduced plants, and in late summer and autumn, when flowers are not common, they take fruit. They also eat many insects and spiders by gleaning trunks, branches and leaves; also by hawking. Female Bellbirds take more insects and less nectar than males do, probably because the more aggressive males exclude them from nectar plants. The chicks are almost entirely fed insects.

Reading: Bartle, J. A. & Sagar, P. M. 1987. *Notornis* 34: 253–306. Craig, J. L. & Douglas, M. E. 1984. *Notornis* 31: 82–86. Gaze, P. D. & Clout, M. N. 1983. *NZ J Ecol* 6: 33–38. Sagar, P. M. 1985. *NZ J Zool* 12: 643–648.

335. CHATHAM ISLANDS BELLBIRD *Anthornis melanocephala* PLATE 85

Other name: Komako

Size: 22cm, 40g

Distribution: Subfossil and historical records suggest that they were formerly throughout the Chatham Islands.

Population: Extinct since about 1906. Common in the 1850s throughout forested parts of the Chatham Islands, including around Waitangi, but by the 1870s it had declined on Chatham and Pitt islands, but remained common on Mangere Island. By 1893, it had gone from Chatham and Pitt islands, but was still present on Mangere Island, however, the arrival of cats soon eliminated that population. The last bird was recorded on Little Mangere Island in 1906, perhaps following ongoing predation by cats whenever birds visited nearby Mangere Island.

Conservation: The decline, and ultimate extinction, was likely caused by habitat loss, and especially by predation by cats and ship rats.

Breeding: Chatham Islands Bellbirds were variously recorded breeding in August to October, and from October into the summer, somewhat earlier than their congener on the mainland of New Zealand. The bulky nest was loosely built of twigs and fibres with a deep cup lined with feathers. Clutch size was *c.* 3 pink eggs (26 x 19mm) with reddish-brown spots and blotches at the larger end.

Behaviour: Bellbirds are territorial in the breeding season but may leave the territory to feed at a nearby nectar source. After breeding, they become nomadic and are usually solitary, and this pattern seems to fit the limited observations on this species.

Feeding: No information is available, but diet was likely to have been a mix of nectar, fruit and invertebrates.

Reading: Tennyson, A. & Martinson, P. 2006. *Extinct Birds of New Zealand.* Wellington: Te Papa Press.

336. TUI *Prosthemadera novaeseelandiae* PLATE 77

Other name: Parson Bird

Size: 30cm; male 120g, female 90g (mainland); male 150g, female 110g (Chathams)

Geographical variation: Two subspecies; the Chatham Islands Tui *chathamensis* breeds on the Chathams only; the nominate race *novaeseelandiae* breeds elsewhere in New Zealand.

Distribution: New Zealand only. Throughout forests and towns in the North, South and Stewart islands and on many offshore islands. They have spread north to the Kermadec Islands, east to the Chatham Islands and south to the Auckland Islands. They are abundant in subfossil and midden deposits in both the North and South islands, and are the main passerine found in middens. Tui are mainly forest and scrub birds; however, outside the breeding season they become partially nomadic and travel to towns and rural gardens and forest patches in search of good sources of nectar or fruit. Each year, some birds regularly occupy a summer breeding territory and winter feeding territories that are 20+km apart.

Population: Common on the Kermadec and Auckland islands, and locally common in the North, South and Stewart islands and on their offshore islands, except scarce east of the Southern Alps. Chatham Islands Tui died out from main Chatham Island in the 1980s, but they have been successfully reintroduced to the Awatotara (2009–10). About 260 breed on South East Island, but many commute to winter on Pitt Island, where some breed; a few are resident on Mangere Island.

Conservation: Protected endemic; however, the Chatham Islands Tui is classified as endangered. Tui have adapted well to human changes in New Zealand. Even though much prime lowland forest has been cleared, the widespread planting of flowering plants (especially gums, banksias, kowhai, flax and puriri) in town and rural areas has probably provided them with a regular year-round food supply. Tui play an important ecological role as pollinators of many native trees, and, being highly mobile, they are one of the main dispersers of seeds of plants with medium-sized fruits.

Breeding: Tui establish their territories in September–October and sing from high perches, especially in the early morning and late evening. The female alone builds the nest. It is a bulky structure of twigs and sticks, lined with fine grasses, in a fork or an outer branch in the canopy or subcanopy. Eggs are laid in September–January, mainly November–December. They lay 2–3–4 eggs (29 x 21mm), which are white or pale pink with reddish-brown spots and blotches, especially at the larger end. The female alone incubates for *c.* 14 days. The young are at first fed by the female, then by both adults, and take *c.* 21 days to fledge. The oldest Tui recorded lived 12+ years.

Behaviour: Tui are usually solitary, but when travelling long distances between feeding sites they usually wheel upwards calling others, and then travel in small loose flocks. In winter, they sometimes form loose communal roosts. Even though several birds may feed simultaneously in the same tree, they have clearly defined territories. Tui are the dominant honeyeater in New Zealand; they are aggressive and pugnacious, particularly near the nest or a prominent food source. They vigorously chase other Tui and other birds from their feeding territory, and chase other Tui from breeding territories in the forest at great speed and with noisy, whirring wings. The notch in the 8th primary, particularly of males, makes the wingtips flutter, which produces the whirring noise in flight.

They also soar above the canopy and then make a noisy, near-vertical dive back into the forest. The song dialect varies in each district. It consists of rich, fluid, melodious notes intermixed with croaks, coughs, clicks, grunts, wheezes and chuckles. An energetic, high-pitched subsong is only partly audible close up.

Feeding: Preferred diet is nectar, honeydew, fruit and invertebrates. When breeding, they often commute 10+km in a day to visit a prime nectar source, such as a stand of kowhai, fuchsia, rewarewa, flax, pohutukawa or rata. Fruit dominates their late summer and autumn diet, with wineberry, fuchsia, mahoe, coprosma, kaikomako, ngaio and puriri commonly eaten. Later, they will shift 20+km to gain regular access to good crops of masting kahikatea or rimu fruit, and then move on to winter-flowering gums, banksias, puriri or kowhai. When breeding, they hawk large flying insects, and jump around beating the outside branches of shrubs and trees to disturb stick insects, cicadas and other large insects. They feed nestlings at first on small insects and nectar, and later also on berries and larger insects and spiders.

In the hand: Juveniles are at first browner (except on wings and tail) and lack the throat tufts for *c.* 6 weeks. Juveniles and first-year birds may be distinguished by the lack of a notch in the 8th primary until their first complete moult in their second autumn. Adult males are larger than adult females, and the sexes can be separated by a combination of wing length, head and bill length, and weight.

Reading: Bergquist, C. A. L. 1985. *NZ J Zool* 12: 569–571. Bergquist, C. A. L. 1987. *NZ J Zool* 14: 299–303. Craig, J. L. 1984. *NZ J Zool* 11: 195–200. Craig, J. L. 1985. *NZ J Zool* 12: 589–597. Craig, J. L. et al. 1981. *NZ J Zool* 8: 87–91. Dilks, P. 2004. *Notornis* 51: 217–226. Onley, D. J. 1986. *Notornis* 33: 45–49. Stewart, A. M. & Craig, J. L. 1985. *NZ J Zool* 12: 649–666.

CUCKOO-SHRIKES and TRILLERS

Campephagidae

About 70 species in Africa, Asia and Australasia; 2 vagrants reach New Zealand.

This family superficially resembles cuckoos by plumage colouring and slender silhouette, and shrikes by their bill shape, but they have no direct connection with either. Their plumage is usually mostly grey and black or, in trillers, black and white. The bill is short, stout and decurved near the tip, and they eat mainly insects. Their flight is undulating.

337. BLACK-FACED CUCKOO-SHRIKE *Coracina novaehollandiae* PLATE 73

Size: 33cm, 120g
Distribution: Breeds in the Lesser Sunda Islands, New Guinea, Australia and the Solomon Islands. Birds in southern Australia migrate northwards to winter in the tropics, and some juveniles and a few adults get caught up in bad weather and stray to New Zealand, mostly in autumn and spring. About 20 records, mostly sight records on or near western coasts: Motueka (1869), Invercargill (1870 and 1976), Westport (*c.* 1895 and 1931), Lake Ellesmere (1904), Greymouth (1914), Okato, Taranaki (1914), Poutu, North Kaipara Heads (1953), Himatangi, Manawatu (1955), Feilding (1965), Okuru, south of Haast (1966), Rotorua (1987), Tarras, Central Otago (1990), Stewart Island (2001 and 2011), New Plymouth (2005) and Kapiti Island (2006).
Behaviour: They feed on insects and fruit in the outer foliage of trees, dart from a prominent perch to catch flying insects, or take earthworms and insects on the ground. Their flight is strong and undulating, distinctly closing their wings at the top of each wave. They repeatedly shuffle their wings after landing on a perch. The main call is a croaky purr.
Reading: Smith, M. H. 1978. *Notornis* 25: 159–160.

338. WHITE-WINGED TRILLER *Lalage tricolor* PLATE 74

Size: 18cm, 25g
Distribution: In Australia, they breed only on the mainland. Some migrate to southern areas in spring to breed and then head north in autumn, reaching New Guinea. They are summer vagrants in Tasmania. There is one New Zealand record, of a male, seen in February–June 1969 at Macandrew Bay, Otago Peninsula.
Behaviour: Trillers feed on insects in the outer foliage of trees, hover close to the ground or alight on the ground to feed on insects. They fly rapidly with slight undulations. The call, heard mostly at dawn and dusk in New Zealand, was 'rather liquid, descending and with a similar pattern to the first part of a Chaffinch's song'.
Reading: McPherson, B. 1973. *Notornis* 20: 46–48.

BULBULS

Pycnonotidae

118 species native to Africa and southern Asia; 1 introduced to New Zealand.

Bulbuls are lively birds with cheerful and attractive songs, and so are common cage birds. Their plumage is mainly a dull brown-green or grey, but with bright patches or red, yellow and/or white. Their most notable feature is a patch of hair-like feathers on the upper nape that sometimes forms a distinct crest.

339. RED-VENTED BULBUL *Pycnonotus cafer* PLATE 79

Size: 20cm, 40g
Distribution: Natural breeding range is the Indian subcontinent, Sri Lanka, Nepal, Myanmar, and southwestern China. Successfully introduced to New Caledonia, Fiji, Samoa, Tonga, Tahiti and Hawai'i. Birds of the subspecies *bengalensis* (originally from northern India and eastern Himalayas, but a popular cage bird in ports of Asia) were liberated in Auckland (probably from a ship) in 1952. They bred well, and by 1954 the population in well-treed suburbs of central Auckland (Mt Eden, Parnell and Remuera) was as high as 50 birds. The Department of Agriculture moved to exterminate them before they firmly established and spread from Auckland. All the birds were apparently killed by 1955; however, around 1984, 2006, and again in 2013 a few birds have been seen in widely spaced localities around Auckland (Manukau, Henderson and North Shore), and so some may have survived, or more may have been released from captivity.
Breeding: One nest has been studied in New Zealand; this contained three pinkish eggs (23.5 x 16mm), closely spotted and blotched with reddish brown, in December. The nest was a compact and relatively shallow cup of fibres and twigs, lined with fine fibres, hanging from branchlets near the tip of a pine branch about 3m from the ground.
Behaviour: The common call note of the Red-vented Bulbul is a cheerful and attractive 'be-care-ful', with the last note stressed. The main note heard in Auckland was a low scratchy double croak: 'cark-cark', but single notes of more musical quality were sometimes uttered.
Feeding: Diet is a mixture of invertebrates, fruits and buds. Because they can inflict serious damage to fruit and flower crops they have been declared an unwanted organism in New Zealand. Stomachs of New Zealand birds contained native burrowing bees, wasps and some fruit.
Reading: Turbott, E. G. 1956. *Notornis* 6: 185–193. Watling, D. 1978. *Notornis* 25: 109–117.

WHISTLERS and ALLIES *Pachycephalidae*

28 species confined to Southeast Asia, Australasia and the southwestern Pacific; 3 species endemic to New Zealand.

These small, robust forest and scrub birds have relatively large rounded heads and short stout bills for catching insects amongst foliage and from crevices in branches and tree trunks. Most species have a loud and varied call, usually melodious but sometimes harsh and scolding.

340. WHITEHEAD *Mohoua albicilla* PLATE 78

Other name: Popokatea
Size: 15cm; male 18.5g, female 14.5g
Distribution: The North Island and some offshore islands only. Subfossil remains of Whiteheads have been found throughout the North Island, and they were still widespread at the time of European settlement. However, they disappeared from Northland in the 1870s, from the Auckland area in the 1880s, and from Great Barrier and Rakitu (Arid) islands since the 1950s. They are now widely but patchily distributed in native forests, some older exotic plantations and older stands of scrub on the mainland south of a line from Te Aroha to Mt Pirongia. They remain abundant on Little Barrier and Kapiti islands, and have been successfully introduced to Tiritiri Matangi, Motuora and Mana islands, and to Zealandia, Tawharanui and Maungatautari sanctuaries.
Population: Widespread and locally common in the North Island, abundant on Little Barrier and Kapiti islands.
Conservation: Protected endemic. Whiteheads declined about the time of European settlement with the loss of much lowland forest, and disappeared from the northern North Island in the late 1800s. They seem to have stabilised in their current distribution and have colonised exotic pine plantations in the central North Island, especially stands with a dense understorey of native shrubs. Successfully introduced to islands and sanctuaries where rats and mustelids have been removed.
Breeding: In late winter, family groups of Whiteheads

start to defend a territory. The group consists of a breeding pair, or sometimes two breeding females, with 0–6 surviving young from previous years. Nest-building starts in early September. The nest is built by the main female in each group in 4–7 days. It is a compact, deep cup of twigs, dry grass, leaves and leaf skeletons, rootlets, strips of bark, moss and lichen, bound with cobwebs and lined with tree-fern fibres, feathers and wool. It is placed in the canopy of the forest or sometimes in a shrub or low tree 1–15m above the ground. During nest-building and the following 2–3 days before eggs are laid, the male closely guards the female. Laying is from late September to late December, mostly between mid-October and mid-November. Usually only one brood is raised each year and most late nests are replacement clutches, but a few true second clutches are laid while helpers feed the fledglings from the first nest.

They lay 2–**3**–4 eggs (20 x 15mm, 2.5g), at 24-hour intervals. The eggs are white, variably speckled orange-brown. Only the main female incubates for 17–**18**–19 days, and broods. The male and any helpers help to feed the chicks during the fledging period of 16–**17**–19 days and after they have flown. The chicks start feeding themselves *c.* 10 days after fledging, but still beg and are fed at up to 9 months old. Young are capable of breeding at 1 year old in low-density populations, but at high densities, such as on Little Barrier Island, breeding is delayed for several years, and most young birds act as helpers instead. Adult survivorship on Little Barrier Island averaged 82%, giving a life expectancy of 5 years, but the oldest recorded bird lived over 16 years.

Whiteheads are the host of the Long-tailed Cuckoo, and family groups can sometimes be seen in summer feeding a cuckoo chick many times larger than themselves.

Behaviour: Gregarious; in small flocks all year. Whiteheads often join feeding parakeets, Saddlebacks or Silvereyes to catch the insects they dislodge. In the breeding season, the strictly territorial groups are usually a main pair and their progeny from previous years, especially young males. In autumn and winter, each group has a larger home range centred on its territory, but home ranges overlap and sometimes groups coalesce to form flocks of up to 30 birds. Whiteheads are vocal all day and all year, except during the late summer moult. Territorial song peaks in spring. Calls help to maintain contact within flocks and to proclaim territories. Only males give the loud territorial calls, usually from a prominent perch. These calls are varied, based on a phrase starting with several chirps, followed by a string of clear canary-like chimes or 'peek-o, peek-o, peek-o' calls and descending slurs and finishing with a chuckle. The contact call in flocks is a single harsh 'cheert', which forms a constant chatter in the distance, and the alarm calls are an excited, loud 'chirrt' and a ringing 'chee-chee-chee'.

Feeding: Diet is mainly invertebrates, but includes some fruit. Main prey are spiders, beetles, caterpillars and moths, gleaned from leaves, twigs and branches in the canopy and understorey, sometimes by hanging upside down. They feed on invertebrates dislodged by other feeding birds, and occasionally on insects under loose bark on trunks and large branches; they rarely feed on the ground. They eat some fruit of native shrubs, especially mahoe, matipo, coprosma and hangehange.

In the hand: Adult males have an almost pure white head and shiny black legs, but the crown and nape is shaded brown in adult females and juveniles of both sexes. Males are larger and heavier than females, and so most birds can be sexed from a combination of wing and weight, even though throughout the North Island there is some overlap: wing 67–**71.5**–77 cf. 62–**66**–70mm, and weight 16–**18.5**–21 cf. 12–**14.5**–19.5g. Juvenile females in their first winter can be separated from adult females by having fleshy rictal flanges and pale grey (not dark grey) legs.

Reading: Gill, B. J. 1993. *Notornis* 40: 141–143. Gill, B. J. & McLean, I. G. 1986. *NZ J Zool* 13: 267–271. Gill, B. J. & McLean, I. G. 1992. *Condor* 94: 628–635. Gill, B. J. & Veitch, C. R. 1990. *Notornis* 37: 141–145. McLean, I. G. & Gill, B. J. 1988. *Emu* 88: 177–182. Moeed, A. & Fitzgerald, B. M. 1982, *NZ J Zool* 9: 391–403. Robertson, H. A. et al. 1983. *NZ J Zool* 10: 87–98. Southey, I. & Gill, B. J. 2003. *Notornis* 50: 235.

341. YELLOWHEAD *Mohoua ochrocephala* PLATE 78

Other names: Mohua, Bush Canary
Size: 15cm; male 30g, female 25g
Distribution: South Island only. In the 1800s, Yellowheads were abundant and conspicuous in the beech forests, particularly red beech, from Nelson and Marlborough to Southland, and in the podocarp-hardwood forests of the West Coast and Stewart Island. They declined throughout the South Island in the late 1800s and

disappeared from Banks Peninsula. However, the dramatic decline of Yellowheads began in *c.* 1890 after ship rats and mustelids were introduced. By 1930, they had disappeared from Stewart Island and the podocarp forests of the West Coast, and subsequently have gone from northwestern Nelson, Nelson Lakes National Park, Lewis Pass, Paparoa Range and many South Island beech forests, including northern and central Westland. They have now gone from nearly 85% of their former range and are well established only in Fiordland and Mount Aspiring national parks, extending east to the Dart Valley; in and near Arthur's Pass National Park, especially in the Hawdon and South Hurunui valleys; the Catlins; the Blue Mountains; and the Landsborough Valley. Small, isolated groups remain in the Rowallan, Takitimu, Longwood and Waikaia forests. Successfully introduced to Pigeon Island, Lake Wakatipu; Breaksea, Chalky, Anchor, Pigeon and Secretary islands in Fiordland; Codfish Island and Ulva Island. A transfer to Nukuwaiata Island, Marlborough Sounds was initially successful, but few birds remain.

Population: 5000–10,000 birds, most numerous in the Catlins, Blue Mountains and Landsborough Valley, and on islands in Fiordland.

Conservation: Protected vulnerable endemic. Forest clearance and selective logging of mature trees removed most of their prime habitat: lowland red beech on fertile river terraces. Stoat and rat predation are probably the main cause of Yellowhead decline. Numbers of rodents explode after beech has flowered and seeded profusely (mast), about every 3–5 years, and the number of stoats also explodes following this boom in their main prey. Yellowheads often feed noisily on or close to the ground, and females incubate and oversee nestlings for long periods in their nest holes; this results in a periodic population crash and a disproportionately high loss of females. Competition with introduced vespulid wasps since the 1940s may have contributed to the dramatic decline of Yellowheads in the northern half of the South Island. The aims of conservation management are to control stoats and rats by trapping or aerial 1080 poison operations at the best remaining breeding sites, and to transfer birds to predator-free islands.

Breeding: Yellowheads breed as pairs or in small groups with one or more helpers. They nest in holes high in mature or rotting trees, usually beech trees. The female builds a cup-shaped nest of moss, rootlets, twigs and spiders' webs, lined with fine grass; this is unusual for hole-nesting birds. Laying is from early October to late January, with peaks in early November and late December corresponding to the two clutches usually laid by each pair in good habitats; however, in places where the habitat is poor, most pairs probably lay just one clutch per year.

They lay 1–3–5 pink eggs (23.5 x 18mm), faintly freckled pale reddish brown. The female alone incubates for *c.* 20 days, and broods. The male and any helpers help to feed the chicks during the *c.* 22-day fledging period and after they have flown. The chicks still beg and get fed right through their first winter. The young usually breed first at 2 years old. Adult Yellowheads at Knobs Flat, Eglinton Valley had an annual survivorship of 83% and life expectancy of 5 years, but the oldest recorded bird lived to at least 16 years old.

Yellowheads and Brown Creepers are the hosts of the Long-tailed Cuckoo, and in late summer Yellowheads can sometimes be seen feeding a cuckoo chick many times larger than themselves.

Behaviour: Gregarious when not breeding. From midsummer to the end of winter, family parties coalesce into roaming feeding flocks of up to 25 Yellowheads; the bigger the flock, the noisier. They often lead mixed-species feeding flocks, and especially join parakeets to feed on insects they have disturbed. They are vocal all day and all year, except during the late summer moult. Territorial song peaks in late spring. Only males give the loud territorial song: musical, canary-like whistles and trills. Other calls are loud and varied, mainly a rapid staccato chatter, musical whistles and slurs, and the female only sometimes utters a buzzing call.

Feeding: Diet is mainly invertebrates, especially caterpillars, but includes some fruit. They search vigorously for and glean insects and spiders, often upside down, in or just under the canopy in the leaves and twigs. They also search cracks and crevices of branches and trunks, pressing with their tail feathers until these are so worn down that they look like spines. Yellowheads sometimes come to ground but prefer to scratch through the leaf litter that accumulates in tree forks.

Reading: Dilks, P. 1999. *Notornis* 46: 323–332. Dilks, P. et al. 2003. *NZ J Ecol* 27: 1–9. Elliott, G. P. 1996. *NZ J Zool* 23: 229–237. Elliott, G. P. 1996. *NZ J Zool* 23: 239–247. Elliott, G. P. et al. 1996. *NZ J Zool* 23: 267–278. Gaze, P. D. 1985. *Notornis* 32: 261–269. Read, A. F. 1987. *Notornis* 34: 11–18. Read, A. F. 1988. *NZ J Zool* 15: 471–480. Read, A. F. & O'Donnell, C. F. J. 1987. *Notornis* 34: 307–315.

342. BROWN CREEPER *Mohoua novaeseelandiae* PLATE 78

Other name: Pipipi
Size: 13cm; male 13.5g, female 11g
Distribution: South Island, Stewart Island and some offshore islands only. Although widespread at the time of European settlement, Brown Creepers have declined with the loss of lowland forest and the introduction of mammalian predators. They are now widely but patchily distributed in native forests, exotic plantations and scrub from sea level to the treeline on the South Island mainland. Most common to the north and west of the Southern Alps, especially at higher altitudes in mountain/silver beech forests; in red/silver beech forest on river flats to the east of the Alps, in Fiordland and on Stewart Island and some of its offshore islands. They are also in dry scrub of Marlborough, Banks Peninsula, and South Canterbury coastal hills; in pine forests of Nelson and Otago; and in native forests around Dunedin and in the Catlins.
Population: Widespread and locally common in forests and scrub on the South Island mainland and some islands in the Marlborough Sounds and in Fiordland; widespread and common on Stewart Island, and its northeastern offshore islands; abundant on Codfish Island.
Conservation: Protected endemic. Brown Creepers declined soon after European settlement with the loss of much lowland forest and the introduction of rats, cats and mustelids. Little is known of population trends, but they seem to have stabilised in their current distribution.
Breeding: Pairs defend their territory all year. From early September, females start building the nest, taking 5–**10**–17 days. The nest is a compact deep cup of strips of bark, small twigs, grasses, moss, leaves and leaf skeletons and lichen, bound with cobwebs and lined with dried grasses, feathers and wool. It is placed in a dense patch of vegetation in the canopy of the forest or sometimes in a shrub or low tree 1–**4**–10m above the ground. During nest-building, the following 2–3 days before eggs are laid and the first part of the laying period, the male closely guards the female. Laying is from late September to late January, with peaks in early October and late November representing the normal two clutches, but up to four clutches can be laid in a season if nests fail early.

They lay 2–**3**–4 eggs (18.5 x 14mm, 1.9g) at 24-hour intervals. The eggs are white to dark pink, variably speckled reddish brown. The female alone incubates for 17–**19**–21 days, and broods. Both sexes feed the young, which fledge at 18–**20**–22 days old. The male cares for the fledged young once the female starts to incubate the next clutch. Young birds are occasionally fed through to the end of winter. The young stay as a group once they have become independent and often coalesce with other juvenile groups to form autumn and winter flocks of up to 60 birds. Brown Creepers are capable of breeding at 1 year old. At Kaikoura, adult survival was over 82%, giving a life expectancy of 5 years.

Brown Creepers are the main host of the Long-tailed Cuckoo in the South and Stewart islands, and a pair can sometimes be seen in summer feeding a cuckoo chick many times larger than themselves.
Behaviour: Adults are normally strongly territorial all year, but some that breed at high altitude move downhill and form flocks in winter. Brown Creepers often associate with other feeding forest birds, especially Silvereyes, parakeets, Grey Warblers and Fantails. They are vocal all day and all year, except during the late summer moult. Territorial song peaks in spring. Only males give the loud territorial song, which varies from bird to bird, and is a phrase including slurs, musical whistles and harsh notes, described as 'chi-roh-ree-roh-ree-ree'. Females sing a rapid sequence of brief notes, the last being high-pitched and prolonged, often in a duet with the male. A wide variety of 'chi's, chatters, trills and harsh 'zick's are given.
Feeding: Diet is mainly invertebrates but includes some fruit. Main prey are beetles, spiders, flies, moths and caterpillars, gleaned from leaves and especially from small branches in the canopy, sometimes by hanging upside down. Brown Creepers occasionally feed on insects under loose bark on trunks and large branches, and only rarely feed on the ground. Some ripe fruit of native shrubs such as coprosma are eaten, especially in autumn.
In the hand: Males are larger and heavier than females. Wing length and weight showed no overlap in a sample of 26 male and 18 females at Kaikoura: 59.5–**61**–64 cf. 54.5–**57**–58.5mm and 12–**13.4**–15 cf. 10.5–**11.0**–12g respectively. Before May, juveniles can be distinguished by their yellow bill flanges and dark brown (not light brown) legs and feet.
Reading: Cunningham, J. B. 1984. *Notornis* 31: 19–22. Cunningham, J. B. 1985. PhD thesis, Uni Canterbury. Gill, B. J. et al. 1980. *Notornis* 27: 129–132.

WOODSWALLOWS and ALLIES *Artamidae*

20 species in Australasia; 1 introduced species and 2 vagrants to New Zealand, although 1 of them bred once.

Woodswallows are not closely related to the swallows (Hirundinidae) and have been grouped with Bell Magpies, Butcherbirds and Currawongs.

Woodswallows are accomplished fliers, soaring and gliding gracefully on long, curved, and stiffly held wings as they catch insects with their short stout bill with a strongly decurved upper mandible. They also feed on the ground and take nectar and pollen. Woodswallows build a flimsy nest of fine twigs in a tree fork. They are gregarious, often roosting huddled in tight bunches even in warm weather.

The bell magpies are medium-to-large crow-like songbirds. They are mostly black, grey and white, and have large, powerful, straight bills. They are omnivorous and feed mainly on the ground in open country. They have loud and tuneful calls.

343. AUSTRALIAN MAGPIE *Gymnorhina tibicen* PLATE 79

Size: 41cm, 350g

Geographical variation: Eight subspecies are recognised in Australia. It seems that three subspecies were brought to New Zealand: white-backed *tyrannica* of southeastern Australia, the smaller white-backed *hypoleuca* of Tasmania, and the black-backed *tibicen* of northern Australia and New Guinea. The subspecies interbreed where they meet in Australia and in New Zealand. The white-backed forms predominate in New Zealand except in Hawke's Bay and in North Canterbury, where up to 95% of birds are of the black-backed form.

Distribution: Natural range is Australia and southern New Guinea. Over 1000 Magpies were introduced into New Zealand by Acclimatisation societies in 1864–74, with the main releases being on Kawau Island and in Hawke's Bay, Wellington, Canterbury and Otago. The Otago liberation failed, but the others were successful, and Magpies spread slowly so that by 1945 there were three discrete populations: from the Bay of Islands to South Auckland, the southern North Island, and the eastern South Island from Kaikoura to near Dunedin. The spread has continued, and Magpies are now common in open pasture, forest patches and suburban areas throughout the North Island and on suitable offshore islands, and common through the eastern South Island from Blenheim to Southland, and are widely distributed and becoming more common around Nelson and on the West Coast from Westport to Franz Josef; still scarce in Golden Bay, South Westland and Stewart Island, and absent from forested parts of Fiordland and above the treeline.

Population: Locally common in hill country and arable farmland with shelterbelts of pines, macrocarpas or eucalypts.

Breeding: The social organisation of Magpies is complex: pairs, family groups of 2–10 birds and unrelated groups of 2–10 birds defend territories all year. There are also non-territorial flocks of up to 80 birds, mainly yearlings and subadults. In each defended territory, there is normally only one breeding pair, but sometimes two females have separate nests within the territory, each attended by a different male. The breeding birds do not receive help at the nest from the other birds in the territory, and breeding success of groups is no better than for pairs. Nest-building begins in June. The nest is a platform of twigs, with a cup lined with small twigs, leaves, grass and wool. It is usually high in tall trees such as pines, poplars, macrocarpas or eucalypts, but sometimes on power poles and in low hedges if tall trees are absent. Laying is in July–November; later nests are mostly replacement clutches but some are true second clutches.

They lay 2–**3**–**4**–5 pale bluish-green eggs (39 x 28mm) with olive blotches. The female alone incubates for 20–21 days. Chicks are fed by both parents and fledge at *c.* 28 days old. A few females breed at 1 year old, but most Magpies are at least 3 years old when they start breeding. In the Manawatu, survivorship of adults averaged 85%, giving a life expectancy of 6 years. In Australia, the oldest banded Magpie lived over 19 years.

Behaviour: Many Magpies are territorial all year, some in pairs but others in groups of related or unrelated birds. During the breeding season, some individuals become fiercely territorial and attack people and other animals approaching the nest. Many yearlings and some subadults remain in non-territorial flocks throughout the year, and, although sometimes termed 'nomadic', these flocks are usually found in the same area year after year. The territorial song is a beautiful, flute-like carolling, described by the poet Denis Glover as 'Quardle oodle ardle wardle doodle', and is most often heard in the early

morning and at dusk when birds are going to roost.
Feeding: Diet is mainly invertebrates, supplemented with some seeds and occasional vertebrates and carrion. Magpies were introduced to New Zealand to control pasture pests and were protected until 1951. They eat many harmful pests including grass grubs, weevils, porina and army worm caterpillars, but probably do not keep these pests under control. They also eat worms, spiders, ants, flies, crickets and snails. Plant material includes seeds and grain. They can attack and kill birds up to the size of White-faced Heron and Pheasant, and eat eggs, nestlings, lizards, mice and sick or dead sheep and lambs, but they have little impact on rural bird populations compared with other predators. Magpies usually feed in open pasture or on ploughed paddocks, and peck prey from the surface, although they can also probe quite deeply.
Reading: McCaskill, L. W. 1945. *Notornis* 1: 86–104. Morgan, D. et al. 2005. *Notornis* 52: 61–74. Morgan, D. et al. 2006: *NZ J Zool* 33: 17–29. Veltman, C. J. 1989. *Ibis* 131: 601–608. Veltman, C. J. & Hickson, R. E. 1989. *Aust J Ecol* 14: 319–326.

344. MASKED WOODSWALLOW *Artamus personatus* PLATE 73

Size: 19cm, 35g
Distribution: Breeds in mainland Australia only. They are found mainly in open forests and scrubland of arid regions, but are migratory and nomadic within Australia, and a pair once reached New Zealand. The birds were seen at Naseby, Central Otago from January 1972 to August 1973, and although a nest was not found, they are believed to have reared two chicks in an exotic pine plantation in the summer of 1972–73.
Breeding: In Australia, most nests are within several metres of the ground. They lay 2–3 pale greyish-white eggs (21 x 17mm), which are profusely marked with brown blotches and smudges, especially at the larger end. Both adults incubate and feed the young. Flying but apparently dependent young were first seen at Naseby in early March 1973.
Behaviour: A persistent twittering and chattering kept the Naseby birds in contact. They often roosted huddled together on a wire or branch.
Reading: Child, P. 1974. *Notornis* 21: 85–87. Child, P. 1975. *Notornis* 22: 67–68. Darby, J. T. 1972. *Notornis* 19: 114–117.

345. WHITE-BROWED WOODSWALLOW *Artamus superciliosus* PLATE 73

Size: 19cm, 35g
Distribution: Breeds in mainland Australia only, especially in eastern states. Found in open woodland, scrub, open country and cities. They are migratory and nomadic, and vagrants have reached New Zealand twice. Four males were seen at Naseby Forest, Central Otago, between December 1971 and July 1973, associating with a pair of Masked Woodswallows that apparently bred there. On 21 September 1991, a single male appeared on the site of the limeworks at Miranda, Firth of Thames.
Reading: Child, P. 1974. *Notornis* 21: 85–87. Child, P. 1975. *Notornis* 22: 67–68. Darby, J. T. 1972. *Notornis* 19: 114–117.

FANTAILS *Rhipiduridae*

About 50 species in Southeast Asia, Australasia and the islands of the south-western Pacific; 1 endemic species (following the extinction of the Lord Howe Island subspecies) and one vagrant.

A varied group of insectivorous forest birds with distinctively long tails that can be fanned, and proportionately large heads and short broad bills with abundant bristles at the base. Most hawk insects in the air with short flights, but some glean insects from the foliage.

346. FANTAIL *Rhipidura fuliginosa* PLATE 78

Other name: Piwakawaka
Size: 16cm (including 8cm of exposed tail); 8g
Geographical variation: Three extant subspecies, all in New Zealand: North Island Fantail *placabilis*, South Island Fantail *fuliginosa*, and Chatham Island Fantail *penita*. The subspecies *cervina* on Lord Howe Island is extinct. The South Island subspecies has two colour forms – pied and black, with the black form making up 12–25% of the population, highest in native forest and at higher altitudes. Black phase birds make up less than 0.1% of North Island birds but are recorded mainly around Wellington, indicating some gene flow across Cook Strait.
Distribution: Breeds widely throughout the North, South and Stewart islands and their offshore islands, and on the Chathams and The Snares. They have not been recorded on any of the other subantarctic islands or on the Kermadecs. Fantails are common in forest, scrub, farmland where there are scattered trees, farm gardens, orchards and suburban gardens from sea level to 1500m, but they are scarce in the dry open country of inland Marlborough, the Mackenzie Basin and Central Otago, which are prone to severe frosts and snow in winter. Some adults are sedentary, but others seem to wander and form loose flocks in winter and early spring. Independent juveniles disperse away from their natal territory.
Population: Widespread and locally abundant, especially on forest edges and second-growth scrub habitats. Fantails are one of the most common and widely distributed native birds on the New Zealand mainland.
Conservation: Protected endemic. The Fantail is one of the few native forest birds to have benefited from the large-scale clearance of forest and the creation of forest edge and scrub habitats. Fantail populations undergo major fluctuations from year to year; crashes especially follow prolonged or severe winter and spring storms. These fluctuations can lead to brief local extinctions on islands (e.g. as seen on South East Island, Chathams), but as their annual productivity is high and juveniles (and possibly some adults) disperse, they quickly recolonise temporarily vacated areas.
Breeding: Fantails remain in pairs all year. Males retain the same territory in successive years, but high mortality means that few pairs remain together in successive seasons. Territorial defence becomes obvious in August, and first nests are built in about a fortnight in late August. In the North Island Fantail, the female apparently builds the nest alone, but in the South Island Fantail the male helps, especially early in the season when not looking after dependent fledglings. The nest is a neat cup of dried grass, strips of bark, moss and cobwebs, lined with fine fern fibres, hair and feathers, and with a tail of nest material hanging about 10cm down from the bottom of the nest. It is usually built about 2–3m above the ground in a slender fork of an understorey shrub, or on the frond of a tree fern; it is often protected from above by overhanging vegetation and is normally above a gap in the shrub layer. On the New Zealand mainland, eggs are laid from late August to February, during which they raise 2–5 broods; one pair raised 15 young from 16 eggs laid in 5 clutches in a season. Island populations (including the Chathams) have a shorter season, with a later start and earlier finish, and raise up to 2 broods per year.

They lay 2–**3–4**–5 white eggs speckled with light brown spots (16 x 12mm). Clutches of three eggs are most common at the start and end of the season, whereas clutches of four are common in November–December. On the mainland, incubation starts with the final egg, but on the Chathams it begins with the laying of the penultimate egg. Both birds incubate for 13–**14**–16 days and brood and feed the nestlings during the fledging period of 11–**13**–16 days. After leaving the nest, the chicks often remain close together and are fed by both parents, but when the female starts building the next nest, the male looks after the fledglings. Some juveniles may breed at *c.* 2 months old, but most breed the next season at *c.* 9 months old. Juvenile and adult mortality is high in New Zealand, and the oldest bird recorded lived only 3 years, however, similar species in Australia have reached 10 years old.
Behaviour: Fantails are strongly territorial while breeding, but territories break down in autumn. Loose flocks and communal roosts of up to 10–20 birds are sometimes seen in winter. Calls of Fantails are simple, with the main territorial call of the male being a harsh rhythmical 'saw-like' song: 'tweet-a-tweet-a-tweet-a-tweet . . .'. The usual contact call is a penetrating, sweet-sounding 'cheet'. Birds regularly call from near the nest during incubation and brooding change-overs and when waiting to feed nestlings. Males are more vocal than females throughout the day, and in the early morning only males sing from song-posts.
Feeding: Diet is mainly invertebrates, occasionally supplemented with fruit. Main prey are moths, flies, wasps, beetles and spiders, taken while fly-catching in the understorey, along tracks, in forest clearings and

on river flats, and sometimes above the canopy. They are very manoeuvrable and use their fanned tail to stop in mid-air and to change direction when hawking and flycatching. Fantails also hop around upside down along tree-fern fronds or among foliage to pick prey from the undersides of leaves. They rarely feed on the ground, except on predator-free offshore islands. Fantails often associate with feeding Silvereyes, Whiteheads, parakeets or Saddlebacks and feed on insects dislodged by feeding birds.

In the hand: Males and females are alike. Juveniles have a tawny (not white) eyestripe, and secondary coverts have large fawn tips, the black throat band is absent and the legs are pale grey, not black.

Reading: Blackburn, A. 1965. *Notornis* 12: 127–137. Blackburn, A. 1966. *Notornis* 13: 189–196. Dennison, T. C. et al. 1979. *Notornis* 26: 392–395. McLean, I. G. 1984. *Notornis* 31: 279–283. McLean, I. G. & Jenkins, P. F. 1980. *Notornis* 27: 105–113. McLean, I. G. & Jenkins, P. F. 1980. *Ibis* 122: 98–102. Moeed, A. & Fitzgerald, B. M. 1982. *NZ J Zool* 9: 391–403. Powlesland, M. H. 1982. *Notornis* 29: 181–195.

347. WILLIE WAGTAIL *Rhipidura leucophrys* PLATE 74

Size: 20cm, 20g

Distribution: Breeds in New Guinea, the Moluccas, Bismarck Archipelago, the Solomons and throughout mainland Australia and on many of its offshore islands, but is rarely recorded in Tasmania. It is a partial migrant, with many birds breeding in Victoria and New South Wales moving north to overwinter in Queensland. One New Zealand record, a first-year bird at Mangere Island, Chatham Islands, in October 1999.

Behaviour: Frequents most habitats, and feeds mainly on flying insects taken on the wing in short flights from a perch like a Fantail, but also hops while feeding on the ground.

Reading: Gummer, H. 2002. *Notornis* 49: 186–188.

CROWS and JAYS *Corvidae*

About 105 species worldwide; 1 introduced to New Zealand.

Medium-to-large birds with mainly black plumage (crows) or more varied colours (jays) with large, powerful, straight bills. They are omnivorous and feed mainly on the ground in open country. They have loud, simple, often harsh calls.

Reading: Madge, S. & Burn, H. 1994. *Crows and Jays: A Guide to the Crows, Jays and Magpies of the World.* London: Christopher Helm.

348. ROOK *Corvus frugilegus* PLATE 79

Size: 45cm; male 425g, female 375g

Distribution: Natural breeding range is Europe and Asia, east to Siberia and Mongolia; many migrate south to winter around the Mediterranean, in Iran and the northern part of the Indian subcontinent. Several hundred birds were introduced into New Zealand by Acclimatisation societies in 1862–74. Liberations in Nelson and Auckland failed, even though some Auckland birds persisted to 1905; however, liberations in Hawke's Bay and Canterbury were successful, even if they spread very slowly at first. In the first 50 years to 1920, Rooks in Hawke's Bay had spread only 30km, although colonies established near Feilding in the 1920s and near Pirinoa, southern Wairarapa, in 1930. The spread was very slow until numbers built up to pest levels in Hawke's Bay, leading to shooting and poisoning in the 1960s and 1970s. Displaced Rooks then spread rapidly and established colonies near Miranda (Firth of Thames), Tolaga Bay (Gisborne) and Waitotara (Taranaki) in the 1960s; in southern Hawke's Bay and at Aokautere (Manawatu) in the 1970s; in southern Waikato in the 1980s; and in the Pohangina Valley, Cheltenham and Taihape area in the 1990s. Rooks in Canterbury spread less than 50km in the first 100 years, except for the establishment of a colony near Middlemarch (North Otago). Rooks are capable of dispersing widely, with mainly juveniles seen in Northland, Wellington, Southland, and on Chatham and Stewart islands.

Population: Locally common in hill country and arable farmland in Hawke's Bay and formerly around Banks Peninsula. The total population in 1978 was just under 30,000 birds, of which *c.* 25,000 were in Hawke's Bay and 2500 in Canterbury. Since then, poisoning, shooting and nest destruction have greatly reduced populations, and made Rooks become very wary, more dispersed, and more nomadic.

Breeding: Occasionally a pair of Rooks nest in isolation, but they usually nest in colonies of 20–100 pairs, and of up to 900 pairs. Even though most birds roost away from their colony in winter, they usually visit the colony each day, in the early morning and sometimes again in the late afternoon. Nest-building begins in August. The nest is a large untidy platform of twigs and lined with small twigs and leaves, in the top of a tall tree such as a pine, macrocarpa or gum. Laying is from late August to mid-November; most late nests are replacement clutches.

They lay 1–**3–4**–7 pale greenish-blue eggs (39 x 28mm, 16g) with brown blotches. The female alone incubates for 15–**17**–19 days and broods the nestlings, but the male feeds both the chicks and the female. The fledging period is 26–**33**–38 days, shorter for smaller broods. Some Rooks breed at 1 year old, especially in establishing colonies or in colonies recently reduced by poisoning, but usually they do not start nesting until 2–3 years old. A Rook banded in Hawke's Bay lived to *c.* 15 years old, but in Europe the oldest Rook lived at least 19 years.

Behaviour: Gregarious all year; breeding in colonies and roosting in 'parishes' (large communal roosts of up to 5000 birds from several colonies) and feeding in flocks. They are extremely wary, especially after being persecuted, and birds quickly take to the wing as danger approaches, and utter their characteristic 'caw' or 'kaah'; an occasional higher-pitched 'kiow' is uttered as the birds circle overhead. The 'caw' call is the usual contact call as Rooks fly in loose flocks.

Feeding: Diet is a mix of invertebrates and vegetable matter. The main prey are beetles (especially grass grubs), flies, caterpillars (especially porina), earthworms, spiders and wasps. When feeding on grass grubs, they uproot infested damaged pasture in their search. Plant matter eaten includes walnuts, acorns, maize, cereals, pumpkins, seeds of peas and beans, stock feed, and occasional leaves of clover and grasses. In autumn, Rooks store walnuts by burying them in a tuft of grass or in a crevice between clods of ploughed soil, and then in late autumn and winter they search for and recover stored nuts. Birds feeding on newly sown crops methodically work their way along rows, extracting each seed in turn. They sometimes also damage ripening peas, and because of this Rooks in Hawke's Bay were declared a 'pest of local importance' in 1971 and nearly 86,000 birds had been poisoned in Hawke's Bay by 1985. The damage was much reduced on the Heretaunga Plains following the removal of several very large colonies, but this control caused the rapid expansion in range of the species and a lower overall density and hence less economic impact by the species.

In the hand: Males are larger than females: wing 305–**322**–338mm cf. 280–**301**–314mm; bill 56–**60**–68mm cf. 46–**56**–64mm. The brood patch of the female in the breeding season is the only consistently reliable feature. Adults have a bare face, whereas juveniles have cheeks and chin covered in black feathers until about August, and nostrils covered in black feathers until about 1 year old. In spring and summer, juveniles have very worn blackish-brown wing feathers, whereas adults have glossy black wings.

Reading: Bull, P. C. 1957. *Notornis* 7: 137–161. Bull, P. C. & Porter, R. E. R. 1975. *NZ J Zool* 2: 63–92. Coleman, J. D. 1971. *NZ J Sci* 14: 494–506. Coleman, J. D. 1972. *Notornis* 19: 118–139. Langham, N. P. E. & Porter, R. E. R. 1991. *NZ J Ecol* 18: 389–397. MacMillan, B. W. H. 1983. *NZ J Agr Res* 26: 139–145. McLennan, J. A. & Porter, R. E. R. 1979. *NZ J Zool* 6: 329–337. Porter, R. E. R. et al. 2008. *J Roy Soc NZ* 38: 25–36. Purchas, T. P. G. 1979. *NZ J Zool* 6: 321–327. Purchas, T. P. G. 1980. *NZ J Zool* 7: 557–578.

MONARCH FLYCATCHERS *Monarchidae*

About 140 species in Africa, southern Asia, Southeast Asia, Australasia and the islands of the southwestern Pacific; 2 are vagrants to New Zealand.

A varied group of largely tropical forest birds with proportionately large heads and short, broad, bills with abundant bristles at the base for detecting insect prey. Tail length varies from medium to very long. Most glean insects from leaves and branches, though some hawk for flying insects with short flights.

349. SATIN FLYCATCHER *Myiagra cyanoleuca* PLATE 74

Size: 16cm, 17g
Distribution: Breeds in eastern Australia from Cape York to Tasmania. They migrate from the southern part of their range to northern Queensland and New Guinea, leaving in late February and March and returning in September. Three New Zealand records: a female seen in Gisborne (June 1963), a male found dead at Motueka Sandspit (December 1988), and one reported from Okarito (March 1992).
Reading: Blackburn, A. 1963. *Notornis* 10: 262–265.

350. BLACK-FACED MONARCH *Monarcha melanopsis* PLATE 74

Size: 17cm, 25g
Distribution: Breeds in coastal eastern Australia from Cape York Peninsula to Victoria, especially in the tropics. They migrate from the southern part of their range to northern Queensland and New Guinea, leaving in February to April, and returning in August and September. One New Zealand record: a juvenile male killed by a cat at Stratford (April 1996).
Reading: Tennyson, A. 1997. *Notornis* 44: 267–269.

AUSTRALASIAN ROBINS *Petroicidae*

About 45 species in Australasia; 4 species endemic to New Zealand.

Australasian robins are small, robust, confiding forest birds with large heads and short necks, an upright stance on moderately long, thin legs. Their bill is short, broad at the base and surrounded with abundant bristles. Males are mostly black, grey and white with patches of red or yellow, whereas females have a duller basic colour and lack bright colours. Although superficially similar, this group is not closely related to the European Robin *Erithacus rubecula*, which belongs to the thrushes Turdidae.

351. TOMTIT *Petroica macrocephala* PLATE 80

Other names: Miromiro, Pied Tit (North Island); Ngirungiru, Yellow-breasted Tit (South Island); Black Tit (The Snares)
Size: 13cm, 11g; 20g (The Snares)
Geographical variation: Five subspecies, each restricted to an island and its offshore islands: North Island Tomtit *toitoi*, South Island Tomtit *macrocephala*, Chatham Islands Tomtit *chathamensis*, Snares Tomtit *dannefaerdi*, and Auckland Islands Tomtit *marrineri*.
Distribution: New Zealand only. Subfossil, midden and historical records show that Tomtits were throughout the mainland of New Zealand at the time of European settlement. In the North Island, they are widespread and locally common from Kaitaia to Cape Palliser, although they are scarce between Whangarei and the southern Waikato, sparsely distributed in the lowlands of Rangitikei, Manawatu and Horowhenua. Moderate numbers on the Hen and Chickens, Little Barrier and Kapiti islands, and a few persist on Great Barrier Island. Successfully introduced to Cape Sanctuary, Cape Kidnappers in 2007.

The South Island Tomtit is common to the west of and in the Southern Alps from Farewell Spit and the western part of the Marlborough Sounds to Fiordland, and on Banks Peninsula, in Southland and the Catlins; throughout Stewart Island and its outliers, and on the Solanders Group.

The Chatham Islands Tomtit was common throughout the group in the 1800s, but disappeared from Chatham Island in the 1970s and was removed from Little Mangere and Mangere islands in 1976 so that they would not compete with the critically endangered Black Robin, leaving the subspecies only on Pitt and South East islands. They were successfully reintroduced to Mangere Island in 1987–89, and have made their way to Little Mangere Island. The Snares Tomtit is throughout the group, and the Auckland Islands Tomtit is on Auckland, Adams, Ocean, Rose, Ewing and Enderby islands.

Throughout New Zealand, Tomtits are in mature native forests, especially open beech forest, in second-growth manuka/kanuka scrub, and in some districts they use older stands of exotic plantations. On The Snares and the Auckland Islands, they feed in tussockland with scattered shrubs, and out onto coastal rocks and even floating kelp.

Population: Widespread and locally common, especially in beech forests of the central North Island and the South Island. The Chatham Islands Tomtit numbered *c.* 850 birds in the late 1990s, and there were *c.* 500 pairs of Snares Tomtits in 1987.

Conservation: Protected endemic. Tomtits declined with the clearance of much lowland forest and the introduction of mammalian predators, but they have adapted well to the changed conditions, and their populations have probably stabilised. The Chatham Islands Tomtit has not adapted so well, and declined through the 1900s to have a very restricted distribution on some predator-free islands. Translocations of Tomtits have had relatively poor success; the Tiritiri Matangi Island transfer in 2004 was not helped by a bird returning over 50km to the source site in the Hunua Ranges.

Breeding: Tomtits have been studied on the mainland, the Chathams and The Snares. They maintain their territory all year, and usually keep the same partner year after year. From July onwards, males start to sing their territorial song, and territorial defence and singing increase markedly in August. The female takes about 4 days to build its bulky cup nest of twigs, bark, fibres and moss, bound together with cobwebs and lined with tree-fern scales, moss, fine grasses and occasionally with feathers or wool. It is 1–**2**–**4**–10m off the ground in a sheltered cavity in a tree where a branch has broken off and rotted out, in a fork, attached to the trunk of a tree fern or in a thick tangle of vines such as *Muehlenbeckia* or bush lawyer.

Mainland subspecies of Tomtits lay in September–January, during which time each pair raises up to three broods, but if their nests fail, they can re-lay up to six times in a season. They lay 3–**4**–6 cream eggs (18 x 15mm) with yellowish-purple spots at the larger end. Eggs are laid daily, usually shortly after sunrise. The female incubates for 15–**16**–17 days, and broods the chicks. She is regularly fed near the nest by the male, and both parents feed the nestlings. The fledging period is 17–**18**–20 days. Fledglings are fed by both birds, but once the female starts re-nesting, the male takes full care of them. Juveniles start foraging at *c.* 28 days old, but continue to be fed until *c.* 35 days old. Once independent, they soon disperse from their natal territory.

Chatham Islands Tomtits lay from late September to mid-December and raise two broods. They lay 2–**3**–4 eggs (19 x 15mm, 2.4g). The female incubates for 17–**19**–21 days, and the chicks fledge at 16–21 days old.

Snares Tomtits have similar breeding behaviour, but most nests are within a metre of the ground in hollows in logs or stumps, or among roots of wind-thrown trees. They lay from mid-October to mid-December and usually raise only one brood each year, but in El Niño years, which are exceptionally windy and wet on The Snares, they may not breed at all. They lay 2–**3** eggs (20 x 15.5mm). The female incubates for 18–20 days, and the chicks fledge at 17–22 days old.

Tomtits start breeding at 1 year old. The oldest Tomtit recorded to date lived just 3 years, but some probably live 10+ years.

Behaviour: Adult Tomtits remain on their territory all year, but only actively defend it from about July to February, when the male patrols his patch and sings from prominent perches. The main territorial song of the male is a loud and clear burst: 'ti-oly oly oly oh', often answered by a neighbouring male; a much softer version of this song is sometimes sung by the female. Tomtits have a variety of other calls, the main ones being a simple, short, high-pitched 'swee' used by males and a reedy 'seet' used by females as a contact call. In aggressive encounters between birds, they raise their crown feathers, but in encounters with other species, including humans, all but Snares Tomtits flash the white frontal spot in the centre of their forehead.

Feeding: Diet is mainly invertebrates, supplemented with small fruits in autumn and winter. Main prey are spiders, beetles, caterpillars, moths, weta, earthworms, flies and wasps. On the mainland and at the Chathams, the main search method is 'watch and wait' – perching and scanning an area, and then flying to catch the prey, usually on a nearby trunk or branch. They also glean insects from leaves and small branches, occasionally hover and only rarely catch insects on the wing. Snares Tomtits often forage on the ground and hop about in the leaf litter, as Robins do elsewhere. They also feed on flies that abound in penguin colonies, and perch on seals and sea lions to catch associated blowflies.

Reading: Best, H. A. 1975. *Wildlife – A Review* 6: 32–37. Fleming, C. A. 1950. *Trans Roy Soc NZ* 78: 14–47, 127–160. Kearton, J. M. 1979. MSc thesis, Uni Canterbury. Knegtmans, J. W. & Powlesland, R. G. 1999. *Notornis* 46: 446–456. McLean, I. G. & Miskelly, C. M. 1988. *NZ Natural Sciences* 15: 51–59. Miskelly, C. M. 1990. *Emu* 90: 24–27. Powlesland, R. G. et al. 2001. *Notornis* 48: 207–216.

352. NORTH ISLAND ROBIN *Petroica longipes* PLATE 80

Other name: Toutouwai
Size: 18cm, 35g
Distribution: New Zealand only. Subfossil, midden and historical records show that North Island Robins were throughout the North Island at the time of European settlement. They disappeared from northern and southern parts in the early 1900s, and, apart from strong populations on Little Barrier and Kapiti islands, they became restricted to a band across the central North Island from Taranaki (but not Mt Taranaki) to the Bay of Plenty and Te Urewera National Park. They have been the subject of many translocations, including successful introductions to Moturua and Moturoa islands (Bay of Islands), Puketi Forest, Tawharanui, Tiritiri Matangi Island, Mayor Island, Mokoia Island, Boundary Stream, Cape Kidnappers, Bushy Park, Mana Island and Zealandia (Wellington).

North Island Robins are found mainly in mature native forests, but in some districts they use older stands of exotic plantations and scrub.

Population: Widespread, but with a patchy distribution; sometimes locally common, and abundant on Little Barrier, Tiritiri Matangi and Kapiti islands.

Conservation: Protected endemic. North Island Robins have declined since European settlement as a result of clearance of much prime lowland forest and the introduction of mammalian predators, especially ship rats, cats and stoats. Robin numbers on Kapiti Island increased rapidly in the decade after the eradication of possums in the 1980s, thus showing that possums may be a serious predator or somehow alter the habitat to the detriment of Robins. Landscape-scale 1080 operations have been shown to have a nett benefit to North Island Robins, despite some accidental mortality, because of improved nesting success following removal of rats, stoats and possums. Over 30 translocations have been done, with varying success.

Breeding: North Island Robins usually keep the same partner year after year. From July, they start courtship feeding and from August the male starts singing his full territorial song. The female takes about 5 days to build its nest, a bulky cup of twigs, bark, fibres and moss, bound together with cobwebs and lined with tree-fern scales, moss, fine grasses and occasionally with feathers or wool. It is usually 1–**4–5**–14m up in a notch in a tree trunk, in the fork between the trunk and a large branch, in the crown of a tree fern, or in an epiphyte, and is usually well hidden by surrounding vegetation. Laying is from September to January, during which time each pair rears 2–3 broods, but if their nests fail, they can re-lay up to 5 times in a season.

They lay 1–**2–3** eggs, with clutch size peaking in November. The eggs (24.5 x 18.5mm, 4.5g) are white with brown or purplish-brown spots concentrated at the larger end. Eggs are laid daily, usually shortly after sunrise. The female incubates for 17–21 days and broods the chicks. She is called off the nest and fed 20–50m away by the male 2–3 times an hour while incubating, but both birds feed the nestlings after about 5 days. The fledging period is 17–22 days. Single fledglings are looked after by the male, but if there are two or more, the parents divide care of the brood. This division continues until the female starts re-nesting 2–4 weeks after fledging, when the male feeds all juveniles. The fledglings start foraging *c.* 2 weeks after leaving the nest, but continue to be fed until 4–7 weeks old and stay in their natal territory until ousted at 7–10 weeks old. They start breeding at 1 year old. The oldest North Island Robin lived over 17 years.

Behaviour: North Island Robins are territorial all year but especially so in the breeding season, when the male patrols his patch and sings from prominent perches. The main territorial song of the male, given from August–December, is loud and clear, and consists of a variety of simple notes strung together and sometimes sustained for half an hour, broken only by short pauses. From March to July, the main song is a simple downscale. They also give a short 'chirp' as a contact call. In aggressive encounters between birds, they raise their crown feathers, but in encounters with other species, including humans, they often flash the white frontal spot in the centre of their forehead. In some areas, Robins are shy and secretive, but elsewhere they are bold and can be induced to come near by clearing a patch of leaf litter and then sitting quietly nearby.

Feeding: Diet is mainly invertebrates, supplemented with small fruits in summer and autumn. Main prey are earthworms, spiders, amphipods, beetles, moths and caterpillars, weta, cicadas, stick insects, snails and slugs. Most are caught on the forest floor. They often perch on a low branch, supplejack or trunk of a sapling, scanning the ground before flying down to grab their prey. When on the forest floor, they sometimes tremble one foot as a means of inducing prey to move in response to the vibrations caused. They sometimes glean insects from leaves or under bark on a branch or trunk, and occasionally take insects or fruit from a tree while hovering, but only rarely catch flying insects on the wing.

In the hand: Because North Island Robin males do not

show sex-specific plumage differences from females until 12–16 months old, juvenile males can be sexed from a combination of tarsus length and maximum wing chord; males generally have a tarsus >35.6mm and wing >87mm.

Reading: Armstrong, D. P. 2001. *Notornis* 48: 76–80. Armstrong, D. P. et al. 2000. *Notornis* 47: 106–118. Fleming, C. A. 1950. *Trans Roy Soc NZ* 78: 14–47, 127–160. Powlesland, R. G. 2002. *Notornis* 49: 263–365. Powlesland, R. G. et al. 1999 *NZ J Ecol* 23: 149–159. Powlesland, R. G. et al. 2000. *Notornis* 47: 95–105.

353. SOUTH ISLAND ROBIN *Petroica australis* PLATE 80

Other name: Toutouwai

Size: 18cm, 35g

Geographical variation: Two subspecies; *australis* on the South Island mainland and offshore islands, and *rakiura* on Stewart Island and its outliers.

Distribution: New Zealand only. Subfossil, midden and historical records show that South Island Robins were widespread in the South Island and Stewart Island before the time of European settlement. In the South Island, they are quite common north of Arthur's Pass National Park, in Buller, Nelson and coastal Marlborough, but south of Arthur's Pass they are patchily distributed, with strongholds in Okarito Forest, the eastern foothills of Fiordland, the Umbrella Mountains of northern Southland, and around Dunedin. They have been successfully introduced to Allports and Motuara Island in the Marlborough Sounds (and have since colonised Long Island); Adele Island (Nelson), Orokonui (Dunedin), and the West Matukituki Valley and Pomona, Hawea, Pigeon, Anchor and Chalky islands in Fiordland.

The Stewart Island Robin is moderately common on Stewart Island and on some outliers, and has been successfully introduced to Ulva and Putauhina islands.

Robins are found mainly in mature beech forests, but in some districts they use mixed podocarp forest and older stands of exotic plantations and scrub.

Population: Widespread, locally common in some parts of the northern South Island, islands in the Marlborough Sounds, and in eastern Fiordland.

Conservation: Protected endemic. South Island Robins have declined since European settlement as a result of clearance of much prime lowland forest and the introduction of mammalian predators. The current distribution of Robins in the South Island is puzzling, because they are rare and patchily distributed south of Arthur's Pass despite no obvious difference in habitat or introduced predators present. At Kowhai Bush, near Kaikoura, a colour-banded population declined from 94 to 16 adults in the space of 10 years, probably as a result of predation of adult birds by mustelids and/or rats.

Breeding: South Island Robins keep their territory all year, and usually keep the same partner year after year. From March to July, the main song is a downscale, but in August–December males sing their full territorial song. From July, they start courtship feeding. The female takes about 5 days to build its nest, a bulky cup of twigs, bark, fibres and moss, bound together with cobwebs and lined with tree-fern scales, moss, fine grasses and occasionally with feathers or wool. It is usually 1–**4**–9m up in the fork of a tree trunk or fork between large branches, and quite often the nest is built in an old nest of a Robin, Song Thrush, Blackbird or Bellbird. Laying is in July–January, during which time each pair may raise up to four broods, but if their nests fail, they can re-lay up to 6 times in a season.

They lay **2**–**3**–4 eggs; first clutches are mainly of 2 eggs, and later clutches mainly of 3. The eggs are cream with purplish-brown spots (25 x 18.5mm, 4.5g) and are laid daily, usually shortly after sunrise. The female incubates for 17–**18**–19 days and broods the chicks. She is called off the nest and fed 20–50m away by the male 2–3 times an hour while incubating, and both birds feed the nestlings. The fledging period is 19–**21**–26 days. Single fledglings are looked after by the male, but if there are two or more, the parents divide care of the brood. This division continues until the female starts re-nesting and then the male feeds all juveniles. They start foraging *c.* 2 weeks after leaving the nest, but continue to be fed by their parents for 25–50 days before being ousted from the territory. Robins start breeding at 1 year old. The average annual survivorship of adult Robins at Kowhai Bush, during a period when they were stable, was about 70%, giving a mean life expectancy of *c.* 3 years, however, the oldest South Island Robin recorded lived over 16 years.

Behaviour: South Island Robins are territorial all year but especially so in the breeding season, when the male patrols his patch and sings from prominent perches. The main territorial song of the male is loud and clear, and consists of a variety of simple notes strung together and sometimes sustained for half an hour, broken only by short pauses. Robins also give a short 'chirp' as a contact call. In aggressive encounters between birds, they raise their crown feathers, but in encounters with other species, including humans, they often flash the white frontal spot in the centre of their forehead. In some areas, South Island Robins are shy and secretive, but elsewhere they are bold and can be induced to come near by clearing a patch of leaf litter and then sitting quietly nearby.

Feeding: Diet is mainly invertebrates, supplemented with small fruits in summer and autumn. Main prey are earthworms, spiders, amphipods, beetles, moths and caterpillars, weta, cicadas, stick insects, snails and slugs. Most are caught on the forest floor. Robins often perch on a low branch, supplejack or trunk of a sapling, scanning the ground before flying down to grab their prey. When on the forest floor, they sometimes tremble one foot as a means of inducing prey to move in response to the vibrations caused. They sometimes glean insects from leaves or under bark on a branch or trunk, and occasionally take insects or fruit from a tree while hovering, but only rarely catch flying insects on the wing.

Reading: Flack, J. A. D. 1975. *Notornis* 23: 90–105. Fleming, C. A. 1950. *Trans Roy Soc NZ* 78: 14–47, 127–160. Powlesland, R. G. 1981. *Notornis* 28: 89–102. Powlesland, R. G. 1981. *NZ J Ecol* 4: 98–105. Powlesland, R. G. 1983. *Notornis* 30: 265–282. Powlesland, R. G. 1983. *NZ J Zool* 10: 225–232.

354. BLACK ROBIN *Petroica traversi* PLATE 80

Size: 15cm; male 25g, female 22g

Distribution: Chatham Islands only. Subfossil and midden records show that Black Robins were once widespread through the Chathams group, but by the 1870s they had become restricted to Mangere and Little Mangere islands. They disappeared from Mangere about 1880, but a few persisted on Little Mangere. In 1976–77, all seven Black Robins were shifted from Little Mangere Island to Mangere, and in the early 1980s some were taken to South East Island, where they subsequently became established. They are now found throughout forest and scrub on Mangere and South East islands.

Population: 274 birds in April 2014: Mangere Island 45, South East Island 229.

Conservation: Protected critically endangered endemic. The intensive management of the Black Robin, by the Wildlife Service and then the Department of Conservation is one of the world's outstanding conservation success stories. When rediscovered on Little Mangere Island in 1938, there were 20–35 pairs. Over the years, the habitat deteriorated and the population had declined to just seven birds in 1976. These five males and two females were transferred to a small forest patch on nearby Mangere Island, which was clear of the cats that had caused their disappearance from the island in the 1880s. The Black Robins continued to decline, and by 1979 there were only five birds left, including just one productive pair.

In 1979–88, the Wildlife Service carried out intensive management, which included supplementary feeding to boost breeding, protection of nests from seabirds and starlings, and, in 1980, the cross-fostering of eggs and chicks to Chatham Island Warblers; however, the warblers were unable to raise Black Robin chicks to fledging age. In 1981, female 'Old Blue' laid three clutches. Two clutches of three eggs were fostered to Tomtit nests on South East Island, and the three resultant chicks were reintroduced to Mangere Island, taking the population to 12 birds. Since then, cross-fostering eggs and chicks to Tomtits to boost Black Robin productivity became an essential part of the recovery programme. Black Robins were permanently introduced to South East Island in 1983. With cross-fostering, the population reached 100 birds by autumn 1989, and since then Black Robins have continued to increase without further intervention to 229 birds in April 2014. A potential threat to their long-term persistence is the very high level of inbreeding, which can affect reproductive success and their ability to deal with new challenges, such as a novel disease.

Breeding: Black Robins maintain their territory all year, and usually keep the same partner year after year. From June onwards, males start to sing their territorial song, and from September they start courtship feeding. The female normally builds 2–3 nests, but only one is completed. It is a neat open cup of twigs, bark, leaves and moss, held together with spider webs, and thickly lined with moss and feathers. They usually build in a shallow cavity such as a hollow branch or a rotten stump, sometimes among rocks, and occasionally in an old Blackbird nest in a tangle of vines. They readily use nest boxes. Most eggs are laid in October–November, and each pair usually raises only one brood a year; however, they re-lay if they lose a clutch, and this behaviour was used to induce Black Robins to lay up to three clutches in a season through to January.

They lay 1–**2**–3 cream eggs (22 x 17mm) with purplish-brown blotches and spots. The eggs are laid at 24-hour intervals, normally in the morning. The female incubates for 17–**18**–19 days and broods the chicks. Both parents feed the chicks during their fledging period of 19–**22**–25 days. Young are capable of breeding at 1 year old, but most do not start until 2 years old. The average annual survivorship of Black Robins from 1980 to 1991 was 78%, giving a mean life expectancy of *c.* 4 years; however, the key female 'Old Blue' lived for 12+ years, and the oldest bird recorded lived to 14 years old.
Behaviour: Black Robins are territorial all year, but especially so in the breeding season, when the male patrols his territory and sings from prominent perches. The main territorial song of the male is a clear, simple and sustained phrase of 5–7 notes. Females sometimes sing brief phrases but never the full song. They also have a high-pitched, single-note contact call.
Feeding: Diet is entirely invertebrates such as caterpillars, spiders, beetles, aphids, fly larvae and weta, mostly taken from the forest floor or from low branches. Black Robins generally hop when feeding and only rarely hawk for insects.
Reading: Ardern, S. L. & Lambert, D. M. 1997. *Molecular Ecol* 6: 21–28. Butler, D. & Merton, D. 1992. *The Black Robin: Saving the World's Most Endangered Bird.* Auckland: OUP. Merton, D. V. 1990. *Forest & Bird* 21: 14–19. Merton, D. V. 1993. *NZ J Ecol* 16: 65–68. Miller, H. C. & Lambert, D. M. 2006. *Molecular Phylogenetics & Evolution* 40: 844–855.

LARKS *Alaudidae*

76 species worldwide except South America; 1 has been introduced to New Zealand.

The larks are small songbirds of open country, especially rough grassland, steppes and undeveloped tussockland. They have moderately long legs, long toes and an especially long hind toe and claw. Their bill is usually stout, and they feed on a mix of invertebrates and seeds. Although larks have erectile crown feathers that can form a short crest, their plumage is otherwise drab to provide camouflage on the ground, where they nest. Their territorial song is a beautiful torrent of trills and runs, often delivered while hovering high overhead.

355. SKYLARK *Alauda arvensis* PLATE 81

Other name: Eurasian Skylark
Size: 18cm, 38g
Geographical variation: Of 13 subspecies, it is likely that the nominate *arvensis* was introduced to New Zealand.
Distribution: Their natural breeding range is Europe, North Africa, the Middle East and northern Asia to China; migrating south to India and northern Africa. At least 1000 birds were introduced into New Zealand by Acclimatisation societies for sentimental reasons, and widely released between 1864 and 1875. They quickly became well established and spread throughout the country.

The Skylark is now very common in all types of open country, such as sand dunes, farmland and tussockland, from North Cape to Stewart Island and on offshore islands, and from sea level to subalpine herb fields at 1900m; it avoids forest and other thick stands of vegetation. They are common on the Chatham Islands and vagrants have reached the Kermadecs, The Snares, Antipodes, Auckland and Campbell islands. In their natural range, most birds migrate south in winter, but in New Zealand most seem to be sedentary or make local movements to flock at good food sources; however, some northward migration from Farewell Spit has been noted in late autumn.
Population: Widespread and locally abundant in open country, especially in drier parts east of the Main Divide in both main islands, in sand-dune country, and on the Chathams. In Canterbury, densities are higher on pastoral sheep farms than on dairy farms or mixed cropping arable farms.
Breeding: Some pairs remain on territory all year and breed together year after year. Other birds, perhaps mainly juveniles, form loose flocks in autumn and winter. Singing by males increases from May, but eggs are not laid until September–January, during which pairs lay 2–3 clutches. The female builds the nest and then lays 2–**3**–**4**–5 eggs (23 x 17mm), greyish white to creamy buff, thickly speckled brown, frequently with a darker zone at the broader end. The nest is a neat

grass-lined cup in a small depression in the ground, especially a hoof-print, and often concealed by an overhanging clump of grass, rush or tussock. The female alone incubates for *c.* 11 days, but both parents feed the nestlings, which leave the nest at 9–10 days old, but do not fly until *c.* 20 days old. Young breed at 1 year old. Few birds have been banded in New Zealand, but in Europe a Skylark lived at least 8 years.
Behaviour: Pairs are strongly territorial during the breeding season, but some form winter flocks, and some migrate within New Zealand. The territorial song of the male, heard mainly in August–January and rarely through to mid-April, is an enthusiastic torrent of variable trills and runs, sustained for up to 5 minutes while the bird soars steeply, hovers at 30–100m facing into the breeze and drops slowly earthwards. They occasionally sing from a post or on the ground. The call note is a liquid 'chirrup', often given in flight.
Feeding: Diet is mainly seeds of grass, cereals, sedges, clover and various weeds, supplemented with moderate quantities of invertebrates such as beetles, flies, spiders, bugs, and larvae of flies, beetles and moths. All food is taken from the ground. Feeding birds scan around them but do not walk far between each food item. Skylarks can cause considerable economic damage to crops by eating sown grain and seeds, and by pulling out or defoliating seedlings of tomatoes, cabbages, wheat and peas.
In the hand: Males have longer wings than females: 105–**110**–116mm cf. 95–**100**–104mm.
Reading: Beauchamp, A. J. 1998. *Notornis* 45: 95–101. Delius, J. D. 1965. *Ibis* 107: 466–492. Garrick, A. S. 1981. *NZ J Ecol* 4: 106–114. Hamel, J. 1972. *Notornis* 19: 20–25. Moeed, A. 1975. *Notornis* 22: 135–142. Niethammer, G. 1971. *J f Orn* 112: 202–206.

REED-WARBLERS *Acrocephalidae*

54 species in Africa, Eurasia, Australasia and on islands of the Pacific; 1 vagrant to New Zealand.

The reed-warblers are small drab songbirds, mainly of swamps but in forest on many Pacific Islands. They have moderately long legs, and can perch sideways on reed stems. Their loud, repeated, territorial song is usually the best clue to their presence, and also to distinguish between the various species.
Reading: Kennerley, P. & Pearson, D. 2010. *Reed and Bush Warblers*. London: Christopher Helm.

356. AUSTRALIAN REED-WARBLER *Acrocephalus australis* PLATE 74

Size: 16cm, 20g
Distribution: Between October and March, they breed widely in western and eastern, but not central Australia, and Tasmania. Disperses widely after breeding, with a partial migration to northern Australia. One New Zealand record: St Anne's Lagoon, North Canterbury (November 2004).
Behaviour: Easily missed unless calling. Skulks in thick wetland vegetation and could be mistaken for a Fernbird at first glance; sometimes clings sideways on a reed at the edge of thick vegetation, but otherwise rarely seen. Insectivorous.

GRASSBIRDS and ALLIES *Megaluridae*

57 species in Africa, Eurasia and Australasia; 2 species endemic to New Zealand, but the Chatham Islands Fernbird (*Bowdleria rufescens*) is believed to have become extinct by 1900, and so is not covered here.

These are small drab songbirds, mainly of tall grassland, swamps and marshes. They have moderately long legs and distinctively long tails. Their loud, repeated, territorial song is usually the best clue to their presence, and also to distinguish between the various species.
Reading: Tennyson, A. & Martinson, P. 2006. *Extinct Birds of New Zealand*. Wellington: Te Papa Press.

357. FERNBIRD *Bowdleria punctata* PLATE 78

Other name: Matata
Size: 18cm, 35g
Geographical variation: Five subspecies, each restricted to a single island and its offshore islands: North Island Fernbird *vealeae*, South Island Fernbird *punctata*, Stewart Island Fernbird *stewartiana*, Codfish Island Fernbird *wilsoni*, and Snares Fernbird *caudata*.
Distribution: New Zealand only. In the North Island, they are widely but patchily distributed north of a line from the Waikanae Estuary to Porangahau, and on Great Barrier Island. Successfully introduced to Tiritiri Matangi Island in 2001–02. In the South Island, they are common west of the Southern Alps from Farewell Spit and Nelson to the Hollyford Valley, including the Open Bay Islands. They are found along the eastern edge of Fiordland to Southland and eastwards to Dunedin, but they are absent from the Marlborough Sounds and most of the eastern side of the Alps as far south as Dunedin. Fernbirds are on Stewart Island and many outliers, and successfully introduced to Kundy Island in 1995. Codfish Island Fernbirds are common and were successfully introduced to Putauhina Island in 1997 when rats were about to be eradicated from Codfish Island. Snares Fernbirds are the most abundant landbird on North East and Broughton islands and Alert Stack. The main habitats used by Fernbirds are low, dense ground vegetation interspersed with emergent shrubs in swamps; pakahi; rush and tussock-covered frost flats; salt marsh; low manuka scrub; and some young pine plantations; from sea level to *c.* 1000m. On the Open Bay Islands they inhabit dense kiekie, and on The Snares they are on the forest floor in open *Olearia* and *Senecio* forests. After becoming independent, juveniles roam away from their natal territory and can turn up in small scrub patches and wetlands 20+km away from the nearest breeding birds.
Population: Widespread and locally common on the mainland, especially in coastal Northland and parts of the Volcanic Plateau, the northern and western South Island, and coastal Southland and Otago. The island populations are moderately abundant. The population on The Snares, was estimated to be *c.* 1500 pairs in 1985–87.
Conservation: Protected endemic. The Fernbird declined about the time of European settlement with the loss of much wetland and fernland through agricultural development, the introduction of mammalian predators, and periodic burning of wetland and scrub habitats. Fernbirds disappeared from most of the southern North Island and most of the eastern South Island by the late 1800s. They seem to have stabilised in their current distribution, mainly on poorer land unsuitable for farming, and have colonised some young stands of exotic forest in the central North Island and Hawke's Bay.
Breeding: Most Fernbirds stay in pairs or small groups all year, and many pairs stay in or near their breeding territory. In spring, territorial disputes and call rates increase. Both birds work together to make the nest, which takes about 3 days to build. It is a neatly woven deep cup of dry grass, sedge and rushes, generally lined with feathers. It is usually placed deep in cutty grass, rushes or tussock 15–75cm above the ground or water level, but occasionally in a small shrub up to 2m off the ground. On the mainland, Stewart Island and Codfish Island, eggs are laid from late August to January, but on The Snares they are laid from mid-October to late February. Probably two or three clutches are laid each year on the mainland, but on The Snares they normally raise only one brood. Clutch size in the North Island is 2–**3**–4 eggs (19.5 x 14.5mm), in the South Island 1–**4**–5 eggs (20.5 x 15mm), on Stewart and Codfish islands 2–3 eggs (22.5 x 15.5mm), and on The Snares 1–**2**–3 eggs (23 x 16.5mm). The eggs, which are laid daily, are pale pink, heavily flecked with purplish brown, especially towards the large end, but the amount of flecking decreases with successive eggs in a clutch. Both adults incubate for 12–**13**–15 days on the mainland, and for 15–**16**–19 days on The Snares. Both parents feed the chicks during the fledging period of 15–**17** days on the mainland and 20–21 days on The Snares. Young can breed at 9 months old. The oldest Fernbird recorded in New Zealand lived 6.5 years.
Behaviour: Fernbirds are usually territorial and sedentary, and their flight is weak. Their calls often reveal their presence in a swamp or in scrub. They are secretive, but sometimes an inquisitive bird appears out of a tangle of vegetation for a moment or two, and equally quickly disappears. They are reluctant to leave cover, but when forced to, they fly low, with their tail hanging down. Territory defence breaks down during the autumn moult and in the early winter, but territorial calls increase in early spring. The main calls are a mechanical double call consisting of a low and a sharp metallic note: 'uu-tick', either given by the male alone or in duet with his mate, who responds very rapidly to the male 'uu' with the 'tick' portion. Other calls include 'tchip', 'tcheong' and 'zrup' notes, and a series of rapid clicks, or 'chittering' and, rarely, a melodic warble. Calls heard occasionally

in the middle of the night, even in heavy rain.
Feeding: Diet is mainly invertebrates, especially caterpillars, spiders, grubs, beetles, flies and moths. They feed in low vegetation or on the ground. On The Snares, Fernbirds eat maggots and flies around dead penguins, and they often perch on the back of a fur seal or sea lion to catch flies.
Reading: Barlow, M. 1983. *Notornis* 30: 199–216. Best, H. A. 1973. MSc thesis, Uni Canterbury. Best, H. A. 1979. *Notornis* 26: 279–287. Best, H. A. 1979. *NZ J Zool* 6: 481–488. Parker, K. A. 2002. MSc thesis, Uni Auckland.

WHITE-EYES *Zosteropidae*

About 100 species in Africa, southern and eastern Asia, Australasia and the islands of the southwestern Pacific; 1 native to New Zealand.

Small, mainly olive-green forest birds, most with a distinctive white ring around each eye. They have a fine, tapered bill and a brush-tipped tongue for drinking nectar, but they also feed extensively on insects and fruits. They help to pollinate flowers and disperse seeds of small fruits, but peck at the flesh and damage larger fruit.

358. SILVEREYE *Zosterops lateralis* PLATE 75

Other names: Tauhou, Waxeye, White-eye
Size: 12cm, 13g
Geographical variation: This species has complex racial variation in Australasia and the southwestern Pacific. Up to nine subspecies are recognised in Australia alone; the Tasmanian subspecies *lateralis* migrates to eastern states of the Australian mainland in winter, and it is this form that colonised New Zealand.
Distribution: Breeds in Australia, Norfolk Island, New Caledonia, Vanuatu, Loyalty Group, Banks Island, Fiji and New Zealand. Silvereyes were recorded in New Zealand as early as 1832, and may have established on Stewart Island and in Southland about then, but it was not until 1856 that they apparently arrived in large numbers in many parts of the country and colonised permanently. The Maori name 'tauhou' means 'stranger', thus implying that Silvereyes were a new bird to New Zealand. It is now among the most abundant of New Zealand birds, being found in native forest and scrub from sea level to the treeline, in exotic plantations, orchards and suburban gardens. Since colonising the mainland of New Zealand, they have spread to all offshore islands, the Kermadecs, Chathams, Antipodes, Snares, Auckland and Campbell islands, and possibly were the birds that colonised Norfolk Island in 1904.

There is considerable local movement of small flocks in autumn and winter, mainly seeking fruit or nectar, and banded individuals are often recorded in the same town gardens or other wintering site, year after year. The pattern of regular seasonal movements is sometimes disrupted by irregular variations in food supply, such as the periodic intense flowering of rata, or in years when there is good fruiting of kahikatea, when several thousand birds can occupy a forest patch for several weeks or months.

Flocks of Silvereyes have been reported flying northwards up the South Island at night in autumn and winter, and at Farewell Spit flocks have been seen on clear, calm mornings flying very high towards the northeast, and heading for Taranaki; however, movement across Cook Strait has not yet been supported by band recoveries.
Population: Widespread and locally abundant. Silvereyes are especially common in podocarp forests and some orchards and vineyards when fruit is available in autumn and winter, also in town gardens in the winter when food (fat, fruit or sugar water) is provided for them. The only places where Silvereyes are relatively scarce are in open habitats such as tussockland and grassland, and on some offshore islands where the forest and native forest bird communities are relatively intact, e.g. the Poor Knights, Little Barrier and Kapiti islands.
Conservation: Protected native. Because the Silvereye colonised New Zealand naturally (although possibly helped by sailing ships), it has been classified as a native species. It is likely that Silvereyes have had a significant impact on native forest habitats by changing the pattern of seed dispersal and by competing with other animals for fruit, nectar and invertebrates. The biomass of Silvereyes in some forests, especially in autumn and

winter, exceeds that of any other bird species. Silvereyes can cause considerable economic damage to grapes and other fruit crops, especially cherries, apricots and figs; although they often feed from fruit already damaged by other birds.

Breeding: Established pairs remain together in winter flocks, but in late winter they leave to set up territories and first-year birds pair up. The nest is a delicate cup suspended like a hammock from twigs and foliage. The nest is woven strongly from fine grasses, rootlets and fibres, with fragments of moss, spider web, lichen and thistledown, which provide camouflage. Nests are from 1–**2–3**–15m above the ground, usually towards the outermost branches of a tree, shrub or tree fern.

Eggs are laid from September to February, during which time pairs can raise two or three broods. Each clutch is of 2–**3**–5 pale blue eggs (17.5 x 13mm), laid at 24-hour intervals. Incubation starts after the second egg is laid and is shared by both parents during the 10–**11**–12-day incubation period. Both parents brood and feed nestlings during the fledging period of 9–**10**–11 days. The family stays together for 2–3 weeks after the chicks leave the nest, but the young then become independent. The interval between successive clutches has been recorded as 47–60 days. Young breed at 9 months old, and pairs remain together year after year. The oldest banded bird recorded in New Zealand lived at least 11.5 years.

Behaviour: Pairs are strongly territorial during the breeding season, but Silvereyes form winter flocks. Within flocks, there are dominance hierarchies, and birds are often seen fluttering their wings aggressively at another bird. The flocking call, often heard in flight, is an excited chirping 'cli-cli-cli', and single birds often give a plaintive 'cree' call. The song of males in the breeding season is similar to that of the Dunnock but is a less powerful and more melodious mix of warbles, trills and slurs, interspersed with occasional high-pitched plaintive notes; it is usually given from a song-post within a tree or shrub, not from the top like a Dunnock. Also, in autumn they also give a Blackbird-like warbling subsong from dense cover.

Feeding: Diet is varied, mainly comprising invertebrates, fruit and nectar, although some birds rely on fat, cooked meat, bread and sugar water provided at bird tables in winter. The main invertebrates eaten include caterpillars, spiders, bugs, flies and beetles. In the early phase of their colonisation of New Zealand, Silvereyes were known as 'Blight-birds' because they fed on woolly aphids that infested apple trees. They feed on a variety of fruit, including commercial fruit and grape crops, but most fruit eaten is taken from native trees and shrubs, such as kahikatea, rimu, *Coprosma*, fuchsia, broadleaf, hangehange and kiekie. They eagerly take nectar from native plants such as rata, fuchsia, kowhai, rewarewa, kiekie and puriri, and from introduced species such as gums and banksias, but they are often excluded by local Tui and Bellbirds. Their specially modified tongue, with bristles, allows them to lap up nectar.

Reading: Dennison, M. D. et al. 1981. *Notornis* 28: 119–120. Fleming, C. A. 1943. *Emu* 42: 193–217. Kikkawa, J. 1961. *Ibis* 103A: 428–442. Kikkawa, J. 1962. *Notornis* 9: 280–291. Kikkawa, J. 1963. *Emu* 63: 32–34. Marples, B. J. 1944. *NZ Bird Notes* 1: 41–48. Moeed, A. & Fitzgerald, B. M. 1982. *NZ J Zool* 9: 391–403. Stead, E. F. 1932. *The Life Histories of New Zealand Birds*. London: Search.

SWALLOWS and MARTINS *Hirundinidae*

About 83 species worldwide; 1 is a recently self-introduced native, and two are vagrants to New Zealand.

Swallows are usually larger than martins, but the two terms are interchangeable and follow no taxonomic lines. They are generally small, graceful, dark blue and white birds, with variable amounts of rusty red on their head and breast. They have a streamlined body with short neck and long, pointed wings with only nine primaries. Most have a deeply forked tail, but some have a square tail. Their flight is graceful and rapid as they wheel and dart to catch aerial insects in their short, wide bill. They are birds of open country, especially hunting over lakes, rivers and grassland; on warm, calm days they often fly high, but in poor weather they hunt close to the ground or water surface where flying insects are concentrated. Their feet are very small, and they shuffle about when they rarely land on the ground; they usually perch between feeding bouts on posts and powerlines. Swallows and martins build distinctive mud nests, formerly mainly in tree cavities or in cliff overhangs, but now often under bridges or culverts, or under the eaves of buildings.

359. WELCOME SWALLOW *Hirundo neoxena* PLATE 72

Size: 15cm, 14g

Geographical variation: Two subspecies, of which *neoxena* breeds in eastern Australia, Tasmania, Lord Howe Island, and New Zealand.

Distribution: Breeds mainly in southern parts of Australia and in Tasmania, and many move north and inland in winter. They colonised Lord Howe Island in 1970 and are a winter visitor to Norfolk Island. They have only recently colonised New Zealand, with breeding first recorded in 1958. Before then, they had been only a rare vagrant: Northland (1920), Auckland Islands (1943), Awhitu Peninsula (1944), Lake Ellesmere (1953), Stewart Island (1953) and, eventually, a Welcome Swallow at Farewell Spit (1955). There were probably several invasions in the late 1950s and early 1960s. They were first recorded breeding at Awanui, near Kaitaia, in 1958, and by 1965 were well established throughout Northland. They bred at Lake Ellesmere in Canterbury in 1961, in Hawke's Bay and Manawatu in 1962, and in Wairarapa in 1964.

The spread of the Welcome Swallow has been spectacular, and they are now abundant in open country of lowland parts of the North and South islands, although less common in Otago and Southland. They are becoming common in high country of the Volcanic Plateau and the Mackenzie Country and Central Otago. They have bred on the Chathams since 1976, and vagrants have reached the Kermadec, Snares, Auckland and Campbell islands.

Welcome Swallows are probably partial migrants in New Zealand, as they are quite often recorded at sea north of New Zealand in autumn and regularly appear at Norfolk Island in winter. Some birds have been seen leaving Farewell Spit for the North Island in late autumn; however, a southwards movement has been recorded in coastal Otago in autumn, and during the colonisation phase moderate numbers of birds appeared in Southland, where few bred.

Population: Widespread and locally common, especially in lowland farmland with numerous small streams or drains, and in wetlands.

Conservation: Protected self-introduced native. Welcome Swallows sometimes cause a minor nuisance by building their nests on houses, and so fouling doorways and patios, but generally live up to their name and are regarded as a welcome addition to our birdlife.

Breeding: Pairs begin prospecting for suitable nest sites in August, and several days are spent courting, including courtship feeding, before nest-building commences. Both birds help to build the half-cup mud nest, which is strengthened with dry grass. It is lined with dry grass, rootlets, hair, wool and a layer of feathers. The nest is attached to a rough vertical surface, usually within 15cm of the top, normally under a small bridge or culvert, under eaves of houses, sheds and garages, inside water tanks, under jetties and in boats. Some nests are built in natural sites such as caves, rock outcrops or under overhanging banks.

Eggs are laid in August–February, during which they raise up to three broods, sometimes in the same nest. The female lays 2–**4**–7 pale pink eggs (18 x 13mm, 1.6g), variably flecked reddish brown. Clutches of up to 10 eggs are probably laid by two females, or a fresh clutch has been laid in an abandoned nest. Clutch size is higher in New Zealand (4.1) than in eastern Australia (3.7) or western Australia (3.2), but seems to have declined as they have become well established. The second clutch of the season (4.7) is larger than the first (3.8) or third (3.3). Eggs are laid daily, usually about an hour after sunrise. The female alone incubates in spells of *c.* 8 minutes, with 4-minute feeding spells, for 15–**17**–19 days. The eggs hatch over 48 hours in the order they were laid. The female broods the young, but both birds feed them during the fledging period of 18–**21**–23 days. For several days after first flying, the young return to the nest to roost. They continue to be fed for *c.* 3 weeks, even though re-nesting may have begun. Welcome Swallows probably breed at 1 year old. The oldest bird recorded in New Zealand lived 6 years.

Behaviour: Welcome Swallows maintain a small territory around their nest and sometimes tolerate other pairs nesting in the same culvert, as close as a metre away, but usually there is just one pair to each site. During the breeding season, juveniles form summer flocks, and from late December adults start to join them; however, some pairs remain close to their breeding site all year. Flocks of up to 500 birds congregate in autumn and winter at good feeding sites such as over sewage ponds, lakes, rivers, sand dunes and root crops. Temporary roosting flocks often form during the day on powerlines, especially in a sheltered spot, but at night they often roost in huge aggregations of several thousand birds in raupo swamps. In the breeding season, pairs indulge in high-level chasing flights or slow, almost hovering flights accompanied by tail-fanning; the male quite often follows the female in these flights. The pair often sit together on a perch and twitter quietly, occasionally rubbing bills. The main call is a twittering 'twsit'.
Feeding: Diet is entirely invertebrates such as flies, including midges and blowflies, small beetles and moths. They catch most of their prey by hawking with their characteristic dipping, diving, darting flight. Sometimes they catch insects from the water surface.
Reading: Crouchley, G. & Crouchley, D. 1979. *Notornis* 26: 309–310. Edgar, A. T. 1966. *Notornis* 13: 27–60. Evans, K. L. et al. 2003. *Emu* 103: 215–220. Michie, R. 1959. *Notornis* 8: 61–62. Park, P. 1981. *Corella* 5: 85–90. Tarburton, M. K. 1993. *Emu* 93: 34–43. Tunnicliffe, G. A. 1968. *Notornis* 15: 228–233. Turbott, E. G. 1965. *Notornis* 12: 241–244.

360. FAIRY MARTIN *Petrochelidon ariel* PLATE 72

Size: 12cm, 11g
Distribution: Endemic to mainland Australia. Birds breeding in southern states migrate north in winter and stragglers reach New Guinea in winter and Tasmania in spring. Vagrants reach Lord Howe Island and New Zealand. Fairy Martins were first recorded in New Zealand in December 1978, when two unusual bottle-shaped nests were found in a pumping shed near Lake Wairarapa. No birds were seen, but the nests had been built in 1977 or 1978. Subsequently seen at Farewell Spit (November 1982), Totaranui (possibly five in February 1983), Taieri Plains (two in February 1983, one in December 1983), Cape Reinga (November 1983), Leigh (November 1984), Papakura (January 1986), Te Paki (August 2001), Rahotu (four in September 2001), Tapora (July 2004), The Snares (November 2004) and Tawharanui (two in March 2008).
Behaviour: In Australia, Fairy Martins nest in colonies and construct distinctive large bottle-shaped nests of mud pellets against the wall or ceiling of a cave, culvert, building or cliff. They form large flocks in open country in late summer to winter, often resting on powerlines by day. They hawk insects on the wing as Welcome Swallows do, but tend to glide more.
Reading: Bell, B. D. 1984. *Notornis* 31: 172–173. Nevill, A. 1984. *Notornis* 31: 173–175.

361. TREE MARTIN *Petrochelidon nigricans* PLATE 72

Other name: Australian Tree Martin
Size: 13cm, 15g
Geographical variation: Three subspecies, of which *nigricans* of Tasmania and *neglecta* of southern Australia could turn up in New Zealand.
Distribution: Breeds in Australasia; southern populations migrate northwards to overwinter in northern Queensland, New Guinea and the Solomon Islands. A few vagrants reach New Zealand in most years, with about 50 records of single birds or flocks of up to 30–35 birds (East Cape, April 1974) since 1851. They have been reported from Little Barrier Island in the north to The Snares in the south and from Chatham Island (November 1988). Some of the early records, including newspaper reports of their breeding in a mill near Oamaru in 1892–93, may have referred to Welcome Swallows. Tree Martins have been recorded in New Zealand in all months, but usually in autumn and early winter when birds are migrating northwards in eastern Australia. Some birds have stayed in one locality for several years or regularly returned to one site over several years, but breeding has not yet been confirmed.
Behaviour: In Australia, Tree Martins nest in mud-lined holes in trees or cliffs, and sometimes in buildings. They form large flocks in open country in late summer to winter, often resting on powerlines by day. When migrating, they wheel high as a large flock

and then head off. They hawk insects on the wing as Welcome Swallows do, but their flight appears slower and more direct. In New Zealand, they often associate with Welcome Swallows.

Reading: Henley, J. C. 1974. *Notornis* 21: 266–267. Nevill, A. 1984. *Notornis* 31: 173–175.

THRUSHES *Turdidae*

About 338 species worldwide; 2 successfully introduced to New Zealand.

A large group of plump songbirds, mostly with brown or black plumage, but sometimes offset with spots and bright colours. Many have musical songs and harsh, staccato alarm calls. They often catch insects and earthworms on the ground, but also eat fruit from trees and disperse the seeds of small- to medium-sized fruits.

362. BLACKBIRD *Turdus merula* PLATE 81

Other name: Eurasian Blackbird
Size: 25cm, 90g
Distribution: Natural breeding range is Europe and northwestern Africa, the Middle East, and Asia south to India and Sri Lanka and east to southern China. About 1000 birds were introduced into New Zealand by Acclimatisation societies for sentimental reasons in 1862–75. They were liberated in both islands and established quickly, so that by 1900 they were distributed widely on the mainland and had colonised the Chatham and Auckland islands. The species is now abundant throughout the mainland and offshore islands, and well established on the Kermadec, Chatham, Snares, Auckland and Campbell islands, and vagrants have reached the Antipodes Islands.

Blackbirds are common in suburban gardens, parks, orchards, paddocks surrounded by hedges, exotic plantations, scrub and native forest, reaching at least 1600m. The only places they are uncommon are on offshore islands with intact native forest bird communities, such as on Little Barrier and Kapiti. In Eurasia, some birds migrate, but there is no evidence of regular long-distance movement in New Zealand; the maximum movement of a banded bird is only 90km, from the Orongorongo Valley to Levin.

Population: Probably the most widespread species within New Zealand, and especially abundant in parks, suburban gardens, orchards and farmland hedgerows where there is a mix of dense cover and open spaces.

Breeding: Males establish territories in April; usually the same territory is used by the same pair year after year. Most eggs are laid from late August to late December, but occasionally as early as June or as late as February. Pairs quickly replace nests that fail, and so most pairs nest 2–5 times each year and raise 2–3 broods, sometimes in the same nest. The female takes over a week to build the nest at the start of the season, but as little as 3 days later in the season. The nest is a substantial cup of twigs, grass, roots and moss, bound together with mud, and roughly lined with grass and leaf skeletons. It is usually built in the fork of a shrub or hedge 1–10m above the ground, but occasionally nests are built on a ledge on a bank, or in a shed.

They lay 2–**3**–**4**–6 eggs (28 x 21mm, 6.5g) at daily intervals. The eggs are bluish green to greenish brown, and are densely freckled and blotched with reddish brown. The female starts incubation before the clutch is completed, and incubation takes 13–14 days. Both parents feed the nestlings, which fledge at 13–15 days old. The young remain near their parents and are occasionally fed for several weeks after fledging. Young can breed at 9 months old. The oldest known Blackbird in New Zealand lived 15 years, but in Europe the record is over 20 years.

Behaviour: Blackbirds defend their territory for 8 months from April to January, but during the autumn moult they often congregate (but do not flock) at good sources of food such as orchards or mast-fruiting kahikatea forests. The territorial song of the male, heard mainly in July–January and delivered from an elevated perch, is loud, fluent and mellow, with notes running into each other. In late summer and early autumn, Blackbirds may sing a soft, warbling subsong while remaining hidden in a shrub or hedge. Alarm notes are an anxious, repeated 'tchook', especially given when a bird is flushed from cover, and a persistent, repeated 'tchink' when a predator is being mobbed.

Feeding: Diet is a mixture of invertebrates and fruits.

The main invertebrates eaten include worms, beetles, amphipods, caterpillars, millipedes and spiders. Small fruits of native and introduced shrubs and weeds are eaten whole, but flesh of larger fruits is pecked from ripe fruit in trees or from fallen fruit. Blackbirds can cause considerable damage to commercial crops of berryfruits, grapes, pipfruit and stonefruit, and tomatoes. They also spread weed seeds into native forest and crops, but in some native forests they help to disperse seeds of fleshy-fruited understorey plants.

Most food is taken on the ground, especially close to cover or from closely mown lawns. When they are searching for insects, leaves are flicked aside with the bill and occasionally scratched away by the feet, but when hunting worms the bird usually takes a few hops, then stops with head cocked 'listening' before moving a step or two to catch the worm and pull it from the ground.

In the hand: Adults can be sexed in the field, but juveniles are difficult; young males tend to have brownish-black upperparts, not olive-tinged as in young females. In autumn, adults moult wing and tail feathers, and so have feathers missing or have fresh feathers, whereas young birds do not moult their primaries until over a year old, and so have very worn primaries by the next breeding season. In the first winter male, the worn brown primaries contrast with the black body feathers acquired in a partial moult in the autumn.

Reading: Bull, P. C. 1946. *Emu* 46: 198–208. Bull, P. C. 1953. *Notornis* 5: 149–156. Flux, J. E. C. 1966. *Notornis* 13: 142–149. Gurr, L. 1954. *Ibis* 96: 225–261. Williams, P. 2006. *NZ J Ecol* 30: 285–291. Williams, P. A. & Karl, B. J. 1996. *NZ J Ecol* 20: 127–145.

363. SONG THRUSH *Turdus philomelos* PLATE 81

Size: 23cm, 70g

Distribution: Natural breeding range is Europe, western and central Asia. Several hundred birds were introduced into New Zealand by Acclimatisation societies in 1862–78. They were released in both main islands and spread quickly, so that by 1900 they were well established. Now they are found throughout the mainland and offshore islands, and have colonised the Kermadecs, Chathams, Antipodes (breeding not confirmed), Snares, Auckland and Campbell islands, and have also reached Lord Howe, Norfolk and Macquarie islands.

Song Thrushes are found in a variety of habitats from sea level to subalpine scrub at 1600m, including suburban gardens, orchards, exotic plantations, scrub and forest, although they are scarce in virgin native forest and on islands such as Little Barrier and Kapiti where original forest bird communities are largely intact. In Eurasia, some migrate, but there is no evidence of regular long-distance movement in New Zealand.

Population: Widespread and one of the most common birds in New Zealand; especially abundant in farmland hedgerows, orchards, parks and suburban gardens.

Breeding: Males establish territories from April; often the same territory is used by the same pair year after year. Most eggs are laid from early August to late December, but occasionally nests are found as early as May, or as late as February. Pairs quickly replace nests that fail, and so most pairs nest 2–5 times each year and raise 2–3 broods, rarely in the same nest. The female takes 1–2 weeks to build the nest, and then it is often left for a few days before she lays 2–3–4–6 eggs (27 x 20.5mm, 6g) at daily intervals. The eggs are a clear greenish blue with small black spots. The nest is a substantial cup of twigs, grass, roots and moss, bound together with mud and smoothly lined with mud or a mixture of rotten wood and saliva. It is usually built in the fork of a shrub or hedge, 1–5m above the ground. The female starts incubating when the clutch is complete, and incubation takes 12–13 days. Both parents feed the nestlings, which fledge at 13–15 days old. The young remain with the parents and are occasionally fed for several weeks after fledging. Young can breed at 9 months old. The oldest Song Thrush recorded in New Zealand lived over 10.5 years, but in Europe the record is over 13 years.

Behaviour: Song Thrushes defend their territory for 9 months from April to January, but during the autumn moult they become secretive and inconspicuous. The territorial song of the male, heard mainly in April–December and delivered from an elevated perch, is an energetic, bold and varied string of repeated musical phrases, each of which is clear-cut with a brief pause between phrases: 'chitty-choo chitty-choo, oo-eee oo-eee . . .'. Sometimes Song Thrushes are mimics, incorporating phrases borrowed from other species. The alarm note is a rapidly repeated 'chuk' or 'chip', and the flight call is a thin, high-pitched 'seep'.

Feeding: Diet is a mixture of invertebrates and fruits. The main invertebrates eaten include snails (garden, mud, marine, flax and native landsnails), insects, worms, amphipods, millipedes and spiders. Small fruits of native and introduced shrubs and weeds are eaten whole, but flesh of larger fruits is pecked from ripe fruit in trees or

from fallen fruit. They can cause some minor damage to commercial crops of berryfruits, grapes, pipfruit and stonefruit, and tomatoes. They also spread weed seeds into native forests and crops. Most food is taken on the ground, especially close to cover or from closely mown lawns. When feeding on snails, they carry the animal to a favourite rock and then bash the snail against the rock with a flick of the head until the shell breaks and the animal comes free; such 'anvils' can be surrounded by the remains of 20+ snails. When hunting worms, the bird usually runs a few paces or takes a few hops, and then stops with head cocked before moving a step or two to catch the worm and pull it from the ground.
In the hand: Adults can be sexed reliably only in the breeding season, when the female has a brood patch. Song Thrushes have a conspicuous yellow gape, even as adults, and so this cannot be used to age birds. In autumn, adults moult their complete wing and tail feathers, but first-year birds moult only some of the smaller wing feathers, and so in winter there is a contrast between the large triangular buff tips of the five outer greater coverts and smaller tips of the five freshly moulted inner ones. The tail feathers of adults have blunter ends than in first-year birds, and in adults the primary coverts have less contrast between the tip and the outer webs. In spring, the primaries of first-year birds are more worn than in adults and the contrast in the greater coverts is still clear.
Reading: Bull, P. C. 1946. *Emu* 46: 198–208. Flux, J. E. C. 1966. *Notornis* 13: 142–149. Nye, P. A. 1975. *Notornis* 22: 248–249. Williams, P. A. & Karl, B. J. 1996. *NZ J Ecol* 20: 127–145.

STARLINGS and MYNAS *Sturnidae*

About 112 species in Africa, Europe, Asia, northern Australia and the South Pacific; 2 introduced to New Zealand.

Medium-sized birds of towns, open country and forest. Most species are dark, sometimes with a glossy sheen of purple, green or blue. The bill is straight and slender, and they are generally omnivorous. Most nest in holes. Their calls are highly varied, and they often mimic other species.

364. STARLING *Sturnus vulgaris* PLATES 79 AND 81

Other name: Common Starling
Size: 21cm, 85g
Distribution: Natural breeding range is northern and central Europe, the Balkans, the Middle East, and in Russia east to the Urals; many migrate south to winter on the Iberian Peninsula, the Mediterranean, North Africa, and Asia Minor east to India. Widely introduced around the world and now established in North America, South Africa, Australia, New Zealand, and on some oceanic islands. About 1000 Starlings were introduced to New Zealand by various Acclimatisation societies and private individuals in 1862–83. Most introductions were successful, and Starlings soon spread throughout the country. Now abundant in cleared parts of the mainland, suitable offshore islands, and the Chathams; in farmland, orchards, rural and suburban gardens, and forest edges. They breed on the Kermadecs, Bounty, Antipodes, The Snares, Auckland and Campbell islands; in these more remote sites they feed along sandy or rocky shores or in grassland, and nest in tree hollows or rocky crevices. They have spread to Tonga, southern Fiji, and Lord Howe, Norfolk and Macquarie islands. There is no evidence of migration within New Zealand. In winter, large flocks are often seen flying purposefully as they depart from or converge at favoured roosts; these flocks can travel 30+km each day. Favoured roosts are in isolated stands of tall trees (especially macrocarpas and pohutukawa) and on cliffs or islands.
Population: Locally abundant and probably one of the most numerous species in New Zealand. Starlings were extremely common up to the 1940s but then declined, probably because of the widespread use of DDT to kill pasture pests. Since that insecticide has been banned, numbers have increased again.
Breeding: Males visit their nest site in the early morning all year, but it is not until August–September that they stay nearby all day and defend the site from other males. The nest is a cup of dry grass, twigs and leaves, usually in a hole of a tree, cliff or building, but sometimes they will nest in the base of a toetoe, pampas or flax, in

tight-growing cypresses or in a thick tangle of vegetation in a pine tree. Starlings readily use 18 x 18 x 30cm-deep nest boxes with a 6cm-diameter entrance, especially if raised 2–3m off the ground in an open situation. Laying is highly synchronised; in most parts of the country first eggs are laid in the second or third week of October, but the start of breeding each year is influenced by prevailing climatic conditions. First breeders usually start a little later, and lost clutches are replaced, producing a second peak in early November. Second clutches are laid by 30–50% of successful breeders, and so there is a third peak from late November to the first week of December. Clutches are of 1–**4–5**–9 eggs, but those over 6 eggs are usually laid by more than one female. First clutches and those laid by experienced pairs are usually larger than replacement or second clutches, or those laid by new pairs.

The clear pale blue eggs (30 x 21mm) are laid daily in the early morning. Incubation begins with the laying of the last egg and is shared by both parents during the day, but by the female alone at night, for 11–**12**–13 days. The chicks are fed by both parents and fledge at 18–**23**–25 days old. The young are often fed for 1–2 weeks after leaving the nest. Many young females breed at 1–2 years old, but males rarely breed until 2–3 years old. In New Zealand, annual adult survivorship is at least 72%, giving a life expectancy of just over 3 years; however, the oldest banded bird lived over 14 years, and in Europe the record is 23 years.

Behaviour: Gregarious in autumn and winter, forming feeding flocks of up to 1000 birds, and they form even larger flocks as they head towards their evening roost. They often stop at staging points before moving on to the final night-time roost, which can include more than 1 million birds. In the breeding season, non-breeders form small flocks of up to 50 birds and juveniles also form small flocks or join non-breeders shortly after becoming independent. During breeding, Starlings do not defend a feeding area but vigorously defend their nest site. The territorial song, usually delivered from a high perch near the nest, with bill pointed upwards and half-opened wings flapping stiffly, is a lively rambling medley of throaty warbling, clicking and gargling notes interspersed with musical whistles and imitations of other species or mechanical noises. The two birds most often imitated are Pukeko and California Quail. At large roosts, Starlings maintain a twittering chorus often late into the night.

Feeding: Diet is a mix of invertebrates and fruit, supplemented with nectar from flowers such as flax (when their forehead becomes covered in orange pollen). Starlings mainly eat small invertebrates, such as grass grub and porina moth caterpillars, worms, snails and spiders, caught by probing in short pasture or grain stubble, occasionally on beaches or mudflats. Starlings sometimes hawk for insects, especially in calm, warm weather. Fallen fruits are eaten in orchards, but Starlings can cause severe localised damage to grapes and other commercial orchard fruit. Roosting Starlings can foul buildings and footpaths in cities. In autumn, flocks of Starlings sometimes descend on bush patches where kahikatea is fruiting well and strip the trees of fruit in weeks, thus depriving New Zealand Pigeons, Tui and Bellbird of a good supply of food through the winter.

In the hand: The sex of most Starlings can be told from eye and bill colours; males have uniformly dark brown or liver-coloured eyes, whereas females have brown eyes with a narrow inner and/or outer margin of yellow or orange. In May–December, when the bill is yellow, the base of the lower bill of males is bluish, whereas it is pink or yellowish in females. Adults moult in December–February, about a month earlier than juveniles. After autumn, adults and first-year birds that have been sexed can be recognised by the length of the iridescent portion of their throat hackles: adult males >12mm, first-year males <10mm; adult females >7mm, first-year females <6mm. In addition, first-year birds rarely have yellow on the tongue, and the tail feathers are rounded, not slightly pointed as in adults.

Reading: Bull, P. C. & Flux, J. E. C. 2000. *Notornis* 53: 208–214. Coleman, J. D. 1973. *Notornis* 20: 324–329. Coleman, J. D. 1977. *Proc NZ Ecol Soc* 24: 94–109. East, R. & Pottinger, R. P. 1975. *NZ J Ag Res* 18: 417–452. Evans, L. E. et al. 2009. *Anim Behav* 78: 671–675. Flux, J. E. C. & Flux, M. M. 1981. *NZ J Ecol* 4: 65–72. Moeed, A. 1980. *NZ J Zool* 7: 247–256. Tryjanowski, P. et al. 2006. *Austral Ecol* 31: 634–637.

365. MYNA *Acridotheres tristis* — PLATE 79

Other names: Indian Myna, Common Myna
Size: 24cm, 125g
Distribution: Natural breeding range is from Afghanistan east through India and Sri Lanka to Bangladesh, but either through introductions or natural range expansion in the 1900s they have reached much of

Southeast Asia. They have been widely introduced around the world and are established in South Africa, Australia, New Zealand, Solomons, New Caledonia, Fiji, Western Samoa, Cook Islands, Hawai'i and some other oceanic islands. Several hundred birds were introduced to New Zealand, mainly to the South Island, by Acclimatisation societies and private individuals between 1870 and 1877.

Mynas persisted in the South Island (especially Nelson, Christchurch and Dunedin) until about 1890, but they fared better in the North Island and by the 1930s they were split into two populations: one from Masterton to East Cape, and the other in the west from Palmerston North to the Waikato. From about 1940, they spread quickly to colonise the Volcanic Plateau and reached Auckland by about 1947, Tauranga and Rotorua about 1950, the Bay of Islands in 1960 and Kaitaia in 1965. At the same time, they were disappearing from the southern North Island. They were once numerous in Wellington, Masterton and Palmerston North, but apart from a small population based at Masterton Refuse Tip and odd other birds, the southern limit is a line from Whanganui to Waipukurau through Ohakune and Turangi. Mynas are locally abundant in the northern North Island in farmland, orchards and suburban gardens, and have colonised some offshore islands such as Poor Knights, Kawau, Waiheke and Great Barrier. They rarely venture far into forests, but can be common on the forest edge. They are largely sedentary. In winter, large flocks are often seen flying purposefully as they converge on favoured roosts; these flocks can travel 10+km between roosting and feeding sites each day. Favoured roosts are in isolated stands of tall trees, especially macrocarpas and pohutukawa.

Population: Locally abundant in northern New Zealand.

Breeding: Pairs stay together year after year and keep the same territory in successive years. The nest is a cup of dry grass, twigs and leaves, usually in a hole of a tree, cliff or building or other structure, but sometimes they will nest in a thick tangle of vegetation in a pine tree. Mynas readily use 20 x 20 x 30cm-deep nest boxes with an 8cm-diameter entrance, especially if raised 2–3m off the ground in an open situation. Laying is from mid-October to early March, mostly in November and January. Each pair usually raises two broods a year. They lay 1–**3–4**–6 greenish-blue eggs (29 x 22mm, 7.5g) daily in the early morning. Incubation starts with the laying of the last egg and is done mainly by the female during the day, but solely by the female at night, for 13–**14**–15 days. Both parents feed the nestlings during the 20–**25**–32-day fledging period and for *c.* 3 weeks after leaving the nest. Many young form pairs when 9 months old, but only a few females attempt to breed in their first year. In Hawke's Bay, some colour-banded Mynas lived over 12 years.

Behaviour: In the breeding season they are strongly territorial, and neighbouring pairs often fight furiously; however, in autumn and winter they often feed in flocks of 5–20 birds. Except for incubating females, Mynas spend the night at communal roosts, some of which are of 1000+ birds. Territorial birds normally have a bout of intense calling for 5–15 minutes when they arrive in their territories in the early morning. Males call more often than females, but pairs sometimes duet. The territorial call is a rowdy medley of notes, raucous, gurgling, chattering, even bell-like in rapid sequence. Adults with young utter a harsh 'skwark', and the calls of flying young are a noisy persistent 'chi-chi-chi'. At their communal roosts, Mynas maintain a noisy chattering well after nightfall and again before dawn.

Feeding: Diet is a mix of invertebrates and fruits, scraps found at rubbish tips, on roads and from places where stock and poultry are fed. They also eat eggs, chicks, and lizards. The main invertebrates eaten include beetle larvae and adults, bugs, caterpillars, worms, flies, snails and spiders, taken mainly from the ground and especially along roads, where many insects are killed by cars. They also feed by pecking from the surface in short pasture and grain stubble. In Hawke's Bay, the main fruit eaten was black nightshade and fallen fruits in orchards, but they occasionally inflict damage to grapes and other commercial fruit crops.

In the hand: Males tend to be larger than females: wing 131–**142**–150mm cf. 127–**135**–145mm.

Reading: Councilman, J. J. 1974. *Notornis* 21: 318–333. Cunningham, J. M. 1948. *Notornis* 3: 57–64. Moeed, A. 1976. *Notornis* 23: 246–249. Wilson, P. R. 1973. PhD thesis, Victoria Uni.

OLD WORLD SPARROWS *Passeridae*

About 40 species in Africa, Europe and Asia; 1 introduced to New Zealand.

Small birds of towns, open country and the fringes of forests. They have heavy, conical bills and powerful gizzards for eating and breaking up seeds. Most build an untidy domed nest, or nest in holes in trees, earth banks, or buildings. Calls are simple and unmusical.

366. HOUSE SPARROW *Passer domesticus* PLATES 82 AND 83

Size: 14cm, 30g

Distribution: Natural range is Europe, North Africa, the Middle East and Asia; introduced to North America, South America, southern Africa, Java, Australia, New Zealand and various islands including Mauritius, New Caledonia and Hawai'i. Over 100 House Sparrows were liberated in New Zealand by various Acclimatisation societies in 1866–71. They quickly became established and were widespread by 1880, at about which time they colonised the Chatham Islands. Now common throughout cleared parts of the mainland and inhabited offshore islands, and vagrants have been recorded from the Antipodes, Snares, Auckland and Campbell islands. They are mainly in arable farmland, rural and suburban gardens, town streets, and around grain-storage or grain-handling facilities. House Sparrows are generally sedentary, but a few long movements have been recorded in New Zealand: 300km from Upper Hutt to Reporoa, 85km from Hawera to Raetihi, and 65km from Ward to Picton.

Population: Abundant, especially in arable farmland and towns.

Breeding: Pairs form in flocks in late winter, and males establish territories in September. The male spends about a week building a bulky, domed nest with a side entrance. It is usually in a hole in a tree, building, cliff or nest box, or near the tops of tall conifers or gums, but sometimes in a low tree. Abandoned Blackbird or Song Thrush nests are occasionally used as a base. Laying is from late September to January, during which time 3–4 broods are raised. They lay 1–**4**–6 greyish-white eggs (22 x 15.5mm, 3g) marked with brown spots and streaks. Eggs are laid daily, shortly after dawn. Both birds incubate, but the female does most, including overnight. Incubation commences from the laying of the penultimate egg, and takes 10–**12**–15 days. The chicks are fed by both parents and fledge at 11–**15**–19 days old. Re-nesting commences a week or two after the previous brood has fledged. Birds can first breed at just under 1 year old. The oldest House Sparrow recorded in New Zealand lived over 15 years.

Behaviour: Gregarious, feeding in flocks of hundreds of birds and roosting in the autumn and winter in their thousands in dense conifers, pohutukawa, bamboo stands, or on buildings. In the breeding season, they defend a small area around the nest, but sometimes form loose colonies where breeding habitat is limited. From late September to January, males call from a perch near their nest a series of unmusical chirps. At roost, the chirping of many birds creates a cacophony.

Feeding: Diet is mainly cereal, grass and weed seeds, and food scraps, supplemented with invertebrates, fruit and nectar. The main seeds eaten are standing or stubble wheat and barley, maize, grasses (especially toetoe), fat hen, redroot and mat amaranth. Invertebrates are rarely eaten by adults but form the most important part of the diet of young nestlings. Main invertebrates eaten are beetles, caterpillars, bugs, aphids, grasshoppers, flies and spiders. In late summer, they sometimes disturb and aerially hawk cicadas. House Sparrows are probably the most economically important bird pest in New Zealand, by causing serious damage to wheat, barley and maize crops, and lesser damage to oats and seedling peas and brassicas. They also attack grapes, cherries and other ripening fruit, feed on grain products being fed to livestock and poultry, and foul buildings and footpaths in cities.

In the hand: Males are slightly larger than females: wing 71–**78**–84mm cf. 70–**75**–80mm. In summer, recently fledged juveniles resemble adult females but have fresh wing and tail feathers. Juvenile males usually have a dusky throat patch, rather like that of the adult female, while juvenile females have a grey throat. In autumn, all birds moult wing and tail feathers, and so after moult is complete, ages are impossible to determine; however, during moult the unmoulted primaries of adults are very worn compared with those of juveniles.

Reading: Baker, A. J. 1980. *Evolution* 34: 638–653.

Dawson, D. G. 1970. *NZ J Ag Res* 13: 681–688. MacMillan, B. H. W. 1981. *NZ J Zool* 8: 93–104. MacMillan, B. H. W. & Pollock, B. J. 1985. *NZ J Zool* 12: 307–317. Summers-Smith, J. D. 1963. *The House Sparrow.* London: Collins.

PIPITS and WAGTAILS *Motacillidae*

About 65 species worldwide; 1 is endemic to New Zealand.

The pipits and wagtails are small birds of open country, especially rough farmland, steppes, undeveloped grassland, beaches and rivers. They resemble larks in having drab plumage to provide camouflage when feeding and nesting on the ground, and like the larks they have long legs and toes, and an exceptionally long hind toe and claw. Their most notable feature is a long tail, which is wagged up and down. Their bill is slender, and they feed mainly on invertebrates. Their calls are loud and unmusical.

367. NEW ZEALAND PIPIT *Anthus novaeseelandiae* PLATE 81

Other name: Pihoihoi

Size: 19cm, 40g

Geographical variation: The taxonomy of pipits is subject to debate. Until recently this species was considered to have a very wide distribution, to Africa and Europe, with many subspecies. Now the New Zealand Pipit is considered to be endemic to New Zealand, with four subspecies: *novaeseelandiae* of the North, South and Stewart islands and their offshore islands; the Chatham Islands Pipit *chathamensis*, of the Chathams, the Antipodes Islands Pipit *steindachneri* of the Antipodes; and the Auckland Islands Pipit *aucklandicus* of the Auckland and Campbell islands.

Distribution: Endemic to New Zealand. On the mainland and offshore islands, they are widely but patchily distributed in open habitats such as beaches, riverbeds, high-country river flats, gravel roads and road verges, rough pasture, tussockland, and cleared compartments in exotic forests. Found from sea level to subalpine tussock and herb fields at 1900m. They are scarce in very dry parts of the South Island and in intensive agricultural districts such as Auckland, Waikato, Bay of Plenty, Taranaki, Manawatu, Canterbury and Southland. They are abundant on the Chatham Islands and common on the Antipodes and Auckland islands, but until rats were eradicated from Campbell Island in 2001 they were restricted to offshore stacks in the Campbell Islands. Stragglers have reached the Kermadecs and The Snares.

Population: Widespread and locally common in open country, especially in Northland, central North Island, the eastern hill country from East Cape to Cape Palliser, Nelson, northern Westland, eastern foothills of the Southern Alps, Stewart Island, Chatham Islands, and the subantarctic islands.

Conservation: Protected endemic. At first, Pipits probably benefited from the clearance of forests and the creation of open habitats, but as pasture improved, pesticides were used and mammalian predators and Magpies were introduced. Pipits declined locally and disappeared from some arable districts. Some people think that the Skylark has ousted them, but there is little overlap in diet and both species can be abundant in rough open country, such as on the Chathams. Auckland Islands Pipits quickly recolonised main Campbell Island, and have become common there following the eradication of rats in 2001, suggesting that rats have a major impact on the species.

Breeding: Some pairs remain on territory all year and breed together year after year. The female builds the nest, which is a deep cup in a bulky structure of dry grass, well hidden at the base of a clump of grass, tussock, bracken fern, manuka bush, or occasionally under fallen logs or in a hollow on a bank or road cutting. Each pair has 2–3 clutches between August and February. They lay 2–**3–4**–5 cream eggs (23 x 17mm), heavily blotched brown with a darker zone at the broader end. The incubation period is 14–15 days. Both parents feed the nestlings, which fledge at 14–16 days old. When visiting the nest, the adults usually alight 5–10m away and walk to it, but they fly directly from the nest.

Behaviour: Pairs are strongly territorial during the breeding season, but some birds, perhaps mainly juveniles, form loose flocks of up to about 20 birds in autumn and winter. The territorial song of the male, heard mainly in August–February, is a repeated, high-pitched and slurred 'pip-it' with a descending first note and a rising second, and a musical trill given from a prominent perch. The common call throughout the year is a shrill 'scree' or drawn-out 'zwee'.

Feeding: Diet is mainly invertebrates, especially beetles (including grass grubs), wasps, flies, spiders, crickets, moths and bugs, and various insect larvae and pupae. On beaches, they eat sandhoppers. Seeds of grasses, clover and weeds make up a small part of the diet. Most food is taken from the ground by walking slowly along with frequent stops to scan the surroundings, but some insects are caught after dashing after them, or are caught on the wing close to the ground.

Reading: Beauchamp, A. J. 1998. *Notornis* 45: 95–101. Beauchamp, A. J. 2007. *Notornis* 54: 112–114. Beauchamp, A. J. 2009. *Notornis* 56: 183–189. Foggo, M. N. 1984. *Notornis* 31: 1–5. Foggo, M. N. et al. 1997. *Ibis* 139: 366–373. Garrick, A. S. 1981. *NZ J Ecol* 4: 106–114. Hamel, J. 1972. *Notornis* 19: 20–25. Moeed, A. 1975. *Notornis* 22: 135–142.

ACCENTORS *Prunellidae*

13 species in Europe, North Africa and Asia; 1 introduced to New Zealand.

These small, rather drab brown birds superficially resemble sparrows (Passeridae), but have a fine pointed bill for catching insects, and they also have a musical song.

368. DUNNOCK *Prunella modularis* PLATE 81

Other name: Hedge Sparrow

Size: 14cm, 21g

Distribution: Natural breeding range is Europe and western Asia; some migrate south to winter around the Mediterranean and in North Africa. Several hundred birds were introduced into New Zealand by Acclimatisation societies and private individuals in 1867–82. They were released in both islands and spread quickly, although some parts of the country, especially Auckland and Northland, were not colonised until the 1930s. The species now breeds throughout New Zealand, including the Chathams, Antipodes, Auckland and Campbell islands; only occasionally recorded at The Snares. They are found in a variety of habitats from sea level to subalpine scrub at 1600m, including suburban gardens, orchards, exotic plantations, scrub and forest. Uncommon on well forested offshore islands such as Little Barrier and Kapiti islands. In Eurasia, they migrate, but there is no evidence of long-distance movement in New Zealand.

Population: Widespread and locally common in scrub, orchards, parks and suburban gardens, places where there is a mix of dense cover and open spaces. They are inconspicuous and so are little known by the public.

Breeding: In England, Dunnocks have a variety of mating arrangements, including simple pairs, a male with several females, a female with several males, or even several males with several females (usually the surplus birds are helpers at the nest of the main pair). In New Zealand, a similar diversity of mating arrangements has been noted, but many seem to live in simple pairs. Eggs are laid in August–January, during which time 2–3 broods are raised. The female takes *c.* 5 days to build the nest, and she is sometimes helped by the male. The nest is usually well concealed in thick undergrowth or a hedge, and normally less than 2m above the ground. It is a neat bowl of twigs, grass and moss, lined with hair, wool, feathers, tree-fern scales and moss. After a gap of *c.* 4 days after the nest is complete, the female lays 2–**4**–5 clear deep blue eggs (20 x 14.5mm) at daily intervals. Incubation is by the female alone, and takes 11–**12**–14 days. Both parents feed the young during the fledging period of 10–**12**–14 days. The oldest Dunnock recorded in New Zealand lived over 6 years.

Behaviour: In England, many territories contain a main pair plus other birds that help to defend the territory and to feed the nestlings. In New Zealand, birds seem to remain on territory all year and do not migrate. The territorial song of the male, heard mainly in April–January, is a hurried warble, faster and stronger than that of a Silvereye, and rendered 'weeso, sissy-weeso, sissy-weeso, sissy-wee'; this lasts a few seconds but is repeated several times in rapid succession. The male often sits high in a tree or on top of a bush to sing. The main call is a sharp, insistent 'tseep'.

Feeding: Diet is mainly small invertebrates, such as

beetles, spiders, flies, aphids, ants and worms. Some small fruits and seeds are also eaten. Most food is taken from the ground, usually not far away from cover.
In the hand: Males and females are virtually identical, with the male tending to have more grey on the head, chin, throat and breast. During breeding, the female has a brood patch and the male has a large bulbous cloacal protuberance. In autumn, adults have a reddish-brown eye, black bill and are often in wing-moult, while juveniles have a dull or greyish-brown eye, dark brown bill and are not moulting wing feathers.
Reading: Birkhead, M. E. 1981. *Ibis* 123: 75–84. Mauersberger, G. 1977. *Zool Abh Mus Tierk Dresden* 34: 101–126. Moeed, A. & Fitzgerald, B. M. 1982. *NZ J Zool* 9: 391–403.

OLD WORLD FINCHES *Fringillidae*

About 144 species around the Northern Hemisphere; 4 introduced to New Zealand.

Small, often colourful birds of towns, open country and sometimes forests. They have short, stout, conical bills and powerful gizzards for eating and breaking up seeds. They have 9 instead of the usual 10 primary flight feathers. Most have small, neat, cup-shaped nests. Their songs are varied and musical.
Reading: Newton, I. 1972. *Finches*. London: Collins.

369. CHAFFINCH *Fringilla coelebs* PLATE 82

Size: 15cm; male 22g, female 21g
Distribution: Natural range is Europe, North Atlantic islands, North Africa, the Middle East, and western and central Asia; introduced to South Africa and New Zealand. Several hundred birds were liberated in New Zealand by various Acclimatisation societies in 1862–80. They were slow to establish, but spread widely in the late 1800s and were well established throughout the whole country by 1920. They are now abundant throughout the mainland and offshore islands, and breeding on the Chatham Islands, The Snares, Auckland and Campbell islands. Vagrants have been recorded at the Kermadecs and Antipodes islands, as well as at Lord Howe Island. They are in farmland, orchards, gardens, exotic plantations and native forest from sea level to alpine scrub at 1400m. Although northern populations in Europe are migratory, there is no evidence of regular migration here; however, Chaffinches flock in autumn and winter and congregate in orchards, on grain stubble, and where grain or hay is being fed to horses or stock.
Population: Common throughout New Zealand; the second most widely distributed bird.
Breeding: Pairs form in early spring as winter flocks break up, and males start singing in late July. The female builds the nest over a period of 1–2 weeks. It is a neat cup of dry grass and moss, camouflaged with lichen and lined with hair, feathers and wool, and is usually firmly placed in the fork of a branch or between the trunk and a side branch 1–**3**–18m above the ground. Manuka, gorse, matagouri, pine and willow are commonly used sites. Laying is from mid-September to late January, with a peak in October–November. They lay 3–**4**–6 greyish blue (occasionally pink) eggs (20 x 14mm) with purplish blotches. The female alone incubates for 11–**13**–15 days, and the eggs hatch over 1–3 days. The chicks are brooded by the female and are frequently fed whole invertebrates by both parents. They continue to be fed by both parents for *c.* 3 weeks after the fledging period of 10–**14**–16 days. The oldest Chaffinch recorded in New Zealand lived almost 10 years, but in Europe the record is 13+ years.
Behaviour: Gregarious in autumn and winter, forming flocks of 100+ birds, often mixed in with House Sparrows and other finches in open farmland. A few join small mixed flocks of insectivorous native passerines. Chaffinch flocks are sometimes just of one sex. From late July to January, males advertise their territory with a distinctive and loud territorial song – a series of short notes ending in a terminal flourish, and rendered 'chip-chip-chip, tell-tell-tell, cherry-erry-erry tissi cheweeo'. This song is repeated persistently from a high perch. Each male has a slightly different call, and regional dialects have already established through New Zealand. The ordinary contact call note is a metallic 'pink' or 'chwink-chwink', and the flight call is a soft 'tsip'.
Feeding: Diet is a mix of seeds, invertebrates and occasional fruits. The main seeds eaten are cereals, oilseed rape and other brassicas, weeds such as redroot and

fat hen, and pine seeds from the ground or pulled from newly opened cones. Invertebrates such as spiders, caterpillars, moths, flies and aphids are most important in the breeding season, and chicks are fed mainly caterpillars. Small fruits of native and adventive shrubs and trees are occasionally eaten. They sometimes cause minor damage to newly sown cereal crops and to fruit buds, but rarely damage commercial fruit crops. Chaffinches feed mainly on the ground, walking about with short quick steps. They are sometimes seen hawking for insects above streams and riverbeds, or on the outer parts of conifers.

In the hand: Sexes are easily distinguished by head and breast colours, and males are larger than females: wing 78–**86**–92mm cf. 76–**81**–88mm. Only adults moult their primaries and tail feathers in autumn. First-winter males have dark grey alula, primary coverts, and occasional greater coverts contrasting with the black inner coverts. In females, the contrast is less obvious. Adults of both sexes have more rounded outer tail feathers than juveniles, and often have a black centre near the tip of the central tail feathers.

Reading: Jenkins, P. F. & Baker, A. J. 1984. *Ibis* 126: 510–524. Sibson, R. B. 1983. *Notornis* 30: 70–72.

370. GREENFINCH *Carduelis chloris* PLATE 83

Other name: European Greenfinch

Size: 15cm, 28g

Distribution: Natural range is Europe, North Africa, the Middle East and western Asia; introduced to the Azores, southeastern Australia and New Zealand. Fewer than 100 Greenfinches were liberated in New Zealand by various Acclimatisation societies in 1862–68. Despite the modest size of the recorded liberations, they soon became numerous and widespread throughout farmland of the whole country, and reached the Chathams before 1920. They are now common throughout the mainland and offshore islands, except in native forests. Uncommon on the Chatham Islands, and vagrants have reached the Kermadecs, Snares and Campbell islands. Birds from New Zealand or Australia have colonised Norfolk Island. Greenfinches favour farmland shelterbelts, edges of pine plantations, orchards and large gardens. There is no evidence of regular internal migration, although a bird banded in Upper Hutt moved to Christchurch. There is considerable local movement and flocking in autumn and winter on open paddocks and to the seashore and associated coastal vegetation.

Population: Widespread and locally common.

Breeding: Pairs form in early spring as winter flocks break up, and males start singing in September. Sometimes Greenfinches nest in loose colonies, with several pairs nesting within a few metres. The nest is 1–2.5–11m off the ground, near the tip of a spreading branch of a large conifer or oak, or in a fork towards the top of a gorse bush, matagouri, boxthorn or other small shrub or tree. It is bulky and untidy, built of twigs, dry grass, moss, rootlets and wool, and lined with finer material. Most eggs are laid between mid-October and early February, with peaks in late October and early January in the North Island, and in late November and mid-January in the South Island, corresponding with the usual two clutches per year, though some can rear three broods. They lay 3–5–6 pale blue eggs (22 x 14.5mm) with scattered brown spots and blotches. The female alone incubates for 11–13–15 days and is fed on the nest by the male. Both parents infrequently feed the chicks by regurgitation during the fledging period of 13–**16**–17 days and for 2–3 weeks after leaving the nest. Birds can first breed at just under 1 year old. The oldest Greenfinch recorded in New Zealand lived over 7.5 years, but in Europe the record is over 12 years.

Behaviour: Gregarious in autumn and winter; flocks of 1000+ birds have been recorded. They often join House Sparrows at grain crops, stubble or storage areas, or Goldfinches at paddocks full of weed or brassica seeds. In the breeding season, males have a characteristic butterfly-like display flight. The distinctive breeding season call of the male is a persistently repeated, harsh drawn-out 'dzwee', reminiscent of a Long-tailed Cuckoo call. A common call, delivered from a prominent perch or in flight, is a pleasant twittering song: 'chi-chi-chi-chi-chit-teu-teu-teu-teu'. Sometimes they simply repeat the 'teu' notes or utter a sweet questioning 'tsooeet' call.

Feeding: Diet is mainly seeds, supplemented with fruit buds and a few invertebrates. The main seeds eaten are maize, cereals, oilseed rape and other seeding brassicas, sunflowers, fodder radish, peas and hops, and weeds such as redroot, chickweed, storksbill and thistles. They also eat pine seeds from the cone or from the ground. Greenfinches are a minor pest of commercial fruit crops because they eat the buds of apricots, peaches, nectarines and apples, but they can inflict damage to brassica and cereal crops. They also eat small fruits of boxthorn and some native shrubs and trees (e.g. kahikatea, beech). Insects such as beetles, flies and wasps are

regularly eaten but never form a large part of the diet.
In the hand: Males are larger than females: wing 82–**87**–92mm cf. 80–**84**–90mm. Males have yellow outer webs of the three outermost primaries, and the yellow on the inner (broad) webs of the three outermost tail feathers clearly reaches the black shaft, whereas in females the yellow does not reach the shaft. Adult males have mainly yellow outer webs of the alula, whereas this is mainly brownish-grey green in first-year males. Females are more difficult to age, but adults have green outer webs to their grey-tipped primary coverts, whereas these feathers are usually olive in first-winter females. First-winter birds often have incomplete moult of tail feathers or wing coverts, and so have contrast between old 'juvenile' feathers and new 'adult' feathers.
Reading: Gillespie, G. D. 1982. *NZ J Zool* 9: 481–486. McLennan, J. A. & MacMillan, B. W. H. 1985. *Notornis* 32: 95–100. MacMillan, B. W. H. 1981. *NZ J Zool* 8: 93–104. MacMillan, B. W. H. 1985. *Notornis* 32: 85–93.

371. GOLDFINCH *Carduelis carduelis* PLATE 82

Other name: European Goldfinch
Size: 13cm; male 16g, female 15g
Geographical variation: The subspecies *britannica* from Europe was introduced to New Zealand.
Distribution: Natural range is Europe, North Africa, the Middle East and western Asia; introduced to Argentina, Bermuda, Australia and New Zealand. About 500 Goldfinches were liberated in New Zealand by various Acclimatisation societies in 1862–83. They quickly established and were widespread by 1900. They are now common throughout the mainland and offshore islands, except in forests; locally common in the Chathams since 1910, and established on The Snares and the Auckland Islands. Vagrants have reached the Kermadecs, Antipodes and Campbell islands. Birds from New Zealand or Australia have colonised Norfolk Island, and vagrants have reached Lord Howe and Macquarie islands. Goldfinches are found in farmland, orchards and gardens from sea level to *c.* 500m asl. Although northern populations in Europe are migratory, there is no evidence of regular migration in New Zealand, but there is some local movement and flocking in autumn and winter.
Population: Common and widespread at lower altitudes.
Breeding: Pairs form in spring after winter flocks break up, and males start singing in late September. The female builds the nest, a delicate cup of dry grass, fine twigs, moss, wool and cobwebs, lined with thistle down, feathers, hair and wool. The nest is usually placed in the fork of a branch near the top of or outside of a shrub 1–**2**–6m from the ground. Many tree species are used, but peach, apple and conifer trees, grape vines, gorse, matagouri and briar are common sites. Laying is from mid-October to mid-February, during which some pairs raise two broods. They lay 2–**4**–**5**–6 pale blue eggs (17 x 12mm) with reddish-brown spots and streaks. The female alone incubates for 11–**12**–13 days and is fed on the nest by the male. The chicks are brooded by the female for the first week, and at first the male feeds the female who in turn feeds the chicks. Later, both parents infrequently feed the chicks by regurgitation during the fledging period of 12–**14**–17 days and for 2–3 weeks after leaving the nest. Birds can first breed at just under 1 year old. The oldest Goldfinch recorded in New Zealand lived nearly 8 years.
Behaviour: Gregarious in autumn and winter, forming flocks of several hundred birds, often mixed in with other finches. In the breeding season, they defend a small area around their nest but do not maintain an exclusive territory. From late September to early February, males sing from a perch near their nest a pleasant, liquid, twittering 'tswitt-witt-witt' which can be elaborated into a vibrant, canary-like song. The call note is a shrill 'pee-yu', and the flight call a soft, rambling version of the full song.
Feeding: Diet is mainly seeds of introduced weeds, grasses and brassicas, supplemented with invertebrates. The main seeds eaten are winged thistles, Scotch thistles, dandelions, ryegrass and chickweed in late spring and summer, rosemary and redroot in autumn and winter, storksbill and meadowgrass in spring. They sometimes damage strawberries when they peck seeds from the outside of ripening fruit, but they cause little damage compared with other introduced birds. Invertebrates such as aphids, bugs, flies, caterpillars and spiders are eaten in small quantities all year, but are more important in spring and are an important part of the diet of young nestlings. When feeding on tall weeds and thistles, birds flutter from plant to plant and hang upside down to extract the seeds.
In the hand: Males are larger than females: wing 72–**77**–82mm cf. 70–**74**–78mm. Males have more

extensive red on the throat and head, especially above and behind the eye. The nasal bristles of adult males are black, whereas they are grey to blackish-grey in adult females. Most first-year males also have black nasal bristles, and most first-year females have light grey bristles, but some intermediate juveniles are not possible to sex. In autumn, adults moult wing and tail feathers, whereas juveniles have slightly worn and distinctly pointed outer tail feathers, and at least some of the greater coverts are not moulted and so are tipped buffish white rather than yellow or white as in adults.

Reading: Campbell, P. O. 1972. MSc thesis, Massey Uni. Middleton, A. L. A. 1970. *Emu* 70: 159–167. Niethammer, G. 1970. *Notornis* 17: 214–222.

372. REDPOLL *Carduelis flammea* PLATE 82

Other name: Common Redpoll

Size: 12cm, 12g

Distribution: Natural range is northern parts of North America, Europe and Asia; many migrate south to winter in lower latitudes in the United States, around the Mediterranean and in southern Asia. About 500 Redpolls were liberated in New Zealand by the various Acclimatisation societies in 1862–75, including over 200 near Auckland in 1872. They quickly established and were widespread by 1900. They are now throughout the mainland and offshore islands, although more common in the South Island than the North Island. They have colonised the Kermadecs, Chathams, Antipodes, Snares, Auckland and Campbell islands, and also Macquarie Island. Vagrants have been reported on Lord Howe Island. Redpolls are found in farmland, orchards, tussockland, coastal dunes, forest and scrub margins, and subalpine scrub to 1750m, more common at higher altitudes and in less developed areas. There is no evidence of regular migration in New Zealand, but there is some local movement and flocking in winter.

Population: Widespread and locally common, especially in higher and drier parts of the South Island.

Breeding: Pairs form in flocks in late winter, and males establish territories and start singing in September. The female builds the nest, which is a small neat cup of dry grass, fine twigs, moss, wool and cobwebs, lined with feathers, willow catkins, wool and hair. It is usually placed in a fork of a low shrub such as gorse, matagouri, briar or lupin, 0.2–**2**–7m from the ground. Laying is from mid-October to early February, during which most pairs probably raise two broods. They lay 3–**4**–6 bluish-green eggs (15 x 11.5mm) with light brown spots and streaks. The female incubates for 10–**11**–15 days and is fed on the nest by the male. The chicks are fed infrequently by regurgitation by both parents and fledge at 12–**13**–15 days old. They continue to be fed for 1–2 weeks after leaving the nest. The oldest Redpoll recorded in New Zealand lived *c.* 8 years.

Behaviour: Gregarious in autumn and winter, sometimes forming huge flocks of several thousand birds. One flock in the King Country was estimated to be of 100,000+ birds. In the breeding season, they defend a small area around the nest, and sometimes they form loose colonies where breeding sites are limited. From late September to early February, males sing a short rippling trill from a perch near their nest. The most common and distinctive call is a harsh, rattling flight call: 'chich-chich-chich-chich', sometimes followed by a 'bizzzz'. The alarm note is a plaintive, questioning 'tsooeet'.

Feeding: Diet is mainly small weed and grass seeds, supplemented with invertebrates and fruit buds; unlike most birds, Redpoll chicks are fed only seeds. The preferred seeds are grass, sedge, tussock, clover, brassica, dock, redroot, fat hen, thistle and evening primrose. Redpolls sometimes cause serious economic damage by destroying fruit buds of apricots and peaches during a brief period in spring, and also damage strawberries when they peck seeds from the outside of ripening fruit.

In the hand: Males are slightly larger than females: wing 64–**69.5**–75mm cf. 62–**67.5**–72mm. In autumn and winter, adult males have a pinkish-red breast, flanks, rump and sides of head, whereas adult females have pinkish-red on the head only. In spring and summer, females develop a brood patch, and birds with pinkish-red breast and flanks are adult males, but birds lacking these pink markings, and without a brood patch, cannot be sexed. Adult males and females can have similar head markings. In autumn, adults moult all wing and tail feathers, whereas juveniles may moult only a few tail feathers, and so in winter, juveniles have wing and most tail feathers looking distinctly worn.

Reading: Fennell, J. et al. 1985. *Notornis* 32: 245–253. Fennell, J & Sagar, P. M. 1985. *Notornis* 32: 254–256. Stenhouse, D. 1962. *Notornis* 10: 61–67.

BUNTINGS and NEW WORLD SPARROWS

Emberizidae

About 326 species worldwide, except Australasia; 2 introduced to New Zealand.

Small, often colourful birds of towns, open country and sometimes forests. They have short, robust, conical bills adapted for husking and crushing seeds. The lower bill is hinged at the base to allow large seeds to be swallowed. Most have a cup-shaped nest. Their songs are simple but varied, and generally not very musical.

373. YELLOWHAMMER *Emberiza citrinella* PLATE 83

Size: 16cm, 27g
Distribution: Natural breeding range is Eurasia from Britain to Siberia; many migrate south to winter in North Africa, the Middle East and southern Asia. About 500 Yellowhammers were introduced into New Zealand by Acclimatisation societies between 1862 and the early 1870s. They were released in both islands and spread quickly so that by 1900 they were well established throughout the mainland. Now they are found throughout the North, South and Stewart islands and on many offshore islands, and have colonised the Kermadecs and the Chathams, although they remain uncommon at those sites. There is no clear evidence of migration within New Zealand, but vagrants have reached The Snares, Campbell and Lord Howe islands. Yellowhammers are found in farmland, orchards and open tussockland from sea level to subalpine herb fields at 1600m.
Population: Widespread and locally common.
Breeding: Males start territorial singing in late August. Laying is in October to mid-February, during which two broods are normally raised. The nest is usually built on or very close to the ground in gorse, blackberry, bracken, long grass or other clump of thick vegetation on a bank or other ungrazed ground. The nest is a cup of dry grass, lined with fine rootlets, moss, grass, hair, wool and feathers. They lay 3–**4**–5 whitish-pink eggs (21 x 16mm) covered in fine scribbling of dark brown lines. The female does most of the incubation during the incubation period of **12**–13 days. Both parents feed the young during the fledging period of 12–**13** days. The oldest Yellowhammer recorded in New Zealand lived 9+ years, but in Europe one lived 11+ years.
Behaviour: Yellowhammers are territorial during breeding, but in autumn and winter they form flocks of up to 300 birds at good food sources such as around stables, grain silos where grain has been spilt, or where stock-food and hay are being fed out. Male Yellowhammers have a distinctive and monotonous song, usually delivered from a conspicuous perch, and rendered 'chitty-chitty-chitty… sweee' or 'a little bit of bread and no cheese'; the 'sweee' or 'cheese' is omitted at the start (August) and end (February) of the singing season. The call note is a ringing 'tink' or 'chip'; a single 'twick' is the usual flight call, and a liquid 'twitup' is characteristic in winter flocks.
Feeding: Diet is a mix of seeds and invertebrates. Seeds are from a variety of introduced weeds, grasses, clover and cereals. Invertebrates include caterpillars, beetles, flies, bugs and spiders. They feed mainly on the ground and hop as they search for food in short grass or on bare soil. Yellowhammers sometimes eat newly sown seeds, but generally they are regarded as a colourful addition to open landscapes rather than as a serious pest.
In the hand: Males are larger than females, but their measurements overlap: wing 82–**87**–97mm cf. 78–**82**–86mm. Adult males are much brighter yellow than females or juveniles, and can be reliably distinguished by having over half of each crown feather yellow with a greyish-green tip and a tiny black spot or streak on the feather shaft near the tip. Adult females and first-year males have broad greyish-brown tips to their crown feathers, a narrow central yellow portion and broad black base, and a narrow black shaft streak, while first-year (and rarely adult) females have little yellow on the crown feathers and a prominent black shaft streak. In autumn, adults moult wing and tail feathers, whereas juveniles do not; and so in winter, adults have fresh rounded feathers, whereas first-year birds have worn feathers.
Reading: Harrison, J. M. 1955. *Notornis* 6: 176–177.

374. CIRL BUNTING *Emberiza cirlus* PLATE 83

Size: 16cm, 25g
Distribution: An uncommon and declining sedentary species of southern Europe, North Africa and Asia Minor, which has its northern limit in southern England. Records indicate that only a few Cirl Buntings were introduced to New Zealand by Acclimatisation societies: seven were liberated in Otago in 1871, and four in Wellington in 1880 (possibly from Otago stock). Cirl Buntings spread widely but are the rarest of the introduced passerines – although they are easily overlooked. They are found in open country from Northland to southern Otago, but mainly in drier pastoral country with scattered trees or hedgerows, or rough grassland with patches of gorse, briar and matagouri, east of the Main Divide from Gisborne to Otago (especially in Marlborough and Central Otago), and near Whangarei and Nelson. There is some local or nomadic movement and winter flocking into suitable coastal grassland and saltmarsh habitats.
Population: Rare, perhaps fewer than 10,000 birds, but locally common in Marlborough and Central Otago, and small winter flocks are recorded each year at coastal sites in Tasman Bay and at Lake Grassmere.
Conservation: Unprotected introduced species. Cirl Buntings have declined significantly in their natural range, especially in Britain (where the population declined from *c.* 300 pairs in 1970 to 167 pairs in 1982), probably because of changes to agricultural practices. Continued persecution of small birds in southern Europe makes their status in Europe tenuous, and so the New Zealand population could be internationally important.
Breeding: Males start territorial singing in late August. Laying is in October–January, during which probably two broods are raised. The nest is built in thick vegetation in a gorse bush, matagouri, briar or macrocarpa 1–5m from the ground. It is a cup of dry grass and moss, lined with fine grass, hair and wool, sometimes placed in the old nest of another species. They lay 2–3–4 bluish-green eggs (21 x 16mm) covered in black streaks and hairlines. The female incubates for 11–13 days and is fed on the nest by the male. Both parents feed the young during the fledging period of 11–13 days.
Behaviour: Cirl Buntings are territorial during breeding, and some seem to remain on territory all year. In February–August, some birds form flocks of 5–15 birds, mainly in coastal wasteland but also recorded in Central Otago, or join winter flocks of Yellowhammers. The territorial call of the male is heard in the early morning and late afternoon from about mid-August and regularly from October. It is a monotonous metallic, rattling buzz, resembling a black cricket, delivered up to 9 times per minute from a high perch in a tree or powerline. Call notes are a thin 'zit' or 'see', sometimes run together to form a strident 'sissi-sissi-sip'.
Feeding: Diet has not been studied in detail in New Zealand, but they have been seen feeding on seeds of barley grass and weeds, and adults feed their young caterpillars and moths.
In the hand: Males are larger than females, but measurements overlap: wing 77–**80**–83mm cf. 76–**78**–79mm. Males have a greyish-black throat and chin rather than dull yellowish, spotted darker, in females. First-year males can be similar to bright adult females, but in January–March adults moult wing and tail feathers, while juveniles moult only a few central tail feathers. In winter, adults therefore have fresh rounded feathers, whereas first-year birds have worn feathers, except for fresh central tail feathers.
Reading: Taylor, T. J. 1978. *Notornis* 25: 249–251.

WHERE TO SEE BIRDS IN NEW ZEALAND

By international standards, New Zealand has a small number of species (the record seen in 24 hours is just over 100 species), but what it lacks in diversity, it makes up for in uniqueness. The 12 sites listed here are not necessarily the best birding places in New Zealand, but they provide a wide geographical spread of good birding sites, often in spectacular or interesting settings. The sites are easily accessible, cover a range of habitat types, and should allow you to see or hear a good variety of native and endemic species during a visit. Many species (e.g. *Swamp Harrier*, *Pukeko*, *Variable Oystercatcher*, *NZ Pigeon*, *Tui* and *Fantail*) can be seen almost anywhere and so they are not usually included in the lists of notable native species you are likely to see at each site. Others are sufficiently rare that the chances of seeing them on a site visit are so low that it would be misleading to raise your hopes too much. The distribution and conspicuousness of birds can vary through the year, so bear this in mind when planning a visit to a particular site.

We have included information about sites that was accurate in 2014, but site conditions, operators, charges, contact information and schedules will change over time. Prices are those for adults; many operators offer substantial discounts for children, senior citizens, family or group bookings. We suggest that you use the websites or other contacts given to check the most up-to-date site information. The international dialling code for New Zealand is +64 and the 0 in the two-digit area code is dropped for international calling.

NORTH ISLAND

Aroha Island, Bay of Islands

This 12ha 'island' in the Bay of Islands is owned by the Queen Elizabeth II National Trust and is the site of the Aroha Island Eco Centre. The island is actually connected to the mainland by a causeway, and is situated about 12km northeast of the Kerikeri Stone Store (one of the oldest buildings in New Zealand). Access is via Landing, Kapiro, Redcliffs, Rangitane and Kurapari roads. The island is open to the general public 9.30 a.m. to 5.30 p.m. with entry by donation; however, various forms of accommodation (self-catering cottage, bed and breakfast, and camping/campervan sites) are available on the island all year round. The Ecological Centre has good educational displays, including material on the star attraction of the site, the *Brown Kiwi*. Guided night walks are available November to July by arrangement at $40 per adult for a maximum of four people. A wide range of bush, wetland and estuarine birds are also seen here, including *Reef Heron*, *Banded Rail*, *Morepork* and *Fernbird*. Contact: www.arohaisland.co.nz, phone: 09 407 5243, email: manager@arohaisland.co.nz.

Tiritiri Matangi Island, Hauraki Gulf

This 220ha island is an open sanctuary run by the Department of Conservation in association with the Supporters of Tiritiri Matangi Inc. It lies 3.5km off the tip of the Whangaparaoa Peninsula and 25km from downtown Auckland. The island has recently been restored from mainly farmland to a forest haven for birds, and so apart from several valleys of mature forest, most vegetation is less than 40 years old. Because mammalian predators have been eradicated, and many bird species reintroduced, the island has a particularly abundant and diverse birdlife. 360 Discovery Cruises (www.360discovery.co.nz, phone: 09 307 8005, email: info@360discovery.co.nz) run a large, comfortable catamaran launch service to the island, departing at 9 a.m. from Pier 4 (downtown Auckland) and 9.50 a.m. from Gulf Harbour (near the tip of the Whangaparaoa Peninsula) from Wednesday to Sunday, arriving at the island at 10.15 a.m.; departing the island at 3.30 p.m. Return fares are $69 per adult from Auckland or $52 per adult from Gulf Harbour. On the journey from Auckland you may see: *Flesh-footed Shearwater*, *Buller's Shearwater*, *Fluttering Shearwater*, *Common Diving Petrel*, *Australasian Gannet*, *Pied Shag* and *Arctic Skua*. The resident rangers will welcome you to the island and explain its history and restoration work, and run a bio-security check to ensure that pests do not re-establish. The Supporters of Tiritiri Matangi (www.tiritirimatangi.org.nz) run guided walks at $5 per adult, and your guide will take you to the best birding sites on the island and share their knowledge of the birdlife. A day visit should reveal *Blue Penguin* (in nesting and roosting boxes along the shore from the wharf), *Brown Teal, Takahe, Red-crowned Parakeet, North Island Kokako, North Island Saddleback, Stitchbird, Bellbird, Whitehead, North Island Robin* and *Fernbird. Spotless Crake* are heard occasionally in swampy areas, especially in Wattle Valley. The Supporters of Tiritiri Matangi run a visitor centre and shop on the island and offer complimentary tea and coffee, but lunches are not available. Limited accommodation is available on the island for overnight stays in a shared cottage at $30 per adult; contact: www.doc.govt.nz/tiritiribunkhouse. Those staying overnight should hear or see *Little Spotted Kiwi* and *Grey-faced Petrel*, in season.

Miranda Shorebird Centre, Firth of Thames

The Firth of Thames, 50km southeast of Auckland, is one of the best and most accessible wader sites in the country. This 'Ramsar wetland' site is approached from Auckland by a scenic but winding route via Takanini or Papakura and Clevedon on the Pacific Coast Highway (watch for *Pied Shag* and *Spotted Shag* along the coast), or more directly by SH1 until the southern side of the Bombay Hills, then along SH2 and SH25. The major roosts are on the western coast between Kaiaua and Miranda, and these shellbanks and freshwater pools are easily accessible. The only bird observatory in New Zealand is situated 2km north of Miranda and 6.5km south of Kaiaua (famed for its excellent fish and chips) and is run by the Miranda Naturalists' Trust. The observatory (www.miranda-shorebird.org.nz, phone: 09 232 2781, email: shorebird@farmside.co.nz) has comfortable 4–6-person bunkrooms and self-catering facilities at $25 per adult, and two self-contained units at $95 for two people. Day entry to the observatory is free and tea and coffee are available for a gold coin donation. The resident manager and shop manager are very knowledgeable and can advise day visitors or overnight guests about the best places to see particular species, and a blackboard lists the species seen recently in the area. A high-tide visit to the observation hides at the old limeworks site at Miranda at any time of year should reveal: *Red Knot, Bar-tailed Godwit, South Island Pied Oystercatcher, Pied Stilt, New Zealand Dotterel, Banded Dotterel, Wrybill* and *Black-billed Gull*, along with numerous Arctic waders from October to March, especially *Turnstone, Red-necked Stint, Sharp-tailed Sandpiper* and *Pacific Golden Plover*, though rarer vagrants are also seen each summer, and *Little Tern* are regular visitors to the area. Many Arctic migrants overwinter, but the diversity is lower. Native waders dominate the winter counts, and *Royal Spoonbill* and *White Heron* are often present.

Rainbow Springs/Sulphur Bay/Wingspan National Bird of Prey Centre, Rotorua

The Rotorua area is famed for its impressive geothermal attractions of geysers, boiling mud and hot pools, and it also has displays of Maori culture, New Zealand agriculture and trout. *Brown Kiwi* are displayed at nocturnal houses at Rainbow Springs and at the Maori Arts and Crafts Institute. Rainbow Springs has a facility known as Kiwi Encounter which incubates a large number of wild-laid Brown Kiwi eggs as part of a highly successful conservation programme known as Bank of New Zealand Operation Nest Egg. A 30-minute guided tour of this facility costs an extra $10 per adult above the normal Rainbow Springs entry fee of $40 per adult (www.rainbowsprings.co.nz).

Lake Rotorua has a wide variety of waterfowl, and the best place to see them is at Sulphur Bay, a wildlife refuge, on the edge of downtown Rotorua. A walkway follows the shoreline from Rotorua City Lakefront Reserve east to Motutara Point and then along the western edge of Sulphur Bay to the Polynesian Spa. The peaceful Government Gardens and active thermal vents provide a unique backdrop to birdwatching. In spring and summer, *Pied Stilt, Banded Dotterel, Spur-winged Plover, Red-billed Gulls* and *Black-billed Gulls* nest on the silica flats in Sulphur Bay. *NZ Scaup, NZ Dabchick, Little Shag, Black Shag* and *Little Black Shag* nest in willows along the shoreline or on the island at Motutara Point. Resident waterfowl include *Black Swan, Paradise Shelduck, Grey Teal* and *Australasian Shoveler*.

About 15 minutes northwest of Rotorua is the Wingspan National Bird of Prey Centre (www.wingspan.co.nz, phone: 07 357 4469), a facility dedicated to education about birds of prey. Turn off SH5 into Paradise Valley Road about 1km south of the Agrodome or 1.5km west of the SH5/SH36 junction at Ngongotaha, and follow that road for about 2km. The centre is open 9 a.m. to 3 p.m. daily, with flight displays of *NZ Falcon* and *Swamp Harrier* at 2 p.m. Entry to the centre, museum and the flight displays is $25 per adult.

Manawatu Estuary/Lake Horowhenua, Manawatu

A visit to the mouth of the Manawatu River at Foxton Beach provides good opportunities to see a wide range of waders and other wetland birds at a small 'Ramsar wetland' site. Turn west off SH1 at Foxton, and a couple of kilometres into Foxton Beach township turn left into Dawick Street, where a small viewing platform offers a view over the estuary. Closer approach to waders at the high-tide roost on the spit opposite the viewing platform is via a basic road through tall trees by the motor camp and then through sand dunes. It is best to park near the pines well above the high-water mark. Species likely to be seen at roost, or on mudflats on either side of high tide include *South Island Pied Oystercatcher*, *Banded Dotterel*, *Wrybill* (January to July), and a variety of Arctic waders, especially *Red Knot*, *Sharp-tailed Sandpiper*, *Bar-tailed Godwit* and *Pacific Golden Plover*. A good variety of terns often call in during the summer and autumn, and *Royal Spoonbill* often feed on mudflats about 1km upstream from the high-tide roost.

About 15km to the south is Lake Horowhenua, a good site to see waterfowl. In Levin, turn west off SH1 into Queen Street West at the traffic lights opposite where SH57 joins. Follow the road 2.5km to the domain, where *NZ Dabchick*, *Paradise Shelduck*, *Grey Teal* and *Australasian Shoveler* are often seen. A few *Black-billed Gulls* roost at the domain in winter.

Kapiti Island/Zealandia, Wellington

Kapiti Island has one of New Zealand's premier nature reserves and some private Maori land. The 1965ha island has been cleared of all mammalian pests, and a large range of native birds abound. The nature reserve is managed by the Department of Conservation and strict conditions apply to visitors to maintain the quality of the reserve; for example, your bags will be inspected to ensure that you are not accidentally taking any rodents to the island. Day visits, including an entry permit and the 15-minute boat trip from Paraparaumu Beach, cost $75–$85 per adult, with an additional $20 per adult for a 1-hour guided walk when you get to the island. Three concessionaires run day trips based on demand: Kapiti Island Nature Tours (www.kapitiislandnaturetours.co.nz, phone: 0800 547 5263 or 021 126 7525), Kapiti Marine Charter (www.kapitimarinecharter.co.nz, phone: 0800 433 779 or 027 442 4850) and Kapiti Tours (www.ngatitoakapititours.co.nz, phone: 0800 527 484 or 027 248 1512). Trips depart at 9 a.m. and return at 3.30 p.m. There are two destinations on the island, which you need to specify at the time of booking: Rangatira Point, in the centre of the island, which provides access through mainly mature forest to the summit; or Waiorua, which provides access to Okupe Lagoon and a bush walk through regenerating forest. Most forest birds can be seen within 500m of the landing site at Rangatira Point, but many visitors enjoy the 521m climb to the summit, where spectacular views of the Cook Strait region can be had on a fine day. A greater diversity of birds is seen at Waiorua, but it lacks some forest specialists, such as *North Island Kokako*, *North Island Saddleback* and *Stitchbird*, that are usually seen or heard on the summit route. Birds likely to be seen during a day trip at any time of year include: *Blue Penguin*, *Fluttering Shearwater*, *Weka*, *Takahe*, *Kaka*, *Red-crowned Parakeet*, *Whitehead*, *Tomtit*, *North Island Robin*, *Bellbird* and *Pipit*, with *Long-tailed Cuckoo* added in summer.

An overnight visit to Waiorua, which usually includes separate days at Rangatira and Waiorua, provides a very good chance of seeing *Little Spotted Kiwi* on a guided night walk. A range of accommodation options is available from Kapiti Island Nature Tours, with prices ranging from $355 per adult, including permits, transport, meals, accommodation and the guided night walk.

Zealandia is a 225ha ecosanctuary just 10 minutes from central Wellington. In 1999, this forested valley was ringed with an 8.6km-long and 2.2m-high predator-proof fence and all mammal pests within were eradicated. Since then, tracks have been built, habitats restored, interpretation provided, and many species have been reintroduced. The sanctuary (www.visitzealandia.com, phone: 04 920 9200) is open 9 a.m. to 5 p.m. daily, with a variety of walks available, along with free guided walks and talks. Entry costs $17.50 per adult. During a day trip at any time of year you should see or hear: nesting or roosting *Little Shag*, *Pied Shag*, *Brown Teal*, *Takahe*, *Kaka*, *Red-crowned Parakeet*, *North Island Saddleback*, *Stitchbird*, *Bellbird*, *Whitehead* and *North Island Robin*, and tuatara are often seen basking outside their burrows in a special enclosure. The sanctuary also runs 2.5-hour guided night walks every night from 1 November to 31 March, or four nights a week 1 April to 30 October, at $75 per adult, during which you have a good chance of seeing *Little Spotted Kiwi* and *Morepork*, but bookings are essential because group size is limited.

SOUTH ISLAND

Kaikoura

This small seaside town lies about halfway between Picton and Christchurch, and is overlooked by the majestic Seaward Kaikoura Mountains (2285m), nesting site of the *Hutton's Shearwater*. A deep marine canyon lies just offshore and upwellings of cold nutrient-rich water make this a highly productive feeding ground for seabirds and marine mammals. Kaikoura is best known for its whale-watching (mainly sperm whale), and opportunities to watch or swim with dusky dolphins and NZ fur seals. Weather permitting, Albatross Encounter (www.albatrossencounter.co.nz, phone: 0800 733 365) runs 2–3 specialist 2.5-hour pelagic seabird cruises each day at 6 a.m. (summer only), 9 a.m. and 1 p.m. at $115 per adult. These trips run all year, and the following species are seen regularly: *Blue Penguin, Wandering Albatross, Antipodean Albatross, Southern Royal Albatross, Northern Royal Albatross, Black-browed Mollymawk, Buller's Mollymawk, White-capped Mollymawk, Salvin's Mollymawk, Southern Giant Petrel, Northern Giant Petrel, Cape Pigeon, Fairy Prion, Grey-faced Petrel, White-chinned Petrel, Westland Petrel, Buller's Shearwater, Flesh-footed Shearwater, Sooty Shearwater, Fluttering Shearwater, Hutton's Shearwater, Common Diving Petrel* and *Arctic Skua*. On shore, the tip of the peninsula has huge colonies of *Red-billed Gull* and *White-fronted Tern*, and *Variable Oystercatcher, Turnstone* and the occasional *Wandering Tattler* feed on the wave platforms among the fur seals, or on kelp-strewn beaches.

Kowhai Bush, on the northern banks of the Kowhai River, has numerous *Bellbird* and small but declining populations of *Rifleman, South Island Robin* and *Brown Creeper*.

Arthur's Pass

This alpine pass is on the main road (SH73) and trans-alpine railway from Christchurch to the West Coast. A variety of accommodation is available in Arthur's Pass village. A stop at the Department of Conservation Visitor Centre is recommended to get advice about various walks available in the adjacent national park and around the village, and for the latest information on particular species. Approaching from Christchurch, look for *Australasian Crested Grebe* on Lake Pearson to the right of SH73 about 25km past Porter's Pass (8km before Cass) and *Black-fronted Tern* on the Waimakariri River. *Yellowhead* and *Orange-fronted Parakeet* are found in beech forest flanking the Hawdon River, accessed from Riversdale Road which turns off SH73 and crosses the Waimakariri River at the Mt White bridge about 25km east of Arthur's Pass, or 3km north of Cass. At night, *Great Spotted Kiwi* are often heard calling from the hills behind the Hawdon Shelter, or around Arthur's Pass village, however, they are unlikely to be seen. Daytime bush walks from the village should reveal *Rifleman, Tomtit, South Island Robin, Brown Creeper* and *Bellbird*. *Kea* are heard and occasionally seen around the village, but some usually hang out at the Otira Gorge viaduct lookout. *Blue Duck* and *Kaka* are best seen in the Otira Valley on the West Coast side of the pass. In summer and autumn, *Rock Wren* are sometimes seen above the bushline in Temple Basin, a 500m (2-hour) climb through beech forest, or at the head of the Otira Valley about 30 minutes beyond the footbridge on the track that heads west of SH73 just north of the Arthur's Pass summit.

Eglinton Valley/Milford Sound

The very scenic drive from Te Anau to Milford Sound, via the Eglinton and upper Hollyford valleys, passes through several very good birdwatching spots, which offer chances to see a wide range of native birds. In summer, *Black-fronted Tern* nest on the Eglinton River. *Blue Duck* are sometimes seen in Monkey Creek, Falls Creek, main Hollyford Valley, or the creek about 1km before Milford Sound village, and *NZ Scaup* are on most lakes. Bush birds include: *NZ Falcon, Kaka, Yellow-crowned Parakeet, Long-tailed Cuckoo, Rifleman, Bellbird, Brown Creeper, Tomtit* and *South Island Robin*; the best places to see them are Smithy Creek, Lake Gunn nature walk, north of the Deer Flat camping area, and at Lake Lochie near 'The Divide'. *Kea* are often seen at either end of the Homer Tunnel and at 'The Chasm' on the Milford side. *Rock Wren* are frequently seen from the nature trail at the eastern portal to the Homer Tunnel, or a short distance up the Gertrude Saddle Track from the Homer Huts (1.5km east of the Homer Tunnel). At Milford Sound, several companies operate cruise boats that take passengers down the spectacular fiord to near the Tasman Sea, and some cruises stop at the Milford Discovery Centre and Underwater Observatory at Harrison Cove, where surprisingly colourful corals, sponges, anemones and fish can be viewed from more than 10m under the surface. During the various 1.5–2.5-hour cruises, which cost $45–$100 per adult depending on the time of day and duration, *Fiordland Crested Penguin* are often seen on the northern shores of the fiord; entry to the underwater observatory is an additional $36 per adult. Contact: www.realjourneys.co.nz, www.southerndiscoveries.co.nz, www.mitrepeak.com or www.jucycruize.co.nz.

Dunedin

Dunedin city and its environs are sometimes referred to as the 'Wildlife Capital of New Zealand' because of the wide range of wildlife and natural habitats within close reach of the city. The Otago Peninsula is the jewel in the crown of the area, and a number of ecotourism operators conduct general wildlife tours (contact: www.

dunedin.govt.nz/isite, phone: 03 474 3300). The Otago Peninsula Trust (www.albatross.org.nz, phone: 03 478 0499) operates a specialist observatory to view the unique *Northern Royal Albatross* colony at Taiaroa Head, right at the tip of the peninsula, where birds come and go all year round. Albatross Centre tours (11 a.m. to 5.30 p.m. daily) can be gained through one of the land-based tours or at the centre itself ($39 per adult); however, in summer and at weekends bookings should be made in advance. The centre also offers a *Blue Penguin* viewing tour at dusk. Monarch Wildlife Cruises (www.wildlife.co.nz, phone: 03 477 4276) operate 1-hour wildlife cruises ($49 per adult) from Weller's Rock wharf to view the colony from offshore, as well as cliff-nesting *Spotted Shag, Stewart Island Shag* and *Red-billed Gull*, penguins and other marine wildlife. Nearby, Penguin Place (www.penguinplace.co.nz, phone: 03 478 0286) on Harrington Point Road, offers good opportunities to get excellent views of *Yellow-eyed Penguin* and *Blue Penguin*. The tours, which run from 10.15 a.m. in summer (October to March) and 3.15 p.m. in winter (April to September), include a talk and a short (<1km) walk to viewing hides; cost $49 per adult.

Orokonui Ecosanctuary (www.orokonui.org.nz, phone: 03 482 1755) is a 307ha predator-free, cloud-forest sanctuary, ringed since 2007 by an 8.7km-long predator-proof fence. It is situated northeast of Dunedin on Blueskin Road, 6km over the hill north of Port Chalmers, or reached off SH1 at Waitati, 20km north of central Dunedin, via Harvey Street and Mount Cargill Road. The Ecosanctuary has *Takahe* and a good range of forest birds, including *Kaka, Rifleman, South Island Saddleback, Brown Creeper, South Island Robin* and *Fernbird*. Entry for self-guided walks is available 9.30 a.m. to 3.30 p.m. daily ($16 per adult), 1-hour and 2-hour guided tours leave the Visitor Centre at 11 a.m. and 1.30 p.m. daily. By arrangement, 2.5-hour twilight tours ($69 per adult) commence half an hour before sunset, during which you may hear or see *Haast Tokoeka* (kiwi) and *Morepork*; bookings are essential because group size is limited.

STEWART ISLAND/RAKIURA

The southernmost of the three main islands of New Zealand is mostly national park, with small enclaves of private or Maori land. The only township is Oban in the northeast of the island. The island is reached by three daily scheduled flights on light aircraft (www.stewartislandflights.com, phone: 03 218 9129) to Oban at $203 return per adult, or by a 1-hour fast-ferry trip across Foveaux Strait from Bluff 1–3 times daily depending on season (www.stewartislandexperience.co.nz, phone: 03 212 7660) at $75 per adult. A wide range of seabirds can sometimes be seen on this crossing, but the ferries usually travel too fast for good birdwatching. Oban is a delightful fishing village of about 500 people, nestled into bush surrounding Halfmoon and Horseshoe bays. A wide variety of accommodation is available, ranging from backpackers to luxury lodges (contact the Oban Visitor Centre: www.stewartisland.co.nz, phone: 03 219 0056). Bush birds such as *Weka, NZ Pigeon, Kaka, Red-crowned Parakeet, Yellow-crowned Parakeet, Morepork, Brown Creeper, Tomtit* and *Bellbird* abound around the village, and *Stewart Island Tokoeka* (kiwi) and *Morepork* can be heard calling at night. On a windy day, from the tip of Akers Point (a 2.5km walk from the village centre) a good range of seabirds can be seen offshore, including *Yellow-eyed Penguin, Blue Penguin, Black-browed Mollymawk, Buller's Mollymawk, White-capped Mollymawk, Southern Giant Petrel, Northern Giant Petrel, Cape Pigeon, Mottled Petrel, Sooty Shearwater, Broad-billed Prion, Fairy Prion, Common Diving Petrel, Stewart Island Shag* and *Spotted Shag*, and the occasional *Antarctic Tern*; however, a charter fishing boat or water taxi via the Oban Visitor Centre should give you a better chance to get among these seabirds and add to this list of species that abound around the northern Muttonbird Islands, around the mouth of Paterson Inlet, and along the east coast of the island. Ulva Island is a 269ha predator-free island a 10-minute water-taxi trip from Golden Bay; in addition to the forest birds seen around Oban it has *Rifleman, South Island Saddleback, Yellowhead* and *South Island Robin*. Bravo Adventure Cruises (www.kiwispotting.co.nz, phone: 03 219 1144) run an excellent 4-hour evening guided tour most nights for parties of 6–30 people at $140 per adult. The trip includes launch travel and a 1.5-hour easy walk to a beach where *Stewart Island Tokoeka* are usually found fossicking among tidal wrack, or seen in the bush on the walk there. Ruggedy Range Wilderness Experience (www.ruggedyrange.com, phone: 03 219 1066) offer a variety of guided nature walks, including a trip to Mason Bay, during which there is a high probability of seeing *Stewart Island Tokoeka* feeding in daylight, or around the Mason Bay Hut at night. A trip to Mason Bay via a water taxi to Freshwater Landing and a 4-hour (sometimes muddy but almost flat) walk to the Department of Conservation's Mason Bay Hut (20 bunk at $5 per adult), and then a 20-minute walk down Duck Creek is a must for seabird enthusiasts. Seabirds are often wrecked on this wild, west-facing, open sandy beach, especially in the 3km section south of Duck Creek. Species often found include *Fiordland Crested Penguin*, *Snares Crested Penguin*, albatrosses and mollymawks, *Mottled Petrel*, *Sooty Shearwater*, *Broad-billed Prion*, *Fairy Prion* and *Common Diving Petrel*, and you should see *Variable Oystercatcher* and *Banded Dotterel* along the coast, and perhaps also *Southern Skua* or *Arctic Tern*. *Southern NZ Dotterel* fly from Paterson Inlet at high tide to roost on dune flats 200m due south of the first creek crossing below the Mason Bay Hut. Charter aircraft from Stewart Island Flights can land on the beach at low tide, and thus reduce the walking time on the outward or return trip.

CHATHAM ISLANDS

This small cluster of islands lying about 800km east of Christchurch has many rare endemic birds, but some are inaccessible on small island nature reserves. The main Chatham Island, with a population of about 500 people, is reached by Air Chathams (www.airchathams.co.nz, phone: 03 305 0209) flights from Wellington, Auckland and Christchurch, with a total of 4–6 flights each week, depending on season, from $754 return. Accommodation, vehicle hire and guided tour options are available from the Chatham Islands Tourism Development office (www.discoverthechathamislands.co.nz, phone: 03 305 0443).

Buff Weka and *NZ Pipit* abound throughout the islands; and *Chatham Islands Shag* and *Pitt Island Shag* are moderately common around the coast, and a mixed colony is found on cliffs at Matarakau Point on the northern coast. *Chatham Islands Oystercatcher* nest on many low rocky headlands and stream mouths on the coast, especially at Cape Pattison, Maunganui Beach and at Taupeka Point, all in the north of the island. *Banded Dotterel*, a variety of Arctic waders, and numerous *Black Swan* are found on the northeastern shores of Te Whanga Lagoon between Hapupu and Ocean Mail. Forest birds such as *Chatham Islands Pigeon*, *Chatham Islands Red-crowned Parakeet* and *Chatham Islands Warbler* can be seen from the road at the Awatotara Valley. The best way to see and learn about bird conservation efforts in the area is on a guided walk or wider conservation tour led by the landowners, Bruce & Liz Tuanui (phone: 03 305 0351), which will include information about the rediscovery and recovery of *Chatham Islands Taiko* on their property, and reintroductions of *Chatham Islands Mollymawk*, *Chatham Islands Petrel*, *Chatham Islands Tui* and *Chatham Islands Tomtit*, some of which you may be lucky enough to see. Sea-watching off Owenga or other promontories, or better still a fishing boat charter from Owenga or Waitangi to Pitt Strait or beyond, should offer views of some of the numerous seabirds that breed in the group, especially *Blue Penguin*, *Northern Royal Albatross*, *Buller's Mollymawk*, *Chatham Islands Mollymawk*, *Northern Giant Petrel*, *Broad-billed Prion*, *Sooty Shearwater*, *Grey-backed Storm Petrel* and *White-faced Storm Petrel*. A visit close to the shore of South East (Rangatira) Island Nature Reserve should permit views of *Shore Plover* and *Southern Skua* on the wave platforms, but landing there is not permitted.

INDEX

Numerals in **bold type** refer to the plate number and its facing text, those in plain type refer to page numbers in the handbook section.

ABOUT THE AUTHORS

Hugh Robertson was educated at Massey University (BSc Hons) and Oxford University (DPhil). He is currently a Principal Science Advisor at the Department of Conservation (DOC) and has worked for the Department of Scientific and Industrial Research (DSIR)/DOC for over 35 years, specialising in kiwi research for the past 23.

Author or co-author of over 60 scientific publications, Robertson is an acknowledged expert in his field, serving as the Oceania representative on the CITES Animals Committee and scientific advisor to the Kakerori Recovery Programme in the Cook Islands, and has won several awards for his work, including the Ornithological Society of New Zealand (OSNZ)'s AT Edgar Junior and Falla Memorial awards. He is a regular commentator on Radio New Zealand National.

Robertson lives in Wellington, and is married with two children and a kiwi-finding labrador.

Barrie Heather (d. 1995) was educated at King's College and University of Auckland (BA and MA Hons) before undertaking a career as a high school teacher and a tutor at the Open Polytechnic.

Heather was editor of the scientific journal *Notornis* for 17 years and authored or co-authored over 35 scientific publications, including the superbly titled 'Welcome Swallow at Farewell Spit'. He also won several OSNZ commendations, including the Falla Memorial Award and being made an Honorary Life Member.

Heather is survived by his wife, four children and a wader-attracting corgi.

ABOUT THE ILLUSTRATOR

Derek Onley moved from the UK to New Zealand in 1972 via Southampton, Swansea, Portugal, Cambridge and Oxford. He lived for many years on the West Coast as an ornithological hippie and among many other things he trapped possums, built a house or two and was active in native forest conservation. After 20 years of wet feet, he moved east to Waitati where he lives with his partner and cat, continues to study birds and grows vegetables, trees and roses. In between he has carried out fieldwork in New Zealand and many offshore islands. His illustrations have appeared in field guides world-wide and he is currently working on a guide to Paraguay birds.

BIRDWATCHING CHECKLIST

This checklist is designed to allow you to maintain a record of the number of different species of New Zealand birds you have seen or heard. The columns could be used to build life lists of different members of your family, your property list, your regional list, to record different visits to New Zealand or to note species on the official New Zealand list that you have seen overseas.

Sp	Species					
1	*Brown Kiwi*					
2	*Rowi*					
3	*Tokoeka*					
4	*Little Spotted Kiwi*					
5	*Great Spotted Kiwi*					
6	*California Quail*					
7	*Helmeted Guineafowl*					
8	*Chukor*					
9	*Red-legged Partridge*					
10	*Grey Partridge*					
11	*Bobwhite Quail*					
12	*Brown Quail*					
13	*Feral Chicken*					
14	*Pheasant*					
15	*Peafowl*					
16	*Wild Turkey*					
17	*Plumed Whistling Duck*					
18	*Mute Swan*					
19	*Black Swan*					
20	*Cape Barren Goose*					
21	*Feral Goose*					
22	*Canada Goose*					
23	*Pink-eared Duck*					
24	*Paradise Shelduck*					
25	*Chestnut-breasted Shelduck*					
26	*New Zealand Merganser*					
27	*Australian Wood Duck*					
28	*Blue Duck*					
29	*Grey Teal*					
30	*Chestnut Teal*					
31	*Brown Teal*					
32	*Auckland Islands Teal*					
33	*Campbell Islands Teal*					
34	*Northern Pintail*					
35	*Mallard*					
36	*Grey Duck*					
37	*Australasian Shoveler*					
38	*Northern Shoveler*					
39	*Australian White-eyed Duck*					
40	*New Zealand Scaup*					

Sp	Species					
41	*Australasian Crested Grebe*					
42	*New Zealand Dabchick*					
43	*Hoary-headed Grebe*					
44	*Australasian Little Grebe*					
45	*Emperor Penguin*					
46	*King Penguin*					
47	*Adélie Penguin*					
48	*Gentoo Penguin*					
49	*Chinstrap Penguin*					
50	*Western Rockhopper Penguin*					
51	*Eastern Rockhopper Penguin*					
52	*Moseley's Rockhopper Penguin*					
53	*Fiordland Crested Penguin*					
54	*Snares Crested Penguin*					
55	*Erect-crested Penguin*					
56	*Macaroni Penguin*					
57	*Royal Penguin*					
58	*Yellow-eyed Penguin*					
59	*Blue Penguin*					
60	*Magellanic Penguin*					
61	*Wandering Albatross*					
62	*Antipodean Albatross*					
63	*Southern Royal Albatross*					
64	*Northern Royal Albatross*					
65	*Laysan Albatross*					
66	*Atlantic Yellow-nosed Mollymawk*					
67	*Indian Ocean Yellow-nosed Mollymawk*					
68	*Grey-headed Mollymawk*					
69	*Black-browed Mollymawk*					
70	*Campbell Islands Mollymawk*					
71	*Buller's Mollymawk*					
72	*White-capped Mollymawk*					
73	*Chatham Islands Mollymawk*					
74	*Salvin's Mollymawk*					
75	*Sooty Albatross*					
76	*Light-mantled Sooty Albatross*					
77	*Southern Giant Petrel*					
78	*Northern Giant Petrel*					
79	*Antarctic Fulmar*					
80	*Antarctic Petrel*					
81	*Cape Pigeon*					
82	*Snow Petrel*					
83	*Kerguelen Petrel*					
84	*Grey-faced Petrel*					
85	*White-headed Petrel*					
86	*Providence Petrel*					
87	*Chatham Islands Taiko*					
88	*Kermadec Petrel*					
89	*Phoenix Petrel*					
90	*Soft-plumaged Petrel*					
91	*Mottled Petrel*					
92	*Juan Fernández Petrel*					
93	*White-naped Petrel*					
94	*Black-winged Petrel*					
95	*Chatham Islands Petrel*					
96	*Cook's Petrel*					

Sp	Species					
97	*Stejneger's Petrel*					
98	*Pycroft's Petrel*					
99	*Gould's Petrel*					
100	*Blue Petrel*					
101	*Broad-billed Prion*					
102	*Salvin's Prion*					
103	*Antarctic Prion*					
104	*Thin-billed Prion*					
105	*Fairy Prion*					
106	*Fulmar Prion*					
107	*Bulwer's Petrel*					
108	*White-chinned Petrel*					
109	*Westland Petrel*					
110	*Black Petrel*					
111	*Grey Petrel*					
112	*Tahiti Petrel*					
113	*Cory's Shearwater*					
114	*Streaked Shearwater*					
115	*Wedge-tailed Shearwater*					
116	*Buller's Shearwater*					
117	*Flesh-footed Shearwater*					
118	*Pink-footed Shearwater*					
119	*Great Shearwater*					
120	*Sooty Shearwater*					
121	*Short-tailed Shearwater*					
122	*Christmas Island Shearwater*					
123	*Newell's Shearwater*					
124	*Manx Shearwater*					
125	*Fluttering Shearwater*					
126	*Hutton's Shearwater*					
127	*Little Shearwater*					
128	*Subantarctic Little Shearwater*					
129	*Wilson's Storm Petrel*					
130	*Grey-backed Storm Petrel*					
131	*White-faced Storm Petrel*					
132	*Kermadec Storm Petrel*					
133	*New Zealand Storm Petrel*					
134	*Black-bellied Storm Petrel*					
135	*White-bellied Storm Petrel*					
136	*Leach's Storm Petrel*					
137	*Common Diving Petrel*					
138	*South Georgian Diving Petrel*					
139	*Red-tailed Tropicbird*					
140	*White-tailed Tropicbird*					
141	*Australian Pelican*					
142	*Cape Gannet*					
143	*Australasian Gannet*					
144	*Brown Booby*					
145	*Masked Booby*					
146	*Little Shag*					
147	*Black Shag*					
148	*Pied Shag*					
149	*Little Black Shag*					
150	*King Shag*					
151	*Stewart Island Shag*					
152	*Chatham Islands Shag*					

Sp	Species					
153	*Bounty Islands Shag*					
154	*Auckland Islands Shag*					
155	*Campbell Islands Shag*					
156	*Spotted Shag*					
157	*Pitt Island Shag*					
158	*Darter*					
159	*Great Frigatebird*					
160	*Lesser Frigatebird*					
161	*Pacific Heron*					
162	*White Heron*					
163	*Cattle Egret*					
164	*Plumed Egret*					
165	*White-faced Heron*					
166	*Little Egret*					
167	*Reef Heron*					
168	*Nankeen Night Heron*					
169	*Australasian Bittern*					
170	*Little Bittern*					
171	*Glossy Ibis*					
172	*Australian White Ibis*					
173	*Straw-necked Ibis*					
174	*Royal Spoonbill*					
175	*Yellow-billed Spoonbill*					
176	*Black Kite*					
177	*Swamp Harrier*					
178	*Nankeen Kestrel*					
179	*Black Falcon*					
180	*New Zealand Falcon*					
181	*Auckland Islands Rail*					
182	*Banded Rail*					
183	*Weka*					
184	*Spotless Crake*					
185	*Marsh Crake*					
186	*Black-tailed Native-hen*					
187	*Dusky Moorhen*					
188	*Pukeko*					
189	*Takahe*					
190	*Australian Coot*					
191	*South Island Snipe*					
192	*Chatham Islands Snipe*					
193	*Snares Snipe*					
194	*Subantarctic Snipe*					
195	*Japanese Snipe*					
196	*Red Knot*					
197	*Great Knot*					
198	*Sanderling*					
199	*Dunlin*					
200	*Curlew Sandpiper*					
201	*Stilt Sandpiper*					
202	*Sharp-tailed Sandpiper*					
203	*Pectoral Sandpiper*					
204	*Baird's Sandpiper*					
205	*White-rumped Sandpiper*					
206	*Little Stint*					
207	*Red-necked Stint*					
208	*Long-toed Stint*					

Sp	Species					
209	*Least Sandpiper*					
210	*Semipalmated Sandpiper*					
211	*Western Sandpiper*					
212	*Broad-billed Sandpiper*					
213	*Buff-breasted Sandpiper*					
214	*Ruff*					
215	*Asiatic Dowitcher*					
216	*Far-eastern Curlew*					
217	*Whimbrel*					
218	*Little Whimbrel*					
219	*Bristle-thighed Curlew*					
220	*Bar-tailed Godwit*					
221	*Black-tailed Godwit*					
222	*Hudsonian Godwit*					
223	*Upland Sandpiper*					
224	*Wandering Tattler*					
225	*Grey-tailed Tattler*					
226	*Common Sandpiper*					
227	*Greenshank*					
228	*Marsh Sandpiper*					
229	*Lesser Yellowlegs*					
230	*Terek Sandpiper*					
231	*Turnstone*					
232	*Grey Phalarope*					
233	*Red-necked Phalarope*					
234	*Wilson's Phalarope*					
235	*Painted Snipe*					
236	*Variable Oystercatcher*					
237	*South Island Pied Oystercatcher*					
238	*Chatham Islands Oystercatcher*					
239	*Pied Stilt*					
240	*Black Stilt*					
241	*Red-necked Avocet*					
242	*Pacific Golden Plover*					
243	*American Golden Plover*					
244	*Grey Plover*					
245	*New Zealand Dotterel*					
246	*Semipalmated Plover*					
247	*Red-capped Plover*					
248	*Banded Dotterel*					
249	*Lesser Sand Plover*					
250	*Greater Sand Plover*					
251	*Oriental Dotterel*					
252	*Wrybill*					
253	*Black-fronted Dotterel*					
254	*Shore Plover*					
255	*Red-kneed Dotterel*					
256	*Spur-winged Plover*					
257	*Oriental Pratincole*					
258	*Southern Skua*					
259	*South Polar Skua*					
260	*Pomarine Skua*					
261	*Arctic Skua*					
262	*Long-tailed Skua*					
263	*Pacific Gull*					
264	*Black-backed Gull*					

Sp	Species					
265	*Franklin's Gull*					
266	*Red-billed Gull*					
267	*Black-billed Gull*					
268	*Brown Noddy*					
269	*Black Noddy*					
270	*Grey Ternlet*					
271	*White Tern*					
272	*Sooty Tern*					
273	*Grey-backed Tern*					
274	*Bridled Tern*					
275	*Little Tern*					
276	*Fairy Tern*					
277	*Gull-billed Tern*					
278	*Caspian Tern*					
279	*White-winged Black Tern*					
280	*Whiskered Tern*					
281	*Black-fronted Tern*					
282	*White-fronted Tern*					
283	*Antarctic Tern*					
284	*Arctic Tern*					
285	*Common Tern*					
286	*Crested Tern*					
287	*Rock Pigeon*					
288	*Barbary Dove*					
289	*Spotted Dove*					
290	*New Zealand Pigeon*					
291	*Chatham Islands Pigeon*					
292	*Kakapo*					
293	*Kaka*					
294	*Kea*					
295	*Sulphur-crested Cockatoo*					
296	*Galah*					
297	*Rainbow Lorikeet*					
298	*Crimson Rosella*					
299	*Eastern Rosella*					
300	*Red-crowned Parakeet*					
301	*Yellow-crowned Parakeet*					
302	*Orange-fronted Parakeet*					
303	*Forbes' Parakeet*					
304	*Antipodes Islands Parakeet*					
305	*Reischek's Parakeet*					
306	*Oriental Cuckoo*					
307	*Pallid Cuckoo*					
308	*Fan-tailed Cuckoo*					
309	*Shining Cuckoo*					
310	*Long-tailed Cuckoo*					
311	*Channel-billed Cuckoo*					
312	*Morepork*					
313	*Laughing Owl*					
314	*Little Owl*					
315	*Barn Owl*					
316	*Spine-tailed Swift*					
317	*Fork-tailed Swift*					
318	*Laughing Kookaburra*					
319	*Kingfisher*					
320	*Dollarbird*					

Sp	Species					
321	*Rifleman*					
322	*Bush Wren*					
323	*Rock Wren*					
324	*North Island Kokako*					
325	*South Island Kokako*					
326	*North Island Saddleback*					
327	*South Island Saddleback*					
328	*Huia*					
329	*Stitchbird*					
330	*North Island Piopio*					
331	*South Island Piopio*					
332	*Grey Warbler*					
333	*Chatham Islands Warbler*					
334	*Bellbird*					
335	*Chatham Islands Bellbird*					
336	*Tui*					
337	*Black-faced Cuckoo-shrike*					
338	*White-winged Triller*					
339	*Red-vented Bulbul*					
340	*Whitehead*					
341	*Yellowhead*					
342	*Brown Creeper*					
343	*Australian Magpie*					
344	*Masked Woodswallow*					
345	*White-browed Woodswallow*					
346	*Fantail*					
347	*Willie Wagtail*					
348	*Rook*					
349	*Satin Flycatcher*					
350	*Black-faced Monarch*					
351	*Tomtit*					
352	*North Island Robin*					
353	*South Island Robin*					
354	*Black Robin*					
355	*Skylark*					
356	*Australian Reed-warbler*					
357	*Fernbird*					
358	*Silvereye*					
359	*Welcome Swallow*					
360	*Fairy Martin*					
361	*Tree Martin*					
362	*Blackbird*					
363	*Song Thrush*					
364	*Starling*					
365	*Myna*					
366	*House Sparrow*					
367	*New Zealand Pipit*					
368	*Dunnock*					
369	*Chaffinch*					
370	*Greenfinch*					
371	*Goldfinch*					
372	*Redpoll*					
373	*Yellowhammer*					
374	*Cirl Bunting*					

Three Kings Is
North Cape
Parengarenga Harbour
Rangaunu Harbour
Ninety Mile Beach
NORTHLAND
Kaitaia
Bay of Islands
Poor Knights Is
Hokianga Harbour
Whangarei
Hen and Chickens Is
Dargaville Beach
Little Barrier I
Great Barrier I
Hauraki Gulf
Kaipara Harbour
Tiritiri Matangi Island
Mercury Is
AUCKLAND
Auckland
COROMANDEL
Manukau Harbour
Mayor I
Miranda
Firth of Thames
Tauranga Harbour
Waikato River
Maketu Estuary
WAIKATO
Ohope Estuary
Raglan Harbour
Tauranga
East Cape
Hamilton
Raukumara Range
BAY OF PLENTY
Kawhia Harbour
Rotorua
Rotorua Lakes
KING COUNTRY
Urewera
Taupo
POVERTY BAY
L Taupo
Gisborne
New Plymouth
L Waikaremoana
VOLCANIC PLATEAU
Mt Taranaki
HAWKE'S BAY
Wairoa
Mahia Peninsula
TARANAKI
Mt Ruapehu
Portland I
Ahuriri Estuary
Napier
Cape Kidnappers
Hastings
Ruahine Range
Waitotara Estuary
Palmerston North
Porangahau Estuary
Manawatu Estuary
Cape Turnagain
Levin
Tararua Range
Mt Bruce
Kapiti Island
WAIRARAPA
Masterton
Mana I
Wellington
L Wairarapa
Cook Strait
Cape Palliser